A Guide to the Study and Use of Military History

A Guide to the Study and Use of Military History

John E. Jessup, Jr. & Robert W. Coakley

Center of Military History
United States Army

Library of Congress Cataloging in Publication Data

Main entry under title:

A Guide to the Study and Use of Military History.

   Bibliography: p.
   Includes index.
   1.   United States—History, Military—Historiography.
2.   History, Military—Historiography.   3.   United
States. Army.   I.   Jessup, John E. II.   Coakley,
Robert W.   III.   Center of Military History.
EI81.G85   973'.07'2   78–606157

For Sale by the Superintendent of Documents
U.S. Government Printing Office   Washington, D.C. 20402
Stock No. 008–029–00105–5   First Printing, 1979

Department of the Army
Historical Advisory Committee
(as of May 1978)

Contents

Four: History Outside the U.S. Army

Appendices

Foreword

OVER the years the study of military history has had its ups and downs within the Army. In the education of the World War II generation of military leaders it played an important part, for the study of past operations held a preeminent place in the Army schools' curricula in the period between the two great world wars. In the years immediately following World War II, it lost that place. This happened partly because the information explosion broadened so greatly the areas in which an officer had to be knowledgeable and partly because of a belief that the pace of change in technology had rendered the study of past experience irrelevant. In the Army's higher schools, military history became largely a matter of using examples from the past in courses dealing with current problems.

On his retirement in 1970 as Chief of Military History, Brig. Gen. Hal C. Pattison voiced his concern to the Army Chief of Staff, General William C. Westmoreland, over "the departure of the Army from its traditional reliance upon the experience of history." General Pattison suggested that the Army had paid the price of this neglect in many of the problems it encountered in the late 1960s and urged the restoration of military history to "its proper place in the importance of things." In response General Westmoreland established an ad hoc committee to "ascertain the Army need for the study of military history" and to "develop recommendations on how any unfulfilled needs can be met." Under the chairmanship of Col. Thomas E. Griess of the U.S. Military Academy and composed of representatives of the higher Army schools, the Continental Army Command, and the Office of the Chief of Military History, the committee met over an extended period at West Point in 1971. The committee concluded that there was indeed a need for study of military history in the Army to contribute to "broadened perspective, sharpened judgment, increased perceptivity, and professional expertise." It included in its recommendations to meet "unfulfilled needs" the publication of a "guide to the study and use of military history" which would be "issued to all officers at the Basic Course and others on request." The Chief of Staff approved this recommendation, entrusted the preparation to the then Office of the Chief of Military History (now Center of Military History), and this *Guide* is the result.

As recommended by the ad hoc committee, the primary audience is the young officer just entering upon a military career. But the *Guide* has been shaped for use throughout that career as he matures and progresses, not as something to be thrown aside after one reading. It should serve the officer in the advanced courses, the Command and General Staff College, and the Army War College, as well as those in basic courses. Perhaps more important, since the time Army schools can allot to military history is limited, it can serve as a most useful tool for self-education at any stage of an officer's career. It should also be of value to instructors in all Army schools and to noncommissioned officers and other enlisted personnel with an interest in the military past. Civilian students and instructors in history, and indeed all those interested in military affairs, should find much of interest and value in this volume. In sum, the *Guide* should become an important tool in the never-ending process of education of both Army officers and civilian students of history. I hope that it will indeed assist in restoring military history to its "proper place in the importance of things."

James L. Collins, Jr.
Brigadier General, USA
Chief of Military History

Preface

O N 6 June 1944, as the allied forces began the invasion of Normandy, General George S. Patton, Jr., wrote to his son, then a cadet at the United States Military Academy, that "to be a successful soldier, you must know history." The number of similar pronouncements from noted military figures, including Napoleon, is almost endless and the basic refrain is the same—to understand the present and to prepare for the future the study of history is vital. This applies most particularly to those who lead men in battle. As Marshal Foch wrote, "no study is possible on the battlefield, one does simply what *one can* in order to apply what one knows." Despite vast changes in technology since World War II, the combat leader may still learn much from the study of past battles and campaigns. Weather, terrain, and intelligence of friendly and enemy dispositions, for instance, are as important today as in the days of Alexander, Frederick the Great, and Napoleon; human reactions in combat remain relatively constant.

Quite beyond vicarious experience of the battlefield, the study of military history affords an understanding of the interplay of forces that have shaped the present and provides the means of viewing current problems against the long perspective of how men have handled similar problems in the past. The immediate utility of a knowledge of history is likely to vary with the situation in which the individual soldier finds himself. Certainly force planners could profit from a study of the varying approaches of General Pershing and General Marshall in the two world wars toward the size and composition of the Army, officers in charge of training from a reminder that the American soldier's traditional outlook was not conducive to fighting a counterinsurgency war in Vietnam, and military leaders and policy makers alike from an appreciation of the long American tradition against drafting men for combat service in anything short of an all-out national war effort. Knowledge of military history cannot produce solutions to all problems, nor can it guarantee success in a military career. But it can provide a foundation for both problem solving and career achievement.

This *Guide to the Study and Use of Military History* is designed to foster an appreciation of the value of military history and explain its uses and the resources available for its study. It is not a work to be read and lightly tossed aside, but one the career soldier should read again or use as a reference at those times during his career when necessity or leisure turns him to the contemplation of the military past.

The *Guide* consists of four parts. Part One is general in nature and deals with the nature of history as a discipline, military history as a branch of that discipline, the uses of military history, and suggested methods of reading and study.

Part Two is a guide to the areas of study and the materials available for study in each. It consists of seven bibliographical essays—one on the great military historians and philosophers with whom all students of military history should have some acquaintance, two on world military history, three specifically on American military history, and a final essay on the merging of American and world military history since the end of World War II. Each of the period essays weaves its bibliographical information into the framework of a discussion of the main military developments of the era covered, introducing, where pertinent, varying historical interpretations of events and issues. Each contains at the end an alphabetical listing of all works mentioned.

Part Three deals with U.S. Army historical programs and activities and how the Army uses or has used military history. This part informs the reader of the resources available within the Army for study and research in military history and some of the practical uses of history in staff work.

Part Four similarly deals, albeit more briefly, with military history outside the Army—in other elements of the Department of Defense, in foreign military establishments, and in the academic world.

Finally two appendices provide annotated listings of reference works and historical periodicals of greatest interest and utility to the student of military history.

The longest part of the *Guide*, Part Two, contains the bibliographical essays, generally modeled on the bibliographical pamphlets published by the American Historical Association Center for Teachers. Like them, each individual essay, written by a specialist in the field, adopts a somewhat different approach. All of them, however, must list many works within a relatively short space to give the reader some understanding of the vast variety of historical literature available. Bibliographic essays seldom make light bedtime reading, and those in the *Guide* are no exception. But the editors do believe these essays can be read initially with interest and profit for a general appreciation of the whole field of military history, and then used later as a more detailed reference when the student develops an interest in a particular period or subject. Except in the essay on the great military historians and philosophers, only works written in English or translated into English have been included. And there is relatively heavy emphasis on American military history as opposed to the broader field of world military history. The reason is simply the belief that books in the national language and on the national experience will be of greatest interest and utility to the American officer.

As the title indicates, the volume is primarily a guide to the study and use of military history and not a guide to research and writing, although certainly parts of it should be useful to the researcher. It is not intended to supplant *The Writing of American Military History: A Guide*, published by the Office of the Chief of Military History (OCMH) as a Department of the Army pamphlet in 1956, although the student should find the bibliographies on American history in this volume more comprehensive and up to date.

The *Guide* is a cooperative work to which many individuals, both in the U.S. Army Center of Military History and outside, have contributed. When the task was first assigned to OCMH in 1972, the office enlisted the aid of the History Department at the U.S. Military Academy, personnel of the U.S. Army Military History Research Collection (now the U.S. Army Military History Institute) at Carlisle Barracks, Pennsylvania, visiting professors of military history at West Point and Carlisle, and others. It has been assembled and edited by personnel at the center in Washington. For the most part, the editors have let authors approach their subjects as they wished, within certain space limitations. The editors and others, however, have made many suggestions to the authors in the course of several reviews of drafts and in some cases have made changes on their own in the interest of a better integrated work. Like all Center of Military History publications, the various chapters have been carefully edited, form and references standardized, and duplication eliminated. Essentially, nonetheless, each chapter remains the work of its author and is intended to stand on its own.

The original conception for this *Guide* was largely the work of Col. John E. Jessup, Jr., who served as the OCMH member of the 1971 Ad Hoc Committee on the Need for the Study of Military

History in the Army and was chief of the OCMH Histories Division when the task of preparing the volume was assigned. With some advice and assistance from others in OCMH and at the Military Academy, Colonel Jessup developed an outline, made the original chapter assignments, and assembled most of the contributions before he retired from the military service in October 1974. For some months thereafter the *Guide* languished in partial rough draft form until Dr. Robert W. Coakley, Deputy Chief Historian of the center, assumed responsibility for it in April 1975. Since that time Dr. Coakley has seen the draft through two main revisions—one before submission to a review panel in September 1975 and the other after the panel had rendered its critique. Both the concept and the draft underwent considerable revision in detail during the two separate processes, but the general scheme of the *Guide* and much of its contents remain as initially shaped by Colonel Jessup.

Preparation and coordination of this work among its many authors has required considerable time. One consequence has been the danger that many sections might become outdated before publication. Even though in the later stages the editor made every effort to have authors update their respective contributions, there has been some time lag as a result of delays in receiving various revisions and time consumed in editing and printing. New works of considerable significance may have appeared since the bibliographic essays were originally prepared. A more serious consequence is in the chapters on the Army and other Department of Defense military history institutions and programs and those of foreign governments. Although the general nature of these programs and activities usually remains constant from year to year, there are frequent changes in detail. Some organizations and practices may have changed since the summer of 1976 when most of the descriptions underwent final revision.

The editors wish to express their great appreciation to the other contributors to the *Guide*, some of whom rendered generously of their time and effort without remuneration, and most particularly to Col. Thomas E. Griess, Professor and Head of the History Department at the United States Military Academy, who chaired the ad hoc committee that gave birth to the idea of the *Guide* and later not only contributed a chapter of his own but secured contributions from two others then at the academy.

All members of the center panel who reviewed the draft in 1975 made valuable suggestions as have others who read and commented on the draft from time to time. Dr. Maurice Matloff, Chief Historian of the center, although a contributor, served as chairman of the review panel; Mr. Joseph R. Friedman, then Editor in Chief, also a contributor, served on it. Other members of the panel from the center were Col. James F. Ransone, Jr., Mr. Robert Ross Smith, and Dr. Alfred M. Beck, and from the outside Mr. Martin Blumenson, then Visiting Professor of Military History at the Army War College, Capt. John R. Miller, Assistant Professor of Military Science at Washington and Lee University, and Dr. Russell F. Weigley of Temple University.

Others who made valuable comments at one time or another have been Dr. Edward M. Coffman of the University of Wisconsin, Dr. Stanley L. Falk, Chief Historian of the Air Force, Dr. Frank Freidel of Harvard University, Dr. Peter Paret of Stanford University, Maj. Gen. Robert C. Hixon, Chief of Staff of the U.S. Army Training and Doctrine Command, and Brig. Gen. Benjamin L. Harrison, Deputy Commandant of the U.S. Army Command and General Staff College. Mr. James McSherry and Ms. Joyce Hardyman of the Center's Editorial Branch performed the detailed editing necessary to prepare this volume for the printer. Mr. Dudley Kruhm of the Typography and Design Section of the Government Printing Office designed the book. The sins of omission and of commission of which this Guide may be guilty, however, must be attributed in the main to the general editors, rather than to the contributors, advisers, or technical editors.

John E. Jessup, Jr.
Robert W. Coakley

One

Military History, Its Nature and Use

Chapter 1

The Nature
of History

Maurice Matloff

BEFORE a reader embarks on the study of military history, he may well ask about the nature of the historical discipline of which it is a part. What is history? Why and how study it? In the swiftly changing world of the 1970s with newspapers, radio, and television pouring out a constant stream of information and news that competes for his attention, why should the reader concern himself about the past? Is the past dead? Is it useful or relevant to the present? Does it have anything to teach? Is history more than a collection of dates and events entombed in a dull textbook that taxed the reader's memory in his school days? By what standards can he judge the merits of historical writings and the contributions of historians? To answer these questions, it is necessary to understand what history is about, what its relations are with other disciplines, how it is written, what purposes and uses it serves, and how the field in general has developed.

History and the Historian

It has been said that it is easier to write history than to define it. Part of the problem is that history has meant different things at different times from the ancient world to the present and that there have been as many varieties of history as there have been schools of sculpture, painting, or philosophy. Historians have differed in method, content, and purpose of their work. Some have been primarily interested in telling a story, others in determining and recording facts or re-creating events as they actually happened, others in interpreting their findings in some

Dr. Matloff (Ph.D., Harvard), Chief Historian of the U.S. Army Center of Military History, has taught or lectured at service institutions and numerous civilian colleges and universities. He wrote *Strategic Planning for Coalition Warfare, 1943-44* (U.S. Army in World War II series), is coauthor of a similar volume for 1941-42, and is general editor of the CMH publication *American Military History*.

cosmic synthesis or thesis. The permutations and combinations in approaches from the beginning of recorded history have been manifold. The problem of definition is also complicated by the fact that in a sense everything has a past, and some would therefore define history as everything that ever happened. By this definition history can be extended to include the study of animate and inanimate objects that have constituted the universe from the beginning of time and have undergone changes—mountains, seas, suns and planets, plants and animals.

Such a broad extension of the definition tends to dilute the meaning of the term. The more common uses of the term history focus on a record of man's past, the study of man's past, and critical thinking about that past. Such usage stresses man and his activities, a concern with his past, particularly the recorded past, and the search for the truth about it. History thus involves a body of recorded materials from that past and a method, a special manner of treating those materials. The historian deals with changes, with time sequences, and with cause and effect relations in human events. He uses dates to peg events in time and help establish such sequences, changes, and relationships. The historian's concern with change has sometimes led to the criticism that he is overly concerned with the "pathology" of the human condition—war, revolution, and other cataclysmic events, rather than its "physiology"—periods or phases of little change, so-called normality. Stressing that the story of man is central to the multifaceted historical discipline, Allan Nevins, one of the foremost recent American historians, suggested a useful definition for the beginning reader in his introductory volume, *The Gateway to History*. "History," he stated, "is any integrated narrative, description or analysis of past events or facts written in a spirit of critical inquiry for the whole truth."[1]

While this definition emphasizes method and content in the modern approach to the field, it is well to caution, as Nevins did, that to enjoy and understand history in its many variations one should not be too dogmatic in defining it. There have been almost as many schools of history as great historians, and in many cases they have disagreed with each other vehemently over conceptions of the nature of the discipline. There are all kinds of history and no reason for the beginner to cut himself off from the rich fare that awaits him as a result of too narrow a definition of the field. A diverse galaxy in different lands and ages have written

1. Allan Nevins, *The Gateway to History*, rev. ed. (Garden City, N.Y.: Doubleday, 1962), p. 39.

from different vantage points and have left an indelible imprint on the field—Herodotus, Thucydides, and Xenophon in the ancient world, Voltaire and Gibbon in eighteenth-century Europe, the German von Ranke, the British Macaulay and Carlyle, and the Americans Prescott, Motley, and Parkman in the nineteenth century, to name but a few. They illustrate the wide variety of tastes and fashions in approach—literary, scientific, popular, patriotic, biographical, philosophical, narrative, and descriptive—that have characterized this discipline over the centuries. They illustrate too that history is made by historians rather than by the actors in the events—"the movers and the shakers" in human experience. Historians select and cull the records and describe, narrate, or interpret the facts in patterns and priorities that seem significant to them rather than to the contemporaries of the events or the actors themselves. While the historian seeks the truth, in human affairs truth is relative, limited by the available materials and filtered through the spectacles with which the scholar views happenings of the past. What is important to one age will seem unimportant to another, and many of the seemingly significant happenings of our own age will undoubtedly be forgotten or viewed in different perspective by scholars a hundred years hence. Since historians and their histories are inseparable, the beginning reader will do well to find out as much as he can about both.

Just as the historian and his product are intertwined, so history has close relations with other disciplines. In method and content it is both a borrower from and a contributor to other fields of knowledge. The best accounts of the development of the specialized branches of learning, geology, medicine, religion, the fine arts, for example, draw on the historian's methods of ascertaining facts and the time framework of events established by the historian. In turn the historian uses the tools and insights offered by skilled practitioners in other fields to broaden his explorations of society, past and present.

History has a foot in the camp of the social sciences as well as the humanities. Indeed scholars are by no means agreed on whether the discipline belongs more to the one or the other. As a branch of the social sciences, history borrows the special approaches to human behavior in such related fields as economics, political science, sociology, anthropology, psychology, law, and statistics. With the aid of psychology, the historian is beginning to probe the human psyche more deeply in biographical and even social history. With the help of anthropology, he is better able to understand cultural differences and similarities among preliterate societies. Political science gives him a special approach to problems in the art of government and decision making; sociology to questions of group dynamics. Statistics permit him to treat and digest masses of data and reach generalizations more securely based on facts—for example, the rich harvest of information gleaned from census tables and analyses of votes in crucial elections. The increased use of statistics in historical work has led to the entry of a new tool, the computer, into the field, and the mastery of the machine and its programming has become an interdisciplinary effort in itself. On the other side of the coin, history as the study of the past is the only laboratory most social scientists have since they cannot, like physical scientists, often set up controlled experiments. They must gather their data from a study of what has happened in given situations in the past, and consequently they must use history.

History has long had a close relationship with the humanities—with such fields as literature and the fine arts, archaeology, philosophy, and linguistics. From the beginning master stylists have contributed to the development of history as a literary art. Virtually all the great historians have been masters of narration. High standards of literary craftsmanship typified by such writers as Carlyle and Gibbon in the old world were carried on by Parkman, Prescott, and Motley in the new and remain an ideal of the discipline to this day.

Whether a master stylist or not, the historian can draw on the discoveries of the archaeologists to enrich his knowledge of civilizations in the old and new worlds in prerecorded times. He benefits from the linguists' studies of word usages and changes that shed light on the differentiation of cultures in various times and places and from the writings on philosophy, literature, and the fine arts that illuminate trends in human thought and artistic achievement. Through such auxiliary means the historian diversifies and strengthens the weapons in his arsenal to probe the past of mankind.

History has especially strong bonds with biography. "A good biography," Allan Nevins, an outstanding practitioner of both arts, has written, "must vividly re-create a character; it must present a full, careful, and unbiased record of his acts and experiences; and it must indicate the place of the hero in history."[2] Indeed some writers have regarded biography as the embodiment and distillation of human experience, the most

---

2. *Ibid.*, p. 364.

important form of history, and even identical with it. History to Carlyle was "the essence of innumerable biographies." Emerson argued there was "properly no history, only biography." Although not all historians would go so far as Carlyle and Emerson, history does deal with human beings, both as individuals and in the aggregate, acting and reacting to impersonal and personal forces. And a first-rate biography will offer not only an accurate account of an individual's life but also project that life against the background of his times and serve as an excellent introduction to that period. Much history may therefore be learned in congenial fashion by reading outstanding biographies of those who have lived in different ages and societies. As the field of biography has broadened to cover nonpolitical as well as political characters, secondary as well as leading figures in all walks of life, and as psychological insights increasingly have been brought to bear, the historian's portrayal of the past has been enriched, humanized, and made concrete. The biographical approach to history, really an old form of the discipline, is today more popular then ever, and the historian and the biographer, two old allies in the field of letters, continue to walk side by side. Indeed, they are often one and the same.

The ties of history extend not only to the social sciences and the humanities but also to natural and applied sciences. In the pursuit of truth modern historians share with scientists the spirit of critical inquiry and utilize scientific procedures and methods to gather reliable data. Furthermore, since man's life is intertwined with his environment, the historian must take into account the impact of geography, climate, and natural resources; the invention of labor-saving devices; the revolution in transportation, communication, agriculture, physics, chemistry, and medical science; and the application of atomic energy. To understand and portray recent American history, for example, the historian must be aware of the effects of the great changes in space and time factors wrought by the new technology in transportation, communications, and weaponry—fast ships, airplanes, communication satellites, and missiles.

Through the nineteenth century, safely ensconced behind the ocean barriers that separated them from Europe and Asia, Americans concentrated on developing the bountiful resources of their continent in relative immunity from troubles abroad. In the shrunken world of the twentieth century Americans are no longer the beneficiaries of the relative isolation, the "free security," they enjoyed during most of their national existence. Once regarded by Americans as the Far East, the Orient has in effect become the Near West. As a result, the historian of contemporary America has to grapple with the apparent conflict between national traditions and present realities accompanying the revolution in the strategic position of the United States in the world since World War II, a revolution largely a consequence of scientific and technological developments. In his never-ending search for important keys to unlock and understand the past and to gain perspective on the present, the historian gathers his allies where he may and enlists whatever help he can find from the pursuit of truth in other fields of inquiry.

How History Is Written

How does the historian go about the task of reconstructing the past? What techniques does he use to produce his written product? Treatises have been written on this subject, but the essential steps may be boiled down to three: gathering the data, criticizing or evaluating the data, and presenting the material in readable form. Each of these processes entails its own special technique and training, but in the hands of experienced practitioners they are interrelated activities. Finding, sifting, and presenting the evidence in combination involve the skills of a detective, a scientist, a judge, and an artist.

History, it has been said, could not have been born without two basic elements—a body of more or less reliable materials and a critical method to deal with them.[3] While the historian relies primarily on documents, his sources also include a variety of other materials: physical remains—roads, fortifications, buildings, pottery, weapons, chiselled stones, coins, tapestries, pictures, sculptures, and other museum pieces; orally transmitted folklore in legends, ballads, and sagas; handwritten papyri and parchment manuscripts; printed books and papers; motion picture films; sound recordings; television and radio broadcasts; and computer tapes. The accumulation of data on man's past is a fascinating story in its own right; it long was a slow process, and only in late modern times did the materials become voluminous and the sources more complex, a process associated with the growth of large repositories in national archives and libraries, and with collections of private papers. To find the data on a given subject, the historian uses a variety of bibliographical compilations and archival finding aids and draws on the skills of archivists, librarians, and museum specialists.

---

3. *Ibid.*, p. 66.

In historical research, sources are divided into two general categories: primary and secondary. Primary sources offer firsthand testimony of a happening, the view of an eyewitness. Secondary sources are descriptions or narrations of the event derived from the primary sources. Thus a letter of George Washington contemporaneous with his Revolutionary War experience and describing an incident in it, for example his first-hand report of 27 December 1776 to the President of the Continental Congress on the previous day's battle of Trenton, is a primary source; a later scholar's reconstruction or account of the event, for instance in Christopher Ward's *The War of the Revolution* (1952), represents a secondary source. Sometimes the line between the two categories may be blurred and the same document may be a primary source from one standpoint and a secondary source from another. A volume like Sir Arthur Bryant's *The Turn of the Tide* (1957) contains a primary source, extracts from the wartime diaries of Field Marshal Lord Alanbrooke, Chief of the British Imperial General Staff in World War II, and also offers commentary by Bryant, the author—a secondary account.

While in many ways modern technology has made printed sources more readily and widely available to the historian, the telephone has proved to be the historian's enemy. Historians of recent events have often commented on how an important trail they could once trace in documents may now disappear in an unrecorded telephone call at high levels of officialdom. But to supplement the written record in contemporary history and to fill gaps in it, the historian may draw on oral history—interviewing his subjects, recording the interview on tape, and using the transcription as a source. This technique is a modern refinement of the process of drawing on the testimony of witnesses utilized by probably the greatest historian writing of his own times, Thucydides, in his study of the Peloponnesian Wars between the Athenians and the Spartans. In this way the contemporary historian generates his own primary sources.

Once he has accumulated his raw data from whatever source, the historian must subject it to the second process, critical examination and evaluation, before he can use it.[4] The term

---

4. For good discussions of the evaluation of data, see Allen Johnson, *The Historian and Historical Evidence* (New York: Scribner's, 1926); Homer C. Hockett, *Introduction to Research in American History*, 2d ed. (New York: Macmillan, 1948), pp. 56-111; Charles V. Langlois and Charles Siegnobos, *Introduction to the Study of History*, trans. G. G. Berry (New York: Barnes and Noble, 1966), pp. 71-208; and Arthur P. Scott and James L. Cate, "Syllabus and Problems for History 201, Introduction to Historical Method and Historiography" (Chicago: Univ. of Chicago, 1945), pp. 33-92.

historical science is used most commonly to refer to the principles of criticism that have been adopted by the historical craft. The application of such critical standards is the heart of the sifting process through which the historian puts his data. Simply put, the principles are really common-sense rules that have evolved to test the validity and reliability of sources.

The historian's critical examination is composed of two basic procedures: external criticism and internal criticism. External criticism involves those tests that seek to establish the authenticity of a particular source. It detects forgeries and false versions and identifies anonymous documents. It attempts to establish where, when, how, and by whom a document was written, for this knowledge is essential to the writing of history. This type of criticism is obviously one which the student of modern history seldom needs to employ. Forgeries and anonymous papers have been comparatively rare since the end of the eighteenth century. External criticism is used most often by historians of earlier periods who have developed elaborate skills to establish the origin of their sources. They can detect counterfeits through tests to determine the age of paper or ink. But as the average American document is easily identified, measures of detection such as comparison with other documents and textual criticism are apt to be less essential.[5]

For the writer of history, internal criticism is an indispensable technique. Once a document has been identified, internal criticism is used to analyze the meaning of statements in the document and to determine their accuracy, truthworthiness, and sincerity. At the risk of oversimplification, external criticism may be said to determine the admissibility of historical evidence, internal criticism its credibility. The properly skeptical historian can put several questions to his sources in the process of internal criticism: Is the writer of a given document a good authority? Was he an eyewitness? If so, can his testimony be relied on? Is he a trained observer? This necessary qualification is demonstrated by the story of the Wall Street explosion in 1920. Of nine eyewitnesses, eight testified that there were several vehicles of various kinds in the block where the explosion occurred, and three of the eight were sure that a red motor truck carried the bomb. But the ninth eyewitness, an Army officer trained to keep his poise under fire, stated that the explosion took place on a small horse-drawn truck and that only one other

---

5. Hockett, *Introduction to Research*, pp. 59–79 and Johnson, *Historian and Historical Evidence*, pp. 50–75 contain discussions of external criticism and cite salient examples.

vehicle, an automobile, was in sight. His testimony was subsequently proved to be correct.[6] If the eyewitnesses are good observers, theirs is the best, in fact the ultimate, testimony. Testimony of one reliable eyewitness is good, but the best evidence is the independent testimony of several eyewitnesses. But caution is needed here. Two eyewitnesses who tell exactly the same story have probably checked their stories and agreed on a common version. Honest, independent testimony from several eyewitnesses will normally contain several variations, variations which tend to indicate that the testimony is sincere and independent.

To pierce the "fog of war," for example, evidence must be carefully weighed. It is obvious that in the tension and confusion of battle the participants do not see, hear, or recollect with absolute clarity. Neither do they see from the same position or angle. Few men in battle have a clear conception of what is going on. Censorship may suppress facts, especially in news dispatches and communiques. Military reports submitted to higher headquarters are not always complete. Important facts may not be known at the time; errors and failures may be glossed over; rumors of dubious origin may spread rapidly and even find their way into the official reports.

Was the writer biased? Here, of course, the writer of any after action report or any other account of an organization's activities is automatically suspect. Even if there is no conscious bias or deliberate attempt to falsify, a certain amount of unconscious bias will manifest itself in any number of ways—playing down mistakes, exaggerating successes, or failing to give credit to others. Participants reporting on their own activities can normally be expected to exaggerate, consciously or unconsciously, their own roles, and in dealing with arguments or disputes to present their own points of view with more sympathy and understanding than those of opponents. Personal memoirs, even those based on diaries, are immediately doubted, for the temptations to justify oneself, to absolve oneself of blame, to claim credit, to get revenge for old scores, and to be wise after the event are all too strong.

To sum up, sound research is fundamental to good history, since history is useless unless it is based on fact. The major problem of historical research is that the historian can ascertain many facts only through the highly fallible testimony of other human beings, and that much, if not most, of this testimony is

---

6. Johnson, *Historian and Historical Evidence*, p. 24.

contained in documents that cannot be taken at face value. He must therefore subject each statement in such documents to critical analysis. In the process he applies rules of evidence, similar to those of a court of law, that are essentially a combination of skepticism and common sense. In this manner he rates his evidence in order of trustworthiness. At each step he puts questions to his evidence—to help answer the "how," "when," "where," and "why," and to arrive at conclusions. While this process may sound tedious and mechanical, actually it calls for imagination and boldness as well as caution and suspicion.[7]

With virtually all the material collected and evaluated, the historian reaches the climax of his critical examination—the careful analysis of the sifted data to determine its meaning and significance and to determine what new knowledge his end product will contribute. The meaning of the history and its contribution constitute its theme. No matter how arduous the research that went into gathering material, the author discards what is not relevant to his subject, determines which aspects of his subject are to be emphasized, and assigns proportionate space in his narrative. With these steps, the processes of research have been practically completed.

The culmination of the historian's work is the production of an accurate and readable account. The historian's efforts will be judged by the final product and his use of the three basic techniques reflected in it. If the historian in his research shows the spirit of the scientist, presenting a synthesis in interesting written form reveals him in the role of creative artist. The presentation represents a special art of its own.

The historian is of necessity an interpreter. Even if he knew all the facts, he could not present the total. He cannot completely reconstruct the past, and if he could the result would be unintelligible. The chances are that he will never have all the facts; documents do not normally reveal all, and if he is using oral testimony, he is dealing with fallible human memories. He therefore selects from the available evidence the facts to be presented. In the process of selecting, he interprets. How does he select? Carl Becker, a well-known American historian, aptly observed that the mark of a good historian is the questions he puts to the evidence. Those questions grow out of the individual historian's experience, reading, training, intellect, and wisdom. He will try to anticipate the questions of his readers and may well also ask what would be useful to the reader as a guide to

---

7. Kent R. Greenfield, "Historical Research: A Critical Approach" (lecture delivered at the Army War College, 4 October 1950).

thought or action about a particular happening. He designs his questions to elicit useful answers, and sometimes he will have to rephrase or narrow them in accord with the evidence available. Basically, in his selection and presentation the historian attempts to bring order out of chaos—to show relationships, emphasize important developments, and establish a pattern. Since the resultant picture can be too orderly and artificial—for example, a description of action on a battlefield—the reader must be aware and beware.

The reader must be aware, too, that it is not easy for the historian to free himself wholly from bias of one kind or another. Even Leopold von Ranke, the leading nineteenth-century German exponent of presenting history "as it really happened," unconsciously wrote from the standpoint of a contemporary conservative Prussian. All the histories of George Bancroft, a strong advocate of American democracy and nationalism, are said to have voted for Andrew Jackson. Difficult as it is for the historian to be completely impartial, his goal must still be the pursuit of truth. As Homer C. Hockett phrased it, "Even though he cannot hope to tell the whole truth he must strive to tell nothing but the truth."[8] He must not prejudge the evidence, and his conclusions should follow, not precede, his study of the evidence.

In presenting his written study, the historian puts it in such a form that the reader can readily see on what evidence he has based his statements of fact. Full and accurate documentation is the stamp of authenticity the scholar places on his work. The character of the sources will do much to establish the author's skill—or lack of it—in the evaluation of evidence and will also reveal to what extent the author has made use of sources previously available and has exploited sources not previously used. The sources utilized are revealed through the mechanics of footnoting that accompany statements in the text and in the bibliography at the back that groups the sources according to type. The reader should easily be able to distinguish between what is presented as fact and the author's own assumptions, opinions, and conclusions. As we have seen, no historian can entirely keep himself out of his history. Nor should he. But the pursuit of truth requires clear distinctions among fact, commentary, and conclusions.

In the final analysis, how wide an audience the study will have and how effective the study will be depend on the author's skill

---

8. Homer C. Hockett, *The Critical Method in Historical Research and Writing* (New York: Macmillan, 1955), p. 10.

in the use of language, the perfection of his style. The historian's style reinforces his interpretation in a presentation that develops according to a recognizable plan and presents its subjects—the answers to the questions the historian has raised—in a logical, coherent, and imaginative literary pattern. Master stylists of vigorous narrative and vivid descriptive power can make the reader feel he is present at great events. With Francis Parkman, he can accompany Braddock's army on its fateful march; with Samuel Eliot Morison, he can participate in a great naval engagement in the Pacific in World War II. In bringing his judgment, perspective, and literary skill to bear on his narrative, the historian adds a sense of style in the larger sense, a contribution to history as a creative art.

The Utility of History

With this background in the nature and methodology of the historical discipline, the reader at this point may well ask what is the use of history? What purposes does it serve? What can history do for the man of thought or action? Of what benefit is it to the average reader? Perhaps the simplest reason for studying history is that man cannot help being interested in his past. He is surrounded by history and is himself a part of it. Just as an individual draws upon recollections of his own past, his personal history, so a nation or race uses history as its collective recollections. The best an individual can do is to learn to choose between good and bad studies of the past in newspapers and novels as well as in more carefully assembled historical works. If the reader is at all intellectually curious about the legacy of the past, if he seeks knowledge for its own sake, history as man's memory can fulfill his quest. History may also be read for entertainment, and the tradition of history as the art of the storyteller is old; it is strongly reflected in the writing of its founding father, Herodotus. Indeed the current popularity of the historical novel and biography attests to the continuing market for interesting stories entertainingly presented. Some readers prefer history for the same reason that others choose detective stories—they simply enjoy it.

But history also serves other and more utilitarian purposes. The study of history is a form of vicarious experience, of learning from the experience of others. "It provides us with the opportunity to profit by the stumbles and tumbles of our forerunners," wrote the British military theorist and historian, Sir Basil Liddell Hart.[9] To study the past in order to understand the present and obtain guidance for the future also has a long and continuing tradition in historical writing. With Thucydides, called "the first truly critical historian." Clio, the Muse of History, began to change from storyteller to instructor. Whereas Herodotus wrote his *History of the Persian Wars* in "the hope of thereby preserving from decay the remembrance of what men have done," Thucydides stressed history as a form of didactic literature, and he wrote his *History of the Peloponnesian War* for those "who desire an exact knowledge of the past as an aid to the interpretation of the future."[10] While Herodotus was particularly interested in causes, Thucydides was especially concerned with lessons.

Some cautions are necessary to bear in mind about history in its utilitarian role. From what has been said about its nature and methodology it is evident that history is not and cannot be an exact science. It is a science only in the sense of being a search for the truth. As an effort to establish natural laws, science is based on two assumptions: that the phenomena concerned are recurrent and identical in each occurrence, and that the exact antecedents of each recurrence can be established and the relationship of cause and effect between natural events can therefore be formulated. Since the chemist or physicist can, by controlled experiments, produce this recurrence under identical conditions, he can predict further recurrence. But cause and effect in human relationships cannot be exactly established. It is not possible to discover all the factors bearing on any event in human history; documents seldom yield complete or precise knowledge of them. Nor do the factors ever reappear in exactly the same combination. In other words, while historians may repeat each other, history never completely repeats itself. For this reason the writing of history is essentially an art. Written history cannot offer a perfect reconstruction of the past of mankind. No two situations are precisely alike, and there is danger as well as value in historical parallels. When one relies on a historical parallel without appreciating all the variations in past and present situations, he does so at his own peril. Suspicious as he is of historical analogies, the historian is apt to be wary of drawing precise or specific lessons from the past.

Nevertheless, studying results of the historian's art is of immense value. By pondering the experience and precedents of the past, by studying methods that have worked well and those

9. *Why Don't We Learn from History?* (London: George Allen & Unwin, 1946), p. 16.

10. Quoted in Louis Gottschalk, *Understanding History* (New York: A. A. Knopf, 1956), pp. 212–13; and Peter Gay and Gerald J. Cavanaugh, eds., *Historians at Work* (New York: Harper and Row, 1972): 1:1, 55.

that have worked badly in known situations, wisdom can be acquired. Although study of the past cannot produce precise directions for the future or a capacity to prophesy, it can broaden human understanding and furnish a breadth of alternatives. Of course, even the broadest knowledge of history will not provide all the answers to the problems of today and tomorrow, but study of the past is man's best path to a better understanding of the present and to some surer guide to the future. It is perhaps clearest in telling him what not to do.

What about the charges that in this swiftly changing world the past is no longer relevant? that history no longer is important? and why identify with the past at all? Why not start afresh and look ahead to some brave new world freed of the baggage of the past? Perhaps the best answer is that to change human affairs one must first understand their present state and how they reached this point. We cannot constructively move forward unless we know where we have been. Without the past, in other words, there is no standard to judge one's contribution to the present and the future.

Devotees of history continue to stress its general value as part of the broad cultural background of a cultivated mind, the mark of an educated man, an asset in communication among professions. But the reader must also be aware that history has at times bent to serve special utilitarian purposes and interests and at times been perverted to propaganda. History may be taught or written to inspire patriotism, a love of country, and respect for its heroes. It may also be presented in such a way as to inspire hatred of other lands and peoples. It may be used or abused—as in Germany under Hitler and Italy under Mussolini—to win support for a political regime. It has been employed to glorify a particular race, religion, economic system, or creed. In Communist countries, where an official meaning is put on the past, it has been enlisted to promote the belief that their peoples are riding the steamroller of history. But these are examples of the history of special pleading.

The way people look at history immensely affects their whole idea system and often determines it. And sometimes judgments are made in ignorance. For instance, students may regard the great American entrepreneurs of the last half of the nineteenth century—Vanderbilt, Carnegie, and others—as vastly talented men who brought the benefits of the industrial revolution to the people or as "robber barons" who seized industrial empires for their own advantage. Either judgment can influence their view of present-day capitalism.

History in its many capacities and at its best remains useful and valuable in diverse ways. Every generation looks to the past for inspiration, wisdom, knowledge, antecedents and precedents, and a source of ideas in meeting its own problems. In its capacity as a tool of research, history has been used not only by historians to study the record of man's past but also by other disciplines as an aid in their research, by political scientists and psychologists for example. As a laboratory of experience, history represents a broad foundation which can be drawn upon not only by other social sciences but also for individual education and training in the practice of an art or profession, as in the case of the military for whom vicarious experience is important. The study of history develops a sense of perspective, of the continuities and discontinuities, and of time in human affairs. A. L. Rowse has put it well: "Not to have a sense of time is like having no ear or sense of beauty—it is to be bereft of a faculty."[11]

To those who cultivate it, history offers pleasures as well as a broadening of intellectual horizons, an appreciation of other peoples' cultures as well as one's own. Much can be learned from defeats and mistakes in national history—as much, if not more, as from successes. The phenomenon of cultural lag, of continuing established ways long after the reasons for doing so have vanished, has appeared again and again in history—often leading to defeat in war. We ignore our past and other peoples' past at our peril.

Changing Fashions in Historical Interpretation

Underlying the historian's never-ending quest to understand and explain the past, to make it more relevant and useful, is the question of interpretation. The search over the centuries for the key to unlock the past, to discover the most penetrating syntheses and meanings in the human story, has given rise to a number of diverse and often conflicting theories of historical interpretation. To understand that story historians have viewed the past through different spectacles—through different approaches to the selection and emphasis among facts and the causes of change. While they agree on the general importance of history, they have disagreed and continue to disagree on which

---

11. A. L. Rowse, *The Use of History* (New York: Collier Books, 1963), p. 127.

approach is the most useful and valuable. Since each historian cannot entirely escape the influences of the period in which he lives, even if he wished to do so, the changing fashions in theory usually reflect the needs and values of the age in which they were produced.

Volumes have been written on philosophies and theories of history. Some ages have stressed theological interpretations. Indeed, history as the gradual unfolding of a divine plan has had a strong influence not only in the ancient and medieval worlds but in colonial America as well, where the early historians saw divine providence at work in the happenings in the "New Canaan." The Enlightenment of the eighteenth century, usually identified as the beginning of modern history, introduced new approaches. Freeing history from theology, the Enlightenment encouraged the pursuit of knowledge for its own sake and nourished the critical spirit in the use of historical sources.

Building on such bases, modern historical theory emerged in the nineteenth century in a number of distinct forms. One may be termed the "great hero" theory—that the most fruitful approach to history is through studying the lives of the great men of the past. But the question whether men make history or history makes men has long been disputed, and before the century was over the "great hero" theory was seriously challenged. Some scholars believe that the "movers and shakers," for example statesmen and generals, are simply products of their times and that their activities are conditioned by the times. Others would argue that great men can influence their times within limits and that the human story is one of interaction between the leaders and their times. They would hold that leaders are sometimes compelled to act the way they do as a result of social and economic factors, but at times they can influence and thereby affect the course of history and that both approaches are valuable.

The search in the nineteenth century for the key principles of historical change led one influential German philosopher to stress the importance of ideas, another of economics. To Georg W. F. Hegel each era was dominated by a specific idea, and the human struggle in each epoch constituted a contest between the idea and its counteraction. The importance of the idea, emphasized by the Hegelian school, came to dominate American historiography in the latter part of the nineteenth century, and the interpretations of history resting on divine intervention and the great hero took second place. Under such influence the ideas of freedom, democracy, and the Union are advanced as the touchstones of American progress.

But to Karl Marx, the German exponent of a materialistic interpretation, who bent Hegel's system to his own purposes, the path to understanding any historical era was the study of its methods of producing and exchanging goods and of the struggle between ruling and oppressed classes. Marx, it has been pointed out, invented neither the economic nor the class interpretation of history but he infused the theory with system and a crusading spirit. The Marxian stress on the inevitability of the historical process—the class struggle, the triumph of the proletariat, and the eventual emergence of a Utopian state—in which Communist doctrine is rooted has led modern Communists to regard history as the center of all the sciences.

In contrast to the Marxian interpretation, the approach to history in the West has remained pluralistic and essentially open-ended. While few American historians adopted a doctrinaire Marxian approach, scholars were influenced to pay more attentioon to economic factors. Charles A. Beard, author of *An Economic Interpretation of the Constitution* (1913), led a host of American historians who focused on economic interest as a central force in shaping political and social change, and many publications have appeared that interpret various phases of American history from an economic standpoint.

Less influential on American historiography to date have been the European theorists, such as Arnold J. Toynbee and Oswald Spengler in the twentieth century, who from time to time have attempted to explain the rise and fall of civilizations. More typical and influential have been the interpretations by American scholars based on specific principles or theses applicable to American circumstances. Two or the most notable have been Frederick Jackson Turner's thesis and Alfred Thayer Mahan's doctrine of sea power. In his provocative essay, "The Significance of the Frontier in American History," presented in 1893, Turner put forth his concept that the westward movement gave American democracy its distinctive characteristics and that the disappearance of the area of free land by 1890 marked the close of an era in American history. While Turner stressed domestic factors to explain American development, Admiral Mahan in his *The Influence of Sea Power upon History, 1660-1783* (1890) and *The Influence of Sea Power upon the French Revolution and Empire, 1793-1812* (1892) put forth his thesis of the role of sea power in determining the destiny of modern nations. Drawing lessons from his studies of naval history, the apostle of sea power called upon the United States to "look outward" and fulfill its mission as a rising world power. As new interests and findings on the American scene

have appeared, the search for special theses or integrating
principles on other fronts has continued in American historiography.

Two schools revolving around opposite views of objectivity in
historical writing deserve special notice. One, the school of
"scientific history" that took Ranke as its hero, argued that
objectivity was an attainable ideal. The accumulation of facts
systematically and objectively set forth in monographs, studies
on particular subjects, would provide the ultimate reality. The
historian should therefore concentrate on collecting and verify-
ing the facts. When properly arranged, the facts would in effect
interpret themselves. Using Ranke's guideline of telling the story
as it really happened, history purported to be scientific and
shared the heady state of science in the last quarter of the
nineteenth century. The establishment of the first seminars in
American universities for training American historians in
stricter canons of historical scholarship arose out of this German
influence. But this school came under increasing fire in the early
twentieth century in Europe and the United States. In the United
States the attack was led by the proponents of the "New
History," who argued that the historian neither could nor should
be objective and that history should serve current interests of
society and be in accord with the historian's own values. The
leading exponent of this approach, James Harvey Robinson,
incorporated his views in The New History (1912). A collabora-
tor with Charles Beard in producing pioneering, broad-ranging
texts in European history covering economic, cultural, and
political affairs, he was influential in persuading teachers of
history to give more attention to contemporary problems. Thus,
the "New History" school opened the door for history and
historians to serve current political ends.

Reinforcement of the attack on "scientific" history came from
the doctrine of "historical relativism" which shared some
elements in common with the "New History." Carl L. Becker, a
contemporary and friend of leading historians of the "New
School" but less convinced than they of the utility of history as a
direct instrument of social change, set forth the case for
"historical relativism" in his presidential address, "Everyman
His Own Historian," before the American Historical Association
in December 1931. Sensitive to the limits of historical knowledge, he argued that historical facts cannot speak for themselves;
that the historian must select and interpret facts, and that the
principles he employs in the process reflect the values and

interests of his own society. "If the essense of history is the memory of things said and done," he contended, "then it is obvious that every normal person, Mr. Everyman, knows some history." As Becker portrayed it, the remembered past is essentially living history. "Being neither omniscient nor omnipresent," he went on, "the historian is not the same person always and everywhere; and for him, as for Mr. Everyman, the form and significance of remembered events, like the extension and velocity of physical objects, will vary with the time and place of the observer."[12]

Like Becker, most American historians today would not subscribe to the idea that history should be deliberately enlisted as an instrument of social change. Certainly historians disagree on the direction social change should take and even the "New History" leaders did not act consistently in practice on the basis of this principle. Most historians today accept the idea that a balance must be struck between history as a carefully researched body of facts and history as an exercise in interpretation. They would agree that interpretation is necessary and inevitable but that objectivity, even if not completely attainable, must remain the goal. They tend to avoid dogmatic theories but to look for insights and hypotheses from whatever quarter to shed light on the facts they gather. Suspicious of neat and easy generalizations or explanations resting on a single cause, they subscribe to multiple causation, a pluralistic approach, to interpret the great changes in man's past.

On the basis of past changes in historical fashions, the rise and fall of successive theories of interpretation, we may be certain that history in the twenty-first century will be written differently from the way it is done today. The changing fashions have come not only in response to new research and findings and new weapons in the historian's arsenal but also to new needs. Each generation rewrites history in terms of its problems, interests, and tastes. It holds up a new mirror to the past it cannot completely recover or, to change the figure, refocuses its lens. The discipline has responded to every great current of ideas in the Western world since its emergence in modern dress in the eighteenth century—to science, evolution, democracy, nationalism, sociology, psychology, and so forth. The contents, as well as the techniques and interpretations, of history reflect the

---

12. Carl L. Becker, *Everyman His Own Historian* (New York: F. S. Crofts and Co., 1935), pp. 235-36, 251-52.

changing influences from generation to generation. Modern history began with a focus largely on politics and war, with kings and their conquests. In recent years there has been more and more interest in economic, social, and cultural matters. New fields of interest have arisen and the older fields have been broadened and enriched. The varieties of history are greater than ever. Political history, religious history, military history, and biographical history exist side by side with social history, intellectual history (sometimes called the history of ideas or cultural history), and economic history and its more specialized forms, labor and business history. There is more interest than ever in contemporary history, the study of the recent past, in comparative history, ethnic history, and urban history. With their connections with other social sciences stronger than ever, the practitioners are adapting interdisciplinary approaches and sociological, psychological, and quantitative techniques to older as well as newer forms of history.

The legacy of ferment left from older debates in historical interpretation continues in the newer guises, particularly over trends in recent history. Thus a dispute rages between those who accept conventional or official interpretations for the outbreak of World War I, World War II, and the Cold War and those who adopt revisionist views, and between those who would emphasize "consensus" in modern history and those who would stress "conflict." Regardless of the outcome of current debates among scholars, we may be sure that the same phenomena looked at from different points of view, in the future as in the past, will produce different interpretations.

The awesome problems of the current dynamic age in the wake of two destructive world conflicts, the spread of nuclear weapons and revolutionary warfare, and doubt raised about the future of mankind have set historians once more to reexamine the past in search of wisdom, understanding, and guidance. That search would appear to underscore H. G. Wells' characterization of history as "more and more a race between education and catastrophe." Once more the inseparability of the past from the present is being demonstrated. Inevitably the turmoil of the twentieth century and the anxiety over national security and survival have led historians to take a fresh look at the military factor, as well as the relations between military affairs and society, in man's past. And the same broadening, deepening, and cross-fertilization in technique, content, and interpretation apparent in other fields of history in this century are increasingly reflected in the area that lies on the frontier between general history and military art and science, the field of military history, to which we now turn.

Bibliography

Barzun, Jacques, and Graff, Henry. The Modern Researcher. New York: Harcourt, Brace and World, 1957.

Becker, Carl L. Everyman His Own Historian. New York: F. S. Crofts, 1935.

Bloch, Marc. The Historian's Craft. New York: A. A. Knopf, 1964.

Carr, Edward H. What is History? New York: A. A. Knopf, 1962.

Cochran, Thomas C. The Inner Revolution: Essays on the Social Sciences in History. New York: Harper and Row, 1964.

Croce, Benedetto. History: Its Theory and Practice. New York: Russell and Russell, 1960.

Freidel, Frank, ed. Harvard Guide to American History. Rev. ed., 2 vols. Cambridge, Mass.: Harvard Univ. Press, Belknap Press, 1974.

Garraty, John A. Interpreting American History: Conversations with Historians. New York: Macmillan, 1970.

——. The Nature of Biography. New York: A. A. Knopf, 1957.

Gay, Peter, and Cavanaugh, Gerald J., eds. Historians at Work, Vol. 1. New York: Harper and Row, 1972.

Gottschalk, Louis. Understanding History. New York: A. A. Knopf, 1956.

Gottschalk, Louis, ed. Generalization in the Writing of History. Chicago: Univ. of Chicago Press, 1963.

Gray, Wood. Historian's Handbook. 2d ed. Boston: Houghton Mifflin, 1964.

Hexter, Jack H. Reappraisals in History. Evanston, Ill.: Northwestern Univ. Press, 1961.

Higham, John; with Krieger, Leonard; and Gilbert, Felix. History. Englewood Cliffs, N.J.: Prentice-Hall, 1965.

Hockett, Homer C. The Critical Method in Historical Research and Writing. New York: Macmillan, 1955.

——. Introduction to Research in American History. 2d ed. New York: Macmillan, 1948.

Hofstadter, Richard. The Progressive Historians: Turner, Beard, Parrington. New York: A. A. Knopf, 1969.

Johnson, Allen. The Historian and Historical Evidence. New York: Scribner's, 1926.

Kent, Sherman. Writing History. 2d ed. New York: Appleton-Century-Crofts, 1967.

Kraus, Michael. The Writing of American History. Norman: Univ. of Oklahoma Press, 1953.

Langlois, Charles V., and Seignobos, Charles. Introduction to the Study of History. Translated by G. G. Berry. New York: Barnes and Noble, 1966.

Liddell Hart, B. H. Why Don't We Learn From History? London: George Allen and Unwin, 1946.

Meyerhoff, Hans. ed. The Philosophy of History in Our Time. Garden City, N.Y.: Doubleday, 1959.

Morison, Samuel E. "History as a Literary Art." In By Land and by Sea: Essays and Addresses by Samuel Eliot Morison. New York: A. A. Knopf, 1954.

Nevins, Allan. The Gateway to History. Rev. ed. Garden City, N.Y.: Doubleday, 1962.

Robinson, James Harvey. *The New History*. New York: Macmillan, 1912.

Rowse, A. L. *The Use of History*. New York: Collier Books, 1963.

Rundell, Walter, Jr. *In Pursuit of American History*. Norman: Univ. of Okla. Press, 1970.

Saveth, Edward N. *Understanding the American Past*. Boston: Little, Brown, 1954.

Saveth, Edward N., ed. *American History and the Social Sciences*. New York: Free Press, 1964.

Stern, Fritz. *The Varieties of History*. New York: Meridian Books, 1957.

Chapter 2

A Perspective on Military History

Col. Thomas E. Griess

NOT infrequently critics charge that history is of marginal value because it has little relevance to the present. They argue that the living present, not the dead past, is important and demands attention. This claim is usually based upon a dangerously narrow and unbalanced view of the present and ignores the everyday use people make of the past. We cannot escape history because the present is an extension of historical events that in some instances are still running their course. Most current problems originated in the past, and the forces working upon contemporary society are better understood by knowing something of the historical roots of those forces. People cannot avoid making judgments or taking sides on controversial issues indefinitely; neither bland, uninformed compromise nor allegedly sophisticated skepticism are suitable substitutes for a knowledge of the past which will assist them in criticizing and reevaluating their assumptions and judgments. Convictions, values, and standards accumulate over time; one generation modifies those passed on by a previous generation, but it also builds upon the earlier standards and passes on to the next generation a changed but still historically growing body of conclusions. Not a few presidents have placed high value on reading and knowing history, and the shelves in bookstores and libraries continue to grow with new works on all types of history. The public demand, at least, does not seem to sustain the pessimistic claim about irrelevance.

Like the general discipline, military history also has its critics and its advocates, as well as a substantial appeal to both civilian and military audiences. The fraternity of scholars has traditionally shown some skepticism toward military history, despite rejoinders from distinguished advocates. That attitude has stemmed from at least two causes. First, hating the futility of

Colonel Griess (Ph.D., Duke), head of the Department of History at the U.S. Military Academy since 1969, is preparing biographies of Dennis Hart Mahan and General Jacob L. Devers.

war, historians have dwelt largely on cause and effect and have shown minimal concern for how war has historically become institutionalized. Second, they have rebelled against the utilitarian aspects of operational military history. Until very recently in America, these two considerations have influenced most writers of general history against incorporating, or at least recognizing, military history as an important element in the broader narratives. Charles Francis Adams recognized this feeling when he advocated higher esteem for military history at the 1899 meeting of the American Historical Association and urged general historians to encourage the writing of factual military history and to rely upon, even incorporate, it in their works.

Indeed, the aggressive, combative nature of man and the historical resort to force by nations has made the study of war inevitable. Sir Charles Oman argued that "one may dislike war just as one dislikes disease; but to decry the necessity for studying it . . . is no less absurd than it would be to minimize the need for medical investigation because one disliked cancer or tuberculosis." Similarly, Cyril Falls later took up the cudgel for studying military history as opposed to studying primarily the laborer, the peasant, or the ruler:[1]

> What I want to urge is that all men, common and uncommon, great and small . . . have been profoundly and unceasingly influenced by war. Our literature, our art and our architecture are stamped with the vestiges of war. Our very language has a thousand bellicose words and phrases woven into its fabric. And our material destinies, our social life and habits, our industry and trade, have assumed their present forms and characteristics largely as the result of war. . . . We are, all of us, indeed, the heirs of many wars.

Thus it has been throughout most of history. Men, sometimes participants, have always written about war in one form or another. The thoughtful professional soldier is well advised to consider what military history encompasses, to appreciate how it properly must remain part of the overall discipline of history, and to understand how study of the subject can be personally meaningful. Frank Craven made the point clearly in 1959:

> Let it be admitted that the modern technological revolution has confronted us with military problems of unprecedented complexity, problems made all the more difficult because of the social and political turbulence of the age in which we live. But precisely because of these

---

1. Sir Charles Oman, *Studies in the Napoleonic Wars* (London: Meuthen, 1930), p. 24. Cyril Falls, *The Place of War in History* (London: Oxford Univ. Press, 1947), p. 7.

revolutionary developments, let me suggest that you had better study military history, indeed all history, as no generation of military men have studied it before.[2]

The Scope of Military History

Not until the early 1800s did military history become a special field apart from general history. Jomini, the nineteenth century Swiss theorist, recognized three kinds of military history. The first he categorized as the pure version—the recounting in minute and pedantic terms of all aspects of a given battle, including such details as hourly locations of small units. This recounting was done without much concern for useful analysis. The second form, he said, used a campaign or battle to examine the principles of waging war; it analyzed the relationship between events and principles, and, applied in broad context, could reveal something of the evolution of the art of war. Jomini's third category was political-military history—the examination of war in its broadest spectrum through association of military with political, social, and economic factors.

While Jomini was thinking and writing essentially about military strategy, the great Prussian military thinker, Karl von Clausewitz, was studying the entire problem of war. Seeking to develop a theory of war, Clausewitz considered and wrote (*On War*) about the basic aspects of conflict between nations. In so doing, he was producing military history which can properly be classified under Jomini's third category. At the same time, he devoted considerable coverage to an examination of principles and generalship through the device of rigorous analysis and criticism. (See Chapter 4.)

Although the study of military history in terms of Jomini's second category (analysis of principles) can benefit the soldier, this approach also has its shortcomings, particularly in more modern times. In the first place, considered from the larger view of war as organized international violence, such analysis is most meaningful if the contest on the battlefield is decisive and overriding in the conflict. For a time in history this was often the case. But once industrialization and war were linked, the battlefield leader found it difficult to bring about the overwhelmingly decisive engagement.[3] Second, this analytically

---

2. W. Frank Craven, *Why Military History?* Harmon Memorial Lecture no. 1 (USAFA, Colorado, 1959), p. 11.

3. Michael Howard, "The Demand for Military History," *Times Literary Supplement*, 13 Nov. 1969, p. 1294.

operational view of military history slights the important institutional developments that take place within an army and the important roles they play during times of peace or prolonged periods of international tension.

Probably for this second reason, about the turn of the twentieth century a few individuals in some European countries expressed interest in a broader view of military history. In a laborious dialectical examination of the term in a 1914 lecture at Cambridge, Sir John W. Fortescue finally concluded that military history "is the history of the external police of communities and nations."[4] Across the North Sea in Germany, Hans Delbrück was questioning the approach of the General Staff which prized and exploited military history as operational history, useful for its examinations of principles and strategy. Delbrück was interested in operations, but his interest was more in general ideas and tendencies than in minute detail or practical principles. He wanted his history of the art of war to analyze the subject within the broader framework of political history. In France during this period, Jean Jaurès, the prominent socialist political leader and theoretician, was articulating the theory that military endeavors could be successful only when military institution's accurately reflected the composition and aspirations of the entire nation.

After World War I, the Russian military theorist, M. V. Frunze, following Marx and Lenin in their acceptance of Clausewitz's dictum that war was an extension of politics, reflected on his nation's experiences and accepted Jaurès's theories as the foundation of a much broader definition of military history. Frunze noted that the actions of persons actually under arms could not be understood without considering the entire social context within which those actions took place. In a number of writings, Lenin denied the purely military character of the First World War, stating in one instance that "appearance is not reality. The more dominated by military factors a war may seem to be, the more political is its actual nature, and this applies equally in reverse."[5] While Stalin attempted to refute Clausewitz in the anti-German atmosphere in the Soviet Union at the end of World War II, he did so only to the extent of abandoning the outdated technical aspects of Clausewitz's theses. To this day, the theory of the interrelationship of military activity and national activity is woven into the fabric of the Soviet approach to military history.

---

4. J. W. Fortescue, *Military History* (Cambridge, 1914), p. 9.

5. V. I. Lenin, quoted in Werner Hahlweg, "Clausewitz, Lenin, and Communist Military Attitudes Today," *Journal of the Royal United Service Institution* 105 (1960):224.

Until World War II most U.S. Army officers thought of military history as being the systematic analysis of how the military forces of a country waged war. As late as the 1940s, for example, Matthew Steele's *American Campaigns*, written expressly for the purpose of analyzing campaigns and battles, was used in Army schools. And in 1937 a Fort Benning reference text termed military history "the professional analysis of events and operations" and envisioned it as being the "laboratory phase of military science." In short, the Infantry School considered military history of most value when it was used to provide historical documentation to support military doctrine. This application of military history bore a striking similarity to ideas advanced in England a decade earlier by J.F.C. Fuller in a seminal work that advocated developing a science of war in order to understand and apply better the art of war.[6]

By the turn of the century, nonetheless, some slight interest in turning military history to broader themes of national policy and strategy had developed in America. This current, somewhat akin to the work of Clausewitz, was characterized by Walter Millis as "the literature of popular education for publics and politicians in strategy, in military policy and in the theory of war."[7] It is best exemplified by Emory Upton's *The Military Policy of the United States Since 1775* (1904) and Alfred Thayer Mahan's *The Influence of Sea Power on History, 1660-1773* (1890). Both authors used military history in an attempt to influence national military policy; at the same time, in other works, both men also wrote military history of the technical variety in an attempt to analyze principles or professional institutions.

Following World War II and the Korean War, a note of despondency concerning the relevance of military history began to be heard. This discouragement, largely voiced by civilian critics, was rooted in the belief that military history, though broadened somewhat, was still too technical and utilitarian in purpose and that if it was to be of more than antiquarian interest it had to become a broad study of war itself. J.F.C. Fuller, the outspoken, earlier advocate of considering war and peace as related phenomena in an inevitable cycle, claimed that since war had become policy itself it had to be studied to "regulate human affairs." Walter Millis went further and argued that nuclear

---

6. *Military History: Methods of Research*, Infantry School Reference Text no. 25 (Fort Benning, Ga. [1937]), pp. 3-4. J.F.C. Fuller, *The Foundations of the Science of War* (London: Hutchison, 1926), pp. 19-24.

7. Walter Millis, *Military History* (Washington: Service Center for Teachers of History, 1961), p. 9. Millis identified three main streams of American military literature historically. The other two were "the literature of recall" and "the literature of technical education for the soldier."

weapons made most of the traditional materials of operational military history inapplicable. Concluding that a nation's use of war as an instrument, now, more then ever, encompassed every aspect of its social, political, and economic order, as well as the purely military factor, he questioned whether a modern commander might not find the study of past generalship actually deleterious. In his view, only if one studied war in its broadest terms—that is, made it less military and more civilian—would the exercise prove useful. Although agreeing that the relationship of war to society was important, Cyril Falls took issue with Millis and perspicaciously observed that "small wars without nuclear weapons have not been avoided and remain a possibility."[8] Falls might have added that from another viewpoint nuclear weapons required formulation of a new doctrine which could only be illuminated, not retarded, by the experience of earlier thinkers who had also grappled with revolutionary weapons. Or, if awesome new weapons now exist, the human being has not changed much and the basic requirements for thoughtful leadership remain and are intensified.

Discussion over the nature of military history has been influenced to some degree by contemporary interpretations of the war in Vietnam. In a thoughtful critique of 1971 on the state of military history, Peter Paret noted that much work was being devoted to civilian rather than military aspects and that too few historians were "interested in war and in military institutions for their own sake."[9] Despite the assumed irrelevance of the subject, the continuing discussion has stimulated an apparently greater interest among civilian scholars in teaching military history in the universities. Paradoxically, the rising civilian interest came at a time when the trend within the Army was toward minimizing military history in its own school system, a trend only partially reversed as a result of an ad hoc committee study in 1971. (See Chapters 17 and 23.) Revived interest has generally involved studying war and its institutions in a broad context, although more meaningful and sophisticated approaches to operational military history are being devised as well. As war has become more industrialized and all-consuming, military historians are broadening their approach to studying and writing about it. The Army's present concept of what comprises military history reflects these shifting tides of opinion.

---

8. J. F. C. Fuller, *A Military History of the Western World* (New York: Funk and Wagnalls, 1954) 1:xi; Fuller, *Decisive Battles of the U.S.A.* (New York: Harper, 1953), p. viii. Millis, *Military History*, pp. 15–18. Cyril Falls, *The Art of War* (New York: Oxford Univ. Press, 1961), pp. 5–6.

9. Peter Paret, "The History of War," *Daedalus* 100, no. 1 (Spring 1971):381–86.

The Army has officially defined military history as an objective, accurate, descriptive, and interpretive record of all activities of the Armed Forces in peace and war. Expressed another way, military history is concerned with how nations prepare for war, how they wage and terminate wars, how preparing for and fighting wars influences society, and how nations assign and regulate the peacetime functions of armed forces. Because historians and readers alike often refer to types of military history, one might offer the following useful categories:

Operational: combat or military aspects; encompasses logistics, tactics, military strategy and leadership; includes campaign studies and operationally oriented biography.

Administrative and Technical: generally functional and professional activities of armed forces; includes studies of doctrine and organizational structure, procurement and training of manpower, and weapons developments; involves both peacetime and wartime developments.

The Military and Society: in an historical sense, considers the entire spectrum of military affairs throughout the cycle of war and peace; deals with national strategy and encompasses the relationship among the military, social, political, economic, and psychological elements at the national level; deals with institutional problems, solutions, and developments; explores the relationship between civil and military authority.

These categories are not mutually exclusive, and they are conceptual in nature rather than exact definitions. Because they are intentionally broad, a given work on military history usually will deal in some degree with each category, although it may emphasize one.

The Value of Military History

Soldiers have traditionally attached utilitarian value to the study of military history while scholars have been more attracted by the educational value of the subject. It actually contributes in both ways to the development of the professional officer, and the discussion that follows deals with both of them. If sharpened judgment, improved perception, and a broadened perspective are valuable to anyone, they are crucially important to soldiers who may be vitally concerned with problems of national importance and who, throughout their lives, deal with the capabilities and limitations of men and women.

Studying military history can also help compensate for deficiencies in individual experience. Soldiers may serve only two or three years in a combat zone during their professional careers. Somehow, they must prepare themselves for waging war without the benefit of much practice. It is almost as if a doctor faced a crucial operation after nothing but medical school observation and practice on animals. Although what one learns from military history will not displace what one has already learned from experience, it will illuminate what is important in that experience. Careful and critical reading of military history permits analyses of operations conducted under varying conditions and broadens and deepens understanding. Moreover, as one continues reading over a period of years, he or she will develop a critical faculty in assimilating material and integrating it with experience. Ultimately, the soldier will sift out those ideas, conceptions, or principles that have gradually come to be most valuable in a personal sense. It is not an exaggeration to claim that individuals who know what was attempted in the past, the conditions under which it was attempted, and what results followed, are less likely to grope haltingly when faced with their own immediate problems. As Ardant du Picq concluded from his studies of battlefield conduct, "whoever has seen, turns to a method based on his own knowledge, his personal experience as a soldier. But experience is long and life is short. The experiences of each cannot therefore be completed except by those of others."[10]

Military history offers soldiers an opportunity to improve their professional qualifications. Indeed, in a world growing ever more complex and in a society which increasingly questions old methods and values, soldiers must study their profession continuously if they expect to meet the challenges which the unlimited liability clause in battle may pose at any time. No one field of study will guarantee success on the battlefield, but lacking actual experience in combat the thoughtful soldier will do well to turn to the study of past wars. And even combat experience unaccompanied by professional study and reflection may not stimulate professional growth. (Frederick the Great characterized some men as having little more imagination than the mule which campaigned with Prince Eugene in the eighteenth century.) Among 4,000 Army officers of all grades surveyed in 1971, two out of three indicated that the study of military history had been professionally beneficial. According to these officers,

---

10. Ardant du Picq, *Battle Studies*, trans. John N. Greely and Robert C. Cotton (Harrisburg: Military Service Publishing Company, 1947), p. 8.

whose appreciation increased with military rank, the principal benefits are insight gained from studying problems which illuminate contemporary difficulties and perception gained from studying military success and failure.[11]

A caveat is necessary, however. History provides no clear cut lessons for the reader. Situations in history may resemble contemporary ones, but they are never exactly alike, and it is a foolish person who tries blindly to apply a purely historical solution to a contemporary problem. Wars resemble each other more than they resemble other human activities, but similarities between wars can be exaggerated. As Michael Howard warned,

> the differences brought about between one war and another by social or technological changes are immense, and an unintelligent study of military history which does not take adequate account of these changes may quite easily be more dangerous than no study at all. Like the statesman, the soldier has to steer between the dangers of repeating the errors of the past because he is ignorant that they have been made, and of remaining bound by theories deduced from past history although changes in conditions have rendered these theories obsolete.[12]

Carefully grounded in military history, the soldier can nevertheless develop useful theories, ideas, and interpretations about the practice of the military profession. This is the immensely stimulating and educational role of the critic, a role in which one explores and tests alternative solutions to a given problem. The person who attempts this exercise will need to know military history well since it will form the base of the criticism, whether the problem is strategic, tactical, logistical, or social. A knowledge of philosophy, political science, and sociology will also be useful to complement the historical base. And our critic will still need much patience, analytical skill, honesty, and objectivity. Such qualifications, exploited by individual brilliance and dedication, produced a Clausewitz. And this type of critical inquiry led Liddell Hart to discover and advocate his "indirect approach." Here we have an example of how military history studied in depth and involving careful research can provide the basis of a doctrinal idea. After considerable study, Liddell Hart wrote Strategy, which was a form of special pleading for the theory of the indirect approach,

11. Ad Hoc Committee, Department of the Army, "Report on the Army Need for the Study of Military History" (West Point, N.Y., 1971), vol. IV.

12. Michael Howard, "The Use and Abuse of Military History," Journal of the Royal United Service Institution 107 (1962):7.

using selected examples to support that theory which earlier research had assured him was universally valid.[13]

But conceptions based upon historical experience do not necessarily guarantee success in the field. A careful study of history will illustrate that principles are not immutable rules which the commander is forbidden to violate. Nor should a theory be based on historical examples arbitrarily selected to support an unfounded preconception. What is necessary is rigorous testing and honest, thorough research. If an historically based principle is fallible, however, it is infinitely better than pure theory ungrounded on historical experience. The French strategic paralysis in 1940, for example, resulted at least as much from faulty, highly theoretical thinking as from lack of resources.

The study of military history, particularly of the operational variety, can inspire many men and women. Because of the tendency to magnify the obstacles and hardships of warfare, soldiers may adjust more quickly to combat if they know that others have overcome similar or worse conditions. Accuracy of depiction is important, however, for inspiration can turn to disillusion if the history is distorted or propagandist. Overly didactic unit histories may paint war romantically and the deeds of the unit in terms more mythical than realistic. When the young soldier of the unit then first experiences war he may find the shock completely demoralizing. And if military history is exploited too often to stimulate a superficial patriotism, it can produce cynicism among throughtful persons.

Historically, pride of profession has been a necessary and foremost characteristic of the soldier. A wide and critical reading of military history can help the soldier define and appreciate the meaning of professionalism. Personal understanding will be shaped by learning what others have used as yardsticks in the past. Broad study and careful reflection on earlier views will also encourage analysis of the military ethic which can stimulate useful discussion of that ethic with others who may be less well informed. What obligations does professionalism require? How do the demands of war determine the nature of military professionalism? How does one educate oneself for the grave responsibilities of leadership on the battlefield? History can help provide answers to these questions.

Professionalism also nurtures the ability to reach conclusions

---

13. Support for this interpretation appears in Jay Luvaas, *The Education of an Army* (Chicago: Univ. of Chicago Press, 1964).

by combining recognition of a sense of duty with a scientific commitment to the determination of cause and effect. Studied in depth, military history can contribute to learning this approach to a problem. The scientist works with matter, energy, and natural laws, but the soldier in addition works with the most unpredictable material of all—human beings. The leader's mental attitude, or professional frame of mind, must accordingly be both tough and compassionate. Studying military history can help one gauge human capabilities and limitations while offering guidelines on how to make the best use of both. It may also help some soldiers learn how to lead faltering human beings to accomplishments they believe beyond them. Speaking to British Staff College candidates, Sir Archibald Percival Wavell advised:

> Study the human side of history . . . to learn that Napoleon in 1796 with 20,000 beat combined forces of 30,000 by something called economy of force or operating on interior lines is a mere waste of time. If you can understand how a young unknown man inspired a half starved ragged, rather Bolshie crowd; how he filled their bellies; how he outmarched, outwitted, outbluffed and defeated men who had studied war all their lives and waged it according to the text-books of their time, you will have learnt something worth knowing.[14]

Personal study for the American troop leader must also include an examination of American institutions, society, customs, and general history since they contribute to beliefs and ideals that motivate subordinates. Study of the American military experience can help a leader gain valuable insights: the changing outlook of citizens who enter the Army and their reactions to military service; views of the regular versus those of the conscript; what subordinates expect of their leaders; and human reactions to adversity. Leadership, an important aspect of professionalism, can be profitably studied by reading history with its many examples, good and bad. The leader who knows his own leadership style learns what to emulate and what to avoid. In learning vicariously about people one perceives that the basic elements of human nature do not change even though society and institutions are in a constant state of flux. This perception requires a critical reading of works which may be self-seeking autobiographies or propaganda offered under the guise of history.

There is a good deal of the visceral in military leadership, but the moral side of leadership is particularly important because it is so influenced by a person's character. By studying military

---

14. Quoted by Major General E. K. G. Sixsmith, "Military History or War Studies?" *The Army Quarterly and Defense Journal* 101 (1971):439.

history one can learn something about strength of character. In all American military annals, there is no better example of contrasting character in battlefield leadership than that of Lee and Hooker at Chancellorsville where the absence of strong leadership doomed a brilliant plan to failure. But leadership involves more than personal resolution or physical courage: It includes a deep and abiding understanding of the traits, weaknesses, and aspirations of subordinates. And it involves personal integrity as well. Beginning with Washington, through Sherman, Lee, Pershing, and beyond, a long, honored list, the student can find a tradition of integrity well worth emulating.

Careful reading of military history can supply a valuable perspective for the critical examination of contemporary problems. Historical perspective leads to a sense of proportion and encourages the long view; it contributes to an awareness that life moves in a channel of continuous change, thus helping to counter excessive optimism or pessimism about current developments. Moreover, it will help one reassess the values used to weigh achievements, methods, and decisions. Shielded from the heat and passion of partisan argument, for example, one can learn something of the wisdom as well as the practical difficulties in our subordination of military forces to civilian direction. Or the thoughtful person may appreciate that the apparent American penchant for absolutes can lead to a tendency to view problems as always susceptible of solution, thereby creating additional problems. Gradually, the student learns that with greater knowledge it is easier to assimilate new material and to associate the new with the old. Judgment grows more discriminatory, and one begins to separate the transitory from the permanent as ideas and concepts are weighed. One becomes aware that discerning differences in the historical flow of events is often more meaningful than establishing similarities through strained analogy.

The sharpening of judgment is part of the total intellectual process to which a study of history contributes. Rather than testing hypotheses in search of predictive models, history deals with cause and effect of individual events. It broadens the soldier's vision and arouses curiosity about specific problems, none of which are exactly like those faced in the past. A careful reading of military history can help develop what Liddell Hart calls "the scientific approach":

> Adaptation to changing conditions is the condition of survival. This depends on the simple yet fundamental question of *attitude*. To cope with the problems of the modern world we need, above all, to see them clearly and analyse them scientifically. This requires freedom from

prejudice combined with the power of discernment and with a sense of proportion. . . . Discernment may be primarily a gift, and a sense of proportion, too. But their development can be assisted by freedom from prejudice, which largely rests with the individual to achieve—and within his power to achieve it. Or at least to approach it. The way of approach is simple, if not easy—requiring, above all, constant self-criticism and care for precise statement.[15]

One can properly question that it is possible to learn strategy from a textbook in the same manner as one learns an academic skill. But history can help the soldier by revealing qualities that other men have found useful in developing independence of mind and by emphasizing that confusion, lack of information, and friction are normal in war. Although no concrete lessons can be learned from history and then blindly applied, there is an argument for the broad deduction of general principles. Based upon a careful analysis of warfare, for example, J. F. C. Fuller articulated the principles of war now generally accepted as doctrine throughout most of the world. Similarly, students learn some basic rules that usually pay dividends (e.g., be stronger at the decisive point, thorough training often compensates for inferior strength, be aggressive). They also learn that these rules are frequently violated, sometimes knowingly and for specific reasons.

Experience improperly gleaned can make one dogmatic and lead to an attempt to apply lessons too literally. But this vicarious experience is the raw material of imagination and can lead to the development of new ideas. Combined with intelligence and ingenuity, imagination can lead to wisdom, sometimes a wisdom more advanced in years than a soldier's age would indicate. In search of either principles or wisdom, however, one must study military history critically and objectively.

Alfred Vagts complained that military men too often looked backward, ignoring changed circumstances, in order to prepare for the future.[16] And indeed historical examples are rarely, if ever, exact enough to allow unquestioning application to specific contemporary problems. By analyzing trends in tactics, strategy, and weapons, however, soldiers can grasp the evolution of warfare and learn something of the basis for doctrine—or devise a rationale for questioning it.

There is, of course, a danger in blithely applying narrowly based historical experience to the general case in search of

15. B. H. Liddell Hart, *Why Don't We Learn From History?* (London: Allen and Unwin, 1946), p. 10.

16. Alfred Vagts, *A History of Militarism* (New York: Meridian Books, 1959), p. 27.

doctrine. Although the historian tries to bring order out of chaos, his use of evidence is necessarily selective. Moreover, war is anything but simple. Weapons change, technology advances, the motivation of human beings to fight varies; the last war may be completely irrelevant to the next one. Yet there are numerous valid examples of the doctrinal application of military history: Studying the ancient art of warfare, Maurice of Nassau devised tactical changes which Gustavus Adolphus brilliantly put to the battlefield test; a War Office committee painstakingly studied the British official history of World War I to confirm or to establish a basis for changing the Field Service Regulations; and, more narrowly, an exhaustive study of the American intelligence failure at Pearl Harbor resulted in a statement of doctrinal principles for command application. Douglas MacArthur understood both the danger and the benefits of this doctrinal application:

> The military student does not seek to learn from history the minutiae of method and technique. In every age these are decisively influenced by the characteristics of weapons currently available and by the means at hand for maneuvering, supplying, and controlling combat forces. But research does bring to light those fundamental principles, and their combinations and applications, which, in the past, have been productive of success. These principles know no limitation of time. Consequently, the Army extends its analytical interest to the dust-buried accounts of wars long past as well as to those still reeking with the scent of battle. It is the object of the search that dictates the field for its pursuit.[17]

As a final comment it is vitally important to reemphasize that the soldier's study of military history must involve more than purely operational accounts. He must also study the institutional aspects of the military and the relationship between civilian and the soldier in peace and war: the development of the American military system within the society which fosters and sometimes berates it, and how military choice in strategy and tactics must conform to American traditions and the constitutional system. And studied in such broad context, military history can tell much about what Sir John Fortescue characterized as the supreme test to which war subjects a nation. The case for the study of military history in its broader milieu was well made by Richard Preston three decades ago:

> War, as is becoming realized in the modern world, is more than a mere clash of arms. The development of armies and of their organization, and the narratives of campaign strategy and of operational tactics, which

---

17. General Douglas MacArthur, *Report of the Chief of Staff U.S. Army, 1935* (Washington: Government Printing Office, 1935), p. 32.

were formerly the military historian's exclusive concern, can be understood only in relation to developments in the world at large, in relation to advances in technology, and in relation to changes in political and economic organization.

In short, as Michael Howard urged, the soldier should study military history in depth to get beneath the historian's necessarily imposed pattern of seeming orderliness and to try to understand what war is really like; in breadth to understand the flow of events and the existence of continuity or discontinuity therein; and in context to appreciate the political, social, and economic factors that exercise important influences on the military part of the equation.[18]

In sum then, the study of military history has both an educational and a utilitarian value. It allows soldiers to look upon war as a whole and relate its activities to the periods of peace from which it rises and to which it inevitably returns. And soldiers who know what was attempted, and what results followed, are better able to deal positively with immediate problems. As their thought process grows more sophisticated, soldiers will attempt, more and more, to analyze critically, conceptualize creatively, and test theories. Military history also helps in developing a professional frame of mind—a mental attitude. In the leadership arena, it shows the great importance of character and integrity. Finally, military history studied in depth helps the soldier to see war, in Clausewitz's time-worn phrase, as a chameleon, a phenomenon that affects and draws its spirit from the society which spawns it.

Select Bibliography

Ad Hoc Committee, Department of the Army. "Report on the Army Need for the Study of Military History." 4 vols. West Point, N.Y., 1971.

Craven, Wesley Frank. Why Military History? Harmon Memorial Lecture no. 1. U.S.A.F. Academy, Colo., 1959.

Du Picq, Ardant. Battle Studies. Translated by John N. Greely and Robert C. Cotton. Harrisburg: Military Service Publishing Company, 1947.

Falls, Cyril. The Place of War in History. London: Oxford Univ. Press, 1947.

Fortescue, Sir John W., Military History. Cambridge, 1914.

Fuller, Maj. Gen. J. F. C. Decisive Battles of the U.S.A. New York: Harper, 1953.

———. The Foundations of the Science of War. London: Hutchinson, 1926.

———. A Military History of the Western World. 3 vols. New York: Funk and Wagnalls, 1954-56.

---

18. Richard A. Preston, "The Teaching of Military History in Canada," Canadian Army Journal 3 (1949):15. Howard, "The Use and Abuse of Military History," pp. 7-8.

Gilbert, Felix, and Graubard, Stephen, R., eds., *Historical Studies Today*, New York: W. W. Norton, 1972.

Guerard, Albert. *France: A Modern History*. Ann Arbor: Univ. of Michigan Press, 1959.

Henderson, Col. George F. R. *The Science of War*. Edited by Captain Neill Malcolm. London: Longmans, Green and Company, 1908.

Howard, Michael. "The Demand for Military History." *Times Literary Supplement,* 13 Nov. 1969.

——. "The Use and Abuse of Military History." *Journal of the Royal United Services Institution.* 107 (1962):4–10.

Liddell Hart, Sir Basil H. *Why Don't We Learn From History?* London: Allen and Unwin, 1946.

Luvaas, Jay. *The Education of an Army*. Chicago: Univ. of Chicago Press, 1964.

Military History: Methods of Research. Infantry School Reference Text no. 25. Fort Benning, Ga. [1937].

Millis, Walter. *Arms and Men: A Study in American Military History*. New York: Putnam's, 1956.

——. *Military History*. Washington: American Historical Association Service Center for Teachers, 1961.

Oman, Sir Charles. *Studies in the Napoleonic Wars*. London: Meuthen, 1930.

Paret, Peter. "The History of War." *Daedalus* 100, no. 1 (Spring, 1971):376–96.

Preston, Richard A. "The Teaching of Military History in Canada." *Canadian Army Journal* 3 (1949):14–15, 30.

Shy, John. "The American Military Experience: History and Learning." *Journal of Interdisciplinary History* 1. no. 2 (Winter, 1971):205–28.

Sixsmith, Major General E. K. G. "Military History or War Studies?" *Army Quarterly and Defence Journal* 101 (1971):437–44.

Smith, Page. *The Historian and History*. New York: Random House, 1966.

Vagts, Alfred. *A History of Militarism*. Rev. ed. New York: Meridian Books, 1959.

Weigley, Russell F., ed. *New Dimensions in Military History*. San Rafael, Calif.: Presidio Press, 1975.

Chapter **3**

An Approach
to The Study
Of Military History

Lt. Col. John F. Votaw

SINCE military history covers vast areas, both topically and chronologically, the student who would enter the field has a wide range of choice. The study of Alexander the Great, for instance, still offers relevant insights into the exercise of power—military economic, and political—at the highest level; and a good biography of King Gustavus Adolphus of seventeenth-century Sweden offers a case history in the application of theory to the problems of reorganizing a military system. Frederick the Great tells us in his own words of tactical genius and the training of eighteenth-century soldiers. Napoleon Bonaparte has filled many bookstore shelves both directly through his memoirs and maxims and indirectly through a mass of idolizing and scathing biographies. From Napoleon the student can learn of generalship and in the process appreciate the crushing burden and responsibility of supreme command; he can better understand the military problems of maintaining an empire won by the sword and the limits of military power in suppressing newly aroused nationalism.

Military history includes biography, fiction, battle narratives, memoirs, theoretical treatises, scientific discourses, philosophy, economic studies—and more. Studying the subject can be somewhat like shopping in a used book store where the books are stacked on many different shelves. If one enters with no idea of what he is looking for, chances are he will leave unsatisfied. But if he enters with some general ideas of what he is seeking, as well as ability to recognize valuable items not presently on his "want list," then the venture will be rewarding.

The study of history is not a great search for details in the pages of dusty books; it involves the discovery of knowledge in the broader sense and the enrichment of the intellect. Military history is history first and military second. Methods of studying it are invariably tied to individual goals and individual concepts

Lt. Colonel Votaw (M.A., California at Davis), was an instructor in history at the U.S. Military Academy when he wrote this contribution.

of what military history is. If directed to prepare a list of the ten most important books of military history, ten different persons would probably draw up ten different lists, each list representing its compiler's values, priorities, and biases, although some titles would appear on more than one list. In using this *Guide* and its extensive book lists, the reader must decide what he is seeking and frame questions to be asked while reading, questions that will deter aimless wandering.

The skills needed to investigate the many dimensions of military history can be tailored to one's concept of the nature of history. The study of military history can be rewarding and exciting, but it can become drudgery if pursued in a methodical but plodding way. Students have a tendency to equate the study of history with the commitment to memory of facts that can be returned to the instructor at examination time little the worse for wear.[1] We are not concerned with this type of historical study. Allan Nevins, one of the most noted American historians, counsels:

> There is but one golden rule in reading history: it should be read by the blazing illumination of a thoroughly aroused intellectual curiosity. . . . A self-stimulated interest, one based upon a fixed ambition to master some select period of history, and to do it by systematic, intensive reading, is of course far more valuable. It represents a steady disciplined impulse, not a transient appetite.[2]

Essentials of a Study Program

Military history should be studied in width, depth, and, most importantly, in context. In this way, according to Professor Michael Howard, "the study of military history should not only enable the civilian to understand the nature of war and its part in shaping society, but also directly improve the officer's competence in his profession." Reading with a purpose to gain a better understanding of the nature of war and the practice of warfare sharpens the intellect and develops perspective to face current problems in an informed manner as well as to plan for the future. But "history has limitations as a *guiding* signpost," said Sir Basil H. Liddell Hart, "for although it can show us the right direction, it does not give detailed information about the road condition."

---

1. This idea was paraphrased from Carl L. Becker's imaginative essay, "Frederick Jackson Turner," in *Everyman His Own Historian* (Chicago: Quadrangle, 1966).

2. Allan Nevins, *The Gateway to History* (Boston: D. C. Heath, 1938), pp. 365–66.

Bertrand Russell also offers some advice that is pertinent to the problem of beginning a study program:[3]

> If history is not necessary to your career, there is no point in reading it unless you enjoy it and find it interesting. I do not mean that the only point of history is to give pleasure—far from it. It has many other uses. . . . But it will not have these uses except for those that enjoy it. The same is true of such things as music and painting and poetry. To study these things either because you must, or because you wish to be cultured, makes it almost impossible to acquire what they have to offer.

Formal graduate training in military history is obviously one way to launch a long, rewarding career of continued study. There are many opportunities to pursue graduate studies in the service, all clearly spelled out in current regulations. You can complete an unfinished degree with Army financial assistance which provides for full-time study as you near graduation. And the Army will share the cost of your gradually accumulating the necessary course work for an advanced degree. You may combine duty as an instructor and formal study in a nearby graduate institution. As long as continued educational development remains a goal in the Army, there will be opportunities for anyone with the determination to take advantage of them.

Academic study is not the only way. Another is self-instruction through reading. It would be difficult if not impossible for anyone to construct a single reading list that would fit all the needs of students whose interests are necessarily diverse; a more fruitful approach is to develop a set of questions around which a reading program may be built. The student must develop his own questions to reflect his goals, values, and personal interests.

How can you formulate that basic list of questions and themes that will govern your reading program? You will discover questions as you read, but, by way of suggestion, some of the fundamental questions involve:

—The formation of armies (militia, conscript, volunteer, mercenary)

—Explaining why armies fight (religion, dynastic interests, nationalism, ideology, discipline)

—Assessing how armies fight (shock tactics, firepower, linear tactics, employment of masses, mobility, position warfare)

---

3. Michael Howard, "The Use and Abuse of Military History," *Journal of the Royal United Service Institution* 107 (1962):4-10. Liddell Hart, *Why Don't We Learn From History?* (London: Allen and Unwin, 1946), p. 15. Bertrand Russell, *Understanding History* (New York: Philosophical Library, 1957), pp. 9-10.

—Investigation of the relationships between the armed forces (naval defense, the army as the first line of defense, geographic position of the state)

—Who directs the employment of the armed forces (soldier king, chief executive, commanding general, general staff, legislature)

—How armies are sustained (logistics, technology, morale, national style, industrial power)

—How wars are ended (exhaustion, negotiated settlement, surrender, destruction)

The ingredients of battle have prompted many soldiers and civilians to write extensively about how combat power is applied on the battlefield; tactics, training, doctrine, and generalship are frequently the subjects of these examinations. The men who wage war—commanders, statesmen, soldiers, guerrillas—are natural subjects of investigation to one interested in gaining a better understanding of war. The general has attracted much attention as the focal point of battlefield activity.

Each period of history has something to offer. Try to determine what is distinctive about the military history of a given period. You might ask, for example, if warfare as practiced by Napoleon's *Grande Armée* was different from warfare in the time of Frederick the Great? Certainly. Armies were larger, battlefields had expanded into theaters of war, logistics became more complex, and the French soldier was part of a more flexible army because he could be trusted not to desert. Frederick's army was dynastic, mercenary, expensive, and effective. Then you might ask what about the Napoleonic period is relevant to military affairs today? The idea is not to apply Napoleonic solutions to our current problems but to try to fathom how Napoleon approached his problems, say with conscription and recruitment, and then armed with new perspective tackle our own problems. History is not an exact science governed by rules, theorems, postulates, and principles. Liddell Hart "always tried to take a projection from the past through the present into the future" in his study of military problems.[4] Sometimes the lens through which we view the past gets a little out of adjustment, distorting the image, but our improved understanding and sharpened perspective can help rectify that.

What nonmilitary factors have affected the course of warfare over the ages? How is the decision to go to war arrived at? Frederick the Great and Napoleon Bonaparte had less of a

---

4. *Why Don't We Learn From History?*, p. 16.

problem in deciding for war than did President Lincoln or President Franklin Roosevelt; in an autocracy the autocrat has powers of decision unchecked by democratic processes. Yet all four men were very sensitive to the opinions of others; in Frederick's case, the concern was for other monarchs, not the Prussian people.

Finance and economics have frequently played important roles in warfare. Frederick depended on British financing during the Seven Years' War. Napoleon understood that economic power can be a successful adjunct to raw military power, but he also appreciated that without a navy it would not be possible to strike directly at Britain's mercantile power. The Continental System employed a type of boycott designed to seal off the European continent and deny markets to British goods. The plan had flaws, but it did squeeze the merchants in mighty Albion.

Political and social factors also play an important role in warfare. Frederick was careful to promote discord among his potential enemies. In the American Civil War, Lincoln played his powerful trump card, the emancipation of Negro slaves in the Southern states, at the propitious moment to enlist support for the Northern cause both at home and abroad. The Emancipation Proclamation was a military instrument, argues John Hope Franklin, that the president wielded only after he had gained a seeming victory at Antietam in September 1862.[5] The assumption of victory disarmed the argument that the slaves were freed as an act of desperation and so helped to sway opinion in England against intervention on the side of the South. In World War II, Roosevelt used the fervor generated by the Japanese attack on Pearl Harbor to carry through full mobilization for war.

Reading biographies of leading soldiers or statesmen is a good way to begin the study of military history. Examination of leadership during periods of great stress and crisis may well be a springboard to a satisfying reading program. A study of Franklin D. Roosevelt as war leader, for instance, can lead to an exploration of most of the aspects of modern war—leadership, political and military; decision making, personal and institutional; mobilization and war production; censorship and propaganda; diplomacy and national strategy. Such a study also illustrates the variety of approaches and interpretations different historians may use in dealing with a strong leader's actions.

---

5. John Hope Franklin, *The Emancipation Proclamation* (New York: Doubleday, Anchor Books, 1965), pp. 129-46.

Examining Roosevelt's part in the coming of war, Charles A. Beard found in 1948 that "At this point in its history the American Republic has arrived under the theory that the President of the United States possesses limitless authority publicly to misrepresent and secretly to control foreign policy, foreign affairs, and the war power." Examining the evolution of American strategy, Maurice Matloff emphasized the different point, that the military planners "had also learned that whatever their theories and plans, they would have to reckon with an active and forceful Commander-in-Chief bent on pursuing his own course".[6]

Although the president's biographer, James MacGregor Burns, seems to agree with this interpretation, he argues that Roosevelt as war leader was intent on immediate tactical moves during the first years of the war rather than on grand strategy. "Roosevelt's utter concentration on the task at hand—winning military victory—raised difficult problems, just as his absorption with winning elections at whatever cost had created difficulties during the peace years." Herbert Feis, on the other hand, finds the president not so capricious as often painted in his decision to support unconditional surrender as the basic Allied war aim. The decision, he says, was not made on the spur of the moment at the Casablanca press conference of 24 January 1943 but was "preceded by discussion." Even though he may have acted on impulse in selecting that particular moment to make the announcement, "the record shows plainly that the idea of doing so had been in his mind for some time."[7] All these interpretations of Roosevelt's actions are not necessarily incompatible; they simply illustrate the many facets of his wartime leadership and the ways in which historians look at them.

Even in very narrow fields of historical study it is now almost impossible to roam through all the available literature in pursuit of your objectives. As far back as 1879, in delivering his inaugural address to the Military Service Institution of the United States, Maj. Gen. John M. Schofield alluded to the information explosion which has continually complicated the labor of the military student.[8] The proliferation of literature has increased many times since General Schofield made his obser-

---

6. Charles A. Beard, *President Roosevelt and the Coming of the War, 1941: A Study in Appearances and Realities* (New Haven: Yale Univ. Press, 1948), p. 598. Maurice Matloff, "The American Approach to War, 1919–1945," in *The Theory and Practice of War*, ed. Michael Howard (New York: Praeger, 1966), p. 236.

7. James MacGregor Burns, *Roosevelt: The Lion and the Fox* (New York: Harcourt, Brace and World, 1956), pp. 459–64. Herbert Feis, *Churchill, Roosevelt, Stalin: The War They Waged and the Peace They Sought* (Princeton, N.J.: Princeton Univ. Press, 1957), pp. 109–10.

8. *Journal of the Military Service Institution of the United States* 1 (1880):8.

vation. It may be necessary to revise your questions and your reading program periodically, both to meet your needs, which certainly may change, and to accomodate the new literature in your field of interest.

The best way to keep your program current is to consult some of the many scholarly historical periodicals such as the *American Historical Review*, the *Journal of Modern History*, and the *Journal of American History*.[9] There are also specialized periodicals such as *Choice* and *Perspective* that are devoted almost entirely to short reviews of the most recent publications. Many weekly newspapers carry book reviews. The *New York Times* provides the Sunday reader with a large selection of reviews and the *Times Literary Supplement* (London— frequently called the *TLS*) even reviews scholarly foreign-language books. There are scores of magazines such as *American History Illustrated* and *History Today* (Great Britain) that you can scan to keep current. *Foreign Affairs* has a handy list of available documents and monographs on a variety of subjects in addition to the useful book review section. The Superintendent of Documents in Washington, D.C., can provide a list of publications available from the U.S. Government Printing Office. It is apparent that the many references available to update your reading program may in themselves be something of an obstacle; you cannot consult all of them.

The Mechanics of Study

Although it is more difficult to describe the mechanics of successful study than to raise questions, there are simple ways of organizing an approach to studying some of the fundamental questions. Ten years ago cadets at the U.S. Military Academy were taught to organize their study of military history around the ubiquitous "principles of war." Many decades of teaching practices had led to that method. A broader concept of military history now forms the basis of study at West Point; cadets organize their inquiries by the device known as the threads of continuity. The ten "threads" presently in use are as follows:

Military theory and doctrine—ideas about war; a generally accepted body of ideas and practices that governs an army's organization, training, and fighting

---

9. For a list of the main scholarly historical journals, see Appendix B. Practically all these journals devote space to book reviews.

Military professionalism—an attitude or state of mind distinguishing the expert from the amateur. The military professional is an expert in the management of violence and is characterized by his sense of responsibility to his men and to the state.

Generalship—the art of command at high levels. Generalship includes both leadership and management (but neither word is a synonym) and many diverse functions involving preparation for combat, supervision during combat, and administration and maintenance of combat strength.

Strategy—the preparation for war and the waging of war; getting to the battlefield as opposed to action on the battlefield. Strategy is a changing concept now generally divided into national (or grand) strategy and military strategy (a component of national strategy).

Tactics—the preparation for combat and the actual conduct of combat on the battlefield

Logistics and Administration—defines the relationship between the state's economic capacity and its ability to support military forces

Technology—in a military sense, the application of science to war. Technology includes not only new ideas, techniques, and equipment but also their application.

Political factors—those characteristic elements or actions of governments affecting warfare

Social factors—those elements affecting warfare that result from human relationships

Economic factors—those elements affecting warfare that result from the production, distribution, and consumption of the resources of the state

Portraying history as a "seamless web" or a "tapestry of man's past" with the woven strands representing the major themes is a commonplace.[10] The threads of continuity have no inherent worth; they function merely as ways to get at information or as that lens used by Liddell Hart to place events in perspective. By examining a portion of the changing nature of war or warfare, for example tactics, over a specific period of time such as 1850 to 1950, one can expect to gain a deeper understanding of the nature of the whole. The ten threads of continuity are not necessarily definitive or final, but they are a useful means of organizing the study of military history.

---

10. See the comments of Bruce Mazlish, general editor of the Macmillan series, Main Themes in European History, in the foreword to Heinz Luzbasz, *The Development of the Modern State* (New York: Macmillan, 1964), p. v.

By the same token, the principles of war still have some utility, but now as part of the military theory and doctrine thread of continuity. Since the purpose of our study of military history is not to search out examples of the valid application of the principles of war and demonstrate that failure generally stemmed from ignorance of or unwillingness to abide by them, we can restore the principles to their proper historical position. Principles of one sort or another have been alluded to by most theorists and successful commanders. There must be some rules, however general, that will allow man to cope with war. Or so thought General J. F. C. Fuller when, from his study of Napoleonic warfare, he constructed the list of principles of war American soldiers now generally recognize. Rear Adm. Joseph C. Wylie describes the principles as "an attempt to rationalize and categorize common sense." As long as a "principle of war" remains a tool and does not become a maxim to be demonstrated as immutable the student can proceed with confidence. Neither the threads of continuity nor the principles of war—or any conceptual device for that matter—can substitute for an intelligent and discriminating search to gain understanding of the past.[11]

Somewhere in your study you will want to assess the strengths and weaknesses of a particular military system, the wisdom of a particular strategic decision, or the generalship in a particular campaign, in short to render critical judgment on military history. Military men are trained to do just that, to solve problems by rational analysis and then choose the best course of action. It is through this process that they use history in formulating doctrine. But recognize that there is a difference between the military historian and the military critic, as the noted German military historian, Hans Delbrück, points out. Ideally the historian is concerned with describing events as accurately as possible in proper sequence and with cause and effect relationships in those events, not with personal judgments on the leading characters. The latter is the province of the military critic. Delbrück made this distinction, Peter Paret explains, not to "impute greater value to one or the other, but to

11. Jay Luvaas, The Education of An Army: British Military Thought, 1815-1940 (Chicago: University of Chicago Press, 1964), p. 338 (for a discussion of Fuller's ideas). Joseph C. Wylie, Military Strategy: A General Theory of Power Control (New Brunswick, N.J.: Rutgers University Press, 1967), p. 21. For some other thoughts on the utility of the principles of war see Cmdr. Bruce Kenner, III, "The Principles of War: A Thesis for Change," U.S. Naval Institute Proceedings 93 (Nov. 1967):27-36; James A. Huston, "Re-examine the Principles of War," Military Review 35 (Feb. 1956):30-36; and Maurice Matloff, gen. ed., American Military History (Washington: Government Printing Office, 1969), pp. 4-13.

establish meaningful standards for both."[12] And the distinction is valid, even though Delbrück's own works reflect much personal judgment, praise, and comdemnation, as do those of many other noted military historians who double as critics.

Military men do need to prepare themselves to be critics and, when called upon, to use judgment sharpened by historical study in formulating Army doctrine. This preparation is clearly one of the uses of military history. But for the student of history to judge past activities and decisions by present standards or to assign praise or condemnation to acts of leadership in combat may result in distortion and injustice. "What is the object of history?" asked Liddell Hart. And his reply to his own rhetorical question was "quite simply, 'truth'."[13] The student of military history should first seek the truth and then base his critical judgments upon it, recognizing that in the latter process he is acting as military critic and not as military historian.

Because the pursuit of military history involves extensive reading, it is worthwhile to cultivate good reading habits. There are many good primers on the subject. How to Study History by Norman F. Cantor and Richard I. Schneider is a good starting point. The Modern Researcher, revised edition, by Jacques Barzun and Henry F. Graff (New York: Harcourt, Brace, and World, 1957), and Understanding History, second edition, by Louis Gottschalk (New York: A. A. Knopf, 1969) are useful introductions to the historical method. Helen J. Poulton's The Historian's Handbook: A Descriptive Guide to Reference Works is indispensable. B. H. Liddell Hart's Why Don't We Learn From History? (London: Allen and Unwin, 1946) provides insight into the method of one of the great modern strategic theorists. For a provocative examination of the historical method in very readable and entertaining style see J. H. Hexter's The History Primer.

Oliver L. Spaulding's advice on how to evaluate books on military history, given in a lecture in 1922 and summarized in an Army pamphlet, is still basically sound. Spaulding stressed the value of book reviews and the use of title page, preface, index, table of contents, and bibliography as clues to the coverage of volumes, the credentials of their authors, and their value to the prospective reader. "A systematic use of book reviews and of the clues . . . will lead to the discard of many books and will direct the student's attention to the particular parts of those he wishes

---

12. Peter Paret, "Hans Delbrück on Military Critics and Military Historians," Military Affairs 30 (Fall 1966):149.
13. Liddell Hart, Why Don't We Learn From History? p. 15.

to study."[14] The ineffective way to read is to plunge in at the beginning and not stop until you reach the objective which lies near the index. There never is enough time to turn this method into an efficient one, but the opposite—scanning the entire work—is as ineffective. You must identify the significant parts of the book and concentrate on detecting, then understanding, the author's theses. Ask your own questions of the book, or no relevant answers will be forthcoming. What the author is trying to convince you of is not nearly so important as what his material and point of view mean to you.

Where does one start with a reading program? Your interest has undoubtedly been stimulated by reading newspapers and magazines. For example, *London Daily Express* and *New York Daily News* articles on Martin Bormann renewed public interest in the final days of World War II when Berlin fell to the Soviet Army. There is a great deal of published material on that subject, as a quick check of the *Reader's Guide to Periodical Literature*, the *New York Times* index, and any library's general card catalog will reveal. If you find Bormann interesting, you might select the most recent article from the *Reader's Guide*. The documentation (footnotes, bibliography, text references) in the article will lead to other sources.

After you have selected your book or article, read for the author's thesis and mentally note his documentation. One way to keep track of what you have read is to start a card file. Enter the author's full name, complete title of the book, place of publication, publisher, and date of publication near the top of the card. Note the number of pages and comments on any unusual features of the book such as particularly well-made maps. Briefly summarize in a sentence or two the topic of the book and the author's thesis. List your own impressions of the book with respect to your areas of interest. If the author is not familiar to you, make a biographical note. Finally, indicate where you located the book and include the library call number. This process sounds tedious, but it will pay off when you discover the limitations of your memory. Identifying the author's thesis will help in evaluating each piece you read.

Along with a framework for study, such as the threads of continuity, and a method of keeping track of what you have read, some suggestions regarding study techniques are in order. Responsible criticism is one way of testing your grasp of the

14. DA Pamphlet 2-200, *The Writing of American Military History: A Guide* (Washington: Government Printing Office, 1956), p. 17-18.

material you study. As military critic you are taking that step beyond merely understanding what happened and why it happened; judgment and assessment of accomplishments and errors are useful to the man interested in sharpening his perspective. Campaign and battle analysis can be conducted mentally only or in a written essay. There are different ways of organizing the analysis, some of which are familiar to any student of warfare. The commander's estimate of the situation is a good format. Ask then answer the questions: (1) who was involved? (2) what happened? (3) when did it happen? (4) where did it happen? (5) how did the action develop? (6) why did things progress as they did? and (7) what was the significance of the action? This will generally lead you systematically through the action.

Another way of making a campaign analysis is the narrative technique, which can be organized in the following fashion:

—Evaluation of the strategic situation (period of history; war; international adversaries; principal events leading up to the battle, campaign, or conflict analyzed)

—Review of the tactical setting (location; any terrain advantages held by either antagonist; approximate force ratios; types of forces if relevant; feasible courses of action available to antagonist)

—List of other factors affecting the event (effects of terrain or weather; special advantages or disadvantages possessed by antagonists)

—Synopsis of the conduct of the event (opening moves; salient features; outcome)

—Statement of the historical lessons provided by the event

—Assessment of the significance of the event

The following analysis of the battle of Gaugamela, in which Alexander the Great defeated the Persian army in 331 B.C., illustrates the narrative format.

Strategic setting: Having secured the eastern Mediterranean with the victory at Issus and the successful siege of Tyre, Alexander marched his army eastward into the heart of the Persian Empire. Darius III was drawn into a decisive battle at Guagamela in the spring of 331 B.C.

Tactical setting: Darius placed his troops on a broad plain and employed chariots with his infantry. Although the terrain favored neither side, the more numerous Persians extended far beyond the Macedonian flanks. Darius attacked forcing Alexander to react. Expecting a Persian envelopment, Alexander had deployed his army to refuse his flanks and to provide all around security. The main striking force was positioned to exploit any gaps that might open in the advancing Persian front.

Other factors: Alexander had scouted the battlefield. The Macedonians were rested; the Persians, perhaps less confident, had remained awake through the night. Weather had no significant effect on the battle. Darius apparently had planned to attack all along the line with no provision to exploit weaknesses in the Macedonian formation.

Conduct of the battle: The Persian army closed with a chariot and cavalry charge. The Macedonians inclined to their right in oblique order and, as the Persians followed, a gap opened near the Persian left. Seizing the opportunity, Alexander drove a wedge of Companion cavalry into the breech and dispersed the Persian infantry. King Darius fled the battlefield close behind them. The Persian cavalry had enveloped the Macedonian left, but Alexander reinforced. The flight of the Persian infantry soon spread to the cavalry and a general retreat began. Alexander relentlessly pursued the remnants of the Persian force through the night, effectively destroying Darius's army.

Lessons: Alexander calculated that the Persian formation would break apart as it attacked and therefore was justified in surrendering the tactical initiative by standing on the defensive. Carefully weighing the terrain conditions, the experience of his army, and the disparity in leadership, Alexander took a calculated risk to offset the advantage in numbers enjoyed by the Persians. The Macedonian commander regained the initiative at the critical point in the battle and exploited the advantage he had created.

Significance: The professional Macedonian army was equal to the difficult task planned by its bold commander. Alexander's decisive victory assured his conquest of the Persian Empire. The Macedonian treasury was swelled with thousands of talents of gold and the palace of Xerxes in Persepolis was burnt. Further consolidation and expansion to India provided more territory to be divided at Alexander's death in 323 B.C. The Persian threat to the Hellenic world was eliminated.

Certainly not every analysis needs to be written. As you study battles, campaigns and wars, thoughtful mental analyses will deepen your understanding of cause and effect in war and will provide a better appreciation of the role of chance or friction. As a military critic you can probe the apparent errors made during the event in order to render your considered judgment and to identify those lessons that have meaning for you. Similarly, you may identify actions that had a positive influence on the outcome of the event. General Sir Edward Bruce Hamley saw his writings as enabling students to study military history "with the confidence of one who does not grope and guess, but surveys and judges."[15]

Analyses can also be organized around the critical decisions made during the course of events under examination. The important thing to remember in making a historical analysis is to organize your investigative process in an orderly fashion and then explore the subject in depth. Regardless of format, the questions you ask yourself are of utmost value. Absorbing information is not your goal, but it is an essential element of your study. Understanding is a legitimate goal of historical study; it is also a personal achievement which comes through hard work. Although there is a need to be systematic, study should not become an overburdening routine, a chore to be accomplished. Seek diversity in your reading and avoid boredom.

Evaluating different versions of historical events and decisions is one of the first hurdles you must clear in your reading. People write books for definite reasons—to inform, to entertain, to chastise, or even to precipitate a desired action by the reader. The reader must evaluate the author's reliability, how well the author supports his thesis with evidence and examples. In this way he can determine whether the book is honestly drawn. As Robin W. Winks observed, "the truth ought to matter."[16]

Physical evidence can be found in places other than books; for example, a Civil War battlefield still holds much information for a student of that conflict. Most of us have made the "tourist sweep" of our National Park Service battlefields, but it is a far different experience to stand on the high ground one hundred yards north of the Bloody Lane at Antietam and look back at the muzzles of the Confederate battery in firing positions above the lane. Lieutenant Thomas L. Livermore of the 5th New Hampshire, which was in line as part of Maj. Gen. Israel Bush Richardson's 1st Division, II U.S. Corps, observed, "in this road there lay so many dead rebels that they formed a line which one might have walked upon as far as I could see. . . . It was on this ghastly flooring that we kneeled for the last struggle."[17]

---

15. Quoted by Jay Luvaas in *Education of an Army*, p. 140. For further information on Alexander's wars of conquest see Chester G. Starr, *A History of the Ancient World* (New York: Oxford Univ. Press, 1965), Chap. 19; J. F. C. Fuller, *The Generalship of Alexander the Great* (New York: Minerva Press, 1968); F. E. Adcock, *The Greek and Macedonian Art of War* (Berkeley: Univ. of Calif. Press, 1962); and J. F. C. Fuller, *A Military History of The Western World*, 3 vols. (New York: Minerva Press, 1967), 1:140.

16. Robin W. Winks, ed., *The Historian As Detective: Essays-on Evidence* (New York: Harper and Row, 1969), p. xiv.

General John M. Schofield in 1899 saw the great object of historical study as "to reduce the 'chances' of war to the minimum; to bring it as nearly as possible within the domain of exact science; ... to learn how to rapidly organize, equip, discipline, and handle new troops, *and then to judge correctly what enterprises may be undertaken with a reasonable expectation of success.*"[18] Schofield concluded that the great value of study of this sort was the cultivation of a habit of thought which tempered hasty decisions and insured proper preliminary plans essential to effective orders. Military history is normally not utilitarian in a direct way. Eighteenth-century Austrian armies were molded in the Prussian image without the understanding that a Frederician system required a Frederick. Armies marched into Belgium and France in 1914 expecting another short war of maneuver culminating in a decisive battle as in 1870. The realities of modern war and faulty strategy soon matured in the trenches.

But if you approach the study of the past with an attitude of growing wise forever rather than clever for the next time, there is a use for history. In battle, as elsewhere, great courage should be attended by sound intellect honed through study. The method you develop must be tied to your conception of military history.

Select Bibliography

Adcock, F. E. *The Greek and Macedonian Art of War.* Berkeley: Univ. of Calif. Press, 1962.

Beard, Charles A. *President Roosevelt and the Coming of the War, 1941: A Study in Appearances and Realities.* New Haven: Yale Univ. Press, 1948.

Burns, James MacGregor. *Roosevelt: The Lion and the Fox.* New York: Harcourt, Brace and World, 1956.

Cantor, Norman F. and Schneider, Richard I. *How to Study History.* New York: Thomas Y. Crowell, 1967.

Commager, Henry S., ed. *The Blue and the Gray.* Indianapolis, Ind.: Bobbs-Merrill, 1950.

---

17. Livermore's story is one of the many contained in Henry Steele Commager, ed., *The Blue and the Gray* (Indianapolis: Bobbs-Merrill, 1950) Livermore is introduced as a member of the 18th New Hampshire Regiment; but Commager does not tell us that Livermore finished his military career as colonel of the 18th, but fought with the 5th New Hampshire at Antietam—the 18th was not there. Colonel Edward E. Cross, commanding the 5th New Hampshire at Antietam, cited Livermore in his report of 18 September 1862. This document can be found in U.S., War Department, *The War of the Rebellion: The Official Records of the Union and Confederate Armies,* Series I, Vol. 19, Pt. 1, p. 288. Using Commager's end notes, Thomas Livermore's recollections of Civil War service, *Days and Events, 1860-1866* (Boston: Houghton Mifflin, 1920), can be located and used to corroborate and expand the small selection provided in *The Blue and the Gray.*

18. "Inaugural Address," *Journal of the Military Service Institution of the United States* 1 (1880):9-10.

Feis, Herbert. *Churchill, Roosevelt, Stalin: The War They Waged and the Peace They Sought.* Princeton, N.J.: Princeton Univ. Press, 1957.

Franklin, John Hope. *The Emancipation Proclamation.* New York: Doubleday, Anchor, 1965.

Fuller, J. F. C. *The Generalship of Alexander the Great.* New York: Minerva Press, 1968.

Hexter, J. H. *The History Primer.* New York: Basic Books, 1971.

Huston, James A. "Re-examine the Principles of War." *Military Review* 35, no. 3 (Feb. 1956):30–36.

Keener, Commander Bruce, III. "The Principles of War: A Thesis for Change." *U.S. Naval Institute Proceedings* 93, no. 11 (Nov. 1967):27–36.

Livermore, Thomas. *Days and Events, 1860–1866.* Boston: Houghton Mifflin, 1920.

Lubasz, Heinz. *The Development of the Modern State.* New York: Macmillan, 1964.

Luvaas, Jay. *The Education of an Army: British Military Thought, 1815–1940.* Chicago: Univ. of Chicago Press, 1964.

Matloff, Maurice. "The American Approach to War, 1919–1945." In *The Theory and Practice of War,* edited by Michael Howard. New York: Praeger, 1966.

Matloff, Maurice, gen. ed. *American Military History.* Army Historical Series. Washington: Government Printing Office, 1969.

Paret, Peter. "Hans Delbrück on Military Critics and Military Historians." *Military Affairs* 30, no. 3 (Fall 1966):148–52.

Poulton, Helen J. *The Historian's Handbook: A Descriptive Guide to Reference Works.* New York: Hawthorn Books, 1971.

Russell, Bertrand. *Understanding History.* New York: Philosophical Library, 1957.

Schofield, John M. "Inaugural Address." *Journal of the Military Service Institution of the United States* 1 (1880):1–19.

Starr, Chester G. *A History of the Ancient World.* New York: Oxford Univ. Press, 1965.

U.S., Department of the Army. *The Writing of American Military History: A Guide.* Pamphlet 20-200. Washington: Government Printing Office, 1956.

U.S., War Department. *The War of the Rebellion: A Compilation of the Official Records of the Union and Confederate Armies.* 3 series, 128 vols. Washington: Government Printing Office, 1880–1901.

Winks, Robin W., ed. *The Historian as Detective: Essays on Evidence.* New York: Harper and Row, 1969.

Wylie, Joseph C. *Military Strategy: A General Theory of Power Control.* New Brunswick, N.J.: Rutgers Univ. Press, 1967.

Two

Bibliographical Guide

Chapter **4**

The Great
Military Historians
and Philosophers

Jay Luvaas

BY a curious paradox military history is one of the oldest and
most prominent fields of history, yet only recently has it acquired respectability in the academic world. Indeed, in a very
real sense history began as military history, for the frequent
wars in classical times provided a popular theme for the
historian no less than the poet. Herodotus gave Greek warfare an
epic quality in his work on the Persian wars, and Thucydides,
who has taught us most of what we know about the Peloponnesian wars—and has much to teach about problems that plague a
democracy at war in our times as well—is a military historian of
the first rank. One has only to think of Xenophon's *Anabasis*,
Caesar's *Commentaries*, and vast portions of Polybius and Livy
to appreciate the significance of military history to the ancients.
The literary style of many of these old books may lack the appeal
of a Bruce Catton or S. L. A. Marshall, but the authors of these
works were often surprisingly modern in their outlook. Their
motives, their fundamental assumptions about human nature
and war, their enlightening descriptions of the minutiae of
military life, and their analysis of problems that they faced can
make for fascinating reading.

Each generation, it is said, writes its own history, which
means simply that each generation is preoccupied with its own
problems and is inclined to read its own experiences into the
past. But the past, even the remote past, can also speak directly
to the present. In his delightfully unpretentious *Pen and Sword
in Greece and Rome* (1937), Col. Oliver L. Spaulding reminds us
that the ancient warrior didn't realize that he was an ancient
warrior; he thought of himself as a modern warrior, and as such
he has much of interest to tell us.

Dr. Luvaas (Ph.D., Duke) is Professor of History at Allegheny College. His
numerous publications include *The Military Legacy of the Civil War, Frederick
the Great on the Art of War* (translator and editor), and *The Education of an
Army*. He wrote this contribution while a visiting professor at the U.S. Military
Academy.

Certainly this would be true of Thucydides, whose *History of the Peloponnesian War*, written in the fifth century B.C., remains one of the great works of history, military or otherwise. As an Athenian general Thucydides was ideally qualified to describe Greek tactics, siege operations, the construction of warships, and even flame throwers. His treatment of Periclean strategy was "so well and clearly detailed," a soldier in the eighteenth century has stated, that the modern general could learn from it how to frame his own plan of campaign.[1]

In addition to providing interesting details of weapons and tactics, Thucydides explains much about human nature. Describing the great plague, he gives not only the physical symptoms of the disease but also the psychological damage to the population of Athens. Citizens lost respect for their gods and for the law, the two major restraints in Greek civilization. "Zeal," Thucydides observes on another occasion, "is always at its height at the commencement of an undertaking," and apparently it was true then, as it is of the political debates in our own day, that "it is the habit of mankind to entrust to careless hope what they long for, and to use sovereign reason to thrust aside what they do not fancy." "The strength of an army lies in strict discipline and undeviating obedience to its officers." "Self-control is the chief element in self-respect, and self-respect is the chief element in courage." "Peace is best secured by those who use their strength justly, but whose attitude shows that they have no intention of submitting to wrong." To these and many similar aphorisms are added Thucydides' profound insights on societies at war. In his day, as in ours, "society became divided into camps in which no man trusted his fellow." An assembly was persuaded to go to war to prevent a series of allies from falling like dominoes; governments experienced delay, mistrust, and difficulty in negotiating an end to conflict; democracies were "very amenable to discipline while their fright lasted."[2] In many respects Thucydides is as relevant today as he was to the next generation of Greeks.

The officer interested in tactics and leadership in the Greek armies should become acquainted with Xenophon, whose *Anabasis* (written about 375 B.C.) relates the story of the march of the Ten Thousand deep into Persia and back again into Greece. This book is more than a record of incredible adventure; it is a fascinating study in command, and the character sketch of Cyrus

---

1. Marshal de Puységur, *Art de la Guerre, par principes et par regles* (Paris, 1748), I, 36.

2. Thucydides, *The History of the Peloponnesian War* (New York: Dutton, 1935), pp, 88, 90, 243, 266, 390.

would pass for suitable reading in any leadership laboratory. The resourcefulness shown by Xenophon and the other Greek commanders in bringing the army intact 1,700 miles through hostile territory has inspired generals for centuries. In his monumental *Art de la Guerre* (The Art of War) published in 1748, Puységur mentions the practical lessons Xenophon's book contains for the eighteenth century, and a few years later British General James Wolfe confessed that the inspiration for a maneuver of his light infantry came from Xenophon's description of a running battle with the Kurds in 401 B.C., when Greek spearmen successfully negotiated a mountain range defended by lightly armed troops.

Xenophon also wrote what probably is the most famous Greek treatise on military theory and practice. In *Cyropaedia* he described an imaginary war in which he gave free rein to his own ideas on organization and administration, tactics and training, weapons and armor. We learn, for example, why the Greeks failed to develop an adequate supply system, which limited their concept of strategy. Frequently they were subject to civil discord, there was no such thing as a trained staff, and the commander, lacking both maps and an accurate method of determining time, found it impossible to coordinate the movements of two or more detachments.[3]

In battle the Spartan general usually kept his principal officers—the equivalent of the modern battalion commanders—close at hand in order to consult with them and issue his orders. Once he had determined the best course of action, these officers returned to their troops and passed the word down the chain of command to the leaders of what today would be called companies, platoons and sections. In the Greek phalanx each file was a self-contained unit led by an officer in the front rank. Each officer knew his men by name, which Xenophon assures us is essential in motivating the common soldier. "Men who think that their officer recognizes them are keener to be seen doing something honorable and more desirous of avoiding disgrace." No officer who could recognize his men "could go wrong." Thanks to Xenophon the figures who comprise the phalanx emerge as modern soldiers. They move, they must eat, they generally respond to orders, they require discipline, and they respond to motivation, and he explains carefully how these things were done. "No one can be a good officer," he comments,

---

3. Xenophon's imaginary "battle of Thyrmbrara" is skillfully analysed by J. K. Anderson, *Military Theory and Practice in the Age of Xenophon* (Berkeley: Univ. of Calif. Press, 1970), pp. 165–91.

"who does not undergo more than those he commands," and he understood the eternal truth that Baron von Steuben later demonstrated again at Valley Forge. "Willing obedience always beats forced obedience."[4]

For a comparable look at the Roman military system, the student should start with *The Histories* of Polybius written in the second century A.D. His treatment of the Punic Wars ranks alongside the history of Thucydides. Convinced "there is no more ready corrective for mankind than the understanding of the past," this unusual Greek prisoner of war combined sound historical research with the insights gained from his own experience in politics and war. Few books have contributed so much to our understanding of the past. His description of the constitution of the Roman Republic had a direct influence upon the framers of our own constitution, and his treatment of the Roman military system influenced military thinkers nearly twenty centuries later. Most of what we know about Scipio Africanus and Hannibal, for instance, comes from Polybius, and his treatment of organization and tactics was sufficiently detailed to encourage a prominent French theorist in the eighteenth century to write six volumes of commentary— Folard's *Histoire de Polybe . . . avec un commentaire* (1727-30). This work in turn triggered a running fight between exponents of the *ordre profond* (deep column) and the *ordre mince* (line). Was depth to be the basic combat order, as it had been with the Romans, or should infantry deploy into lines to take advantage of firepower? In answering this question some eighteenth- and nineteenth-century soldiers still looked to the Romans.

Polybius describes military operations in sufficient detail to permit later historians to reconstruct the battles intelligently, and sometimes with a practical purpose. Although we do not know exactly where Hannibal's elephants crossed the Alps, enough is known of his dispositions at Cannae to have inspired a German general a little over seventy years ago. At the strategical level, Count Alfred von Schlieffen devised a plan for enveloping the French army employing the same principles that Hannibal evidently followed in enveloping Varro's legions. Convinced that Germany must win a quick victory over France before the Russians had time to concentrate overwhelming numbers for an invasion of East Prussia, Schlieffen found his inspiration in the first volume of Hans Delbrück's *History of the Art of War* (1900).

---

4. Robert D. Heinl, *Dictionary of Military and Naval Quotations* (Annapolis: U.S. Naval Institute, 1966), p. 217.

Delbrück's account of Cannae suggested to Schlieffen's fertile imagination the idea of a battle of annihilation through envelopment. Later he developed his own doctrine in a series of articles, many of which were later translated and published in a work entitled *Cannae* (1913). The Schlieffen plan was the ultimate result, and if it would be naive and misleading to claim any sort of cause and effect relationship, we may at least point to Schlieffen as an example of a strategist who discovered that the classics remain instructive even in modern times.

The military student would expect to learn something from the first of the Great Captains to write of his own campaigns, but Julius Caesar's *Commentaries* is disappointing in this respect. Whereas Thucydides and Polybius wrote for the enlightenment of future generations, Caesar intended his book to serve a more immediate purpose. He hoped to convince his fellow Romans not only that he was a great general but also that his policies in Gaul were less violent and rapacious than his political opponents charged. For centuries his work has been useful in teaching young boys Latin, but as for imparting anything of value to the professional soldier we can believe Frederick the Great when he claims that Caesar "scarcely teaches us anything."[5]

A more fruitful source for the student interested in problems of command in Roman times is Onasander's monograph *The General (Strategicus)*. Written in the first century A.D., this interesting treatise contains many pithy remarks upon generalship in all phases, from the selection of officers and staff to specific formations to be used on the march and in battle. Onasander deals with the use of terrain, matters of camp hygiene, the value of drill, and the conferring of rewards. Although he wrote primarily for other Roman soldiers, his observations on the character, temperament, and training of a good commander are so generally philosophical that many of them are valid even today. Translations appeared in England, Spain, France, and the states of Germany and Italy by the sixteenth century. Marshal Maurice de Saxe, one of the foremost commanders of the eighteenth century, testified "that he owed his first conceptions of the conduct of a commander-in-chief to Onasander," and Frederick the Great almost certainly was familiar with the work. Captain Charles Guischardt, a member of Frederick's military retinue, included a translation of *The General* in his own *Memoirs militaires sur les Grecs et les Romains* (1760), and Frederick's own *Military Instructions*

---

5. Jay Luvaas, trans. and ed., *Frederick the Great on the Art of War* (New York: Free Press, 1966), p. 52.

written a few years earlier resemble Onasander's treatise both in subject matter and treatment, although this could be said of much of the military literature that appeared in the eighteenth century. Problems of command and control had not changed much between the time of Onasander and Frederick, which might help to explain why the cult of antiquity was common among soldiers at the time of the Enlightenment. Indeed, on the eve of World War II, Oliver L. Spaulding observed: "We can read Onasander in the regulations of many countries, and hear him in the lectures of many school commandants to their successive classes."[6]

Of all the military works from antiquity, *The Military Institutions of the Romans* by Vegetius is probably the best known. Certainly over the centuries it has been the most influential. Copies were carried by Charlemagne's commanders and by at least two English kings in the Middle Ages, Henry II and Richard the Lion Hearted. Even before the advent of printing the book was translated into several vernacular languages, and published editions appeared in Cologne, Paris, and Rome and in England before the end of the fifteenth century. Vegetius inspired Machiavelli and Saxe, both of whom borrowed heavily from his description of Roman military institutions, and his work was an important element in the theoretical education of many later commanders. A well known Austrian general in the Seven Years' War, the Prince de Ligne, wrote facetiously that God had not inspired the legion, as Vegetius had claimed, but He probably had inspired Vegetius.[7]

Vegetius made no such claim. His information came from a careful and systematic reading of all the military works of antiquity, and by making this collective wisdom available he hoped to contribute to an improvement of the Roman army in his own day, late in the fourth century A.D. Because he failed to distinguish between the armies that won the Punic Wars, or conquered under Caesar, or pacified the later Empire, Vegetius is not a reliable source about the military institutions of the Romans for any particular period in history. What he wrote about the cavalry is more relevant to the Roman forces after the battle of Adrianople (A.D. 378) than to the legions at the time of Marius nearly five centuries earlier (106 B.C.). On the other hand his description of Roman methods of recruiting, training, and

---

6. Oliver L. Spaulding, *Pen and Sword in Greece and Rome* (Princeton, N.J.: Princeton Univ. Press, 1937), p. 90.

7. Thomas R. Phillips, *Roots of Strategy* (Harrisburg: Military Service Publishing Co., 1940), p. 67.

building discipline may well reflect practices that lasted for several centuries. The modern reader will find that his maxims have no time limit upon them at all: "Who wishes peace, let him prepare for war." "What is necessary to be performed in the heat of action should be constantly be practiced in the leisure of peace." "Few men are born brave; many become so through training and force of discipline." "Valor is superior to numbers."[8] (This last idea, however, can be carried to excess, as many Japanese commanders demonstrated in World War II.)

The wisdom of the ancient military writers finds ultimate expression in Sun Tzu's *Art of War*. Introduced to the West only in the late eighteenth century, this Chinese classic has attracted wide attention in our own day, especially now that it has been established that Sun Tzu "strongly influenced" Mao Tse-tung and the recent doctrine of revolutionary warfare.[9] The book is surprisingly modern in outlook, perhaps due as much to Brig. Gen. Samuel B. Griffith's translation as to the timeless quality of Sun Tzu's thought, but it is rich in insight and loaded with striking aphorisms. The book is probably as instructive, in a general sense, today as when it was written nearly twenty-five centuries ago.

The Middle Ages produced no military treatise to rival that of Vegetius and the other Greek and Roman studies on war or Sun Tzu. Even though military institutions formed the foundation for political and social institutions and the eventual decline of feudalism was directly influenced by military developments, western Europe from the fourth to the fifteenth century offers no military literature worthy of the name. The student will get a much better feeling for warfare during this period by reading the secondary works by John Beeler, Charles Oman or R. C. Smail (see Chapter 5) than by clawing his way through some medieval chronicle. "Nothing is to be learned" from all of the medieval wars, declared Frederick the Great contemptuously. And in his erudite treatise on the art of war, Puységur jumped from Vegetius to Montecuccoli, an Imperial general of the late seventeenth century.

Like the gentler and more cultured arts, the art of war was transformed during the Renaissance. The French army of Charles VIII that invaded the Italian states in 1494 was medieval in its organization, equipment, tactics, and above all in its outlook, but by the end of the Italian wars some thirty-five years

---

8. *Ibid.*, p. 71; Spaulding, *Pen and Sword in Greece and Rome*, p. 101.
9. Samuel B. Griffith's Introduction to *The Art of War*, by Sun Tzu (New York: Oxford Univ. Press, 1963), pp. 45–56.

later kings were served by trained standing armies, firearms had become as common among infantry as the pike, cavalry had diminished both in relative numbers and in importance, and artillery had forced changes in fortifications. As the pilgrim still journeyed to Rome and the apprentice painter to Florence, military engineers from northern Europe now visited Italy to learn the latest developments in their profession. The increased importance of fortifications can be seen in the writings of Niccolo Machiavelli (1469–1527), who in 1513 claimed that a ruler with a strong army had no need for fortresses; yet seven years later Machiavelli considered it necessary to devote an entire book in his *Art of War* to the subject.

Machiavelli's treatise on war is the first modern military classic. Like the typical humanist in his day, Machiavelli looked to the classics for inspiration and most of his ideas on training, tactics, organization, and command are little more than attempts to adapt practices described by Livy, Polybius, and Vegetius to conditions prevailing in the fifteenth century. Looking over his shoulder at the Romans, it is scarcely surprising that he failed to appreciate the importance of firearms, nor was he any better than Vegetius in distinguishing between the military institutions of Republican and Imperial Rome. Machiavelli therefore is not a particularly good source for the military practices of either the Romans or their Italian descendants.

His unique contribution is his recognition that war is essentially a branch of politics and that armies normally reflect the qualities of their respective societies. Convinced that he lived in a decadent age, compared with the Roman Republic, Machiavelli called for a citizen army to replace the mercenary forces hired by most Italian princes. He considered citizens more reliable politically and more efficient in tactics and also hoped that a citizen army might become an instrument for restoring civic virtues lost to society. Already in *The Prince* he had urged his patron to discard the undisciplined and unreliable mercenary armies in favor of a militia. In *The Discourses* he wrote at length upon the citizen soldier of Republican Rome. *The Art of War* reveals his plan for a citizen army that would infuse the other citizens with *virtu*, that hard to define characteristic of the good soldier embracing such qualities as courage, discipline, loyalty, obedience, and self-sacrifice.

This is an intriguing theory, particularly coming from a man whose political maxims have been distorted by oversimplification into a philosophy of "might makes right," and "the end justifies the means." Instead of viewing the soldier and the civilian as two separate and distinct individuals, often with conflicting aims, Machiavelli saw them as two sides of the same man. The soldier served the citizen, but each citizen was at some time a soldier. This argument that the army can serve as the school of the nation resurfaced in the nineteenth century, when advocates of the nation in arms used it to justify universal military service.

Machiavelli should be consulted, therefore, for the insights he can provide on war as one of the collective activities of mankind. It is not necessary to accept his theory that military power is the foundation of civil society to appreciate the relationships he established between war and politics three centuries before Clausewitz blazed a new path in military literature by discussing war as an instrument of policy.

Not until the French Revolution, in fact, did other military writers dwell on the reciprocal action of political and military institutions, although the idea is implicit in the reforms suggested in Saxe's *Reveries* (1757) and is the point of departure for Jacques Guibert in his *General Essay on Tactics* (1775). Probably the most profound military writer of the eighteenth century, Guibert began his study with an account of the ways in which the character of a people and the nature of their government influenced tactics. No significant improvement in armies was possible, he contended, until there first occurred some fundamental changes in society. But let there "spring up a vigorous people, with genius, power, and a happy form of government," a people with virtue in a state where the subjects are citizens, "where they cherish and revere government, where they are fond of glory, where they are not intimidated at the idea of toiling for the general good," and armies would become invincible.[10] The army of Guibert's dreams did in fact materialize fifteen years later as a result of the French Revolution.

Nearly all of the military books written between the time of Machiavelli and Guibert belong to the realm of theory, although authors usually did not bother to distinguish between military history and theory. Saxe and Guibert drew heavily upon history in formulating their theories; Frederick wrote history for the purpose of instructing his successors just as he wrote military theory for the purpose of instructing his generals. And General Henry Lloyd, an Englishman who fought for the Austrians against Frederick, in his *History of the Late War in Germany* (1766-81) was concerned as much with examining the art of war

---

10. Comte de Guibert, *A General Essay on Tactics* . . . (London, 1781), Vol. I, pp. vii–viii; xxiii–xxv, lxvii.

as narrating the facts of battles and campaigns. Those who endeavored to write military history and ignore theory had so little to say that Guibert once wrote of historians: "I see nothing in respect to military events that can be relied on but the names of Generals and the dates of battles."[11]

On the other hand, the use of the word *theory* in describing the military literature of the eighteenth century is somewhat misleading. The Chevalier de Folard created his system of tactics from a study of the classics, while another well known military writer, Mesnil-Durand, reduced tactics to a series of mathematical formulas. But most of the so-called theorists were merely practical soldiers trying to record their knowledge, acquired largely through extensive personal experience, for the benefit of younger officers. They described in detail their camps and sieges; they specified the correct practices to follow in surprising enemy posts and convoys; they explained the problems often encountered in skirmishes and ambuscades; and they discussed the various methods to be employed in conducting marches to and from cantonments, flank marches, or retreats. Above all they were concerned with practical matters in tactics and organization. Strategy as we use the term did not attract much attention.

The reasons for this neglect of strategy are varied. The word itself had not yet been coined, and when military writers turned their thoughts from the mechanical movement of bodies of troops to that "higher art" of generalship known to later generations as strategy, the term they used was "plan of campaign." And here, instead of establishing any theoretical framework or body of knowledge, they treated each "plan" as a unique project that had to be shaped according to a particular enemy, the terrain, the nature of the war, and the rivers and fortified cities serving as obstacles or as lines of communication and depots. In each instance, just as in the deployment of armies for battle, rules decreed by experience had to be followed—effective ways to defend a river line, established methods of determining the order of march, basic problems to consider when establishing camps, and so forth. There were general rules for offensive and defensive warfare, for the use of detachments, and for precautions to avoid being caught by surprise. Frederick even listed fourteen measures to prevent desertion, perhaps the most consuming concern of an Army commander before the French Revolution transformed subjects into citizens with a cause.

---

11. *Ibid.*, p. 5.

There is, however, no body of theoretical knowledge about strategy in these eighteenth-century treatises; for that it would be necessary to imitate Jomini and study the actual campaigns. Puységur and Frederick were typical of their day when they resorted to hypothetical situations to communicate their thoughts on strategy, one describing the measures to be taken in a theater bounded by the Seine and the Loire and the other depicting imaginary wars against the French and the Austrians. Frederick in fact wrote his *History of the Seven Years' War* in 1763 primarily to "leave an authentic record of the advantageous [military] situations as they occurred in the provinces . . . where war was made." He hoped that his successors in the next war with Austria (and he always assumed that there would be another) would benefit from his experiences. "All positions, all camps, all marches are known and made. It is only a question of using them correctly and playing everything to its advantage."[12]

It follows, then, that most eighteenth-century treatises, reflecting then current military practices as well as useful "lessons" gleaned from recent campaigns, will provide the modern reader with a clearer insight into the spirit and nature of eighteenth-century warfare than he might hope to gain from the average secondary account of some war or battle. Indeed, this literature should be approached solely with this purpose in mind, for Frederick and his contemporaries were far too pragmatic to worry about formulating maxims that would apply for all time. Occasionally they did glimpse some eternal principle, but this has been true of every military writer of substance since Sun Tzu. One should read Frederick, Saxe, and Guibert for what they tell us of military problems in their own day, for that was their persistent purpose in writing. If their observations provoke reflection upon some similar problem today, this merely proves the wisdom of Emerson's observation a century ago: "Tis the good reader that makes the good book."[13]

Among the military writers of the eighteenth century, Vauban and Frederick the Great stand out because of their practical accomplishments. Vauban designed over one hundred great fortresses and harbor installations and conducted nearly fifty sieges, establishing in the process the basic rules that came to dominate strategy in the "war of positions" until the day of Napoleon. And Frederick, easily the foremost field commander of his age, represents the apogee of the military art as it was practiced before Napoleon.

---

12. *Frederick the Great on the Art of War*, pp. 48–49.
13. *The Complete Works of Ralph Waldo Emerson*, 12 vols. (Boston, 1930), 7:296.

Saxe's *Reveries*, on the other hand, are a refreshing curiosity. Although his ideas for improving military efficiency did carry considerable weight with nineteenth-century reformers, his influence upon Napoleon is often exaggerated. "Among many extremely mediocre matters" in Saxe's *Reveries*, Napoleon did find "some good ideas" on ways to make the enemy pay for the French war effort.[14] Guibert, who has properly been called a military philosopher, is well worth reading, but the only English edition was published late in the eighteenth century. Unless the student has access to a good rare book collection or possesses a reading knowledge of French, he is not likely to become acquainted at first hand with the most important of all military writers of eighteenth-century France.

Fortunately Vauban's *Manual of Siegecraft and Fortification* is available, the most recent translation being in 1968; this major work contains his formula for the attack and defense of fortified cities. Perhaps, in order fully to appreciate Vauban's contribution, one should also read Eugene Viollet-le-Duc's *Annals of a Fortress* (1876), which traces the evolution of fortification to 1870 by describing in detail seven sieges representative of the successive stages. A casual visit to any fort constructed in this country before the Civil War, when the introduction of heavy rifled artillery made the existing system of coastal defense obsolete, will reveal the debt that our own military engineers have owed to Vauban. And aerial photographs of German defenses on the western front in 1916 demonstrate the application of Vauban's principles even in our own century: The bastions and curtains were made of barbed wire rather than brick or stone, but the trace (ground plan)—and the principle—remained the same.

This is true also of siege warfare. A hundred years after the death of Vauban, sieges were being conducted in the Spanish peninsula exactly as he prescribed, and a glance at any military map of the siege of Sevastopol in 1854–55, the approaches to Battery Wagner in Charleston Harbor in 1863, or the works thrown up by the Japanese at Port Arthur in 1904, will reveal that Vauban's principles were still applicable in the modern era. His *Manual* should be read therefore not only for the light it throws upon military operations in the eighteenth century but also because of his persistent influence upon fortification and siegecraft.

Vauban's influence is also evident in the writings of Frederick

---

14. Lt. Col. Ernest Picard, *Preceptes et jugements de Napoleon* (Paris: Berger-Levrault, 1913), pp. 545–56.

the Great, who applied these same rules of siegecraft to tactics and strategy in the field. To Frederick the attack in battle was similar to the attack against a modern fortress:

> Anyone in a siege thinks of beginning not with the third parallel, but with the first. Provision depots are laid out and all the works that are pushed forward must be supported by those in the rear. Similarly, in battles, the only good dispositions are those that provide mutual support, where a corps of troops never is risked all alone but is constantly supported by the others.[15]

Frederick would treat strategy in the same way, advancing methodically with a river, a mountain chain, or a line of fortresses serving the same purpose as Vauban's parallels, each sure step bringing his army closer to the object of his plan of campaign, which he compared to the breach in the enemy's walls. Above all, Frederick contended, avoid making a deep penetration into enemy territory with an army or even with a detachment—to do so is as fatal as to rush an enemy fortress without first laying siege to the place, establishing parallels to bring the guns close enough to blast a breach in the fortress walls, and moving troops forward in relative safety to a point from which they can rush the breach.

Frederick is best known for his *Military Instructions*, which he wrote early in his military career, before the close of the Silesian Wars (1740-45). His mature thoughts are to be found only in a recent translation of selected writings from his collected works entitled *Frederick the Great on the Art of War* (1966). Here we find Frederick's views on mobility, discipline and firepower, his peacetime experiments with new tactical forms and maneuvers, his penetrating analysis in 1759 of the changing Austrian methods of waging war, and his belated recognition of the new role of artillery and the growing importance of intrenched camps in what is probably his most significant work, "Elements of Castrametation and Tactics" (1770).[16]

Frederick wrote more to clarify his own thoughts than to contribute ideas to ours, and he never presented his ideas in a unified system. Nevertheless his views are essential to any understanding of eighteenth-century warfare, and none of the others Napoleon considered Great Captains—Alexander, Hannibal, Caesar, Gustavus Adolphus, Prince Eugene, or even Turenne—has enabled us to share his thoughts and the motives

---

15. *Frederick the Great on the Art of War*, p. 312.

16. *Ibid.*, pp. 276-305, for the most significant portions of this essay.

underlying his actions. Napoleon himself never wrote fully on the subject of war. Although the thirty-two volumes of his published *Correspondance* contain a wealth of information on tactics, strategy, organization, logistics, command, and the military occupation of conquered territories, Napoleon's thoughts on these subjects are generally expressed with some specific situation in mind.

In contrast, *The Military Maxims of Napoleon*[17] is nothing more than a collection of random thoughts expressed by Napoleon at St. Helena (1815-21) and compiled by an admiring general. We do not know the basis for General Burnod's selections, whether he chose passages that seemed to him an honest reflection of Napoleon's views or whether he selected those maxims—some of them out of context—that he thought would have lasting value. In any event the *Military Maxims* represent Napoleon's final thoughts rather than his reactions to military situations as he confronted them over a period of twenty years. If read on the heels of Frederick's *Military Instructions*, which appeared near the beginning of an even longer career, the reader can easily exaggerate the differences between the two generals. In many respects Napoleon's earlier thoughts on such subjects as artillery represent a logical extension of Frederick's last views on the subject.

Napoleon's *Military Maxims* were quickly translated into German, English, Spanish, and Italian, and in one form or another they permeated the formal education of most soldiers in the nineteenth century. Stonewall Jackson always carried a copy in the field. Others were introduced to Napoleon's maxims through secondary works like Henry Halleck's *Elements of Military Art and Science* (1846), P. L. MacDougall's *Theory of War* (1856), Sir Edward Hamley's *Operations of War* (1866), and a host of lesser but similar works that attempted to recast the great campaigns of history into a mold formed by the principles of Napoleon and his worthy opponent, the Archduke Charles.

The most celebrated and influential student of Napoleon's generalship was of course Baron Henri Jomini, who in numerous books endeavored to distill from Napoleon's campaigns the essence of his tactical and particularly of his strategical doctrine. Napoleon's greatness as a commander resulted above all from his preeminence in the field of strategy, and it was not until his day that military writers began to think in strategic

---

17. There have been many editions of the *Maxims* since this small book was first published in 1827; the most readily available is probably that contained in Phillips, *Roots of Strategy*, pp. 407-41.

terms. Jomini was the first to grasp the significance of Napoleon's new methods and the principles underlying his actions; indeed, it was Jomini who gave to the nineteenth century a working definition of strategy. Originally the term was taken to mean "the science of military movement beyond the visual circle of the enemy, or out of cannon shot," but Jomini expanded it to signify "the art of bringing the greatest part of the forces of an army upon the important point of the theater of war, or of a zone of operations,"[18] and so it was understood by the generals who guided the armies in the American Civil War and the German wars for unification.

Indeed, Jomini commanded the field of military theory to such an extent in the nineteenth century that no student of military history can disregard either his ideas or influence. The claim that our Civil War generals surged into battle with a sword in one hand and a copy of Jomini in the other is a naive but pardonable exaggeration; whether or not most officers in 1861 were familiar with the writings of Jomini, nearly all of them initially shared his fundamental assumptions about tactics. Formal instruction in military art and science at West Point had been based largely upon the study of Napoleonic warfare as analyzed in the writings of Jomini and his American pupils, and the ideal battle in the mind of the average general in 1861 probably differed little from the classic Napoleonic formula. The drill manuals in use at that time prepared each arm for its role in the kind of battle envisaged by Jomini, and it required several campaigns before most Civil War tacticians could appreciate the fact that American terrain, increased firepower, and a faulty organization made it impossible to fight the kind of battle described so enticingly in the pages of Jomini or Halleck.

The railroad, telegraph, and steamboat were similarly destined to change the dimensions of Jomini's strategy, but here the transition was far less abrupt. Jomini would have been delighted with Lee's generalship during the Seven Days' battles, when the Confederate commander tried "to throw by strategic movements the mass of his army upon the communications of the enemy" (a cherished principle of Jomini), and where McClellan, in changing his line of communications to Harrison's Landing, had pulled off the type of maneuver Napoleon himself had described as "one of the most skillful of military maneuvers."[19] And surely he would have been delighted with Jackson's Valley

18. Baron de Jomini, *Summary of the Art of War* (New York, 1864), p. 326.
19. Phillips, *Roots of Strategy*, p. 413.

campaign, in many respects an "instant replay" of Napoleon's early campaigns in Italy when it came to the exploitation of "interior lines."

But what sense could Jomini have made of Grant's unorthodox movements before Vicksburg, when he deliberately disregarded Jomini's one great principle: "To throw by strategic movements the mass of an army . . . upon the decisive points of a theater of war, and also upon the communications of the enemy as much as possible *without compromising one's own*."[20] How would he have reacted to Sherman's march through Georgia, or explained away the fact that in 1862 and 1863 Lee occasionally had violated Jomini's principles and still had managed to win convincing victories? Granted that Jomini recognized that every maxim has its exceptions, the fact remains that the battles of the Civil War were won by generals who wrote their own rules.

And in 1866 the Prussian generals took further liberties with Jomini's maxims. "Let history and principles go to the devil!" one of them snorted when confronted by an unexpected situation a few days before the crucial battle at Königgrätz. "After all, what is the problem?"[21] Moltke himself described strategy as "common sense applied to the art of war," and his formula for victory was simple: seek out and destroy the enemy army with superior forces made available by mobilization of the nation's manpower, meticulous peacetime planning, and the well-developed German rail system. The military student may understand Napoleon's campaigns after reading Jomini, but the Swiss theorist could easily distort a person's view of the Civil War and would be of no help whatever in explaining the generalship of Moltke. For this the writings of Karl von Clausewitz are more instructive.

Jomini and Clausewitz are often contrasted and usually it is Jomini who suffers by comparison. This is manifestly unfair, for each wrote with a quite different purpose in mind and each has contributed uniquely to our knowledge of war. Jomini's *Art of War* is a systematic treatise on strategy; Clausewitz's *On War* is essentially a philosophical inquiry into the phenomenon of mass struggle. Jomini seeks to explain, Clausewitz to explore. You could probably compare both of them to instructors you have seen in the classroom. Jomini is the lecturer concerned with explaining his material in well-organized, practical lessons. Clausewitz, on the other hand, is the ivory-towered scholar

---

20. *Jomini and his Summary of the Art of War* . . ., ed. J. D. Hittle (Harrisburg: Military Services Publishing Co., 1947), p. 67.

21. Quoted in Marshal Ferdinand Foch, *The Principles of War* (London: H. K. Fly Co., 1918), p. 14.

constantly wrestling with some challenging and perhaps insoluble problem, in the classroom as well as in his book-lined study. Jomini is popular for the tidy lectures he delivers year after year (every fraternity has a set of his notes, often yellow with age but still helpful in the course). Clausewitz is constantly fumbling for his notes, never seems well-organized, and rarely if ever completes his course because he is perpetually adding new material. You can feel comfortable with Jomini; Clausewitz will remind you of your own inadequacies. You leave Jomini convinced that you have mastered "the course," but probably not until you are an old grad will you appreciate the wisdom of the old Prussian professor. Jomini seemed relevant at the time, but as the years pass, and conditions change, and as your interests and responsibilities grow, it is probably some passage from Clausewitz that will march to your assistance when needed. For Clausewitz did not look for any fixed laws or principles, and his conclusions therefore were less exposed than the maxims of Jomini to the progressive totalitarianism of warfare and the acceleration of technical invention in industrial society.

Clausewitz made a profound impression upon the Prussian army. Contending that war properly belonged to the province of chance rather than calculation, he convinced a generation of Prussian generals that the overriding aim in war should be the destruction of the enemy's armed forces and that this was best achieved through the offensive, provided the army enjoyed the edge in numbers and moral and intellectual forces. He did not leave behind a rational system of maxims such as those expounded by Jomini, but his penetrating insights into the nature of modern war helped to educate the judgment of Moltke and his disciples, and Moltke's doctrine as it was understood and applied after 1871 was built upon the foundation laid originally by Clausewitz.

This is not to say that Clausewitz was completely understood even in his own army. German generals, generous always in the lip service they paid to his theories, often tended to overlook, if not deliberately overturn, his basic premise that war is an instrument of policy. Moltke, for example, insisted that strategic considerations should determine policy in time of war. And Prince Kraft Hohenlohe, one of the most respected German theorists in the late nineteenth century, insisted that national policy must go hand in hand with strategy, which places him closer to Ludendorff than Clausewitz in this respect.

Even in the purely military sphere, the meditative ideas of Clausewitz have served many interests over the years. For instance, convinced that "battle is the only argument in war, therefore the only end that must be given to strategical operations,"[22] the future Marshal Foch responded to those passages in Clausewitz that seemed to reflect his own beliefs. A generation was convinced that the next war would be an immense armed drama, beginning with the mobilization of vast armies, their strategic deployment along the frontiers, and then a rapid and sustained advance to those bloody acres where victory would follow short, violent combat. Clausewitz did indeed appear as the prophet if not the uncompromising advocate of total war. It would be strange if he had not evoked this brutal response.

But read On War with different assumptions in mind, read Clausewitz for what light he can cast upon our recent experience in Vietnam, and a quite different set of passages will snap to attention: "The probable character and general shape of any war should mainly be assessed in the light of political factors and conditions." Clausewitz points to significant differences between wars: "Every age has its own kind of war, its own limiting conditions and its own peculiar preconceptions,"[23] and he has something relevant to say about the peculiarities of war in our time, the relationship between war and politics, even the distinction between limited and total war. Like Machiavelli or Plato, he can always reward the thoughtful reader although his speculations, like theirs, are easily distorted.

After 1871 the military world was inundated with technical and theoretical literature. New professional journals gave soldiers everywhere an opportunity to air their views; new military schools stimulated the study of war and gave direction to doctrine; revised tactical manuals tried in vain to keep pace with technological change; and even military history became the captive of historical sections of the various general staffs or else served as a vehicle to prove the validity of some particular point of view. The unwary reader who picks up a campaign history written anytime between 1871 and 1914 would do well to remember Bronsart von Schellendorf's observation, "It is well known that military history, when superficially studied, will furnish arguments in support of any theory or opinion."[24]

---

22. Ibid., p. 43.

23. Karl von Clausewitz, On War, ed. and trans. Michael Howard and Peter Paret (Princeton, N.J.: Princeton Univ. Press, 1976), pp. 593, 607.

24. Quoted in Prince Kraft Hohenlohe, Letters on Artillery (London: E. Stanford, 1890), p. 108.

Most of this literature was inspired by some recent development or problem and can safely be set aside by today's soldier without any sense of loss. A few titles, however, are worth remembering for the comprehensive insights they continue to give into the military thoughts and institutions that dominated the period. Jean Colin's *Transformation of War* (1912), for example, remains indispensable for understanding the evolution of warfare since Napoleon. Sir Frederick Maurice's essay "War" (1891), which he wrote originally for the *Encyclopaedia Britannica*, contains a useful annotated bibliography of the best of the military literature produced in the nineteenth century. Spencer Wilkinson, *The Brain of an Army* (1890), is a gem that remains the best source for the ways in which the German General Staff functioned under Moltke. Elihu Root, the American Secretary of War who was instrumental in founding our own Army War College and the general staff, has acknowledged his indebtedness to this unusual book. Anything by G.F.R. Henderson will repay reading. Henderson excelled both as historian and military critic. He used history to stimulate independent thought rather than to illustrate conventional views, and he wrote with unusual sensitivity and imagination. *The Science of War* (1905) is probably still the most original and provocative book on the development of tactics during the Napoleonic wars, the Civil War, the German wars for unification, and the South African war, while *Stonewall Jackson and the American Civil War* (1898) remains a military classic, embodying Henderson's own views on tactics and command and representing a novel approach to the study of strategy.

Probably the most complete tactical studies are Arthur Wagner's *Organization and Tactics* (1895) and William Balck's *Tactics* (1897-1903). The latter is a useful compilation of tactical thought and practice in the major armies of Europe, and illustrates the hold that the Prussian campaigns against Austria and France had upon soldiers thirty years later. Prince Kraft zu Hohenlohe-Ingelfingen's popular *Letters on Artillery* (1890), *Letters on Cavalry* (1889), and *Letters on Infantry* (1892), are more original and less technical essays on the performances of the three arms in the German wars for unification. Useful summaries can also be found in E.M. Lloyd, *A Review of the History of Infantry* (1908), George T. Denison, *A History of Cavalry* (1913) and A.F. Becke, *An Introduction to the History of Tactics, 1740-1905* (1909).

In the field of military history, in contrast to the theoretical and technical literature, Hans Delbrück's *History of the Art of*

War (1900-1920) still stands in the front rank. The first volume was published appropriately in 1900, for Delbrück's work is at once a synthesis of the best military and historical literature of the nineteenth century and a bold first step in the direction of a more sophisticated and scholarly brand of military history.

Delbrück shared Clausewitz's interest in the relationship between war and politics, and indeed in many respects his research on the links between the state and tactics and strategy from the time of the Greeks until Frederick and Napoleon tend to confirm the more selective observations of Clausewitz. He did not, however, agree with what the enthusiastic disciples of Clausewitz were writing about the total nature of modern warfare. Whereas most professional soldiers, at least on the continent, were advocating a strategy of annihilation by the end of the century (and distorting much of what Clausewitz had to say in the process), Delbrück advocated what he called a strategy of exhaustion. For his study of the campaigns of Pericles, Belisarius, Wallenstein, Gustavus Adolphus and Frederick the Great revealed that battle was not necessarily the only pay off in war: It was but one of several means to the end, that being the achievement of the political objectives of the war. Great commanders like Alexander, Caesar, and Napoleon had aimed at the complete military subjection of the enemy, and most soldiers in Delbrück's day were similarly committed to the doctrine that the enemy army was the main object of strategy and that there was no alternative to the decisive battle. Delbrück outraged conventional military opinion by constantly pointing to campaigns and wars where the destruction of a detachment, skillful maneuver, and a successful blockade or siege were likewise effective in bringing a war to a successful conclusion.

The reader today will not be so much interested in Delbrück's debates with the German General Staff over strategies of exhaustion and of annihilation as in Delbrück's unusual approach to the study of military history. What he can best learn from Delbrück is that military history is but one of many branches in history: It has the same values, the same shortcomings, and to be understood properly it must be studied in much the same way. Delbrück maintained that the value of military history was enhanced when it was treated as but one of many branches of history that "flow together . . . and cross-fertilize one another,"[25] which probably explains why he was the first to

---

25. Hans Delbrück, *Geschichte der Kriegskunst im Rahmen der politischen Geschichte*, 4 vols. (Berlin, 1900-1920). Col. Walter J. Renfroe of the Military Academy has recently completed his excellent translation of the first volume with the others to follow: *History of the Art of War Within the Framework of Political History* (Westport, Conn.: Greenwood Press, 1975), quotation from p. 11.

establish military history as a respectable academic discipline.

The reader will also benefit from Delbrück's methodology, for by combining meticulous research with the practical military knowledge of his own day he demolished many of the legends that survived antiquity. Thus when Herodotus claimed that the Athenians charged into the Persians at Marathon after running for some 1,500 meters, Delbrück consulted his own experience as a reserve officer and the most recent pamphlets on military training and tactics before stating this to be a physical impossibility. A large unit in his own day could cover at most 150 meters at a run during maneuvers (Prussian regulations in fact permitted the soldier with all field equipment to run for only two minutes, or 350 meters). From his study of Greek society he knew that the Athenian army comprised men of fifty as well as youths in their prime, and personal experience taught him that a closed mass (the Greek phalanx) runs with much more difficulty than an individual. Finally, an incident in the 1864 war between Prussia and Denmark provided a useful example of what can happen when a body of troops enters hand to hand combat after a forced run of 400 paces. He rejected therefore the version of Herodotus, and a personal study of the terrain enabled him to revise the traditional version so that it might make more sense to the modern soldier.

He similarly used his knowledge of demography and of Persian and Greek society to demonstrate that instead of being outnumbered six to one, the Athenians probably fought the battle with something approaching even odds. Only then, he contended, do the tactical decisions of both commanders make the slightest sense. Delbrück's method enabled him to reject the story that ten years later the Persians returned with an army of 4,200,000 men! Instead of merely scaling down the numbers to a more reasonable figure, which most modern historians have done, Delbrück shows why this too was an absolute impossibility:

> An army corps of 30,000 covers, in the German march order, some 14 miles, without its supply train. The march column of the Persians would therefore have been 2,000 miles long, and when the head of the column was arriving before Thermopylae, the end of the column might have been just marching out . . . on the far side of the Tigris.[26]

In this manner Delbrück worked his way through 2,300 years of military history, providing fresh insights on familiar campaigns

---

26. *Ibid.*, p. 35.

and leaving behind a work that is as valuable today as when it was first written.

No survey of military literature can ignore Adm. Alfred Thayer Mahan, who approached the past with an entirely different point of view than Delbruck. Mahan treated the history of sea power as "largely a military history," and he searched the period from 1660 to 1815 for "inferences applicable to one's own country and service." Jomini provided his methodology, although he was a far better historian than the Swiss pundit. Mahan's principles of naval strategy are comparable to Jomini's maxims for land warfare; both believed that "the organized forces of the enemy are ever the chief objective," and Mahan shared Jomini's faith in the validity of unchanging principles. "The battles of the past," he claimed, "succeeded or failed according as they were fought in conformity with the principles of war."[27]

Because Mahan wrote didactic history, it really makes little difference which of his books on the influence of sea power one reads: The lessons will be the same. *The Influence of Sea Power Upon History, 1660-1783*, which appeared in 1890, and its sequels dealing with the wars of the French Revolution, Napoleon, and the war of 1812, had a profound influence upon both naval theory and history. Mahan constantly applied his principles to contemporary military and commercial control of the seas. Because he made the past speak to the present in meaningful terms, his theories became immensely popular not only in the United States, then emerging as a major naval and colonial power, but also in Germany and England, where there was an intense interest in naval power. No American military writer—and few American authors in any field—can match his international reputation. Mahan found naval history "a record of battles, and left it as a subject that was intimately connected with foreign policy and the general history of the nation state."[28]

Works devoted to strategy before 1914 are disappointing and surprisingly lacking in originality. In *The Development of Strategical Science During the 19th Century* (1904), Rudolf von Caemmerer traces the influence of Clausewitz, Jomini and Moltke but deadens the interest of the student in the process. After 1871 strategy became pragmatic and nationalized as most writers turned away from the purely theoretical and focussed attention upon specific problems that their respective military

27. A. T. Mahan, The Influence of Sea Power Upon History 1660-1783 (Boston: Little, Brown, 1890), pp. 1, 9, 83.

28. D. M. Schurman, The Education of a Navy: The Development of British Naval Strategic Thought, 1867-1914 (Chicago: Univ. of Chicago Press, 1965), p. 82.

forces faced. Strategy also became increasingly dominated by tactics, which is suggested by the title of one of General Jules Lewal's treatises, *Strategie de Combat* (1895). According to Lewal, familiar definitions seemed to have lost their meaning; old rules could not be extended to cover the new conditions created by the railroad, telegraph, mass army, and modern weapons. "The unexpectancy of combat is inevitable, and in view of this fact he who invokes the memory of the glorious maneuvers that led to Marengo, Austerlitz and Jena is open to censure. . . . Now one arrives on the ground and one fights there: that is the war of the future."[29] As the alliance structure and arms race increased international tensions and limited the options of strategy, the significant work in the field was inevitably directed toward the elaborate plans produced in the operations sections of the various general staffs. German strategic thought finally came to rest in the much publicized Schlieffen plan, while the spirit of the offensive that dominated French military thought by the turn of the century found its ultimate expression in the ill-fated Plan XVII.

There are some excellent studies of the soldier in modern battle. In his famous *Battle Studies* (1880), Ardant du Picq examined the Latin classics to gain fresh understanding of men and morale in ancient combat, which he then applied to modern battle. By the use of a questionnaire which he sent to many of his fellow officers, he acquired much the same kind of data on the behavior of soldiers in the Crimean War and the Italian War of 1859 that S. L. A. Marshall was later to glean from his extensive after-action interviews in World War II, Korea, and Vietnam.

The infantryman of World War I is the subject of Lord Moran's fascinating account of his medical experiences on the Western Front, *The Anatomy of Courage* (1945). Easily overlooked, this book should be required reading for all who would understand what men went through in the trench war of 1914-18. More recently John Baynes has investigated the morale of the front-line soldier in a work entitled *Morale: A Study of Men and Courage* (1967). Commencing with the 2d Battalion of the Cameronians in 1914, he follows the men of his father's old unit through the battle of Neuve Chapelle.

By far the most stimulating study of human behavior in battle is John Keegan's *The Face of Battle* (1976). This is not just another book about battles. Keegan has re-created the fighting at Agincourt (1415), Waterloo (1815), and the Somme (1916) to

---

29. J. L. Lewal, *Strategie de combat* (Paris: Baudion, 1895), 1:3, 35; 2:189.

demonstrate how soldiers have reacted to three sorts of weapons, namely the sword and lance, the musket, and the machine gun and poison gas. How did men in such varied circumstances "control their fears, staunch their wounds, go to their deaths"? Unlike the others, Keegan is not a professional soldier nor has he seen combat, but he has made brilliant use of his sources, and his approach will influence the thinking of any serious scholar interested in battle.

Any soldier who takes his profession seriously will benefit from these studies, for as Napoleon reminds us, "morale makes up three quarters of the game." "Remember also," Admiral Farragut advised his son, "that one of the requisite studies for an officer is *man*," and General George S. Patton, Jr., wrote long before his name became a household word, "wars may be fought with weapons, but they are won by men."[30]

For the problems inherent in the mass army, the curious student would be well advised to browse through General Friedrich von Bernhardi's *On War of To-day* (1912). Written only three years before the outbreak of war in 1914, this work gives probably the best insight into the assumptions that guided soldiers into the first battles. In two surprisingly readable volumes, Bernhardi probes the secrets of modern war—the relation of force to numbers, technical appliances, march techniques, supplies and lines of communication, principles of command, and the essential elements of superiority in war. His discussion of military operations includes fortress warfare and naval warfare. His mistakes are the mistakes of the generals who fought the First World War, but it is always well to remind ourselves that had the Germans won the first battle of the Marne—and it was a near thing at that—military writers like Bernhardi would probably be honored as prophets today.

World War I produced a flood of analytical literature, much of it prophetic, about the nature and shape of wars to come. Giulio Douhet, an Italian artillery officer who early developed a belief in air power as the dominant factor in modern war, was such a writer. Douhet was not alone in his observation that in a war of attrition it is not so much armies as whole populations that determine the outcome. Despite their military victories, the Germans had eventually suffered a complete general collapse, which could only have happened as the result of "a long and onerous process of disintegration, moral and material, of an essential nature—a process which came about almost independently of the purely military conduct of the war."

---

30. Farragut and Patton are quoted in R. D. Heinl, *Dictionary of Military and Naval Quotations*, p. 178.

According to Douhet, the airplane could strike an enemy far behind his fortified lines without every having to repeat the ghastly assaults seen on every front in the 1914–18 war. In the future a massive air assault against enemy population centers would destroy civilian morale and hence win the war. Command of the air was as fundamental in his thinking as command of the sea had been to Mahan, and while he urged that the military, naval, and air forces should be "thoroughly co-ordinated," he insisted upon an independent air force which could "always operate in mass." And once this independent air force had won command of the air, "it should keep up violent, uninterrupted action against surface objectives, to the end that it may crush the material and moral resistance of the enemy."[31]

Douhet's theories may seem old hat to the military reader familiar with the great bomber offensives of the Second World War and the more recent experiences in Korea and Vietnam, although few informed soldiers today would share Douhet's faith that civilian morale and even enemy ground forces could be destroyed as easily as bridges and buildings. But Douhet makes good reading, both for his insights into the nature of the First World War and the reasoning that led him to believe completely in the victory of air power in any future conflict.

There is, however, a pitfall here that is by no means unique to Douhet. The casual reader of history often is likely to assume a cause and effect relationship between an idea that is forcefully articulated and some subsequent event. While Douhet undoubtedly reinforced the arguments of apostles of air power in other countries, his book, unlike those of Mahan, did not change the direction of military thinking. The United States Army after all had its own Billy Mitchell, and the printed evidence makes it clear that Douhet had no influence upon British doctrines of air bombardment that evolved between the two wars. The complete version of *Command of the Air* was not even translated into English until 1942.

The next two writers whose books belong on the shelf of any well educated officer are deservedly recognized as prophets who, shortly before their deaths, had won high honor even in their own country. J. F. C. Fuller and B. H. Liddell Hart are easily the most prolific, controversial, and influential military writers produced by the First World War. Lifelong students of war, they dedicated themselves to the cause of army reform and mechani-

---

31. Giulio Douhet, *The Command of the Air* (New York: Coward-McCann, 1942), pp. 128–29, 151. First Italian publication 1921.

zation. They attempted to find order in history as a realistic basis for their theories; between them they developed the concept of *Blitzkrieg*, which made them true revolutionaries.

Liddell Hart bears a striking resemblance to Jomini. Both were interested primarily in strategy, both assumed that their historical studies could be boiled down to a few basic principles valid in all times and under most situations, both were addicted to method and fond of coining words (Jomini is responsible for *logistics*, Liddell Hart for *baited gambit, alternative objectives,* and the strategy of *indirect approach*). Above all, both believed in their theories to the extent that they taught the same lessons throughout their long and prolific careers. It is almost true that if you have read one book by Jomini you have read them all, while Liddell Hart's celebrated strategy of indirect approach provides a consistent theme in practically every one of his writings after about 1928.

Both theorists, incidentally, prided themselves on the influence they exerted from time to time on military policy and strategy. Jomini was an adviser to the Russian Tsar and probably more than any other individual was responsible for the French strategy in the war of 1859 against Austria. Liddell Hart's advice was solicited by several governments and frequently by friends in high places within the British military and political establishment. As a theorists, military correspondent, historian, and reformer he exerted a powerful influence upon military developments throughout his active life.

Fuller on the other hand may be compared with Clausewitz. He was interested more in the phenomenon of war than in the elements of stratey. He too approached the subject philosophically, relying upon Hegel rather than Kant and, like Clausewitz, Fuller never completely synthesized his dissonant and roving thoughts on war. *The Conduct of War* (1961) represents his mature reflections on war and policy, but it does not show the unconventional staff officer wrestling with our modern principles of war (which he recovered, incidentally, from the *Correspondance* of Napoleon), searching out solutions to military problems aggravated by industrialization, or endeavoring to comprehend the universal meaning of war as a scientist, social scientist, philosopher, and historian. Here perhaps Fuller would differ from Clausewitz, for his writings have a basic integrity that transcends the worth—or the weakness—of any single volume, whereas the essence of Clausewitz is contained, if not necessarily in final form, in *On War*.

Since between them Fuller and Liddell Hart wrote some sixty

to seventy volumes, it is possible here only to suggest those that are more representative of their thought—or provocative in stimulating the thought of others. *On Future War* (1928) more than any other single book imparts the spirit of Fuller's inquiries in the 1920s, when he was struggling to formulate a theory of mechanized warfare and at the same time to induce the British army to catch up with the march of technical civilization. *Armoured Warfare* (1943), known originally as *Lectures on Field Service Regulations III* (1931), remains his most important work on mechanization. Although most of Fuller's basic ideas were realized in the Blitzkrieg of 1940 and the subsequent campaigns in North Africa, the reader should remember that he wrote before 1931 and that significant improvements were made in both tanks and aircraft before his theories could be put to the test of war. *The Army in My Time* (1935) shows Fuller at his irreverent best (or worst, depending upon the degree to which one associates himself with the Establishment). Better than any other single work, this book gives Fuller's devastating criticisms of the institutions and leaders of the British Army from the Boer War to the time of his retirement. None of Fuller's books merited attention as history until he produced his monumental three-volume *Decisive Battles of the Western World and Their Influence upon History* (first edition, 1940). After the Second World War he was less interested than before in using history us a vehicle to carry his own theories to the public.

Liddell Hart's *Great Captains Unveiled* (1927) provides a fascinating glimpse of the actions of Ghenghis Khan, Saxe, Gustavus Adolphus, Wallenstein, and Wolfe; it also reveals the thought of the author as he sought to apply certain lessons from history to military problems of his own day. This book effectively illustrates the use of historical analogies in the evolution of armored warfare. His biography of *Sherman* (1929) remains the best military study of Sherman's campaigns, but it is of even greater importance in tracing the development of Liddell Hart's own theories. In the process of writing this volume, Liddell Hart first worked out the elements of his strategy of indirect approach, which he then developed by searching history for proof of the validity of his theories. *Strategy* (first edition, 1954), perhaps his best-known work today, is the last of a long line of philosophical (rather than strictly historical) works illustrating by well-chosen examples the successful application of the strategy of indirect approach. His good friend and admirer, Field Marshal Archibald P. Wavell, once chided him gently for searching for "the military philosopher's stone" and suggested rather slyly that with his intelligence and command of the pen, Liddell Hart could have written just as convincingly on the strategy of the direct approach. *The British Way in War* (1932) and *Thoughts on War* (1944) contain Liddell Hart's reflections on nearly every aspect of war; *The Tanks* (1959) is a superb history of the evolution of the tank, the development of a theory of mechanized warfare, and the role of the Royal Tank Corps in World War II. *The Ghost of Napoleon* (1933), which Wavell once described as "an excellent mental irritant," is a provocative series of lectures on military thought in the eighteenth and nineteenth centuries, and *The Real War 1914-1918* (1930) remains one of the finest single volumes on World War I. Unlike the great majority of earlier writers, both Fuller and Liddell Hart wrote autobiographies that contain not only the essence of their respective theories, but also a revealing glimpse of the trials and tribulations of the military reformer.

Bibliography

Anderson, John K. *Military Theory and Practice in the Age of Xenophon.* Berkeley: Univ. of Calif. Press, 1970.

Balck, William. *Tactics.* Translated by Walter Krueger. 4th ed., 2 vols. Fort Leavenworth, Kans.: U.S. Cavalry Association, 1911-14. originally published in German, 6 vols., 1897-1903.

Baynes, John. *Morale: A Study of Men and Courage: The Second Scottish Rifles at the Battle of Neuve Chapelle, 1915.* New York: Praeger, 1967.

Becke, A. F. *Introduction to the History of Tactics, 1740-1905.* London: Hugh Rees, 1909.

Bernhardi, Friedrich A. J. von. *On War of Today.* Translated by Karl von Donat. Edited by Trumbull Higgins. New York: Global Publications, 1972. Originally published in German, 1912.

Caemmerer, Rudolf von. *The Development of Strategical Science During the 19th Century.* Translated by Karl von Donat. London: Hugh Rees, 1905. Originally published in German, 1904.

Caesar, Gaius Julius. *War Commentaries: De Bello Gallico et De Bello Civile.* Edited and translated by John Warrington. New York: Dutton, 1953.

Clausewitz, Karl von. *On War.* Edited and translated by Michael Howard and Peter Paret, Princeton, N.J.: Princeton Univ. Press, 1976.

Colin, Jean L. A. *Transformation of War.* Translated by Brevet Major H. R. Pope-Hennessey. London: H. Rees, 1912.

Delbrück, Hans. *History of the Art of War Within the Framework of Political History.* Translated by Col. Walter J. Renfree. Vol I: *Antiquity.* Westport, Conn.: Greenwood Press, 1975. Other volumes to follow. Complete work in German, *Geschichte der Kriegskunst im Rahmen der Politischen Geschichte,* 4 vols. (Berlin, 1900-20).

Denison, George T. *A History of Cavalry from the Earliest Times With Lessons for the Future.* 2d ed., London: Macmillan, 1913. Originally published 1877.

Douhet, Giulio. *The Command of the Air.* Translated by Dino Ferrari. New York: Coward-McCann, 1942. Originally published in Italian, 1921, 1927.

Du Picq, Ardant. *Battle Studies: Ancient and Modern Battle*. Translated from 8th French ed. by Col. John M. Greely and Maj. Robert C. Cotton. New York: Macmillan, 1921. Originally published 1880.

Foch, Ferdinand. *The Principles of War*. Translated by J. Morimini. London: H. K. Fly Co., 1918. Originally published in French, 4th ed., Paris, 1917.

Folard, Jean Charles, Chevalier de. *Histoire de Polybe . . . avec un commentaire*. 6 vols. Paris: P. Gardovici, 1727-30. No English translation available.

Frederick the Great. *See* Luvaas, Jay.

Fuller, J. F. C. *The Army in My Time*. London: Rich and Cowan, 1935.

——. *The Conduct of War, 1789-1961*. London: Eyre and Spottiswoode, 1961.

——. *Decisive Battles of the Western World and Their Influence Upon History*. 3 vols. London: Eyre and Spottiswoode, 1954-56.

——. *On Future War*. London: Sifton Praed, 1928.

——. *Lectures on Field Service Regulations III*. London: Sifton Praed, 1931. Republished as *Armoured Warfare*. Harrisburg: Military Services Publishing Co., 1943.

Guibert, Jacques, Comte de. *A General Essay on Tactics With an Introductory Discourse Upon the State of Politics*. London, 1781. Originally published in French, 2 vols., Liege, 1775.

Guischardt, Charles. *Memoirs militaires sur les Grecs et les Romains*. Paris: De L. Baudion, 1760.

Halleck, Henry W. *Elements of Military Art and Science*. Westport, Conn.: Greenwood Press, 1971. Originally published 1846.

Hamley, Sir Edward Bruce. *The Operations of War Explained and Illustrated*. Edinburg and London: Blackwood, 1907. First published 1866.

Heinl, Robert D., comp. *Dictionary of Military and Naval Quotations*. Annapolis, Md.: U.S. Naval Institute, 1966.

Henderson, G. F. R. *The Science of War: A Collection of Essays and Lectures, 1892-1903*. Edited by Capt. Neill Malcolm. London: Longmans, Green, 1905.

——. *Stonewall Jackson and the American Civil War*. London and New York: Longmans, Green, 1898.

Herodotus. *The History of Herodotus*. 2 vols. New York: Dutton, Everyman's Library, 1936-37.

Hohenlohe-Ingelfingen, Kraft Karl, Prince zu. *Letters on Artillery* (1890), *Letters on Cavalry* (1889), and *Letters on Infantry* (1892). All translated from German by Maj. N. L. Wolford and published in London by E. Stanford.

Jomini, Henri, Baron. *Summary of the Art of War*. New York, 1864. New edition in French as *Precis de l'art de la guerre*, Paris, 1838.

——. *Jomini and His Summary of the Art of War: A Condensed Version*. Edited by J. D. Hittle. Harrisburg: Military Services Publishing Co., 1947.

Keegan, John. *The Face of Battle*. New York: Viking Press, 1976.

Lewal, Jules Louis. *Strategie de Combat, 2ieme extrait des Journal des sciences militaires*. Paris: De L. Baudion, 1895-96.

Liddell Hart, B. H. *The British Way in War: Adaptability and Mobility*. London: Faber and Faber, 1932.

——. *The Ghost of Napoleon*. London: Faber and Faber, 1933.

——. *The Great Captains Unveiled*. London: W. Blanchard and Sons, 1927.

——. *The Real War, 1914-1918*. London: Faber and Faber, 1930. Published also as *A History of the World War*.

——. *Sherman: Soldier, Realist, American*. New York, Dodd, Mead, 1929.

——. *Strategy*. 2d ed. New York: Praeger, 1967.

——. *The Tanks: The History of the royal Tank Regiment and Its Predecessors . . . 1914-1945*. New York: Praeger, 1959.

Livy. *The War with Hannibal.* Translated by Aubrey de Selincourt. Edited by Betty Radice. Harmondsworth: Penguin Books, 1965.

Lloyd, E. M. *A Review of the History of Infantry.* London: Longmans, Green, 1908.

Lloyd, Henry. *Henry of the Late War in Germany.* 2 vols. London: 1766–81.

Luvaas, Jay, trans. and ed. *Frederick the Great on the Art of War.* New York: Free Press, 1966.

MacDougall, P. L. *The Theory of War.* London: Longman, 1856.

Machiavelli, Niccolo. *The Art of War.* 2 vols. London: D. Nutt, 1905.

──── . *The Prince and the Discourses.* Introduction by Max Lerner. New York: Modern Library, 1940.

Mahan, Alfred Thayer. *The Influence of Sea Power Upon History, 1660–1783.* Boston: Little, Brown, 1890.

Maurice, Sir Frederick B. *Governments and War: A Study of the Conduct of War.* London: Heinemann, 1926.

Moran, Charles, Lord. *The Anatomy of Courage.* London: Constable, 1945.

Onasander. *Strategicus* (The General). English translation in *Aeneas Tacticus, Asclepiodotus, Onasander,* translation by members of the Illinois Greek Club and texts mainly prepared by W. A. Oldfather. New York: Putnam's, 1923.

Phillips, Thomas R. *The Roots of Strategy.* Harrisburg: Military Services Publishing Co., 1940.

Picard, Ernest. *Precèptes et jugements de Napoleon recueillés et classés par Lieut. Col. Ernest Picard.* Paris, Nancy: Berger-Levrault, 1913.

Polybius. *The Histories of Polybius.* Translated from the text of F. Huitisch by Evelyn S. Shuckburgh. 2 vols. Bloomington: Univ. of Ind. Press, 1962.

Puységur, Jacques de Castenet. *Art de la Guerre, par Principes et Par Régles.* Paris: C. A. Jombert, 1748. No English translation available.

Saxe, Maurice, Comte de. *Reveries or Memoirs on the Art of War.* Westport, Conn.: Greenwood Press, 1971. Original published in French in 1757.

Schlieffen, Alfred, Count von. *Cannae.* Fort Leavenworth, Kans.: Command and General Staff School Press, 1936. Orginally published in German, 1913.

Schurman, D. M. *The Education of a Navy: The Development of British Naval Strategic Thought, 1867–1914.* Chicago: Univ. of Chicago Press, 1965.

Spaulding, Col. Oliver L. *Pen and Sword in Greece and Rome.* Princeton, N.J.: Princeton Univ. Press, 1937.

Sun Tzu. *The Art of War.* Translated with an Introduction by Samuel B. Griffith. New York: Oxford Univ. Press, 1963.

Thucydides. *The Complete Writings of Thucydides.* New York: Modern Library, 1934.

──── . *The History of the Peloponnesian War.* New York: Dutton, 1935.

Vauban, M. de Sebastien Le Prestre de. *Manual of Siegecraft and Fortifications.* Translated by George A. Rotrock. Ann Arbor: Univ. of Mich. Press, 1968. Originally published in French in 1737.

Vegetius, Flavius Renatus. *The Military Institutions of the Romans.* Harrisburg: Military Services Publishing Co., 1943.

Viollet-le-Duc, Eugene Emmanuel. *Annals of a Fortress.* Translated by Benjamin Bucknell. Boston: J. R. Osgood, 1876. Originally published in French in 1874.

Wagner, Arthur L. *Organization and Tactics.* London and New York: B. Westermann, 1895.

Wilkinson, Spencer. *The Brain of an Army: A Popular Account of the German General Staff.* New ed. London: Constable, 1895. Originally published 1890.

Xenophon. *Cyropaedia.* With an English Translation by Walter Miller. 2 vols. New York: Macmillan, Leob Classical Library, 1914.

──── . *The Persian Expedition.* Harmondsworth: Penguin Books, 1949.

Chapter **5**

Military History to the End of the Eighteenth Century

Theodore Ropp

MILITARY history's peaks are its great wars, battles, and captains. Underneath are the strata which relate them to political, socioeconomic, and technological developments. The military history of the long years from the first appearance of primitive man to the death of Frederick the Great in 1786 may be broken down into four general periods. The earliest is the millennia before 1000 B.C. when our first civilizations began competing with one another. The following sixteen centuries cover the Iron Age empires from Assyria to Rome; eight more, from 600 to 1400, belong to our Middle Ages, and the final four fit our early gunpowder era.

Over 2,400 years ago the Greek historian Herodotus wrote his *History of the Persian Wars* (c. 444 B.C.) so that "men's actions may not be effaced by time, nor the great and wonderous deeds" of "Greeks and barbarians deprived of renown" and to show "for what causes they waged war upon each other" (p. 1 of translation listed in bibliography). A century later and thousands of miles distant, the Chinese philosopher Sun Tzu taught that "war is a matter of vital importance to the state; the province of life and death. . . . It is mandatory that it be thoroughly studied" (*The Art of War*, p. 63). Since that time men have written at length about the great wars, battles, and captains and have tried with varying success to relate them to the political, social, economic, and technological developments of each era. Most have recognized the limitations as well as the advantages of such work. It is difficult to imagine what made an eighteenth-century redcoat fight or how his government worked, and even harder to understand the motives of a Greek hoplite or his Persian foe. Thus, while political scientists may usefully apply historical insights to present problems, the complexities of such transferences should not be underestimated.

Dr. Ropp (Ph.D., Harvard), Professor of History at Duke University, is the mentor of many leading American military historians. His works include *War in the Modern World*. Dr. Ropp wrote this contribution while a visiting professor at the Army War College.

89

General Works

The one work that covers Western military history to the death of Frederick the Great is Oliver L. Spaulding, Jr., Hoffman Nickerson, and John W. Wright's *Warfare: A Study of Military Methods from the Earliest Times* (1939). Thomas R. Phillips's (ed.) *Roots of Strategy* (1940) is equally useful, although the author left out Vegetius's books on fortification and naval operations as "of interest only to military antiquarians." The writings of Sun Tzu, Vegetius, Maurice de Saxe, and Frederick go very well with the Spaulding, Nickerson, and Wright text. Lynn Montross's *War Through the Ages* (1960) is fine battle history. Richard A. Preston, Sidney F. Wise, and Herman O. Werner's shorter *Men in Arms: A History of Warfare and its Interrelationships with Western Society* (1970) is a better study of the underlying factors of war. The best general reference work is R. Ernest and Trevor N. Dupuy's, *Encyclopedia of Military History from 3500 B.C. to the Present* (1970). Half of its 1,400 pages cover the years before 1800. Each regionally oriented chronological chapter begins by surveying general trends; the battle descriptions, maps, and line drawings are excellent. Viscount Montgomery of Alamein's *History of Warfare* (1968) is the best illustrated general work. Two-thirds of it carries the story to 1789; the author's quirks are most apparent in his treatment of the later period. The narrative does not quite match the quality of J.F.C. Fuller's *Military History of the Western World* (1954), an expansion of his 1940 *Decisive Battles: Their Influence upon History and Civilization*. Frank A. Kiernan, Jr., and John K. Fairbank (eds.) cover *Chinese Ways in Warfare* (1974), and Bernard and Fawn Brodie's little *From Crossbow to H-Bomb* (1962) is the book on deliberate weapons development. Melvin Kranzberg and Carroll W. Pursell, Jr's. (eds.) *Technology in Western Civilization* (1967) has sections on technology and warfare, Maurice Dumas's (ed.) *History of Technology and Invention* (1971) is better on non-Western societies and cultures, and Thomas Wintringham's, *The Story of Weapons and Tactics* has been updated and reissued (1974).

There is no good general military historical atlas nor any general survey of military literature, whether defined as purely military or as a literary treatment of warfare. Louis C. Peltier and G. Etzel Pearcy's fine short *Military Geography* (1966) is concerned primarily with the ways in which geography has affected modern strategy, tactics, and logistics. And modern social scientists have produced so many works on war that any list would be longer than this chapter. Kenneth N. Waltz's *Man, the State, and War: A Theoretical Analysis* (1959) classifies social scientists by their optimistic or pessimistic assumptions about men, states, and international systems. Robert Ardrey's *Territorial Imperative* (1971) is balanced by Anthony Storr's *Human Aggression* (1968) or by Leon Bramson and George W. Goethals, Jr.'s (ed.) *War: Studies from Psychology, Sociology, Anthropology* (1964); and John Winthrop Hackett's *The Profession of Arms* (1963) and Stanislav Andreski's *Military Organization and Society* (first printing 1954) are modern classics.

Andreski analyzed military organizations in terms of military participation ratios ("the proportion of militarily utilized individuals in the total population"), their subordination to hierarchial authority, and internal cohesion. Subordination implies cohesion but not the reverse as in the case of the medieval crusaders. If Andreski's variables are combined with modern technological, political, and social factors, the resulting model of technological resources, political organization, social cohesion, military participation, military subordination, and weapons technology takes in the factors developed in Quincy Wright's 1942 *Study of War* for a pioneering University of Chicago war seminar. Wright later helped to edit the English meteorologist Lewis Fry Richardson's *Statistics of Deadly Quarrels* (1960), but his figures have been used widely without noting their shaky sources or extending them back to 1820, where the lack of sound statistics hampers studies of the role of war and armaments in economic development. The same problem was also faced by another Chicago seminar member, John U. Nef, whose *War and Human Progress: An Essay on the Rise of Industrial Civilization* (1963) questioned the existence of any symbiotic relationship between military conflict and human advancement.

Weapons tend to be hard, preservable, and even magical objects. Both archaeological evidence and illustrated books are abundant. P. E. Cleator's *Weapons of War* (1968), Howard I. Blackmore's *Arms and Armour* (1965) and *Firearms* (1964), O. F. G. Hogg's *Clubs to Cannon: Warfare and Weapons before the Introduction of Gunpowder* (1968), Edwin Tunis's *Weapons: A Pictorial History* (1954), and Joseph Jobe's *Guns: An Illustrated History* (1971) are worthwhile. Romola and R. C. Anderson's *The Sailing Ship* (1947), R. C. Anderson's *Oared Fighting Ships* (1962), O. F. G. Hogg's *Artillery* (1970), E. M. Lloyd's *A Review of the History of Infantry* (1908), George T. Denison's *History of Cavalry* (1913), Sidney Toy's *History of Fortifications From 3000 B.C. to A.D. 1700* (1955), Quentin Hughes's *Military*

Architecture (1975), and George F. Bass's (ed.) *A History of Seafaring Based on Underwater Archaeology* (1972) cover those subjects.

Ralph H. Major's *Fatal Partners: War and Disease* (1941) is a story of the frustration felt by medical personnel in wartime. There are no good short general histories of military medicine, engineering, logistics, or long- or short-range communications. And in spite or because of Alfred Thayer Mahan's influence on historians, this is also true for sea power, navies, and amphibious operations. Björn Landström's *The Ship: An Illustrated History* (1961) is, however, a useful reference on types of naval vessels through the ages, and Robert B. Asprey's, *War in the Shadows* (1975) tells all that you wanted to know about *The Guerrilla in History*.

Primitive War and the First Civilizations

While agriculture could usually support more people than hunting, food-gathering, or herding, farmers might not be superior in weaponry, and hunters or herdsmen might be superior in fighting skill and mobility. Harry Holbert Turney-High's classic study, *Primitive War* (1971), shows that better military organization might follow an advance to agricultural civilization but that organizing large-scale military operations was not beyond the capabilities of many preliterate peoples. The Old Stone, New Stone (Neolithic), Copper, Bronze, and Iron "stages" used by early prehistorians (archaeologists) have in some ways confused things. Polished stone or metal tools and weapons might be no more important to human progress than many other innovations. Plants and animals were domesticated in Southeast Asia by 1300 B.C., and copper and bronze cast there by 4000 B.C., but there was no breakthrough to civilization. Stuart Piggott, *Ancient Europe* (1965, pp. 17ff.), sees "*innovating and conserving societies*" in "remote antiquity." In the latter "the *modus vivendi* for the community within its natural surroundings" produced "no urgent need to alter the situation" or was "too delicately adjusted . . . and too rigidly conceived" to admit of it. He contends that east Asia's uplands were too friendly and protected to demand further social innovation, though the technical skill of their craftsmen is still observable. If these matters seem far removed from the problems of modern military historians, it may warn them against seeing military history as a simple tale of great captains, great states, or decisive battles and technological innovations.

Most thrown, propelled, and hand weapons and protective devices were invented by preliterate peoples. Our protocities were in the Near Eastern uplands, where food gatherers exploited the natural grainfields and herded sheep, goats, pigs, and cattle away from them. Catal Huyuk in Anatolia, for example, had ten thousand people; its linked mudbrick house walls repelled attackers from 6500 to 5650 B.C. Though its security may have come from its being a neutral trading post or shrine, the problems of attacking a maze of dark chambers accessible only by ladder from the roof are apparent in many later fortifications. Catal Huyuk's people had three wheats, two vetches, barley, peas, and oil plants and made or traded for beer, wine, flints, shells, obsidian weapons and mirrors, copper, iron, and lead beads, and fertility objects. The challenges which produced the first civilizations, however, did not arise or were not met in the Asian uplands but in the fertile valleys of the Nile, Tigris, Euphrates, Indus, and Yellow rivers.

Irrigation made Mesopotamia. The Egyptians had the even more difficult task of taming the Nile to use its annual gifts of new soil, fish protein, and antimalarial scouring. Written records were probably created to predict annual floods. Recovering landmarks and laying out ditches and fortifications demanded engineers and surveyors in both areas. Mesopotamia's political pattern was one of small, fortified, warring cities; an occasional conqueror united them and extended his control over potential upland and desert marauders. Egypt's single ruler had varying degrees of control over local landowners. Professional soldiers served as royal guards for frontier defense and foreign wars, and local militia beefed up last-ditch defenses and furnished local transport. And more metals meant better tools for working wood and stone.

In his *Art of Warfare in Biblical Lands in the Light of Archaeological Study* (1963), Israeli soldier-archaeologist Yigael Yadin uses the first pictured Egyptian battles (Megiddo, 1469 B.C., and Kadesh, 1292 B.C.) to show that special foot, horse, engineer, transport, and marine units already existed when these battles were fought, and that weapons were only recombined and refined until the heavy cavalry revolution at the end of the classical era. Key innovations in this final period were iron weapons, armor, chariots, and cavalry. Yadin discusses mobility, firepower, personal protection, and fortifications for each biblical period. The era before Abraham (4000-2100 B.C.) saw the first civilizations, and the periods from the Patriarchs through the Exodus (2100-1200 B.C.) saw the rise of a common

Near Eastern art of war and the rise and fall of Minoan or Cretan civilization. But military history is not a continuous story until after new land and sea invaders had been absorbed during the era of the Judges and the United Monarchy (1200-920 B.C.).

Egyptians may have invented oars, but their ships were river boats, and the keel plank, ribs, fixed mast, and sail furling gear of the classical "round" trader were Levantine. Arab dhows and Indonesian outrigger canoes sailed their adjacent oceans, but all early sea or caravan traders depended on the goodwill and sometimes on the military aid of powers with greater agricultural resources. The Minoans killed interlopers and bad customers or denied them trade goods until their fragile maritime empire was wrecked by a tidal wave around 1400 B.C. With the Mediterranean people under sail—but surely with some stowed sweeps or oars—round ships appear in the first pictured sea fight off the Nile delta in 1194 B.C. The classical warship, a galley strong enough for ramming, was a later Phoenician or Greek development. The best books are William Culican's *The First Merchant Venturers: The Ancient Levant in History and Commerce* (1966), Michael Grant's *The Ancient Mediterranean* (1969), and Lionel Casson's *Ships and Seamanship in the Ancient World* (1971).

The Classical Iron Age Empires

Assyria dominated the Near East from the tenth through the seventh century B.C. with spearmen, archers, charioteers, and cavalry—city-smashers who massacred or transported whole peoples. The Persians, who took over in the sixth century, were Middle Eastern archers and heavy cavalrymen who relied on water transport from subject Greek or Phoenician cities. Greek heavy hoplite pikemen were formidable foes for horsemen in wooded mountains with many defensible positions. The decisive battles of the wars between Greece and Persia (499-448 B.C.) were Salamis and Plataea about 480 B.C. The former was the occasion of the destruction of the Persian fleet supporting the occupation of Athens, allegedly on the same day that the Sicilian Greeks defeated the Persians' Carthaginian allies off Himera. The latter, Plataea, marked the defeat of Xerxes's land army and the end of the Persian threat to Greece. The best books are Yadin on the Assyrians and Babylonians, Harold Lamb's popularized *Cyrus the Great* (1960), and Peter Green's *Xerxes at Salamis* (1970).

Greek then fought Greek in the Peloponnesian Wars (460–404 B.C.) that destroyed the Athenian maritime empire and established even shorter lived Spartan and Theban hegemonies. J. K. Anderson's *Military Theory and Practice in the Age of Xenophon* (1970) shows how Sparta dominated military affairs in Greece during a period when the country was exporting soldiers to the whole civilized world. But the first great captain who can be linked with a specifically new maneuver was Epaminondas of Thebes, whose oblique order of attack at Leuctra in 371 B.C. ended Sparta's domination.

Philip of Macedon had been a hostage in Thebes, and the close ties between him, his son Alexander (356–323), and the Greek city-states have obscured their similarity to traditional oriental conquerors. The Macedonian conquerors used a deeper phalanx formation and more heavy cavalry than the Greeks, added allies as they advanced, and imposed a new layer of soldiers, bureaucrats, traders, and gods on existing civilizations. Among the best books are F. E. Adcock's *The Greek and Macedonian Art of War* (1957), A. M. Snodgrass's *Arms and Armour of the Greeks* (1967) and E. W. Marsden's *Greek and Roman Artillery* (1969), and F. E. Winter's *Greek Fortifications* (1971). Peter Green's *Armada from Athens* (1970) relates the disastrous expedition against Syracuse, and J. F. C. Fuller's *The Generalship of Alexander the Great* (1960) and Peter Green's *Alexander the Great* (1970) are good studies of a great captain whose empire fell apart when he died but who profoundly influenced history, partly because he inspired so many would-be imitators.

The Romans, or their successors in Constantinople, ruled the Mediterranean from their victories over Carthage, Macedonia, and Syria at the turn of the third century B.C. to the victories of Heraclius I over Sassanid Persia in the seventh century A.D., just before the Arab explosion. But we know much about only a few Roman leaders of these eight centuries; as little, for example, about Heraclius as about Dionysius of Syracuse, whose hegemony in Sicily and Greek Italy was contemporaneous with that of Sparta in Greece proper.

Hollywood storytelling has aided moralizing on Rome's rise and fall, but more general factors are historically safer. Mediterranean metals technology was not as advanced as that of the northern barbarians, but Mediterranean agriculture could support more people. Rome's social cohesion was relatively high. Her great innovation was the political organization of a "Latin League" in which allied or colonial citizens had the same private rights as Romans. With each legion paired with an allied one,

Rome expanded by adding allies, founding colonies, and making more Romans; landless citizens received captured lands in return for long military services. The molding of the central Italian peoples into a united society was also promoted by their related cultures and common enemies. During the Second Punic War, 219–202 B.C., Rome could call on 750,000 men; 250,000 were in her legions from a population of 3,750,000, a military participation ratio of men trained to common standards of military subordination which was seldom reached again before 1786.

In contrast, Greek or Carthaginian colonists had no special rights at home, and Corcyrans were soon fighting their mother city of Corinth. By the third century B.C., deforestation and erosion were affecting the Greek lands, while Carthage never had as much farmland as Rome. Slavery was also a complicating factor. Sparta's military participation ratio seems high until the Messenian helots are counted. The farms and mines of Carthage were worked by bonded peasants or slaves with uncaught relatives in the backlands. Some of them joined rebel mercenaries in the social war which followed the First Punic War of 265–241 B.C.; but when Rome's slaves revolted in 135–132, a Syrian on a Sicilian plantation was far from outside assistance.

The Greek historian Polybius stressed the quality of Roman weapons—how the no-return javelin hooked when it hit; the strength of the iron-edged, iron-bossed shield against heavy Celtic swords and axes; and the effectiveness of the short, two-edged sword against the overlong Eastern pike. The Roman army's nightly camps, their usually good scouting, and their march discipline reflected years of campaigning. They had adopted Greek ships, siege engines, and heavy cavalry spears, and Polybius found them expert at imitating better practice. Modern research has confirmed his position as a great historian, those of Hannibal and Scipio as great captains, and that of Cannae in 216 B.C. as a model battle. Two biographies of Hannibal by Gavin de Beer (1969) and Leonard Cottrell (1961), and H. H. Scullard's *Scipio Africanus* (1970), supplement E. Badian's abridged *Polybius: The Histories* (1966), F. E. Adcock's *The Roman Art of War Under the Republic* (1963), and Chester G. Starr, Jr.'s *The Emergence of Rome as Ruler of the Western World* (1953).

The Roman soldiery was fully professional by the end of the second century B.C. The three-line phalangial legion—with the third line's veterans using short pikes—was replaced by the more uniform and flexible ten-cohort "checkerboard" legion in which all men carried two javelins and a sword. Men enlisted for up to sixteen years to get land and citizenship from the political generals who fought the civil wars of 88-30 B.C., while winning more foreign land, slaves, and booty. On their greatest captain, Matthias Gelzer's *Caesar* (1968) is better than J. F. C. Fuller's *Julius Caesar* (1969).

Octavian or Augustus Caesar (31 B.C. -14 A.D.) cut the army to about 300,000 men, not many more than during the Second Punic War two centuries earlier, although the population base of "Rome" had increased tenfold, totalling 50-70 million. By the time of Marcus Aurelius (161-80), marking the height of the Empire, this force had grown to almost 400,000 men drawn from a population of 50-100 million. But two centuries later, a Roman field force of 200,000, supplemented by 350,000 militia, faced growing pressure from barbarian tribes who were shifting from the north and east as their lands were farmed out by a system better suited to the Mediterranean. Rome had abandoned the swamp, deep forest, and steppe lands of central Europe and stabilized its frontier on the Rhine, Main, and Danube behind walls fronted by subsidized tribesmen and backed by settled legionaries, refortified cities, and cavalry, river, and coastal patrols. The process tended to barbarize Romans and Romanize barbarians, some of whom were allowed to settle on lands depopulated by plague and soil exhaustion. The best books are G. R. Watson's *The Roman Soldier* (1969), Graham Webster's *The Roman Imperial Army* (1970), Chester G. Starr, Jr.'s *The Roman Imperial Navy* (1941), E. A. Thompson's *The Early Germans* (1965), and, on one frontier, David Divine's *Hadrian's Wall* (1969).

Hadrian's (117-38) idea of two emperors harks back to that of two consuls, but the boundaries of the four civilian prefectures better suggest the geopolitical structure of the later empire. Gaul included Britain and Spain. Africa (Carthage) and the provinces that covered the eastern Alpine passes were part of Italy. Illyria included the southern Balkans and Greece. The East included Thrace, Asia Minor, Syria, and Egypt. Constantine's conversion in 312 A.D. added Christians to Rome's defenders. In making Byzantium (Constantinople) his capital, he recognized the importance of the land-sea bastion that channeled invaders west and from which Persian attacks on Syria and Egypt could be countered. In 376 the Huns destroyed an Eastern or Ostrogothic steppe "empire" and pushed the Western or Visigoths into the Roman domain. After the heavy Gothic cavalry with saddles, stirrups, bows, swords, and lances defeated the Eastern emperor's legions at Adrianople in 378, his successor, Theodosius the Great, began to make heavy "cataphract" mounted archers the main East Roman missile and shock force.

Then the Western Empire collapsed. The invaders, like the Imperial tax farmers, did more damage to the dying cities than to the self-sufficient landlords. Alaric the Visigoth sacked Rome in 410, and his tribesmen later set up a kingdom in Spain. In Gaul, the Franks and Romans defeated Attila's Huns at Chalons in 451; Attila was bought off in Italy in 452, and his horde broke up on the Danube. The Vandals—only 80,000 of them for the whole tribe—were pushed from Spain to Africa but returned to sack Rome in 455 for an emperor's widow. The last Western emperor was deposed in 476, the traditional beginning of the West's Middle Ages. Theodoric the Great, an Ostrogoth educated at Constantinople, was sent to recover Italy, and he set up his own kingdom. On what lay behind these movie scenarios, the best book is Frank William Walbank's *The Awful Revolution: The Decline of the Roman Empire in the West* (1969).

Justinian (527-65) reconquered those parts of the empire within range of his naval forces: Africa, Carthaginian Spain from Cadiz to Cartagena, and Italy. His professional army of 150,000 men was also fighting on the Danubian and Persian frontiers. New churches, religious orders, palaces, roads, fortifications, and trading posts showed the recuperative power of an empire which was still larger than those of Alexander's successors nine centuries before. John Barker's *Justinian and the Later Roman Empire* (1966) can be read before books on the cautious emperor, his ex-prostitute wife Theodora, the great captain Belisarius, and the eunuch-soldier Narses, all of which are just as racy as those on Philip, Alexander, and Olympias, or on Caesar, Cleopatra, Antony, and Octavian.

The Middle Ages

The Middle Ages may have begun with the Arab conquests in the century after Mohammed's death in 632. Greek fire, probably a mixture of naphtha or some petroleum product with sulphur and lime, projected from galley bow tubes, saved Constantinople in 672, and the Eastern Roman Empire continued for another eight centuries. Leo the Isaurian repelled the last Arab assault against the city in 722, and, at the other end of Europe, Charles Martel checked the Moslems at Tours ten years later. John Bagot Glubb's *The Great Arab Conquests* (1963) is a good overview. The great medieval captains—Charles Martel's grandson

Charlemagne, Otto the Great, William the Conqueror, Saladin, Bibars, Murad I, and others—were more local figures in a scene dominated tactically by heavy cavalry and strategically by fortifications, an easy military investment for localized agrarian economies. In the east, the steppe cavalryman's era began with the Mongols' Genghis Khan (1180-1227) and closed with Kublai Khan (1280-1294) and the Tartar Tamerlane (1381-1405); these nomads had adopted the principles of discipline and administration previously used by settled peoples to build and hold their empires. Glubb's *The Great Arab Conquests*, Rene Grousset's *Conqueror of the World*, and Harold Lamb's *Tamerlane* are the best books. But the cavalry's dominance was ending even before the battle of Nicopolis in 1396, about the time that gunpowder began to affect siegecraft.

The West's economic decline began before the barbarian invasions. Lynn White, Jr.'s *Medieval Technology and Social Change* (1962) links its revival with a new three-field farming system and the concept of a power technology. Economic localization and military feudalization, a system of landholding in return for service, was accentuated by new wars and invaders in all three worlds after the reigns of Charlemagne (771-814), the Eastern Roman Emperor Nicephorus I (802-11), and the Caliph Harun al-Rashid (763-809). By 1000 the Northmen's double-ended, shallow-draft, oared sailers had taken them by river to the Black and Caspian seas and by sea to America. Viking raiding parties were seldom large. Norse Iceland, as big as north Italy, had only 60,000 people, a few more than the Magyar "horde" of 955 A.D. or the city of Venice. By the time the Vikings were converted to Christianity, the Arabs controlled much of the western Mediterranean, although the Normans managed to win Sicily and southern Italy. Gwynn Jones's *A History of the Vikings* (1968), David C. Douglas's *The Norman Achievement* (1969), Romilly Jenkins's *Byzantium: The Imperial Centuries* (1966), Archibald R. Lewis's *Naval Power and Trade in the Mediterranean* (1951), Bernard S. Bachrach's *Merovingian Military Organization, 481-751* (1972), and Robert S. Lopez's *The Birth of Europe* (1967) are fine general works on this era.

At Hastings (14 October 1066)—one battle on which we have some details—William of Normandy had 3,000 cavalry with chain mail tunics, conical caps, and kite shields light enough for dismounted fighting, 1,000 archers, and 4,000 other footmen from as far away as Italy. His opponent, King Harold, repulsed a Viking invasion at Stamford Bridge and then marched south with 2,000 axemen, a few archers, and no cavalry, picked up

6,000 militia on the way, and was in turn defeated at Hastings. After William's death, the Normans covered a previously unfortified England with motte-and-bailey castles that resembled Roman cantonments.

Manzikert, where the Greeks lost their Anatolian recruiting base to the Seljuk Turks in 1071, was as decisive as Hastings. Eight crusades (1095-1271) helped the Latins set up a kingdom, a principality, and two counties in an area the size of modern Israel, and a Latin empire (1205-1261) in Constantinople. The net effect was to hasten the destruction of the Eastern emperor they professed to have come to save. Christians lost Jerusalem in 1187 and Acre in 1291, but Greeks, Latins, and Ottoman Turks were still fighting over the empire's ruins at Nicopolis in 1396. John Beeler's *Warfare in Feudal Europe, 730-1200* (1971) shows that a mixed force of mounted knights and infantry was always better than a purely cavalry one in the West. The other best books on medieval warfare are Beeler's edition of Charles W. C. Oman's *Art of War in the Middle Ages, A.D. 378-1515* (1953), R. C. Smail's *Crusading Warfare, 1097-1193* (1967), Steven Runciman's *A History of the Crusades* (1951-55), Aziz S. Atiya's *Crusade, Commerce, and Culture* (1966), and Joshua Prawer's *The World of the Crusaders* (1972).

While the Crusades drew some of the Western aristocracy to the tasks of recovering the Holy Land, Spain, and Africa, converting Baltic pagans, and uprooting heretics, other nobles and townsmen blanketed Europe with Crusader castles. A typical garrison post might number forty men-at-arms, forty crossbowmen, forty pikemen, and two gunners. Trebuchets and other war engines brought higher angle fire against them, while bolts and arrows forced lancers and horses into plate armor and reduced the former's effectiveness when dismounted. Although "fire pot" guns had little to do with the infantry revival and early firearms could do little more than scare horses and set fires inside fortifications, contemporary seige artillery soon included all types of homemade cannon and explosives.

The English longbow has been overrated. It was feudal ideas of social superiority and honor that led French knights to ride down their Genoese crossbowmen at Crecy in 1346 and to scorn scouting at Nicopolis, and the Teutonic Knights to stop at Tannenberg in 1410 for a battle of champions. The English had 20,000 men at Crecy, on the first of the dynastic raids which later historians saw as an Anglo-French Hundred Years' War (1338-1453). The crusading force at Nicopolis was somewhere between the 50,000 men who had reached Constantinople and the

12,000 who had taken Jerusalem on the First Crusade. Back home, Saint Louis (Louis IX, 1226-70) had more success trading French lands against their inhabitants' wishes and backing his brother Charles of Anjou's schemes for reviving the Latin empire from Sicily. Some good books are Fredrick Heer's *The Medieval World* (1970), Steven Runciman's *The Sicilian Vespers* (1958), H. J. Hewitt's *The Organization of War under Edward III* (1966), Eduoard Perroy's *The Hundred Years' War* (1965), C. T. Allmand's *Society at War* (1973), and Richard Vaughan's *Philip the Bold* (1962). It was Philip who parlayed his father's and wife's resources into a semi-independent Burgundian state.

The Crusades and the Mongols had put Westerners in contact with the technology of the Eastern, Arabic, and Chinese empires. From these sources they borrowed the lateen sail, windmill, poundlock gate, compass, gunpowder, and papermaking. The use of printing, the crank, and the stored-weight trebuchet (catapult) was fostered by labor shortages and unrest, war, the Black Death (1347-), famine, and an agricultural crisis of the Little Ice Age of the fourteenth to nineteenth centuries. The last factor drove the Atlantic fisheries south, doomed Norse Greenland, and drove lesser nobles into the pay of greater ones or into the free companies which were devastating France. The French population did not recover until the eighteenth century, but there were some islands of relative peace and prosperity in the Netherlands, the Rhineland, south Germany, and Italy. Discharged veterans who wandered or were driven into Italy contributed to social stability by making contracts (*condottas*) with town oligarchs to replace less reliable and efficient militia. Some condottieri battles were bitter; others were tournaments because captains would not risk their men and, unlike prisoners, dead foes could not be ransomed. Florentine militia service was commuted for cash in 1351, just before the peasant Sforza Attendiolo (1364-1424) was kidnapped into a wandering band, became its captain, and laid the foundations of a Milanese dynasty. Three good books are C. C. Bayley's *War and Society in Renaissance Florence: The De Militia of Leonardo Bruni* (1961), Geoffrey Trease's *The Condottieri: Soliders of Fortune* (1971), and Michael Mallett's *Mercenaries and Their Masters: Warfare in Renaissance Italy* (1974).

If the Roman historian Tacitus could have visited Germania in 1400, he might have been impressed by the barbarians' personal independence, glass-walled buildings, armorers, mechanics, lands won from the sea, and Latin readers from Iceland to Riga. But he would have been appalled by their indiscipline, roads, and the discomforts of their castles. Rome was now a provincial town, while Constantinople, Alexandria, and Quinsay (in China) were still metropoli. Tacitus might well have read one of the travel books then firing Latin imaginations, that of Marco Polo the Venetian, "as told to" a fellow prisoner, the professional writer Rustician of Pisa, in Genoa in 1298.

The Early Modern Era

In 1786 the funeral of Frederick the Great honored the last dynastic great captain. By that time Western armies and navies were all armed with guns, and Tacitus would have been impressed by their discipline, Latin readers and villas on five continents, and Gaul's roads and canals. Since 1400 Westerners had conquered the Atlantic Ocean and two continents; their added stocks of food, materials, power, and bullion had fueled further economic and technological development. In 1814, twenty-eight years later, Tacitus could have seen the abdication of a self-made Alexander who had lost a field army twice as large as Augustus's whole force after taking a city as far from Paris as Carrhae—where the Triumvir Marcus Crassus had lost his legions and life in 53 B.C.—had been from Rome.

In *The Rise of the West* (1963, p. 587), William H. McNeill attributes Europe's early sixteenth-century "command of all the oceans" and conquest of "the most highly developed regions of the Americas" to "(1) a deep-rooted pugnacity and recklessness; . . . (2) a complex military technology, most notably in naval matters; and (3) a population inured to" many Old World diseases. Carol. M. Cipolla's *Guns, Sails and Empires: Technological Innovation and the Early Phases of European Expansion* (1965) stresses weapons, though Old World diseases killed more American Indians than did guns. But Western pugnacity and technology do not explain Ottoman Turks taking Constantinople with guns in 1453, defeating Mameluke Egypt in 1517, attacking Vienna in 1529, or raiding Western Mediterranean coasts and commerce after 1533. While the Ottomans took Christian tribute boys into their elite Janissaries and bureaucracy, military participation ratios remained low. But the stream of equally pugnacious Western townsmen and peasants into Turkish frontier areas seems to have conferred no particular military advantage on the West.

The fifteenth century's greatest captains were Murad II (1421-51), who rearmed some archers with handguns, and Mohammed II (1451-81), whose big guns helped to take

Constantinople. The Bohemian Hussites' armored wagons had less influence on war than better quality grained or "corned" gunpowder for siege guns, mines, and matchlock handguns. Firearms were more effective against armor than crossbows or longbows, though their operators also had to be protected by pikemen because of short ranges and slow rates of fire. The best books are David Ayalon's *Gunpowder and Firearms in the Mamluk Kingdom: A Challenge to a Medieval Society* (1956), Frederick G. Heymann's *John Ziska and the Hussite Revolution* (1969), Steven Runciman's *The Fall of Constantinople* (1969), Eric Brockmann's *The Two Sieges of Rhodes* (1969) for the Turkish artillery's failure in 1480 and success in 1522, and Bertrand Gille's *Engineers of the Renaissance* (1966) for an amazing variety of civil and military engines and devices.

Better political organization meant better weapons and better subordinated men. Louis XI of France (1461-83) and Ferdinand II of Aragon (1476-1516), whom Niccolo Machiavelli saw as the ablest of the "new" princes, used methods like those of a Venetian Republic which was neither subverted nor conquered from 1310, when a Council of Ten was set up to secure social order, if not cohesion, to 1797. Venetian "great galleys" met rigid construction standards; bowmen and gunners were chosen by public competition. New navigational methods allowed even slow ships to make two Levant trips a year; greater loading capacities and lower costs generated bulk trade in alum, wheat, and cotton. By 1500 the galleys were bringing 1,500 tons of spices from Mameluke Egypt each fall; up to 1,000 percent profits financed the long Turkish wars. On this model of political and financial organization for the new national monarchs, or Machiavelli's proposed Prince for Italy, who came to dominate Europe, the best books are D. S. Chamber's *The Imperial Age of Venice, 1380-1580* (1971), Frederick C. Lane's *Venetian Ships and Shipbuilders of the Renaissance* (1934), and John F. Guilmartin, Jr.'s *Gunpowder and Galleys* (1974).

The English won another Crecy at Agincourt in 1415, but Charles VII of France (1422-61) regained Paris in 1436, after Joan of Arc had made the repulse of the English invader a national cause. The French king's *compagnies d'ordonnance* (regulations or standards) that constituted the first permanent or standing army were bands of men-at-arms and mounted archers whose quality was insured by peacetime payments from a permanent tax. A new artillery corps helped Charles recover everything but Calais by 1453. It was marriage, not conquest, however, that united the Austrian and Spanish empires and made the

Habsburg Emperor Charles V (1519-55) the most powerful prince in Europe. The details of the dynastic wars or of the English Wars of the Roses (1453-1485) are less important than the appearance of new monarchs who, like Henry VII, were primarily administrators and felt less compelled to lead, or be captured or killed, in battle. Those who find William Shakespeare's or Jean Froissart's (1337-1410) genealogies hard to follow can read Richard Vaughan's *John the Fearless* (1966) or *Philip the Good* (1970) on Burgundy and Paul Murray Kendall's *Louis XI* (1972), *Richard the Third* (1956), or *Warwick the Kingmaker* (1957).

In 1494 Charles VIII of France opened nearly four centuries of foreign intervention in Italy by reclaiming Naples. Though their guns were the best in Europe, by 1559 the French had forced Italy and the Church to seek Habsburg protection, were allied with Suleiman the Magnificent (1520-66), and were defending Paris against Philip II of Spain. Philip had inherited Charles V's Spanish, Italian, and Burgundian possessions while his uncle shouldered the problems of the Viennese emperorship, Germany's Protestants, and the Turks on the Danube. Gonzalo de Cordoba, whose story is told in Mary Purcell's *Great Captain* (1962), devised the Spanish square of pikemen and countermarching handgunners, a formation perfected by the Duke of Parma. Cavalry with wheellock pistols got volume fire by caracoling (making a half turn to right or left), and fortifications were thickened and lowered to take more guns and given outworks against attacking gunners, sappers, and miners. Some good books are Charles W. C. Oman's *A History of the Art of War in the Sixteenth Century* (1937), F. L. Taylor's *The Art of War in Italy, 1494-1529* (1921), Jean Giono's *The Battle of Pavia* (1963) (where Francis I of France was captured in 1525), C. G. Cruickshank's *Army Royal: Henry VIII's Invasion of France, 1513* (1969), and Harold Lamb's *Suleiman the Magnificent* (1951). *The Pirotechnia of Vannoccio Biringuccio* (modern reprint, 1959) is a fine example of the illustrated printed books which were spreading technological, scientific, military, and religious ideas.

Indian allies and Spanish armor, crossbows, guns, horses, and diseases that killed nine-tenths of Mexico's 25 million people from 1519 to 1568 explain the Spanish conquest of that country. Mercury amalgam refining added silver to the gold which supported Philip in Europe. The classics are Bernal Diaz del Castillo's *The Conquest of New Spain* (written in the sixteenth century), Francisco Lopez de Gomara's *Cortes* (1965), William H.

Prescott's *History of the Conquest of Mexico* (1843) and *History of the Conquest of Peru* (1847), and Samuel Eliot Morison's *Admiral of the Ocean Sea* (1942). Other fine works are Björn Landström's *Columbus* (1967), John Hemming's *The Conquest of the Incas* (1970), and J. H. Parry's *The Establishment of the European Hegemony, 1415-1715* (1961) and *The Spanish Seaborne Empire* (1966). The Portuguese destroyed some lighter Arab dhows at Diu, India, in 1509 and reached the Spice Islands by 1513 to cut prices and increase volume and profits by substituting one voyage for several. The Turks, Persians, Chinese, and Japanese confined Westerners to a few port "factories," but the Mogul Empire in India was breaking up when Dutch, English, and French traders later appeared. After Sebastian I of Portugal was killed by the Moors at Alcazar in 1578, Philip cashed in his dynastic claims and by the time Portugal recovered her independence in 1640, the Dutch had taken over most of her Eastern trade. Some good books are Elaine Sanceau's *Henry the Navigator* (1969), E. W. Bovill's *The Golden Trade of the Moors* (1968) and *The Battle of Alcazar* (1952), and C. R. Boxer's *The Portuguese Seaborne Empire, 1415-1825* (1970) and *The Dutch Seaborne Empire, 1600-1800* (1965).

In 1571 the Italians and Spanish defeated the Turks in the last great galley battle at Lepanto. Garrett Mattingly's *The Armada* (1959) is the book on Philip's attempt to invade England in 1588 and the first great sailing ship fight; Geoffrey Marcus's work is now called *The Naval History of England* (1971-). Blaise de Monluc's *The Habsburg-Valois Wars and the French Wars of Religion* (1972) captures the spirit of those conflicts, which ended in 1590 when Henry IV defeated a Spanish-backed army at Ivry. The Netherlands had revolted against Philip in 1568, but by the time William the Silent was assassinated in 1584, Parma had confined the rebels to seven waterlaced Dutch provinces. William's son, Maurice of Nassau, used infantry cohorts with more firepower than the heavier Spanish squares and used canals as Gustavus Adolphus of Sweden, the first of Elbridge Colby's *Masters of Mobile Warfare* (1943), was to use rivers in the Thirty Years' War (1618-1648) which devastated Germany. Trevor N. Dupuy's *Military Life of Gustavus Adolphus* (1970) discusses his salvo-firing musketeers, pikemen with shorter ironclad pikes, light guns, and sabre-armed cavalry. The Swedish King defeated the Austrian Emperor's best general, Count Albrecht von Wallenstein, at Lützen in 1632 but lost his own life in the process. Two years later Wallenstein was assassinated for allegedly plotting for the Bohemian crown.

Francis Watson's *Wallenstein* (1938) and Fritz Redlich's *The German Military Enterpriser and His Work Force* (1965) are the best works on this extraordinary soldier, while Thomas M. Barker discusses Raimondo Montecuccoli in *The Military Intellectual and Battle* (1975).

The entrance of France into the war on behalf of the German Protestants only complicated what began as a religious struggle and ended in 1659 when Louis XIV (1645-1715) married a Spanish princess who brought along a claim to the Spanish throne. At about the same time, Oliver Cromwell's son was removed as Lord Protector by the rump of a Parliament which had executed Charles I of England in 1649, and in Russia, Michael Romanov ended the Time of Troubles (1604-13) by beating back Swedish and Polish invaders and establishing the beginnings of a stable dynasty.

J. H. Elliott's *Imperial Spain* (1964) and John Lynch's *Spain Under the Hapsburgs* (1946-69) stress the nearly insoluble communications problems that afflicted the Spanish Empire and complement Geoffrey Parker's fine *The Army of Flanders and the Spanish Road, 1567-1659: The Logistics of Spanish Victory and Defeat in the Low Countries Wars* (1972). Spain's colonists, like the self-sufficient Roman Gauls, increasingly evaded regulation. While convoys saved most ships from French, Dutch, and English interlopers, their stragglers were so rich that James I began his dynasty's financial woes by ending Elizabeth's long war with Spain. C. G. Cruickshank's *Elizabeth's Army* (1968), Kenneth R. Andrews's *Elizabethan Privateering* (1964), Julian S. Corbett's *Drake and the Tudor Navy* (1898), Cyrus H. Karraker's *Piracy Was a Business* (1953), T. Rayner Unwin's *The Defeat of John Hawkins* (1960), and Charles H. Firth's *Cromwell's Army* (1962) supplement Correlli Barnett's general *Britain and Her Army, 1509-1970* (1970). Georges Pages, in *The Thirty Years' War* (1971), saw that war as modernizing. But C. V. Wedgwood's *Thirty Years' War* (1961), like Hans J. C. von Grimmelshausen's novel *Simplicius Simplicissimus* (1669), held that it "settled nothing worth settling."

The two best short works on an era when Europe was as near anarchy as it had been in the fourteenth century are Trevor Aston's (ed.) *Crisis in Europe, 1560-1660* (1956) and Michael Roberts's *The Military Revolution, 1560-1660* (1956). They are also the best introductions to the demands for religious, political, financial, international, and military order that supported the centralizing and standardizing efforts of the so-called enlightened despots of an era that began with Louis XIV's personal assumption of power in 1661 and ended with the financial collapse of the French monarchy in 1789. The political and military achievements of the most important monarchs are treated in Pierre Goubert's *Louis XIV and Twenty Million Frenchmen* (1970), Vasili Klyuchevsky's *Peter the Great* (1961), Gerhard Ritter's *Frederick the Great* (1968), and by Frederick himself in *Frederick the Great on the Art of War* (1966, translated and edited by Jay Luvaas). Geoffrey Symcox's (ed.) *War, Diplomacy, and Imperialism* (1974) is a more general survey, and Paul W. Bamford's *Fighting Ships and Prisons* (1973) covers the Sun King's Mediterranean galley fleets.

The financial genius of Louis XIV's "mercantilist" adviser, Jean Baptiste Colbert, allowed France to raise the largest army and navy in Europe and to pay the allies who helped Louis attack the exposed Spanish Hapsburg and Imperial lands on his northeastern frontiers. Vauban then worked each conquest into an offensive-defensive fortifications system which covered all of France and provided the protected magazines from which the armies raised and trained by the Marquis of Louvois could make their next carefully prepared forays.

International law and regular supplies and pay limited the looting which had marked previous wars, looting which had done as much damage to the armies themselves as to the economy of occupied areas. Infantry tactics became simpler when socket bayonets made flintlock muskets into pikes as well as firearms. The eighteenth-century Prussian doubled-ended iron ramrod increased loading speed and firepower and the need for march and fire discipline. Unarmored men could carry more rounds for the volume fire that preceded the decisive bayonet charges; uniformed soldiers were easier to identify and direct and less likely to desert in battle. Men wintered better in barrack workshops than when quartered on civilians. Their noble officers had to spend more time with their soldiers or at courts where the monarch could watch them for disloyalty. Hosts of royal inspectors cut down fraud and assured more regular pay and better supplies to armies which were still recruited from the lowest classes of society so that more productive small farmers, artisans, and merchants could add to the state's wealth.

The result was a series of dynastic wars that were more limited in their effects on civilian populations than those of the previous era and established the international balance of power for most of the next two centuries. Louis XIV's aggressions were finally checked in the War of the League of Augsburg, 1689-98. The War of the Spanish Succession, 1700–1714, placed a French prince on the Spanish throne but gave Gilbraltar, Minorca, Newfoundland, Hudson's Bay, and Acadia to Britain and the Spanish Netherlands and major Italian territories to Austria. It also bankrupted the French monarchy. The disorders noted in Lee Kennett's *French Armies in the Seven Years' War* (1967) were as much a result of Louis XIV's selling offices and the right to collect taxes as of Louis XV's ineptitude from 1715 to 1774. Sweden's enemies forced Charles XII to disgorge his earlier conquests in a Great Northern War, 1700–1721, which gave Peter the Great of Russia his Baltic "window" to the west and made Russia a European power. Frederick the Great of Prussia barely kept his gains from the War of the Austrian Succession, 1740–48, in the Seven Years' War, 1756–63, which made Britain the paramount power in North America and India. The biggest losers besides Spain and Sweden were Poland and Turkey. Russia, Austria, and Prussia began to partition Poland in 1772 and completed their work in 1793 and 1795. Eugene of Savoy captured all of Hungary, Transylvania, Croatia, and Slavonia for Austria in 1699, and, after a series of wars, Russia obtained the right to protect Christians in the Ottoman Empire in 1774 and in 1781 agreed with Austria on a future division of all Turkish European territories. And France, Spain, and other powers made Britain less great overseas by helping some British Americans win their independence in 1783.

Technological development continued in areas which, as in the fourteenth century, saw little fighting. Religious uniformity increased local social cohesion; John Prebble's *Culloden* (1962) and *Glencoe* (1968) show the savagery with which the divine-right kings might keep order. One in forty Frenchmen served in Louis's forces and thirty-five Prussians supported every soldier, so military participation was still under Roman Punic War ratios. But there was now no question of the military subordination of the soldiery to monarchs. Winston Churchill's *Marlborough* (1933–38) and Nicholas Henderson's *Prince Eugen of Savoy* (1965) cover Britain's and Austria's greatest captains in the wars of Louis XIV. Reginald Blomfield's *Sebastien le Prestre de Vauban* (1938) treats an engineer in the French king's service who was also an economist, but technology's application to warfare was still largely one of adopting such "random" craft innovations as bayonets, iron ramrods, antiscurvy agents, copper-bottomed ships, and better roads, bridges, and waterways to get more men and guns to more distant targets. Other fine books are John Stoye's *The Siege of Vienna* (1964), R. E. Scouller's *The Armies of Queen Anne* (1966), Frans G. Bengtsson's *The Life of Charles XII* (1960), Jon Manchip White's *Marshal of France: The Life and Times of Maurice, Comte de Saxe* (1962), and Reginald Savory's *His Britannic Majesty's Army in Germany During the Seven Years' War* (1966).

Alfred Thayer Mahan's *The Influence of Sea Power Upon History 1660-1783* (1890), Herbert Richmond's *Statesmen and Sea Power* (1946), Gerald S. Graham's *Empire of the North Atlantic* (1958), and Geoffrey Marcus's *Heart of Oak* (1975) only suggest the developments in gunnery, fleet and convoy and amphibious tactics, logistics, and medicine which enabled Britain to throw 32,000 men—Hannibal's force at Cannae or Caesar's at Pharsalus—at New York in 1776. Geoffrey Marcus's *Quilberon Bay: The Campaign in Home Waters, 1795* (1960) and Charles P. Stacey's *Quebec, 1759* (1959) are fine studies of an earlier war (1756-1763) in which the British pocketed twelve ships of the line and five million dollars in money and goods at Havana, a ransom of four million for Manila, and seven million dollars in treasure from two galleons in 1762. Shelford Bidwell's *Swords for Hire* (1972), Desmond Young's *Fountain of the Elephants* (1959), and Michael Edwardes's *Plassey: The Founding of an Empire* (1970) deal with the adventurers who established a new European empire in India, while the forces that brought down the old systems of statecraft and war in Europe proper are best seen in the first volume of Robert R. Palmer's *The Age of the Democratic Revolution* (1959). The Comte de Guibert, who disowned his ideas for larger and more popular and national armies after meeting Frederick, was only one of many reformers discussed in Robert S. Quimby's *The Background of Napoleonic Warfare* (1957) who wanted reform rather than revolution in what Karl von Clausewitz many years later described as a restricted, shriveled-up form of war.

Bibliography

Adcock, Frank E. *The Greek and Macedonian Art of War*. Berkeley: Univ. of Calif. Press, paperback, 1957.
——. *The Roman Art of War Under the Republic*. Rev. ed. New York: Barnes and Noble, 1963.
Allmand, C. T., ed. *Society at War: The Experience of England and France During the Hundred Years' War*. New York: Harper and Row, 1973.
Anderson, J. K. *Military Theory and Practice in the Age of Xenophon*. Berkeley: Univ. of Calif. Press, 1970.
Anderson, R. C. *Oared Fighting Ships: From Classical Times to the Coming of Steam*. London: Percival Marshall, 1962.
Anderson, Romola, and Anderson, R. C. *The Sailing Ship: Six Thousand Years of History*. New York: Robert M. McBride, 1947.

Andreski, Stanislav. *Military Organization and Society*. 2nd ed. Berkeley: Univ. of Calif. Press, paperback, 1968.

Andrews, Kenneth R. *Elizabethan Privateering: English Privateering During the Spanish War, 1585-1603*. New York: Cambridge Univ. Press, 1964.

Ardrey, Robert. *The Territorial Imperative: A Personal Inquiry Into the Origins of Property and Nations*. New York: Atheneum, 1966. Dell paperback, 1971.

Asprey, Robert B. *War in the Shadows: The Guerrilla in History*. 2 vols. Garden City, N.Y.: Doubleday, 1975.

Aston, Trevor, ed. *Crisis in Europe, 1560-1660*. New York: Basic Books, 1965. Doubleday-Anchor paperback.

Atiya, Aziz S. *Crusade, Commerce, and Culture*. Bloomington: Ind. Univ. Press, 1962. New York: Wiley, paperback, 1966.

Ayalon, David. *Gunpowder and Firearms in the Mamluk Kingdom: A Challenge to a Medieval Society*. London: Valentine, Mitchell, 1956.

Bachrach, Bernard S. *Merovingian Military Organization, 481-751*. Minneapolis: Univ. of Minn. Press, 1972.

Bamford, Paul W. *Fighting Ships and Prisons*. Minneapolis: Univ. of Minn. Press, 1973.

Barker, John W. *Justinian and the Later Roman Empire*. Madison: Univ. of Wisc. Press, 1966.

Barker, Thomas M. *The Military Intellectual and Battle: Raimondo Montecuccoli and the Thirty Years' War*. Albany: State Univ. of N.Y. Press, 1975.

Barnett, Correlli. *Britain and Her Army, 1509-1970: A Military, Political, and Social Survey*. New York: William Morrow, 1970.

Bass, George F., ed. *A History of Seafaring Based on Underwater Archaeology*. New York: Wallace, 1972.

Bayley, C. C. *War and Society in Renaissance Florence: The De Militia of Leonardo Bruni*. New York: Oxford Univ. Press, 1961.

Beeler, John. *Warfare in Feudal Europe, 730-1200*. Ithaca, N.Y.: Cornell Univ. Press, 1971.

Bengtsson, Frans G. *The Life of Charles XII, King of Sweden, 1697-1718*. Translated by Naomi Walford. New York: St. Martin's Press, 1960.

Bidwell, Shelford. *Swords for Hire: European Mercenaries in Eighteenth Century India*. New York: Transatlantic Arts, 1972.

Blackmore, Howard L. *Arms and Armour*. London: Studio Vista, 1965. New York: Dutton, paperback.

———. *Firearms*. London: Studio Vista., 1964. New York: Dutton, paperback.

Blomfield, Reginald. *Sebastien le Prestre de Vauban 1633-1707*. London: Mathsun, 1938.

Bovill, E. W. *The Battle of Alcazar: An Account of the Defeat of Don Sabastion of Portugal at El-Ksar el kebir*. London: Batchworth Press, 1952.

———. *The Golden Trade of the Moors*. 2nd ed. New York: Oxford Univ. Press, 1968.

Boxer, Charles R. *The Dutch Seaborne Empire, 1600-1800*. New York: A. A. Knopf, 1965.

———. *The Portuguese Seaborne Empire, 1415-1825*. New York: A. A. Knopf, 1970.

Bramson, Leon, and Goethals, George W., Jr., eds. *War: Studies from Psychology, Anthropology, Sociology*. New York: Basic Books, 1964.

Brockman, Eric. *The Two Sieges of Rhodes, 1480-1522*. London: John Murray, 1969.

Brodie, Bernard, and Brodie, Fawn. *From Crossbow to H-Bomb*. New York: Dell, paperback, 1962.

Casson, Lionel. *Ships and Seamanship in the Ancient World*. Princeton, N.J.: Princeton Univ. Press, 1971.

Chambers, D. S. *The Imperial Age of Venice, 1380-1580*. New York: Harcourt Brace Jovanovich, paperback, 1971.

Churchill, Winston. *Marlborough: His Life and Times*. 4 vols. London: Harrap, 1933-38.

Cipolla, Carlo M. *Guns, Sails and Empires: Technological Innovation and the Early Phases of European Expansion, 1400-1800*. New York: Patheon Books, paperback, 1965.

Cleator, P. E. *Weapons of War*. New York: Thomas Y. Crowell, 1968.

Colby, Elbridge. *Masters of Mobile Warfare*. Princeton, N.J.: Princeton Univ. Press, 1943.

Corbett, Julian S. *Drake and the Tudor Navy*. 2nd ed. London: Longmans, 1898.

Cottrell, Leonard. *Hannibal: Enemy of Rome*. New York: Holt, Rinehart and Winston, paperback, 1961.

Cruickshank, Charles Grieg. *Army Royal: Henry VIII's Invasion of France, 1513*. New York: Oxford Univ. Press, 1969.

――――. *Elizabeth's Army*. 2nd ed. New York: Oxford Univ. Press, paperback, 1968.

Culican, William. *The First Merchant Venturers: The Ancient Levant in History and Commerce*. New York: McGraw-Hill, paperback, 1966.

De Beer, Gavin. *Hannibal: Challenging Rome's Supremacy*. New York: Viking Press, 1969.

Denison, George T. *History of Cavalry*. 2nd ed. London: Macmillan, 1913.

Diaz del Castillo, Bernal. *The Conquest of New Spain*. Translated by J. M. Cohen. Baltimore: Penguin, paperback, 1963.

Divine, David. *Hadrian's Wall: A Study of the North-West Frontier of Rome*. Boston: Gambit, 1969.

Douglas, David C. *The Norman Achievement 1050-1100*. Berkeley: Univ. of Calif. Press, 1969.

Dumas, Maurice, ed. *History of Technology and Invention: Progress Through the Ages*. Multivolume. New York: Crown 1971-.

Dupuy, R. Ernest, and Dupuy, Trevor N. *The Encyclopedia of Military History from 3500 B.C. to the Present*. New York: Harper and Row, 1970.

Dupuy, Trevor N. *The Military Life of Gustavus Adolphus: Father of Modern War*. New York: Franklin Watts, 1970.

Edwardes, Michael. *Plassey: The Founding of an Empire*. New York: Taplinger, 1970.

Elliott, John H. *Imperial Spain: 1469-1716*. New York: St. Martin's Press, paperback, 1964.

Firth, Charles H. *Cromwell's Army*. 2nd ed. London: Metheun, 1962.

Frederick the Great on the Art of War. Translated and edited by Jay Luvaas. New York: Free Press, 1966.

Fuller, J. F. C. *Decisive Battles: Their Influence upon History and Civilization*. New York: Scribner's, 1940.

――――. *The Generalship of Alexander the Great*. New Brunswick, N.J.: Rutgers Univ. Press, 1960. New York: Funk and Wagnalls, paperback, 1968.

――――. *Julius Caesar: Man, Soldier, and Tyrant*. New York: Funk and Wagnalls, paperback, 1969.

――――. *A Military History of the Western World*. 3 vols. New York: Funk and Wagnalls, paperback, 1954.

Garlan, Yvon. *War in the Ancient World: A Social History*. London: Chatto and Windus, 1975.

Gelzer, Matthias. *Caesar: Politician and Statesman.* Translated by Pete Needham. Cambridge, Mass.: Harvard Univ. Press, 1968.

Gille, Bertrand. *Engineers of the Renaissance.* Cambridge, Mass.: MIT Press, 1966.

Giono, Jean. *The Battle of Pavia: 24th February, 1525.* Translated by A. E. Murch. New York: Fernhill, 1963.

Glubb, John Bagot. *The Great Arab Conquests.* London: Hodder and Stoughton, 1963.

Gomara, Francisco Lopez de. *Cortes.* Translated and edited by Lesley Byrd Simpson. Berkeley: Univ. of Calif. Press, 1965.

Goubert, Pierre. *Louis XIV and Twenty Million Frenchmen.* Translated by Anne Carter. New York: Pantheon Books, paperback, 1970.

Graham, Gerald S. *Empire of the North Atlantic: The Maritime Struggle for North America.* 2nd ed. Toronto: Univ. of Toronto Press, 1958.

Grant, Michael. *The Ancient Mediterranean.* New York: Scribner's, 1969.

Green, Peter. *Alexander the Great.* New York: Praeger, 1970.

———. *Armada from Athens.* Garden City, N.Y.: Doubleday, 1970.

———. *Xerxes at Salamis.* New York: Praeger, 1970.

Grimmelshausen, Hans J. C. von. *Simplicius Simplicissimus.* Translated by Helmuth Weissenborn and Lesley Macdonald. London: J. Calder, 1965.

Grousset, Rene. *Conqueror of the World.* Translated by M. McKellar and D. Sinor. New York: Orion, 1966.

Guilmartin, John F., Jr. *Gunpowder and Galleys: Changing Technology and Mediterranean Warfare at Sea in the Sixteenth Century.* New York: Cambridge Univ. Press, 1974.

Hackett, John Winthrop. *The Profession of Arms.* London: Times Publishing Co., 1963.

Heer, Friedrich. *The Medieval World.* New York: Praeger, 1970.

Hemming, John. *The Conquest of the Incas.* New York: Harcourt Brace Jovanovich, 1970.

Henderson, Nicholas. *Prince Eugen of Savoy: A Biography.* New York: Praeger, 1965.

Herodotus. *The Histories of Herodotus.* Translated by George Rawlinson. Edited by E. H. Blakeney. New York: Dutton, 1964.

Hewitt, H. J. *The Organization of War under Edward III, 1338–1362.* New York: Barnes and Noble, 1966.

Heymann, Frederick G. *John Ziska and the Hussite Revolution.* New York: Russell and Russell, 1969.

Hogg, Oliver F. G. *Artillery: Its Origin, Heyday and Decline.* Hamden, Conn.: Archon, 1970.

———. *Clubs to Cannon: Warfare and Weapons before the Introduction of Gunpowder.* London: Duckworth, 1968.

Hughes, Quentin. *Military Architecture.* London: Hugh Evelyn, 1975.

Jenkins, Romilly. *Byzantium: The Imperial Centuries, A.D. 610–1071.* New York: Random House, 1966.

Jobé, Joseph, ed. *Guns: An Illustrated History of Artillery.* New York: Crown, 1971.

Jones, Gwyn. *A History of the Vikings.* New York: Oxford Univ. Press, 1968.

Karraker, Cyrus R. *Piracy Was a Business.* Rindge, N.H.: Richard R. Smith, 1953.

Kendall, Paul Murray. *Louis XI: The Universal Spider.* New York: W. W. Norton, 1972.

———. *Richard the Third.* New York: W. W. Norton, 1956.

———. *Warwick the Kingmaker.* London: George Allen and Unwin, 1957.

Kennett, Lee. *The French Armies in the Seven Years' War: A Study in Military Organization and Administration.* Durham, N.C.: Duke Univ. Press, 1967.

Kiernan, Frank A., Jr., and Fairbank, John K., eds. *Chinese Ways in Warfare.* Cambridge, Mass.: Harvard Univ. Press, 1974.

Klyuchevsky, Vasili. *Peter the Great.* Translated by Lilian Archibald. New York: Vintage, paperback, 1961.

Kranzberg, Melvin and Pursell, Carroll W., eds. *Technology in Western Civilization.* 2 vols. New York: Oxford Univ. Press, 1967.

Lamb, Harold. *Cyrus the Great.* Garden City, N.Y.: Doubleday, 1960.

———. *Suleiman the Magnificent: Sultan of the East.* Garden City, N.Y.: Doubleday, paperback, 1951.

———. *Tamerlane: The Earth Shaker.* New York: H. M. McBride, 1928.

Landström, Björn. *Columbus.* New York: Macmillan, 1967.

———. *The Ship: An Illustrated History.* Garden City, N.Y.: Doubleday, 1961.

Lane, Frederick C. *Venetian Ships and Shipbuilders of the Renaissance.* Baltimore: Johns Hopkins Univ. Press, 1934.

Lewis, Archibald R. *Naval Power and Trade in the Mediterranean, A.D. 500-1000.* Princeton, N.J.: Princeton Univ. Press, 1951.

Lloyd, E. M. *A Review of the History of Infantry.* London: Longmans, Green, 1908.

Lopez, Robert S. *The Birth of Europe.* New York: M. Evans, 1967.

Luvaas, Jay. See *Frederick the Great on the Art of War.*

Lynch, John. *Spain Under the Hapsburgs.* 2 vols. New York: Oxford Univ Press, 1964-69.

McNeill, William H. *The Rise of the West: A History of the Human Community.* Chicago: Univ. of Chicago Press, paperback, 1963.

Mahan, Alfred Thayer. *The Influence of Sea Power upon History.* Boston: Little, Brown, 1890. New York: Hill and Wang, paperback, 1957.

Major, Ralph H. *Fatal Partners: War and Disease.* Garden City, N.Y.: Doubleday, 1941.

Mallett, Michael Edward. *Mercenaries and Their Masters: Warfare in Renaissance Italy.* Totowa, N.J.: Rowman and Littlefield, 1974.

Marcus, Geoffrey. *Heart of Oak.* New York: Oxford Univ. Press, 1975.

———. *A Naval History of England.* Boston: Little, Brown, 1962-.

———. *Quiberon Bay: The Campaign in Home Waters, 1759.* London: Hollis and Carter, 1960.

Marsden, E. W. *Greek and Roman Artillery: Historical Development.* New York: Oxford Univ. Press, 1969.

Mattingly, Garrett. *The Armada.* Boston: Houghton Mifflin, paperback, 1959.

Monluc, Blaise de. *The Habsburg-Valois Wars and the French Wars of Religion.* Edited by Ian Roy. Military Memoirs, edited by Peter Young. Hamden, Conn.: Archon, 1972.

Morison, Samuel Eliot. *Admiral of the Ocean Sea: A Life of Christopher Columbus.* Boston: Little Brown, 1942.

Montgomery, Field Marshal Bernard L., Viscount. *A History of Warfare.* Cleveland: World, 1968.

Montross, Lynn. *War Through the Ages.* 3d ed. New York: Harper, 1960.

Nef, John U. *War and Human Progress: An Essay on the Rise of Industrial Civilization.* Cambridge, Mass.: Harvard Univ. Press, 1950. As *Western Civilization Since the Renaissance.* New York: Harper Torchbook, 1963.

Oman, Charles W. C. *The Art of War in the Middle Ages, A.D. 378-1515.* Revision edited by John H. Beeler, Ithaca, N.Y.: Cornell Univ. Press, 1953.

———. *A History of the Art of War in the Sixteenth Century.* New York: Dutton, 1937.

Pages, Georges. *The Thirty Years' War, 1618-1648*. Translated by D. Maland and J. Hooper. New York: Harper and Row, 1971.

Palmer, Robert R. *The Age of the Democratic Revolution: A Political History of Europe and America, 1760-1800*. 2 vols. Princeton, N.J.: Princeton Univ. Press, paperback, 1959.

Parker, Geoffrey. *The Army of Flanders and the Spanish Road, 1567-1659: The Logistics of Spanish Victory and Defeat in the Low Countries War*. New York: Cambridge Univ. Press, 1972.

Parry, J. H. *The Establishment of the European Hegemony, 1415-1715: Trade and Exploration in the Age of the Renaissance*. New York: Harper, 1961.

——. *The Spanish Seaborne Empire*. New York: A. A. Knopf, 1966.

Peltier, Louis C. and Pearcy, G. Etzel. *Military Geography*. Princeton, N.J.: Van Nostrand, paperback, 1966.

Perroy, Eduoard. *The Hundred Years' War*. Translated by W. B. Wells. New York: Capricorn, paperback, 1965.

Phillips, Thomas R., ed. *Roots of Strategy: A Collection of Military Classics*. Harrisburg: Military Service Publishing Co., 1940.

Piggott, Stuart. *Ancient Europe from the Beginnings of Agriculture to Classical Antiquity*. Chicago: Aldine, 1965.

The Pirotechnia of Vannoccio Biringuccio. Introduction and notes by Cyril Stanley Smith and Martha Teach Gnudi. New York: Basic Books, 1959.

Polybius. *The Histories*. Translated by Mortimer Chambers. Edited and abridged by E. Badian. New York: Washington Square, paperback, 1966.

Prawer, Joshua. *The World of the Crusaders*. New York: Quadrangle, 1972.

Prebble, John. *Culloden*. New York: Atheneum, paperback, 1962.

——. *Glencoe: The Story of the Massacre*. Harmondsworth: Penguin, 1968.

Prescott, William H. *History of the Conquest of Mexico*. Original in 3 vols., 1843. Abridged by C. H. Gardiner. Chicago: Univ. of Chicago Press, 1966.

——. *History of the Conquest of Peru*. Original in 2 vols., 1847. New York: Heritage, 1957.

Preston, Richard A.; Wise, Sidney F.; and Werner, Herman O. *Men in Arms: A History of Warfare and Its Interrelationships with Western Society*. 2d rev. ed. New York: Praeger, paperback, 1970.

Purcell, Mary. *The Great Captain: Gonzalo Fernandez de Cordoba*. Garden City, N.Y.: Doubleday, 1962.

Quimby, Robert S. *The Background of Napoleonic Warfare: The Theory of Military Tactics in the Eighteenth Century*. New York: Columbia Univ. Press, 1957. AMS Press, 1968.

Redlich, Fritz. *The German Military Enterpriser and His Work Force: A Study in European Economic and Social History*. 2 vols. Wiesbaden: Franz Steiner, 1964-65.

Richardson, Lewis Fry. *Statistics of Deadly Quarrels*. Edited by Quincy Wright and C. C. Lienau. Pittsburgh: Boxwood, 1960.

Richmond, Herbert. *Statesmen and Sea Power*. Oxford: Clarendon Press, 1946.

Ritter, Gerhard. *Frederick the Great: A Historical Profile*. Translated with introduction by Peter Paret. Berkeley: Univ. of Calif. Press, 1968.

Roberts, Michael. *Essays in Swedish History*. London: Weidenfeld and Nicolson, 1967.

——. *The Military Revolution, 1560-1660*. Belfast: Queens Univ. Press, 1956.

Runciman, Steven. *The Fall of Constantinople, 1453*. London: Cambridge Univ. Press, paperback, 1969.

——. *A History of the Crusades*. 3 vols. London: Cambridge Univ. Press, paperback, 1951-55.

——— . *The Sicilian Vespers: A History of the Mediterranean World in the Later Thirteenth Century*. London: Cambridge Univ. Press, paperback, 1958.

Sanceau, Elaine. *Henry the Navigator: The Story of a Great Prince and His Times*. Hamden, Conn.: Shoe String Press, Archon, 1969.

Savory, Reginald. *His Britannic Majesty's Army in Germany During the Seven Years' War*. New York: Oxford Univ. Press, 1966.

Scouller, R. E. *The Armies of Queen Anne*. New York: Oxford Univ. Press, 1966.

Scullard, H. H. *Scipio Africanus: Soldier and Politican*. Ithaca, N.Y.: Cornell Univ. Press, 1970.

Smail, R. C. *Crusading Warfare, 1097-1193*. London: Cambridge Univ. Press, 1967.

Snodgrass, A. M. *Arms and Armour of the Greeks*. Ithaca, N.Y.: Cornell Univ. Press, 1967.

Spaulding, Oliver L., Jr.; Nickerson, Hoffman; and Wright, John W. *Warfare: A Study of Military Methods from the Earliest Times*. Washington: Infantry Journal Press, 1939.

Stacey, Charles P. *Quebec, 1759: The Siege and the Battle*. New York: St. Martin's Press, 1959.

Starr, Chester G., Jr. *The Emergence of Rome as Ruler of the Western World*. Ithaca, N.Y.: Cornell Univ. Press, paperback, 1953.

——— . *The Roman Imperial Navy, 31 B.C.-A.D. 324*. Ithaca, N.Y.: Cornell Univ. Press, 1941.

Storr, Anthony. *Human Aggression*. New York: Atheneum, 1968.

Stoye, John. *The Siege of Vienna*. London: Collins, 1964.

Sun Tzu. *The Art of War*. Translated with an introduction by Samuel B. Griffith. New York: Oxford Univ. Press, 1963.

Symcox, Geoffrey, ed. *War, Diplomacy, and Imperialism, 1618-1763*. New York: Harper and Row, 1973.

Taylor, F. L. *The Art of War in Italy, 1494-1529*. London: Cambridge Univ. Press, 1921.

Thompson, E. A. *The Early Germans*. New York: Oxford Univ. Press, 1965.

Toy, Sidney. *A History of Fortification from 3000 B.C. to A.D. 1700*. London: Heinemann, 1955.

Trease, Geoffrey. *The Condottieri: Soldiers of Fortune*. New York: Holt, Rinehart and Winston, 1971.

Tunis, Edwin. *Weapons: A Pictorial History*. Cleveland: World, 1954.

Turney-High, Harry Holbert. *Primitive War: Its Practice and Concepts*. 2d ed. Columbia: Univ. of S.C. Press, paperback, 1971.

Unwin, T. Raynor. *The Defeat of John Hawkins: A Biography of His Third Slaving Voyage*. New York: Macmillan, 1960.

Vaughan, Richard. *John the Fearless: The Growth of Burgundian Power*. New York: Barnes and Noble, 1966.

——— . *Philip the Bold: The Formation of the Burgundian State*. Cambridge, Mass.: Harvard Univ. Press, 1962.

——— . *Philip the Good: The Apogee of Burgundy*. New York: Barnes and Noble, 1970.

Walbank, Frank William. *The Awful Revolution: The Decline of the Roman Empire in the West.* Toronto: Univ. of Toronto Press, paperback, 1969.

Waltz, Kenneth N. *Man, the State, and War: A Theoretical Analysis*. New York: Columbia Univ. Press, 1959.

Watson, Francis. *Wallenstein: Soldier Under Saturn*. London: Chatto and Windus, 1938.

Watson, G. R. *The Roman Soldier*. Ithaca, N.Y.: Cornell Univ. Press, 1969.

Webster, Graham. *The Roman Imperial Army*. New York: Funk and Wagnalls, 1970.

Wedgwood, C. V. *The Thirty Years War*. Harmondsworth: Penguin, 1961.

White, Jon Manchip. *Marshal of France: The Life and Times of Maurice, Comte de Saxe (1696-1750)*. Chicago: Rand McNally, 1962.

White, Lynn, Jr. *Medieval Technology and Social Change*. 2d ed. New York: Oxford Univ. Press, paperback, 1962.

Winter, F. E. *Greek Fortifications*. Toronto: Univ. of Toronto Press, 1971.

Wintringham, Thomas Henry. *The Story of Weapons and Tactics*. Updated by J. N. Blashford-Snell. Hardmonsworth: Penguin, 1974.

Wright, Quincy. *A Study of War*. Abridged and edited by Louise L. Wright. Chicago: Univ. of Chicago Press, paperback, 1965.

Yadin, Yigael. *The Art of Warfare in Biblical Lands in the Light of Archaeological Study*. 2 vols. New York: McGraw-Hill, 1963.

Young, Desmond. *Fountain of the Elephants*. New York: Harper, 1959.

Chapter **6**

World Military History, 1786-1945

Jeffrey J. Clarke

NATIONALISM, technology, and the democratic revolution have been major themes of the nineteenth and twentieth centuries. Each has reflected a fourth phenomenon of the modern world, the acceleration or "institutionalization" of change, and together they have taken military history down roads that neither Alexander nor Frederick had ever dreamt existed. Major authors dealing with the theme of change are Carlton J. H. Hayes (*A Generation of Materialism*, 1941, and other works on nationalism), William L. Langer (editor of the "Rise of Modern Europe" series), and William McNeill (*Rise of the West*, 1963), while Robert R. Palmer and Joel Colton's *A History of the Modern World* (1971) is one of the best texts covering the entire period and boasts an excellent bibliography. Other key studies include Edmund Wilson's *To The Finland Station* (1940) and sociologist Barrington Moore, Jr.'s *Social Origins of Dictatorship and Democracy* (1966). Wilson traces the rise of socialism and emphasizes the power of individuals and ideas. Moore, from a different perspective, sees the varying growth rates of economic classes as the source of all social conflict. Both studies offer a good foundation for the comparatively short but incredibly complex period of Western development and expansion from 1786 to 1945.

Important works focusing more closely on military affairs are Theodore Ropp's *War in the Modern World* (1962), Michael Howard's *Studies in War and Peace* (1970), Gordon Craig's *War, Politics and Diplomacy* (1966), and John U. Nef's pessimistic *War and Human Progress* (1950). All would agree with Ropp's definition of war as "a complex social phenomenon" that is more than just "a tale of great states, key inventions, or great captains." Edward Mead Earle's (ed.) *Makers of Modern Strategy* (1943) is the best work on military thought and a

Dr. Clarke (Ph.D., Duke) is a historian with the Current History Branch of CMH and is preparing a volume on the American advisory effort in South Vietnam, 1965-73.

pioneering classic in the field. Gordon Turner's *A History of Military Affairs Since the Eighteenth Century* (1956), a source book of carefully selected readings, and J.F.C. Fuller's *The Conduct of War, 1789-1961* (1961) are also good introductions, and, for unconventional warfare, Lewis H. Gann's *Guerrillas in History* (1971) is short, but still the best study.

Two major works in the field of civil-military relations are historian Alfred Vagts' *Defense and Diplomacy* (1956) and the American political scientist Samuel Huntington's *The Soldier and the State* (1957) Huntington examines the growing speciali-zation and professionalization of the military and the ensuing change in its relationship to the state from a "subjective" one of shared goals to a more realistic "objective" one of master and servant. Vagts approaches the problem from a European point of view, the Prusso-Germanic experience, and the conclusions reached in his earlier work, *A History of Militarism* (1937). From his corner, military concerns have become almost inseparable from the domestic and foreign affairs of the national state, and the influence of military professionals has expanded accord-ingly. David Ralston's (ed.) *Soldiers and States* (1966) and Samuel Edward Finer's *The Man on Horseback* (1962) grapple with much the same problem. Finer, a British political theorist, complements Vagts by pointing out the danger of separating the military from society and stresses the importance of shared values and a "common political culture."

The sea and air arms have usually been treated separately. The mechanization of the former has received excellent coverage in Bernard Brodie's *Sea Power in the Machine Age* (1941), but ideas on air and naval strategy have been more partisan. The gist of the classic "command of the sea" concept, first broadcast by Alfred Thayer Mahan in 1890 and last by Brodie in *A Guide to Naval Strategy* (1942), was the overwhelming importance of the liquid medium as both the conduit and generator of national power. Since then, more modest authors have analyzed military power in terms of weapons delivery systems originating in one of the three mediums. In this respect, L. W. Martin's *The Sea in Modern Strategy* (1967), stressing the utility of "waterborne" forces, and Brodie's excellent *Strategy in the Missile Age* (1959) have much in common. Giulio Douhet made the first overstatement of airpower capabilities in *The Command of the Air* (1921, see Chapter 4), and the early chapters of *Strategy in the Missile Age* take the story from there. Other key works are Eugene Emme's (ed.) *The Impact of Air Power* (1959) and I. B. Holley's *Ideas and Weapons* (1953). Harold Lasswell's venerable *Propaganda*

Technique in the World War (1927) and David Kahn's The Codebreakers (1967) also treat specialized topics and are complemented by an almost infinite number of "nuts-and-bolts" works on military hardware. But the effort to study the interplay of history and technology is only just beginning.

The Age of European Revolution, 1789-1850

The French Revolution ushered in an era of profound and often violent change in Western civilization. Louis Gottschalk's The Era of the French Revolution (1929), Palmer's Twelve Who Ruled (1941), and Crane Brinton's A Decade of Revolution 1789-1799 (1934) introduce an event that has developed a massive audience. Underlying this attention has been the use of the French experience as a model for future revolutions by scholars and practitioners alike. All have noted the tendency of the revolution to become more radical, the problems posed by the Thermidorian Reaction and the "man on horseback," and the relationship between rapid internal change and conventional war. It was the antiquated Frederician armies parading at France's doorstep that both intensified and justified the revolution and linked the myth of the people's uprising with that of the nation-in-arms. Lazare Carnot, a middle-class engineer officer, led Palmer's twelve in organizing French resources and applying the total war concept to defend the revolutionary gains already made. Conscription (levée en masse), promotions by merit, food rationing, price and wage controls, and the centralization of arms production were all part of a new national system for waging war. Carnot's efforts are chronicled in Huntly Dupre's Lazare Carnot, Republican Patriot (1940), and the reorganization and performance of the army in Ramsay W. Phipp's The Armies of the First French Republic (five volumes, 1926-39) and Katherine Chorley's Armies and the Art of Revolution (1943). By 1789 all the critical elements of the Napoleonic system of waging war were present (Ropp outlines these elements as command decentralization, massed artillery, emphasis on pursuit, and use of mixed line and column formations).

Robespierre's successors failed to remedy France's economic ills and restrain her most ambitious general. In 1799 Napoleon Bonaparte overthrew the government and by 1804 had himself declared absolute ruler of France. The upstart emperor brought internal peace to France and marshaled all her resources in an effort to achieve lasting French hegemony on the continent.

Three recent biographies are Pieter Geyle's remarkable *Napoleon, For and Against* (1949), James M. Thompson's *Napoleon Bonaparte: His Rise and His Fall* (1951), and F. M. H. Markham's *Napoleon* (1963); his string of decisive battle victories are ably discussed in W. G. F. Jackson's *Attack in the West* (1953) and David G. Chandler's *The Campaigns of Napoleon* (1966). But in Iberia, on the Atlantic, and east of the Niemen, French eagles encountered Spanish nationalism, British seapower, and some of the most barren lands in Europe. In Russia Napoleon lost a half-million men, and his failure encouraged the fourth and final coalition against France. The best firsthand account of the 1812 adventure is the Count de Segur's *Napoleon's Russian Campaign* (1825). The three-day Battle of Nations in October 1813 completed the turnabout, and the hundred days that preceded Waterloo only spooked the jittery statesmen of Vienna. Long before Bonaparte's final exile, what Liddell Hart titled *The Ghost of Napoleon* (1933) could be seen throughout Europe.

The key British military leaders were Arthur Wellesley (Duke of Wellington) and Horatio Nelson. Sir Charles Petrie's *Wellington: A Reassessment* (1956) is one of many good treatments of the duke, and the standard work on Britain's greatest sea captain is Carola Oman's *Nelson* (1946). W. F. P. Napier's *History of the War in the Peninsula* (six volumes, 1828–40) is the classic account of Britain's effort to succor Spain and Portugal, and is seconded by Charles Oman's superlative study, *Wellington's Army* (1912). *The War in the Mediterranean, 1803–1810* (1957) is covered by Piers Mackesy, *The Battle of the Nile* (1960) by Oliver Warner, and Nelson's decisive victory over the combined fleets of France and Spain by Dudley Pope's *Decision at Trafalgar* (1960). Michael Lewis's *A Social History of the Navy, 1793–1815* (1960) is a deeper analysis of Britain's wood and sail technicians and is a gold mine of information.

Napoleon's travels into Central Europe speeded up the awakening of German nationalism. While Freiherr vom Stein "junked" much of Prussia's rigid social and economic structure, Scharnhorst, Gneisenau and others sought to make the army more modern, professional, and democratic, and Hardenberg and Yorck maneuvered the small state on to the winning side of the Viennese conference table. The medley of reformers is covered by William O. Shanahan's *Prussian Military Reforms, 1786–1813* (1945) and Peter Paret's comprehensive *Yorck and the Era of Prussian Reform 1807–1815* (1966). Tsar Alexander I was an eighteenth-century monarch of a medieval state, and this may explain Russia's bizarre response to the whole affair. But both Catherine's Suvarov and Alexander's Kutuzov responded to the French military challenge and gave Russians their first national experience. In *The Art of Victory*, Philip Longworth treats *The Life and Achievements of Field Marshal Suvarov, 1729-1800* (1965), while Roger Parkinson's *The Fox of the North* (1976) covers his successor.

The Congress of Vienna restored a European balance of power and inaugurated a century without a general European war. Led by the Austrian prime minister, Prince Klemens von Metternich, the restoration of the monarchical system was approved by all the great powers, including France; liberalism, nationalism, and democracy were correctly regarded as subversive to the established order and were rigorously opposed. The best accounts are Harold Nicolson's *The Congress of Vienna* (1946) and Henry A. Kissinger's *A World Restored* (1957). The liberal cause of the 1820s is treated in Christopher M. Woodhouse's *The Greek War for Independence* (1952) and the Russian fiasco in Anatole Mazour's *The First Russian Revolution, 1825* (1937). Revolutionaries were also crushed in England, Germany, and Spain, the last with French troops, but Latin America maintained its independence when London vetoed Russian proposals for massive European intervention. For an introduction see John B. Trend's *Bolivar and the Independence of Spanish America* (1946) and Jay Kinsbrunner's *Bernardo O'Higgins* (1968).

In the early 1830s revolutions again broke out across the continent. Their success in Western Europe—a constitutional monarch for the French, independence for the Belgians, and the right to vote for the English upper middle class—was balanced by their complete failure in the east. The revolutions of 1848 repeated the same pattern. While in France socialism divided the revolutionaries and delivered the bourgeoisie to Louis Napoleon, nationalism remained the dominant theme east of the Rhine and south of the Alps. Assorted dukes and princes were booted from Italy, the Habsburg Empire temporarily disintegrated, Metternich was forced into exile, and Frederick William IV hurriedly granted a constitution to his bewildered Prussian subjects. But by the end of the spring the revolutions had run their course. In Prussia the vacillating monarch refused the imperial German crown, and to the south Austria's "counterinsurgency" generals—Benedek, Radetsky, Windischgrätz, and the Croat Jellachich—crushed the Italian and Slav rebels and, with Russian aid, destroyed Kossuth's Magyar armies.

After brushing aside the Decembrists, Alexander's brother,

Nicholas I, established the most reactionary regime in Europe, crushed the Polish nationalists in 1831 (but was unable to send expeditions to Belgium or France), and sent over 100,000 troops to aid the Austrians in 1849. But as events would prove five years later, the Russian Army was little better than a massive police force. Priscilla Robertson's *Revolutions of 1848: A Social Study* (1952) is the best book on 1848, and *The Russian Army Under Nicholas I* (1965) by John Shelton Curtiss is a trenchant work on the decline of the tsar's legions and an indispensable background to the Crimean War.

The Rise of Nation-States, 1850-1914

As long as Britain led the industrial revolution, she also led in technological innovations, or at least was able to make the fullest use of them to uphold the Atlantic *Pax Britannica*. Throughout the nineteenth century, British yards built good ships faster than any other two powers combined and allowed London to steer a "blue water" course free from European entanglements while promoting what it considered a balance of power on the continent. The critical later period is treated by Arthur T. Marder's excellent *The Anatomy of British Sea Power* (1940), and Christopher Lloyd's *The Navy and the Slave Trade* (1949) discusses one matter that American and French revolutionaries left unsolved. For Britain's greatest challenge, see Ernest Woodward's *Great Britain and the German Navy* (1935) and Alfred von Tirpitz's *My Memoirs* (1919).

Like the French, British generals did well fighting non-European military forces abroad but never mastered the art of amphibious operations. Wellington's ghost may account for the Crimean and Gallipoli debacles. In the first case, both sides had critical supply problems, and mutual ineptitude produced a war of attrition. The best account is Col. Edward Hamley's *The War in the Crimea* (1890). Hamley, a participant, and G.F.R. Henderson were the foremost British military critics of the nineteenth century, and both are discussed in Jay Luvaas's *The Education of an Army* (1964). C. B. Woodham-Smith's *Florence Nightingale* (1951) and *The Reason Why* (1953) are probing biographies and are eminently readable, as is Donald Morris's *The Washing of the Spears* (1965), a re-creation of the tragic Zulu wars. Brian Bond's (ed.) recent *Victorian Military Campaigns* (1967), however, is all one needs on Britain's "small wars."

Late nineteenth-century European imperialism only reflected

growing continental rivalries. From 1899 to 1902 South African Dutch waged a guerrilla war against British expansion and barely managed to force what amounted to a draw. Works like Rayne Kruger's *Good-Bye Dolly Gray* (1960) are fine narratives but emphasize campaign history and tend to romanticize a "popular" war that saw the incarceration of 120,000 Boer women and children, of whom an estimated 20,000 perished through disease and neglect. For the ensuing period, John K. Dunlop's *The Development of the British Army, 1899-1914* (1938) provides background, and key figures are treated in Philip Magnus' *Kitchener* (1958) and Dudley Sommer's *Haldane of Cloan* (1960).

While Britain was ruling the seas, the "great questions" of Europe were being settled by "blood and iron." What the revolutionaries had failed to do in 1789, 1830, and 1848, great statesmen and great armies would accomplish, or so it seemed. While neither Jomini nor Clausewitz bequeathed any magic formula to the Prussian generals, the latter were the first to marry the military staff system with "higher" military education. Their most notable offspring, the "Grosser Generalstab," or General Staff, was composed of the country's brightest officers and charged with formulation of doctrine and war plans independent of the traditional chain of command. The best treatment is Gordon Craig's *The Politics of the Prussian Army, 1640-1945* (1955) which emphasizes the development of German militarism and its deleterious effects on the nation's future. Although Craig sought the origins of the Nazi phenomenon in Prussia's military tradition, Barrington Moore may be closer to the truth when he explores the impact of revolutions from above and their stifling effect on Germany's social growth—*Social Origins of Dictatorship and Democracy* (1966).

Both Italy and Germany were unified under comparatively liberal constitutional regimes after three short, decisive wars between 1859 and 1871; Britain had received the message earlier and began granting self-governing dominion status to her most powerful possessions at the same time, but the rest of Europe had to wait until World War I. Other ingredients in the Prussian story can be found in E. A. Pratt's *The Rise of Rail-Power in War and Conquest, 1853-1914* (1915) and Eugene N. Anderson's *The Social and Political Conflict in Prussia, 1858-1864* (1954), while Jay Luvaas's *The Military Legacy of the Civil War* (1959) is also valuable. Napoleon III emerged intact from the Crimea, supported Count Camillo di Cavour with troops in 1859, but lost his nerve after Solferino. The emperor fared no better in Mexico, where the end of America's Civil War precipitated a rapid French withdrawal leaving the romantic Archduke Maximilian to face the traditional Latin American music. Cavour's long struggle to unify Italy ended successfully in 1870, and John Parris's *The Lion of Caprera: A Biography of Giuseppe Garibaldi* (1962) treats his unexpected and colorful ally. To the north, Prussia's seven-week triumph over Austria is covered by Gordon Craig's excellent *The Battle of Königgrätz* (1964) and her decisive defeat of Louis Napoleon in Michael Howard's fine *The Franco-Prussian War* (1961). Behind everything seemed to be the hand of the Prussian Chancellor, Otto von Bismarck.

In France, the defeat of the Second Empire's highly paid, professional army in 1870 discredited the concept of an all-volunteer military force for the immediate future. Complications arose when Parisian republicans objected to Prussia's harsh peace terms, refused to recognize the newly elected National Assembly, and established their own revolutionary government, the Commune, to continue the war effort. But the conservative Assembly—most of its members were royalists—saw the municipal body as a threat to the existing social order and directed its remaining armies against it. While the Prussians stepped aside, French regulars crushed the Commune in some of the cruelest fighting ever seen in Western Europe. In the wake of the battle, some 38,000 suspected Communards were arrested, 20,000 put to death, and 7,500 deported to New Caledonia. The tragedy is covered in Melvin Kranzberg's *The Siege of Paris, 1870-1871* (1950).

Better known is the explosive Dreyfus Affair that divided France in the 1890s. Guy Chapman's *The Dreyfus Case: A Reassessment* (1955) is one of the better works addressing the case of a young Jewish general staff officer falsely accused of espionage and the efforts of individuals, both in and outside of the defense establishment, to protect or expose the Army's original error. But the passions of the affair were soon forgotten in the upsurge of nationalism that spread throughout Europe. Richard Challener's *The French Theory of the Nation in Arms, 1866-1939* (1955) examines the close relationships between internal politics, foreign policy, and military strategy and doctrine, including the arguments for professional and draftee armies. Although the great Socialist leader Jean Jaurès championed a short-term, defensive militia in his *L'Armée nouvelle* published in 1910 (the abridged English version is *Democracy and Military Service*, 1916), until World War I other ideas held sway. David Ralston's fine *The Army of the Republic* (1967) covers the period before 1914, and Paul-Marie de La Gorce's *The*

French Army: A Military-Political History (1963) sketches the story up to Algeria. By then even the French were beginning to realize that France was no longer a great power.

The Great European War, 1914-1918

The First World War was essentially a continental affair. The war's origins, a point of heated debate, were also European. Popular democracy had fueled intense national rivalries which in turn had produced governments that sought national objectives through complex alliances and expanded armaments. A general war had been almost inevitable. One of the most balanced accounts is by an American scholar, Laurence Lafore, whose *The Long Fuse: An Interpretation of the Origins of World War I* (1965) avoids the tangle over war guilt and concentrates on unraveling and weighing the multiple factors involved.

Perhaps even more fascinating is Dwight E. Lee's survey of the more partisan literature in *The Outbreak of the First World War: Who was Responsible?* (1963). Because the treaty of Versailles fixed the blame for the war on Germany and its allies, basic primary source material on the origins of the war became available far earlier than historians had reason to expect. Anxious to refute the Allied verdict, the Germans quickly published documents from their diplomatic archives, an act which prompted other governments to open their records in response. From a study of this evidence, one early revisionist, Harry Elmer Barnes, in *The Genesis of the World War* (1926), concluded that "direct and immediate responsibility for its outbreak" fell upon Serbia, France, and Russia, with Germany and Britain "tied for last place." Other respected historians, like Bernadotte E. Schmitt in *The Coming of the War, 1914* (two volumes, 1930), insisted that Germany had to bear the main share of the blame for the war. But in a work that has stood the test of time remarkably well, *The Origins of the World War* (two volumes, 1930), Sidney Bradshaw Fay determined that "all the European countries, in a greater or less degree, were responsible." In the 1960s the controversy was fueled by two leading German historians, Gerhard Ritter and Fritz Fischer. Ritter's *The Sword and the Scepter* (1954-70) develops his earlier analysis in the *Schlieffen Plan* (1956) and accuses Germany's war planners of ignoring political factors. Fischer, in *Germany's Aims in the First World War* (1967) and his recent expansion of the same topic, *War of Illusions: German Policies from 1911 to 1914* (1975), has a broader target. The author portrays 1914 as a

German war of conquest, a "Griff nach der Weltmacht," and a cruel substitute for greatly needed social and political reforms at home.

The war brought European military participation, subordination, and cohesion to a high pitch. Aspects of the home front struggle are treated in the international Carnegie Endowment series, *Economic and Social History of the World War*, edited by James T. Shotwell (150 volumes, 1921-40) which includes superior works like William H. Beveridge's *British Food Control* (1928) and Albrecht Mendelssohn-Bartholdy's *The War and German Society: The Testament of a Liberal* (1937). Frank P. Chamber's *The War Behind the War, 1914-1918* (1939) is the best general study and traces the gradual centralization of social and economic controls necessitated by the war.

The immediate benefits of "war socialism" were dubious. Each sacrifice, each political, economic, or social concession to the war effort, ran the bidding up and made it more difficult to withdraw from the game without losing everything. The deepening commitment to total military victory was never seriously questioned. In the end, the struggle took the lives of at least ten million individuals, incapacitated about twenty million more, ruined Europe's economy, and discredited a culture that would allow such a slaughter to take place. Both René Albrecht-Carrié's *The Meaning of the First World War* (1965) and editor Jack J. Roth's *World War I: A Turning Point in Modern History* (1967) address the war's significance. Histories of its conduct have been more numerous. Two excellent short studies are Cyril Falls's *The Great War* (1959) and B. H. Liddell Hart's *A History of the World War, 1914-1918* (a 1970 revision of his *The Real War, 1930*). In the latter, the British military critic exposes the failure of Allied generalship and presents his indirect approach thesis (see Chapter 4). Falls gives greater weight to strategic and tactical problems facing commanders on the Western Front and also supplies a broader coverage of the war. Of the official operational histories, Britain's *The Great War* (edited by Sir James Edward Edmonds, Wilfrid Miles, and Henry Rodolph Davies, forty-five volumes, 1927-47), although not without bias, is the best, and C. E. W. Bean's excellent *Anzac to Amiens* (1946), a semiofficial summary of the Australian effort, is the most readable (see Chapter 22).

Basic works on command and strategy within the Allied camp are Paul Guinn's *British Strategy and Politics, 1914 to 1918* (1965), Jere Clemens King's *Generals and Politicians: Conflict between France's High Command, Parliament and Government,*

1914-1918 (1951), and Sir Frederick Maurice's *Lessons of Allied Co-operation* (1942). Once the promised quick victories failed to materialize, the war councils of the western democracies were taken over by strong civilian leaders headed by France's Georges Clemenceau and Britain's David Lloyd George. On the formulation of British strategy, *Great Britain and the War of 1914-1918* (1967) by Sir Ernest Woodward is supplemented by Maurice Hankey's *The Supreme Command, 1914-1918* (two volumes, 1961) and *Field Marshall Sir Henry Wilson: His Life and Diaries* (1927) edited by Charles E. Callwell. The last is lively and caustic and is complemented by a sympathetic biography, Basil Collier's *Brasshat* (1961), and a harsh criticism, General Sir Hubert Gough's *Soldiering On* (1954).

The opening plays are reported in Barbara Tuchman's fascinating and popular *The Guns of August* (1962). For a more detailed review of the initial war of movement in the west, see Sewell Tyng's *The Campaign of the Marne, 1914* (1935) and John Terraine's *Mons: The Retreat to Victory* (1960). For the other end of Europe, the standard English language battle study is Sir Edmund Ironside's *Tannenberg: The First Thirty Days in East Prussia* (1925). Of all the offensives, the German came closest to success, but was thwarted by French stubbornness and German overconfidence. Thereafter, mutual exhaustion and trench warfare ended the war of movement, and the struggles described in Alistair Horne's *The Price of Glory* (1962) and Leon Wolff's *In Flanders Fields* (1958) are more typical of what followed. For a tactical overview, see P. M. H. Lucas's *The Evolution of Tactical Ideas in France and Germany During the War of 1914-1918* (1925) and, at the ground level, read Charles Carrington's *A Subaltern's War* (1929) or Charles Douie's *The Weary Road* (1929). Some of the better anthologies are Eugene Löhrke's *Armageddon* (1930) and Guy Chapman's *Vain Glory* (1937), while Arthur Marwick examines changing British attitudes toward the war in *The Deluge: British Society and the First World War* (1965).

Generalship has been hotly debated. Correlli Barnett's *The Swordbearers* (1963) and Liddell Hart's earlier *Through the Fog of War* (1938) are two of many that take up the British commander, Sir Douglas Haig. Haig came to personify the strategy of attrition, and favorable treatments include Maj. Gen. Sir John Davidson's *Haig, Master of the Field* (1953), but to Alan Clark he was just another one of *The Donkeys* (1961) whose strategy threatened Britain's chance to survive even a final victory. Other important works are Hugh M. Urquhart's angry

Arthur Currie: The Biography of a Great Canadian (1950) and Hubert Gough's story in *The Fifth Army* (1931); both were key subordinates to Haig.

Good studies of French generalship are few. Edward L. Spears's *Liaison 1914* (1930) and Jean de Pierrefeu's *French Headquarters, 1915-1918* (1924) complement Marshal Joseph Joffre's translated *Personal Memoirs* (1932), Liddell Hart's *Foch: The Man of Orleans* (1931), and Jan Tanenbaum's recent biography, *General Maurice Sarrail* (1974). Joffre claims credit for the Marne, Liddell Hart feels Foch was a slow learner, and there are no good histories of Nivelle, Pétain, or the mutinies of 1917. After the disastrous Nivelle offensive on the Aisne, French morale crumbled and some fifty-four divisions were affected by "collective indiscipline." There was little organized violence, disturbances were generally confined to the rear, and the Germans never realized the scope of the affair. In the end some 23,000 soldiers were court-martialed, but only 432 received death sentences, 55 were shot, and, under a more cautious commander in chief, the army was saved from total collapse.

The German generals were no more successful than their opponents. Erich von Falkenhayn, who relieved Moltke (the younger) in 1914 and was replaced two years later, gives an overview in *The German General Staff and Its Decisions, 1914-1916* (1920). The exploits of his successors, the Hindenburg-Ludendorff team, are discussed in Donald J. Goodspeed's *Ludendorff: Genius of World War I* (1966) and John W. Wheeler-Bennett's *Wooden Titan: Hindenburg in Twenty Years of German History* (1936). Ludendorff later supervised the German war effort but was unable to transfer his tactical genius to other areas. One of his most brilliant staff officers, Max Hoffmann, was also his worst critic in *War Diaries and Other Papers* (1929).

There is no account of the shrewd Austrian Commander, Conrad von Hotzendorff, but Russia's best leader, Alexei Brusilov, has written *A Soldier's Notebook, 1914-1918* (1930), which complements Sir Alfred Knox's standard *With the Russian Army, 1914-1917* (1921). The best study on the decline of the tsarist state is Hugh Seton-Watson's *The Russian Empire, 1801-1917* (1967), while the 1905 Revolution is examined in Sidney Harcave's excellent *First Blood* (1964) and director Sergei Eisenstein's *Potemkin* (1926), a classic silent film. Two wars showed that the Russian tsar could suppress internal dissent and wage war, but not at the same time. By the end of 1916, with "Nicky" running the ill-provisioned armies, and Rasputin and the empress heading the state, the collapse was almost inevitable. The revolutionary period is introduced by William Henry Chamberlin's standard *The Russian Revolution, 1917–1921* (1935) and Isaac Deutscher's superb biographies, *Trotsky* (three volumes, 1954–63) and *Stalin* (1949), but there are many gaps.

The collapse of the Eastern Front failed to end the war, and the naval and southern theaters were indecisive. The desert war is covered by T. E. Lawrence's classic *Seven Pillars of Wisdom* (1926) and Field Marshal Archibald P. Wavell's *Allenby: A Study in Greatness* (1940–43) and his earlier *The Palestine Campaigns* (1928). The latter are excellent campaign and leadership analyses, but, like the African campaigns, they have little to do with Europe, and Allied forces in Italy and the Balkans remained stalemated. In 1915 Churchill directed Britain's massive amphibious campaign against the Straits but was unable to cut the Turkish knot. The full story of the Allied disaster is told in *Gallipoli Diary* (1920) by the British Commander-in-Chief, Sir Ian Hamilton, and *Gallipoli* (1929–32), the superb official account by C. F. Aspinall-Oglander. For the defending side, there is Hamilton's opposite, Otto Liman von Sanders and his *Five Years in Turkey* (1927).

To the north, the Royal Navy kept the lid on German sea power. Arthur J. Marder's sweeping *From the Dreadnought to Scapa Flow* (five volumes, 1961–70) is the best account, and R. H. Gibson and Maurice Pendergast's *The German Submarine War, 1914–1918* (1931) is best on Germany's greatest threat. The German high seas admirals were unwilling to risk a major encounter and sat out the war on the wrong side of the Kiel Canal. Their one major engagement with the British Grand Fleet off the coast of Danish Jutland was accidental. Good stories of what was the largest naval encounter to that date are Donald Macintyre's fine *Jutland* (1958) and, for the German side, Reinhard Scheer's *Germany's High Seas Fleet in the World War* (1920). Scheer piloted the Kaiser's fleet and matched wits with Britain's finest captains whose stories are told in A. Temple Patterson's *Jellicoe* (1969) and Admiral W. S. Chalmers's *The Life and Letters of David Earl Beatty* (1951). Moving away from the traditional biographies and battle studies is Daniel Horn's *The German Naval Mutinies of World War I* (1969), one of several recent works combining history and sociology.

Military technology offered another way to end the stalemate in the west. Defenses could be paralyzed by poison gases, shattered by armored "land battleships," or bypassed by flying machines. But these alternatives were never thoroughly pursued—aircraft design was still primitive, gas indiscriminate, and both the submarine and tank used hesitantly by their respective employers. Most air literature is romantic, but Raymond H. Fredette's *The Sky on Fire* (1966) is sound, as is Maj. Gen. Alden H. Waitt's *Gas Warfare* (1942). The tank, or armored fighting vehicle, was more of a "felt need" than either the airplane or submarine, and its origin is well documented in Liddell Hart's excellent *The Tanks* (1959), which covers both world wars from the British point of view. But despite the massive employment of thousands of these devices, the essential nature of World War I remained unchanged.

World War II and the Decline of Europe, 1919-1945

The failure of Western leaders to develop a community of interest and deal with a series of worldwide financial crises were major contributing factors to the Second World War. Laurence Lafore's recent *The End of Glory: An Interpretation of the Origins of World War II* (1970) introduces the problem with a good discussion of A. J. P. Taylor's controversial *The Origins of The Second World War* (1961). Taylor portrayed Hitler as a popular leader pursuing traditional German goals. His efforts to revise the harsh Versailles peace settlement were encouraged by the vacillating policies of London and Paris and the ensuing war was a colossal blunder that stronger statesmen could have avoided. In contrast, Taylor's opponents would agree with Ernest Nolte's *Three Faces of Fascism* (1966) that totalitarian Germany represented something new and threatening to Western culture, and the irrational use of force was implicit in its ideological underpinnings. Robert G. Waite sees *The Free Corps Movement in Post War Germany, 1918-1923* as the *Vanguard of Nazism* (1952) and a training ground for paramilitary politics. The German Army did not intervene openly in Weimar's political process, but its impact was heavy until subordinated by Hitler. Some fine studies are Francis L. Carsten's *The Reichswehr and Politics, 1918-1933* (1966) and Wheeler-Bennett's *The Nemesis of Power* (1953), complemented by Reichswehr chief Hans von Seeckt's *Thoughts of a Soldier* (1930).

Spain was the first real sample of Hitler's political-military methods and a warning to Russia and the West. The Western democracies were too divided to aid the Republic and, with only limited assistance from the Soviet Union and the International Brigades, the Loyalists fell to General Francisco Franco's better equipped legions after a bitter three-year struggle. Hugh

Thomas's impartial *The Spanish Civil War* (1961) and Gabriel Jackson's more comprehensive *The Spanish Republic and the Civil War, 1931-1939* (1965) are both excellent. Gerald Brenan's *The Spanish Labyrinth* (1943) discusses the war's background, while the more exciting firsthand accounts are George Orwell's disillusioned *Homage to Catalonia* (1938) and the well-known interpretations of Hemingway and Malraux. All fought for the Republic.

General European war began in September 1939. While Britain and France expected another long war of attrition, the German dictator destroyed or intimidated his opponents with a series of quick, decisive victories. Poland, Norway, Denmark, Holland, Belgium, and France fell to the mechanized blitzkrieg with surprising speed, and Churchill's England barely managed to weather the storm that followed. Unable to defeat Britain and fearing an eventual Anglo-American coalition in the west, Hitler needed military security in the east and assured supplies of food and raw materials. To secure this, he launched an invasion of Russia in mid-1941. Stubborn resistance by both Russia and Britain finally ended the Nazi war of movement and, with the American entrance, turned the struggle into a war of technological attrition in the West and manpower attrition in the East, with Germany the loser. The Western Allies made up for Gallipoli by a dazzling series of amphibious invasions more reminiscent of Foch's strategy of 1918 than of the indirect approach. Once the huge Russian armies began rolling in from the steppes, Germany was overwhelmed and Europe divided between American and Soviet spheres of influence.

The best single-volume study is Gordon Wright's *The Ordeal of Total War, 1939-1945* (1968). Other fine histories include Brigadier Peter Young's *World War* (1966), Basil Collier's *A Short History of the Second World War* (1967) and Fuller's *The Second World War* (1948). Official histories of the war were produced by the United States, Great Britain, Australia, New Zealand, Canada, South Africa, the Soviet Union, and others. All are narratives based on official documents, and most are more balanced and professional than their World War I predecessors. The most comprehensive foreign series is the United Kingdom's *History of the Second World War* which includes separate civil (twenty-nine volumes), medical (twenty-one volumes), and military (twenty-nine volumes) series, although, unlike their U.S. counterparts, they are devoid of both citations and bibliographical notes (see Chapter 22). Soviet historians, not unexpectedly, have been plagued by ideological intrusions and are currently making at least their second attempt at an officially acceptable version. Even these massive projects have been dwarfed by a vast outpouring of popular literature—paperback memoirs, biographies, small-unit operations, technical histories, many of which are based on the official histories and the sources noted in James E. O'Neill and Robert W. Krauskopf (eds.) *World War II: An Account of Its Documents* (1976).

Interwar French leaders had rejected the idea of a quick-strike, mechanized, professional army and opted for a larger draftee force with more depth. Whatever can be said of their strategy, there was no immediate invasion and France was given eight months to prepare for the expected assault. The army was lost when its commander, General Maurice Gamelin, committed his mobile reserves prematurely; the country was lost when his successors lost the will to fight. The sideshows were the deceptive Winter War between Russia and Finland, and *The Campaign in Norway* treated officially by Thomas K. Derry (1952). The standard battle studies are Col. Adolphe Goutard's *The Battle of France, 1940* (1959) and Lionel F. Ellis's official *The War in France and Flanders* (1953), with a good firsthand account by Spears in *Assignment to Catastrophe* (two volumes, 1954-55). A more searching study of France's psychological collapse is Marc Bloch's brilliant *Strange Defeat* (1949), and, for the Army's thrust into the political arena, Philip Bankwitz's *Maxime Weygand and Civil-Military Relations in Modern France* (1967) is excellent.

Weygand succeeded Gamelin and prepared the way for Pétain's armistice. But as de Gaulle predicted, France had lost a battle but not the war, and both he and Churchill were guided by their broader vistas of history. De Gaulle's *The Edge of the Sword* (1932), together with his *War Memoirs* (five volumes, 1955-60), and Churchill's *The Second World War* (six volumes, 1948-53) are autobiographical testaments to their strengths and weaknesses. Lord Hankey's *Diplomacy by Conference* (1946) and Liddell Hart's *Memoirs* (1965-66) and *The British Way in Warfare* (1932) reflect the island's prewar yearning for the "blue water" strategy which the fall of France now made inevitable. For the war, Churchill's histories are complemented by the official series and balanced by Sir Arthur Bryant's *A History of the War Years Based on the Diaries of Field-Marshal Lord Alanbrooke, Chief of the Imperial General Staff* (two volumes, 1957-59).

Britain's command of the air and sea insured her immediate survival. The development of the Royal Air Force is covered in

Philip Joubert de la Ferte's *The Third Service* (1955) and Peter Townsend's *Duel of Eagles* (1970), and operations are presented by Denis Richards and Hilary A. Saunders' *Royal Air Force, 1939-1945* (three volumes, 1953-54). The official account of Britain's *Strategic Air Offense Against Germany* (four volumes, 1961) by Charles Kingsley Webster and Noble Frankland is supplemented by the U.S. Air Force histories and Anthony Verrier's *The Bomber Offensive* (1968). The results were controversial, and indiscriminate bombing may have only stiffened resistance on both sides.

For the Royal Navy, Stephen W. Roskill's *The War at Sea* (three volumes, 1954-61) is the excellent official study and is supplemented by his shorter *White Ensign* (1960) and Samuel Eliot Morison's official histories of the American effort. Two key biographies by William S. Chalmers are *Full Cycle: The Biography of Admiral Sir Bertram Home Ramsay* (1959), which includes the Dunkirk episode, and *Max Horton and the Western Approaches* (1954), and, on the development of British amphibious warfare, Brigadier Bernard Fergusson's *The Watery Maze* (1961) is valuable.

On the ground, the larger implications are discussed in William McNeill's *America, Britain and Russia: Their Cooperation and Conflict, 1941-1946* (1953) and Herbert Feis's *Churchill-Roosevelt-Stalin: The War They Waged and the Peace They Sought* (1957). Operational differences between British and American commanders are brought out in Field Marshal Montgomery's *Memoirs* (1958) and Maj. Gen. Hubert Essame's *The Battle for Germany* (1969). More balanced are the official history, *Victory in the West* (1962-68) by Ellis, and Reginald W. Thompson's recent *Montgomery, the Field Marshal* (1969).

The role of the Mediterranean theater is difficult to analyze. Trumbull Higgins explores the matter in *Soft Underbelly: The Anglo-American Controversy over the Italian Campaign, 1939-1945* (1968), but the best book is Michael Howard's *The Mediterranean Strategy in the Second World War* (1968). British interest "east of Suez" was hard to shake off. The Balkans and Crete are taken up in Walter Ansel's *Hitler and the Middle Sea* (1972), and the Mediterranean war is covered broadly but apologetically by Marc Antonio Bragadin's *The Italian Navy in World War II* (1957) and by Admiral Paul Auphan and Jacques Mordal's extremely biased *The French Navy in World War II* (1959). None of the avant-garde dictatorships had aircraft carriers or adequate radar. Britain's master stroke—a naval air attack against an anchored Italian fleet—is described in Don

Newton and A. Cecil Hampshire's *Taranto* (1959) and the local British sea lords in Admiral Andrew B. Cunningham's *A Sailor's Odyssey* (1951), Admiral Philip Vian's *Action This Day* (1960), and Macintyre's *Fighting Admiral: The Life of Admiral of the Fleet Sir James Somerville* (1961). The antagonists in North Africa are dealt with in Robert John Collins's *Lord Wavell* (1947), John Robertson's *Auchinleck* (1959), Alan Moorehead's *Montgomery* (1946) and Ronald Lewin's *Rommel as Military Commander* (1968), the last complementing *The Rommel Papers* (1953), edited by Liddell Hart, and all evaluated in Barnett's *The Desert Generals* (1960). See also J. A. I. Agar-Hamilton and L. C. F. Turner's *Crisis in the Desert, May–July 1942* (1952), and Dereck Jewell's (ed.) experimental *Alamein and the Desert War* (1968). On the mainland, the painfully slow advance up the Italian peninsula is plotted in General W. G. F. Jackson's *The Battle for Italy* (1967) supplemented by Field Marshal Albert Kesselring's *A Soldier's Record* (1954) and General Frido von Senger und Etterlin's *Neither Fear Nor Hope* (1964).

Allan Bullock's *Hitler: A Study in Tyranny* (1952) is a good introduction to the Nazi leadership, and operational decisions are taken up in Liddell Hart's *The Other Side of the Hill* (1951). Heinz Guderian's *Panzer Leader* (1952), Friedrich von Mellenthin's *Panzer Battles, 1939–1945* (1955), and Erich von Manstein's *Lost Victories* (1958) represent the younger and more energetic generals and marshals. Another new element, Germany's tactical air force, lacked a strategic capability. Good accounts are Richard Suchenwirth's *Historical Turning Points in the German Air Force War Effort* (1959) and Adolf Galland's eyewitness *The First and the Last: The Rise and Fall of the German Fighter Forces* (1954). The real fall came when Germany failed to replace her first generation of pilots and aircraft.

The neglected Navy is discussed in Admiral Friedrich Ruge's fine *Der Seekrieg* (1957, in English), and the best work on Germany's cross-channel invasion plans is Ansel's *Hitler Confronts England* (1960). In *Struggle for the Sea* (1959), German naval chief Erich Raeder describes his mistaken efforts to create a new battle fleet, while his successor, "U-boat" Admiral Karl Doenitz, related his trials in *Memoirs: 10 Years and 20 Days* (1959). German submarine production peaked in the winter of 1944/45, but by then Germany had lost the technological race.

Expecting a short war, the Nazi leaders had not begun to mobilize their economic resources until the end of 1943. The problem is discussed in Alan S. Milward's *The German*

Economy at War (1965); the turnabout is documented in Albert Speer's *Inside the Third Reich* (1970); and books like Rudolf Lusar's *German Secret Weapons of the Second World War* (1959) show how slim the margin of victory may have been. Other elements of the Hitlerian formula are discussed in Louis de Jong's *The German Fifth Column in the Second World War* (1956), Gerard Reitlinger's *The SS* (1956), and George H. Stein's *The Waffen SS* (1966).

On the Eastern Front, the survival of Russian military professionalism was a question mark. For the early period see John Erickson's *The Soviet High Command* (1962), D. Fedotoff White's *The Growth of the Red Army* (1944), Z. K. Brzezinski's (ed.) *Political Controls in the Soviet Army* (1954), and Robert Conquest's *The Great Terror: Stalin's Purge of the Thirties* (1968). Germany's excursion into Russia is treated in Allan Clark's *Barbarossa* (1965), and the retreat in Earl F. Ziemke's excellent *Stalingrad to Berlin* (1968). The last is part of a three-volume series on the Eastern Front to be published by the U.S. Army Center of Military History, which has also sponsored about a dozen specialized studies on the same campaign. Alexander Werth has written the best popular history, *Russia at War* (1964), and Seweryn Bialer's (ed.) *Stalin and his Generals: Soviet Military Memoirs of World War II* (1969) covers some of the internal bickering. Leon Goure's *The Siege of Leningrad* (1962) is a Rand research project that complements Harrison Salisbury's excellent *The 900 Days* (1969). To the south, Ronald Seth's informal *Stalingrad, Point of Return* (1959) treats the operational turning point marked by the loss of the entire German Sixth Army, while, behind the lines, Alexander Dallin's *German Rule in Russia* (1957) presents a broad coverage of Nazi Germany's insane occupational policies.

The underground opposition to Hitler's New Order is treated in M. R. D. Foot's *Resistance* (1977), while Charles Delzell's *Mussolini's Enemies* (1961) and Peter Hoffmann's *The History of the German Resistance, 1933-1945* (1977) cover the internal dissenters. Also falling into the "unconventional" category are Paul Leverkuehn's *German Military Intelligence* (1954) and Robert M. Kennedy's *German Antiguerrilla Operations in the Balkans* (1954). For frustrated cryptologists, F. W. Winterbotham's *The Ultra Secret* (1974) and Anthony Cave Brown's *Bodyguard of Lies* (1975) tell how the German codes were cracked and have stirred up a lively historical controversy about both the reliability of their stories and the relative importance of this intelligence success in winning the war. Taking a broader

view, former Central Intelligence Agency Executive Director
Lyman Kirkpatrick's *Captains Without Eyes: Intelligence
Failures in World War II* (1969) includes discussions of
Barbarossa (the Russians), Pearl Harbor (the Americans),
Dieppe, Market Garden and the Bulge.

Asia and the West, 1800-1945

Western expansion into Africa, Asia, and South America
introduced ferment and instability into what had been areas of
high social, economic, and political continuity. Basic descriptions of the Far Eastern experience are O. Edmund Clubb's
Twentieth Century China (1964), Edwin O. Reischauer's *The
United States and Japan* (1950), and John K. Fairbanks's *The
United States and China* (1958). In the nineteenth century,
military forces opened China to economic invasion, but the
Middle Kingdom was too large for Europe to swallow. Led by the
crafty dowager Tz'u Hsi, the ruling dynasty managed to stave off
a final collapse until 1911. Peter Ward Fay's *The Opium War,
1840-1842* (1975) introduces the period, Chester C. Tan's *The
Boxer Catastrophe* (1955) tells the story of the regime's last
stand, and Ralph L. Powell's *The Rise of Chinese Military Power,
1895-1912* (1955) covers the final years. Once national cohesion
disintegrated, power fell to local generals like Yüan Shih-k'ai,
and, despite his tremendous prestige, Sun Yat-sen had little
authority even within his own party. The warlord period is
discussed in James E. Sheridan's *Chinese Warlord* (1966) and
Donald Gillan's *Warlord: Yen Hsi-shan in Shansi Province,
1911-1949* (1967) (most were reformers as well as generals).
Sun's successor, Chiang Kai-shek, was also a general and
received the nominal allegiance of most of China by the end of
1928. The small Chinese Communist party was mismanaged by
Moscow, which had little use for agrarian reformers, and Mao
Tse-tung, Chu Teh, Lin Piao, and others made their 6,000-mile
Long March in 1934 to escape pursuing Nationalist armies. But
once Japan occupied Chiang's coastal power base, the Kuomintang deteriorated and Mao began his guerrilla war behind both
Japanese and Nationalist lines.

Key works on the 1920s are Conrad Brandt's *Stalin's Failure in
China* (1958), Harold Isaac's classic *The Tragedy of the Chinese
Revolution* (1938), and Benjamin I. Schwartz's *Chinese Commu-
nism and the Rise of Mao* (1951). For a feel of the revolution, read
Pearl Buck's *The Good Earth* (1931), then Edgar Snow's key *Red
Star Over China* (1937), and Mao's nonpolitical *Basic Tactics*

(1938). His *Selected Works* (four volumes, 1961-65) include *Strategic Problems of the Anti-Japanese Guerrilla War* and *On the Protracted War*, both written in 1938. The 1945-50 period is reported by Derk Bodde in *Peking Diary* (1950), A. Doak Barnett in *China on the Eve of Communist Takeover* (1963), and Jack Belden in his eyewitness *China Shakes the World* (1949). For the struggle against Japan, F. F. Liu's comprehensive *A Military History of Modern China, 1924-1949* (1956), Graham Peck's lively *Two Kinds of Time* (1967), Harold Scott Quigley's *Far Eastern War, 1937-1941* (1942), and Belden's *The New Fourth Army* (1938) are the best accounts of a gigantic but generally undocumented struggle.

The Japanese experience was different. In 1868 Japan's leading families established a "Western" government and made the emperor the symbolic head of the new nation. Under clan leadership, the feudal Samurai system was replaced by a modern national army, the country was industrialized from above, and the small but sturdy middle class expanded. During the next forty years the islanders took Formosa, occupied Korea, and decisively defeated one of the great European powers. The Russo-Japanese war is reported in Frederick Palmer's firsthand *With Kuroki in Manchuria* (1904) and the American *Reports of Military Observers Attached to the Armies in Manchuria during the Russo-Japanese War* (five volumes, 1906-7), but there is no good general history.

World War I made Japan the dominant power in the Far East, and Tokyo's policy makers continued to expand Japanese regional hegemony. Although conservative military leaders crushed the ultranationalist young officers' movement in 1936, they continued to exploit Chinese weakness. Manchuria had been occupied in 1931, and China was openly invaded six years later. By 1941 the Japanese had seized most of China's urban areas, including her coastal ports, shut up the remnants of Chiang's army in central China, and organized several local puppet governments. But China was too big. The Nationalists survived in Chungking, Mao expanded his control in the countryside, and all awaited the outcome of the war in the Pacific. Francis C. Jones's *Japan's New Order in East Asia* (1954) points out the absence of any master blueprint for conquest, and the army's domination of national policy is highlighted in Robert Butow's *Tojo and the Coming of the War* (1961). The earlier period is treated in Takehiko Yoshihashi's *Conspiracy at Mukden* (1963) and the young officers by Hugh Byas's journalistic *Government by Assassination* (1942), but there are hardly any English treatments of Japanese military operations on the mainland.

Japan's Pacific offensive was tactically brilliant, operationally superb, but strategically disastrous. Good introductions are Emmanuel Andrieu-D'Albas's *Death of a Navy* (1957), Masonari Ito's *The End of the Imperial Navy* (1962), and Saburo Hayashi's *Kogun: The Japanese Army in the Pacific War* (1959). In *Singapore: The Japanese Version* (1960), Masanobu Tsuju, former Military Operations Director for the 25th Army, tells how it was done. *Midway, the Battle That Doomed Japan* (by Mitsuo Fuchida and Masataka Okumiya, 1955) occurred only six months after Pearl Harbor; Japan's best aircraft (see *Zero* by Okumiya and designer Jiro Horikoshi, 1956) remained competitive throughout the war, but her skilled aviators were slowly replaced by the suicidal pilots described in Rikihei Inoguchi and Tadashi Nakajima's *The Divine Wind* (1958). The kamikaze effort highlighted the continued singularity of what should have been the most "Westernized" culture in Asia and represented the high-watermark of the total war concept. *Japan's Economy in War and Reconstruction* (1949), by Jerome B. Cohen, is the chief work on that subject, and all the above are supplemented by the fine volumes in the American, British, Indian, New Zealand, and Australian official histories and the host of associated memoirs and special studies. Of these, Sir William Slim's *Defeat Into Victory* (1956), treating the Burma campaign, is perhaps the best memoir by a general officer and is an excellent introduction to the field.

The war's end left both nationalism and democracy exhausted across the globe, and only technology, the third member of the trio, seemed to have emerged stronger. Whether a new balance could ever be created between the three, or whether rampant technology would tilt the world into some terrible historical chasm, remained to be seen. The explosion of two great atomic bombs in crowded urban centers did not augur well for the future. Total war had now twice almost destroyed Europe and, in the process, had reduced Western pugnacity to a shadow of its former self. Although the prognosis was bad, it was not hopeless. Yet the heady confidence that had propelled the West through the eighteenth and nineteenth centuries was not likely to repeat itself again.

Bibliography

Agar-Hamilton, John A. I., and Turner, Leonard C. F. *Crisis in the Desert, May-July 1942*. Capetown: Oxford Univ. Press, 1952.

Albrecht-Carrié, René. *The Meaning of the First World War*. Englewood Cliffs, N.J.: Prentice-Hall, 1965.

Anderson, Eugene N. *The Social and Political Conflict in Prussia, 1858-1884*. Lincoln: Univ. of Neb. Press, 1954.

Andrieu-d'Albas, Emmanuel. *Death of a Navy: Japanese Naval Action in World War II*. Translated by Anthony Rippon. New York: Devin-Adair, 1957.

Ansel, Walter. *Hitler and the Middle Sea*. Durham, N.C.: Duke Univ. Press, 1972.

———. *Hitler Confronts England*. Durham, N.C.: Duke Univ. Press, 1960.

Aspinall-Oglander, Cecil Faber. *History of the Great War: Military Operations, Gallipoli*. 2 vols. London: Heinemann, 1929-32.

Auphan, [Gabriel A. J.] Paul, and Mordal, Jacques. *The French Navy in World War II*. Translated by A. J. C. Sabalot, Annapolis, Md.: U.S. Naval Institute, 1959.

Bankwitz Philip. *Maxime Weygand and Civil-Military Relations in Modern France*. Cambridge, Mass.: Harvard Univ. Press, 1967.

Barnes, Harry Elmer. *The Genesis of the World War: An Introduction to the Problem of War Guilt*. New York: A. A. Knopf, 1926.

Barnett, A. Doak. *China on the Eve of Communist Takeover*. New York: Praeger, 1963.

Barnett, Correlli. *The Swordbearers: Studies in Supreme Command in the First World War*. London: Eyre and Spottiswoode, 1963.

———. *The Desert Generals*. London: Kimber, 1960.

Bean, Charles E. W. *Anzac to Amiens: A Shorter History of the Australian Fighting Services in the First World War*. Canberra: Australian War Memorial, 1946.

Belden, Jack, *China Shakes the World*. New York: Harper, 1949.

———. *The New Fourth Army*. Shanghai: Post-Mercury, 1938. Reprinted from a series of articles in the *Shanghai Evening Post and Mercury*.

Beveridge, William Henry. *British Food Control*. New Haven: Yale Univ. Press, 1928.

Bialer, Seweryn, ed. *Stalin and His Generals: Soviet Military Memoirs of World War II*. New York: Pegasus, 1969.

Bloch, Marc L. B. *Strange Defeat: A Statement of Evidence Written in 1940*. Translated by Gerard Hopkins. New York: Oxford Univ. Press, 1949.

Bodde, Derk. *Peking Diary: A Year of Revolution*. New York: Schuman, 1950.

Bond, Brian, ed. *Victorian Military Campaigns*. New York: Praeger, 1967.

Bragadin, Marc' Antonio. *The Italian Navy in World War II*. Translated by Gale Hoffman. Annapolis, Md.: U.S. Naval Institute, 1957.

Brandt, Conrad. *Stalin's Failure in China, 1924-27*. Cambridge, Mass.: Harvard Univ. Press, 1958.

Brenan, Gerald. *The Spanish Labyrinth: An Account of the Social and Political Background of the Civil War*. London: Cambridge Univ. Press, 1943.

Brinton, Crane. *A Decade of Revolution, 1789-1799*. New York: Harper, 1934.

Brodie, Bernard. *A Guide to Naval Strategy*. Princeton, N.J.: Princeton Univ. Press, 1944. First published as *A Layman's Guide to Naval Strategy* in 1942.

———. *Sea Power in the Machine Age*. Princeton, N.J.: Princeton Univ. Press, 1941.

———. *Strategy in the Missile Age*. Princeton, N.J.: Princeton Univ. Press, 1959.

Brown, Anthony Cave. *Bodyguard of Lies*. New York: Harper and Row, 1975.

Brusilov, Alexei A. *A Soldier's Notebook, 1914-1918*. London: Macmillan, 1930.

Bryant, Arthur. *A History of the War Years Based on the Diaries of Field-Marshal Lord Alanbrooke, Chief of the Imperial General Staff.* 2 vols. Garden City, N.Y.: Doubleday, 1957-59. (1) *The Turn of the Tide, 1939-1943*; (2) *Triumph in the West, 1943-1946.*

Brzezinski, Zbigniew K., ed. *Political Controls in the Soviet Army: A Study Based on Reports by Former Soviet Officers.* New York: Research Program on the USSR, 1954.

Buck, Pearl. *The Good Earth.* New York: John Day, 1931.

Bullock, Alan L. C. *Hitler, A Study in Tyranny.* Rev. ed. New York: Harper and Row, 1962.

Butow, Robert J. C. *Tojo and the Coming of the War.* Princeton, N.J.: Princeton Univ. Press, 1961.

Byas, Hugh. *Government by Assassination.* New York: A. A. Knopf, 1942.

Callwell, Charles E., ed. *Field-Marshal Sir Henry Wilson, bart., G.C.B., D.S.O.: His Life and Diaries.* 2 vols. New York: Scribner's, 1927.

Carnegie Endowment for International Peace, Division of Economics and History. *Economic and Social History of the World War.* Edited by James T. Shotwell. Multivolume. New Haven, Yale Univ. Press, 1921-40.

Carrington, Charles Edmund [Charles Edmonds]. *A Subaltern's War: Being Memoirs of the Great War, etc.* London: Davies, 1929.

Carsten, Francis Ludwig. *The Reichswehr and Politics, 1918-1933.* London: Oxford Univ. Press, 1966.

Challener, Richard D. *The French Theory of the Nation in Arms 1866-1939.* New York: Columbia Univ. Press, 1955.

Chalmers, William Scott. *Full Cycle: The Biography of Admiral Sir Bertram Home Ramsey.* London: Hodder and Stoughton, 1959.

——. *The Life and Letters of David, Earl Betty, Admiral of the Fleet, etc.* London: Hodder and Stoughton, 1951.

——. *Max Horton and the Western Approaches: A Biography of Admiral Sir Max Kennedy Horton.* London: Hodder and Stoughton, 1954.

Chamberlin, William Henry. *The Russian Revolution, 1917-1921.* 2 vols. New York: Macmillan, 1935.

Chambers, Frank Pentland. *The War Behind the War, 1914-1918: A History of the Political and Civilian Fronts.* New York: Harcourt, Brace, 1939.

Chandler, David G. *The Campaigns of Napoleon.* New York: Macmillan, 1966.

Chapman, Guy. *The Dreyfus Case: A Reassessment.* New York: Reynal, 1955.

Chapman, Guy, ed. *Vain Glory: A Miscellany of the Great War, 1914-1918: Written by Those Who Fought in It on Each Side and on All Fronts.* London: Cassell, 1937.

Chorley, Katherine. *Armies and the Art of Revolution.* London: Faber and Faber, 1943.

Churchill, Winston Leonard Spencer. *The Second World War.* 6 vols. Boston: Houghton Mifflin, 1948-53. (1) *The Gathering Storm* (1948), (2) *Their Finest Hour* (1949), (3) *The Grand Alliance* (1950), (4) *The Hinge of Fate* (1950), (5) *Closing the Ring* (1951), (6) *Triumph and Tragedy* (1953).

Clark, Alan. *Barbarossa: The Russian-German Conflict, 1941-1945.* New York: William Morrow, 1965.

——. *The Donkeys.* London: Hutchinson, 1961.

Clubb, O. Edmund. *Twentieth Century China.* New York: Columbia Univ. Press, 1964.

Cohen, Jerome B. *Japan's Economy in War and Reconstruction.* Minneapolis: Univ. of Minn. Press, 1949.

Collier, Basil. *Brasshat: A Biography of Field-Marshal Sir Henry Wilson.* London: Secker and Warburg, 1961.

——. *A Short History of the Second World War.* London: Collins, 1967.

Collins, Robert John. *Lord Wavell, 1883–1941: A Military Biography.* London: Hodder and Stoughton, 1947.

Connell, John. *See* Robertson, John Henry.

Conquest, Robert. *The Great Terror: Stalin's Purge of the Thirties.* Rev. ed. Harmondsworth: Penguin, 1971.

Craig, Gordon. *The Battle of Königgrätz: Prussia's Victory Over Austria, 1866.* Philadelphia: Lippincott, 1964.

——. *The Politics of the Prussian Army, 1640–1945.* Rev. ed. New York: Oxford Univ. Press, 1964.

——. *War, Politics, and Diplomacy: Selected Essays.* New York: Praeger, 1966.

Cunningham, Andrew B. *A Sailor's Odyssey: The Autobiography of Admiral of the Fleet, Viscount Cunningham of Hyndhope.* New York: Dutton, 1951.

Curtiss, John Shelton, *The Russian Army Under Nicholas I, 1825–1855.* Durham, N.C.: Duke Univ. Press, 1965.

Dallin, Alexander. *German Rule in Russia, 1941–1945: A Study of Occupation Policies.* New York: St. Martin's Press, 1957.

Davidson, John Humphrey. *Haig, Master of the Field.* London: Nevill, 1953.

de Gaulle, Charles. *The Edge of the Sword.* Translated by Gerard Hopkins. New York: Criterion, 1960. French edition 1932.

——. *War Memoirs.* 5 vols. New York: Simon and Schuster, 1955–60. (1) *The Call to Honor, 1940–1942,* translated by J. Griffin (1955); (2) *Unity, 1942–1944,* translated by R. Howard (1959); (3) *Salvation, 1944–46,* translated by R. Howard (1960); (4) *Unity, 1942–1944* (documents), translated by J. Murchie and H. Erskine (1959); (5) *Salvation, 1944–1946* (documents), translated by J. Murchie and H. Erskine (1960).

Delzell, Charles F. *Mussolini's Enemies: The Italian Anti-Fascist Resistance.* Princeton, N.J.: Princeton Univ. Press, 1961.

Derry, Thomas Kingston. *The Campaign in Norway.* London: H.M. Stationery Office, 1952.

Deutscher, Isaac. *The Prophet Armed: Trotsky, 1879–1921.* New York: Oxford Univ. Press. 1954.

——. *The Prophet Unarmed: Trotsky, 1921–1929.* New York: Oxford Univ. Press, 1959.

——. *The Prophet Outcast: Trotsky, 1929–1940.* New York: Oxford Univ. Press, 1963.

——. *Stalin: A Political Biography.* New York: Oxford Univ. Press, 1949.

Doenitz, Karl. *Memoirs: 10 Years and 20 Days.* Translated by R.H. Stevens. Cleveland: World Publishing Company, 1959.

Douhet, Giulio. *The Command of the Air.* Translated by Dino Ferrari. London: Faber and Faber, 1943. First Italian edition 1921.

Douie, Charles. *The Weary Road: Recollections of a Subaltern of Infantry.* London: Murray, 1929.

Dunlop, John K. *The Development of the British Army, 1899–1914: From the Eve of the South African War to the Eve of the Great War, With Special Reference to the Territorial Force.* London: Methuen, 1938.

Dupre, Huntley. *Lazare Carnot: Republican Patriot.* Oxford, Ohio: Mississippi Valley Press, 1940.

Earle, Edward Mead, ed. *Makers of Modern Strategy: Military Thought from Machiavelli to Hitler.* Princeton, N.J.: Princeton Univ. Press, 1943.

Edmonds, Charles. *See* Carrington, Charles Edmund.

Ellis, Lionel F. *Victory in the West.* 2 vols. London: H.M. Stationery Office, 1962–68. (1) *The Battle for Normandy,* (2) *The Defeat of Germany.*

——. *The War in France and Flanders, 1939–1940.* London: H.M. Stationery Office, 1953.

Emme, Eugene M., ed. *The Impact of Air Power: National Security and World Politics.* Princeton, N.J.: Van Nostrand, 1959.

Erickson, John. *The Soviet High Command: A Military-Political History.* New York: St. Martin's Press, 1962.

Essame, Hubert. *The Battle for Germany.* New York: Scribner's, 1969.

Fairbanks, John K. *The United States and China.* Rev. ed. Cambridge, Mass.: Harvard Univ. Press, 1958.

Falkenhayn, Erich G. von, *The German General Staff and Its Decisions, 1914–1916.* New York: Dodd, Mead, 1920.

Falls, Cyril B. *The Great War.* New York: Putnam's, 1959.

Fay, Peter Ward. *The Opium War, 1840–1842.* Chapel Hill: Univ. of N.C. Press, 1975.

Fay, Sidney Bradshaw. *The Origins of the World War.* 2 vols. New York: Macmillan, 1928.

Fedotoff-White, Dimitri. *The Growth of the Red Army.* Princeton, N.J.: Princeton Univ. Press, 1944.

Feis, Herbert. *Churchill-Roosevelt-Stalin: The War They Waged and the Peace They Sought.* Princeton, N.J.: Princeton Univ. Press, 1957.

Fergusson, Bernard. *The Watery Maze: The Story of Combined Operations.* New York: Holt, Rinehart and Winston, 1961.

Finer, Samuel Edward. *The Man on Horseback: The Role of the Military in Politics.* New York: Praeger, 1962.

Fischer, Fritz. *Germany's Aims in the First World War.* (New York: W.W. Norton, 1967.

——. *War of Illusions: German Policies from 1911 to 1914.* Translated by Marion Jackson. New York: W.W. Norton, 1975.

Foot, M. R. D. *Resistance: European Resistance to Nazism, 1940–1945.* New York: McGraw-Hill, 1977.

Fredette, Raymond H. *The Sky on Fire: The First Battle of Britain, 1917–1918, and the Birth of the Royal Air Force.* New York: Holt, Rinehart and Winston, 1966.

Fuchida, Mitsuo, and Okumiya, Masatake. *Midway, the Battle That Doomed Japan: The Japanese Navy's Story.* Edited by Clark H. Kawakami and Roger Pineau. Annapolis, Md.: U.S. Naval Institute, 1955.

Fuller, J. F. C. *The Conduct of War, 1789–1961: A Study of the Impact of the French, Industrial, and Russian Revolutions on War and Its Conduct.* New Brunswick, N.J.: Rutgers Univ. Press, 1961.

——. *The Second World War, 1939–1945: A Strategical and Tactical History.* London: Eyre and Spottiswoode, 1948.

Galland, Adolf. *The First and the Last: The Rise and Fall of the German Fighter Forces, 1938–1945.* Translated by Mervyn Savill. New York: Holt, 1954.

Gann, Lewis H. *Guerrillas in History.* Stanford, Calif.: Hoover Inst. Press, 1971.

Geyl, Pieter. *Napoleon: For and Against.* Translated by Olive Renier. New Haven: Yale Univ. Press, 1949.

Gibson, Richard Henry, and Pendergast, Maurice. *The German Submarine War, 1914–1918.* New York: R.R. Smith, 1931.

Gillan, Donald. *Warlord: Yen Hsi-shan in Shansi Province, 1911–1949.* Princeton, N.J.: Princeton Univ. Press, 1967.

Goodspeed, Donald James. *Ludendorff: Genius of World War I*. Boston: Houghton Mifflin, 1966.

Gottschalk, Louis. *The Era of the French Revolution (1715–1815)*. Boston: Houghton Mifflin, 1929.

Gough, Hubert. *The Fifth Army*. London: Hodder and Stoughton, 1931.

———. *Soldiering On*. London: Barber, 1954.

Gouré, Leon. *The Siege of Leningrad*. Stanford, Calif.: Stanford Univ. Press, 1962.

Goutard, Adolphe. *The Battle of France, 1940*. Translated by A. R. P. Burgess. New York: Ives Washburn, 1959.

Guderian, Heinz. *Panzer Leader*. Translated by Constantine Fitzgibbon. New York: Dutton, 1952.

Guinn, Paul. *British Strategy and Politics, 1914 to 1918*. New York: Oxford Univ. Press, 1965.

Hamilton, Ian S. M. *Gallipoli Diary*. 2 vols. London: Arnold, 1920.

Hamley, Edward. *The War in the Crimea*. New York: Scribner and Welford, 1890.

Hankey, Maurice P. *Diplomacy by Conference: Studies in Public Affairs, 1920–1946*. London: Benn, 1946.

———. *The Supreme Command 1914–1918*. 2 vols. London: Allen and Unwin, 1961.

Harcave, Sidney. *First Blood: The Russian Revolution of 1905*. New York: Macmillan, 1964.

Hayashi, Saburo (with Alvin Coox). *Kogun: The Japanese Army in the Pacific War*. Quantico, Va.: Marine Corps Association, 1959.

Hayes, Carlton J. H. *A Generation of Materialism, 1871–1900*. New York: Harper, 1941.

Hemingway, Ernest. *For Whom the Bell Tolls*. New York: Scribner's, 1940.

Higgins, Trumbull. *Soft Underbelly: The Anglo-American Controversy Over the Italian Campaign, 1939–1945*. New York: Macmillan, 1968.

Hoffman, Max. *War Diaries and Other Papers*. Translated by Eric Sutton. 2 vols. London: Secker, 1929.

Hoffmann, Peter. *The History of the German Resistance, 1933–1945*. Translated by Richard Barry. Cambridge, Mass.: MIT Press, 1977.

Holley, Irving Brinton, Jr. *Ideas and Weapons: Exploitation of the Aerial Weapon by the United States During World War I: A Study in the Relationship of Technological Advance, Military Doctrine, and the Development of Weapons*. New Haven: Yale Univ. Press, 1953.

Horn, Daniel. *The German Naval Mutinies of World War I*. New Brunswick, N.J.: Rutgers Univ. Press, 1969.

Horne, Alistair. *The Price of Glory: Verdun, 1916*. New York: St. Martin's Press, 1962.

Howard, Michael Eliot. *The Franco-Prussian War: The German Invasion of France*. New York: Macmillan, 1961.

———. *The Mediterranean Strategy in the Second World War*. New York: Praeger, 1968.

———. *Studies in War and Peace*. London: Temple, Smith, 1970.

Huang Chen-hsia and Whitson, William. *The Chinese High Command: A History of Communist Military Politics, 1927–71*. New York: Praeger, 1973.

Huntington, Samuel Phillips. *The Soldier and the State: The Theory and Politics of Civil-Military Relations*. Cambridge, Mass.: Harvard Univ. Press, 1957.

Inoguchi, Rikihei, and Nakajima, Tadashi (with Roger Pineau). *The Divine Wind: Japan's Kamikaze Force in World War II.* Annapolis, Md., U.S. Naval Institute, 1958.

Ironside, Edmund. *Tannenberg: The First Thirty Days in East Prussia.* London: Blackwood, 1925.

Isaacs, Harold R. *The Tragedy of the Chinese Revolution.* Stanford, Calif.: Stanford Univ. Press, 1951.

Ito, Masonari (with Roger Pineau). *The End of the Imperial Japanese Navy.* New York: W. W. Norton, 1962.

Jackson, Gabriel. *The Spanish Republic and the Civil War, 1931-1939.* Princeton, N.J.: Princeton Univ. Press, 1965.

Jackson, William G. F. *Attack in the West: Napoleon's First Campaign Re-Read Today.* London: Eyre and Spottiswoode, 1953.

———. *The Battle for Italy.* New York: Harper and Row, 1967.

Jaurès, Jean Léon. *L'Armée nouvelle: l'organisation socialiste de la France.* Paris: Rouff, 1911. Abridged English translation is *Democracy and Military Service.* Edited by G. G. Coulton. London: Simpkin, Marshall, Hamilton and Kent, 1916.

Jewell, Dereck, ed. *Alamein and the Desert War.* New York: Ballantine Books, 1968.

Joffre, Joseph. *The Personal Memoirs of Joffre, Field Marshal of the French Army.* Translated by T. Bentley Mott. 2 vols. New York: Harper, 1932.

Jones, Francis Clifford. *Japan's New Order in East Asia: Its Rise and Fall, 1937-1945.* New York: Oxford Univ. Press, 1954.

Jong, Louis de. *The German Fifth Column in the Second World War.* Translated by C. M. Geyle. Chicago: Univ. of Chicago Press, 1956.

Joubert de la Ferte, Philip B. *The Third Service: The Story Behind the Royal Air Force.* London: Thames, Hudson, 1955.

Kahn, David. *The Codebreakers: The Story of Secret Writing.* New York: Macmillan, 1967.

Kennedy, Robert M. *German Antiguerrilla Operations in the Balkans, 1941-1944.* DA Pamphlet. Washington: Government Printing Office, 1954.

Kesselring, Albert. *Kesselring: A Soldier's Record.* Translated by Lynton Hudson. New York: William Morrow, 1954.

King, Jere Clemens. *Generals and Politicians: Conflict Between France's High Command, Parliament and Government, 1914-1918.* Berkeley: Univ. of Calif. Press, 1951.

Kinsbrunner, Jay. *Bernardo O'Higgins.* New York: Twayne, 1968.

Kirkpatrick, Lyman B. *Captains Without Eyes: Intelligence Failures in World War II.* New York: Macmillan, 1969.

Kissinger, Henry A. *A World Restored: Metternich, Castlereagh and the Problems of Peace, 1812-22.* Boston: Houghton Mifflin, 1957.

Knox, Alfred W. *With the Russian Army, 1914-1917: Being Chiefly Extracts from the Diary of a Military Attache.* 2 vols. New York: Dutton, 1921.

Kranzberg, Melvin. *The Siege of Paris, 1870-1871: A Political and Social History.* Ithaca, N.Y.: Cornell Univ. Press, 1950.

Kruger, Rayne. *Good-Bye Dolly Gray: The Story of the Boer War.* Philadelphia: Lippincott, 1960.

Lafore, Laurence D. *The End of Glory: An Interpretation of the Origins of World War II.* 2d ed. Philadelphia: Lippincott, 1970.

———. *The Long Fuse: An Interpretation of the Origins of World War I.* Philadelphia: Lippincott, 1965.

La Gorce, Paul-Marie de. *The French Army: A Military-Political History.* New York: Braziller, 1963.

Langer, William L. *The Diplomacy of Imperialism, 1890-1902.* 2 vols. New York: A. A. Knopf, 1935.

Lasswell, Harold Dwight. *Propaganda Technique in the World War.* New York: A. A. Knopf, 1927.

Laurence, T[homas]. E[dward]. *Seven Pillars of Wisdom: A Triumph.* London: Pike and Hodgson, 1926. Abridged version is *Revolt in the Desert.*

Lee, Dwight E., ed. *The Outbreak of the First World War: Who was Responsible?* Rev. ed. Boston: Heath, 1963.

Lenanton, Carola M. A. See Oman, Carola.

Leverkuehn, Paul. *German Military Intelligence.* Translated by R. H. Stevens and Constantine Fitzgibbon. New York: Praeger, 1954.

Lewin, Ronald. *Rommel as Military Commander.* Princeton, N.J.: Van Nostrand, 1968.

Lewis, Michael A. *A Social History of the Navy, 1793-1815.* London: Allen and Unwin, 1960.

Liddell Hart, B. H. *Foch: The Man of Orleans.* London: Eyre and Spottiswoode, 1931.

———. *The British Way in Warfare.* London: Faber and Faber, 1932.

———. *The Ghost of Napoleon.* London: Faber and Faber, 1933.

———. *Through the Fog of War.* New York: Random House, 1938.

———. *The Other Side of the Hill.* London: Cassell, 1951. Smaller edition, *The German Generals Talk,* published by William Morrow in 1948.

———. *The Tanks: The History of the Royal Tank Regiment and Its Predecessors, Heavy Branch Machine-Gun Corps, Tank Corps, and Royal Tank Corps, 1914-1945.* 2 vols. New York: Praeger, 1959.

———. *Memoirs.* 2 vols. New York: Putnam's, 1965-66.

———. *A History of the World War, 1914-1918.* Enlarged ed. Boston: Little, Brown, 1970. Revision of *The Real War.* Boston: Little, Brown, 1930.

Liman von Sanders, Otto V. *Five Years in Turkey.* Translated by Carl Reichmann. Annapolis, Md.: U.S. Naval Institute, 1927.

Liu, F. F. *A Military History of Modern China, 1924-1949.* Princeton, N.J.: Princeton Univ. Press, 1956.

Lloyd, Christopher. *The Navy and the Slave Trade.* New York: Longmans, Green, 1949.

Löhrke, Eugene W., ed. *Armageddon: The World War in Literature.* New York, Cape and Smith, 1930.

Longworth, Philip. *The Art of Victory: The Life and Achievements of Field Marshal Suvarov, 1729-1800.* London: Constable, 1965.

Lucas, Pascal Marie Henri. *The Evolution of Tactical Ideas in France and Germany During the War of 1914-1918.* Translated by P. V. Kieffer. Paris: Berger-Levrault, 1925 (?).

Lusar, Rudolf. *German Secret Weapons of the Second World War.* Translated by R. P. Heller and M. Schindler. New York: Philosophical Library, 1959.

Luvaas, Jay. *The Education of an Army: British Military Thought, 1815-1914.* Chicago: University of Chicago Press, 1964.

———. *The Military Legacy of the Civil War: The European Inheritance.* Chicago: Univ. of Chicago Press, 1959.

Macintyre, Donald G. F. W. *Fighting Admiral: The Life of Admiral of the Fleet Sir James Somerville, etc.* London: Evans, 1961.

———. *Jutland.* New York: W. W. Norton, 1958.

Mackesy, Piers. *The War in the Mediterranean, 1803-1810.* Cambridge, Mass.: Harvard Univ. Press, 1957.

McNeill, William H. *America, Britain, and Russia: Their Cooperation and Conflict, 1941-1946.* London: Oxford Univ. Press, 1953.

———. *The Rise of the West: A History of the Human Community*. Chicago: Univ. of Chicago Press, 1963.

Magnus, Philip M. *Kitchener: Portrait of an Imperialist*. London: Murray, 1958.

Malraux, André. *L'Espoir*. Paris: Gallimard, 1937. Translated as *Man's Hope* and *Days of Hope*.

Manstein, Erich von. *Lost Victories*. Edited and Translated by Anthony G. Powell. Chicago: Henry Regnery, 1958.

Mao Tse-tung. *Basic Tactics*. Translated by Stuart R. Schram. New York: Praeger, 1966. Chinese edition ca. 1938.

———. *Selected Works*. 4 vols. Peking: Foreign Languages Press, 1961-65. Chinese edition 1951-?.

Marder, Arthur J. *The Anatomy of British Sea Power: A History of British Naval Policy in the Pre-Dreadnought Era, 1880-1905*. New York: A. A. Knopf, 1940.

———. *From the Dreadnought to Scapa Flow: The Royal Navy in the Fisher Era, 1904-1919*. 5 vols. New York: Oxford Univ. Press, 1961-70.

Markham, Felix. *Napoleon*. London: Weidenfeld and Nicolson, 1963.

Martin, Laurence W. *The Sea in Modern Strategy*. New York: Praeger, 1967.

Marwick, Arthur. *The Deluge: British Society and the First World War*. London: Bodley Head, 1965.

Maurice, Frederick Barton. *Lessons of Allied Co-operation: Naval, Military and Air, 1914-1918*. New York: Oxford Univ. Press, 1942.

Mazour, Anatole G. *The First Russian Revolution, 1825: The Decembrist Movement, Its Origins, Development, and Significance*. Berkeley: Univ. of Calif. Press, 1937.

Mellenthin, Friedrich Wilhelm von. *Panzer Battles: A Study of the Employment of Armor in the Second World War, 1939-1945*. Edited by L. C. F. Turner. Translated by H. Betzler. London: Cassell, 1955.

Mendelssohn-Bartholdy, Albrecht. *The War and German Society: The Testament of a Liberal*. New Haven: Yale Univ. Press, 1937.

Milward, Alan S. *The German Economy at War*. London: Athlone Press, 1965.

Montgomery, Bernard Law. *The Memoirs of Field-Marshal the Viscount Montgomery of Alamein, K.G.* Cleveland: World Publishing Co., 1958.

Moore, Barrington, Jr. *Social Origins of Dictatorship and Democracy: Lord and Peasant in the Making of the Modern World*. Boston: Beacon Press, 1966.

Moorehead, Alan. *Montgomery: A Biography*. New York: Coward-McCann, 1946.

Morris, Donald R. *The Washing of the Spears: A History of the Rise of the Zulu Nation under Shaka and Its Fall in the Zulu War of 1879*. New York: Simon and Schuster, 1965.

Napier, William Francis Patrick. *History of the War in the Peninsula and in the South of France from A.D. 1807 to A.D. 1814*. 5 vols. New York: AMS Press, 1970. First edition, 6 vols. London: Boone, 1828-40; revised by author in 1856.

Nef, John Ulric. *War and Human Progress: An Essay on the Rise of Industrial Civilization*. Cambridge: Harvard Univ. Press, 1950.

Newton, Don, and Hampshire, A. Cecil. *Taranto*. London: Kimber, 1959.

Nicolson, Harold G. *The Congress of Vienna: A Study in Allied Unity*. London: Constable, 1946.

Nolte, Ernst. *Three Faces of Fascism*. Translated by Leila Vennewitz. New York: Holt, Rinehart and Winston, 1966.

Okumiya, Masatake, and Horikoshi, Jiro (with Martin Caidin). *Zero!* New York: Dutton, 1956.

Oman, Carola. *Nelson*. Garden City, N.Y.: Doubleday, 1946.

Oman, Charles William Chadwick. *Wellington's Army*. New York: Longmans, Green, 1912.

O'Neill, James E., and Krauskopf, Robert W., eds. *World War II: An Account of Its Documents*. Washington: Howard Univ. Press, 1976.

Orwell, George. *Homage to Catalonia*. London: Secker and Warburg, 1938.

Palmer, Frederick. *With Kuroki in Manchuria*. New York: Scribner's, 1904.

Palmer, Robert R. *Twelve Who Ruled: The Committee of Public Safety During the Terror*. Princeton, N.J.: Princeton Univ. Press, 1941.

Palmer, Robert R., and Colton, Joel. *A History of the Modern World*. 2d rev. ed. New York: A. A. Knopf, 1971.

Pares, Bernard. *The Fall of the Russian Monarchy: A Study of the Evidence*. New York: A. A. Knopf, 1939.

Paret, Peter. *Yorck and the Era of Prussian Reform, 1807-1815*. Princeton, N.J.: Princeton Univ. Press, 1966.

Parkinson, Roger. *The Fox of the North: The Life of Kutuzov, General of War and Peace*. New York: David McKay, 1976.

Parris, John. *The Lion of Caprera: A Biography of Giuseppe Garibaldi*. New York: David McKay, 1962.

Patterson, Alfred Temple. *Jellicoe: A Biography*. New York: St. Martin's Press, 1969.

Peck, Graham. *Two Kinds of Time*. Rev. ed. Boston: Houghton Mifflin, 1967.

Petrie, Charles Alexander. *Wellington: A Reassessment*. London: Barrie, 1956.

Phipps, Ramsay W. *The Armies of the First French Republic and the Rise of the Marshals of Napoleon I*. 5 vols. London: Oxford Univ. Press, 1926-39.

Pierrefeu, Jean de. *French Headquarters, 1915-1918*. Translated by C. J. C. Street. London: Bles, 1924.

Pope, Dudley. *Decision at Trafalgar*. Philadelphia: Lippincott, 1960.

Powell, Ralph L. *The Rise of Chinese Military Power, 1895-1912*. Princeton, N.J.: Princeton Univ. Press, 1955.

Pratt, Edwin A. *The Rise of Rail-Power in War and Conquest, 1833-1914*. London: King, 1915.

Quigley, Harold Scott. *Far Eastern War, 1937-1941*. Boston: World Peace Foundation, 1942.

Raeder, Erich. *Struggle for the Sea*. Translated by Edward Fitzgerald. London: Kimber, 1959.

Ralston, David B. *The Army of the Republic: The Place of the Military in the Political Evolution of France, 1871-1914*. Cambridge, Mass.: MIT Press, 1967.

Ralston, David B., ed. *Soldiers and States: Civil Military Relations in Modern Europe*. Boston: Heath, 1966.

Reischauer, Edwin O. *The United States and Japan*. Cambridge, Mass.: Harvard Univ. Press, 1950.

Reitlinger, Gerald. *The SS: Alibi of a Nation, 1922-1945*. London: Heinemann, 1956.

Reports of Military Observers Attached to the Armies in Manchuria During the Russo-Japanese War. 5 vols. Washington: Government Printing Office, 1906-7.

Richards, Denis, and Saunders, Hilary A. *Royal Air Firce, 1939-1945*. 3 vols. London: H.M. Stationery Office, 1953-54.

Ritter, Gerhard. *The Schlieffen Plan: Critique of a Myth*. Translated by Andrew and Eva Wilson. New York: Praeger, 1958. German edition 1956.

——. *The Sword and the Scepter: The Problem of Militarism in Germany*. Translated by Heinz Norden. 3 vols. Coral Gables, Fla.: Univ. of Miami Press, 1969-. German edition 1954-70.

Robertson, John Henry [John Connell]. *Auchinleck: A Biography of Field-Marshal Sir Claude Auchinleck.* London: Cassell, 1959.

Robertson, Priscilla [Smith]. *Revolutions of 1848: A Social Study.* Princeton, N.J.: Princeton Univ. Press 1952.

Robertson, William Robert. *Soldiers and Statesman, 1914-1918.* 2 vols. New York: Scribner's 1926.

Rommel, Erwin. *The Rommel Papers.* Edited by B. H. Liddell Hart. Translated by Paul Findlay. New York: Harcourt, Brace, 1953.

Ropp, Theodore. *War in the Modern World.* Rev. ed. New York: Collier, 1962.

Roskill, Stephen W. *The War at Sea, 1939-1945.* 3 vols. London: H.M. Stationery Office, 1954-61.

———. *White Ensign: The British Navy at War, 1939-1945.* Annapolis, Md.: U.S. Naval Institute, 1960.

Roth, Jack Joseph, ed. *World War I: A Turning Point in Modern History.* New York: A. A. Knopf, 1967.

Ruge, Friedrich. *Der Seekrieg: The German Navy's Story, 1939-1945.* Translated by M. G. Saunders. Annapolis, Md.: U.S. Naval Institute, 1957.

Salisbury, Harrison E. *The 900 Days: The Siege of Leningrad.* New York: Harper and Row, 1969.

Scheer, Reinhard. *Germany's High Seas Fleet in the World War.* New York: Cassell, 1920.

Schmitt, Bernadotte. *The Coming of the War, 1914.* 2 vols. New York: Scribner's, 1930.

Schwartz, Benjamin I. *Chinese Communism and the Rise of Mao.* Cambridge, Mass.: Harvard Univ. Press, 1951.

Seeckt, Hans von. *Thoughts of a Soldier.* Translated by Ian Hamilton. London: Benn, 1930.

Ségur, Phillipe Paul de. *Napoleon's Russian Campaign.* Translated by J. David Townsend. Boston: Houghton Mifflin, 1958. French edition 1825.

Senger und Etterlin, Fridolin von. *Neither Fear nor Hope: The Wartime Career of General Frido von Senger und Etterlin, Defender of Cassino.* Translated by George Malcolm. New York: Dutton, 1964 German edition 1960.

Seth, Ronald. *Stalingrad, Point of Return: The Story of the Battle, August 1942-February 1943.* New York: Coward-McCann, 1959.

Seton-Watson, Hugh. *The Russian Empire, 1801-1917.* New York: Oxford Univ. Press, 1967.

Shanahan, William O. *Prussian Military Reforms, 1786-1813.* New York: Columbia Univ. Press, 1945.

Sheridan, James E. *Chinese Warlord: The Career of Feng Yu-hsiang.* Stanford, Calif.: Stanford Univ. Press, 1966.

Slim, William Joseph. *Defeat Into Victory.* London: Cassell, 1956.

Snow, Edgar. *Red Star Over China.* London: Gollancz, 1937.

Sommer, Dudley, *Haldane of Cloan: His Life and Times, 1856-1928.* London: Allen and Unwin, 1960.

Spears, Edward L. *Assignment to Catastrophe.* 2 vols. New York: Wyn, 1954-55.

———. *Liaison, 1914: A Narration of the Great Retreat.* Rev. ed. New York: Stein and Day, 1968.

Speer, Albert. *Inside the Third Reich: Memoirs.* Translated by Richard and Clara Winston. New York: Macmillan, 1970.

Stein, George H. *The Waffen SS: Hitler's Elite Guard at War, 1939-1945.* Ithaca, N.Y.: Cornell Univ. Press, 1966.

Suchenwirth, Richard. *Historical Turning Points in the German Air Force War Effort.* Translated by Patricia Klamerth. Maxwell Air Force Base, Ala.: USAF Historical Division, 1959.

Tan, Chester C. *The Boxer Catastrophe.* New York: Columbia Univ. Press, 1955.

Tanenbaum, Jan Karl. *General Maurice Sarrail, 1856–1929: The French Army and Left-Wing Politics.* Chapel Hill: Univ. of N.C. Press, 1974.

Tantum, William H., and Hoffschmidt, E. J., eds. *The Rise and Fall of the German Air Force, 1933–1945.* Old Greenwich, Conn.: WE Press, 1969.

Taylor, A[lan]. J[ohn]. P[ercivale]. *The Origins of the Second World War.* London: Hamilton, 1961.

Terraine, John. *Mons: The Retreat to Victory.* New York: Macmillan, 1960.

Thomas, Hugh. *The Spanish Civil War.* New York: Harper, 1961.

Thompson, James Matthew. *Napoleon Bonaparte.* New York: Oxford Univ. Press, 1952.

Thompson, Reginald W. *Montgomery, the Field Marshal: A Critical Study of the Generalship of Field-Marshal the Viscount Montgomery of Alamein, K.G., and of the Campaign in North-West Europe 1944/45.* London: Allen and Unwin, 1969.

Tirpitz, Alfred von. *My Memoirs.* 2 vols. New York: Dodd, Mead, 1919.

Townsend, Peter. *Duel of Eagles.* New York: Simon and Schuster, 1970.

Trend, John Brande. *Bolivar and the Independence of Spanish America.* London: Hodder and Stoughton, 1946.

Tsuji, Masanobu. *Singapore: The Japanese Version.* Edited by A. V. Howe. Translated by Margaret E. Lake. Sydney: R. Smith, 1960.

Tuchman, Barbara. *The Guns of August.* New York: Macmillan, 1962.

Turner, Gordon B., ed. *A History of Military Affairs Since the Eighteenth Century.* Rev. ed. New York: Harcourt, Brace, 1956.

Tyng, Sewell T. *The Campaign of the Marne, 1914.* New York: Longmans, 1935.

Urquhart, Hugh M. *Arthur Currie: The Biography of a Great Canadian.* Toronto: Dent, 1950.

Vagts, Alfred. *Defense and Diplomacy: The Soldier and the Conduct of Foreign Relations.* New York: King's Crown Press, 1956.

———. *A History of Militarism: Romance and Realities of a Profession.* Rev. ed. New York: Meridian, 1959.

Verrier, Anthony. *The Bomber Offensive.* London: Batsford, 1968.

Vian, Philip. *Action this Day: A War Memoir.* London: Muller, 1960.

Waite, Robert G. L. *Vanguard of Nazism: The Free Corps Movement in Post War Germany, 1918–1923.* Cambridge, Mass.: Harvard Univ. Press, 1952.

Waitt, Alden H. *Gas Warfare.* New York: Duell, Sloan, and Pearce, 1942.

Warner, Oliver. *The Battle of the Nile.* New York: Macmillan, 1960.

Wavell, Archibald Percival. *Allenby: A Study in Greatness: The Biography of Field-Marshal Viscount Allenby of Megiddo and Felixstowe, G.C.B., G.C.M.G.* 2 vols. London: Harrap, 1940–43.

———. *The Palestine Campaigns.* London: Constable, 1928.

Webster, Charles Kingsley, and Frankland, Noble. *The Strategic Air Offensive Against Germany, 1939–1945.* 4 vols. London: H.M. Stationery Office, 1961.

Werth, Alexander. *Russia at War, 1941–1945.* New York: Dutton, 1964.

Wheeler-Bennett, John W. *The Nemesis of Power: The German Army in Politics, 1918–1945.* New York: Macmillan, 1953.

———. *Wooden Titan: Hindenburg in Twenty Years of German History, 1914–1934.* New York: William Morrow, 1936. Republished 1967 as *Hindenburg: The Wooden Titan.*

Wilson, Edmund. *To the Finland Station: A Study in the Writing and Acting of History*. New York: Harcourt, Brace, 1940.

Winterbotham, Frederick W. *The Ultra Secret*. New York: Harper and Row, 1974.

Wolff, Leon. *In Flanders Fields: The 1917 Campaign*. New York: Viking Press, 1958.

Woodham-Smith, Cecil B. [FitzGerald]. *Florence Nightingale*. New York: McGraw-Hill, 1951.

——. *The Reason Why*. London: Constable, 1953.

Woodhouse, Christopher Montague. *The Greek War for Independence: The Historical Setting*. London: Hutchinson's University Library, 1952.

Woodward, Ernest Llewellyn. *Great Britain and the German Navy*. Oxford: The Clarendon Press, 1935. Republished 1964.

——. *Great Britain and the War of 1914-1918*. New York: Barnes and Noble, 1967.

Wright, Gordon. *The Ordeal of Total War, 1939-1945*. New York: Harper and Row, 1968.

Yoshihashi, Takehiko. *Conspiracy at Mukden: The Rise of the Japanese Military*. New Haven: Yale Univ. Press, 1963.

Young, Peter. *World War 1939-45: A Short History*. New York: Thomas Y. Crowell 1966

Ziemke, Earl F. *Stalingrad to Berlin: The German Defeat in The East*. Washington: Government Printing Office, 1968.

Chapter 7

American Military History: The Early Period, 1607-1815

Robert W. Coakley

THIS chapter and the two that follow deal with individual periods of American military history to the end of World War II. As an introduction the student needs to know something of the writings on the whole course of that history and of the principal themes and controversies that historians and writers have developed in dealing with it. These topics can be dealt with only briefly.

To the earliest American historians, military history was not considered a field separate from that of the general history of the United States. George Bancroft, the most noted of the nineteenth-century group, contributed a great deal to the military as well as political history of America. And if his simplistic belief in the story of America as the triumph of liberty under divine guidance no longer appeals to the critical mind of the twentieth century, Bancroft still left an important legacy to historians of all phases of American life, including the military. His successors in writing general histories of the United States—men like Justin Winsor, John B. McMaster, Richard Hildreth, and Edward Channing—likewise did not neglect military history. The general run of analytical and "scientific" historians of the early twentieth century, however, shifted the focus away from military events and institutions to the social and economic structure beneath political development. Academic historians of the 1920s and 1930s were apt to stress the causes and consequences of war to the exclusion of either the course of American wars or military institutions as a part of American life. Only after World War II was the balance in some measure redressed.

Around the turn of the twentieth century, then, military history became to some extent divorced from general American

Dr. Coakley (Ph.D., Virginia) is Deputy Chief Historian of the Center of Military History and coauthor of two volumes on *Global Logistics and Strategy* (U.S. Army in World War II series) and a CMH bicentennial publication on *The American Revolution.*

history and became the province of military professionals and gifted amateur historians with military interests; only a few of the new "scientific" historians made contributions. The pioneer in the field of military policy was a Regular Army officer and Civil War veteran with a confirmed faith in the superiority of the military professional over the citizen soldier. Emory Upton's *Military Policy of the United States*, published posthumously by the War Department at the instigation of Secretary Elihu Root in 1904, exerted a powerful influence for decades on both Army officers and military historians. Upton's thesis was that the United States, because of lack of appreciation of the value of trained military professionals, had blundered unprepared into its wars at a scandalous cost in time, human life, and natural resources. Upton was contemptuous of hastily trained citizen soldiers and politicians in Congress and the Presidency whom he held responsible for the nation's inept military policies. Upton's account stopped at the end of the Civil War. Frederic L. Huidekoper's *Military Unpreparedness of the United States* (1915), relying on Upton for the earlier years, covered the period through the Spanish-American War in essentially Uptonian fashion. C. Joseph Bernardo and Eugene H. Bacon in *American Military Policy: Its Development Since 1775* (1955) have brought Upton's thesis past the Second World War. The first comprehensive histories of the United States Army that appeared between World War I and World War II, William A. Ganoe's *History of the United States Army* (1924) and Oliver L. Spaulding's *The United States Army in War and Peace* (1937), both written by Army officers and still very useful, show strong Uptonian influence.

The Uptonians did not have the field all to themselves. John A. Logan, one of those "political" generals of the Civil War, in 1887 published *The Volunteer Soldier of America*, a massive and ill-organized tome but one that used American military history to argue the superiority of the citizen soldier over the professional. A more up-to-date statement of Logan's thesis is to be found in Jim Dan Hill's *The Minute Man in Peace and War: A History of the National Guard* (1964). The most balanced and effective counterargument to Upton came from a fellow professional and distinguished military scholar, John McAuley Palmer, and was presented in its most comprehensive form in *America in Arms: The Experience of the United States with Military Organization* (1941). Using the same historical examples as Upton, Palmer argued that the great defect in American policy had not been the use of citizen soldiers but the failure to train them well in an organized reserve. Palmer cited Washington's support of a "well regulated militia" after the Revolution in support of his contention much as Upton had used Washington's tirades against ill-trained militia in the Revolution to make his case for the professionals.

The contrasting Upton and Palmer theses have provided much of the central theme for the history of the United States Army, its wars and battles. Since World War II the whole controversy has been placed within a broader context. Walter Millis's *Arms and Men* (1956) is an excellent and readable account of the development of American military policy within the broader context of technological change and political shifts in the world around us. Millis adds a naval dimension to the story of the development of American military policy and ends with a discussion of the dilemma that the development of air power and of atomic weapons has brought about, suggesting that under modern conditions war can no longer serve any useful purpose. Russell Weigley in two books, *Towards an American Army* (1962) and *History of the United States Army* (1967), deals with the development of the Army as an institution, candidly recognizing that he is writing the history of two armies, one the professional and the other the citizens' reserve, and that the tension between them is well illustrated by the writings of Upton and his critics. Unlike his predecessors, Ganoe and Spaulding, Weigley deals little with military operations. A recent amalgam of both institutional history of the Army and its role in battles and wars is to be found in Maurice Matloff's (ed.) *American Military History* (1969, revised 1973) produced by the U.S. Army Center of Military History primarily as an ROTC text. In a third work, *The American Way of War* (1973), Weigley traces the development of American strategy beginning with the American Revolution and concludes, much like Millis, that the traditional American concept of war has been outdated by post-World War II developments. T. Harry Williams's *Americans at War* (1956) is a very readable treatise on military organization and policy, although weak on developments in the twentieth century. Two useful books on the development of American military policy and thought are Millis's (ed.) *American Military Thought* (1966) and Raymond O'Connor's (ed.) *American Defense Policy in Perspective* (1965).

The U.S. Navy theorists, sparked by Alfred Thayer Mahan's writings, have generally dealt with broader themes of world naval history rather than confining themselves strictly to

American military developments. There are, however, numerous useful histories of the U.S. Navy; the earliest, by novelist James Fenimore Cooper, appeared in 1854. In 1893 Edgar S. Maclay published a two-volume *History of the Navy*, expanded into three volumes after the Spanish-American War. Like many of its successors, it is in the heroic tradition. Dudley Knox's *History of the United States Navy*, first published in 1936 with an updated and enlarged edition in 1948, is better balanced, as is the work of Naval Academy teachers Carroll S. Alden and Allen Westcott, *The United States Navy: A History* (1943). The best scholarly work on the history of the United States Navy to the end of World War I is Harold and Margaret Sprout's *The Rise of American Naval Power* (1939), a work that puts Mahan in proper context as Millis and Weigley put Upton in context. E. B. Potter's (ed.) *The United States and World Sea Power* (1955) follows the Mahan tradition of treating U.S. naval history within the framework of the long story of developments in sea warfare.

There are a number of general histories of the Marine Corps, the most notable, all written by Marine officers, are Clyde H. Metcalfe's *A History of the United States Marine Corps* (1939), Robert D. Heinl's *Soldiers of the Sea: The United States Marine Corps, 1775-1962* (1962), and Edwin H. Simmons's, *The United States Marine Corps, 1775-1975* (1975). The most recent and detailed Marine Corps history is J. Robert Moskin's *The U.S. Marine Corps Story* (1977), essentially a combat narrative.

For general coverage of battle history, the old classic, Matthew Steele's *American Campaigns* (1909), is now largely outdated; but neither J.F.C. Fuller's *Decisive Battles of the U.S.A.* (1942) nor Robert Leckie's *Wars of America* (1968) really supplant it. The battles of our wars can in fact be studied best in the more specialized literature. An indispensable adjunct to their study, in whatever sources, is *The West Point Atlas of American Wars* (two volumes, 1959) edited by Brig. Gen. Vincent Esposito.

Civil-military relations have attracted a great deal of attention in the post-World War II era, and both historians and political scientists have explored the historical dimensions of the problem. Louis Smith's *American Democracy and Military Power* (1951) is a solid, relatively impartial account. Samuel P. Huntington's *The Soldier and the State* (1957) is more provocative, a study quite sympathetic to the military that stresses the need for strict military professionalism and what Huntington designates as "objective civilian control." In contrast, a strong antimilitary bias shows in Arthur E. Ekirch's *The Civilian and the Military* (1956), a work that stresses what Ekirch considers increasing military dominance since World War II.

James A. Huston in *Sinews of War: Army Logistics 1775–1953* (1966) gives comprehensive treatment to an area of American military history long neglected. The only other work in the logistics area on a comparable scale, but more specialized, is Erna Risch's *Quartermaster Support of the Army* (1962). In the field of military education the best work is by John W. Masland and Lawrence I. Radway, *Soldiers and Scholars: Military Education and National Policy* (1957). On the oldest American military educational institution, perhaps the best recent history is Stephen Ambrose's *Duty, Honor, Country: A History of West Point* (1966).

An ambitious series covering both American wars and military policy and institutions is the Macmillan Wars of the United States series under the general editorship of Louis Morton. Individual volumes from this series, all written by outstanding scholars in their respective fields, will be cited in connection with the specific periods they cover.

To turn now to the first of these periods, in the two centuries that elapsed between the first English settlements at Jamestown in 1607 and the end of the second American war with Britain in 1815, military affairs played an important part in American life and development. As colonists, Americans fought thousands of engagements with the Indians, took part in half a dozen European wars that spread to the American continent, and engaged in a certain amount of strife among themselves. As rebels they fought an eight-year war to break their bonds to the mother country. As citizens of a free and independent state, they established a framework for national military policies, pushed the Indian frontier westward, and pursued a precarious neutrality in the wars that wracked Europe between 1792 and 1815. They finally went to war with Britain for a second time in 1812, providing a test for the military institutions that had taken shape during the colonial and early national experience. The peace that ended this war also ended an epoch in American military history when the country, as colony and nation, had been inextricably embroiled in the affairs of European states; it marked the beginning of a new era, to last until 1898, during which the United States would concentrate on internal development and westward expansion across the continent.

The Colonial Experience

In 1955 Clarence C. Clendenen characterized the colonial era as "A Little Known Period of American Military History" and decried the lack of attention of military historians to this period except as "background."[1] In a comparative sense, Clendenen was right. There has been much less written on the military history of the colonial period, particularly in recent years, than on the Revolution and the subsequent development of the United States as a nation. Yet neglect is a relative matter, and there is ample historical literature on the colonial wars, both of a summary and specialist nature. The coverage of colonial military institutions is somewhat less adequate, and no single book provides a thorough summary of both colonial wars and military institutions.

The military institutions of the American colonists owed much to a European heritage that went back to Greek and Roman times; but this European heritage was modified greatly in an American wilderness where land was plentiful and labor to work it scarce and where the Indians with whom the English colonists had first to vie for control fought in a different fashion from Europeans. The essential feature of the military system of colonial America was the requirement for militia service on the part of every able-bodied male. The militia was an ancient English institution going back to the Middle Ages; by the end of the seventeenth century, however, it no longer had the same importance in England as in the colonies. In America the militia system was well adapted to the environment, for a professional army was probably not the most effective instrument for the intermittent and scattered warfare with the aborigines of North America, nor could the colonies afford one.

Some of the older works still contain the best accounts of the militia. Herbert L. Osgood's *The American Colonies in the Seventeenth Century* (three volumes, 1904–07) and *The American Colonies in the Eighteenth Century* (four volumes, 1924) offer some of the best treatments of militia institutions. *Backgrounds of Selective Service*, edited by Arthur Vollmer (two volumes, Volume II in nine parts, 1947) as part of the historical effort of the Selective Service System headquarters, contains both a summary and a convenient compilation of the militia laws of all of the original thirteen colonies. More recently

---

1. Clarence C. Clendenen, "A Little Known Period of American History," *Military Affairs* 19, no. 1 (Spring 1955):37.

Daniel Boorstin has provided a provocative sketch of the militia and the "minuteman" tradition in Part 13 of *The Americans: The Colonial Experience* (1958), dealing more in the realm of ideas than in the complications of militia practices.

A more detailed view of the colonial militia as an institution and of these practices in different colonies must be sought in institutional histories of the various individual colonies, in the literature on the colonial wars, and in a large number of articles on various aspects of the militia that have appeared in scholarly journals since World War II, of which only a few can be cited. Philip Alexander Bruce's *Institutional History of Virginia in the Seventeenth Century* (1910) contains one of the better studies of the militia in a southern colony. Louis Morton in "The Origins of American Military Policy," *Military Affairs* 22 (1958-59), deals with the early development of militia institutions in both New England and Virginia. Jack S. Radabaugh in "The Militia of Colonial Massachusetts," *Military Affairs* 18 (1954), and E. Milton Wheeler in "Development and Organization of the North Carolina Militia," *North Carolina Historical Review* 41 (1964) treat the militia of these two colonies in some detail. Morison Sharp, in "Leadership and Democracy in the Early New England System of Defense," *American Historical Review* 50 (1945), stresses the extent to which the militia organization was an integral part of a whole social system. Benjamin Quarles in "The Colonial Militia and Negro Manpower," *Mississippi Valley Historical Review* 45 (1959) treats the role of blacks in the militia system.

And colonial military institutions were really not so simple as they have frequently been painted, a point effectively made by John Shy in "A New Look at the Colonial Militia," *William and Mary Quarterly*, 3d Series, Volume 20 (1963). Shy points out that there were great differences in military practices in the thirteen individual colonies, that the quality of militia varied from colony to colony and by regions within colonies, and finally that many of the forces employed by the colonies were not, strictly speaking, militia at all but volunteers enlisted for particular terms of service. These volunteer forces, he says, included indentured servants and drifters not enrolled in the common militia, and he speculates that the poor character of some of these volunteers had much to do with the miserable performance of some colonial units in the French and Indian War.

Shy's preliminary conclusions draw attention to the need for further investigation of the whole spectrum of colonial military practices if we are to understand fully the roots of American military policy. The ordinary militia organization practically never took the field as a unit. It was rather a base for volunteers or draftees who were formed into special organizations for specific incidents or campaigns. Then, outside this regular organization, some militiamen formed volunteer organizations, purchased uniforms, and undertook special drills; these units would form the basis for the nineteenth-century development of the National Guard. Similarly, the volunteer units noted by Shy, with their officers appointed not elected, and their men enlisted for specific terms of service, were not militia but the predecessors of the Continental Army and the state volunteers of the Mexican and Civil wars. The last element in this picture was of course the British regular, who appeared in America only in isolated instances up to 1755 but played an important role after that date, first as defender and then as a threat to American liberties. American colonists also served, though infrequently, in the ranks of British regular units, as in the Cartegena expedition in 1741 and in the French and Indian War. The best reference on the weapons and uniforms of all these types of forces and of their enemies is Harold L. Peterson's *Arms and Armor in Colonial America, 1526-1783* (1956).

The wars and battles provincials and redcoats fought have been the subject of more historical literature than have the military institutions of the colonists. Both early wars with the Indians and internal conflicts were normally localized within individual colonies or regions, but the Indian wars eventually merged into the wars between France and England for the control of North America—King William's War (1689-97), Queen Anne's War (1701-13), King George's War (1744-48), and the French and Indian War (1754-63), to use their American nomenclature. The climax of colonial military history came in the last of these wars, known in Europe as the Seven Years' War (1756-63) and rechristened by Lawrence Gipson, historian of the old British Empire, as the Great War for Empire.

Several good modern works cover, in whole or in part, localized Indian wars of the seventeenth century. Douglas E. Leach's *Flintlock and Tomahawk: New England in King Philip's War* (1958) treats the major and decisive encounter of the New England colonists with the Indians of that region. Alden T. Vaughan's *New England Frontier: Puritans and Indians, 1620-1675* (1965) extends the coverage further back in time while Leach's *The Northern Colonial Frontier, 1607-1763* (1966), in a new series entitled Histories of the American Frontier, covers other matters relating to frontier life as well as Indian fighting over a longer period. Verner W. Crane's *The Southern Frontier, 1670-1732* (1928) is an older work considered standard on the Indian wars of the Carolinas. On Indian warfare, intertribal as well as with the whites, along the lake and river chain between New York and Canada, see George T. Hunt's *The Wars of the Iroquois* (1940) and Allen W. Trelease's *Indian Affairs in Colonial New York: The Seventeenth Century* (1960). Wilcomb E. Washburn's *The Governor and the Rebel: A History of Bacon's Rebellion in Virginia* (1957) deals both with the problem of the Indian frontier and with internal conflict in seventeenth-century Virginia, treating the rebellion as an outgrowth of a crisis in defense policy rather than in the traditional manner as an incident in the struggle for political liberty. A good introduction to the methods of Indian warfare is John K. Mahon's "Anglo-American Methods of Indian Warfare, 1676-1794," *Mississippi Valley Historical Review* 45 (1958).

In covering the epic struggle between France and England for control of North America, and the Indian warfare that accompanied it, Francis Parkman was the pioneer. Although Parkman did not have access to all the sources that the present day historian has, his firsthand knowledge of the terrain and of the North American Indian have never been surpassed. He wrote with consummate literary skill and his nine-volume series on France and England in North America, published between 1865 and 1892, constitutes a stirring and dramatic account full of the personality of the leaders and the clash of arms in the wilderness. Parkman was above all a good storyteller, not an analytical historian, but his stories have formed the basis of the traditional view of the events of this long conflict.

Another military classic, Sir John Fortescue's *History of the British Army* (Volume II, 1899) covers the colonial wars in outline with the main emphasis on the French and Indian War, the only one in which sizable British Army units operated on the American mainland. A modern scholarly work on a grand scale is Lawrence H. Gipson's *The British Empire Before the American Revolution* in fifteen volumes (1936-70), which in selected portions deals with the colonial wars from the viewpoint of the British administrators in London. A compact summary, reflecting the modifications of Parkman's accounts by modern scholars, is Howard H. Peckham's *The Colonial Wars, 1689-1762* (1964), a volume in the University of Chicago's History of American Civilization series. The most recent summary work, Douglas Leach's *Arms for Empire: A Military History of the British Colonies in North America* (1973) in the

Macmillan Wars series, treats the colonial wars in broader social context than did the earlier histories; it is in fact the nearest thing to an adequate overall treatment of both the colonial wars and military institutions, and it contains the best bibliography for those who want to investigate the colonial period in depth.

Perhaps the most noted colonial military exploit was the capture of the French fortress at Louisbourg in 1745, one of the few cases where colonial military forces successfully mounted an offensive outside their borders. G. A. Rawlyk's *Yankees at Louisbourg* (1967) has superseded earlier accounts of this expedition. In the southern colonies, the struggle was with Spain rather than France, and the thirteenth colony, Georgia, was founded primarily as a British outpost against Spain. The wars on the southern frontier have had no Parkman to recount them. Two valuable recent studies are J. Leitch Wright's *Anglo-Spanish Rivalry in North America* (1971) and Larry E. Ivers's *British Drums on the Southern Frontier . . . 1733-1749* (1973).

The war waged with France from 1754 to 1763 was the climax of colonial military history. Gipson's view of the "Great War for Empire" (covered in Volumes VI-VIII of his work), as the designation implies, is that it was not a defensive but an offensive war waged by the British to expand their empire. Writing from a different vantage point, a French Canadian scholar, Guy Fregault, thoroughly agrees; in *Canada: The War of the Conquest* (1955, reprint 1969) he emphasizes the effects of the British imperial drive on the French culture of the province. The British threw their full energies into the conflict in North America and after early defeats emerged completely victorious, banishing the French threat to the British colonies forever. In this war the direction, financing, and the greater part of the military forces were furnished by the British, but all types of colonial forces described earlier participated. Many Americans, including George Washington, got the military experience that was to stand them in good stead in the American Revolution. Stanley Pargellis has written the most authoritative account of the whole range of affairs relating to the British conduct of the war in *Lord Loudoun in North America* (1933) and has provided a judicious selection of documents in *Military Affairs in North America, 1748-1765: Selected Documents from the Cumberland Papers in Windsor Castle* (1936). From another vantage point John A. Schutz has covered the early campaigns in the north in his biography of *William Shirley, King's Governor of Massachusetts* (1961).

Two events in the French and Indian War attract particular attention—the ambush and utter defeat of General Edward Braddock's force approaching Fort Duquesne in 1755, and the victory of General James Wolfe over the Marquis de Montcalm on the Plains of Abraham before Quebec in 1759, clinching a British victory in the war. They may be used to dispel certain myths about the inability of British regulars to adapt to warfare in America. Braddock's defeat supposedly proved the unsuitability of traditional linear tactics of eighteenth-century warfare in America, yet Wolfe's climactic victory on the Plains of Abraham was gained almost exclusively by his use of these same tactics. In truth, the victory of the vastly inferior French and Indian forces over Braddock on the Monongahela was a singular event, not to be repeated in the nine years that followed. Although the British learned their lessons from it, they did not reduce their emphasis on rigid discipline or abandon regular line of battle tactics, even in the American wilderness. But they did modify these tactics under particular conditions in the American environment as described by J.F.C Fuller in *British Light Infantry in the Eighteenth Century* (1925) and, more recently, by Eric Robson in "British Light Infantry in the Mid-Eighteenth Century: The Effect of American Conditions," *Army Quarterly* 63 (1952). Peter Paret argues, on the contrary, in "Colonial Military Experience and European Military Reform at the End of the Eighteenth Century," *Bulletin of the Institute of Historical Records* 37 (1964), that the influence of colonial experience on the tactics of European armies was slight.

In any case the traditional picture of Braddock's defeat as a result of the blunders of the British general has undergone considerable transformation at the hands of modern scholars, though few completely absolve him of blame for the debacle. But Stanley Pargellis in "Braddock's Defeat," *American Historical Review* 41 (1936) and Lee McCardell in *Ill-Starred General: Braddock of the Coldstream Guards* (1958) show him as more unlucky than inept. The role of the young George Washington in the war, including his part in Braddock's expedition, is treated realistically in Volume II of Douglas Freeman's *George Washington* (1950) and in James Flexner's *George Washington: The Forge of Experience, 1732-1775* (1965). Both volumes also treat extensively the difficulties besetting the Virginia military effort in the war, problems also covered in Louis K. Koontz's *Robert Dinwiddie* (1925), written from the viewpoint of the Virginia colonial governor. On Montcalm and Wolfe a Canadian historian, C.P. Stacey, has brought the best of modern scholarship to bear on the events on the Plains of Abraham in his *Quebec, 1759: The Siege and the Battle* (1959). Stacey corrects many old myths and dispels much of the heroic aura that has always surrounded the tragic figures of Wolfe and Montcalm, showing them in all their true human dimensions—as men with many frailties playing out a great historic drama, men whom their contemporaries regarded with a certain ambivalence.

The war did not really end with the defeat of the French. The Indian tribes along the western frontier undertook a desperate effort in 1763 to salvage something of what they had lost with the defeat of their French allies, an episode to which Howard Peckham has given full treatment (revising and updating Parkman) in *Pontiac and the Indian Uprising* (1947). Viewing the long Anglo-French struggle in broader perspective, the decisive factor was probably not superior British land forces but the control of the seas by the British Navy. The best works on the role of the naval war are Michael Lewis's *The Navy of Britain* (1948) and Gerald Graham's *Empire of the North Atlantic: The Maritime Struggle for North America* (1950).

British success in the "Great War for Empire" led directly to the American Revolution: Administering and defending the new territories produced the policy of maintaining British regulars in America and taxing the colonists to support them, a policy that found its first expression in the Stamp Act. The story of British military policy in this connection and that of the British Army that served in America and its part in provoking the conflict is well told in John Shy's *Toward Lexington: The Role of the British Army in the Coming of the Revolution* (1965).

The American Revolution

The American Revolution was a great event, not only in American but in world history. It brought into being a nation that became, in less than two centuries, the most powerful in the western world. And it marked the beginnings of vast changes that would sweep that western world in the century following, thrusting aside old monarchical institutions in favor of parliamentary democracy and *laissez faire* economics. Albeit fought on the main battlefields much like other eighteenth-century wars, it also carried within it the seeds of change that would sprout and grow in the French Revolution less than two decades later. It was, in this sense, a transition between limited wars fought by professional armies and people's wars fought by the "nation in arms."

The literature on the military history of the Revolution, quite apart from that on its political, economic, and social aspects, is voluminous—the product of several generations of historians collectors, memoir writers, and journalists. Although the military history of the war has not generated so much controversy or changing interpretation as that of its causes or the extent of internal revolution, successive generations of historians have looked at it somewhat differently.[2]

The nineteenth century was a period of rampant American nationalism, and American historiography of the Revolution, seldom critical or impartial, for the most part portrayed the war in terms of the heroic deeds of Washington and his comrades in arms, enshrining them in a special pantheon of American heroes. While some writers benefited from personal knowledge of men and events, nearly all lacked written source material since collecting and printing documents was a slow process. Some of the earliest histories of the Revolution, for instance those by Rev. William Gordon (1788) and Dr. David Ramsay (1793), contained large sections copied almost verbatim from the accounts published each year during the conflict in the British *Annual Register*.

There was a good deal of originality, however, in Benson J. Lossing's *Pictorial Field Book of the Revolution* (two volumes, 1851-60), an encyclopedia-like book based on a tour of the sites of Revolutionary events which is still quite useful. Also useful is the great amount of source material collected and published by state governments, historical societies, and private individuals during the course of the nineteenth century, including many soldiers' journals, diaries, and memoirs. The biographies of the period, although generally laudatory, also included much original material. There were many good articles and monographs covering battles and campaigns, an especially significant number appearing in the course of the centennial celebration between 1875 and 1883. Some battle and campaign histories that merit particular attention are Henry P. Johnston's *Campaign of 1776 Around New York* (1878) and *The Yorktown Campaign and the Surrender of Cornwallis* (1881), Lyman C. Draper's *King's Mountain and Its Heroes* (1881), Henry B. Carrington's *Battles of the American Revolution* (1876), and William S. Stryker's *The Battles of Trenton and Princeton* (1898).

---

2. For an excellent essay on this topic, see Don Higginbotham, "American Historians and the Military History of the American Revolution," *American Historical Review* 70 (Oct. 1965):18–34.

Indeed, the nineteenth-century nationalist historians established a good factual basis for the history of battles and campaigns and for the contributions of various leaders. But they incorporated little critical analysis of the generalship on either side, of the nature of American or British military policy and strategy, or of the reasons for American victory and British defeat. The new professional "scientific" historians of the first four decades of the twentieth century, in their study of the Revolution, with some few exceptions, concentrated on economic, social, and political changes, virtually ignoring the extent to which the military course of the war affected these areas.

The military professionals or talented amateur historians who did continue to study the military aspects of the struggle adopted a critical approach quite different from that of their romantic nationalist predecessors. Emory Upton drew heavily on the Revolution to produce his examples of the inefficiency of militia. Frances Vinton Greene's *The Revolutionary War and the Military Policy of the United States* (1911), a short military history of the Revolution, was largely Uptonian in spirit. And Charles Francis Adams, a member of the famous family and a Civil War veteran, in *Studies Military and Diplomatic* (1911), established some of the principal lines the military critique of the war was to follow for some time to come. He described the battle of Bunker Hill as an epic of blunders on both sides, found Washington's conduct of the New York campaign in 1776 little short of disastrous, and charged that the American Commander-in-Chief's lack of appreciation of cavalry cost the patriots dearly. The message of the writings of Adams, Upton, Greene, and like critics was that the Americans had won more because of British blunders and French aid than because of their own wise policies or intelligent leadership. While some, like Adams, criticized Washington, most, like Upton, concentrated their fire on an inept Continental Congress. Both lines of thought found their way into the debunking biographies and popular histories of the 1920s and 1930s.

Despite slight attention in academic circles, some solid scholarly works were produced on the military side of the Revolution in the first four decades of the twentieth century. Louis C. Hatch's *Administration of the American Revolutionary Army* (1904), though unsatisfactory in many respects, is still the best work dealing with what we would today call personnel administration. Charles K. Bolton's study, *The Private Soldier under Washington* (1902), falls into a similar category. Justin Smith's two-volume work, *Our Struggle for the Fourteenth*

Colony: Canada and the American Revolution (1907) is still the only full treatment of American efforts to conquer Canada. Admiral Alfred Thayer Mahan turned his skills to analysis of the naval operations on both sides in *Major Operations of the Navies in the War of Independence* (1913). Gardner Allen produced what is still the standard history of the Continental Navy in *Naval History of the American Revolution* (two volumes, 1913). E. E. Curtis's *Organization of the British Army in the American Revolution* (1926) was one of the first studies to call attention to the immense difficulties the British faced in raising, transporting, and supplying an army to fight the war in America.

A number of other studies of the period laid greater stress on the ineptitude of British ministers and commanders than on any inherent difficulties they faced. William M. James's *British Navy in Adversity* (1926) emphasized the incompetence of Lord Sandwich, the First Lord of the Admiralty. Hoffman Nickerson's *The Turning Point of the Revolution* (1928), a classic study of the Saratoga campaign by an Army officer, blamed much of the British failure in the 1777 campaign on the blundering of Lord George Germain. Allen French's *The Day of Lexington and Concord* (1925) and *The First Year of the American Revolution* (1934), meticulously researched accounts of the events of 1775-76, stressed the ineptitude of the king's ministers and his commanders in America in the revolutionary crisis. Troyer S. Anderson in *The Command of the Howe Brothers During the American Revolution* (1936) pictured the Howes as caught in a dilemma between their peacemaking and warmaking missions.

World War II seemingly reminded American professional historians, many of whom served in the conflict, that how wars are fought can be as important as the causes and consequences of them and indeed must in any case vitally affect the latter. The 1950s saw the appearance of a number of general histories of land warfare during the American Revolution—Willard Wallace's *Appeal to Arms* (1951); Lynn Montross's *Rag, Tag, and Bobtail: The Story of the Continental Army* (1952); Christopher Ward's *The War of the Revolution*, edited by John R. Alden (two volumes, 1952); George F. Scheer and Hugh F. Rankin's *Rebels and Redcoats* (1957); and Howard Peckham's *The War for Independence: A Military History* (1958). A voluminous documentary collection by Henry S. Commager and Richard B. Morris, *The Spirit of '76: The Story of the American Revolution as told by Participants* (two volumes, 1958), by no means slighted the military events of the war itself.

These various general histories provide the student today with more than adequate general coverage of the campaigns and battles of the war. Meanwhile, scholars in more specialized areas have produced a large number of new studies, and new balanced biographies have supplanted both the romanticized works of the nineteenth century and the debunking biographies of the 1920s and 1930s. The most recent general military history of the Revolution, Don Higginbotham's *The War of American Independence: Military Attitudes, Policies, and Practices* (1971), contains the best synthesis of all this recent scholarship. Higginbotham adds little to Ward or Wallace insofar as the course of battles and campaigns is concerned, but he does add a dimension in treating the military policies and institutions of Revolutionary America in an attempt to show how they grew out of the colonial past and influenced the future of American military policy. In similar fashion, Mark M. Boatner's *Encyclopedia of the American Revolution* (1966, revised in 1974) is an indispensable reference work that incorporates, in topical entries, much of the results of scholarly study of the Revolution since Lossing's time. Also useful as reference works are two bicentennial publications sponsored by the Clements Library at the University of Michigan—Howard H. Peckham's (ed.) *The Toll of Independence: Engagements and Battle Casualties of the American Revolution* (1974) and Charles H. Lesser's (ed.) *The Sinews of Independence: Monthly Strength Reports of the Continental Army* (1976).

The picture of the Revolution that emerges from this welter of new scholarship is neither the nineteenth-century one of righteous patriots triumphing over villainous redcoats nor of an American victory explained solely in terms of British blunders and French aid. If there is any one theme running through much of the recent literature produced on both sides of the Atlantic it is the emphasis on the sheer physical difficulty the British faced in subduing the American revolt. The British had to recruit an army or buy one in Germany, transport and supply it over 3,000 miles of ocean, and then use it effectively to reestablish control over a vast and sparsely populated territory. If British generals seemed slow and lethargic and constantly worked at cross purposes with their colleagues, their naval counterparts, and the government at home, much of this was owing to the great difficulties of transport, supply, and communication over long distances.

This point of view is ably presented in the British historian Eric Robson's brilliant series of essays, *The American Revolution in Its Political and Military Aspects* (1955). Another British scholar, Piers Mackesy, has also faced the question of why the

British defeat in a study of British policy and strategy at the cabinet level in London, *The War for America, 1775–1783* (1964). Mackesy feels that a British military victory would have been possible on a number of occasions, and particularly in 1780 when war weariness had set in among the Americans, had the British been able to put about 10,000 more troops in America. Mackesy admits, however, that such a military victory would have had little political value unless the British could have found a native Tory element capable of governing the country. Mackesy finds the French and Spanish contribution in contesting control of the seas the really vital factor, a judgment not very different from that of Admiral Mahan in 1913. In contrast to Mackesy, John R. Alden in his *The American Revolution* (1954) contends that the British task was so difficult that the Americans could probably have won without French aid.

Those who, like Mackesy, believe the British might have won admit that the victory would have been possible only if they could have used the "good Americans," the Tories, to control the "bad" ones—Washington, Jefferson, and the other rebels. No question in the historiography of the Revolution is more difficult than that of the Tories. Who and how numerous were they? William H. Nelson in an excellent philosophical analysis, *The American Tory: A Study of the Loyalists in the American Revolution* (1961), argues that the Tories were usually local minorities and that they were about one quarter of the "politically active" population. Wallace Brown in *The Good Americans: The Loyalists in the American Revolution* (1969), based largely on a study of Loyalists who claimed compensation from the British after the war, places their number within the broad range of fifteen to thirty percent of the population. Paul H. Smith's *Loyalists and Redcoats: A Study in British Revolutionary Policy* (1964) shows how the British failed in their effort to make effective use of the Tories.

The new emphasis upon the difficulties the British faced and the importance of the Tories has forced some re-evaluation of Upton's strictures on the militia during the Revolution. For the militia, after all, maintained control of the countryside, put the Tories in their place, and harried the British armies that moved too far away from their coastal bases. Walter Millis has put it quite succinctly:

> While the regular armies marched and fought more or less ineffectually, it was the militia which presented the greatest single impediment to Britain's only practicable weapon, that of counter-revolution. The militia were often much less than ideal combat troops and they have

come in for hard words ever since. But their true military and political significance may have been underrated.[3]

As the United States itself became involved, in Vietnam, in wrestling with a problem of control of a countryside and its population, appreciation of the difficulties the British faced in the Revolution and of the importance of the militia has increased. Yet in all the welter of scholarship on the American Revolution, no good work treats the Revolutionary militia nor indeed provides a satisfactory account of the Continental Army as a military institution, though the subjects are covered with varying accuracy in the standard military histories of the Revolution and of the United States Army.

Whatever the militia's contribution, the final victory still had to be won on the land and sea by regular American and French military forces. The detailed study of battles and leaders of the Revolution continues therefore to hold its importance and allure. A few of the modern studies in these areas need to be noted. Arthur B. Tourtellot's *William Diamond's Drum: The Beginnings of the War of the American Revolution* (1959) is the best account of Lexington and Concord. Alfred H. Bill's *Valley Forge: The Making of an Army* (1952) treats the battles of Germantown and Monmouth as well as the great winter ordeal of the Continental Army. Rupert Furneaux's *The Battle of Saratoga* (1971), Russell F. Weigley's *The Partisan War: The South Carolina Campaign of 1780-1782* (1970), and Harold Larrabee's *Decision at the Chesapeake* (1964) on the Yorktown campaign are all valuable studies. Samuel S. Smith's four books on the battles of Trenton (1965), Princeton (1967), Monmouth (1964), and the Delaware forts (1970) are readable and relate the events of these battles to present-day landmarks. Jack M. Sosin's *The Revolutionary Frontier, 1763-1783* (1967) and Dale Van Every's *A Company of Heroes: The American Frontier 1775-1783* (1962) are modern accounts of the war along the fringes of settlement. Intelligence activities are the central feature of Carl Van Doren's *Secret History of the American Revolution* (1941) which, along with James Flexner's *The Traitor and the Spy* (1953), contains a full account of Benedict Arnold's treason drawn from new sources in British archives. Harold Peterson's *The Book of the Continental Soldier* (1968) is a well illustrated treatment of uniforms, weapons, practices, and customs of the Continental Army. Benjamin Quarles's *The Negro in the American Revolution*

---

3. Walter Millis, *Arms and Men* (New York: Putnam's, 1956), pp. 34–35.

(1961) treats the role of blacks in winning American independence—a long-neglected subject.

Contributions to American naval history during the Revolution have been made by William Bell Clark in a series of works on various Continental Navy officers and privateers, typical of which is Ben Franklin's Privateers (1956), and by William J. Morgan in Captains to the Northward: The New England Captains in the Continental Navy (1959). Good short treatments of the British Navy during the Revolution are to be found in the two works mentioned earlier, Lewis's Navy of Britain and Gerald Graham's Empire of the North Atlantic. As a reference on the naval vessels, tactics, weapons, and crews, see Jack Coggins's Ships and Seamen of the American Revolution (1969). The Naval History Division is engaged in a massive project of editing and publishing Naval Documents of the American Revolution (1964-); the seven volumes completed at the end of 1976 cover the period 1774-77.

The prosaic field of logistics has in the past attracted few writers, though logistics were of transcendent importance in determining the outcome of the conflict, as Eric Robson noted in his essays. Supporting Robson's view of the role of logistics in British defeat are two recent studies on British supply and transport problems, David Syrett's Shipping in the American War, 1775-1783 (1970) and R. Arthur Bowler's Logistics and the Failure of the British Army in America (1975). There have been no comparable analyses of American logistics. The student must rely primarily on articles and chapters in broader works such as Huston's Sinews of War and Risch's Quartermaster Support of the Army. Victor L. Johnson's The Administration of the American Commissariat During the Revolutionary War (1941) covers a specialized area. A comprehensive treatment of finances, certainly the Achilles' heel of the American war effort, is to be found in Elmer J. Ferguson's The Power of the Purse: A History of American Public Finances, 1776-1790 (1961). A most useful compilation of maps for the student of either logistics or battles is the Rand McNally Atlas of the American Revolution (1974, edited by Kenneth Nebenzabel).

Many of the most significant recent works on the Revolution have been biographies of American and British military leaders. On the American side, the laudatory tone of the nineteenth-century biographies and the debunking tone of those of the twenties and thirties have been supplanted by a realistic approach which leaves Washington and his principal lieutenants as heroes but of quite human proportions. Douglas Freeman's

massive eight-volume biography of George Washington devotes
three volumes to his role as leader of the Revolution, while James
T. Flexner covers this part of his career in one volume, *George
Washington in the American Revolution, 1775-1783* (1968). The
Washington of Freeman and Flexner (and the portrait of the two
differs in some respects) is a great leader, but not the marble-like
god of the nineteenth century. Few any longer deny that his
conduct of the New York campaign, as Charles Francis Adams
contended in 1911, left much to be desired or that he made other
mistakes in his military conduct of the war. His strength lay
more in his character and perseverance in the face of almost
insuperable obstacles than in any innate military genius. A
dissident on this score, however, is Dave R. Palmer, who in *The
Way of the Fox: American Strategy in the War for America* (1975)
paints Washington as a consummate strategist whose moves in
each of four phases of the war were carefully calculated to
produce American victory. For those who may wish an
iconoclastic view of the great man, see Bernhard Knollenberg's
Washington and the Revolution (1940), which poses some
interesting questions about such key episodes as the court-
martial of Charles Lee and the alleged Conway cabal.

Theodore Thayer's *Nathanael Greene: Strategist of the Revolution* (1960) paints Greene as the best of the military minds
among Washington's subordinates and in so doing presents an
account of the southern campaign. North Callahan's *Henry
Knox: George Washington's General* portrays sympathetically
another of the Commander-in-Chief's principal assistants. Two
biographies of Daniel Morgan appeared at roughly the same
time, Don Higginbotham's *Daniel Morgan, Revolutionary
Rifleman* (1961) and Callahan's *Daniel Morgan, Ranger of the
Revolution* (1961). Willard M. Wallace in *Traitorous Hero: The
Life and Fortune of Benedict Arnold* (1954) tells anew the
amazing tale of the exploits and eventual apostasy of a most
contradictory character. John R. Alden in *General Charles Lee:
Traitor or Patriot* (1951) treats another controversial character
and exonerates him of anything worse than bad judgment at
Monmouth. An older work by a military scholar, John M.
Palmer's *General Von Steuben* (1937), is the best on the German
pseudobaron who did so much to train the Continental Army. In
a trilogy, *Lafayette Comes to America* (1935), *Lafayette Joins the
American Army* (1937), and *Lafayette and the Close of the
American Revolution* (1942), Louis R. Gottschalk has dispelled
much of the myth that has surrounded the young French
marquis. Samuel Eliot Morison's *John Paul Jones: A Sailor's
Biography* (1959) is the best as well as the liveliest and most

readable account of the life of the greatest American naval hero of the war.

The treatments of British commanders have generally been less biographies than accounts of their roles in the Revolution. John R. Alden's *General Gage in America* (1948) treats sympathetically the first in the succession of British commanders-in-chief in America. In *The Howe Brothers and the American Revolution* (1972), Ira D. Gruber emphasizes their efforts at conciliation, contending that in this pursuit they sacrificed the "ministry's best prospect for regaining the colonies." William B. Willcox's *Portrait of a General: Sir Henry Clinton in the War of Independence* (1964) is of particular significance as a study in the psychology of the British commander who held the position longer than any other during the Revolution and as a treatment of the quarrels and misunderstandings that continually beset the British command in America. If Gruber finds the secret of British failure in 1776–78 in the futile efforts of the Howe Brothers to conciliate rather than to fight, Willcox finds it in 1778–81 in the indecisive character of Sir Henry Clinton and the de facto divided command that cost the British dearly in both north and south. Franklin B. and Mary Wickwire's *Cornwallis, the American Adventure* (1970) portrays with considerable sympathy the character and career of the British general who lost his army at Yorktown, stressing the difficulties he faced and holding Clinton largely responsible for his failure. Gerald Saxon Brown's *The American Secretary: The Colonial Policy of Lord George Germain* (1963) does much to rehabilitate the character of the British cabinet minister whose alleged muddling has generally been held largely responsible for the British disaster at Saratoga. George Martelli has done much the same for the First Lord of the Admiralty in *Jeremy Twitcher: A Life of the Fourth Earl of Sandwich* (1962).

In two volumes, George A. Billias, as editor, has brought together sketches of the major military leaders on both sides, each essay written by a different author. The first volume, *George Washington's Generals* (1964), contains sketches of Washington himself, and of ten of his principal subordinates; the second, *George Washington's Opponents: British Generals and Admirals of the American Revolution* (1969), has essays on a dozen British generals and admirals. Though the sketches in these volumes vary a great deal in approach and quality, their final effect is clear. They show the American leaders as more energetic and resourceful and call attention again to the ineffectiveness of British leaders and the divided counsels that plagued the development of British strategy. The net impact of the newer biographies of both English and American leaders is thus not so different from that of the less sophisticated hero-worshipping idylls of the nineteenth century.

The writings of several generations of historians have served to illuminate but not to resolve completely the whys of American victory and British defeat or even the military meaning of the American victory. Tactical innovations were not extensive, but they did represent a culmination of the trend toward employment of light troops as skirmishers that had begun in the French and Indian War. In general Americans tried to adapt to the linear tactics of the British army as the British adapted to the guerrilla tactics of the American forest. At one time American success was ascribed to a superior weapon, the so-called Kentucky rifle, which was far more accurate than the smoothbore musket with which the British, and indeed most Americans, were equipped. Colonel John W. Wright in "The Rifle in the American Revolution," *American Historical Review* 29 (1924), laid this theory to rest by pointing out that though the rifle was useful in wooded areas it was unsuitable for open-field fighting because of its slow rate of fire and lack of a bayonet. Wright made it clear that the rifle played only a subsidiary role in American victory; it was useful at Saratoga but not at Yorktown.

Walter Millis in *Arms and Men* contends that the real significance of the American Revolution for later military development was not in tactics at all but in the concept, inherent in the thinking of Washington and other leaders, of a national army to which every citizen owed service in war and peace. This concept was but imperfectly realized in the Continental Army and the militia of the American Revolution, but it came to full fruition in the "nation in arms" of the French Revolution.

The Early National Period

In the Uptonian tradition, the period between the Revolution and the end of the War of 1812 is a sort of "Dark Age" in American military history. In that view, the American people, imbued with an unreasoning prejudice against standing armies in time of peace and mindful of government economy, emasculated their military forces. The Continental Army (or the Regular Army as it was to be called after 1788), after practical disbandment in 1783, survived only as a very small force, not very professional at that, largely employed on the frontiers against the Indians. The Navy, which disappeared entirely at the end of the Revolution, was revived in 1796 during the troubles with revolutionary France but barely survived the Jeffersonian economy drive in the early 1800s. The country came to rely on an unwieldy militia system, inherited from Colonial times, and entered the War of 1812 completely unprepared. The militia proved a weak reed, and American performance in that war was miserably inept.

This "Dark Age" was hardly so dark as the Uptonians would paint it. Whatever may have been the defects in American military institutions, and they were undoubtedly great, the country had singular success in achieving the longer range goals of its foreign policy and in insuring domestic security, the ends military policy normally serves. The new nation established a central government with the powers of taxation and of raising military forces that the Confederation had sadly lacked. The Constitution, in its army, navy, and militia clauses, laid the foundation of American military power. The Indians along the frontier were subdued or pushed westward, opening the area between the Appalachians and the Mississippi to unlimited settlement. The Louisiana Purchase extended American boundaries westward, and military explorers carried the flag to the top of the Rockies and to the Pacific Coast. Internal threats to disrupt the union, such as the Whiskey Rebellion in 1794 and the several conspiracies to separate the trans-Appalachian west from the union, were successfully frustrated. One could hardly say the United States won the War of 1812 in any literal meaning of that word, yet the end of the war did herald the beginning of American supremacy on the continent. In truth, Americans paid few penalties beyond local defeats for the military inefficiency and ineptitude with which military critics, with some justice, have charged them. The military history of 1783–1815 has its share of ironies.

Works dealing exclusively with military history of the interwar period, 1783–1812, are not numerous. Military affairs of the period have been treated quite extensively in both general military histories of the United States and in general histories of the particular period. Henry Adams's *History of the United States During the Administrations of Jefferson and Madison* in nine volumes (1889–91) is still perhaps the best detailed work for military as well as political and diplomatic history of the 1800–1815 period. The studies of Leonard White on the administrative structure of the federal government, *The Federalists* (1948) and the *Jeffersonians* (1951), are indispensable aids to the study of the military organization and policies during the period. Harry M. Ward's more specialized *The Department of*

War, 1781-1795 (1962) covers military administration in a transition period.

The best work on the early years of the Army in the field, as opposed to departmental administration, is James R. Jacobs's *The Beginnings of the U.S. Army* (1947). Marshall Smelser has done a similar job for the early years of the Navy in *The Congress Founds the Navy* (1959). Jacobs has also provided in *Tarnished Warrior* (1938) a biography of James Wilkinson, the ranking officer of the Regular Army during most of these years, whose devious dealings with the Spanish and in the Burr conspiracy have never yet been completely unraveled.

The most significant work to appear recently on military policy in the post-Revolutionary period, however, is Richard H. Kohn's *Eagle and Sword: The Beginnings of the Military Establishment in America* (1975). Kohn stresses the importance of the national defense issue in the twenty years after 1783 and shows that it was the Federalists who actually won the day in the battle over the establishment of a national army, although they destroyed their party in the process.

William H. Goetzmann's *Army Exploration in the American West, 1803-1863* (1959) covers the military expeditions into the territory of the Louisiana Purchase. John Bakeless's *Lewis and Clark, Partners in Discovery* (1947) deals more specifically with the most important of these expeditions. Gardner Allen has provided coverage of naval operations in *Our Naval War With France* (1909) and *Our Navy and the Barbary Corsairs* (1905).

One of the few works dealing exclusively with that most important military institution of the period, the militia, is John K. Mahon's *The American Militia: Decade of Decision 1789-1800* (1960), covering a time when the basic militia laws that were to govern to 1903 took shape. Francis Prucha's *The Sword of the Republic: the United States Army on the Frontier, 1783-1846* (1969) contains a good account of the Harmer, St. Clair, and Wayne expeditions against the Indians, as well as the frontier fighting during the War of 1812. Dale Van Every's *The Ark of Empire, 1784-1803* (1963) and *Final Challenge: The American Frontier 1804-1845* (1964) deal more fully with the militia campaigns as well as those of the regulars against the Indians both north and south. Randolph C. Downes's *Council Fires on the Upper Ohio: A Narrative of Indian Affairs in the Upper Ohio Valley Until 1795* (1940) treats this period against the background of the earlier conflicts in the area with far greater sympathy for the Indians than most of the military historians show. Leland D. Baldwin's *Whiskey Rebels: The Story of a*

Frontier Uprising (1939) devotes at least some attention to the militia expedition dispatched by President Washington to western Pennsylvania in 1794 to insure compliance with the tax laws—the great precedent for use of federal military force in civil disturbances in this country.

The War of 1812 itself has been the subject of considerably more historical literature than the formative period of the Union, although the war has not attracted as much attention as the Revolution, the Civil War, or the two great world wars of the twentieth century. The best writing on the war as a whole has come since the post-World War II renaissance of interest in military history, but many of the older works are still valuable. Benson J. Lossing's *Pictorial Field Book of the War of 1812* (1868), a companion piece to his similar book on the Revolution, is still quite useful. And the sections from Henry Adams's nine-volume history edited by Harvey A. DeWeerd and reprinted as *The War of 1812* (1944) remains perhaps the best general history, though one must guard against Adams's prejudices against both the British and the Republican administrations. It was Adams who perhaps did most to create the image of bungling and misman-agement in American conduct of the war. The best account of naval operations is Alfred Thayer Mahan's *Sea Power in Its Relation to the War of 1812* (1905), though his emphasis on the importance of heavy ships of the line and a fleet in being can be disputed as the best policy for the Americans. Theodore Roosevelt's *Naval War of 1812* (1882) is generally reliable and more readable than Mahan.

Since World War II there has been a rash of general accounts. Francis F. Beirne's *The War of 1812* (1949) relies heavily on Adams and Lossing, while Glenn Tucker's *Poltroons and Patriots: A Popular Account of the War of 1812* (1954), which emphasizes the blundering, draws equally heavily on contem-porary newspapers. J. MacKay Hitsman's *The Incredible War of 1812* (1965) presents a modern Canadian view of the war, and Reginald Horsman in *The War of 1812* (1969) presents a relatively balanced account for both sides. Harry L. Coles's *The War of 1812* (1965), a volume in the Chicago History of American Civilization series, and John K. Mahon's *The War of 1812* (1972) are the best modern accounts and the most profitable reading for the military student.

On particular aspects of the war, Alec R. Gilpin treats the campaigns along the northern front in *The War of 1812 in the Old Northwest* (1958); Neil H. Swanson's *The Perilous Fight* (1945) tells of the British inroads in the Chesapeake Bay area in August and September of 1814 and the seriocomic American flight from the capital city. Charles F. Brooks's *The Siege of New Orleans* (1961) and Wilburt S. Brown's *The Amphibious Campaign for West Florida and Louisiana: A Critical Review of Strategy and Tactics at New Orleans* (1969) supplant older accounts of the last battle of the war and the only one that produced a decisive American victory (though fought after the signing of the treaty of peace). As usual, biographies contain some of the most useful treatments of events of the war. Among those of importance are Marquis James's *Andrew Jackson, the Border Captain* (1933), Freeman Cleaves's *Old Tippecanoe: William Henry Harrison* (1939), Charles J. Dutton's *Oliver Hazard Perry* (1935), Charles W. Elliot's *Winfield Scott, the Soldier and the Man* (1937), and Glenn Tucker's *Tecumseh: Vision of Glory* (1956).

What conclusions emerge from modern historical scholarship with regard to the War of 1812? The conflict was once called the Second War of American Independence, and this is not entirely unjustified. It is not, as early American historians assumed, that the British were trying to reverse the verdict of 1783 and reconquer the United States. The British accepted the independence of the United States and sought only to limit the nation's growth and influence. But the war did mark the end of dependence on the European system and the beginning of an era when the country could turn toward its own internal development and expansion on a continent where it was clearly dominant. Even if this development was mainly a result of the European peace that followed the exhaustive wars of the Napoleonic era, it still was a most significant one. As Harry Coles remarks, "From the Revolution onward a basic aim of American statesmen had been to achieve freedom of action so that the United States could choose peace or war as its interest might dictate. With the settlement of 1815 this aim became a reality to a degree that the early statesmen had hardly dared to hope."[4]

This success was achieved despite much ineptitude and blundering in the American conduct of the war, particularly in the first year, and the United States did not win in the military sense. The Peace of Ghent (1815) was essentially our first peace without victory. But Britain did not win the war either, and the issues like impressment of seamen, over which it supposedly was fought, simply disappeared with the peace in Europe. During the first two years, while the Americans were most inept,

---

4. Harry L. Coles, *The War of 1812* (Chicago: Univ. of Chicago Press, 1965), pp. 270-71.

Britain had to devote her greatest efforts to the campaigns against Napoleon in Europe and treated the war in America as a sideshow. With Napoleon's exile to Elba in 1814, the British could make a more serious effort in North America, but the Americans had found new and effective military leaders in such men as Jacob Brown, Winfield Scott, and Andrew Jackson. British goals were still limited, and Britain had the same disadvantages to overcome in terms of terrain and geography as in the Revolution. And although the central government in Washington exercised its power weakly and many Americans opposed the war with England, the United States was now a populous and strong country with a going central government and no Tories.

Perhaps victory was impossible for either side for reasons quite apart from the virtues of men or military systems. Harry Coles put it this way:

> The answer seems to be that both sides were attempting to carry out operations that were simply beyond the technical means of the day. In Canada to a degree, and much more so in the United States, there was much brute strength but nowhere did there exist either the public or private means to organize resources and bring them to bear in an effective war effort.

Or, as Reginald Horsman puts it, "Throughout the war neither power was able to solve the problems of offensive warfare on the North American continent, and defence predominated."[5]

This verdict hardly conforms to that of critics who found in the War of 1812 a failure that was the direct result of a faulty military policy—reliance on the militia. There can be little question that the militia failed on many occasions, and above all it was a most imperfect instrument for offensive operations against Florida and Canada. Since the British did not really attempt to subjugate the country in the War of 1812, the rising of the militia in local areas for defense of their homes had not the same effect it had in the Revolution. Nor was the militia needed to maintain control over the countryside, for there was no British "fifth column" such as the Tories had represented during the Revolution. And when we consider the operations of militia in the field, we must admit too that the results were not entirely negative. Regular forces were defeated and humiliated in the early stages of the war just as militia were, and militia performed well, just as they had in the Revolution, under certain

---

5. Coles, *War of 1812*, pp. 258–59. Reginald Horsman, *The War of 1812* (New York: A. A. Knopf, 1969), p. 265.

circumstances. Maryland militia did well in the defense of
Baltimore in 1814 (in contrast to the performance in the defense
of Washington at Bladensburg in the same year), Kentucky
volunteers did well at the Thames, and some militia units were
among the victors in Jackson's lines at New Orleans.

Yet, on balance, there can be no question that the old militia
system did prove ill suited for fighting the kind of war waged
between 1812 and 1815, and Americans tacitly recognized it.
After 1815 the old militia system fell into decay, to be replaced by
volunteers of two sorts: those who trained in special companies
in peacetime and were eventually known as the National Guard,
and volunteers who enlisted in wartime in state units for specific
periods of time. Volunteers rather than militia were to be the
principal American reliance in the Mexican War, the Civil War,
and the Spanish American War. But volunteers of this sort were
nothing new—they had been used in the colonial period for many
expeditions, and the Continental Army was, of course, composed
of them. On the emergence of the volunteer spirit as the core of
the American military system see Marcus Cunliffe's *Soldiers
and Civilians: The Martial Spirit in America, 1775-1865* (1968).

Bibliography: General

Alden, Carroll S., and Westcott, Allan. *The United States Navy: A History*. Rev.
    ed. Chicago and Philadelphia: Lippincott, 1945.

Ambrose, Stephen. *Duty, Honor, Country: A History of West Point*. Baltimore:
    Johns Hopkins Univ. Press, 1966.

Bancroft, George. *History of the United States of America From the Discovery of
    the Continent*. 10 vols. Boston: Little, Brown, 1834-75.

Bernardo, C. Joseph, and Bacon, Eugene H. *American Military Policy: Its
    Development since 1775*. Harrisburg: Stackpole, 1955.

Channing, Edward, *A History of the United States*. 6 vols. New York: Macmillan,
    1905-25.

Cooper, James Fenimore. *History of the Navy of the United States of America*.
    New York: Putnam's 1854.

Ekirch, Arthur E. *The Civilian and the Military*. New York: Oxford Univ. Press,
    1956.

Esposito, Vincent, ed. *The West Point Atlas of American Wars*. 2 vols. New York:
    Praeger, 1959.

Fuller, J. F. C. *Decisive Battles of the U.S.A.* New York: Harper, 1942.

Ganoe, William A. *History of the United States Army*. New York: Appleton-
    Century, 1924.

Heinl, Robert D. *Soldiers of the Sea: The United States Marine Corps, 1775-1962*.
    Annapolis, Md.: U.S. Naval Institute, 1962.

Hill, Jim Dan. *The Minute Man in Peace and War: A History of the National
    Guard*. Harrisburg: Stackpole, 1964.

Hildreth, Richard. *The History of the United States of America From the Discovery of the Continent to the Organization of Government Under the Federal Constitution*. 6 vols. New York: Harper and Brothers, 1863.

Huidekoper, Frederic L. *The Military Unpreparedness of the United States: A History of American Land Forces From Colonial Times Until June 1, 1915.* New York: Macmillan, 1915.

Huntington, Samuel P. *The Soldier and the State: The Theory and the Politics of Civil-Military Relations*. Cambridge, Mass.: Harvard Univ. Press, Belknap Press, 1957.

Houston, James. *Sinews of War: Army Logistics, 1775-1953*. Army Historical Series. Washington: Government Printing Office, 1966.

Knox, Dudley. *A History of the United States Navy*. Rev. ed. New York: Putnam's, 1948.

Leckie, Robert. *The Wars of America*. New York: Harper and Row, 1968.

Logan, John A. *The Volunteer Soldier of America*. Chicago and New York: R. S. Pell, 1887.

Maclay, Edgar S. *History of the Navy from 1775 to 1901*. 3 vols. New York: D. Appleton-Century, 1901-2.

McMaster, John B. *A History of the People of the United States From the Revolution to the Civil War*. 8 vols. New York: D. Appleton-Century, 1883-1913.

Mahan, Alfred Thayer. *The Influence of Sea Power on History, 1660-1783*. Boston: Little, Brown, 1890.

Masland, John W., and Radway, Laurence I. *Soldiers and Scholars: Military Education and National Policy*. Princeton, N.J.: Princeton Univ. Press, 1957.

Matloff, Maurice, ed. *American Military History*. Rev. ed. Army Historical Series. Washington: Government Printing Office, 1973.

Metcalf, Clyde H. *A History of the United States Marine Corps*. New York: Putnam's, 1939.

Millis, Walter. *Arms and Men: A Study in American Military History*. New York: Putnam's, 1956.

Millis, Walter, ed. *American Military Thought*. Indianapolis, Ind.: Bobbs-Merrill, 1966.

Moskin, J. Robert. *The U.S. Marine Corps Story*. New York: McGraw-Hill, 1977.

O'Connor, Raymond G., ed. *American Defense Policy in Perspective: From Colonial Times to the Present*. New York: Wiley, 1965.

Palmer, John McAuley. *America in Arms: The Experience of the United States with Military Organization*. New Haven: Yale Univ. Press. 1941.

Potter, E. B., ed. *The United States and World Sea Power*. Englewood Cliffs, N.J.: Prentice-Hall, 1955.

Risch, Erna. *Quartermaster Support of the Army: A History of the Corps, 1775-1939*. Washington, Government Printing Office, 1962.

Simmons, Edwin H. *The United States Marine Corps, 1775-1975*. New York: Viking Press, 1975.

Smith, Louis. *American Democracy and Military Power: A Study of Civil Control of the Military Power in the United States*. Chicago: Univ. of Chicago Press, 1951.

Spaulding, Oliver L. *The United States Army in War and Peace*. New York: Putnam's, 1937.

Sprout, Harold, and Sprout, Margaret. *The Rise of American Naval Power, 1776-1918*. Princeton, N.J.: Princeton Univ. Press, 1939.

Steele, Matthew Forney. *American Campaigns*. 2 vols. Washington: Byron S. Adams, 1909.

Upton, Emory. *The Military Policy of the United States From 1775.* Washington: Government Printing Office, 1904.

Weigley, Russell F. *The American Way of War: A History of the United States Military Strategy and Policy.* New York: Macmillan, 1973.

——. *History of the United States Army.* New York: Macmillan, 1967.

——. *Towards an American Army: Military Thought from Washington to Marshall.* New York: Columbia Univ. Press, 1962.

Williams T. Harry. *Americans at War: The Development of the American Military System.* Baton Rouge: La. State Univ. Press, 1956.

Winsor, Justin. *Narrative and Critical History of America.* 8 vols. Boston and New York: Houghton Mifflin, 1884-89.

Bibliography: 1607-1815

Adams, Charles Frances. *Studies Military and Diplomatic, 1775-1865.* New York: Macmillan, 1911.

Adams, Henry. *History of the United States During the Administrations of Jefferson and Madison.* 9 vols. New York: Scribner's, 1889-91.

——. *The War of 1812.* Edited by Harvey A. DeWeerd. Harrisburg: Infantry Journal Press, 1944.

Alden, John R. *The American Revolution.* New York: Harper, 1954.

——. *General Gage in America: Being Principally a History of His Role in the American Revolution.* Baton Rouge: La. State Univ. Press, 1948.

——. *General Charles Lee: Traitor or Patriot?* Baton Rouge: La. State Univ. Press, 1951.

Allen, Gardner W. *Naval History of the American Revolution.* 2 vols. Boston: Houghton Mifflin. 1913.

——. *Our Naval War with France.* Boston: Houghton Mifflin, 1909.

——. *Our Navy and the Barbary Corsairs.* Boston: Houghton Mifflin, 1905.

Anderson, Troyer S. *The Command of the Howe Brothers During the American Revolution.* New York: Oxford Univ. Press, 1936.

Bakeless, John. *Lewis and Clark, Partners in Discovery.* New York: William Morrow, 1947.

Baldwin, Leland D. *Whiskey Rebels: The Story of a Frontier Uprising.* Pittsburgh: Univ. of Pittsburgh Press, 1939.

Beirne, Francis F. *The War of 1812.* New York: Dutton, 1949.

Bill, Alfred H. *Valley Forge: The Making of an Army.* New York: Harper, 1952.

Billias, George A., ed. *George Washington's Generals.* New York: William Morrow, 1964.

——, ed. *George Washington's Opponents: British Generals and Admirals of the American Revolution.* New York: William Morrow, 1969.

Boatner, Mark M. *Encyclopedia of the American Revolution.* New York: David McKay, 1966.

Bolton, Charles K. *The Private Soldier Under Washington.* New York: Scribner's 1902.

Boorstin, Daniel. *The Americans: The Colonial Experience.* New York: Random House, 1958.

Bowler, R. Arthur. *Logistics and the Failure of the British Army in America, 1775-1783.* Princeton, N.J.: Princeton Univ. Press, 1975.

Brooks, Charles F. *The Siege of New Orleans.* Seattle: Univ. of Wash. Press, 1961.

Brown, Gerald Saxon, *The American Secretary: The Colonial Policy of Lord George Germaine, 1775-1778.* Ann Arbor: Univ. of Mich. Press, 1963.

Brown, Wallace. *The Good Americans: The Loyalists in the American Revolution.* New York: William Morrow, 1969.

Brown, Wilburt S. *The Amphibious Campaign for West Florida and Louisiana: A Critical Review of Strategy and Tactics at New Orleans.* University, Ala.: Univ. of Ala. Press, 1969.

Bruce, Philip Alexander. *Institutional History of Virginia in the Seventeenth Century.* New York: Putnam's, 1910.

Callahan, North. *Daniel Morgan, Ranger of the Revolution.* New York: Holt, Rhinehart, and Winston, 1961.

——. *Henry Knox, George Washington's General.* New York: Rhinehart, 1958.

Carrington, Henry B. *Battles of the American Revolution.* New York and Chicago: A. S. Barnes, 1876.

Clark, William Bell. *Ben Franklin's Privateers: A Naval Epic of the American Revolution.* Baton Rouge: La. State Univ. Press, 1956.

——. *Captain Dauntless: The Story of Nicholas Biddle of the Continental Navy.* Baton Rouge: La. State Univ. Press, 1949.

——. *George Washington's Navy: Being an Account of His Excellency's Fleet in New England Waters.* Baton Rouge: La. State Univ. Press, 1960.

——. *Lambert Wickes, Sea Raider and Diplomat: The Story of a Naval Captain of the Revolution.* New Haven: Yale Univ. Press, 1932.

Clark, William Bell, and Morgan, William J., eds. *Naval Documents of the American Revolution.* Vols. 1-6 published. Washington: Government Printing Office, 1964-72.

Cleaves, Freeman. *Old Tippecanoe: William Henry Harrison.* New York: Scribner's 1939.

Clendenen, Clarence C. "A Little Known Period of American Military History." *Military Affairs* 19. no. 1 (Spring 1955):37-38.

Coggins, Jack. *Ships and Seamen of the American Revolution: Vessels, Crews, Weapons, Gear, Naval Tactics, and Actions of the War for Independence.* Harrisburg: Stackpole, 1969.

Coles, Harry L. *The War of 1812.* Chicago: Univ. of Chicago Press, 1965.

Commager, Henry S., and Morris, Richard B. *The Spirit of '76: The Story of the American Revolution as told by Participants.* 2 vols. Indianapolis, Ind.: Bobbs-Merrill, 1958.

Crane, Verner W. *The Southern Frontier, 1670-1732.* Durham, N.C.: Duke Univ. Press, 1928.

Cunliffe, Marcus. *Soldiers and Civilians: The Martial Spirit in America, 1775-1865.* Boston: Little, Brown, 1968.

Curtis, E. E. *Organization of the British Army in the American Revolution.* New Haven: Yale Univ. Press, 1926.

Downes, Randolph C. *Council Fires on the Upper Ohio: A Narrative of Indian Affairs in the Upper Ohio Valley Until 1795.* Pittsburgh: Univ. of Pittsburgh Press, 1940.

Draper, Lyman C. *King's Mountain and Its Heroes: History of the Battle of King's Mountain.* Cincinnati, Ohio: P. G. Thomson, 1881.

Dutton, Charles J. *Oliver Hazard Perry.* New York: Longmans, Green, 1935.

Elliot, Charles W. *Winfield Scott, the Soldier and the Man.* New York: Macmillan, 1937.

Ferguson, Elmer James. *The Power of the Purse: A History of American Public Finance, 1776-1790.* Chapel Hill: Univ. of N.C. Press, 1961.

Flexner, James T. *George Washington: The Forge of Experience, 1732-1775.* Boston: Little, Brown, 1965.

——. *George Washington in the American Revolution, 1775-1783.* Boston, Little, Brown, 1968.

——. *The Traitor and the Spy: Benedict Arnold and John Andre.* New York: Harcourt, Brace, 1953.

Fortescue, Sir John. *History of the British Army.* 13 vols. London and New York: Macmillan, 1899-1930.

Freeman, Douglas. *George Washington.* 8 vols. New York: Scribner's, 1948-57.

Fregault, Guy. *Canada: The War of the Conquest.* Translated by Margaret Cameron. New York: Oxford Univ. Press, 1969.

French, Allen. *The Day of Lexington and Concord, the Nineteenth of April 1775.* Boston: Little, Brown, 1925.

——. *The First Year of the American Revolution.* Boston: Houghton Mifflin, 1934.

Fuller, J. F. C. *British Light Infantry in the Eighteenth Century.* London: Hutchison, 1925.

Furneaux, Rupert. *The Battle of Saratoga.* New York: Stein and Day, 1971.

Gilpin, Alec R. *The War of 1812 in the Old Northwest.* East Lansing: Mich. State Univ. Press, 1958.

Gipson, Lawrence H. *The British Empire Before the American Revolution.* 15 vols. New York: A. A. Knopf, 1936-70.

Goetzmann, William H. *Army Exploration in the American West, 1803-1863.* New Haven: Yale Univ. Press, 1959.

Gordon, William. *The History of the Rise, Progress, and Establishment of the Independence of the United States of America: Including an Account of the Late War and of the Thirteen Colonies From Their Origin to that Period.* 4 vols. London, 1788.

Gottschalk, Louis R. *Lafayette Comes to America.* Chicago: Univ. of Chicago Press, 1935.

——. *Lafayette Joins the American Army.* Chicago: Univ. of Chicago Press, 1937.

——. *Lafayette and the Close of the American Revolution.* Chicago: Univ. of Chicago Press, 1942.

Graham, Gerald S. *Empire of the North Atlantic: The Maritime Struggle for North America.* Toronto: Univ. of Toronto Press, 1950.

Greene, Frances Vinton. *The Revolutionary War and the Military Policy of the United States.* New York: Scribner's, 1911.

Gruber, Ira D. *The Howe Brothers and the American Revolution.* New York: Atheneum, 1972.

Hatch, Louis C. *The Administration of the American Revolutionary Army.* New York: Longmans, Green, 1904.

Higginbotham, Don. "American Historians and the Military History of the American Revolution." *American Historical Review* 60 (Oct. 1965):18-34.

——. *Daniel Morgan, Revolutionary Rifleman.* Chapel Hill: Univ. of N.C. Press, 1961.

——. *The War of American Independence: Military Attitudes, Policies, and Practices.* New York: Macmillan, 1971.

Hitsman, J. MacKay. *The Incredible War of 1812: A Military History.* Toronto: Univ. of Toronto Press, 1965.

Horsman, Reginald. *The War of 1812.* New York: A. A. Knopf, 1969.

Hunt, George T. *The Wars of the Iroquois: A Study in Intertribal Trade Relations.* Madison: Univ. of Wisc. Press, 1940.

Ivers, Larry E. *British Drums on the Southern Frontier: The Military Colonization of Georgia, 1733-1749.* Chapel Hill: Univ. of N.C. Press, 1973.

Jacobs, James R. *The Beginnings of the U.S. Army.* Princeton, N.J.: Princeton Univ. Press, 1947.

———. *Tarnished Warrior, Major General James Wilkinson.* New York: Macmillan, 1938.

James, Marquis. *Andrew Jackson, the Border Captain.* Indianapolis, Ind.: Bobbs-Merrill, 1933.

James, William M. *British Navy in Adversity: A Study in the American War of Independence.* London and New York: Longmans, Green, 1926.

Johnson, Victor L. *. . . the Administration of the American Commissariat During the Revolutionary War.* Philadelphia (1939, Univ. of Pa. Ph.D. thesis), 1941.

Johnston, Henry P. *The Campaign of 1776 Around New York and Brooklyn.* Brooklyn: Long Island Historical Society, 1878.

———. *The Yorktown Campaign and the Surrender of Cornwallis.* New York, Harper, 1881.

Knollenberg, Bernhard. *Washington and the Revolution, a Reappraisal: Gates, Conway, and the Continental Congress.* New York: Macmillan, 1940.

Kohn, Richard H. *Eagle and Sword: The Beginnings of the Military Establishment in America.* New York: Free Press, 1975.

Koontz, Louis K. *Robert Dinwiddie: His Career in American Colonial Government and Westward Expansion.* Glendale, Calif.: Arthur H. Clark Co., 1925.

Larrabee, Harold A. *Decision at the Chesapeake.* New York: C. N. Potter, 1964.

Leach, Douglas E. *Arms for Empire: A Military History of the British Colonies in North America.* New York: Macmillan, 1973.

———. *Flintlock and Tomahawk: New England in King Phillip's War.* New York: Macmillan, 1958.

———. *The Northern Colonial Frontier, 1607-1763.* New York: Holt, Rhinehart, and Winston, 1966.

Lesser, Charles H., ed. *The Sinews of Independence: Monthly Strength Reports of the Continental Army.* Chicago: Univ. of Chicago Press, 1976.

Lewis, Michael. *The Navy of Britain: A Historical Portrait.* London: Allen and Unwin, 1948.

Lossing, Benson J. *The Pictorial Field Book of the Revolution . . .* 2 vols. New York: Harper, 1851-60.

———. *The Pictorial Field Book of the War of 1812.* New York: Harper, 1868.

McCardell, Lee. *Ill-Starred General: Braddock of the Coldstream Guards.* Pittsburgh: Univ. of Pittsburgh Press, 1958.

Mackesy, Piers. *The War for America, 1775-1783.* Cambridge, Mass.: Harvard Univ. Press, 1964.

Mahan, Alfred Thayer. *Major Operations of the Navies in the War of Independence.* Boston: Little, Brown, 1913.

———. *Sea Power in Its Relation to the War of 1812.* 2 vols. London: S. Low, Marston, 1905.

Mahon, John K. *The American Militia: Decade of Decision, 1789-1800.* Gainesville: Univ. of Fla. Press, 1960.

———. "Anglo-American Methods of Indian Warfare." *Mississippi Valley Historical Review* 45 (1958):254-75.

———. *The War of 1812.* Gainesville: Univ. of Fla. Press, 1972.

Martelli, George. *Jeremy Twitcher: A Life of the Fourth Earl of Sandwich, 1718-1792.* London: Cape, 1962.

Montross, Lynn. *Rag, Tag, and Bobtail: The Story of the Continental Army, 1775-1783.* New York: Harper, 1952.

Morgan, William J. *Captains to the Northward: The New England Captains in the Continental Navy.* Barre, Mass.: Barre Gazette, 1959.

Morison, Samuel Eliot. *John Paul Jones: A Sailor's Biography.* Boston: Little, Brown, 1959.

Morton, Louis. "The Origins of American Military Policy." *Military Affairs* 22 no. 2 (Summer 1958):75-82.

Nebenzabel, Kenneth, ed. *Rand McNally Atlas of the American Revolution.* Text by Don Higginbotham. Chicago: Rand McNally, 1974.

Nelson, William H. *The American Tory: A Story of the Loyalists in the American Revolution.* New York: Oxford Univ. Press, Clarendon, Press, 1961.

Nickerson, Hoffman. *The Turning Point of the American Revolution, or Burgoyne in America.* Boston: Houghton Mifflin, 1928.

Osgood, Herbert L. *The American Colonies in the Seventeenth Century.* 3 vols. New York: Macmillan, 1904-7.

——. *The American Colonies in the Eighteenth Century.* 4 vols. New York: Columbia Univ. Press, 1924.

Palmer, Dave R. *The Way of the Fox: American Strategy in the War for America.* Westport, Conn.: Greenwood Press, 1975.

Palmer, John M. *General Von Steuben.* New Haven: Yale Univ. Press, 1937.

Paret, Peter. "Colonial Experience and European Military Reform at the End of the Eighteenth Century." *Bulletin of the Institute of Historical Research* 37 (May 1964):47-59.

Pargellis, Stanley. "Braddock's Defeat." *American Historical Review* 41 (Jan. 1936):253-69.

——. *Lord Loudoun in America.* New Haven: Yale Univ. Press, 1933.

——. *Military Affairs in North American, 1748-1765: Selected Documents From the Cumberland Papers in Windsor Castle.* New York: D. Appleton-Century, 1936.

Parkman, Francis. *France and England in North America.* 9 vols. Boston: Little, Brown, 1865-92. The following individual volumes: *Pioneers of France in the New World* (1865); *The Jesuits in North America* (1867); *LaSalle and the Discovery of the Great West* (1869); *The Old Regime in Canada* (1874); *Count Frontenac and New France Under Louis XIV* (1877); *Montcalm and Wolfe.* 2 vols. (1884); *A Half Century of Conflict,* 2 vols. (1892).

Peckham, Howard H. *Pontiac and the Indian Uprising.* Princeton, N.J.: Princeton Univ. Press, 1947.

——. *The Colonial Wars, 1689-1762.* Chicago: Univ. of Chicago Press, 1964.

——. *The War for Independence: A Military History.* Chicago: Univ. of Chicago Press, 1958.

Peckham, Howard H., ed. *The Toll of Independence: Engagements and Battle Casualties of the American Revolution.* Chicago: Univ. of Chicago Press, 1974.

Peterson, Harold L. *Arms and Armor in Colonial America, 1526-1783.* Harrisburg: Stackpole, 1956.

——. *The Book of the Continental Soldier . . .* Harrisburg: Stackpole, 1968.

Prucha, Francis. *The Sword of the Republic: The United States Army on the Frontier, 1783-1846.* New York: Macmillan, 1969.

Quarles, Benjamin. "The Colonial Militia and Negro Manpower." *Mississippi Valley Historical Review.* 45 (1959):643-52.

——. *The Negro in the American Revolution.* Chapel Hill: Univ. of N.C. Press, 1961.

Radabaugh, Jack S. "The Militia of Colonial Massachusetts." *Military Affairs* 18, no. 1 (Spring 1954):1-18.

Ramsay, David. *The History of the American Revolution.* 2 vols. London: John Stockdale, 1793.

Rawlyk, G. A. *Yankees at Louisbourg.* Orono: Univ. of Maine Press, 1967.

Robson, Eric. *The American Revolution in Its Political and Military Aspects.* New York: Oxford Univ. Press, 1955.

––––––. "British Light Infantry in the Mid-Eighteenth Century: The Effect of American Conditions." *Army Quarterly* 63 (Jan. 1952):209–22.

Roosevelt, Theodore. *The Naval War of 1812: Or the History of the United States Navy During the Last War With Great Britain.* New York: Putnam's, 1882.

Scheer, George F., and Rankin, Hugh F. *Rebels and Redcoats.* Cleveland: World Publishing Co., 1957.

Schutz, John A. *William Shirley, King's Governor of Massachusetts.* Chapel Hill: Univ. of N.C. Press, 1961.

Sharp, Morison. "Leadership and Democracy in the Early New England System of Defense." *American Historical Review.* 50, no. 2 (Jan. 1945):244–60.

Shy, John W. "A New Look at the Colonial Militia." *William and Mary Quarterly.* 3d Series, vol. 20 (Apr. 1963):175–85.

––––––. *Toward Lexington: The Role of the British Army in the Coming of the American Revolution.* Princeton, N.J.: Princeton Univ. Press, 1965.

Smelser, Marshal. *The Congress Founds the Navy, 1787-1798.* Notre Dame, Ind.: Univ. of Notre Dame Press, 1959.

Smith, Justin. *Our Struggle for the Fourteenth Colony: Canada and the American Revolution.* 2 vols. New York: Putnam's, 1907.

Smith, Paul H. *Loyalists and Redcoats: A Study in British Revolutionary Policy.* Chapel Hill: Univ. of N.C. Press, 1964.

Smith, Samuel Stelle. *The Battle of Monmouth.* Monmouth Beach, N.J.: Philip Freneau Press, 1964.

––––––. *The Battle of Princeton.* Monmouth Beach, N.J.: Philip Freneau Press, 1967.

––––––. *The Battle of Trenton.* Monmouth Beach, N.J.: Philip Freneau Press, 1965.

––––––. *Fight for the Delaware, 1777.* Monmouth Beach, N.J.: Philip Freneau Press, 1970.

Sosin, Jack M. *The Revolutionary Frontier, 1763-1783.* New York: Holt, Rhinehart, and Winston, 1967.

Stacey, C. P. *Quebec, 1759: The Siege and the Battle.* New York: St. Martin's Press, 1959.

Stryker, William S. *The Battles of Trenton and Princeton.* Boston: Houghton Mifflin, 1898.

Swanson, Neil H. *The Perilous Fight.* New York: Farrar and Rhinehart, 1945.

Syrett, David. *Shipping in the American War, 1775-1783: A Study of the British Transport Organization.* London: Athlone Press, 1970.

Thayer, Theodore. *Nathanael Greene: Strategist of the Revolution.* New York: Twayne Publishers, 1960.

Tourtellot, Arthur B. *William Diamond's Drum: The Beginnings of the War of the American Revolution.* Garden City, N.Y.: Doubleday, 1959.

Trelease, Allen W. *Indian Affairs in Colonial New York: The Seventeenth Century.* Ithaca, N.Y.: Cornell Univ. Press, 1960.

Tucker, Glenn. *Poltroons and Patriots: A Popular Account of the War of 1812.* Indianapolis, Ind.: Bobbs-Merrill, 1954.

––––––. *Tecumseh: Vision of Glory.* Indianapolis, Ind.: Bobbs-Merrill, 1956.

Van Doren, Carl. *Secret History of the American Revolution.* New York: Viking Press, 1941.

Van Every, Dale. *A Company of Heroes: The American Frontier 1775-1783.* New York: William Morrow, 1962.

––––––. *The Ark of Empire, 1784-1803.* New York: William Morrow, 1963.

———. *The Final Challenge: The American Frontier, 1804-1845*. New York: William Morrow, 1964.

Vaughan, Alden T. *New England Frontier: Puritans and Indians, 1620-1675*. Boston: Little, Brown, 1965.

Vollmer, Arthur, ed. *Backgrounds of Selectice Service*. Selective Service Special Monograph No. 1, 2 vols. Washington: Selective Service System, 1947.

Wallace, Williard M. *Appeal to Arms: A Military History of the American Revolution*. New York: Harper, 1951.

———. *Traitorous Hero: The Life and Fortunes of Benedict Arnold*. New York: Harper, 1954.

Ward, Christopher. *The War of the Revolution*. Edited by John R. Alden. 2 vols. New York: Macmillan, 1952.

Ward, Harry M. *The Department of War, 1781-1795*. Pittsburgh: Univ. of Pittsburgh Press, 1962.

Washburn, Wilcomb E. *The Governor and the Rebel: A History of Bacon's Rebellion*. Chapel Hill: Univ. of N.C. Press, 1957.

Weigley, Russell F. *The Partisan War: The South Carolina Campaign of 1780-82*. Columbia: Univ. of S.C. Press, 1970.

Wheeler, E. Milton. "Development and Organization of the North Carolina Militia." *North Carolina Historical Review* 41 (1964):307-23.

White, Leonard. *The Federalists: A Study in Administrative History*. New York: Macmillan, 1948.

———. *The Jeffersonians: A Study in Administrative History, 1801-1829*. New York: Macmillan, 1951.

Wickwire, Franklin B., and Wickwire, Mary. *Cornwallis, the American Adventure*. Boston: Houghton Mifflin, 1970.

Willcox, William B. *Portrait of a General: Sir Henry Clinton in the War of Independence*. New York: A. A. Knopf, 1964.

Wright, J. Leitch, Jr. *Anglo-Spanish Rivalry in North America*. Athens: Univ. of Ga. Press, 1971.

Wright, John W. "The Rifle in the American Revolution." *American Historical Review* 29 (1924):293-99.

Chapter **8**

American Military History: The Middle Years, 1815–1916

Richard J. Sommers

ANDREW Jackson's decisive victory at New Orleans on 8 January ushered in the year 1815. This battle that began a year also ended an era during which several of the great powers of Europe had threatened the interests, sometimes even the security, of the fledgling United States. For the next hundred years European countries directly posed no serious threat to America's vital interests, and the United States, in turn, did not actively involve itself in the European state system. Friction with foreign nations that did arise was usually settled with a maximum of diplomacy and a minimum of force.

This absence of major foreign threats, together with the natural protection afforded by vast oceans, profoundly influenced the course of American history in these middle years. This "era of free security," as one scholar has termed it,[1] enabled the nation to concentrate on domestic political and economic development, free from concern over danger from abroad. The armed forces generally played a relatively minor role during this period. Except during emergencies they were small, consumed few resources, embraced only a minuscule fraction of the population, and basically remained outside popular consciousness.

Yet, however small, armed forces did exist during these years, so they do have a military history. Understanding the national context in which they functioned is essential to comprehending that history. But following their experiences and development is equally important. The Army's prime responsibility throughout this period was the long, slow, grinding task of advancing and securing the frontier against the Indians, thereby establishing the degree of safety in which westward expansion could

Dr. Sommers (Ph.D., Rice) is an archivist-historian at the U.S. Army Military History Institute. He has published numerous articles on the Civil War and a book, *Richmond Redeemed*, on the siege of Petersburg.

1. C. Vann Woodward, "The Age of Reinterpretation," *American Historical Review* 66 (1960):1–19.

flourish. And on the rare occasions when this expansion or other factors brought the country into conflict with foreign states, Mexico and Spain, the regulars provided the nucleus around which large numbers of volunteers rallied to secure national objectives. These foreign wars themselves mark significant points of study in U.S. military history. Even more of a milestone in the national life was the greatest conflict of this era, the Civil War, which definitively resolved the long controversy over the nature of the federal union—the high point of American military history in the middle years.

The Navy during the same period was the first line of defense against potential overseas foes and a combatant service when wars did erupt. It was also the principal instrument for limited U.S. participation in military ventures in Asia and Africa. And as the country became more involved abroad around the turn of the century, the Navy's responsibilities correspondingly mounted.

In addition to fighting, the armed forces performed other important functions. Both the Army and Navy made major contributions to medicine and science. The Army also did much civil engineering work and, more importantly, was the principal educator of civil engineers in the country. The service academies, indeed, served as general colleges for many young men who could not afford advanced private education. Some of these graduates enriched their civilian communities after limited tours of duty. Those who remained in service correspondingly enriched the armed forces, whose high command came increasingly to be entrusted to them.

As the Army and Navy underwent these experiences, they progressively grew in strength, organization, technique, and professionalism. The American armed forces that re-entered Europe's wars in 1917 were far different from those that had last been embroiled in world conflict in 1812–15. That growth and the experiences along the way make up American military history in the middle years.

The preceding chapter lists general histories, compilations, documents, and interpretations of American military operations, organizations, institutions, personnel, and policies. Portions of such works, of course, pertain to events of the middle years. Other works listed here may start before or extend beyond the middle years. William Goetzmann's study covers *Army Exploration in the American West, 1803–1863* (1959); Clarence Clendenen's *Blood on the Border* (1969) deals with disturbances along the Mexican border after 1848; and J. P. Dunn's *Massacres of the Mountains* (1886), Rupert Richardson's *Comanche Barrier* (1933), John Tebbel and Keith Jennison's *The American Indian Wars* (1960), and Tebbel's *Compact History* (1966) each relate to conflicts with the red men. In the field of technology and weaponry, William Birkhimer's *Historical Sketch of the Organization, Administration, Materiel and Tactics of the Artillery* (1884) is still useful; Claud Fuller's *The Breech-Loader in the Service, 1816-1917* (1965) recounts the long and controversial rise of that weapon to pre-eminence; and Arthur Van Gelder and Hugo Schlatter trace the *History of the Explosives Industry in America* (1927). Other informative volumes on ordnance include Frank Comparato's *Age of Great Guns* (1965) and Arcadi Gluckman's *United States Muskets, Rifles, and Carbines* (1948).

1815-1846

The end of the War of 1812 found the United States with an army of 38,000 regulars and nearly 200,000 militia. The return of peace brought a reduction to some 10,000 regulars. This small force was expected to face recalcitrant Spaniards in the south and southwest, guard against hostile Indians in the west and northwest, and confront potentially troublesome British in the north as well as protect the Atlantic coast. Such requirements appeared impossible for this little army, yet time-honored political and economic doctrines made large standing armies anathema to nineteenth-century America. The small body of regulars would have to make do as best it could between wars and then rely on a large influx of poorly trained volunteers or militia to help it fight major conflicts.

No such big war with another country erupted for thirty years. Friction with Britain over the militarization of the Great Lakes, the Canadian revolt of 1837, the Aroostook frontier, and the Oregon country were settled by diplomacy before occasional border incidents could flare into open war. Spanish Florida, a haven for renegade Indians and slaves, proved more troublesome, but Andrew Jackson's unauthorized invasion of the region in 1818 led to a collapse of Spanish rule. Resulting negotiations not only secured that territory but defined the southwestern frontier as well.

Not foreign states but Indian tribes represented the major problem for the United States military from 1815 to 1846. The Seminoles in Florida turned out to be more formidable than the erstwhile Spanish rulers and remained a thorn in the side of the country throughout the period. Under a succession of commanders including the able Winfield Scott, Zachary Taylor, and William J. Worth, both regulars and volunteers found it difficult to cope with those elusive swamp dwellers, even after their great chief, Osceola, was captured and died in prison. Worth, however, did eventually devastate the country enough to bring many of the Seminoles to terms. Chief Black Hawk's Sacs and Foxes of the Midwest proved less dangerous. When they left Iowa in 1832 to reoccupy their former lands in Illinois and Wisconsin, the Army decisively defeated them to end the last major Indian war east of the Mississippi, outside Florida.

The Indian frontier moved out of the woodlands and prairies onto the Great Plains during this period. Louisiana, Missouri, Arkansas, and Iowa all became states before the Mexican War, and to secure their western borders the Army established a string of posts from Fort Snelling, Minnesota, to Fort Jesup, Louisiana. These posts were essentially defensive. Except for guarding the wagon trails to Oregon and Santa Fe, troops did not yet venture westward in hopes of conquering the plains. This "Great American Desert" was to be left to the Indians. Indeed, many tribes living east of the Mississippi—principally the semicivilized Cherokees, Creeks, Chickasaws, and Choctaws, plus some Seminoles—were forcibly removed to the supposedly worthless plains to make their former lands available for white settlers. The Army superintended this removal and then garrisoned posts throughout the new Indian Territory west of Arkansas, both to keep the Indians under surveillance and to protect them from the more savage "blanket Indians" of the west.

The best studies of the Army on the frontier during this period are Francis Prucha's three excellent works: *American Indian Policy* (1962), *Sword of the Republic* (1969), and *Broadax and Bayonet* (1953). Fairfax Downey's *Indian Wars . . . 1776-1865* (1963) is also useful for the fifty years following the War of 1812. Henry Beers's *Western Military Frontier* (1935) is older but still of value.

The ablest treatment of a particular operation is John Mahon's *Second Seminole War* (1967). No good modern works are available for the Black Hawk War, so older volumes must be used: Reuben Gold Thwaites's brief but scholarly *Story of the Black Hawk War* (1892), Perry Armstrong's *The Sauks and the Black Hawk War* (1887), and Frank Stevens's *The Black Hawk War* (1903). Donald Jackson's edition of Black Hawk's *Autobiography* (1964) is also in print. Grant Foreman's *Indian Removal* (1932) provides a good account of the transfer of the Five Nations to the Indian Territory, and Thurman Wilkins's *Cherokee*

Tragedy (1970) and Wilson Lumpkin's *The Removal of the Cherokee Indians from Georgia* (1907) concentrate on the Cherokee aspect of that operation. A useful study of various Canadian border affairs, necessarily more diplomatic history than military, is Kenneth Bourne's *Britain and the Balance of Power in North America* (1967).

Biographical material is extensive on Andrew Jackson. Two works which focus on his military career are James Parton's *General Jackson* (1892) and Marquis James's more recent *Border Captain* (1933). His correspondence was published by John Spencer Bassett in 1927, and a comparable project for Monroe's Secretary of War, John C. Calhoun, has been under way since 1959 under the editorship of Robert Meriwether and Edwin Hemphill. The standard biography, *Calhoun*, is by Charles Wiltse (1944-51). Another useful biography of a prominent military figure of this period is Roger Nichols's *General Henry Atkinson* (1965).

Wars With Mexico, 1836-1848

Indians were not the only ones to move beyond the western states in the 1830s. Increasingly large numbers of Americans emigrated to Texas, then part of Mexico. These residents of a province distant from Mexico City felt more in common with their former homeland than with their nominal government. In 1836 they revolted in a fight initially for rights within Mexico that soon became a full-fledged war for independence. Numerous American volunteers, particularly from the South, flocked to Texas to aid their kinsmen. Initial defeats at the Alamo and Goliad were eclipsed by the decisive victory at San Jacinto that virtually secured Texan independence.

Irregular hostilities continued along the Texas-Mexico frontier for the next decade, but major fighting resumed only after the Lone Star Republic joined the Union in 1845. In acquiring Texas the United States accepted the Texans' claim to the Rio Grande boundary, rather than the more northerly Nueces, and ordered a sizable portion of the Regular Army to occupy the disputed region—a decision which worsened U.S.-Mexican relations already complicated by Mexican failure to pay debts. The unwillingness of either side to compromise made negotiations futile, and in April 1846, fighting broke out as Mexican forces crossed the Rio Grande and attacked a U.S. patrol. The Americans rapidly counterattacked and within a monthly completely secured both sides of the lower Rio Grande.

Congress, meantime, declared war, and President James Knox Polk once more followed American practice by calling on the states for large numbers of volunteers. Despite opposition to the war in certain areas, particularly New England, the volunteer units and ten new regular regiments were enthusiastically raised and sent to the war zone.

The first reinforcements to reach the Rio Grande bolstered Zachary Taylor's army sufficiently to enable it to press into northern Mexico and capture Monterrey in September. The American drive did not continue much farther south, however, because of logistical considerations and because Polk feared the political consequences to his Democratic Party of allowing the Whig Taylor to continue building his reputation. The president's decision altered the course of the war but not of politics. Even after the departure of most of his regulars and many of his volunteers for Tampico and Vera Cruz left his little army vulnerable, Taylor repulsed a Mexican counterattack at Buena Vista, 22–23 February, and on the basis of this victory he went on to win the Presidency in 1848. The triumph ended major fighting in that theater, although farther north operations continued as some American units from New Mexico took El Paso and invaded Chihuahua. The main force that had overrun New Mexico and moved on to California in 1846, meantime, spent the second year of the war cooperating with the Navy in conquering the Pacific coast.

The principal operations in 1847 occurred farther south. Most of Taylor's veterans plus considerable bodies of newly raised regulars and volunteers made up a new army under America's foremost soldier of the first half of the century, Winfield Scott, the Commanding General of the Army. In the most brilliant American campaign to that time, he took Vera Cruz, plunged westward into the heart of enemy country, and scored a series of triumphs that led to the capture of Mexico City in September. These victories, along with the resulting collapse of the Mexican government, virtually ended fighting. Early the following year a definitive treaty was signed, and in mid-1848 the U.S. Army evacuated Mexico.

The Mexican War ranks as an important milestone in the development of the United States and its armed forces. The nation not only secured all its stated prewar objectives but also conquered a vast domain in the far west. The key to this victory was the armed forces, which enjoyed almost unbroken success against an opponent that had gone into the war with considerable reputation—a big improvement over America's decidedly uneven performance in the War of 1812. Many factors contributed to this improved performance: the generalship of Scott, Taylor, and Stephen Watts Kearny and the fighting quality of the troops, both regular and volunteer. Another major element was the increasing professionalism of much of the junior officer corps, graduates of West Point. The conduct of war was, to be sure, not without flaws. Political considerations continued to influence the appointment of field and general officers. And the short term of service of many volunteer units meant that most of them were mustered out about the time they finally became proficient. Yet, on balance, it is clear that the Army that fought the Mexican War had considerably improved over its counterpart of thirty years before.

The Texans' fight for freedom generated quite a heritage and some writing. Andrew Houston's *Texas Independence* (1938) and Richard Santos's *Santa Anna's Campaign Against Texas* (1968) cover the entire independence movement; Frank Tolbert's *The Day of San Jacinto* (1959) concentrates on the decisive battle of the conflict. *The Writings of Sam Houston* (1938-42), edited by Amelia Williams and Eugene Barker, contains source material on Texas's foremost commander. Official sources on various Mexican leaders are brought together in Carlos Castaneda's *The Mexican Side of the Texas Revolution* (1928). The border fighting that followed San Jacinto is discussed in Joseph Nance's sound volumes, . . . *The Texas-Mexican Frontier* (1963-64).

The Mexican War proper produced considerable literature. Numerous general accounts, often written by participants, were published, some shortly after the fighting ended: Nathan Brooks's *Complete History of the Mexican War* (1849), Philip St. George Cooke's *Conquest of New Mexico and California* (1878), and Roswell Ripley's *War With Mexico* (1849). Another veteran, Cadmus M. Wilcox, brought out his major *History of the Mexican War* in 1892. Only in the early twentieth century, though, did the first scholarly history appear, Justin Smith's two-volume *War With Mexico* (1919), a work distinguished for its research, its coverage of operations, and its refutation of old partisan criticism that the war was unjustified and disgraceful. In many ways, it remains the best study. Three decades later two useful short histories were written: Alfred Hoyt Bill's *Rehearsal for Conflict* (1947) and Robert Selph Henry's *The Story of the Mexican War* (1950); and a spate of small volumes have come out in recent years: Otis Singletary's *The Mexican War* (1960), Charles Dufour's *The Mexican War, A Compact History, 1846-1848* (1968), Donald Chidsey's *The War with Mexico*

(1968), and Seymour Connor and Odie Faulk's *North America Divided* (1971). Most important of the new studies is K. Jack Bauer's volume in the Macmillan series, *The Mexican War (1846-1848)* (1974).

Besides these general accounts, there is a considerable body of primary and secondary literature on the principal commanders on both sides. Useful works include Winfield Scott's *Memoirs* (1864) and Charles Elliott's *Scott* (1937), Zachary Taylor's *Letters* (1908) and Holman Hamilton's *Taylor* (1941), Dwight Clarke's *Kearny* (1961), Edward Wallace's *Worth* (1953), and Antonio Santa Anna's *Autobiography* (1967). Some reminiscences were also published by junior officers and enlisted men but much less extensively than for the Civil War. Such sources as are available have been compiled into three useful anthologies by modern scholars: *To Mexico with Taylor and Scott* by Grady and Sue McWhiney (1969), *Chronicles of the Gringos* by George Winston Smith and Charles Judah (1968), and *To Conquer a Peace* by John Weems (1974). Unit histories are even scarcer, but a fine modern work, *Zach Taylor's Little Army* (1963), has been written by Edward Nichols.

Operations outside the two main theaters are treated in James Cutts's *Conquest of California and New Mexico* (1847) and Ralph Twitchell's *Military Occupation of the Territory of New Mexico from 1846 to 1851* (1909), and George Gibson's *Journal of a Soldier under Kearny and Doniphan* (1935) provides a firsthand account of Alexander Doniphan's expedition into Chihuahua. Bauer's *Surfboats and Horse Marines* (1969) gives good coverage of naval operations.

1848-1860

The Mexican War not only sealed American claims to Texas but also secured a huge region extending west to the Pacific. At the same time the Buchanan-Pakenham Treaty of 1846 confirmed U.S. title to the southern part of the Oregon country. This expansion of the nation across the continent brought new missions for the Army. The need to guard already settled regions in Texas, New Mexico, California, and Oregon put the Army into conflict with the Comanches, Navajoes, Rogue River Indians, Yakimas, and other tribes. At the same time, the necessity of linking these westerly settlements with the main part of the nation meant that the Great Plains could no longer be left to hostile tribes, especially the Sioux. Throughout the 1850s the Army increasingly made its presence felt against these Indians.

But despite a number of local victories, it did not succeed in pacifying the tribes. In addition to fighting Indians, the Army also had to guard the border with Mexico, not so much against an organized invasion as against raiding bandits and caudillos who flourished in this period of Mexican instability. The Army also found itself engaged in an abortive campaign against the Mormons in Utah in 1858.

Yet neither confronting a refractory sect, chasing bandits, nor fighting Indians constituted the Army's most trying task in the 1850s. The vast territories acquired during 1846-48 became enbroiled in the mounting political controversy that was rending the nation. Nor were men content merely to debate whether the west should be "free soil" or slave territory. Partisans from both sides rushed in to occupy the region with a vehemence that soon resulted in increasing violence. To the Army fell the vain and thankless task of trying to maintain order in "bleeding Kansas." In earlier domestic disturbances, the Army had given effect to Andrew Jackson's overawing of the Nullifiers of South Carolina in 1832 and had stood by, ready to act if needed, during Dorr's Rebellion in Rhode Island in 1840. But Kansas was different. This time the opponents were too determined and guidance from Washington was too irresolute to enable the Army to settle the crisis. Kansas was an ominous portent of things to come.

The Army of the 1850s was again the small peacetime establishment that characterized America's interwar years. The volunteers and many regulars were demobilized following the Mexican War, and the Army was reduced almost to its prewar level. Its growing responsibilities, however, led to a relatively significant increase in the middle of the decade. An able Secretary of War, Jefferson Davis (1853-57), moreover, saw to it that key assignments went increasingly to officers of proven ability and promise—many of whom were to hold major commands in the Civil War.

Like the Army, the Navy had many able junior officers who would prove themselves in the 1860s. The small squadrons still consisted of wooden vessels, but their mobility greatly improved through increased adoption of screw propellors for steamships. Moreover, America's first iron warship, completed in 1844, now sailed Lake Erie. The primary duty of these vessels was patrolling the west African coast for slave traders and showing the flag around the world—important and demanding tasks but ones rarely entailing hostile action.

The best account of Indian fighting during 1848-65 is Robert Utley's *Frontiersmen in Blue* (1967). Philip St. George Cooke's

Scenes and Adventures in the Army (1857), Randolph Marcy's
Thirty Years of Army Life on the Border (1866), Hazard
Stevens's Life of Isaac Ingalls Stevens (1900), and Stanley
Crocchiola's Summer (1968) concern some of the principal
Indian fighters of the period. Perspective from the ranks is
provided by Percival Lowe's Five Years a Dragoon (1906). No
adequate scholarly biography of Jefferson Davis has yet been
written, despite many attempts; Hudson Strode's three volumes
(1955-64) are the best available. Clendenen's Blood on the Border
here picks up its continuing subject of Mexican border
disturbances, and Norman Furniss covers The Mormon Conflict,
1850-1859 (1960). Useful modern studies of civil conflict in
Kansas are Jay Monaghan's Civil War on the Western Border,
1854-1865 (1955) and James Rawley's "Bleeding Kansas" (1969).
The earlier Nullification crisis in South Carolina is the subject of
William Freehling's Prelude to Civil War (1966). All this internal
strife, plus other disturbances of the period, are recounted in
Frederick Wilson's general study, Federal Aid in Domestic
Disturbances, 1787-1903 (1903). On naval matters, Samuel
Morison's Matthew C. Perry (1967) covers the prominent naval
officer of the Mexican War who opened Japan to the western
world in 1854.

The Civil War, 1861-1865

The election of Abraham Lincoln in 1860 precipitated the long-
brewing crisis between the sections. seven Southern states
seceded before his inauguration; four more plus the Indian
Territory joined them early in 1861, and elements in Missouri,
Kentucky, Maryland, and Arizona also found representation in
the resulting Confederate States of America. Irresolution
marked the initial Northern response to secession, but the firing
on Fort Sumter in April 1861 galvanized the Federals into action.
Factionalism temporarily subsided, or was overwhelmed, in the
North as men flocked to the colors to preserve the Union and
defeat the Southerners who had so long seemed to dominate the
country. Some individuals also went to war to free the slaves,
but this was not a major war aim in 1861, and for most of the men
who were actually to fight the war it never became one. The
Confederates, meantime, took the field to give substance to their
claim to the independence they considered necessary to preserve
their way of life.

To wage this war, President Lincoln nearly doubled the

Regular Army, yet he continued to rely on the old system of mobilizing short-term, mostly inexperienced volunteers to make up the overwhelming majority of Northern units. Volunteering initially produced more than enough manpower, but as the war continued bounties and then the draft became necessary to bring men into service. These varying approaches raised some 2,778,000 soldiers for the Union Army. Over a million of these men were in service at the end of the war.

The Confederacy, too, at first relied on volunteering to raise troops, but by early 1862 a draft was instituted. Over 600,000 men (peak strength) served in the Confederate Army. Unlike the Federal force, whose numbers progressively grew, the Southern army reached its maximum level in 1863. Thereafter, casualties, war weariness, and a dwindling manpower pool steadily eroded its strength. One continuing advantage, however, was that once the war was under way, the South, far more than the North, channeled new recruits and draftees into existing units rather than into new outfits, thus letting the new men benefit from serving alongside veterans.

Another great advantage the South enjoyed was the high quality of its top military leadership. Robert E. Lee, "Stonewall" Jackson, and Bedford Forrest stand preeminent among a galaxy of able Conferederate generals. The North, too, increasingly entrusted responsibility to superior commanders as the war progressed—Ulysses S. Grant, William T. Sherman, Philip H. Sheridan—but many of the earlier generals were singularly unqualified. Both sides suffered from some professional officers of doubtful competence, but the Union, much more than the Confederacy, paid the price for following the old practice of giving major commands to ambitious but inexperienced politicians.

The ability of generals and the availability and experience of manpower affected the course of the war. Geography, in turn, set the context in which these other variables functioned. The Appalachians divided the Confederacy into eastern and western theaters, and the "Father of Waters" set apart the trans-Mississippi region. The Atlantic and Gulf coasts represented lesser fronts.

The proximity of the rival capitals governed fighting in the east. The Federal army repeatedly drove for Richmond but always looked also to the security of Washington. For three years the secessionists, usually led by Lee, brilliantly parried these thrusts but failed to secure long-range advantages from their successes. Southern invasions of the North, moreover, were invariably defeated. Grant broke this stalemate in 1864 with a combination of relentless strategic pressure and powerful tactical blows that deprived the Confederates of strategic mobility and then pummeled them into submission. Absorbing terrible losses of his own, the Union General in Chief dominated the strategic situation in the east from the Wilderness through Petersburg. At Appomattox he reaped the fruits of this mode of warfare.

Federal troops achieved earlier success in the west. Many navigable rivers there facilitated penetration of the Southern heartland by early 1862. A great Confederate offensive all along the line from Virginia to Missouri that autumn only temporarily halted the Northern drive and was eventually defeated on all fronts. The following year saw major Federal victories at Vicksburg and Chattanooga, and 1864 was highlighted strategically by Sherman's drive from Chattanooga to Savannah and tactically by George H. Thomas's victory at Nashville. The fourth year of the war also saw Northern armies no longer acting disjointedly. Grant made sure that western armies took the offensive simultaneously with his own advance in the east. The resulting pressure on all major fronts denied the Confederates the opportunity to carry out their old practice of weakening quiescent areas to concentrate against a single, advancing Union army. Eventually the pressure proved too great, and the Confederacy collapsed. It is no coincidence that the two major western armies east of the Mississippi surrendered less than a month after Lee did.

Only in the trans-Mississippi country did the Confederates enjoy limited success. Their first-class forces, admittedly, lost Missouri, northern Arkansas, and small portions of Louisiana and Texas and were repeatedly repulsed in attempting to retake those areas. Even so, they did frustrate Union efforts to overrun the entire region, and eventually the Northerners settled for a strategic stalemate and drew forces off to more crucial regions east of the river. Victories in those more important theaters, in turn, rendered illusory the fancied security of the Trans-Mississippi Department. Finally, faced with the prospect of taking on the entire Federal army, Confederate forces there simply disintegrated in May and June 1865 in one of the greatest collapses in American military history.

Like the trans-Mississippi area, the coastal regions were not fronts for major Northern advances. The Union army's primary effort was devoted to closing off ports—the only sure way of making the blockade effective. From these coastal enclaves the

Federals occasionally raided the interior but rarely launched major offensives. Once Grant became General in Chief, moreover, he withdrew many units from these seaboard operations to join the main effort in Virginia. The end of the war, nevertheless, found most Confederate ports in Union hands.

In addition to these successes on the fighting fronts, the Union came off better in the foreign and domestic arenas. Northern diplomatic efforts to reduce European aid to the South succeeded far better than Confederate attempts to secure foreign recognition and intervention. On the home front, too, the strong and thriving Union economy proved better suited to fighting a protracted war than did its Confederate counterpart. Heroic Southern efforts to overcome shortages could not surmount the handicap of a weak economic base, overwhelmingly agricultural, minimally industrial. The resulting shortages weakened both civilian and military morale, and the government only worsened the problem by allowing dissent to spread. The North, in contrast, showed little reluctance in suppressing those who undermined the war effort.

These relative strengths and weaknesses, at home and at the fighting front, led to total Federal victory by the spring of 1865. The Confederacy was dead and with it the doctrine of secession. Slavery, too, died with the end of the conflict. From the war emerged a true union—not merely a union preserved but a union strengthened militarily, politically, economically, and diplomatically, a force increasingly to be reckoned with in world affairs.

The magnitude of the Civil War and the significance of its results make it the most important event in American military history in the middle years. As such, it deserves much study and has generated a rich literature. The war, in fact, is one of the most written-about events in history. The government itself entered the military history field for the first time by publishing several massive documentary compilations: *War of the Rebellion: A Compilation of the Official Records of the Union and Confederate Armies* (1880-1901), *Official Records of the Union and Confederate Navies* (1894-1922), *Medical and Surgical History of the War of the Rebellion* (1870-88), and *Official Army Register of the Volunteer Force of the United States* (1865-67). Although far from exhaustive, these splendid sources form the starting place for all scholarly research on the subject.

Synthesized general histories of the war appeared hard on the close of the conflict and have continued ever since. *History of the Civil War in America* by the Count of Paris (1875-88), *The Story of the Civil War* by John Codman Ropes (1894-1913), and *History*

of the United States from the Compromise of 1850 by James Ford
Rhodes (1928) stand out among these early works. Best of the
modern studies is Allan Nevins's eight-volume *Ordeal of the
Union* (1947-71). Frank Vandiver's *Their Tattered Flags* (1970)
offers a superb account of all facets of Confederate history,
especially military history. E. Merton Coulter's *The Confederate
States of America* (1950), in contrast, virtually ignores military
aspects but is good for other dimensions of the Confederate
experience. James G. Randall and David Donald have prepared a
standard textbook, *The Civil War and Reconstruction* (1961).
Useful general reference works, though not synthesized histories, are Mark Boatner's *Civil War Dictionary* (1959) and E. B.
Long's *Civil War Day by Day* (1971). A good overview of
changing historiographic interpretations in such writings—from
the postwar nationalist school, through the reconciliationists at
the turn of the century and the "needless war" revisionists of the
1930s, to the more sympathetic scholars since World War II—is
provided by Thomas Pressly's *Americans Interpret Their Civil
War* (1954).

Closely related to general histories are campaign and battle
narratives. The chief collective works of that genre are *Battles
and Leaders of the Civil War* (1887-88), edited by R. U. Johnson
and C. C. Buel, Scribner's *Campaigns of the Civil War* (1881-83),
and the *Military Historical Society of Massachusetts Papers*
(1885-1918). The *Southern Historical Society Papers*
(1876-1959), *Confederate Veteran* (1893-1932), and publications
of various commanderies of the Military Order of the Loyal
Legion contain both battle accounts and personal narratives.
Among individual battle studies, John Bigelow's *Chancellorsville* (1910) is a classic. Good recent works are Edwin
Coddington's *Gettysburg* (1968), Glenn Tucker's *Chickamauga*
(1961), and Ludwell Johnson's *Red River Campaign* (1958).

Besides that class of work, numerous volumes are available on
personalities. Many prominent commanders on both sides wrote
their reminiscences: Grant's *Personal Memoirs* (1885-86),
Sherman's *Memoirs* (1875), Sheridan's *Personal Memoirs*
(1902), Benjamin F. Butler's *Book* (1892), George B. McClellan's
Own Story (1887), David D. Porter's *Incidents and Anecdotes*
(1885), John M. Schofield's *Forty-Six Years in the Army* (1897),
Oliver Otis Howard's *Autobiography* (1907), to name but a few
Unionists.

From the Southern side we have Jefferson Davis's *Rise and Fall
of the Confederate Government* (1881), Joseph E. Johnston's
Narrative of Military Operations (1874), Alfred Roman's

Military Operations of General Beauregard (ghost-written by General Beauregard himself—1884), Porter Alexander's *Military Memoirs of a Confederate* (1907), Jubal A. Early's *Autobiographical Sketch* (1912), John B. Hood's *Advance and Retreat* (1880), James Longstreet's *From Manassas to Appomattox* (1896), Raphael Semmes's *Memoirs of Service Afloat* (1869), and Richard Taylor's *Destruction and Reconstruction* (1879).

Even more plentiful are biographies of major leaders. Douglas Southall Freeman's *Lee* (1934-35) and *Lee's Lieutenants* (1942-44) are but the best of such studies. Other noteworthy biographies are T. Harry William's *Beauregard* (1955), Grady McWhiney's *Bragg* (1969-), William C. Davis's *Breckinridge* (1974), Charles Lewis's *Farragut* (1941-43), John Wyeth's and also Robert Henry's *Forrest* (1899 and 1944, respectively), Lloyd Lewis's *Grant* (1950) and Bruce Catton's *Grant* (1960-69), Francis A. Walker's *Hancock* (1894), Nathaniel Hughes's *Hardee* (1965), Hall Bridge's *Harvey Hill* (1961), G. F. R. Henderson's and also Frank Vandiver's *Jackson* (1898 and 1957, respectively), Charles Roland's *Albert Sidney Johnston* (1964), Carl Sandburg's and also John G. Nicolay and John Hay's *Lincoln* (1925-39 and 1890, respectively), Warren Hassler's *McClellan* (1957), Albert Castel's *Price* (1968), William Lamers's *Rosecrans* (1961), Lloyd Lewis's *Sherman* (1932), Joseph Park's *Kirby Smith* (1954), Francis McKinney's and also Wilbur Thomas's *Thomas* (1961 and 1964, respectively), and Robert Hartje's *Van Dorn* (1967). Ezra Warner's *Generals in Gray* (1959) and *Generals in Blue* (1964) are indispensible collective biographies of all Confederate and Union general officers. Provocative interpretative studies of the Northern high command are found in *Lincoln and His Generals* by T. Harry Williams (1952) and *Lincoln Finds a General* by Kenneth P. Williams (1949-59).

Besides these works on leaders, numerous personal narratives of junior officers and enlisted men are available. Two fine modern studies are Bell Wiley's *Johnny Reb* (1943) and *Billy Yank* (1952). Closely related to all such books on persons are collections of letters and diaries. Foremost of numerous such volumes are ongoing editions of *The Papers of Jefferson Davis*, edited by Haskell Monroe and James McIntosh (1971-); *The Papers of Ulysses S. Grant*, edited by John Simon (1967-); plus the earlier *Collected Works of Abraham Lincoln*, edited by Roy Basler (1953-55).

Battle studies and personal narratives blend in another genre, the unit history. From company level to army level, veterans wrote histories of their outfits—particularly for Federal commands; Secessionists, surprisingly, published far fewer such works. Modern writers, in addition, have occasionally undertaken such studies, of which Catton's *Army of the Potomac* trilogy (1951-53), Thomas Connelly's *Army of Tennessee* (1967-71), and Leslie Anders's *Eighteenth Missouri* (1968) are among the best. Charles Dornbusch's three-volume bibliography (1961-72) is a good, though not complete, guide to these numerous works.

Several other classes of publication may be touched upon briefly. Fred A. Shannon's *Organization and Administration of the Union Army* (1928) and Frederick Dyer's *Compendium* (1908) are useful works on the Northern army. Nothing comparable exists for Southern forces; *Confederate Military History* (edited by Clement Evans in 1899) is worthwhile in its way but hardly fills the void. Francis Miller's *Photographic History* (1911) remains preeminent among several pictorial histories of the war. Virgil Jones's recent *Civil War at Sea* (1960-62) plus the U.S. Navy's official *Civil War Naval Chronology* (1961-66) are helpful introductions to naval operations. The technological development and procurement of weapons are treated in *Lincoln and the Tools of War* by Robert Bruce (1956) and *Arming the Union* by Carl Davis (1973), while Warren Ripley thoroughly catalogs *Artillery and Ammunition of the Civil War* (1970). Dudley Cornish's *Sable Arm* (1956), James McPherson's *The Negro's Civil War* (1965), and Benjamin Quarles's *The Negro in the Civil War* (1953) all cover black soldiers in blue. Annie Abel's study is still the best on *The American Indian as Slaveholder and Secessionist* (1915). Frank Owsley's *King Cotton Diplomacy* (1959) is a standard history. His *States Rights in the Confederacy* (1925), along with Charles Ramsdell's *Behind the Lines* (1944), Albert Moore's *Conscription and Conflict* (1924), and Mary Massey's *Refugee Life* (1964) shed light on the Confederate domestic front, while James McCague's *Second Rebellion* (1968) covers the New York city draft riots that were the most flagrant manifestation of Northern dissent. Finally, David Donald compiled five challenging essays, *Why the North Won the Civil War* (1960).

The foregoing summary is but a brief introduction to the literature on the Civil War. Several bibliographies offer ready guides to further reading: Dornbusch's work, *Civil War Books* by Allan Nevins et al. (1967-69), and *Civil War History*'s continuing annual listing of articles.

1865-1898

The end of the Civil War left the United States with a large, experienced, well-led Army. For the first time, leaders in Washington considered keeping a good part of this force on duty to achieve additional national aims: garrisoning the South, confronting the French in Mexico, and conquering the western Indians. This new approach, in turn, introduced what would become a recurring response after subsequent American wars— overwhelming pressure from the civilian populace and from the volunteers themselves to release the soldiers now that the war was over. Getting volunteer units to go west to fight Indians proved virtually impossible, and only a relatively few regiments remained to occupy the old Confederacy. The War Department had no recourse but to disband the volunteers in 1865-66. Although these units were mustered out, many individual soldiers wanted to remain in service and were used to double the size of the Regular Army from thirty to sixty regiments—the largest percentage expansion of a peacetime U.S. Army until the 1940s. Congressional parsimony later led to the disbanding of some new units and the skeletonizing of others, but, even so, the Regular Army was larger than ever before. Still more important, its officer corps of battle-tested Civil War veterans was almost fully professional.

For a time many regular units found themselves garrisoning the South, particularly during Congressional Reconstruction. But as more states were "redeemed," the Army was withdrawn, and by 1877 occupation duty had ceased. Troops—more often militia than regulars—were also used occasionally to guard against striking laborers in the years following the Civil War. Other units had to be kept on the Mexican border, once more to protect the frontier from the consequences of the turmoil that followed the collapse of the empire of Maximilian, whose overthrow was itself a result of a powerful American show of force against his French supporters in 1865.

But all these duties were incidental to the Army's principal mission after the Civil War, pacifying the west. Insufficient manpower and equipment and continuing vacillation in Washington between taking a stern or conciliatory approach toward the Indians handicapped but did not halt efforts to pacify the frontier. Once determined campaigns against them began, the prominent warlike tribes—Sioux, Cheyenne, Arapaho, Kiowa,

Comanche, Apache—under such able chiefs as Red Cloud, Gall, Crazy Horse, Satanta, Cochise, and Geronimo could not hold their own against Indian fighters like George Crook, Nelson A. Miles, and Ranald S. Mackenzie. Fetterman's massacre, the murder of General E. R. S. Canby, and Little Big Horn were but aberrations from the main course of events, which saw the Army, more by strenuous campaigning than by pitched battles, defeat and confine to reservations every hostile tribe. Much of the west was pacified and was receiving statehood by the 1880s. The crushing of the last major Indian uprising in 1890–91 symbolized the end of the struggle for control of the continent which had raged for nearly four hundred years.

As land warfare in the United States drew to a close, foreign involvement grew. The acquisition of some Pacific islands (principally Hawaii in 1898), the quest for others, and the mounting insistence on European respect for the Monroe Doctrine in the western hemisphere increased American presence abroad and occasionally led to disputes with other countries. The conflicts were largely diplomatic, not military, but the Navy, as the available forward force, sometimes lent credibility to statesmen's declarations. Increasing conversion to modern armored vessels greatly improved the Navy's strength during this period. Important technological changes came to the Army, too, late in these years through adoption of magazine rifles, Gatling guns, and smokeless powder. Tactical doctrine also improved. Both services, moreover, became more professional through development of branch and applied practice schools, through the growth of military literature, and, indeed, through rising consciousness among regular officers of their own special professional status.

The literature on Reconstruction is extensive, much of it of recent origin. Two works concentrate on military aspects of that period, James Sefton's *The United States Army and Reconstruction* (1967) and Otis Singletary's *Negro Militia and Reconstruction* (1957). Frederick Wilson, too, touches on the Army's role in Reconstruction and in labor disturbances in the 1870s and 1890s, and Robert Bruce sets the context for the bloody strikes during the Hayes administration in *1877: Year of Violence* (1959). Brian Jenkins's study of *Fenians and Anglo-American Relations During Reconstruction* (1969) centers around the abortive Irish invasion of Canada from the United States. The story of the rise and fall of Maximilian lies outside the scope of this chapter, but the related American show of force is covered in Sheridan's own memoirs, Carl Rister's *Border Command* (1944), and Clendenen's 1969 work.

Numerous books have been written on the Indian wars, besides many historical and ethnological studies of the various tribes. Robert Utley's *Frontier Regulars . . . 1866-1891* (1974) provides the best overall account of the Army's conquest of the hostile tribes. Two other modern studies are S. L. A. Marshall's *Crimsoned Prairie* (1972) and Odie Faulk's *Crimson Desert* (1974), the former somewhat marred by errors. Other useful general accounts are Robert Athearn's *William Tecumseh Sherman and the Settlement of the West* (1956), Fairfax Downey's *Indian-Fighting Army* (1941), Stephen Longstreet's *War Cries on Horseback* (1970), Martin Schmitt and Dee Brown's *Fighting Indians of the West* (1948), and Paul Wellman's *Indian Wars of the West* (1954). Modern treatments of specific operations include Merrill Beal's *Chief Joseph and the Nez Perce War* (1963), Harvey Chalmers's *The Last Stand of the Nez Perce* (1962), Faulk's *The Geronimo Campaign* (1969), Ralph Ogle's *Federal Control of the Western Apaches, 1848-1886* (1970), Keith Murray's *The Modocs and Their War* (1959), William Leckie's *The Military Conquest of the Southern Plains* (1963), Wilbur Nye's *Plains Indian Raiders* (1968), Utley's *The Last Days of the Sioux Nation* (1963), and J. W. Vaughn's *The Reynolds Campaign on Powder River* (1961). The extensive literature on Little Big Horn and George A. Custer is virtually a separate genre; William Graham's *The Story of Little Big Horn* (1962) and *The Custer Myth* (1953) may be noted. The Indian point of view, overemphasized to the detriment of balanced perspective, is presented in Dee Brown's *Bury My Heart at Wounded Knee* (1970).

Prominent Indian fighting commanders like Andrew S. Burt, Eugene A. Carr, Crook, Howard, Mackenzie, Miles, Sheridan, and John Pope are represented through autobiographies, recollections by their subordinates, and studies by modern scholars: Merrill Mattes's *Burt* (1960), James King's *Carr* (1963), Crook's *Autobiography* (1960), John G. Bourke's and also Charles King's *Crook* (1891 and 1890, respectively), Howard's *Autobiography* and *Life and Experiences among our Hostile Indians* (both 1907), Ernest Wallace's edition of Mackenzie's correspondence (1967) and Robert G. Carter's *Mackenzie* (1935), Miles's *Recollections* (1896) and *Memoirs* (1911), Sheridan's *Personal Memoirs*, Carl Rister's *Border Command* (1944), and Richard Ellis's *Pope* (1970). The men in the ranks who fought Indians are covered excellently in Don Rickey's *Forty Miles a Day on Beans and Hay* (1963). John Carroll's *Black Military Experience in the American West* (1971), Arlen Fowler's *Black Infantry in the West* (1971), and Leckie's *Buffalo Soldiers* (1967) each deal with the Negro soldier on the frontier. Jack Foner's *The*

United States Soldier between Two War (1970) is a general
treatment of enlisted men throughout the Army during 1865-98
from the perspective of improving conditions of service.

The flowering of military professionalism is traced in many
works. One example of military writing which was quite
influential during this period is Emory Upton's *The Armies of
Asia and Europe* (1878). The various military schools established at Fort Leavenworth in these years are treated in the
appropriate chapter of Elvid Hunt and Walter Lorence's history
of that post (1937). Albert Gleaves's *Stephen B. Luce* (1925)
concerns the founder of the Naval War College, established in
1884. Luce is one of many officers of "the naval aristocracy,"
covered in Peter Karsten's book of that title (1972). Richard
West's *Admirals of American Empire* (1948) deals with four
prominent naval officers of the period, while B. F. Cooling's
Tracy (1973) focuses on Benjamin Harrison's Secretary of the
Navy, who helped develop the major naval shipbuilding
program. Such changes in naval technology and doctrine are
more broadly treated in Walter Herrick's *American Naval
Revolution* (1966). Increasing involvement of the United States
in the Pacific and the Caribbean—in outlook, rationale, and
practice—is the subject of Kenneth Hagan's *American Gunboat
Diplomacy and the Old Navy, 1877-1889* (1973), Ernest May's
Imperial Democracy (1961), and John Grenville and George
Young's *Politics, Strategy, and American Diplomacy . . .
1873-1917* (1966).

Spanish-American War and Philippine Insurrection, 1898-1907

The seven years following the battle of Wounded Knee were
relatively quiet for the Army. But 1898 brought a new challenge,
fighting a European power overseas. The recently modernized
Navy played the major role in this war with Spain in winning the
decisive battles of Manila Bay and Santiago. The Army, too,
readied itself for a major conflict, once more accepting large
numbers of volunteers, but only a small proportion of troops,
mostly regulars, actually embarked for the war zone. The major
expedition hardly distinguished itself in Cuba, although it did
receive the surrender of Santiago. Spain's increasing realization
of the futility of continued fighting once her fleets were
destroyed meanwhile assured the success of other Army

expeditions to Puerto Rico and the Philippines. Military leadership in this conflict, mostly by aging Civil War veterans, was not spectacular, and scandals in the War Department plus the frightful mortality caused by tropical diseases clouded the luster of victory. The benefits of the Spanish-American War were less military than social and diplomatic. The willingness of Southerners, many of them ex-Confederates, to don the blue and fight their country's battles underscored the healing of the divisive wounds of civil war. At the same time the acquisition of an overseas empire, along with a growing consciousness of national power, interjected the United States more actively into the world arena.

This new imperial role gave the Army more responsibilities after the Spanish-American War than during it. The temporary occupation of Cuba until 1902 and the permanent acquisition of Puerto Rico created the need for military government of civilian areas. And the decision to annex the Philippines brought America into conflict with Filipinos aspiring for independence. Smoldering animosity between the two sides erupted into open warfare in 1899 and continued intermittently for nearly a decade. The insurrectionists proved no match for the regulars and state and U.S. volunteers in major battles and soon resorted to guerrilla tactics. This irregular warfare, far different from what the Army had known against the Indians, raised new problems of bringing the enemy to terms. Dissension in the United States over the conduct of operations—indeed over the desirability of acquiring an empire—further complicated the Army's task. Even so, it managed to pacify the Philippines early in the twentieth century, often by stern measures. Once peace returned, the Army, the civil government, and the natives came increasingly to cooperate in what would become growing amity between the two peoples.

No comprehensive history of the Spanish-American War, drawing together all available sources, has been written. Allan Keller's recent work (1969) in the Compact History series, however, is adequate as a survey, and French E. Chadwick's three volumes, *The Relations of the United States and Spain* (1909–11), still command respect as the best of the immediate postwar studies. Walter Millis's *Martial Spirit* (1931), though often cited, is flawed with the antimilitary prejudices so fashionable in the 1930s. Two other noteworthy works, general in time span but more specific in theme, are Frank Freidel's pictorial *Splendid Little War* (1958) and H. W. Morgan's *America's Road to Empire* (1967). In addition, numerous documentary sources—Miles's *Annual Report, 1898* (1898), The Adjutant General's Office's *Correspondence Relating to the War with Spain . . . Including the Insurrection in the Philippines and the China Relief Expedition* (1898–1902), and congressional documents on the investigation of the War Department (1900) and on the court of inquiry into Admiral Winfield Schley's service in the Caribbean in 1898 (1902)—are rich with primary material from which the reader may begin synthesizing his own understanding of the war.

Besides these general and official sources, many personal narratives and unit histories by participants are in print. Several works have also come from modern scholars: Virgil Jones's *Roosevelt's Rough Riders* (1971) and Willard Gatewood's *"Smoked Yankees"* (1971), for example. Graham Cosmas's *Army for Empire* (1971) offers a fine account of American land forces as a whole. Major naval leaders are well represented by memoirs and biographies: John Long's *New American Navy* (1903), George Dewey's *Autobiography* (1913), Adelbert Dewey's *Life and Letters of Admiral Dewey* (1899), Ronald Spector's *Dewey* (1974), and Winfield Schley's *Forty-five Years Under the Flag* (1904). Surprisingly, few comparable works have come from the Army high command. Russell Alger, Nelson Miles, Joe Wheeler, and James Harrison Wilson, however, have published their recollections: *The Spanish-American War* (1901), *Serving the Republic* (1911), *Santiago Campaign* (1898), and *Under the Old Flag* (1912), respectively.

A good account of the occupation of Puerto Rico is yet to be written. Most campaign studies focus on Cuba; of these, Herbert Sargent's three-volume *Campaign of Santiago de Cuba* (1907) and Jack Dierks's more recent *Leap to Arms* (1970) are among the best. F. D. Millet's *Expedition to the Philippines* (1899) concentrates on the capture of Manila, but most accounts of fighting in the archipelago cover the insurrection as well as the Spanish-American War. Almost all such studies were written shortly after the conflict: James Blount's *American Occupation of the Philippines, 1898–1912* (1913), Charles B. Elliott's *The Philippines to the End of the Military Regime* (1916), Karl Faust's *Campaigning in the Philippines* (1899), James LeRoy's *The Americans in the Philippines* (1914), and Alden March's *Conquest of the Philippines* (1899). Teodoro Kalaw's *The Philippine Insurrection* and William Sexton's *Soldiers in the Sun* appeared in 1925 and 1939, respectively. Unit histories and personal memoirs, such as Frederick Funston's autobiographical *Memories of Two Wars* (1911), are necessarily old, and few biographies have been written recently; Hermann Hagedorn's life of Leonard Wood came out in 1931. More recent studies include Uldarico Baclagon's *Philippine Campaigns* (1952) from the Filipino perspective and the Garel Grunder and William Livezey volume, *The Philippines and the United States* (1951), a useful overview of nearly five decades of American presence in the islands. But the latter book, like Ernest Dupuy and William Bauman's *Little Wars . . . 1798 to 1920* (1968), surveys a broad period and does not concentrate on the insurrection. Two other recent publications—Leon Wolff's anti-imperialist account, *Little Brown Brother* (1960), and the Marxist interpretation of William Pomeroy's *American Neo-Colonialism* (1970)—are clearly inadequate as military history. Much other writing of late has been less military than political and concerns the domestic debate over imperialism; a useful summary of the arguments of the original protagonists is found in Richard Welch's compilation, *Imperialists vs. Anti-Imperialists* (1972). Of modern studies which are military, the best is John Gates's *Schoolbooks and Krags* (1973), which ably focuses on the Army's means for pacifying the islands but does not provide a comprehensive account of operations. A good scholarly military history of warfare in the Philippines during 1898-1907, drawing upon all available sources, remains to be written. Several such studies are under way, however.

1900-1916

The first sixteen years of the new century brought the Army and Navy ever-mounting responsibilities in foreign lands. Besides pacifying the islands, American troops joined the European powers and Japan in raising the siege of the Peking legations in 1900. Closer to home, the Army, Navy, and Marines gave effect to the expanded interpretation of the Monroe Doctrine, whereby the United States intervened in Latin American countries to end disorder that might otherwise result in European intervention. Such intervention also protected the United States' own strategic, political, and economic interests in the Caribbean. Mexico in particular proved troublesome as the civil wars that followed the ouster of Porfirio Diaz repeatedly embroiled American interests. United States forces occupied Vera Cruz in 1914 to facilitate the overthrow of Victoriano Huerta, and two years later John J. Pershing, the rising man of the Army, led a major punitive expedition deep into northern Mexico in pursuit of bandits who had raided into New Mexico. At the same time a large army of regulars and National Guardsmen concentrated in the southwest in case full fledged war should break out. But the difficulty of bringing the bandits to battle, President Woodrow Wilson's reluctance to press operations in the face of official Mexican displeasure, and growing concern over the war then raging in Europe prevented a second Mexican war. But the Mexican border disturbances did give the Army, including the National Guard, valuable experience in mobilizing and assembling large bodies of troops; this proved useful when the United States entered the First World War in 1917.

The availability of the National Guard, newly brought under more uniform federal standards, was but one of many reforms which stand out even more than field operations in American military history of 1900-1916. Emory Upton's far-reaching interpretive study, *The Military Policy of the United States*, written in 1880, was resurrected in 1904 and came increasingly to influence military thinking. Secretary of War Elihu Root modernized the War Department, replaced the Commanding General of the Army with a General Staff modeled on European patterns, improved the structure and content of the Army school system, and founded the Army War College for advanced study and planning in military theory and practice. Conducting large-scale field maneuvers and creating organic peacetime brigades and divisions were other major advances of this period. Even outside the armed forces, civilians concerned over limited readiness to fight a major foreign power voluntarily underwent military training in the so-called Plattsburg Movement. Despite presidential reservations, the Army actively cooperated in this program to improve military capabilities.

Most military operations of this period have been covered by modern authors. William Braisted's two volumes trace the role of *The U.S. Navy in the Pacific, 1897-1922* (1958, 1971). Chester Tan's *Boxer Catastrophe* (1955) and Victor Purcell's *Boxer Uprising* (1963) each give fine accounts of the China Relief Expedition. Monro MacCloskey's *Reilly's Battery* (1969) and William Carter's *Life of Lieutenant General Chaffee* (1917) are also useful on the China episode. Allan Millett's able study of the *Military Occupation of Cuba, 1906-1909* (1968), Robert Quirk's account of *Woodrow Wilson and the Occupation of Vera Cruz* (1967), and Jack Sweetman's narrative, *The Landing at Vera Cruz* (1968), cover specific American interventions in Latin America, while Dana Munro provides a more general account in *Intervention and Dollar Diplomacy in the Caribbean, 1900-1921* (1964). Clendenen's works, *The United States and Pancho Villa* (1961) as well as *Blood on the Border*, remain the best on the

Mexican border disturbances. Frank Tompkins's *Chasing Villa* (1934) and Herbert Mason's more recent *Great Pursuit* (1970) also provide good accounts of the punitive expedition. The world tour of the American battle fleet in 1907 is covered in Samuel Carter's *Great White Fleet* (1971); the fleet's commander, Robley D. Evans, also published two volumes of reminiscences of that operation and his other service (1901 and 1911). The intellectual theory underlying that cruise and other naval shows of force is discussed in works by and about America's great advocate of sea power around the turn of the century, Alfred Thayer Mahan: W. D. Puleston's *Mahan* (1939), William Livezey's *Mahan on Sea Power* (1947), and Mahan's own writings—especially the far-reaching *Influence of Sea Power Upon History* and also the modern three-volume edition of his *Letters and Papers* (1975). The Army's comparable advocate is treated in Stephen Ambrose's *Upton and the Army* (1964). Some of the changes implemented early in the twentieth century are treated in James Hewes's *From Root to McNamara: Army Organization and Administration, 1900-1963* (1975), Jim Dan Hill's *History of the National Guard* (1964), Otto Nelson's *National Security and the General Staff* (1946), and George S. Pappas's *Prudens Futuri: the U.S. Army War College, 1901-1967* (1967). The later Plattsburg Movement is recounted in John Clifford's *The Citizen Soldiers* (1972).

Philip Jessup in 1938 and Richard Leopold in 1954 published biographies of Secretary Root, who implemented many of these reforms, and Mabel Deutrich gives a fine account of the controversial Adjutant General of the period, Fred Ainsworth, in *Struggle for Supremacy* (1962). The autobiographical *Reminiscences* of Adolphus W. Greely (1927) and *Memories of Hugh Scott* (1928) offer insight into the careers of two prominent generals of that era. The role of these and other senior military leaders in influencing and supporting involvement abroad is investigated in Richard Challener's *Admirals, Generals, and American Foreign Policy* (1973). Presidents, too, affect foreign policy. The two most influential of the early twentieth century, Theodore Roosevelt and Woodrow Wilson, have been written on voluminously. Two studies giving valuable perspective on their roles in military affairs are Howard Beale's *Theodore Roosevelt and the Rise of America to World Power* (1956) and Arthur Link's continuing biography, *Wilson* (1947-). Complementing material on leaders is Marvin Fletcher's work on Negro troops at the turn of the century, *The Black Soldier and Officer in the United States Army, 1891-1917* (1974).

The war of 1898 (with the resulting empire), the increasing involvement in the Caribbean, and the confrontations with Mexico underscored the new direction of American interest. The middle years, which had witnessed the expansion and solidification of the nation, were drawing to a close, and portents of active reinvolvement in foreign affairs became ever more numerous. World War I starkly emphasized this new trend, and thereafter the essence of United States military history centers around the nation's active or passive role on the world scene. The year 1916 marked the dividing line between the middle years and the modern period of American military history.

The middle years had seen the armed forces grow from 16,743 men in 1816 to 179,376 a century later. Quality, professionalism, and national rather than state orientation, too, had markedly increased over that period. The growth both derived from and facilitated the corresponding development of the country itself into a political and economic giant spanning the continent, strong at home and increasingly influential abroad. Conquering and pacifying the vast domain in which this expansion occurred—and playing a decisive role in resolving the sectional differences which threatened national development—were the armed forces' great achievements of these years. The military accomplishments of the period were important and far reaching. The literature on the subject is correspondingly rich.

Bibliography

Abel, Annie H. The American Indian as Slaveholder and Secessionist . . . 3 vols. Cleveland: Arthur H. Clark, 1915.

Alexander, Edward Porter. Military Memoirs of A Confederate . . . New York: Scribner's 1907.

Alger, Russell A. The Spanish-American War. New York and London: Harper, 1901.

Ambrose, Stephen E. Upton and the Army. Baton Rouge: La. State Univ. Press, 1964.

Anders, Leslie. The Eighteenth Missouri. Indianapolis, Ind.: Bobbs-Merrill, 1968.

Armstrong, Perry A. The Sauks and the Black Hawk War . . . Springfield, Ill.: H. W. Rokker, 1887.

Athearn, Robert G. William Tecumseh Sherman and the Settlement of the West. Norman: Univ. of Okla. Press, 1956.

Baclagon, Uldarico. Philippine Campaigns. Manila: Graphic House, 1952.

Bauer, K. Jack. The Mexican War (1846-1848). New York: Macmillan, 1974.

———. Surfboats and Horse Marines: U.S. Naval Operations in the Mexican War, 1846-1848. Annapolis, Md.: United States Naval Institute, 1969.

Beal, Merrill D. "I Will Fight No More Forever": Chief Joseph and the Nez Perce War. Seattle: Univ. of Wash. Press, 1963.

Beale, Howard. *Theodore Roosevelt and the Rise of America to World Power.* Baltimore: Johns Hopkins Univ. Press, 1956.

Beers, Henry P. *The Western Military Frontier, 1815-1846.* Philadelphia: Henry P. Beers, 1935.

Bigelow, John. *The Campaign of Chancellorsville . . .* New Haven: Yale Univ. Press, 1910.

Bill, Alfred H. *Rehearsal for Conflict: The War with Mexico, 1846-1848.* New York: A. A. Knopf, 1947.

Birkhimer, William E. *Historical Sketch of the Organization, Administration, Materiel and Tactics of the Artillery, United States Army.* Washington: James J. Chapman, 1884.

Black Hawk. *Black Hawk: An Autobiography.* Edited by Donald Jackson. Urbana: Univ. of Ill. Press, 1964.

Blount, James H. *The American Occupation of the Philippines, 1898-1912.* New York and London: Putnam's, 1913.

Boatner, Mark. *The Civil War Dictionary.* New York: David McKay, 1959.

Bourke, John G. *On the Border With Crook.* New York: Scribner's 1891.

Bourne, Kenneth. *Britain and the Balance of Power in North America, 1815-1908.* Berkeley: Univ. of Calif. Press, 1967.

Brady, Cyrus Townsend. *Northwestern Fights and Fighters.* New York: McClure, 1907.

Braisted, William R. *The U.S. Navy in the Pacific, 1897-1922.* 2 vols. Austin: Univ. of Texas Press, 1958-71.

Bridges, Hal. *Lee's Maverick General, Daniel Harvey Hill.* New York: McGraw-Hill, 1961.

Brooks, Nathan Covington. *A Complete History of the Mexican War: Its Causes, Conduct, and Consequences . . .* Reprint. Chicago: Rio Grande Press, 1965.

Brown, Dee. *Bury My Heart at Wounded Knee: An Indian History of the American West.* New York: Holt, Rinehart, and Winston, 1970.

Bruce, Robert V. *1877: Year of Violence.* Indianapolis, Ind.: Bobbs-Merrill, 1959.

——. *Lincoln and the Tools of War.* Indianapolis, Ind.: Bobbs-Merrill, 1956.

Butler, Benjamin F. . . . *Butler's Book.* Boston: A. M. Thayer, 1892.

Calhoun, John C. *The Papers of John C. Calhoun.* Edited by Robert L. Meriwether and W. Edwin Hemphill. Columbia: Univ. of S.C. Press, 1959-.

Campaigns of the Civil War. 16 vols. New York: Scribner's 1881-83.

Carroll, John M., ed. *The Black Military Experience in the American West.* New York: Liveright, 1971.

Carter, Robert G. *On the Border with Mackenzie. . .* Washington: Eynon Printing Company, Inc., 1935.

Carter, Samuel. *The Incredible Great White Fleet.* New York: Crowell-Collier Press, 1971.

Carter, William H. *The Life of Lieutenant General Chaffee.* Chicago: Univ. of Chicago Press, 1917.

Castaneda, Carlos E., trans. *The Mexican Side of the Texas Revolution [1836] by the Chief Mexican Participants . . .* Dallas: P. L. Turner, 1928.

Castel, Albert. *General Sterling Price and the Civil War in the West.* Baton Rouge: La. State Univ. Press, 1968.

Catton, Bruce. *The Army of the Potomac.* Garden City, N.Y.: Doubleday, 1951-53. Vol. 1, *Mr. Lincoln's Army;* Vol. 2, *Glory Road;* Vol. 3, *A Stillness at Appomattox.*

——. *Grant Moves South.* Boston: Little, Brown, 1960.

——. *Grant Takes Command.* Boston: Little, Brown, 1969.

Chadwick, French E. *The Relations of the United States and Spain: Diplomacy and The Spanish-American War*. 3 vols. New York: Scribner's, 1909-11.

Challener, Richard D. *Admirals, Generals, and American Foreign Policy*. Princeton, N.J.: Princeton Univ. Press, 1973.

Chalmers, Harvey. *The Last Stand of the Nez Perce* . . . New York: Twayne Publishers, 1962.

Chidsey, Donald B. *The War with Mexico*. New York: Crown, 1968.

Civil War History, 1955-.

Civil War Times Illustrated, 1959-.

Clarke, Dwight L. *Stephen Watts Kearny, Soldier of the West*. Norman: Univ. of Okla. Press, 1961.

Clendenen, Clarence C. *Blood on the Border: The United States Army and the Mexican Irregulars*. New York: Macmillan, 1969.

———. *The United States and Pancho Villa* . . . Ithaca, N.Y.: Cornell Univ. Press, 1961.

Clifford, John G. *The Citizen Soldiers: The Plattsburg Training Camp Movement, 1913-1920*. Lexington: Univ. Press of Ky., 1972.

Coddington, Edwin B. *The Gettysburg Campaign: A Study in Command*. New York: Scribner's 1968.

Comparato, Frank E. *Age of Great Guns* . . . Harrisburg: Stackpole, 1965.

The Confederate Veteran. 1893-1932.

Connelly, Thomas L. . . . *The Army of Tennessee* . . . 2 vols. Baton Rouge: La. State Univ. Press, 1967-71.

Connor, Seymour V., and Faulk, Odie B. *North America Divided: The Mexican War, 1846-1848*. New York: Oxford Univ. Press, 1971.

Cooke, Philip St. George. *The Conquest of New Mexico and California* . . . New York: Putnam's, 1878.

———. *Scenes and Adventures in the Army* . . . Philadelphia: Lindsay and Blakiston, 1857.

Cooling, B. F. *Benjamin Franklin Tracy* . . . Hamden, Conn.: Shoe String Press, Archon Books, 1973.

Cornish, Dudley T. *The Sable Arm* . . . New York: Longmans, Green, 1956.

Cosmas, Graham A. *An Army for Empire* . . . Columbia: Univ. of Mo. Press, 1971.

Coulter, Ellis Merton. *The Confederate States of America, 1861-1865*. Baton Rouge: La. State Univ. Press, 1950.

Crocchiola, Stanley. *E. V. Sumner* . . . *1797-1863*. Borger, Tex.: J. Hess, 1968.

Crook, George. *General George Crook, His Autobiography*. Edited by Martin F. Schmitt. Norman: Univ. of Okla. Press, 1960.

Cutts, James M. *The Conquest of California and New Mexico by the Forces of the United States* . . . Reprint. Albuquerque, N.M.: Horn and Wallace, 1965.

Davis, Carl. *Arming the Union: Small Arms in the Union Army*. Port Washington, N.Y.: Kennikat Press, 1973.

Davis, Jefferson. *The Papers of Jefferson Davis*. Edited by Haskell Monroe and James McIntosh. Baton Rouge: La. State Univ. Press, 1971-.

———. *The Rise and Fall of the Confederate Government*. 2 vols. New York: D. Appleton, 1881.

Davis, William C. *Breckinridge: Statesman, Soldier, Symbol*. Baton Rouge: La. State Univ. Press, 1974.

Deutrich, Mabel E. *Struggle for Supremacy: The Career of General Fred C. Ainsworth*. Washington: Public Affairs Press, 1962.

Dewey, Adelbert M. *The Life and Letters of Admiral Dewey* . . . New York: Woolfall, 1899.

Dewey, George. *Autobiography of George Dewey, Admiral of the Navy.* New York: Scribner's, 1913.

Dierks, Jack Cameron. *A Leap to Arms: The Cuban Campaign of 1898.* Philadelphia: Lippincott, 1970.

Donald, David. *Why the North Won the Civil War.* Baton Rouge: La. State Univ. Press, 1960.

Dornbusch, Charles E., comp. *Regimental Publications and Personal Narratives of the Civil War . . .* 3 vols. New York: New York Public Library, 1961-72.

Downey, Fairfax. *Indian-Fighting Army.* New York: Scribner's 1941.

———. *Indian Wars of the U.S. Army, 1776-1865.* Garden City, N.Y.: Doubleday, 1963.

Dufour, Charles L. *The Mexican War, a Compact History, 1846-1848.* New York: Hawthorn Books, 1968.

Dunn, J. P. *Massacres of the Mountains: A History of the Indian Wars of the Far West, 1815-1875.* New York: Harper, 1886.

Dupuy, R. Ernest, and Bauman, William H. *The Little Wars of the United States: A Compact History from 1798 to 1920 . . .* New York: Hawthorn Books, 1968.

Dyer, Frederick. *A Compendium of the War of the Rebellion . . .* Des Moines, Iowa: Dyer Publishing Company, 1908.

Early, Jubal A. . . . *Autobiographical Sketch and Narrative of the War between the States . . .* Philadelphia and London: Lippincott, 1912.

Elliott, Charles B. *The Philippines to the End of the Military Regime . . .* Indianapolis, Ind.: Bobbs-Merrill, 1916.

Elliott, Charles W. *Winfield Scott, the Soldier and the Man.* New York: Macmillan, 1937.

Ellis, Richard N. *General Pope and U.S. Indian Policy.* Albuquerque: Univ. of N.M. Press, 1970.

Evans, Clement A., ed. *Confederate Military History . . .* 12 vols. Atlanta: Confederate Publishing Company, 1899.

Evans, Robley D. *An Admiral's Log.* New York: D. Appleton, 1910.

———. *A Sailor's Log.* New York: D. Appleton, 1901.

Faulk, Odie B. *Crimson Desert: Indian Wars of the American Southwest.* New York: Oxford Univ. Press, 1974.

———. *The Geronimo Campaign.* New York: Oxford Univ. Press, 1969.

Faust, Karl Irving. *Campaigning in the Philippines.* San Francisco: Hicks-Judd, 1899.

Fletcher, Marvin E. *The Black Soldier and Officer in the United States Army, 1891-1917.* Columbia: Univ. of Mo. Press, 1974.

Foner, Jack. *The United States Soldier between Two Wars: Army Life and Reforms, 1865-1898.* New York: Humanities Press, 1970.

Foreman, Grant. *Indian Removal: The Emigration of the Five Civilized Tribes of Indians.* Norman: Univ. of Okla. Press, 1932.

Fowler, Arlen. *The Black Infantry in the West, 1869-1891.* Westport, Conn.: Greenwood Publishing Corp., 1971.

Freehling, William W. *Prelude to Civil War: The Nullification Controversy in South Carolina, 1816-1836.* New York: Harper and Row, 1966.

Freeman, Douglas Southall. *R. E. Lee: A Biography.* 4 vols. New York: Scribner's, 1934-35.

———. *Lee's Lieutenants: A Study in Command.* 3 vols. New York: Scribner's, 1942-44.

Freidel, Frank. *The Splendid Little War.* Boston: Little, Brown, 1958.

Fuller, Claud E. *The Breech-Loader in the Service, 1816-1917 . . .* New Milford, Conn.: N. Flayderman, 1965.

Funston, Frederick. *Memories of Two Wars* . . . New York: Scribner's, 1911.

Furniss, Norman. *The Mormon Conflict, 1850–1859.* New Haven: Yale Univ. Press, 1960.

Gates, John M. *Schoolbooks and Krags: The United States Army in the Philippines, 1898–1902.* Westport, Conn.: Greenwood Press, 1973.

Gatewood, Willard, ed. *"Smoked Yankees" and the Struggle for Empire: Letters from Negro Soldiers, 1898–1902.* Urbana: Univ. of Ill. Press, 1971.

Gibson, George R. *Journal of a Soldier Under Kearny and Doniphan.* Edited by Ralph P. Bieber. Glendale, Calif.: Arthur H. Clark, 1935.

Gleaves, Albert. *Life and Letters of Rear Admiral Stephen B. Luce* . . . New York and London: Putnam's, 1925.

Gluckman, Arcadi. *United States Muskets, Rifles, and Carbines.* Buffalo: Otto Ulbrich, 1948.

Goetzmann, William H. *Army Exploration in the American West, 1803–1863.* New Haven: Yale Univ. Press, 1959.

Graham, William A. *The Custer Myth: A Source Book of Custeriana.* Harrisburg: Stackpole, 1953.

———. *The Story of the Little Big Horn* . . . New York and London: Century Co., 1926.

Grant, Ulysses S. *The Papers of Ulysses S. Grant* . . . Edited by John Y. Simon. Carbondale: Southern Ill. Univ. Press, 1967–.

———. *Personal Memoirs of U. S. Grant.* 2 vols. New York: C. L. Webster, 1885–86.

Greely, Adolphus W. *Reminiscences of Adventure and Service* . . . New York: Scribner's 1927.

Grenville, John, and Young, George B. *Politics, Strategy, and American Diplomacy: Studies in Foreign Policy, 1873–1917.* New Haven: Yale Univ. Press, 1966.

Grunder, Garel, and Livezey, William. *The Philippines and the United States.* Norman: Univ. of Okla. Press, 1951.

Hagan, Kenneth J. *American Gunboat Diplomacy and the Old Navy, 1877–1889.* Westport, Conn.: Greenwood Press, 1973.

Hagedorn, Hermann. *Leonard Wood, a Biography.* 2 vols. New York: Harper, 1931.

Hamilton, Holman. *Zachary Taylor.* Indianapolis, Ind.: Bobbs-Merrill, 1941.

Hartje, Robert. *Van Dorn* . . . Nashville, Tenn.: Vanderbilt Univ. Press, 1967.

Hassler, Warren W. *General George B. McClellan* . . . Baton Rouge: La. State Univ. Press, 1957.

Henderson, George F. R. *Stonewall Jackson and the American Civil War.* 2 vols. New York: Longmans, Green, 1898.

Henry, Robert S. *"First with the Most" Forrest.* Indianapolis, Ind.: Bobbs-Merrill, 1944.

———. *The Story of the Mexican War.* Indianapolis, Ind.: Bobbs-Merrill, 1950.

Herrick, Walter. *The American Naval Revolution.* Baton Rouge: La. State Univ. Press, 1966.

Hewes, James E., Jr. *From Root to McNamara: Army Organization and Administration, 1900–1963.* Center of Military History, Special Studies. Washington: Government Printing Office, 1975.

Hill, Jim Dan. *The Minute Man in Peace and War: A History of the National Guard.* Harrisburg: Stackpole, 1964.

Hood, John B. *Advance and Retreat* . . . New Orleans: Hood Orphan Memorial Fund, 1880.

Houston, Andrew Jackson. *Texas Independence.* Houston: Anson Jones Press, 1938.

Houston, Sam. *The Writings of Sam Houston* . . . Edited by Amelia Williams and Eugene C. Barker. 7 vols. Austin: Univ. of Texas Press, 1938–42.

Howard, Oliver Otis. *Autobiography of Oliver Otis Howard* . . . 2 vols. New York: Baker and Taylor, 1907.

———. *My Life and Experiences Among Our Hostile Indians* . . . Hartford, Conn.: A. D. Worthington, 1907.

Hughes, Nathaniel C. *General William J. Hardee* . . . Baton Rouge: La. State Univ. Press, 1965.

Hunt, Elvid, and Lorence, Walter. *History of Fort Leavenworth, 1827–1937.* Fort Leavenworth: Command and General Staff School Press, 1937.

Jackson, Andrew. *Correspondence of Andrew Jackson.* Edited by John Spencer Bassett. 7 vols. Washington: The Carnegie Institution of Washington, 1927.

James, Marquis. *Andrew Jackson, the Border Captain.* Indianapolis, Ind.: Bobbs-Merrill, 1933.

Jenkins, Brian. *Fenians and Anglo-American Relations During Reconstruction.* Ithaca, N.Y.: Cornell Univ. Press, 1969.

Jessup, Philip C. *Elihu Root.* 2 vols. New York: Dodd, Mead, 1938.

Johnson, Ludwell H. *Red River Campaign: Politics and Cotton in the Civil War.* Baltimore: Johns Hopkins Univ. Press, 1958.

Johnson, Robert U., and Buel, Clarence, eds. *Battles and Leaders of the Civil War* . . . 4 vols. New York: Century Co., 1887–88.

Johnston, Joseph E. *Narrative of Military Operations* . . . New York: D. Appleton, 1874.

Jones, Virgil C. *The Civil War at Sea.* 3 vols. New York: Holt, Rinehart, and Winston, 1960–62.

———. *Roosevelt's Rough Riders.* Garden City, N.Y.: Doubleday, 1971.

Kalaw, Teodoro M. *The Philippine Revolution.* Reprint. Kawilihan, Mandaluyong, and Rizal: Jorge B. Vargas Filipiniana Foundation, 1969.

Karsten, Peter. *The Naval Aristocracy: The Golden Age of Modern American Navalism.* New York: Free Press, 1972.

Keller, Allan. *The Spanish-American War: A Compact History.* New York: Hawthorn Books, 1969.

King, Charles. *Campaigning with Crook.* Reprint. Norman: Univ. of Okla. Press, 1964.

King, James T. *War Eagle: A Life of General Eugene A. Carr.* Lincoln: Univ. of Neb. Press, 1963.

Lamers, William W. *The Eagle of Glory: A Biography of General William S. Rosecrans* . . . New York: Harcourt, Brace, 1961.

Leckie, William H. *The Buffalo Soldiers: A Narrative of the Negro Cavalry in the West.* Norman: Univ. of Okla. Press, 1967.

———. *The Military Conquest of the Southern Plains.* Norman: Univ. of Okla. Press, 1963.

Leopold, Richard. *Elihu Root and the Conservative Tradition.* Boston: Little, Brown, 1954.

LeRoy, James A. *The Americans in the Philippines: A History of the Conquest and First Years of Occupation with an Introductory Account of the Spanish Rule.* Reprint. New York: AMS Press, 1970.

Lewis, Charles L. *David Glasgow Farragut* . . . 2 vols. Annapolis, Md.: United States Naval Institute, 1941–43.

Lewis, Lloyd. *Captain Sam Grant.* Boston: Little, Brown, 1950.

——. *Sherman, Fighting Prophet.* New York: Harcourt, Brace, 1932.

Lincoln, Abraham. *The Collected Works of Abraham Lincoln.* 9 vols. Edited by Roy P. Basler. New Brunswick, N.J.: Rutgers Univ. Press, 1953-55.

Link, Arthur. *Wilson . . .* Princeton, N.J.: Princeton Univ. Press, 1947-.

Livezey, William. *Mahan on Sea Power.* Norman: Univ. of Okla. Press, 1947.

Long, E. B. *The Civil War Day by Day . . .* Garden City, N.Y.: Doubleday, 1971.

Long, John D. *The New American Navy.* New York: Outlook Co., 1903.

Longstreet, James. *From Manassas to Appomattox . . .* Philadelphia: Lippincott, 1896.

Longstreet, Stephen. *War Cries on Horseback . . .* Garden City, N.Y.: Doubleday, 1970.

Lowe, Percival. *Five Years a Dragoon ('49 to '54) and Other Adventures on the Great Plains.* Kansas City: F. Hudson Publishing Co., 1906.

Lumpkin, Wilson. *The Removal of the Cherokee Indians From Georgia, 1827-1841.* Reprint. Clifton, N.J.: Augustus M. Kelley, 1971.

McCague, James. *The Second Rebellion: The Story of the New York City Draft Riots of 1863.* New York: Dial Press, 1968.

McClellan, George B. *McClellan's Own Story . . .* New York: C. L. Webster, 1887.

MacCloskey, Monro. *Reilly's Battery: A Story of the Boxer Rebellion.* New York: Richards Rosen Press, 1969.

Mackenzie, Ranald S. *Ranald S. Mackenzie's Official Correspondence Relating to Texas, 1871-1873.* Edited by Ernest Wallace. Lubbock: West Texas Museum Association, 1967.

McKinney, Francis F. . . . *The Life of George H. Thomas . . .* Detroit: Wayne State Univ. Press, 1961.

McPherson, James M. *The Negro's Civil War . . .* New York: Pantheon Books, 1965.

McWhiney, Grady. *Braxton Bragg and Confederate Defeat.* New York: Columbia Univ. Press, 1969-.

McWhiney, Grady, and McWhiney, Sue., eds. *To Mexico with Taylor and Scott, 1845-1847.* Waltham, Toronto, and London: Blaisdell, 1969.

Mahan, Alfred Thayer. *The Influence of Sea Power Upon History, 1660-1783.* Boston: Little, Brown, 1890.

——. *Letters and Papers of Alfred Thayer Mahan.* Edited by Robert Seager and Doris Maguire. 3 vols. Annapolis, Md.: U.S. Naval Institute Press, 1975.

Mahon, John K. *History of the Second Seminole War, 1835-1842.* Gainesville: Univ. of Fla. Press, 1967.

March, Alden. *The History and Conquest of the Philippines and Our Other Island Possessions . . .* Reprint. New York: Arno Press, 1970.

Marcy, Randolph B. *Thirty Years of Army Life on the Border . . .* New York: Harper, 1866.

Marshall, S. L. A. *Crimsoned Prairie.* New York: Scribner's, 1972.

Mason, Herbert M. *The Great Pursuit.* New York: Random House, 1970.

Massey, Mary Elizabeth. *Refugee Life in the Confederacy.* Baton Rouge: La. State Univ. Press, 1964.

Mattes, Merrill J., ed. *Indians, Infants, and Infantry: Andrew and Elizabeth Burt on the Frontier.* Denver: Old West Publishing Company, 1960.

May, Ernest R. *Imperial Democracy: The Emergence of America as a Great Power.* New York: Harcourt, Brace, and World, 1961.

Miles, Nelson A. *Annual Report of the Major-General Commanding the Army to the Secretary of War, 1898.* Washington: Government Printing Office, 1898.

——. *Personal Recollections and Observations of General Nelson A. Miles . . .* Chicago and New York: Werner, 1896.

————. *Serving the Republic: Memoirs of the Civil and Military Life of Nelson A. Miles* . . . New York and London: Harper, 1911.

Military Historical Society of Massachusetts Papers. Boston, 1895-1918.

Military Order of the Loyal Legion of the United States. Volumes and individual papers were published by the following commanderies: California, District of Columbia, Illinois, Indiana, Iowa, Kansas, Maine, Massachusetts, Michigan, Minnesota, Missouri, Nebraska, New York, Ohio, Oregon, and Wisconsin. The Rhode Island Soldiers and Sailors Historical Society has also published numerous reminiscences of wartime service.

Miller, Francis T., ed. *The Photographic History of the Civil War* . . . 10 vols. New York: Review of Reviews, 1911.

Millet, F. D. *The Expedition to the Philippines.* New York and London: Harper, 1899.

Millett, Allan R. *The Politics of Intervention: The Military Occupation of Cuba, 1906-1909.* Columbus. Ohio State Univ. Press, 1968.

Millis, Walter. *The Martial Spirit: A Study in Our War with Spain.* Boston: Houghton Mifflin, 1931.

Monaghan, Jay [James]. *Civil War on the Western Border, 1854-1865.* Boston: Little, Brown, 1955.

Moore, Albert B. *Conscription and Conflict in the Confederacy.* New York: Macmillan, 1924.

Morgan, Howard Wayne. *America's Road to Empire: The War with Spain and Overseas Expansion.* New York: Wiley, 1967.

Morison, Samuel E. *"Old Bruin," Commodore Matthew C. Perry.* Boston: Little, Brown, 1967.

Munro, Dana. *Intervention and Dollar Diplomacy in the Caribbean, 1900-1921.* Princeton, N.J.: Princeton Univ. Press, 1964.

Murray, Keith A. *The Modocs and Their War.* Norman: Univ. of Okla. Press, 1959.

Nance, Joseph M. *After San Jacinto: The Texas-Mexican Frontier, 1836-1841.* Austin: Univ. of Texas Press, 1963.

————. *Attack and Counterattack: The Texas-Mexican Frontier, 1842.* Austin: Univ. of Texas Press, 1964.

Nelson, Otto. *National Security and the General Staff.* Washington: Infantry Journal Press, 1946.

Nevins, Allan. *Ordeal of the Union.* 8 vols. New York: Scribner's, 1947-71.

————, et al. *Civil War Books: A Critical Bibliography.* 2 vols. Baton Rouge: La. State Univ. Press, 1967-69.

Nichols, Edward J. *Zach Taylor's Little Army.* Garden City, N.Y.: Doubleday, 1963.

Nichols, Roger L. *General Henry Atkinson* . . . Norman: Univ. of Okla. Press, 1965.

Nicolay, John George, and Hay, John. *Abraham Lincoln: A History.* 10 vols. New York: Century Co., 1890.

Nye, Wilbur S. *Plains Indian Raiders* . . . Norman: Univ. of Okla. Press, 1968.

Ogle, Ralph H. *Federal Control of the Western Apaches, 1848-1886.* Albuquerque: Univ. of N.M. Press, 1970.

Owsley, Frank L. *King Cotton Diplomacy* . . . Chicago: Univ. of Chicago Press, 1959.

————. *States Rights in the Confederacy.* Reprint. Gloucester, Mass.: Peter Smith, 1961.

Pappas, George S. *Prudens Futuri: The U.S. Army War College, 1901-1967.* Carlisle Barracks: The Association of the U.S. Army War College, 1967.

Paris, Louis Philippe Albert d'Orleans, Comte de. *History of the Civil War in America*. 4 vols. Philadelphia: Porter and Coates, 1875–88.

Parks, Joseph H. *General Edmund Kirby Smith . . .* Baton Rouge: La. State Univ. Press, 1954.

Parton, James. *General Jackson*. New York: D. Appleton, 1892.

Pomeroy, William J. *American Neo-Colonialism, Its Emergence in the Philippines and Asia*. New York: International Publishers, 1970.

Porter, David Dixon. *Incidents and Anecdotes of the Civil War*. New York: D. Appleton, 1885.

Pressly, Thomas J. *Americans Interpret Their Civil War*. Princeton, N.J.: Princeton Univ. Press, 1954.

Prucha, Francis Paul. *American Indian Policy in the Formative Years . . . 1790-1834*. Cambridge, Mass.: Harvard Univ. Press, 1962.

——. *Broadax and Bayonet: The Role of the United States Army in the Development of the Northwest, 1815-1860*. Madison: State Historical Society of Wisconsin, 1953.

——. *The Sword of the Republic: The United States Army on the Frontier, 1783-1846*. New York: Macmillan, 1969.

Puleston, W. D. *Mahan . . .* New Haven: Yale Univ. Press, 1939.

Purcell, Victor. *The Boxer Uprising . . .* New York: Cambridge Univ. Press, 1963.

Quarles, Benjamin. *The Negro in the Civil War*. Boston: Little, Brown, 1953.

Quirk, Robert. *Affair of Honor: Woodrow Wilson and the Occupation of Vera Cruz*. New York: W. W. Norton, 1967.

Ramsdell, Charles W. *Behind the Lines in the Southern Confederacy*. Baton Rouge: La. State Univ. Press, 1944.

Randall, James G., and Donald, David. *The Civil War and Reconstruction*. Boston: Heath, 1961.

Rawley, James A. *Race and Politics: "Bleeding Kansas" and the Coming of the Civil War*. Philadelphia: Lippincott, 1969.

Rhodes, James Ford. *History of the United States from the Compromise of 1850 to the End of the Roosevelt Administration*. 9 vols. New York: Macmillan, 1928.

Richardson, Rupert N. *The Comanche Barrier to South Plains Settlement . . .* Glendale, Calif.: Arthur H. Clark, 1933.

Rickey, Don. *Forty Miles a Day on Beans and Hay: The Enlisted Soldier Fighting the Indian Wars*. Norman: Univ. of Okla. Press, 1963.

Ripley, Roswell Sabine. *The War with Mexico*. Reprint. New York: Burt Franklin, 1970.

Ripley, Warren. *Artillery and Ammunition of the Civil War*. New York: Van Nostrand Reinhold, 1970.

Rister, Carl C. *Border Command: General Phil Sheridan in the West*. Norman, Univ. of Okla. Press, 1944.

Roland, Charles P. *Albert Sidney Johnston . . .* Austin: Univ. of Texas Press, 1964.

Roman, Alfred. *The Military Operations of General Beauregard . . .* 2 vols. New York: Harper, 1884.

Ropes, John Codman. *The Story of the Civil War . . .* 4 vols. New York: Putnam's, 1894–1913.

Sandburg, Carl. *Abraham Lincoln . . .* 6 vols. New York: Harcourt, Brace, 1925–39.

Santa Anna, Antonio. *The Eagle: The Autobiography of Santa Anna*. Edited by Ann Fears Crawford. Austin: Pemberton Press, 1967.

Santos, Richard G. *Santa Anna's Campaign Against Texas, 1835-1836 . . .* Waco: Texian Press, 1968.

Sargent, Herbert H. *The Campaign of Santiago de Cuba.* 3 vols. Chicago: A. C. McClurg, 1907.

Schley, Winfield Scott. *Forty-five Years Under the Flag.* New York: D. Appleton, 1904.

Schmitt, Martin F., and Brown, Dee. *Fighting Indians of the West.* New York: Scribner's, 1948.

Schofield, John M. *Forty-six Years in the Army.* New York: Century Co., 1897.

Scott, Hugh L. *Some Memories of A Soldier.* New York: Century Co., 1928.

Scott, Winfield. *Memoirs of Lieut.-General Scott, LL.D., Written by Himself.* 2 vols. New York: Sheldon Co., 1864.

Sefton, James E. *The United States Army and Reconstruction, 1865–1877.* Baton Rouge: La. State Univ. Press, 1967.

Semmes, Raphael. *Memoirs of Service Afloat During the War Between the States.* Baltimore: Kelly, Piet, 1869.

Sexton, William Thaddeus. *Soldiers in the Sun: An Adventure in Imperialism.* Harrisburg: Military Service Publishing Company, 1939.

Shannon, Fred A. *The Organization and Administration of the Union Army, 1861–1865.* 2 vols. Cleveland: Arthur H. Clark, 1928.

Sheridan, Philip H. *Personal Memoirs of Philip Henry Sheridan . . .* 2 vols. New York: D. Appleton, 1902.

Sherman, William T. *Memoirs of General William T. Sherman.* 2 vols. New York: D. Appleton, 1875.

Singletary, Otis A. *The Mexican War.* Chicago: Univ. of Chicago Press, 1960.
———. *Negro Militia and Reconstruction.* Austin: Univ. of Texas Press, 1957.

Smith, George Winston, and Judah, Charles, eds. *Chronicles of the Gringos: The U.S. Army in the Mexican War, 1846–1848: Accounts of Eyewitnesses and Combatants.* Albuquerque: Univ. of N.M. Press, 1968.

Smith, Justin H. *The War with Mexico.* 2 vols. New York: Macmillan, 1919.

Southern Historical Society Papers. 1876–1959.

Spector, Ronald. *Admiral of the New Empire: The Life and Career of George Dewey.* Baton Rouge: La. State Univ. Press, 1974.

Stevens, Frank E. *The Black Hawk War . . .* Chicago: Frank E. Stevens, 1903.

Stevens, Hazard. *The Life of Isaac Ingalls Stevens.* Boston: Houghton Mifflin, 1900.

Strode, Hudson. *Jefferson Davis . . .* 3 vols. New York: Harcourt, Brace, and World, 1955–64.

Sweetman, Jack. *The Landing at Veracruz: 1914 . . .* Annapolis, Md.: United States Naval Institute Press, 1968.

Tan, Chester C. *The Boxer Catastrophe.* New York: Columbia Univ. Press, 1955.

Taylor, Richard. *Destruction and Reconstruction . . .* New York: D. Appleton, 1879.

Taylor, Zachary. *Letters of Zachary Taylor from the Battle-Fields of the Mexican War.* New York: Kraus Reprint, 1970.

Tebbel, John. *The Compact History of the Indian Wars.* New York: Hawthorn Books, 1966

Tebbel, John, and Jennison, Keith. *The American Indian Wars.* New York: Bonanza Books, 1960.

Thomas, Wilbur D. *General George H. Thomas . . .* New York: Exposition 1964.

Thwaites, Reuben Gold. *The Story of the Black Hawk War.* Madison: Wisconsin State Historical Society, 1892.

Tolbert, Frank X. *The Day of San Jacinto.* New York: McGraw-Hill, 1959.

Tompkins, Frank. *Chasing Villa . . .* Harrisburg: Military Service Publishing Co., 1934.

Tucker, Glenn. *Chickamauga: Bloody Battle in the West.* Indianapolis, Ind.: Bobbs-Merrill, 1961.

Twitchell, Ralph Emerson. *The History of the Military Occupation of the Territory of New Mexico from 1846 to 1851* . . . Reprint. Chicago: Rio Grande Press, 1963.

U.S., Adjutant General's Office. *Correspondence Relating to the War With Spain* . . . *Including the Insurrection in the Philippine Islands and the China Relief Expedition . . . 1898-1902.* Washington: Government Printing Office, 1902.

———. *Official Army Register of the Volunteer Force of the United States Army for the Years 1861, '62, '63, '64, '65.* 8 vols. Washington: Superintendent of Public Printing, 1865-67.

U.S., Congress, Senate. *Report of the Commission Appointed by the President to Investigate the Conduct of the War Department in the War with Spain.* 56th Cong., 1st sess. Washington: Government Printing Office, 1900.

U.S., Congress, House. *Record of Proceedings of a Court of Inquiry in the Case of Rear-Admiral Winfield S. Schley, U.S. Navy.* 57th Cong., 1st sess. Washington: Government Printing Office, 1902.

U.S., Navy Dept. *Official Records of the Union and Confederate Navies in the War of the Rebellion.* 31 vols. Washington: Government Printing Office, 1894-1922.

U.S., Navy Dept., Division of Naval History. *Civil War Naval Chronology, 1861-1865.* 6 vols. Washington: Government Printing Office, 1961-66.

U.S., War Dept. *The War of the Rebellion: A Compilation of the Official Records of the Union and Confederate Armies.* 128 vols. Washington: Government Printing Office, 1880-1901.

U.S., War Dept., Surgeon General's Office. *The Medical and Surgical History of the War of the Rebellion.* 6 vols. Washington: Government Printing Office, 1870-88.

Upton, Emory. *The Armies of Asia and Europe* . . . New York: D. Appleton, 1878.

———. *The Military Policy of the United States.* Washington: Government Printing Office, 1904.

Utley, Robert. *Frontier Regulars: The U.S. Army and the Indian, 1866-1891.* New York: Macmillan, 1974.

———. *Frontiersmen in Blue: The United States Army and the Indian, 1848-1865.* New York: Macmillan, 1967.

———. *The Last Days of the Sioux Nation.* New Haven: Yale Univ. Press, 1963.

Vandiver, Frank E. *Mighty Stonewall.* New York: McGraw-Hill, 1957.

———. *Their Tattered Flags: The Epic of the Confederacy.* New York: Harper's Magazine Press, 1970.

Van Gelder, Arthur, and Schlatter, Hugo. *History of the Explosives Industry in America.* New York: Columbia Univ. Press, 1927.

Vaughn, J. W. *The Reynolds Campaign on Powder River.* Norman: Univ. of Okla. Press, 1961.

Walker, Francis A. . . . *General Hancock.* New York: D. Appleton, 1894.

Wallace, Edward. *General William Jenkins Worth* . . . Dallas: Southern Methodist Univ. Press, 1953.

Warner, Ezra J. *Generals in Blue* . . . Baton Rouge: La. State Univ. Press, 1964.

———. *Generals in Gray* . . . Baton Rouge: La. State Univ. Press, 1959.

Weems, John E. *To Conquer a Peace* . . . Garden City, N.Y.: Doubleday, 1974.

Welch, Richard E., comp. *Imperialists vs. Anti-Imperialists: The Debate over Expansionism in the 1890's.* Itasca, Ill.: F. E. Peacock, 1972.

Wellman, Paul I. *The Indian Wars of the West.* Garden City, N.Y.: Doubleday, 1954.

West, Richard S. *Admirals of American Empire*. Indianapolis, Ind.: Bobbs-Merrill, 1948.

Wheeler, Joseph. *The Santiago Campaign, 1898*. Reprint. Freeport, N.Y.: Books for Libraries Press, 1970.

Wilcox, Cadmus Marcellus. *History of the Mexican War*. Washington: Church News Publishing Co., 1892.

Wiley, Bell I. *The Life of Billy Yank* . . . Indianapolis, Ind.: Bobbs-Merrill, 1952.

———. *The Life of Johnny Reb* . . . Indianapolis, Ind.: Bobbs-Merrill, 1943.

Wilkins, Thurman. *Cherokee Tragedy: The Story of the Ridge Family and the Decimation of a People*. New York: Macmillan, 1970.

Williams, Kenneth P. *Lincoln Finds a General* . . . 5 vols. New York: Macmillan, 1949–59.

Williams, T. Harry. *Lincoln and His Generals*. New York: A. A. Knopf, 1952.

———. *P. G. T. Beauregard: Napoleon in Gray*. Baton Rouge: La. State Univ. Press, 1955.

Wilson, Frederick T. *Federal Aid in Domestic Disturbances, 1787–1903*. Washington: Government Printing Office, 1903.

Wilson, James Harrison. *Under the Old Flag* . . . 2 vols. New York: D. Appleton, 1912.

Wiltse, Charles M. *John C. Calhoun* . . . 3 vols. Indianapolis, Ind.: Bobbs-Merrill, 1944–51.

Wolff, Leon. *Little Brown Brother* . . . Garden City, N.Y.: Doubleday, 1960.

Woodward, C. Vann. "The Age of Reinterpretation." *American Historical Review* 66, no. 1 (Oct. 1960):1–19.

Wyeth, John A. *That Devil Forrest* . . . Reprint. New York: Harper, 1959.

Chapter **9**

The United States
and the
Two World Wars

Charles B. MacDonald

World War I

HOWEVER much the Spanish-American War, increasing involvement in the Caribbean and the Pacific, and confrontations with Mexico presaged a new era of American participation in foreign affairs, the United States put on the mantle of international responsibility only reluctantly. As World War I raged in Europe, President Woodrow Wilson called on the American people to remain "impartial in thought as well as in action." Yet in the previously unknown context of a world at war, American involvement may have been inevitable. Despite that seeming inevitability, in much the same way they have argued the background of the coming of war in Europe, historians have engaged in a process of recurring revisionism in their study of American intervention. Richard W. Leopold has treated the process perceptively in an essay in *World Politics*, "The Problem of American Intervention" (1950), as has Ernest R. May in a pamphlet, *American Intervention: 1917 and 1941* (1960).

A flood of works appearing immediately after the war, such as John B. McMaster's *The United States in the World War* (1918-20, two volumes), and John S. Basset's *Our War With Germany* (1919), tended to agree with President Wilson's pronouncement that German recourse to unrestricted submarine warfare left the United States no alternative to war. The first serious scholar to contradict that view was Harry Elmer Barnes, who included a long chapter on American intervention in his *Genesis of the World War* (1926); Barnes in effect accepted the German contention that submarine warfare had been a last resort to save the German people from starvation. C. Hartley

Mr. MacDonald (B.A., Litt.D., Presbyterian) is CMH's Deputy Chief Historian for Southeast Asia. His works include *Company Commander, The Battle of the Huertgen Forest, Airborne, The Mighty Endeavor*, and in the U.S. Army in World War II series, *Three Battles, The Siegfried Line Campaign*, and *The Last Offensive*.

Grattan in *Why We Fought* (1929) reinforced Barnes's thesis while attributing much of the onus for the intervention to American economic entanglements, Allied propaganda, and inept American statesmanship. The first solid challenge to that thesis came with Charles Seymour's *American Diplomacy During the World War* (1934). While avowing that submarine warfare was the cause of American intervention, Seymour maintained persuasively that Germany's resort to the submarine was less retaliation or desperation than unmitigated determination to win the war.

Less than a year later appeared an explosive reassessment that, as a best seller, attracted far more attention than did Seymour's work. Written by an astute journalist, Walter Millis, *The Road to War: America, 1914-1917* (1935) was a paean to the senselessness of force and may have contributed to the isolationist fervor that gripped the U.S. Congress over the next few years. To Grattan's earlier charges, Millis added that of greed. A spate of writings blaming economic entanglements followed, none more hard hitting than *American Goes to War* (1938) by Charles C. Tansill. Edwin M. Borchard and William P. Lage, in *Neutrality for the United States* (1937), explored another angle, sharply denouncing Wilson's preoccupation with freedom of the seas.

Yet in the meantime works more in keeping with the Wilsonian thesis continued to appear. Restudying the issue of intervention, Charles Seymour in a series of essays, *American Neutrality, 1914-1917* (1935), asserted that Germany launched the unrestricted submarine campaign with the conscious expectation that war with the United States might result. Harley F. Notter, in *The Origins of the Foreign Policy of Woodrow Wilson* (1937), came to much the same conclusion. In a slim volume, *The Devil Theory of War* (1936), Charles A. Beard put the onus on multiple causes. Frederick L. Paxson, in *Pre-War Years, 1914-1917* (1936), skillfully blended the stories of domestic and foreign affairs.

Early in a renaissance of World War I study that began some thirty years after the war, Hans J. Morgenthau in *In Defense of the National Interest* (1951) and George F. Kennan in *American Diplomacy, 1900-1950* (1950) attacked Wilson and his advisers for having gone to war for the wrong reasons; rather than legal and moral issues, the true goals should have been to rescue the balance of power and to protect American security. Edward H. Buehrig in *Woodrow Wilson and the Balance of Power* (1955) argued that the accusations were unfounded, that for all the concern with moralism and legalism, Wilson was sharply conscious of the balance of power. Yet two of the most significant of the new works returned basically to the Charles Seymour thesis of German determination to win even at the cost of bringing the United States into the war. Both Ernest R. May in *The World War and American Isolation* (1959) and Arthur S. Link in *Wilson: The Struggle for Neutrality, 1914-1915* (1960) showed that Wilson followed a flexible and conciliatory course but that with the German decision to force a crisis no real option other than war existed. A valuable study of American war aims is David F. Trask's *The United States in the Supreme War Council: American War Aims and Inter-Allied Strategy, 1917-1918* (1961).

Many of the recent general histories of the war provide good summaries of the origins of American intervention, in most cases drawing heavily on earlier scholarship. Particularly readable is S. L. A. Marshall's *The American Heritage History of World War I* (1964). Harvey A. DeWeerd in *President Wilson Fights His War* (1968) sketches events before American entry and follows developments in other than American sectors while still focusing on the American role. Edward M. Coffman's *The War to End All Wars* (1968) is specifically directed toward the American experience and provides a useful bibliographical essay. An earlier account, Frederick L. Paxson's *America at War: 1917-1918* (1939), provides an amalgam of political, diplomatic, economic, social, and military events, while Laurence Stallings in *The Doughboys: the Story of the AEF, 1917-1918* (1963) gives the flavor of what it was like in France, a flavor that could be imparted only by one who had been a part of the scene.

Few works deal with specific American battles, although Coffman's provides considerable detail on them, much of it gleaned from unit records previously unexploited. An exception to the lack of focus on specific battles is a study of the baptism of fire of American troops, Robert B. Asprey's *At Belleau Wood* (1965). The journalist Frederick Palmer, who served in France and wrote extensively on various aspects of the war, told of the Meuse-Argonne campaign in *Our Greatest Battle* (1919), but that largest American campaign of the war needs restudying. Three works tell the story of American forces in the international expedition into Asiatic Russia: Betty Miller Unterberger's *America's Siberian Expedition, 1918-1920* (1956), John Albert White's *The Siberian Intervention* (1950), and William Sidney Graves's (who commanded U.S. Forces) *America's Siberian Adventure, 1918-1920* (1931). An unusual study of small unit actions with analytical critiques was produced by the Infantry School at Fort Benning, Georgia, *Infantry in Battle* (1934), while another unusual and valuable approach to the study of battles and campaigns is to be found in two volumes by Douglas W. Johnson, *Topography and Strategy* (1917) and *Battlefields of the World War* (1921), in which strategy and tactics are closely related to the influence of geography and terrain.

No single work covers the logistical side of the war in its entirety, but two of the general histories mentioned earlier, Huston's *Sinews of War* and Risch's *Quartermaster Support of the Army*, provide essential information. Constance M. Green, Harry C. Thomson, and Peter C. Roots's *The Ordnance Department: Planning Munitions for War* (1955), though focused on World War II, gives interesting background on Army ordnance in World War I. On the work of the War Department in industrial mobilization, manpower management, and the support of the overseas war in France, a six-volume work produced shortly after the war, Benedict Crowell and Robert Wilsons's *How America Went to War* (1921), reflects the experience and viewpoint of Crowell as Assistant Secretary of War. Far more critical in approach is a modern scholarly work, Daniel F. Beaver's *Newton D. Baker and the American War Effort* (1966). A similarly critical study of industrial mobilization for war is Robert D. Cuff's *War Industries Board: Business-Government Relations During World War I* (1973). Irving B. Holley has explored American development of the air weapon during World War I in *Ideas and Weapons* (1953), emphasizing the extent to which technical knowledge outpaced weapons development. An excellent work depicting the continuing opposition to the war after American entry and the excessive repression of civil liberties that characterized the period is Horace Peterson and Gilbert Fite's *Opponents of War, 1917-1918* (1957).

Almost every major military figure penned his memoirs, including the commander of the American Expeditionary Forces, John J. Pershing, and the U.S. Army Chief of Staff, Peyton C. March. The wartime differences between the two over prerogatives resulted in a measure of vituperation that has been called the battle of the memoirs and, some say, persuaded a later Chief of Staff, General George C. Marshall, not to write his. Pershing's title is *My Experiences in the World War* (1931); March's is *The Nation at War* (1932). Useful memoirs on the logistical support of the American Expeditionary Force are James G. Harbord's *American Army in France, 1917-1919* (1936) and Johnson Hagood's *The Services of Supply* (1927).

Among a number of accounts by officers and men of lesser rank, of particular interest are one by a Marine Corps captain, John W. Thomason, Jr., *Fix Bayonets!* (1926), and another by Thomas A. Boyd, who vividly recounted his life as an infantryman in the form of a novel, *Through the Wheat* (1923). Long after the war another novelist, Anton Myrer, in *Once an Eagle* (1968) created some memorable World War I battle scenes as part of the story of an Army officer's career from a lieutenant in World War I to a general in World War II.

The better biographies are the product of recent scholarship, such as Donald Smythe's *Guerrilla Warrior: The Early Life of John J. Pershing* (1973—a projected second volume will cover the World War I period), Edward M. Coffman's *The Hilt of the Sword: The Career of Peyton C. March* (1966), Forrest C. Pogue's *George C. Marshall: Education of a General, 1880-1939* (1963), and Martin Blumenson's *The Patton Papers: 1885-1940* (1972), the last depicting a young George S. Patton, Jr., as an ambitious tank commander in France. The role of an equally ambitious Douglas MacArthur as a brigade commander in the 42d Division forms a part of D. Clayton James's *The Years of MacArthur, Volume I: 1880-1941* (1970). The story of the war's premier air power enthusiast is told in Alfred T. Hurley's *Billy Mitchell: Crusader for Air Power* (1964); and Elting E. Morison provides an introspective study of the U.S. naval commander, William S. Sims, in *Admiral Sims and the Modern American Navy* (1968).

Although no official narrative histories of the war exist, there are a number of official publications. A selection of official orders and documents of the American Expeditionary Forces was published in 1948 by the Government Printing Office in seventeen volumes under the title *United States Army in the World War, 1917-1919*. Of value for detailed study of American battles is the American Battle Monuments Commission's *American Armies and Battlefields in Europe* (1938), which is a kind of veteran's or tourist's guide. The commission also prepared for each U.S. division a *Summary of Operations of the World War*.

A concise summary of the American role in the fledgling air war in France is given in James Lea Cate's "The Air Service in World War I," in *The Army Air Forces in World War II*, Volume I: *Plans and Early Operations* (1947). A good nonofficial work is James J. Hudson's *Hostile Skies: A Combat History of the American Air Service in World War I* (1968).

In addition to the biography of Admiral Sims, cited earlier, valuable material on the role of the U.S. Navy is to be found in

Josephus Daniels's *Our Navy at War* (1922) and two compen-
dious works by Harold and Margaret Sprout, *The Rise of
American Naval Power: 1776-1918* (1939) and *Toward a New
Order of Sea Power: American Naval Policy and the World
Scene, 1918-1922* (1943).

World War II

Military developments in the period between the two world
wars can best be studied in general works on American military
history (see Chapter 7), in biographies of such leaders as
Marshall, MacArthur, Mitchell, and Patton, and in background
sections of official histories of World War II. Several works do
deal directly with U.S. Marine Corps intervention in Latin
America, most notably Samuel Flagg Bemis's *The Latin
American Policy of the United States* (1943) and Hans Schmidt's
The United States Occupation of Haiti, 1914-1934 (1971). The
emergence of the Army Air Forces is covered in James Lea Cate's
"The Army Air Arm Between Two Wars, 1919-39," in the official
history previously cited, *The Army Air Forces in World War II*,
Volume I: *Plans and Early Operations*, and in Alfred Goldberg's
(ed.) *A History of the United States Air Force, 1907-1957* (1957).
Some material on U.S. Army developments is to be found in
several of the official World War II histories, United States Army
in World War II: Stetson Conn and Byron Fairchild's *The
Framework of Hemisphere Defense* (1960); Maurice Matloff and
Edwin M. Snell's *Strategic Planning for Coalition Warfare,
1941-1942* (1953); volumes dealing with the Chemical Corps,
Ordnance Department, and other technical services; and Kent
Roberts Greenfield's "Origins of the Army Ground Forces:
General Headquarters, United States Army, 1940-1942," in
Greenfield, Robert R. Palmer, and Bell I. Wiley's *The Organiza-
tion of Ground Combat Troops* (1947). Early developments in
amphibious warfare are treated in an unofficial work, Philip A.
Crowl and Jeter A. Isley's *The U.S. Marines and Amphibious
War* (1951).

Even though the United States was propelled into World
War II by the surprise Japanese attack on Pearl Harbor and
declarations of war by Germany and Italy, revisionists were
soon in print. Charles A. Beard, for example, espoused the same
"devil theory" he had accorded to American entry into World
War I. In *American Foreign Policy, 1932-1940* (1946) and
President Roosevelt and the Coming of War, 1941 (1948), Beard
charged that even as Franklin D. Roosevelt was assuring the

American people that he meant to avoid war, he was deliberately abandoning neutrality by such methods as trading old destroyers to Britain in exchange for bases, promoting lend-lease, and escorting convoys to Britain. He went so far as to charge that Roosevelt deliberately provoked Japan into attacking.

Another revisionist, Charles C. Tansill, took up much the same arguments in a more intemperate book, *Back Door to War* (1952), and George Morgenstern also argued the provocation thesis in *Pearl Harbor: The Story of the Secret War* (1947). Paul W. Shroeder in *The Axis Alliance and Japanese-American Relations* (1958) maintained that if the United States had not imposed an oil embargo on Japan or if President Roosevelt had agreed to meet with the Japanese premier, a détente might have been possible.

In the face of a host of studies by other historians, many working with official records, the credibility of the revisionists was severely strained. Samuel Eliot Morison contributed to the rebuttal with *The Rising Sun in the Pacific* (1950), the third of fifteen volumes in the semiofficial series, History of United States Naval Operations in World War II, written with research assistance by official U.S. Navy historians. Working with Department of State cooperation, William L. Langer and S. Everett Gleason covered the whole broad diplomatic canvas in *The Challenge to Isolation, 1937-1940* (1952) and *The Undeclared War, 1940-1941* (1953).

A later work taking a broad look at the coming of war is Robert A. Divine's *The Reluctant Belligerent: American Entry into World War II* (1965), while a number of studies focus on the start of the war with Japan: Robert J. C. Butow's *Tojo and the Coming of the War* (1961), which concentrates on the rise to power of General Hideki Tojo and the Japanese military; David J. Lu's *From the Marco Polo Bridge to Pearl Harbor: Japan's Entry into World War II* (1961); Walter Lord's *Day of Infamy* (1957), an eminently readable account of the Pearl Harbor attack; Herbert Feis's *The Road to Pearl Harbor* (1950), which views the onset of war in terms of classical tragedy not unlike the position of recent historians on the coming of World War I; George M. Waller's *Pearl Harbor: Roosevelt and the Coming of the War* (1953); and John Toland's *The Rising Sun: The Decline and Fall of the Japanese Empire, 1936-1945* (1970), the last a detailed look at events primarily from the Japanese viewpoint, based in part on postwar interviews with Japanese officials. In *Pearl Harbor: Warning and Decision* (1962), Roberta Wohlstetter focused on the intelligence failure.

Historians have directed less attention to the coming of war between the United States and the Axis powers in Europe, but Saul Friedlaender in *Prelude to Downfall: Hitler and the United States, 1939-1941* (1967) perceived nothing to refute Langer's and Gleason's early finding that even though the German dictator, Adolf Hitler, made determined efforts to avoid provoking the United States, he did so only to avert a showdown until he had solidified his position in Europe. In the official series, United States Army in World War II, Conn and Fairchild in *The Framework of Hemisphere Defense*, previously cited, revealed how seriously the United States viewed the vulnerability of the western hemisphere to possible Axis attack. Alton Frye in *Nazi Germany and the American Hemisphere, 1933-1941* (1967) examined Nazi activities in North and South America and concluded that the threat to the Americas was real.

Two brief but excellent accounts of diplomacy immediately preceding and during the war are John L. Snell's *Illusion and Necessity: The Diplomacy of Global War, 1939-1945* (1963) and Gaddis Smith's *American Diplomacy during the Second World War, 1941-1945* (1965). For broad looks at worldwide American strategy, see Samuel Eliot Morison's *Strategy and Compromise* (1958), Alfred H. Burne's *Strategy in World War II* (1947), and a brief treatise by the former chief historian of the U.S. Army, Kent Roberts Greenfield, under whose general direction many of the official Army histories were written, *American Strategy in World War II: A Reconsideration* (1963).

More detailed examinations of strategy are found in the official Army series: Matloff and Snell, *Strategic Planning for Coalition Warfare, 1941-1942*, previously cited; Maurice Matloff, *Strategic Planning for Coalition Warfare, 1943-1944* (1959); Richard M. Leighton and Robert W. Coakley, *Global Logistics and Strategy, 1940-1943* (1955) and *Global Logistics and Strategy, 1943-1945* (1969); and Ray S. Cline, *Washington Command Post: The Operations Division* (1951). A perceptive unofficial work that surveys the high-level conduct of the war is Herbert Feis's *Churchill, Roosevelt, Stalin: The War They Waged and the Peace They Sought* (1957). Hanson Baldwin is critical of American policy in *Great Mistakes of the War* (1950), and a number of strategic decisions are scrutinized carefully in Kent Roberts Greenfield's (ed.) *Command Decisions* (1959), a collection of essays by U.S. Army historians.

A number of official publications other than the service histories and some commercial printings of official material are of broad interest. Of first importance is a series of documentary volumes published by the Department of State on the various wartime conferences of Allied political and military chiefs: Casablanca, Cairo, Teheran, Malta, Yalta, and Potsdam. The wartime reports of the chiefs of staff of the Army and Army Air Forces and the Chief of Naval Operations have been published in one volume: *War Reports of George C. Marshall, H. H. Arnold and Ernest J. King* (1947). The official report of the supreme commander in Europe, Dwight D. Eisenhower, was published as *Report by the Supreme Commander to the Combined Chiefs of Staff on the Operations in Europe of the Allied Expeditionary Force, 6 June 1944 to 8 May 1945* (1945). General Eisenhower's wartime papers have been published with valuable commentary in Alfred D. Chandler's (ed.) *The Papers of Dwight David Eisenhower: The War Years* (1970, five volumes).

Some of the memoirs and biographies of officials in the Roosevelt administration and at high command levels are particularly illuminating. Henry L. Stimson and McGeorge Bundy in *On Active Service in Peace and War* (1948) and Elting E. Morison in *Turmoil and Tradition: A Study of the Life and Times of Henry L. Stimson* (1960) cover the role of the Secretary of War. The imposing role of the U.S. Army's chief of staff, George C. Marshall, is abundantly clear from the second and third volumes of the authorized biography, Forrest C. Pogue's *Ordeal and Hope, 1939-1942* (1966) and *Organizer of Victory, 1943-1945* (1973), and from several volumes in the official history, particularly Mark S. Watson's *Chief of Staff: Prewar Plans and Preparations* (1950). The activities of the Secretary of State are covered in *The Memoirs of Cordell Hull* (1948). The Army Air Forces chief of staff, Henry H. Arnold, wrote *Global Mission* (1949), while the Chief of Naval Operations told his story (with Walter M. Whitehill) in *Fleet Admiral King: A Naval Record* (1952). The admiral whom Roosevelt added as a fourth member of the Joint Chiefs of Staff to serve as a kind of personal chief of staff to the president, William D. Leahy, wrote *I Was There* (1950).

Among the extensive literature on President Roosevelt, three of the more important works are James MacGregor Burns's *Roosevelt: The Lion and the Fox* (1956), the same author's *Roosevelt: The Soldier of Freedom* (1971), and Robert E. Sherwood's *Roosevelt and Hopkins* (1948), the last constituting something of a source book on the relationship of the president with his principal wartime confident and alter ego.

Possibly because of the inherent difficulty in writing a

meaningful chronicle in one or two volumes of even the American role alone in such a far-ranging conflict, few historians have tried to tell of the entire war. Several short accounts appeared soon after the war but were rapidly dated as new information became available. The first scholarly account to focus on the American role is A. Russell Buchanan's *The United States and World War II* (1964), which is comprehensive and accurate, the author having leaned heavily on the official histories; but the writing is uninspiring and lacks critical analysis. More effective as literature but lacking the trappings of formal scholarship is Kenneth S. Davis's *The Experience of War: The United States in World War II* (1965). A study covering the entire war by the eminent British military historian, B. H. Liddell Hart, was published posthumously, *History of the Second World War* (1971). Graphically impressive is C. L. Sulzberger, et al., *The American Heritage Picture History of World War II* (1966).

The only broad, overall account of the American role in the Mediterranean and Europe is Charles B. MacDonald's *The Mighty Endeavor: American Armed Forces in the European Theater in World War II* (1969). The study begins with prewar planning and the developing command structure in the United States and covers the air, sea, and ground wars through V-E Day.

Memoirs and biographies also provide a broad view of events throughout the Mediterranean and Europe. The supreme Allied commander, General Eisenhower, wrote *Crusade in Europe* (1948). The best biographies covering his wartime years are Kenneth Davis's *Eisenhower: American Hero* (1969) and Stephen Ambrose's *The Supreme Commander: The War Years of General Dwight D. Eisenhower* (1970). Omar N. Bradley, one of Eisenhower's top deputies, wrote *A Soldier's Story* (1951), one of the more outspoken of the memoirs. The viewpoint of the controversial George S. Patton, Jr., commander first of the Seventh Army and then the Third, is in the second of two volumes based on Patton's diary and other material, Martin Blumenson's *The Patton Papers: 1940-1945* (1974). The best of a number of biographies of Patton are Henry H. Semmes's *Portrait of Patton* (1955) and Ladislas Farago's *Patton: Ordeal and Triumph* (1964). The commander of the Fifth Army and subsequently of Allied armies in Italy, Mark W. Clark, wrote *Calculated Risk* (1950), while a good account by a division and later corps commander is Lucian K. Truscott, Jr.'s *Command Missions* (1954).

The standard work on the invasion of North Africa is the

official U.S. Army history, George F. Howe's *Northwest Africa: Seizing the Initiative in the West* (1957). Writing with a lively style, Martin Blumenson studied the German counteroffensive against U.S. and British forces in Tunisia in *Kasserine Pass* (1967).

The standard work on the invasion of Sicily is again the official history, Albert N. Garland and Howard McGaw Smyth's *Sicily and the Surrender of Italy* (1965). A number of other historians studied the complex and intriguing story of Italian surrender, but none produced much not already revealed in that volume. Martin Blumenson wrote *Sicily: Whose Victory?* (1969), while the airborne phase of the Sicilian invasion and all other World War II airborne operations are covered in John R. Galvin's *Air Assault* (1970).

The first phase of the campaign in Italy, up to the stalemates at Monte Cassino and on the Anzio beachhead, is told in the official history, Martin Blumenson's *Salerno to Cassino* (1969), while a second volume, Ernest F. Fisher's *Cassino to the Alps* (1977) carries the story to the end of the war. Blumenson told the Anzio story through the breakout offensive of May 1944 in an unofficial work, *Anzio: The Gamble That Failed* (1963), and took a look from the viewpoint of the responsible commanders at the costly crossing of the Rapido River in *Bloody River* (1970). Several studies in another official U.S. Army series called American Forces in Action, creditably done although written as interim publications before the official histories were ready, deal with the war in Italy: *Salerno: American Operations from the Beaches to the Volturno* (1944), *From the Volturno to the Winter Line* (1944), *Fifth Army at the Winter Line* (1945), and *Anzio Beachhead* (1947).

On the American effort in northwest Europe, Forrest Pogue's *The Supreme Command* (1954) is the volume in the official U.S. Army series focusing on Eisenhower's headquarters and decisions. Roland G. Ruppenthal's two volumes, *Logistical Support of the Armies* (1953 and 1959), in the same series provide one of the few relatively complete logistical histories of any American campaign. Technological aspects of the war in Europe and elsewhere are well covered in the official histories of the technical services: Chemical Warfare Service, Corps of Engineers, Medical Department, Ordnance Department, Quartermaster Corps. Signal Corps, and Transportation Corps.

The official account of D-Day and operations in Normandy through the fall of Cherbourg is Gordon A. Harrison's *Cross-*

Channel Attack (1951). Portions of the Normandy story were told earlier in three studies in the American Forces in Action series: *Omaha Beachhead* (1945), *Utah Beach to Cherbourg* (1947), and *St. Lô* (1946). Cornelius Ryan's *The Longest Day* (1959), a popular account of people caught up in the D–Day invasion, is an example of a form of human interest history based in part on postwar interviews that has attracted tremendous numbers of readers. Chief and most successful practitioners of the form have been Ryan and John Toland. No one wrote more vividly of combat than S. L. A. Marshall, as exemplified by his account of American airborne landings on D–Day in *Night Drop* (1962).

The official account of the breakout from Normandy and the drive to the German frontier is Martin Blumenson's *Breakout and Pursuit* (1961). Blumenson covered much the same ground in an unofficial account, *The Duel for France* (1963). Two works dealing specifically with liberation of the French capital are Willis Thornton's *The Liberation of Paris* (1962) and Dominique LaPierre and Larry Collins's *Is Paris Burning?* (1965), the latter of the Ryan-Toland school of popular history. The official U.S. Army history of the invasion of southern France is still in preparation.

The official accounts of the fall campaigns of 1944 along the German frontier are Hugh M. Cole's *The Lorraine Campaign* (1950), which covers the Third Army, and Charles B. MacDonald's *The Siegfried Line Campaign* (1963), which covers the First and Ninth Armies and the big airborne assault in the Netherlands, Operation Market-Garden. Cornelius Ryan in *A Bridge Too Far* (1974) told of the airborne attack in detail. An unofficial account of another phase of the autumn fighting is Charles B. MacDonald's *The Battle of the Huertgen Forest* (1963), while MacDonald and Sidney T. Mathews take a detailed look at combat at the small unit level in an official work, *Three Battles: Arnaville, Altuzzo, and Schmidt* (1952).

As might be expected, the literature on the Battle of the Bulge, the German counteroffensive in the Ardennes in December 1944, is fairly extensive. The official account is Hugh M. Cole's *The Ardennes: Battle of the Bulge* (1965). In *The Bitter Woods* (1969) John S. D. Eisenhower, son of the supreme commander, provided fresh insight into the nature and thinking of senior commanders on both sides. An early account still stands as the best study of the encirclement and siege of the road center of Bastogne: S. L. A. Marshall, *Bastogne: The First Eight Days* (1946). The official history dealing with liquidation of the bulge and the remainder of the war is Charles B. MacDonald's The Last Offensive (1973). John Toland covered many of the same events in his eminently readable The Last 100 Days (1966), while the definitive work on the First Army's capture of a bridge over the Rhine River is Ken Hechler's The Bridge at Remagen (1957).

Supplementing the memoirs of senior commanders are several by junior officers and enlisted men, such as World War II's most decorated American soldier, a platoon sergeant and platoon leader, Audie Murphy, who wrote To Hell and Back (1949); a platoon leader, Paul Boesch, who wrote Road to Huertgen— Forest in Hell (1962); and Charles B. MacDonald, who wrote Company Commander (revised edition, 1961). The soldier cartoonist, Bill Mauldin, provided lucid commentary on combat and his famous drawings in Up Front (1945).

The volumes in the official Air Forces history, Wesley Frank Craven and James Lea Cate's (eds.) The Army Air Forces in World War II, that deal with the war against Germany are Vol. I: Plans and Early Operations (January 1939 to August 1942) (1948), Vol. II: Europe: Torch to Pointblank (August 1942 to December 1943) (1949), and Vol. III: Europe: Argument to V-E Day (January 1944 to May 1945) (1951). Also of particular interest is the multivolume series prepared by the U.S. Strategic Bombing Survey that examined the effectiveness of air operations in Europe and Asia, published (1945-47) by the Government Printing Office. A feel for what it was like to participate in the air war in Europe may be gleaned from an account by a former B-17 pilot, Bert Stiles's Serenade to the Big Bird (1952).

In Samuel Eliot Morison's semiofficial U.S. Navy series, volumes dealing with the war against Germany are: Vol. I The Battle of the Atlantic (September 1939-May 1943) (1951), Vol. II: Operations in North African Waters (October 1942-June 1943) (1950), Vol. IX: Sicily—Salerno—Anzio (January 1943-June 1944) (1952), Vol. X: The Atlantic Battle Won (May 1943-May 1945) (1956), and Vol. XI: The Invasion of France and Germany (1944-1945) (1957).

For the war against Japan, the closest to a general account is John Toland's The Rising Sun, previously cited, but it tells the story in large measure from the Japanese viewpoint. Not so comprehensive but also noteworthy is Thomas M. Coffey's Imperial Tragedy: Japan in World War II, the First Days and the Last (1970). The definitive work on Allied strategy in the Pacific through the end of 1943 is Louis Morton's Strategy and Command: The First Two Years (1962), in the official U.S.

Army series. There is no sequel covering the last year and a half of the Pacific war.

As might be expected, the literature is considerable on the controversial Douglas MacArthur, commander in chief of the Southwest Pacific Area and later Far East commander in Tokyo and United Nations commander in Korea. MacArthur's memoirs are entitled *Reminiscences* (1964). Very pro-MacArthur are Courtney H. Whitney's *MacArthur: His Rendezvous With Destiny* (1956) and Charles A. Willoughby and John Chamberlain's *MacArthur, 1941-1951* (1954). More objective are the second volume of D. Clayton James's *The Years of MacArthur, 1941-45* (1975) and John Gunther's *The Riddle of MacArthur* (1951). An equally colorful personality, the commander of the South Pacific Area and later of the Third Fleet, William F. Halsey, wrote (with Joseph Bryan) *Admiral Halsey's Story* (1947).

Another sector of the war against Japan, the China-Burma-India Theater, has attracted special attention, probably because of the nature of the leading American figure there, Joseph W. ("Vinegar Joe") Stilwell, and because of the enigma of American relations with China and its generalissimo, Chiang Kai-shek. The experience is well covered in three volumes of the official U.S. Army history, all by Charles F. Romanus and Riley Sunderland: *Stilwell's Mission to China* (1953), *Stilwell's Command Problems* (1956), and *Time Runs Out in the CBI* (1959). Barbara W. Tuchman in *Stilwell and the American Experience in China, 1911–1945* (1971) drew heavily on those volumes for the World War II portion of her work. General Stilwell's personal story is found in a posthumous publication, Theodore H. White's (ed.) *The Stilwell Papers* (1948). The exciting story of a Ranger-type force of volunteers in Burma is told in Charlton Ogburn, Jr.'s *The Marauders* (1959).

The official U.S. Army history of the Japanese conquest of the Philippines is Louis Morton's *The Fall of the Philippines* (1953), good historical scholarship despite a shortage of contemporary documentation. The definitive account of the Americans captured on the Bataan peninsula is Stanley L. Falk's *Bataan: The March of Death* (1962), and the fall of Corregidor is covered in James H. and William H. Belote's *Corregidor: The Saga of a Fortress* (1967). The early fighting is also covered in John Toland's *But Not in Shame: The Six Months After Pearl Harbor* (1961); William Ward Smith's *Midway: Turning Point in the Pacific* (1966) and Walter Lord's *Incredible Victory* (1967) tell the story of the decisive naval battle of Midway.

The official histories recounting the reconquest of the Philippines are M. Hamlin Cannon's *Leyte: The Return to the Philippines* (1954) and Robert Ross Smith's *Triumph in the Philippines* (1963), the latter covering the Sixth and Eighth Armies on Luzon and the Eighth Army's reoccupation of the southern Philippines. Smith also wrote *The Approach to the Philippines* (1953), covering Allied operations in the Southwest Pacific from April to October 1944. In an unofficial work, *Decision at Leyte* (1966), Stanley Falk combined in a single volume the air, naval, and ground campaigns for Leyte and in *Liberation of the Philippines* (1971) the entire Philippine campaign. Good accounts of the naval fighting in Philippine waters are C. Vann Woodward's *The Battle for Leyte Gulf* (1947) and James A. Field, Jr.'s *The Japanese at Leyte Gulf* (1947).

The official U.S. Army histories covering the island-hopping campaign through the Pacific are Samuel Milner's *Victory in Papua* (1957), John Miller, Jr.'s *Guadalcanal: The First Offensive* (1949) and *Cartwheel: The Reduction of Rabaul* (1959), Philip A. Crowl and Edmund G. Love's *Seizure of the Gilberts and Marshalls* (1955), and Philip A. Crowl's *Campaign in the Marianas* (1960).

A colorfully written unofficial account focusing on one phase of the Papuan campaign is Lida Mayo's *Bloody Buna* (1973). S. L. A. Marshall used group after-action interviews to provide a detailed story of the fight for Kwajalein in the Marshall Islands in *Island Victory* (1944), and Henry I. Shaw, Jr., wrote *Tarawa: A Legend is Born* (1969). Brian Garfield wrote of a remote corner of the Pacific in *The Thousand-Mile War: World War II in Alaska and the Aleutians* (1969), and considerable material on the Aleutians, including the invasion of Attu, is also to be found in the official U.S. Army history, Stetson Conn, Rose C. Engleman, and Byron Fairchild's *Guarding the United States and Its Outposts* (1964).

The official history recounting the final ground campaign is Roy E. Appleman, James M. Burns, Russell A. Gugeler, and John Stevens's *Okinawa: The Last Battle* (1948). Unofficial versions are Benis M. Frank's *Okinawa, Capstone to Victory* (1969) and James H. and William M. Belote's *Typhoon of Steel: Battle of Okinawa* (1970).

The best personal experience chronicles by men and officers of lesser rank are by a Navy enlisted man who served on a light cruiser, James F. Fahey, in *Pacific War Diary, 1942-1945* (1963);

a Marine Corps company commander who fought on Peleliu, George P. Hunt, in *Coral Comes High* (1946); and an enlisted marine recounting his experiences from boot camp through several island campaigns, Robert Leckie, in *Helmet for My Pillow* (1957). The war's best fictional account was also set in the Pacific, Norman Mailer's *The Naked and the Dead* (1948).

The official Air Forces histories dealing with the war in the Pacific are Vol. IV: *The Pacific: Guadalcanal to Saipan (August 1942 to July 1944)* (1950) and Vol. V: *The Pacific: Matterhorn to Nagasaki (June 1944 to August 1945)* (1953). Those of Morison's naval series are Vol. III: *The Rising Sun in the Pacific (1931–April 1943)* (1950), Vol. IV: *Coral Sea, Midway, and Submarine Actions (May 1942–August 1942)* (1950), Vol. V: *The Struggle for Guadalcanal (August 1942–February 1943)* (1951), Vol. VI: *Breaking the Bismarcks Barrier (22 July 1943– 1 May 1944)* (1950), Vol. VII: *Aleutians, Gilberts, and Marshalls (June 1942–April 1944)* (1951), Vol. VIII: *New Guinea and the Marianas (March 1944–August 1944)* (1953), Vol. XII: *Leyte (June 1944–January 1945)* (1958), Vol. XIII: *The Liberation of the Philippines: Luzon, Mindinao, the Visayas (1944–1945)* (1959), and Vol. XIV: *Victory in the Pacific (1945)* (1961). Morison later provided a synthesis of the series in *The Two Ocean War* (1963).

Historians of the U.S. Marine Corps first produced a series of pamphlets or monographs covering various actions in the Pacific, then published the five-volume History of U.S. Marine Corps Operations in World War II. The volumes are as follows: Frank O. Hough, Verle E. Ludwig, and Henry I. Shaw, Jr., *Pearl Harbor to Guadalcanal* (1961); Henry I. Shaw, Jr., and Douglas T. Kane, *Isolation of Rabaul* (1963); Henry I. Shaw, Jr., Bernard C. Nalty, and Edwin T. Turnbladh, *Central Pacific Drive* (1966); George W. Garand and Truman R. Strobridge, *Western Pacific Operations* (1971); and Benis M. Frank and Henry I. Shaw, Jr., *Victory and Occupation* (1968).

A definitive account of the black soldier in World War II is in the official U.S. Army series, Ulysses Lee's *The Employment of Negro Troops* (1966), which also provides a comprehensive essay on the experience of black soldiers in earlier times. A good unofficial work carries the study of the black soldier through the Korean War, Richard M. Dalfiume's *Desegregation of the U.S. Armed Forces: Fighting on Two Fronts, 1939–1953* (1969). The role of women in the U.S. Army is told in the official history, Mattie E. Treadwell's *The Women's Army Corps* (1954). Of particular value in any concerted effort to study the nature, attitudes, and motivations of the American soldier is a four-volume series entitled Studies in Social Psychology in World War II. Prepared by Samuel A. Stouffer, et al., the series is based on data accumulated during the war by the Research Branch of the Information and Education Division of the War Department. The volumes are Vol. I: *The American Soldier: Adjustment During Army Life* (1949), Vol. II: *The American Soldier: Combat and Its Aftermath* (1949), Vol. III: *Experiments on Mass Communication* (1949), and Vol. IV: *Measurement and Prediction* (1950).

The massive logistical effort required in supporting battlefronts strung around the world absorbs better than half of the volumes in the U.S. Army in World War II series and has been the subject of numerous other official and semiofficial histories of the war produced under auspices of government agencies. In the Army series, the Leighton and Coakley volumes on *Global Logistics and Strategy* cover the problems of allocation of resources at the highest levels; John D. Millett's *Organization and Role of the Army Service Forces* (1954) describes the work of the Army's central logistical organization; R. Elberton Smith's *The Army and Industrial Mobilization* (1959) deals with the massive procurement program for all varieties of equipment; Irving B. Holley's *Buying Aircraft* (1964) treats procurement of air materiel; and Byron Fairchild and Jonathan Grossman's *The Army and Industrial Manpower* (1959) covers the Army's role in handling labor during the war. The various technical service histories, too numerous to list individually, cover the nuts and bolts of research and development, production, and distribution, both at home and overseas. (For a convenient listing, see any of the more recent volumes of the U.S. Army in World War II series.) The best overview of Navy logistics is Duncan S. Ballantine's *U.S. Naval Logistics in the Second World War* (1947). Robert N. Connery offers a companion volume in *The Navy and Industrial Mobilization During World War II* (1951). Julius Furer wrote the official volume, *Administration of the Navy Department in World War II* (1959). Air Force logistics are covered in Volumes VI and VII of the official series, *Men and Planes* (1955) and *Services Around the World* (1958).

The conscious linking of scientific research and waging war began during World War I but reached much greater heights during World War II. The best general treatment of the scientific effort is James Phinney Baxter's *Scientists Against Time* (1946). The ultimate scientific achievement of the war was, of course, the atomic bomb. The volume of the U.S. Army in World War II series covering the development of the bomb will appear soon, and two historians of the Atomic Energy Commission, Richard G. Hewlett and Oscar Anderson, have published the story of the beginnings of atomic energy in *The New World* (1962), and General Leslie Groves, who headed the Army's Manhattan project, related his story in *Now It Can Be Told* (1962). Two works dealing with the momentous decision to drop the atomic bomb on Japan, thus to usher in a new era in warfare, are Michael Amrine's *The Great Decision: The Secret History of the Atomic Bomb* (1959) and Herbert Feis's *The Atomic Bomb and the End of World War II* (1966).

Bibliography: World War I

American Battle Monuments Commission. *American Armies and Battlefields in Europe.* Washington: Government Printing Office, 1938.

Asprey, Robert B. *At Belleau Wood.* New York: Putnam's, 1965.

Barnes, Harry Elmer. *Genesis of the World War.* New York: A. A. Knopf, 1962.

Bassett, John S. *Our War With Germany.* New York: A. A. Knopf, 1919.

Beard, Charles A. *The Devil Theory of War.* New York: Vanguard Press, 1936.

Beaver, Daniel R. *Newton D. Baker and the American War Effort.* Lincoln: Univ. of Neb. Press, 1966.

Blumenson, Martin. *The Patton Papers: 1885-1940.* Boston: Houghton Mifflin, 1972.

Borchard, Edwin M., and Lage, William P. *Neutrality for the United States.* New Haven: Yale Univ. Press, 1937.

Boyd, Thomas A. *Through the Wheat.* New York: Scribner's, 1923.

Buehrig, Edward H. *Woodrow Wilson and the Balance of Power.* Bloomington: Ind. Univ. Press, 1955.

Cate, James Lea. "The Air Service in World War I." In The Army Air Forces in World War II, edited by Cate and Wesley Frank Craven, vol. I, *Plans and Early Operations.* Chicago: Univ. of Chicago Press, 1948.

Coffman, Edward, M. *The Hilt of the Sword: The Career of Peyton C. March.* Madison: Univ. of Wisc. Press, 1966.

———. *The War to End All Wars.* New York: Oxford Univ. Press, 1968.

Crowell, Benedict, and Wilson, Robert F. *How America Went to War: An Account From the Official Sources of the Nation's War Activities, 1917-1920.* 6 vols. New Haven: Yale Univ. Press, 1921.

Cuff, Robert D. *War Industries Board: Business-Government Relations During World War I.* Baltimore: Johns Hopkins Univ. Press, 1973.

Daniels, Josephus. *Our Navy at War.* Washington: Pictorial Bureau, 1922.

DeWeerd, Harvey A. *President Wilson Fights His War.* New York: Macmillan, 1968.

Grattan, C. Hartley. *Why We Fought.* New York: Vanguard Press, 1929.

Graves, William Sidney. *America's Siberian Adventure, 1918-1920.* New York: J. Cape and H. Smith, 1931.

Green, Constance McLaughlin; Thomson, Harry C.; and Roots, Peter C. *The Ordnance Department: Planning Munitions for War*. U.S. Army in World War II. Washington: Government Printing Office, 1955.

Hagood, Johnson. *The Services of Supply: A Memoir of the Great War*. Boston: Houghton Mifflin, 1927.

Harbord, James G. *The American Army in France, 1917-1919*. Boston: Little, Brown, 1936.

Holley, Irving B. *Ideas and Weapons*. New Haven: Yale Univ. Press, 1953.

Hudson, James J. *Hostile Skies: A Combat History of the American Air Service in World War I*. Syracuse, N.Y.: Syracuse Univ. Press, 1968.

Hurley, Alfred T. *Billy Mitchell: Crusader for Air Power*. New York: Watts, 1964.

Huston, James A. *The Sinews of War: Army Logistics, 1775-1953*. Army Historical Series. Washington: Government Printing Office, 1966.

The Infantry School. *Infantry in Battle*. Washington: Infantry Journal Press, 1934.

James, D. Clayton. *The Years of MacArthur*. Vol. I, 1880-1941. Boston: Houghton Mifflin, 1970.

Johnson, Douglas W. *Battlefields of the World War*. New York: Oxford Univ. Press, 1921.

———. *Topography and Strategy*. New York: Henry Holt, 1917.

Kennan, George F. *American Diplomacy, 1900-1950*. Chicago: Univ. of Chicago Press, 1950.

Leopold, Richard W. "The Problem of American Intervention." *World Politics* 2 (1950):405-25.

Link, Arthur S. *Wilson: The Struggle for Neutrality, 1914-1915*. Princeton, N.J.: Princeton Univ. Press, 1960.

McMaster, John B. *The United States in the World War*. 2 vols. New York: Appleton, 1918-20.

March, Peyton C. *The Nation at War*. Garden City, N.Y.: Doubleday, 1932.

Marshall, S. L. A. *The American Heritage History of World War I*. New York: American Heritage Publishing Co., 1964.

May, Ernest R. *American Intervention: 1917 and 1941*. Washington: Service Center for Teachers of History, 1960.

———. *The World War and American Isolation*. Cambridge, Mass.: Harvard Univ. Press, 1959.

Millis, Walter. *The Road to War: America, 1914-1917*. Boston: Houghton Mifflin, 1935.

Morgenthau, Hans J. *In Defense of the National Interest*. New York: A. A. Knopf, 1951.

Morison, Elting E. *Admiral Sims and the Modern American Navy*. New York: Russell and Russell, 1968.

Myrer, Anton. *Once an Eagle*. New York: Holt, Rinehart, and Winston, 1968.

Notter, Harley F. *The Origins of the Foreign Policy of Woodrow Wilson*. Baltimore: Johns Hopkins Univ. Press, 1937.

Palmer, Frederick. *Our Greatest Battle*. New York: Dodd, Mead, 1919.

Paxson, Frederic L. *Pre-War Years, 1914-1917*. Boston: Houghton Mifflin, 1936.

———. *America at War, 1917-1918*. Boston: Houghton Mifflin, 1939.

Pershing, John J. *My Experiences in the World War*. 2 vols. New York: Stokes, 1931.

Petersen, Horace C., and Fite, Gilbert C. *Opponents of War, 1917-1918*. Madison: Univ. of Wisc. Press, 1957.

Pogue, Forrest C. *George C. Marshall: Education of a General 1880-1939*. New York: Viking Press, 1963.

Risch, Erna. *Quartermaster Support of the Army: A History of the Corps 1775-1939*. Washington: Government Printing Office, 1962.

Seymour, Charles. *American Diplomacy During the World War*. Baltimore: Johns Hopkins Univ. Press, 1934.

———. *American Neutrality, 1914-1917*. New Haven: Yale Univ. Press, 1935.

Smythe, Donald. *Guerrilla Warrior: The Early Life of John J. Pershing*. New York: Scribner's, 1973.

Sprout, Harold, and Sprout, Margaret. *The Rise of American Naval Power, 1776-1918*. Princeton, N.J.: Princeton Univ. Press, 1939.

———. *Toward a New Order of Sea Power: American Naval Policy and the World Scene, 1918-1922*. Princeton, N.J.: Princeton Univ. Press, 1943.

Stallings, Laurence. *The Doughboys: The Story of the AEF, 1917-1918*. New York: Harper and Row, 1963.

Tansill, Charles C. *America Goes to War*. Boston: Little, Brown, 1938.

Thomason, John W., Jr. *Fix Bayonets!* New York: Scribner's, 1926.

Trask, David F. *The United States in the Supreme War Council: American War Aims and Inter-Allied Strategy, 1917-1918*. Middletown, Conn.: Wesleyan Univ. Press, 1961.

Unterberger, Betty Miller. *America's Siberian Expedition, 1918-1920*. Durham, N.C.: Duke Univ. Press, 1956.

White, John Albert. *The Siberian Intervention*. Princeton, N.J.: Princeton Univ. Press, 1950.

Bibliography: World War II

Ambrose, Stephen. *The Supreme Commander: The War Years of General Dwight D. Eisenhower*. Baltimore: Johns Hopkins Univ. Press, 1970.

American Forces in Action. 14 pamphlets. Washington: Government Printing Office, 1943-47.

Amrine, Michael. *The Great Decision: The Secret History of the Atomic Bomb*. New York: Putnam's, 1959.

Appleman, Roy E.; Burns, James M.; Gugeler, Russell A.; and Stevens, John. *Okinawa: The Last Battle*. U.S. Army in World War II. Washington: Government Printing Office, 1948.

Arnold, Henry. *Global Mission*. New York: Harper, 1949.

Baldwin, Hanson. *Great Mistakes of the War*. New York: Harper, 1950.

Ballantine, Duncan S. *U.S. Naval Logistics in the Second World War*. Princeton, N.J.: Princeton Univ. Press, 1947.

Baxter, James Phinney. *Scientists Against Time*. Boston: Little, Brown, 1946.

Beard, Charles A. *American Foreign Policy, 1932-1940*. New Haven: Yale Univ. Press, 1946.

———. *President Roosevelt and the Coming of War, 1941*. New Haven: Yale Univ. Press, 1948.

Belote, James H., and Belote, William M. *Corregidor: The Saga of a Fortress*. New York: Harper and Row, 1967.

———. *Typhoon of Steel: Battle of Okinawa*. New York: Harper and Row, 1970.

Bemis, Samuel Flagg. *The Latin American Policy of the United States*. New York: Harcourt, Brace, 1943.

Blumenson, Martin. *The Patton Papers, 1940-1945*. Boston: Houghton Mifflin, 1974.

——. *Kasserine Pass*. Boston: Houghton Mifflin, 1967.

——. *Sicily: Whose Victory?* New York: Ballantine Books, 1969.

——. *Salerno to Cassino*. U.S. Army in World War II. Washington: Government Printing Office, 1969.

——. *Anzio: The Gamble That Failed*. Philadelphia: Lippincott, 1963.

——. *Bloody River*. Boston: Houghton Mifflin, 1970.

——. *Breakout and Pursuit*. U.S. Army in World War II. Washington: Government Printing Office, 1961.

——. *The Duel for France*. Boston: Houghton Mifflin, 1963.

Boesch, Paul. *Road to Huertgen—Forest in Hell*. Houston: Gulf Publishing Co., 1962.

Bradley, Omar N. *A Soldier's Story*. New York: Henry Holt, 1951.

Buchanan, A. Russell. *The United States and World War II*. 2 vols. New York: Harper and Row, 1964.

Burne, Alfred H. *Strategy in World War II*. Harrisburg: Military Service Publishing Co., 1947.

Burns, James MacGregor. *Roosevelt: The Lion and the Fox*. New York: Harcourt, Brace, and World, 1956.

——. *Roosevelt: The Soldier of Freedom*. New York: Harcourt Brace Jovanovich, 1971.

Butow, Robert J. C. *Tojo and the Coming of the War*. Princeton, N.J.: Princeton Univ. Press, 1961.

Cannon, M. Hamlin. *Leyte: The Return to the Philippines*. U.S. Army in World War II. Washington: Government Printing Office, 1954.

Cate, James Lea. "The Army Air Arm Between Two Wars, 1919-39." In The Army Air Forces in World War II, edited by Cate, and Wesley Frank Craven, vol. I, *Plans and Early Operations*. Chicago: Univ. of Chicago Press, 1947.

Chandler, Alfred D., ed. *The Papers of Dwight David Eisenhower: The War Years*. 5 vols. Baltimore: Johns Hopkins Univ. Press, 1970.

Clark, Mark W. *Calculated Risk*. New York: Harper, 1950.

Cline, Ray S. *Washington Command Post: The Operations Division*. U.S. Army in World War II. Washington: Government Printing Office, 1951.

Coakley, Robert W., and Leighton, Richard M. *Global Logistics and Strategy, 1943-45*. U.S. Army in World War II. Washington: Government Printing Office, 1969.

Coffey, Thomas M. *Imperial Tragedy: Japan in World War II: The First Days and the Last*. Cleveland: World Publishing Co., 1970.

Cole, Hugh M. *The Lorraine Campaign*. U.S. Army in World War II. Washington: Government Printing Office, 1950.

——. *The Ardennes: Battle of the Bulge*. U.S. Army in World War II. Washington: Government Printing Office, 1965.

Conn, Stetson, and Fairchild, Byron. *The Framework of Hemisphere Defense*. U.S. Army in World War II. Washington: Government Printing Office, 1960.

Conn, Stetson; Engelman, Rose C.; and Fairchild, Byron. *Guarding the United States and Its Outposts*. U.S. Army in World War II. Washington: Government Printing Office, 1964.

Connery, Robert H. *The Navy and Industrial Mobilization in World War II*. Princeton, N.J.: Princeton Univ. Press, 1951.

Craven, Wesley Frank, and Cate, James Lea, eds., *The Army Air Forces in World War II*. 7 vols. Chicago: Univ. of Chicago Press, 1948-58.

Crowl, Philip A. *Campaign in the Marianas*. U.S. Army in World War II. Washington: Government Printing Office, 1960.

Crowl, Philip A., and Isley, Jeter A. *The U.S. Marines and Amphibious War*. Princeton, N.J.: Princeton Univ. Press, 1951.

Crowl, Philip A., and Love, Edmund G. *Seizure of the Gilberts and Marshalls*. U.S. Army in World War II. Washington: Government Printing Office, 1955.

Dalfiume, Richard M. *Desegregation of the U.S. Armed Forces: Fighting on Two Fronts, 1939-1953*. Columbia: Univ. of Mo. Press, 1969.

Davis, Kenneth. *Eisenhower: American Hero*. New York: McGraw-Hill, 1969.

———. *The Experience of War: The United States in World War II*. Garden City, N.Y.: Doubleday, 1965.

Divine, Robert A. *The Reluctant Belligerent: American Entry Into World War II*. New York: Wiley, 1965.

Eisenhower, Dwight D. *Crusade in Europe*. Garden City, N.J.: Doubleday, 1948.

———. *Report by the Supreme Commander to the Combined Chiefs of Staff on the Operations in Europe of the Allied Expeditionary Force, 6 June 1944 to 8 May 1945*. Washington: Government Printing Office, 1945.

Eisenhower, John S. D. *The Bitter Woods*. New York: Putnam's, 1969.

Fahey, James J. *Pacific War Diary, 1942-1945*. Boston: Houghton Mifflin, 1963.

Fairchild, Byron, and Grossman, Jonathan. *The Army and Industrial Manpower*. U.S. Army in World War II. Washington: Government Printing Office, 1959.

Falk, Stanley L. *Bataan: The March of Death*. New York: W. W. Norton, 1962.

———. *Decision at Leyte*. New York: W. W. Norton, 1966.

———. *Liberation of the Philippines*. New York: Ballantine Books, 1971.

Farago, Ladislas. *Patton: Ordeal and Triumph*. New York: Astor-Honor, 1964.

Feis, Herbert. *The Atomic Bomb and the End of World War II*. Princeton, N.J.: Princeton Univ. Press, 1966.

———. *Churchill, Roosevelt, Stalin: The War They Waged and the Peace They Sought*. Princeton, N.J.: Princeton Univ. Press, 1957.

———. *The Road to Pearl Harbor*. Princeton, N.J.: Princeton Univ. Press, 1950.

Field, James A., Jr. *The Japanese at Leyte Gulf*. Princeton, N.J.: Princeton Univ. Press, 1947.

Fisher, Ernest F. *Cassino to the Alps*. U.S. Army in World War II. Washington: Government Printing Office, 1977.

Frank, Benis M. *Okinawa, Capstone to Victory*. New York: Ballantine Books, 1969.

Frank, Benis M., and Shaw, Henry I., Jr. *Victory and Occupation*. U.S. Marine Corps in World War II. Washington: Government Printing Office, 1968.

Friedlander, Saul. *Prelude to Downfall: Hitler and the United States, 1939-1941*. New York: A. A. Knopf, 1967.

Frye, Alton. *Nazi Germany and the American Hemisphere, 1933-1941*. New Haven: Yale Univ. Press, 1967.

Furer, Julius A. *Administration of the Navy Department in World War II*. Washington, Government Printing Office, 1959.

Galvin, John R. *Air Assault*. New York: Hawthorne Books, 1970.

Garand, George W., and Strobridge, Truman R. *Western Pacific Operations*. U.S. Marine Corps in World War II. Washington: Government Printing Office, 1971.

Garfield, Brian. *The Thousand-Mile War: World War II in Alaska and the Aleutians*. Garden City, N.Y.: Doubleday, 1969.

Garland, Albert N., and Smyth, Howard McGaw. *Sicily and the Surrender of Italy*. U.S. Army in World War II. Washington: Government Printing Office, 1965.

Goldberg, Alfred, ed. *A History of the United States Air Force*. New York: Van Nostrand, 1957.

Greenfield, Kent Roberts. *American Strategy in World War II: A Reconsideration*. Baltimore: Johns Hopkins Univ. Press, 1963.

———— "Origins of the Army Ground Forces; General Headquarters, United States Army, 1940-1942." In *The Organization of Ground Combat Troops*, by Greenfield, Robert R. Palmer, and Bell I. Wiley, U.S. Army in World War II. Washington: Government Printing Office, 1947.

————, ed. *Command Decisions*. Washington: Government Printing Office, 1959.

Greenfield, Kent Roberts, and Conn, Stetson, general eds. *The United States Army in World War II*. Washington: Government Printing Office, 1948-.

Groves, Leslie. *Now It Can Be Told*. New York: Harper, 1962.

Gunther, John. *The Riddle of MacArthur*. New York: Harper, 1951.

Halsey, William F. (with Joseph Bryan). *Admiral Halsey's Story*. New York: Whittlesey House, 1947.

Harrison, Gordon A. *Cross-Channel Attack*. U.S. Army in World War II. Washington: Government Printing Office, 1951.

Hechler, Ken. *The Bridge at Remagen*. New York: Ballantine Books, 1957.

Hewlett, Richard G., and Anderson, Oscar. *The New World*. University Park: Penn State Univ. Press, 1962.

Holley, Irving B., Jr. *Buying Aircraft: Materiel Procurement for the Army Air Forces*. U.S. Army in World War II. Washington, Government Printing Office, 1964.

Hough, Frank O.; Ludwig, Verle E.; and Shaw, Henry I., Jr. *Pearl Harbor to Guadalcanal*. U.S. Marine Corps in World War II. Washington: Government Printing Office, 1958.

Howe, George F. *Northwest Africa: Seizing the Initiative in the West*. U.S. Army in World War II. Washington: Government Printing Office, 1957.

Hull, Cordell. *The Memoirs of Cordell Hull*. Edited by Robert E. Sherwood. New York: Macmillan, 1948.

Hunt, George P. *Coral Comes High*. New York: Harper, 1946.

James, D. Clayton. *The Years of MacArthur, 1941-45*. Boston: Houghton Mifflin, 1975.

King, Ernest J. (with Walter M. Whitehill). *Fleet Admiral King: A Naval Record*. New York: W. W. Norton, 1952.

Langer, William L., and Gleason, S. Everett. *The Challenge to Isolation, 1937-1940*. New York: Harper, 1952.

————. *The Undeclared War, 1940-1941*. New York: Harper, 1953.

LaPierre, Dominique, and Collins, Larry. *Is Paris Burning?* New York: Simon and Schuster, 1965.

Leahy, William D. *I Was There*. New York: Whittlesey House, 1950.

Leckie, Robert. *Helmet for My Pillow*. New York: Random House, 1957.

Lee, Ulysses. *The Employment of Negro Troops*. U.S. Army in World War II. Washington: Government Printing Office, 1966.

Leighton, Richard M., and Coakley, Robert W. *Global Logistics and Strategy, 1940-1943*. U.S. Army in World War II. Washington: Government Printing Office, 1955.

Liddell Hart, B. H. *History of the Second World War*. New York: Putnam's, 1971.

Lord, Walter. *Day of Infamy*. New York: Henry Holt, 1957.

————. *Incredible Victory*. New York: Harper and Row, 1967.

Lu, David J. *From the Marco Polo Bridge to Pearl Harbor: Japan's Entry into World War II*. Washington: Public Affairs Press, 1961.

MacArthur, Douglas. *Reminiscences*. New York: McGraw-Hill, 1964.

MacDonald, Charles B. *The Battle of the Huertgen Forest*. Philadelphia: Lippincott, 1963.

———. *Company Commander.* Rev. ed. New York: Ballantine Books, 1961.

———. *The Last Offensive.* U.S. Army in World War II. Washington: Government Printing Office, 1973.

———. *The Mighty Endeavor: American Armed Forces in the European Theater in World War II.* New York: Oxford Univ. Press, 1969.

———. *The Siegfried Line Campaign.* U.S. Army in World War II. Washington: Government Printing Office, 1963.

MacDonald, Charles B., and Mathews, Sidney T. *Three Battles: Arnaville, Altuzzo, and Schmidt.* U.S. Army in World War II. Washington: Government Printing Office, 1952.

Mailer, Norman. *The Naked and the Dead.* New York: Rinehart, 1948.

Marshall, S. L. A. *Bastogne: The First Eight Days.* Washington: Infantry Journal Press, 1946.

———. *Island Victory.* Washington: Infantry Journal Press, 1944.

———. *Night Drop.* Boston: Little, Brown, 1962.

Matloff, Maurice. *Strategic Planning for Coalition Warfare, 1943-1944.* U.S. Army in World War II. Washington: Government Printing Office, 1959.

Matloff, Maurice, and Snell, Edwin M. *Strategic Planning for Coalition Warfare: 1941-1942.* U.S. Army in World War II. Washington: Government Printing Office, 1953.

Mauldin, Bill. *Up Front.* New York: Henry Holt, 1945.

Mayo, Lida. *Bloody Buna.* Garden City, N.Y.: Doubleday, 1973.

Miller, John, Jr. *Guadalcanal: The First Offensive.* U.S. Army in World War II. Washington: Government Printing Office, 1949.

———. *Cartwheel: The Reduction of Rabaul.* U.S. Army in World War II. Washington: Government Printing Office, 1959.

Millett, John D. *The Organization and Role of the Army Service Forces.* U.S. Army in World War II. Washington: Government Printing Office, 1954.

Milner, Samuel. *Victory in Papua.* U.S. Army in World War II. Washington: Government Printing Office, 1957.

Morgenstern, George. *Pearl Harbor: The Story of the Secret War.* New York: Devin-Adair, 1947.

Morison, Elting E. *Turmoil and Tradition: A Study of the Life and Times of Henry L. Stimson.* Boston: Houghton Mifflin, 1960.

Morison, Samuel Eliot. *History of United States Naval Operations in World War II.* 15 vols. Boston: Little, Brown. 1947-62.

———. *Strategy and Compromise.* Boston: Little, Brown, 1958.

———. *The Two Ocean War.* Boston: Little, Brown, 1963.

Morton, Louis. *The Fall of the Philippines.* U.S. Army World War II. Washington: Government Printing Office, 1953.

———. *Strategy and Command: The First Two Years.* U.S. Army in World War II. Washington: Government Printing Office, 1962.

Murphy, Audie. *To Hell and Back.* New York: Henry Holt, 1949.

Ogburn, Charlton, Jr. *The Marauders.* New York: Harper, 1959.

Pogue, Forrest C. *George C. Marshall: Ordeal and Hope, 1939-1942.* New York: Viking Press, 1966.

———. *George C. Marshall: Organizer of Victory, 1943-1945.* New York: Viking Press, 1973.

———. *The Supreme Command.* U.S. Army in World War II. Washington: Government Printing Office, 1954.

Romanus, Charles F., and Sunderland, Riley. *Stilwell's Mission to China.* U.S. Army in World War II. Washington: Government Printing Office, 1953.

——. *Stilwell's Command Problems*. U.S. Army in World War II. Washington: Government Printing Office, 1956.

——. *Time Runs Out in the CBI*. U.S. Army in World War II. Washington: Government Printing Office, 1959.

Ruppenthal, Roland G. *Logistical Support of the Armies, May 1941–September 1944*. U.S. Army in World War II. Washington: Government Printing Office, 1953.

——. *Logistical Support of the Armies, September 1944–May 1945*. U.S. Army in World War II. Washington: Government Printing Office, 1959.

Ryan, Cornelius. *The Longest Day*. New York: Simon and Schuster, 1959.

——. *A Bridge Too Far*. New York: Simon and Schuster, 1974.

Schmidt, Hans. *The United States Occupation of Haiti, 1914–1934*. New Brunswick, N.J.: Rutgers University Press, 1971.

Semmes, Henry H. *Portrait of Patton*. New York: Appleton-Century-Crofts, 1955.

Shaw, Henry I., Jr. *Tarawa: A Legend Is Born*. New York: Ballantine Books, 1969.

Shaw, Henry I., Jr., and Kane, Douglas T. *Isolation of Rabaul*. U.S. Marine Corps in World War II. Washington: Government Printing Office, 1963.

Shaw, Henry I., Jr.; Nalty, Bernard C.; and Turnbladh, Edwin T. *Central Pacific Drive*. U.S. Marine Corps in World War II. Washington: Government Printing Office, 1966.

Sherwood, Robert E. *Roosevelt and Hopkins*. New York: Harper, 1948.

Shroeder, Paul W. *The Axis Alliance and Japanese-American Relations*. Ithaca, N.Y.: Cornell Univ. Press, 1958.

Smith, Gaddis. *American Diplomacy During the Second World War, 1941–1945*. New York: Wiley, 1965.

Smith, R. Elberton. *The Army and Economic Mobilization*. U.S. Army in World War II. Washington: Government Printing Office, 1959.

Smith, Robert Ross. *The Approach to the Philippines*. U.S. Army in World War II. Washington: Government Printing Office, 1953.

Smith, William Ward. *Midway: Turning Point in the Pacific*. New York: Thomas Y. Crowell, 1966.

Snell, John L. *Illusion and Necessity: The Diplomacy of Global War, 1939–1945*. Boston: Houghton Mifflin, 1963.

Stiles, Bert. *Serenade to the Big Bird*. New York: W. W. Norton, 1952.

Stimson, Henry L. and Bundy, McGeorge. *On Active Service in Peace and War*. New York: Harper, 1948.

Stouffer, Samuel, et al. *Studies in Social Psychology in World War II*. 4 vols, Princeton, N.J.: Princeton Univ. Press, 1949–50.

Sulzberger, C. L., et al. *The American Heritage Picture History of World War II*. New York: American Heritage Publishing Co., 1966.

Tansill, Charles C. *Back Door to War*. Chicago: Henry Regnery, 1952.

Thornton, Willis. *The Liberation of Paris*. New York: Harcourt, Brace, and World, 1962.

Toland, John. *The Last 100 Days*. New York: Random House, 1966.

——. *But Not in Shame: The Six Months After Pearl Harbor*. New York: Random House, 1961.

——. *The Rising Sun: The Decline and Fall of the Japanese Empire, 1936–1945*. New York: Random House, 1970.

Treadwell, Mattie. *The Women's Army Corps*. U.S. Army in World War II. Washington: Government Printing Office, 1954.

Truscott, Lucian K., Jr. *Command Missions*. New York: Dutton, 1954.

Tuchman, Barbara. *Stilwell and the American Experience in China, 1911-1945*. New York: Macmillan, 1971.

Waller, George M. *Pearl Harbor: Roosevelt and the Coming of the War*. Boston: Heath, 1953.

War Reports of George C. Marshall, H. H. Arnold, and Ernest J. King. Philadelphia: Lippincott, 1947.

Watson, Mark S. *Chief of Staff: Prewar Plans and Preparations*. U.S. Army in World War II. Washington: Government Printing Office, 1950.

White, Theodore H., ed. *The Stilwell Papers*. New York: W. Sloane Associates, 1948.

Whitney, Courtney H. *MacArthur: His Rendezvous with Destiny*. New York: A. A. Knopf, 1956.

Willoughby, Charles A., and Chamberlain, John. *MacArthur, 1941-1951*. New York: McGraw-Hill, 1954.

Wohlstetter, Roberta. *Pearl Harbor: Warning and Decision*. Stanford, Calif.: Stanford Univ. Press, 1962.

Woodward, C. Vann. *The Battle for Leyte Gulf*. New York: Macmillan, 1947.

Zeimke, Earl F. *The U.S. Army in the Occupation of Germany, 1944-1946*. Washington: Government Printing Office, 1975.

Chapter **10**

The United States and the World Military Scene Since 1945

Robert W. Coakley and
Charles B. MacDonald

WORLD WAR II marked the end of an era in the military history of the world. After Hiroshima and Nagasaki, all nations would live under the shadow of atomic power, with its potential destructiveness multiplied enormously by the development of the hydrogen or thermonuclear bomb and increasingly sophisticated methods of delivery by plane and missile. Yet if the development of nuclear weapons threatened to change the whole nature of warfare, it failed to do so immediately. Wars continued to be fought by the older conventional methods and with conventional weapons, even while a nuclear arms race between the United States and the Soviet Union proceeded apace, and other nations acquired nuclear weapons. Much of the arena of conflict was in Asia, Africa, and the Middle East, as native peoples threw off the dominance of their European colonial masters; and indeed a good deal of this conflict featured the least sophisticated of methodology—guerrilla war.

The development of increasingly varied and terrible nuclear weapons was justified largely in terms of their effect in deterring war, rather than in prospect of waging it. Under the panoply of this "great deterrent," even the United States and the Soviet Union pursued their rivalry in other ways. In contrast to its prewar isolation, the United States became intimately involved in the affairs of nations in all corners of the globe—so much so that the most practicable approach to the postwar era for the American student of military history is to consider United States and world military history as a single entity.

There has been a veritable avalanche of literature produced in the United States since 1945 which both develops new military theories to meet new conditions and details the course of military events. Much of this literature belongs to the realm of the political scientist, the journalist, the military theorist, the operations analyst, the sociologist, and the economist rather

---

For notes on the authors, see the first pages of Chapters 7 and 9.

than to that of the historian. Definitive histories are yet scarce. They must await the passage of time to give perspective and allow historians access to documents still classified in the files of various governments. Even then the immense complexity of technology and the rapidity of both technological and social change in the post-1945 era may well defy the simple analyses that historians have often applied to earlier epochs. From the vantage point of the late-1970s, in any case, it is far easier to find historical literature on almost any conceivable aspect of the postwar period than to select the works of greatest value to the student of military history, the difficult task to which this chapter must perforce turn.

Occupation

The immediate aftermath of World War II saw the occupation of Germany, Austria, Japan, and Korea by the victorious Allies. On the American occupation in Europe, Harold Zink's *American Military Government in Germany* (1947) and a volume edited by Carl J. Friedrich, *American Experiences in Military Government in World War II* (1948), are contemporary accounts by scholars that retain much value for their insights. Earl F. Ziemke in a volume in the Army Historical Series, *The U.S. Army in the Occupation of Germany, 1944-1946* (1975), provides a thorough study of the evolution of policy and of the first year of the occupation. A similar work from the British viewpoint is F. S. V. Donnison's *Civil Affairs and Military Government, Northwest Europe, 1944-1946* (1961). The head of the American military government in Germany, General Lucius D. Clay, has rendered his own account of stewardship in *Decision in Germany* (1950). John Gimbel's two works, one a general account, *The American Occupation of Germany: Politics and the Military, 1945-1949* (1968), and the other a study of a locality, *A German Community under Occupation: Marburg, 1945-1952* (1961), are both good studies. The occupation of Austria is covered in William B. Bader's *Austria Between East and West, 1945-1955* (1966). On the occupation of Japan, William J. Sebold's *With MacArthur in Japan* (1965) is essentially the memoir of the Supreme Commander's political adviser. The best general accounts of that occupation are Kazue Kawai's *Japan's American Interlude* (1960) and Shiguru Yoshida's *The Yoshida Memoirs: The Story of Japan in Crisis* (1973). Most of the general histories of the Korean War provide, as background, material on the American occupation of Korea between 1945 and 1948 (see below under Korean War).

The Cold War

Occupation soon merged into what came to be known as the cold war between the United States and the Soviet Union that involved both a nuclear arms race and a struggle for influence, with the United States assuming the leadership of an alliance of free nations of the Atlantic area in the North Atlantic Treaty Organization (NATO) in 1949. The most dramatic early episode of the cold war came a year earlier, in 1948, when the Russians blocked overland access to Berlin, a crisis covered by W. Philipps Davison in *The Berlin Blockade* (1958) and by Jean E. Smith in *The Defense of Berlin* (1963).

The origins of the cold war have given rise to one of the more spirited historical controversies of the postwar epoch. The standard American interpretation, first developed contemporaneously with the events, was that the cold war was an outgrowth of the Soviet effort at military and ideological expansion and the American response a brave and necessary one. Most of the American participants who have written memoirs, including Harry S. Truman in *Years of Decision* (1955) and *Years of Trial and Hope* (1958), have espoused this view. This interpretation was further developed in such scholarly writings as William McNeill's *America, Britain, and Russia* (1953), George F. Kennan's *Russia, the Atom and the West* (1957), John Lukacs's *A History of the Cold War* (1961), Louis Halle's *The Cold War as History* (1967), and Herbert Feis's *From Trust to Terror: The Onset of the Cold War* (1970), all of which support, in greater or lesser degree, the thesis of Soviet intransigence.

Beginning in the 1960s a school of revisionist historians, usually characterized as belonging to the New Left, challenged this view and charged that the economic imperialism of the United States and not the expansionist drive of Soviet communism was responsible for the cold war. Truman was as much villain to this group as he was hero to the other. The spiritual father of the New Left interpretation was William Appleman Williams, a diplomatic historian whose *Tragedy of American Diplomacy* appeared in 1959. Williams's attack was closely followed by a two-volume work by D. F. Fleming, *The Cold War and Its Origins* (1961). And in the era of the Vietnam

War a veritable flood of books found what the authors considered an unwise American Vietnam involvement stemming from the foreign policy that originated with the Truman administration in 1945. Representative are Gabriel Kolko's two books, The Roots of American Foreign Policy (1969) and The Limits of Power (1972); Walter LaFeber's America, Russia, and the Cold War (second edition 1972); Gar Alperowitz's Atomic Diplomacy: Hiroshima and Potsdam (1965); and Thomas G. Paterson's Soviet-American Confrontation: Post War Reconstruction and the Origins of the Cold War (1975).

Rebuttals have come from Robert W. Tucker in The Radical Left and American Foreign Policy (1971) and Robert J. Maddox in The New Left and the Origins of the Cold War (1973), the first of which questions the ideological assumptions and the second the sound scholarship of the New Left school. In the United States and the Origins of the Cold War (1972), a work that lays the blame for the cold war on both sides, John L. Gaddis also points up the basic ideological assumptions that lay behind the New Left writings and questions whether their conclusions do not derive almost automatically from their assumptions. In all the writing on the origins of the cold war the essential element lacking is any research in Soviet sources that would permit something more than conjecture on the motives of Soviet leaders.

The cold war has had many aspects, diplomatic and military, and has generated much writing on its course as well as its origins. On the broad aspects of the course of the cold war, Paul Y. Hammond's The Cold War Years (1969) and Cold War and Detente (1975) are solid works; other works of this genre are George Quester's Nuclear Diplomacy: The First Twenty-Five Years (1970), David Rees's The Age of Containment: The Cold War 1945-1965 (1967), and Ronald Steel's Pax Americana (revised edition, 1970). Of these works, David Rees's is most outspoken in support of the theme of Communist aggression, while Ronald Steel's is highly critical of American policy.

The best accounting of the nuclear balance up to 1971, based entirely on unclassified sources, is a Brookings Institution study by Harland B. Moulton, From Superiority to Parity: The United States and the Strategic Arms Race (1971); Edgar Bottome covers much the same ground in The Balance of Terror: A Guide to the Arms Race (1972). Both demolish the myth of a "missile gap" in the early 1960s and stress the reality of the increase in Soviet nuclear capabilities in the late 1960s and early 1970s that has created virtual nuclear parity between the superpowers.

Of the numerous crises that the cold war has produced, beginning with the Berlin blockade in 1948, the most chilling was the confrontation in the Cuban missile crisis of 1962. Robert F. Kennedy's *Thirteen Days* (1969) is a firsthand account of American policy making. The most complete and balanced secondary accounts are Elie Abel's *The Missile Crisis* (1966) and Graham T. Allison's *Essense of Decision: Explaining the Cuban Missile Crisis* (1971).

The obverse side of the coin from the arms race has been the effort to limit the growth of armaments, particularly nuclear armaments, and prevent the spread of nuclear weapons. Bernhard Bechhoefer's *Postwar Negotiations for Arms Control* (1961) is an excellent detailed history and analysis of the first decade and a half of postwar negotiations; Chalmers M. Roberts, an observant newspaperman, has covered an additional decade in *The Nuclear Years: The Arms Race and Arms Control, 1945-70* (1970). Mason Willrich presents a thoughtful study of the effort to prevent the spread of nuclear weapons in *Non-Proliferation Treaty: Framework for Nuclear Arms Control* (1969), and John Newhouse in *Cold Dawn: The Story of SALT* (1973) deals effectively with the development of policy on strategic arms limitation within the United States government and talks with the Soviet government leading to the first strategic arms limitation treaty.

New Military Philosophies

The new postwar technology raised questions about military theory that had hardly been visualized in the writings of the classical military philosophers from Sun Tzu to Clausewitz (see Chapter 4). With technological developments came new theories of war and new strategies, and, in contrast to the pre-World War II period, the majority of theorists were Americans. Few were actually practitioners of the military art; most came from either the academic world or the operational research organizations, think tanks as they were called, that proliferated in the 1950s to produce studies under government contract.

P. M. S. Blackett, a British Nobel prize winning physicist, and Vannevar Bush, an American scientist prominent in military research in World War II, were among the first to theorize about the future of war in the atomic age. Bush in *Modern Arms and Free Men* (1949) and Blackett in *The Military and Political Consequences of Atomic Energy* (1948) argued that in the immediate future atomic energy would not affect warfare as much as laymen thought. Blackett, however, did note that whereas the chief purpose of military establishments in the past had been to win wars, in the future their *raison d'etre* would be to avert them. And Bernard Brodie's essay in a collection called *The Absolute Weapon* published in 1946 was prescient enough to explore many of the implications of the use of atomic power as a deterrent to war.

The appearance of the hydrogen bomb, with its vastly greater destructive power, and its possession by both the United States and the Soviet Union, stimulated the search for a new military philosophy and brought the whole idea of deterrence into its own. The decade of the 1950s was a period of great intellectual ferment in the study of defense policy in Great Britain and the United States. Both countries adopted deterrence as the basis of their military policies, the Eisenhower administration espousing a "new look" philosophy which stressed the threat of "massive retaliation" not only to deter atomic attack but also to prevent Communist expansion in outlying areas in Asia and Africa. Sir John Slessor, then the chairman of the British Chiefs of Staff, gave expression to the fundamental ideas of deterrence in 1953 when he pointed to the bomber as the "great deterrent." His book under that title appeared in 1957.

The theory of massive retaliation to deter small wars was unpalatable in a growing number of academic defense studies institutes that sprang up in the 1950s. There is, in fact, no good theoretical defense of massive retaliation in all the military literature of the fifties. And there soon appeared a barrage of books whose primary theme was that limited war rather than massive retaliation was the only way to prevent Soviet encroachments in many parts of the world (in contrast to a massive attack on the West). The two most influential of these books appeared in 1957, Robert E. Osgood's *Limited War: The Challenge to American Strategy* and Henry Kissinger's *Nuclear Weapons and Foreign Policy*. By adopting massive retaliation, the Eisenhower administration had sought to avoid future Koreas. But Osgood, in particular, pointed to the Korean War as an example of the uses of limited war in a period when resort to massive nuclear weapons could only produce mutual destruction. Both Osgood and Kissinger stressed that large nuclear weapons could not be effective (as the massive retaliation doctrine seemed to imply) for the conduct of foreign policy in peripheral areas. Both argued that American policy had been traditionally too rigid in waging absolute war for absolute peace and that the nuclear age would no longer permit it; given the destructive power of hydrogen bombs, no absolute war was possible. Kissinger went somewhat further than Osgood in advocating the waging of limited war with the smaller tactical nuclear weapons then being developed. Indeed, some of the force of his logic for limited war was vitiated by a highly unrealistic scenario of a nuclear "tournament" in central Europe in which limitations on the nature and size of weapons would be observed.

The doctrine of limited war gained an almost complete dominance in intellectual circles in the late 1950s and in somewhat modified form became the basis of the Kennedy-McNamara "flexible response" policies. And almost all the theorists of the fifties favored use of tactical nuclear weapons in limited conflicts, a doctrine that led to the development of the Pentomic division in the U.S. Army with an emphasis on capability for either conventional or nuclear warfare. Bernard Brodie, whose 1959 book summed up much of the thinking at the leading operational research organization, the Rand Corporation, concluded that the theory "that nuclear weapons must be used in limited wars has been reached by too many people, too quickly, on the basis of too little analysis of the problem" (*Strategy in the Missile Age*, p. 330). A reaction soon set in. In *The Strategy of Conflict* (1960) Thomas Schelling, a Harvard political scientist, argued forcefully that the break between conventional and nuclear weapons was the natural dividing line between limited and absolute war. Kissinger himself at least partially recanted his earlier enthusiasm for limited nuclear war in *The Necessity for Choice* (1961). The pendulum by the early sixties had thus swung the other way, and the limited war forces of the Kennedy-Johnson period were largely geared to the use of conventional weapons, with the Pentomic division giving way to the ROAD (Reorganization Objective Army Division). But the debate did not end; Brodie in 1966 *(Escalation and Nuclear Option)* defended the use of tactical nuclear weapons under certain circumstances.

Meanwhile, the work of other Rand specialists on the technical requirements of deterrence shifted some of the emphasis from limited war to the question of nuclear balance. The limited war theorists of the fifties had generally assumed that mere possession of the thermonuclear bomb and means of delivery by one side created a "balance of terror" with the other. That this assumption was not necessarily valid was demonstrated by Albert Wohlstetter of Rand in an article entitled "The Delicate Balance of Terror" in *Foreign Affairs* in early 1958. Wohlstetter stressed the vulnerability of the American bomber force and first generation missiles to surprise attack and maintained that a deterrent force existed only if it could absorb this first strike and then inflict reprisals. He laid down a number of requirements for such a deterrent force, and his line of thought heavily influenced the Kennedy-McNamara defense policies.

This thinking also led to the theory of Oscar Morgenstern, set forth in The Question of National Defense (1959, pp. 75–76), that it was "in the interest of the United States for Russia to have an invulnerable retaliatory force and vice versa." This theory of mutual deterrence, with the conflicts of the cold war taking lesser forms under the umbrella of nuclear stalemate, dominated the military thinking of the sixties. One of the leading practitioners of operations research did dare to tackle the unthinkable—what if deterrence failed and thermonuclear war did break out? Herman Kahn in On Thermonuclear War (1960) predicted that the social and political structure of the United States and a large proportion of its population would survive a thermonuclear exchange, particularly if necessary civil preparations were made. Kahn's rather optimistic and light approach to such a macabre subject produced something of a revulsion against his work, but in reality much of his argument was on the need for military forces to meet a whole range of options in what he viewed as a world of continuing conflict between nations.

During the 1960s the emphasis shifted to conflict at the lowest point on the spectrum—wars for national liberation pursued primarily by guerrilla methods, what the French writer, Raymond Aron, aptly characterized as "poor man's total war." The theories of this type of war were in fact much older and originated mainly with the Chinese Communist leader Mao Tse-tung whose Selected Works, written much earlier, appeared in English translation in 1954–55. A translation of the North Vietnamese General Vo Nguyen Giap's People's War, People's Army appeared in 1962 and Ho Chi Minh's On Revolution: Selected Writings, translated and edited by Bernard Fall, in 1967. The theorist of revolutionary guerilla warfare in the western hemisphere was the Cuban leader Che Guevara, whose Guerrilla Warfare (1961) contains the essence of his doctrines.

Mao's thought (the other writers were essentially disciples who adapted his philosophy to areas outside China) was based on the Marxist-Leninist world view but adapted to the conditions of a peasant society. The mobilization of the people behind Communist leadership to overthrow oppressive colonial or capitalist overlords was the central theme of Mao's doctrine.

"With the common people of the whole country mobilized," he wrote, "we shall create a vast sea of humanity and drown the enemy in it, remedy our shortage in arms and other things, and secure the prerequisites to overcome every difficulty in war."[1] Once the masses had been indoctrinated and mobilized, Mao postulated certain stages of conflict beginning with guerrilla war, proceeding through positional warfare during which the revolutionary forces would organize a conventional army and pursue a war of attrition, and ending with a conventional army taking the offensive and achieving final victory. While Mao's doctrine was not one of exclusive guerrilla war, he and his successors (particularly Che Guevara) emphasized the use of guerrilla tactics in all stages and the waging of protracted war in which the indomitable spirit of the masses would finally prevail against any odds. As Giap wrote:

> Guerrilla warfare is the form of fighting of the masses of people, of the people of a weak and badly equipped country who stand up against an aggressive army which possesses better equipment and technique. . . . Success in many small fights added together gradually wears out the enemy manpower while little by little fostering our forces.[2]

The doctrines of Mao, Giap, and Ho Chi Minh came to be studied in the West largely in an effort to find means of combating what appeared to be a new and diabolical method of spreading Communist power and influence. In formulating doctrine, it was the French, with bitter experience in wars of national liberation in Indochina and Algeria, who took the lead. French writers coined the term *revolutionary war* to describe this type of conflict and developed a theory of combating it by destroying the base of guerrilla support with a combination of force and an effort to meet the legitimate grievances of the people. Their views are well summarized in Roger Trinquier's *Modern Warfare: A French View of Counterinsurgency* (1964) and Peter Paret's *French Revolutionary Warfare from Indo-China to Algeria* (1964).

The theories of revolutionary war and of counterinsurgency took their place in the intellectual scene of the sixties—in a scenario that saw a whole range of conflict, from relatively primitive yet politically sophisticated revolutionary war at the lowest end of the scale to full-blown thermonuclear war at the highest. The French scholar Raymond Aron's *On War* (1959)

---

1. Mao Tse-tung, *Selected Works* (New York: International Publishers, 1954-55), 2:204.
2. Vo Nguyen Giap, *People's War, People's Army* (New York: Praeger, 1962), p. 105.

covered much of this range and neatly fitted the French theory of
revolutionary war with the limited war theories of writers such
as Kissinger and Osgood.

For those interested in a quick summary of the strategic
thinkers of the postwar period, Michael Howard has provided a
cogent analysis in "The Classical Strategists," *Adelphi Papers* 54
(February, 1969). Another overlook is that of Harry Coles,
"Strategic Studies since 1945: The Era of Overthink" in *Military
Review* (April, 1973). A book-length treatment is Roy Licklider's
The Private Nuclear Strategists (1971); Urs Schwartz, in
*American Strategy, a New Perspective: The Growth of Politico-
Military Thinking in the United States* (1966), provides a look by
a European at American strategic thinking and doctrine both
before and after World War II. Morton Halperin's *Defense
Strategies for the Seventies* (1971) is a good summary of the state
of American strategic thinking as the Vietnam War was drawing
to a close. And Alexander George and Richard Smoke's
Deterrence in American Foreign Policy (1974) includes a series of
case studies which serve as a basis for analyzing the deterrence
theory as applied to limited wars.

American Defense Organization and Policy

The new role of the United States in world affairs after 1945
brought unprecedented problems in defense organization and
policy. Reorganization in 1947 produced a single Department of
Defense and a separate Department of the Air Force to join the
Departments of the Army (formerly War) and the Navy. But the
powers of the Secretary of Defense actually to direct the
activities of the three services were only gradually strengthened
in successive defense reorganizations. These culminated, in
legislative terms, with the Defense Reorganization Act of 1958,
but Robert S. McNamara's term as secretary saw many
innovations and a significant strengthening of the Secretary of
Defense's position within the framework of the 1958 legislation.
On the broader patterns of defense organization, the best works
are Paul Y. Hammond's *Organizing for Defense* (1961), which
covers the period since 1900; William Kintner's *Forging a New
Sword* (1958); and C. W. Borkland's *The Department of Defense*
(1968). On the original unification act of 1947, the most
important study is that of Demetrios Caraley, *The Politics of
Military Unification: A Study of Conflict and the Policy Process*
(1966). Edward Kolodziej details the congressional role in

making defense policy in *The Uncommon Defense and Congress 1945-1963* (1966).

The emphasis in most of the writing by political scientists has been on political factors in the making of defense policy. Samuel P. Huntington's *The Common Defense: Strategic Programs in National Politics* (1961) is a provocative study of policy making in the Truman and Eisenhower administrations. Studies by Hammond, Warner R. Schilling, and Glen H. Snyder of major decisions leading to a new national security policy during the Korean War and of the genesis and meaning of Eisenhower's "new look" appeared in *Strategy, Politics, and Defense Budgets* (1962). More thorough studies are unlikely until the basic documents have been declassified. Morton Halperin's *Bureaucratic Politics and Foreign Policy* (1974) is another provocative study ranging over the entire postwar period and emphasizing organizational factors. Harold Stein's case book of essays by various authorities, *American Civil-Military Decisions* (1963), and the collaborative work of Stein with Walter Millis and Harvey C. Mansfield, *Arms and the State: Civil-Military Elements in National Policy* (1958), both develop the theme of interaction of civilian and military officials in making decisions on national defense.

For the early postwar period and the problem of defense policies, Walter Millis has edited *the Forrestal Diaries* (1951), revealing on the dilemmas faced by the first Secretary of Defense. Arnold A. Rogow's *James Forrestal: A Study of Personality, Politics, and Policy* (1963) is the only full-length scholarly biography of a Secretary of Defense yet to appear, although the journalist Carl W. Borklund has presented brief sketches of the secretaries from Forrestal to McNamara in *Men of the Pentagon* (1966). The work and thought of Robert S. McNamara have attracted much attention, but no biography of any worth has yet emerged. William W. Kaufman's *The McNamara Strategy* (1964) represents an early effort to appraise the direction of the secretary's policies. A later work by two of his aides, Alain C. Enthoven and K. Wayne Smith, *How Much is Enough? Shaping the Defense Program, 1961-1969* (1971), is more comprehensive though less objective. The work of another aide, Charles J. Hitch, *Decision Making for Defense* (1965), is best on the economics of defense policy making in the McNamara regime. Hitch's earlier work with Roland N. McKean, *The Economics of Defense in the Nuclear Age* (1960), a product of research at Rand, is essential to understanding the whole McNamara approach. Henry L. Trewhitt's *McNamara: His*

Ordeal in the Pentagon (1971) is an early appraisal by an outsider. McNamara's own *The Essence of Security* (1968) consists mainly of his official statements.

All of the American presidents between 1945 and 1968 have written memoirs except John F. Kennedy, and these memoirs, although by their nature not unbiased, form a basic source for the study of defense policy during their administrations. On the Kennedy period, works by his close associates, Arthur M. Schlesinger, Jr.'s *A Thousand Days* (1965) and Theodore Sorenson's *Kennedy* (1966) are a partial substitute.

A number of books by Army leaders who participated in decision making on defense policy in the period mix argument and memoir, reflecting particularly the controversies of the 1950s. Most notable are the works of two former Chiefs of Staff: Matthew B. Ridgway, *Soldier* (1956), and Maxwell D. Taylor, *The Uncertain Trumpet* (1960), *Responsibilities and Response* (1967), and *Swords and Ploughshares* (1972). Both were in the forefront of the struggle for adequate forces for limited war. Two other works by lesser figures, James M. Gavin's *War and Peace in the Space Age* (1958) and John B. Medaris's *Countdown for Decision* (1960), deal primarily with the Army's struggle to find a role in the development and use of missile technology.

NATO

In the post-World War II years, the United States became involved in a whole series of alliances, the most important and binding with the nations of western Europe in the North Atlantic Treaty Organization (NATO). This alliance became the centerpiece of American policy, and its history, as well as controversies regarding NATO strategy, have generated a considerable literature. Lord Ismay, one of the founders, presented a factual account of NATO's origins and early history in *NATO: The First Five Years, 1949-1954* (1955). An especially interesting appraisal is the British military theorist B. H. Liddell-Hart's *Deterrent or Defense: A Fresh Look at the West's Military Position* (1960). (On Liddell-Hart as military philosopher and historian see Chapter 4.) Other analyses of the continuing problems of NATO include Edgar McInnis's *The Atlantic Triangle and the Cold War* (1959); Alastair Buchan's *NATO in the 1960's: The Implications of Interdependence* (1960); a book of essays edited by Klaus Knorr, *NATO and American Security* (1959); Robert E. Osgood's *NATO: The Entangling Alliance* (1962); Henry A. Kissinger's

The Troubled Partnership: A Re-Appraisal of the Atlantic Alliance (1965); William T. R. and Annette Fox's NATO and the Range of American Choice (1967); and a series of essays edited by William Fox and Warner R. Schilling, European Security and the Atlantic System (1967).

The World of Limited and Revolutionary War

New theories of limited and revolutionary war reflected the real world, for the incidence of armed conflict continued high in the thirty years following World War II, although there were no wars between major powers. Seymour Deitchman in Limited War and American Defense Policy (1964) counted over thirty in various parts of the world in the 1945–63 period, and there have been many more since. The most important of these wars were the civil war in China after World War II,[3] the Arab-Israeli Wars, the Korean War, the long conflict in Indochina involving first France and then the United States, and the revolutionary uprising against France in Algeria. But there were also others, including civil conflicts in Africa, Asia, and Latin America, and brief wars involving India and Pakistan.

Reserving for the moment consideration of those wars in which American forces were involved in Korea and Vietnam, there is a considerable body of literature on the others, although practically none of it can be called definitive history. The four Arab-Israeli wars occured in 1948–49, 1956, 1967, and 1973. All but the first were extremely brief and were waged with conventional weapons using traditional Western battlefield tactics. The best work on the 1948–49 war in which the Jewish state was won is Nathaniel Lorch's The Edge of the Sword (1961). There are a number on the Suez War of 1956, including S. L. A. Marshall's Sinai Victory (1956), A. J. Barker's Suez: The Seven Day War (1965), and Paul Johnson's The Suez War (1957). Edgar O'Ballance has written on the first three wars: The Arab-Israeli War, 1948 (1958), The Sinai Campaign of 1956 (1959), and The Third Arab-Israeli War (1972). J. Bowyer Bell's The Long War: Israel and the Arabs since 1946 (1969) also covers the first three wars. Michael Howard and Robert Hunter deal with the 1967 war in its overall context in Israel and the Arab World: The Crisis of 1967 (1967), and the London Times Insight Team has provided the best coverage to date of the 1973 conflict in The

---

3. This civil war actually began in the 1920s, and the 1945–48 war was simply the last stage. For coverage see Chapter 6.

Yom Kippur War (1974). Chaim Herzog in *The War of Atonement: October 1973* (1975) offers an Israeli view.

French defeat in Indochina (covered in connection with the American involvement there) was followed by the long ordeal of the French Army in Algeria where it was able to defeat armed rebellion but never to win a war of national liberation. The Algerian War, following so closely on the defeat in Vietnam, brought home to the French more than to any other nation the difficult problems involved in combating revolutionary war. And it led to the crisis that ended the Fourth Republic and brought General Charles de Gaulle back into power. De Gaulle disappointed the very military figures who had placed him at the head of the French government, provoking an army revolt against the Fifth Republic he founded. The fighting in Algeria is best covered in Michael K. Clark's *Algeria in Turmoil* (1959), and Jean Gillespie's *Algeria: Rebellion and Revolution* (1960). The vicissitudes of the French Army throughout the period are explored in John Stewart Ambler's *The French Army in Politics, 1945-1962* (1966), and the specific crisis arising out of the withdrawal from Algeria in Edgar S. Furniss's *De Gaulle and the French Army* (1964) and in Orville D. Menard's *The Army and the Fifth Republic* (1967).

There are useful works on conflicts where insurgency was not always successful. Sir Robert Thompson's *Defeating Communist Insurgency* (1966) is an account of the British success in Malaya by a principal director of the counterinsurgency effort. An outsider's view is Lucien Pye's *Guerrilla Communism in Malaya* (1956). Uldarico S. Baclagon's *Lessons from the Huk Campaign in the Philippines* (1960) and Col. N. D. Valeriano and Lt. Col. C. T. R. Bohannan's *Counter-Guerrilla Operations: The Philippine Experience* (1962) treat the successful antiguerrilla campaign in the Philippines. Richard Gott's *Guerrilla Movements in Latin America* (1971) deals with a broad range of conflict in the American subcontinent including some uprisings that were not successful as well as the Castro revolution in Cuba. John De St. Torre covers a major civil war in Africa in *The Brothers War: Biafra and Nigeria* (1972). J. Bowyer Bell attempts to dispel the legend of invariable guerrilla success engendered by Vietnam and Algeria in *The Myth of the Guerrilla: Revolutionary Theory and Malpractice* (1971). Perhaps the most sophisticated treatment of guerrilla warfare is Walter Laqueur's *Guerrilla: A Historical and Critical Study* (1976).

The Korean War

From the American viewpoint, the wars in Korea and Vietnam were the major conflicts of the post-1945 period and the best examples of the persistence of limited war in the nuclear age. The U.S. Army plans five official volumes on the Korean War, of which three have been published: James F. Schnabel's *Policy and Direction: The First Year* (1972), which chronicles the major policy decisions and planning actions in Washington and Tokyo until the start of truce negotiations in mid-1951; Roy E. Appleman's *South to the Naktong, North to the Yalu* (1961), a detailed account of the first five months of the fighting; and Walter G. Hermes's *Truce Tent and Fighting Front* (1966), which covers the frustrating truce negotiations at Kaesong and Panmunjom from mid-1951 and the fighting that took place during that time. A projected fourth volume will tell of the fighting from the Chinese Communist intervention in November 1950, to the start of truce negotiations, and a fifth volume will be devoted to logistics. The Army has also published three separate studies: Maj. Robert K. Sawyer's *Military Advisors in Korea: KMAG in Peace and War* (1963); Russel A. Gugeler's *Combat Actions in Korea* (revised edition, 1970), a series of representative small unit actions; and John G. Westover's *Combat Support in Korea* (1955), an account of the work of small combat support units.

The official U.S. Navy history is in one volume, James A. Field, Jr.'s *History of United States Naval Operations, Korea* (1962), as is that of the U.S. Air Force, Frank B. Futrell's *The United States Air Force in Korea, 1950-1953* (1961). The Marine Corps published five volumes: Lynn Montross and Capt. Nicholas A. Canzona, *The Pusan Perimeter* (1954), *The Inchon-Seoul Operation* (1955), and *The Chosin Reservoir Campaign* (1957); Major Hubard D. Kuokka and Major Norman W. Hicks, *The East-Central Front* (1962); and Lt. Col. Pat Meid and Maj. James M. Yingling, *Operations in West Korea* (1972).

Among several good one-volume surveys of the war, David Rees's *Korea: The Limited War* (1964) is the best treatment of policy in its relation to military operations. Harry J. Middleton's *The Compact History of the Korean War* (1965) is brief but well written and reliable. Robert Leckie's *Conflict: The History of the Korean War, 1950-53* (1962), largely combat history, is up to the author's usual standards of style and accuracy. T. R. Fehrenbach's *This Kind of War* (1963) focuses in the main on the men who fought and depends in large measure on postwar interviews and personal narratives. Glen D. Paige's *The Korean Decision* (1968) is a valuable detailed study of America's week of decision in June 1950.

The memoir literature is important, including President Truman's *Years of Trial and Hope*, previously cited, and President Eisenhower's *Mandate for Change* (1956). The Secretary of State during most of the Korean War years, Dean Acheson, covers political and diplomatic aspects of the war in *Present at the Creation* (1969), while Douglas MacArthur's account is in *Reminiscences* (1964). The U.S. Army's Chief of Staff during the period, J. Lawton Collins, wrote *War in Peacetime* (1969), which is less a reflection of General Collins's personal views and actions than a general history from the Washington viewpoint. Matthew B. Ridgway's *The Korean War* (1967) is a similar work from the viewpoint of the Eighth Army commander and MacArthur's successor as United Nations commander.

In addition to biographies of MacArthur noted under World War II writings, three other works make noteworthy contributions to the controversy resulting from his relief. In his usual readable style, Trumbull Higgins provides a penetrating analysis of the conduct of the war in terms of MacArthur's role in *Korea and the Fall of MacArthur* (1960). Richard H. Rovere and Arthur M. Schlesinger, Jr.'s *The General and the President and the Future of American Foreign Policy* (1951) is less than favorable to MacArthur. The most exhaustive and probably the most balanced treatment of the controversy is John W. Spanier's *The Truman-MacArthur Controversy and the Korea War* (1959).

The best educated guesses on the reasoning of the Chinese Communists in entering the Korean War are in Allen S. Whiting's *China Crosses the Yalu* (1960). Although without reliable evidence from China itself, Whiting assumes that the Chinese leaders carefully calculated the risks and arrived at a rational decision. Robert R. Simmons in a more recent work, *The Strained Alliance: Peking, Pyongyang, Moscow, and the Politics of the Korean Civil War* (1975), approaches the Korean conflict from the Communist side, treating it in rather novel fashion as a civil war, not as an eruption of the larger cold war.

Except for the official histories, battle narratives are few. Particularly well done are two by S. L. A. Marshall, *The River and the Gauntlet* (1953) which focuses on the 2d Infantry Division's fierce fighting against Chinese Communist attack across the Congchon River in November 1950, and *Pork Chop Hill* (1956), a detailed account of a battle for outposts by the 7th

Infantry Division in April 1953. Robert D. Heinl, Jr., provides an account of the Inchon invasion and capture of Seoul in *Victory at High Tide* (1968).

Two differing views of the controversial conduct of Americans held captive by the Communists are available. Eugene Kinkaid in *In Every War But One* (1959) suggests that almost a third of the prisoners collaborated actively and that a majority yielded in some degree to Communist pressure, arguing, as the title implies, that American soldiers in Korea behaved quite differently from those in other wars. A sociologist, Albert D. Biderman, in a much more careful study, *March to Calumny* (1963), effectively refutes Kinkaid, concluding that the conduct of American prisoners in Korea differed little from that of prisoners of war, American or otherwise, in other times and places, and that brainwashing affected them little.

The War in Vietnam

Spanning about a score of years, depending upon when one chooses to begin counting, the war in Vietnam spawned a plethora of writings, and because of controversy surrounding American involvement, many of the works are polemical. Yet for all the abundance, a sound military history of American participation has yet to appear. Although all the services are working on official histories (the U.S. Army plans around twenty volumes), only one has been published, Edwin Bickford Hooper, Dean C. Allard, and Oscar P. Fitzgerald's *The Setting of the Stage to 1959* (1976), the first volume of The United States Navy and the Vietnam Conflict.

There have been a number of preliminary monographs. An Army publication is John A. Cash, John N. Albright, and Allan W. Sandstrum's *Seven Firefights in Vietnam* (1970), which consists of lively accounts of representative small unit actions. The Navy's History Division published *Riverine Warfare: The U.S. Navy's Operations on Inland Waters* (1968). The Office of Air Force History published a comprehensive account of mammoth air operations in support of the besieged U.S. Marine Corps combat base at Khe Sanh: Bernard C. Nalty, *Air Power and the Fight for Khe Sanh* (1973). The Marine Corps covered the Khe Sanh fight in Moyers S. Shore, II's *The Battle for Khe Sanh* (1969), and also published Francis J. West, Jr.'s *Small Unit Action in Vietnam, Summer 1966* (1967).

The official reports of the two senior American commanders

during the early years of major American commitment—U.S. Grant Sharp, Commander in Chief, Pacific, and William C. Westmoreland, Commander, U.S. Military Assistance Command, Vietnam—were published in one volume, *Report on the War in Vietnam* (1969). The Department of State from time to time published speeches by government officials and special reports on various aspects of the war, and printed reports of hearings of a number of congressional committees are also available.

Despite some serious limitations, the so-called Pentagon Papers constitutes an invaluable source. This is a detailed study of the involvement in Vietnam from the Washington viewpoint prepared in 1967–68 at the direction of Secretary of Defense Robert McNamara by a committee of officers and scholars with no attempt at overall assimilation and with minimum coordination among the writers. Not intended for publication, the narrative is of uneven quality and on occasion reflects the persuasion of the authors; but extensive quotations from original documents and a number of reproduced documents nevertheless make the study an indispensable aid for any serious student of the war.

Following unauthorized disclosure of the study to a number of newspapers, three "editions" were published, all in 1971. The New York *Times* produced a truncated version known simply as *The Pentagon Papers*, in essence a summary of the original study done by members of the *Times* staff, who added a heavy layer of personal attitude. After entering a copy of the original study in the official record of a Senate subcommittee, U.S. Senator Mike Gravel arranged publication under the title *The Senator Gravel Edition—the Pentagon Papers: The Defense Department History of United States Decisionmaking on Vietnam*. The third edition is an offset reproduction of the original typescript study, officially released by the Department of Defense under the title *United States-Vietnam Relations, 1945-1967*. An occasional paragraph or page that was deleted for security reasons from the official version may be found in the Gravel edition.

The works of three historians have come to be accepted as standard for the early history of Vietnam and for the French Indochina War of 1945–54: Ellen Hammer's *The Struggle for Indochina* (1954), which focuses on the failure of the French to come to terms with the rising nationalism of the Indochinese states; Bernard B. Fall's *Street Without Joy: Indochina at War* (1961) and *The Two Viet-Nams: A Political and Military Analysis* (1967), which explain French failures in the words of a naturalized American who was a former French guerrilla fighter; and Joseph Buttinger's *Vietnam: A Political History* (1968). The last is in effect a distillation of two of the author's somewhat wordy earlier works, *A Smaller Dragon* (1958) and *Vietnam: A Dragon Embattled* (two volumes, 1967), but with an added look at what Buttinger calls "The Americanization of the War," the period following the death of the South Vietnamese leader Ngo Dinh Diem in November 1963 to the beginning of peace talks in mid-1968, a period about which the author is critical. Another excellent study of events leading to the French Indochina War is John T. McAlister, Jr.'s *Vietnam: The Origins of Revolution* (1971), and Bernard Fall contributed the definitive account of the final French battlefield defeat in *Hell in a Very Small Place: The Siege of Dien Bien Phu* (1967).

A scholarly look at an early event, President Eisenhower's decision to resist French pressures to intervene militarily at Dien Bien Phu, is Melvin Gurtov's *The First Vietnam Crisis: Chinese Communist Strategy and U.S. Involvement, 1953-1954* (1967). Victor Bator in *Vietnam: A Diplomatic Tragedy* (1965) focuses on the Geneva Accords of 1954 which unintentionally but actually created two Vietnams, as do George McT. Kahin and John W. Lewis in *The United States in Vietnam* (1967), the latter containing valuable documents in an appendix. Also valuable for its documents is Marvin E. Gettleman's (ed.) *History, Documents, and Opinions on a Major World Crisis* (1965). Robert Scigliano studied the early problems of the Republic of Vietnam in *South Vietnam: Nation Under Stress* (1963). A fascinating sociological look at Vietnamese culture is in Gerald Hickey's *Village in Vietnam* (1964).

Two diametrically opposite views of the American role are Frank Trager's *Why Vietnam?* (1966), which applauds American intervention, and Theodore Draper's *Abuse of Power* (1967), which theorizes that "the escalation of force required an escalation of theory" until the United States was no longer defending the freedom of South Vietnam but engaging in another "war to end all wars, this time 'national liberation' wars."

There are five good works on the enemy. Douglas Pike became established as an authority in this field with *The Viet Cong* (1966), *War, Peace, and the Viet Cong* (1969), and a monograph written for the United States Mission in Saigon, *The Viet Cong Strategy of Terror* (1970). Also noteworthy are George Tanham's *Communist Revolutionary Warfare: The Vietminh in Indochina* (1961) and *Communist Revolutionary Warfare: From the Vietminh to the Viet Cong* (1967).

Questions of legality and morality run through much of the literature. The student who wishes to delve seriously into the matter should turn to two works, John Norton Moore's *Law and the Indochina War* (1972) and Richard A. Falk's (ed.) *The Vietnam War and International Law* (three volumes, 1968–72), an anthology of varied writings on the subject. Although both Professors Falk and Moore are authorities on international law, it would be difficult to find two more divergent views on American involvement in Vietnam, Falk deeming it illegal, Moore arguing its legality.

Some of the most informative and, in some cases, provocative books on the war are by journalists, many of whom worked long assignments in Saigon. After close to twenty years' experience in Vietnam, Robert Shaplen wrote an astute and objective account of the French era and early American involvement, *The Lost Revolution: The U.S. in Vietnam, 1946–1966* (1966). Highly critical of early American policy yet in general sympathetic to the American presence is David Halberstam's *The Making of a Quagmire* (1965), which covers the period immediately preceding Diem's death, a period for which Halberstam shared a Pulitzer Prize for reporting. In a later work, *The Best and the Brightest* (1972), Halberstam can find little right with the American role. Through sharp, sometimes severe portraits of Presidents Kennedy and Johnson and their aides and through dialogue that is more inferred than actual, he tells the story of growing American involvement from the Washington viewpoint generally up to mid-1965 and the decision to commit U.S. combat troops. A well-written book is Frances Fitzgerald's *Fire in the Lake* (1972). Ms. Fitzgerald provides a detailed description of Vietnamese culture but strays outside her field when she analyzes military strategy and tactics.

A number of journalists have dealt with specific events. Among several who visited Hanoi, Harrison Salisbury reported on the effect of American bombing in *Behind the Lines—Hanoi* (1967). Jonathan Schell in *The Village of Ben Suc* turned a critical eye on the evacuation of residents of a Communist-dominated village and the razing of their homes. Seymour M. Hersh dealt with American atrocities in *My Lai 4* (1970), but Richard Hammer told the story better in *One Morning in the War* (1970).

One of the better books by a journalist and the only authoritative account of the enemy's violent *Tet* offensive of 1968 is Don Oberdorfer's *Tet!* (1971). Oberdorfer is sometimes critical of the methods of some of his colleagues in press and television. The definitive work on the reaction of the news media to the *Tet* offensive is Peter Braestrup's *Big Story: How the American Press and Television Reported and Interpreted the Crisis of Tet 1968 in Vietnam and Washington* (1976). Braestrup also is sharply critical. Herbert Y. Schandler focused on the *Tet* offensive in *The Unmaking of a President: Lyndon Johnson and Vietnam* (1976) but from the viewpoint of decision makers in Washington.

The war spawned a series of hybrid memoir-histories written, for the most part, by men who served for varying periods at the second or third echelon of government. The most notable is Walt W. Rostow's *The Diffusion of Power* (1972). Under President Kennedy, Rostow was chairman of the State Department's Policy Planning Council; and under President Johnson, first a deputy to the President's special assistant for national security affairs and later the special assistant. One of the main architects of Johnson's Vietnam policy, Rostow defends it vigorously.

In *To Move a Nation* a former Assistant Secretary of State for Far Eastern Affairs, Roger Hilsman, deals only partly with Vietnam, but the work is important as a sober, straightforward account of the decision making process during the brief Kennedy era, including the decision to give tacit support to a coup to overthrow President Diem. Similarly useful is a study by one who held various special assignments with the State Department and the White House, including attendance at a number of international conferences dealing with Indochina, Chester L. Cooper's *The Lost Crusade: America in Vietnam* (1970).

Several other works are more in the true memoir tradition. President Johnson's *The Vantage Point* (1971) contains a host of information but is less candid that one might have hoped for; the frontier flavor of the president fails to emerge. More satisfying is the memoir of a former U.S. Army Chief of Staff, Maxwell D. Taylor, U.S. Ambassador to Saigon at the time of President Johnson's decision to commit American combat troops. In *Swords and Plowshares* (1972) he takes issue with the strategy of "graduated response," noting that it predictably assured "a prolonged war which gave time not only for more men to lose their lives but also for the national patience to wear thin, the antiwar movement to gain momentum and hostile propaganda to make inroads at home and abroad."

The American military commander in Saigon during 1964-68, General William C. Westmoreland, wrote *A Soldier Reports* (1976), in which he defends his fighting a "large-unit" war because large North Vietnamese units could not be ignored. His strategy of attrition, he writes, was the only strategy open to him in view of the restrictions imposed by political authorities in Washington. Written after the South Vietnamese defeat, the memoir contains one of the few authoritative accounts yet published of the final collapse.

For tactical studies the reader must depend almost entirely on the workhorse of battlefield historians, S. L. A. Marshall. His first and most comprehensive work on Vietnam, *Battles in the Monsoon* (1967), provides detailed accounts of a number of engagements in the Central Highlands during the summer of 1966. An intriguing work is Francis J. West, Jr.'s *The Village* (1972), the story of the efforts over seventeen months of a U.S. Marine Corps combined action platoon, composed of marines and South Vietnamese militia, to defend a village and win the confidence of the villagers. West's is a human story, told without ideological filter, of the actions and motivations of men at war. Marine Col. William R. Corson's *The Betrayal* (1968), generally highly critical of the American effort in Vietnam, found a ray of hope in the methods of these combined action platoons. In *A Rumor of War* (1977), a firsthand account of the experiences of a Marine Corps platoon leader, Philip Caputo provides a searing indictment of the brutalizing effect of the war on the men who fought it. Two works of fiction that provide insight into tactical methods are Josiah Bunting's *The Lionheads* (1972) and William Turner Huggett's *Body Count* (1973).

Robin Moore's *The Green Berets* (1965) is nominally fiction, but it is based in large measure on fact, the story of the U.S. Army's Special Forces in their early days in South Vietnam. The incredibly harsh ordeal of those Americans who were prisoners of war of the North Vietnamese is told in Stephen A. Rowan's *They Wouldn't Let Us Die; The Prisoners of War Tell Their Story* (1974).

Military Sociology and the Social Impact of the Military

The new and important place of the military establishment in American government and society after 1945 generated both analysis and criticism. Critics charged that the United States was becoming a militaristic state dominated by a power elite with vested interests in the perpetuation of cold war and its attendant arms race. While the wave of criticism of the military establishment and of the military industrial complex that supported it reached its height during the Vietnam War, it had antecedents. The spiritual godfather of the critics was the sociologist C. Wright Mills, whose *Power Elite* (1956) and *The Causes of World War III* (1958) painted a picture of an "establishment" of capitalists and military men who together ruled the country. Other works of this genre include Fred J. Cook's *The Warfare State* (1962), Ralph E. Lapp's *The Weapons Culture* (1968) and *Arms Beyond Doubt* (1970), Noam Chomsky's *American Power and the New Mandarins* (1969), and Richard J. Barnet's *The Economy of Death* (1970). The economist Seymour Melman's *Pentagon Capitalism: The Political Economy of War* (1970) holds a special place in the critical literature in that Melman directs his main fire at the "overkill" capacity of the American nuclear weapons arsenal.

Although some of the critics generated more heat than light, they outproduced explicit defenders of the military establishment by a considerable margin. John Stanley Baumgartner, however, does undertake the defense of Mills's power elite in *The Lonely Warriors: Case for the Military-Industrial Complex* (1970). Various books of essays and readings—Herbert I. Schiller and Joseph D. Phillips's (eds.) *Readings in the Military Industrial Complex* (1970), Sam Sarkesian's (ed.) *The Military Industrial Complex: A Reassessment* (1972), Carroll W. Pursell, Jr.'s (ed.) *The Military Industrial Complex* (1972), and Steven Rosen's *Testing the Theory of the Military Industrial Complex* (1973)—attempt to present balanced assessments. And Adam Yarmolinsky, a civilian Defense Department official in the Kennedy years, analyzes the whole problem of the military's place after World War II in *The Military Establishment: Its Impact on American Society* (1971).

Among the works on the sociology of the military profession itself (a relatively new field of investigation) Morris Janowitz's *The Professional Soldier* (1960) holds a special place as an analysis of the career military officer in the period since 1945. Charles C. Moskos, Jr. has attempted to do something of the same thing for the ordinary soldier in *The American Enlisted Man: The Rank and File in Today's Military* (1970). Maureen Mylander's *The Generals* (1974) and Ward Just's *Military Men* (1970) are both iconoclastic and popular in tone but not without a measure of realism.

The status of blacks in the armed forces underwent momentous change in the postwar era. Jack D. Foner's *Blacks and the Military in American History* (1974) accurately though briefly summarizes these changes. Richard M. Dalfiume's *Desegregation of the U.S. Armed Forces* (1969) is a more comprehensive account that emphasizes the role of the civilians, particularly in the Truman administration, in promoting racial equality in the military services. An official Department of Defense volume, *The Integration of the Armed Forces* by Morris MacGregor of the U.S. Army Center of Military History, focuses on the services themselves, analyzing in considerable detail the often conflicting influences of the civil rights movement and military tradition on their evolving racial policies.

Bibliography

Abel, Elie. *The Missile Crisis*. Philadelphia: Lippincott, 1966.

Acheson, Dean. *Present at the Creation*. New York: W. W. Norton, 1969.

Allison, Graham T. *Essence of Decision: Explaining the Cuban Missile Crisis*. Boston: Little, Brown, 1971.

Alperowitz, Gar. *Atomic Diplomacy: Hiroshima and Potsdam*. New York: Simon and Schuster, 1965.

Ambler, John Stewart. *The French Army in Politics, 1945-1962*. Columbus: Ohio State Univ. Press, 1966.

Appleman, Roy E. *South to the Naktong, North to the Yalu*. U.S. Army in the Korean War. Washington: Government Printing Office, 1961.

Aron, Raymond. *On War*. Garden City, N.Y.: Doubleday, 1959.

Baclagon, Uldarico S. *Lessons from the Huk Campaign in the Philippines*. Manila: N. Colcol and Co., 1960.

Bader, William B. *Austria Between East and West, 1945-1955*. Stanford, Calif.: Stanford Univ. Press, 1966.

Barker, A. J. *Suez: The Seven Day War*. New York: Praeger, 1965.

Barnet, Richard J. *The Economy of Death*. New York: Atheneum, 1970.

Bator, Victor. *Vietnam: A Diplomatic Tragedy*. Dobbs Ferry, N.Y.: Oceana Publications, 1965.

Baumgartner, John Stanley. *The Lonely Warriors: Case for the Military-Industrial Complex*. Los Angeles: Nash Publishing, 1970.

Bechhoefer, Bernard. *Postwar Negotiations for Arms Control*. Washington: Brookings Institution, 1961.

Bell, J. Bowyer. *The Long War: Israel and the Arabs Since 1946*. Englewood Cliffs, N.J.: Prentice-Hall, 1969.

———. *The Myth of the Guerrilla: Revolutionary Theory and Malpractice*. New York: A. A. Knopf, 1971.

Biderman, Albert D. *March to Calumny: The Story of the American POWs in the Korean War*. New York: Macmillan, 1963.

Blackett, P. M. S. *The Military and Political Consequences of Atomic Energy*. London: Turnstile Press, 1948.

Borklund, Carl W. *The Department of Defense*. New York: Praeger, 1968.

———. *Men of the Pentagon: From Forrestal to McNamara*. New York: Praeger, 1966.

Bottome, Edgar. *The Balance of Terror: A Guide to the Arms Race*. Boston: Beacon Press, 1972.

Braestrup, Peter. *Big Story: How the American Press and Television Reported and Interpreted the Crisis of Tet 1968 in Vietnam and Washington.* 2 vols. Boulder, Colo.: Westview Press, 1976.

Brodie, Bernard. *Escalation and Nuclear Option.* Princeton, N.J.: Princeton Univ. Press, 1966.

——. *Strategy in the Missile Age.* Princeton, N.J.: Princeton Univ. Press, 1959.

Brodie, Bernard, ed. *The Absolute Weapon.* New York: Harcourt, Brace, 1946.

Buchan, Alastair. *NATO in the 1960's: The Implications of Interdependence.* New York: Praeger, 1960.

Bunting, Josiah. *The Lionheads.* New York: Braziller, 1972.

Bush, Vannevar. *Modern Arms and Free Men.* New York: Simon and Schuster, 1949.

Buttinger, Joseph. *Vietnam: A Political History.* New York: Praeger, 1968.

Caputo, Philip. *A Rumor of War.* New York: Holt, Rinehart, and Winston, 1977.

Caraley, Demetrios. *The Politics of Military Unification: A Study of Conflict and the Policy Process.* New York: Columbia Univ. Press, 1966.

Cash, John A.; Albright, John N.; and Sandstrum, Allan W. *Seven Firefights in Vietnam.* Washington: Government Printing Office, 1970.

Chomsky, Noam. *American Power and the New Mandarins.* New York: Pantheon Books, 1969.

Clark, Michael K. *Algeria in Turmoil: A History of the Rebellion.* New York: Praeger, 1959.

Clay, Lucius D. *Decision in Germany.* Garden City, N.Y.: Doubleday, 1950.

Coles, Harry L. "Strategic Studies Since 1945: The Era of Overthink." *Military Review* 53, no. 4 (April 1973):3-16.

Collins, J. Lawton. *War in Peacetime.* Boston: Houghton Mifflin, 1969.

Cook, Fred J. *The Warfare State.* New York: Macmillan, 1962.

Cooper, Chester L. *The Lost Crusade: America in Vietnam.* New York: Dodd, Mead, 1970.

Corson, William R. *The Betrayal.* New York: W. W. Norton, 1968.

Dalfiume, Richard M. *Desegregation in the U.S. Armed Forces.* Columbia: Univ. of Mo. Press, 1969.

Davison, W. Phillips. *The Berlin Blockade: A Study in Cold War Politics.* Princeton, N.J.: Princeton Univ. Press, 1958.

Deitchman, Seymour. *Limited War and American Defense Policy.* Cambridge, Mass.: MIT Press, 1964.

De St. Torre, John. *The Brothers War: Biafra and Nigeria.* Boston: Houghton Mifflin, 1972.

Donnison, F. S. V. *Civil Affairs and Military Government, Northwest Europe, 1944-1946.* London: H.M. Stationery Office, 1961.

Draper, Theodore. *Abuse of Power.* New York: Viking Press, 1967.

Eisenhower, Dwight D. *Mandate for Change, 1953-1956.* Garden City, N.Y.: Doubleday, 1956.

——. *Waging Peace, 1956-1961.* Garden City, N.Y.: Doubleday, 1965.

Enthoven, Alain C., and Smith, K. Wayne. *How Much Is Enough? Shaping the Defense Program, 1961-1969.* New York: Harper and Row, 1971.

Falk, Richard A., ed. *The Vietnam War and International Law.* 3 vols. Princeton, N.J.: Princeton Univ. Press, 1968-72.

Fall, Bernard B. *Hell in a Very Small Place: The Siege of Dien Bien Phu.* Philadelphia: Lippincott, 1967.

——. *Street Without Joy: Indo-China at War, 1946-1954.* Harrisburg: Stackpole, 1961.

——— . *The Two Vietnams: A Political and Military Analysis.* 2d rev. ed. New York: Praeger, 1967.

Fall, Bernard B., ed. *Ho Chi Minh on Revolution: Selected Writings.* New York: Praeger, 1967.

Fehrenbach, T. R. *This Kind of War.* New York: Macmillan, 1963.

Feis, Herbert. *From Trust to Terror: The Onset of the Cold War, 1945-1950.* New York: W. W. Norton, 1970.

Field, James A., Jr. *History of United States Naval Operations, Korea.* Washington: Government Printing Office, 1962.

Fitzgerald, Frances. *Fire in the Lake: The Vietnamese and the Americans in Vietnam.* Boston: Atlantic-Little Brown, 1972.

Fleming, D. F. *The Cold War and Its Origins.* Vol. I: *1917-1950*; Vol. II: *1950-1960.* Garden City, N.Y.: Doubleday, 1961.

Foner, Jack D. *Blacks and the Military in American History.* New York: Praeger, 1974.

Fox, William T. R., and Fox, Annette. *NATO and the Range of American Choice.* New York: Columbia Univ. Press. 1967.

Fox, William T. R., and Schilling, Warner R., eds. *European Security and the Atlantic System.* New York: Columbia Univ. Press, 1967.

Friedrich, Carl J., ed. *American Experiences in Military Government During World War II.* New York: Rinehart and Co., 1948.

Furniss, Edgar S. *DeGaulle and the French Army: A Crisis in Civil-Military Relations.* New York: Twentieth Century Fund, 1964.

Futrell, Frank B. *The United States Air Force in Korea, 1950-1953.* New York: Duell, Sloan, and Pearce, 1961.

Gaddis, John Lewis. *The United States and the Origins of the Cold War, 1941-1947.* New York: Columbia Univ. Press, 1972.

Gavin, James M. *War and Peace in the Space Age.* New York: Harper, 1958.

George, Alexander, and Smoke, Richard. *Deterrence in American Foreign Policy: Theory and Practice.* New York: Columbia Univ. Press, 1974.

Gettleman, Marvin E., ed. *History, Documents, and Opinions on a Major World Crisis.* New York: Fawcett, 1965.

Giap, General Vo Nguyen. *People's War, People's Army.* New York: Praeger, 1962.

Gillespie, Jean. *Algeria: Rebellion and Revolution.* London: Benn, 1960.

Gimbel, John. *The American Occupation of Germany: Politics and the Military, 1945-1949.* Stanford, Calif.: Stanford Univ. Press, 1968.

——— . *A German Community Under American Occupation: Marburg, 1945-1952.* Stanford, Calif.: Stanford Univ. Press, 1961.

Gott, Richard. *Guerrilla Movements in Latin America.* Garden City, N.Y.: Doubleday, 1971.

Guevara, Che. *Guerrilla Warfare.* New York: Monthly Review Press, 1961.

Gugeler, Russell A. *Combat Actions in Korea.* Rev. ed. Army Historical Series. Washington: Government Printing Office, 1970.

Gurtov, Melvin. *The First Vietnam Crisis: Chinese Communist Strategy and U.S. Involvement, 1953-1954.* New York: Columbia Univ. Press, 1967.

Halberstam, David. *The Best and the Brightest.* New York: Random House, 1972.

——— . *The Making of a Quagmire.* New York: Random House, 1965.

Halle, Louis J. *The Cold War as History.* New York: Harper and Row, 1967.

Halperin, Morton. *Bureaucratic Politics and Foreign Policy.* Washington: Brookings Institution, 1974.

——— . *Defense Strategies for the Seventies.* Boston: Little, Brown, 1971.

Hammer, Ellen Joy. *The Struggle for Indo-China.* Stanford, Calif.: Stanford Univ. Press, 1954.

Hammer, Richard. *One Morning in the War.* New York: Coward-McCann, 1970.

Hammond, Paul R. *Cold War and Detente.* New York: Harcourt Brace Jovanovich, 1975.

──── . *The Cold War Years: American Foreign Policy Since 1945.* New York: Harcourt, Brace and World, 1969.

──── . *Organizing for Defense: The American Military Establishment in the Twentieth Century.* Princeton, N.J.: Princeton Univ. Press, 1961.

Heinl, Robert D., Jr. *Victory at High Tide.* Philadelphia: Lippincott, 1968.

Hermes, Walter G. *Truce Tent and Fighting Front.* U.S. Army in the Korean War. Washington: Government Printing Office, 1966.

Hersh, Seymour M. *My Lai 4.* New York: Random House, 1970.

Herzog, Chaim. *The War of Atonement: October 1973.* Boston: Little, Brown, 1975.

Hickey, Gerald. *Village in Vietnam.* New Haven: Yale Univ. Press, 1964.

Higgins, Trumbull. *Korea and the Fall of MacArthur: A Precis in Limited War.* New York: Oxford Univ. Press, 1960.

Hilsman, Roger. *To Move a Nation: The Politics of Foreign Policy in the Administration of John F. Kennedy.* Garden City, N.Y.: Doubleday, 1967.

Hitch, Charles J. *Decision-Making for Defense.* Berkeley: Univ. of Calif. Press, 1965.

Hitch, Charles J., and McKean, Roland N. *The Economics of Defense in the Nuclear Age.* Cambridge, Mass.: Harvard Univ. Press, 1960.

Hooper, Edwin Bickford; Allard, Dean C.; and Fitzgerald, Oscar P. *The Setting of the Stage to 1959.* The United States Navy and the Vietnam Conflict, vol. I. Washington: Government Printing Office, 1976.

Howard, Michael. "The Classical Strategists" in "Problems of Modern Strategy," Part One. *Adelphi Papers* no. 54 (Feb. 1969). London: Institute of Strategic Studies.

Howard, Michael, and Hunter, Robert. *Israel and the Arab World: The Crisis of 1967.* London: Institute of Strategic Studies, 1967.

Huggett, William Turner. *Body Count.* New York: Putnam's, 1973.

Huntington, Samuel P. *The Common Defense: Strategic Programs in National Politics.* New York: Columbia Univ. Press, 1961.

Ismay, Hastings L. *NATO: The First Five Years, 1949-1954.* New York: Acme Code Co., 1955.

Janowitz, Morris. *The Professional Soldier: A Social and Political Portrait.* Glencoe, Ill.: Free Press, 1960.

Johnson, Lyndon B. *Vantage Point: Perspective of the Presidency 1963-1969.* New York: Holt, Rinehart, and Winston, 1971.

Johnson, Paul. *The Suez War.* New York: Greenberg, 1957.

Just, Ward. *Military Men.* New York: A. A. Knopf, 1970.

Kahin, George McT., and Lewis, John W. *The United States in Vietnam.* New York: Dial Press, 1967.

Kahn, Herman. *On Thermonuclear War.* Princeton, N.J.: Princeton Univ. Press, 1960.

Kaufman, William W. *The McNamara Strategy.* New York: Harper and Row, 1964.

Kawai, Kazue. *Japan's American Interlude.* Chicago: Univ. of Chicago Press, 1960.

Kennan, George F. *Russia, the Atom and the West.* New York: Harper, 1957.

Kennedy, Robert F. *Thirteen Days: A Memoir of the Cuban Missile Crisis*. New York: W. W. Norton, 1969.

Kinkaid, Eugene. *In Every War but One*. New York: W. W. Norton, 1959.

Kintner, William R. *Forging a New Sword: A Study of the Department of Defense*. New York: Harper, 1958.

Kissinger, Henry A. *The Necessity for Choice: Prospects of American Foreign Policy*. New York: Harper, 1961.

——. *Nuclear Weapons and Foreign Policy*. New York: Council on Foreign Relations, 1957.

——. *The Troubled Partnership: A Re-Appraisal of the Atlantic Alliance*. New York: McGraw-Hill, 1965.

Knorr, Klaus, ed. *NATO and American Security*. Princeton, N.J.: Princeton Univ. Press, 1959.

Kolko, Gabriel. *The Limits of Power: The World and United States Foreign Policy, 1945-1954*. New York: Harper and Row, 1972.

——. *The Roots of American Foreign Policy: An Analysis of Power and Purposes*. Boston: Beacon Press, 1969.

Kolodziej, Edward A. *The Uncommon Defense and Congress, 1945-1963*. Columbus: Ohio State Univ. Press, 1966.

Kuokka, Hubard D., and Hicks, Norman W. *The East-Central Front*. U.S. Marine Operations in Korea. Washington: Government Printing Office, 1962.

LaFeber, Walter. *America, Russia, and the Cold War, 1945-1971*. 2d ed. New York: Wiley, 1972.

Lapp, Ralph E. *Arms Beyond Doubt: The Tyranny of Weapons Technology*. New York: Cowel Book Co., 1970.

——. *The Weapons Culture*. New York: W. W. Norton, 1968.

Laqueur, Walter. *Guerrilla: A Historical and Critical Study*. Boston: Little, Brown, 1976.

Leckie, Robert. *Conflict: The History of the Korean War, 1950-1953*. New York: Putnam's, 1962.

Licklider, Roy E. *The Private Nuclear Strategists*. Columbus: Ohio State Univ. Press, 1971.

Liddell Hart, B. H. *Deterrent or Defense: A Fresh Look at the West's Military Position*. New York: Praeger, 1960.

London *Times* Insight Team. *The Yom Kippur War*. Garden City, N.Y.: Doubleday, 1974.

Lorch, Nathanel. *The Edge of the Sword*. New York: Putnam's, 1961.

Lukacs, John A. *A History of the Cold War*. Garden City, N.Y.: Doubleday, 1961.

McAlister, John T., Jr. *Vietnam: The Origins of Revolution*. Garden City, N.Y.: Doubleday, 1971.

MacArthur, Douglas. *Reminiscences*. New York: McGraw-Hill, 1964.

McInnis, Edgar. *The Atlantic Triangle and the Cold War*. Toronto: Univ. of Toronto Press, 1959.

McNamara, Robert S. *The Essence of Security: Reflections in Office*. New York: Harper and Row, 1968.

McNeill, William M. *America, Britain, and Russia: Their Cooperation and Conflict*. London: Oxford Univ. Press, 1953.

Maddox, Robert James. *The New Left and the Origins of the Cold War*. Princeton, N.J.: Princeton Univ. Press, 1973.

Mao Tse-tung. *Selected Works*. 3 vols. Translated from Chinese. New York: International Publishers, 1954-55.

Marshall, S. L. A. *Battles in the Monsoon*. New York: William Morrow, 1967.

——. *Pork Chop Hill*. New York: William Morrow, 1956.

————. *The River and the Gauntlet.* New York: William Morrow, 1953.

————. *Sinai Victory: Command Decisions in History's Shortest War, Israel's Hundred Hour Conquest of Egypt East of Suez, Autumn, 1956.* New York: William Morrow, 1958.

Medaris, John B. (with Arthur Gordon). *Countdown for Decision.* New York: Putnam's, 1960.

Meid, Pat, and Yingling, James M. *Operations in West Korea.* U.S. Marine Operations in Korea. Washington: Government Printing Office, 1972.

Melman, Seymour. *Pentagon Capitalism: The Political Economy of War.* New York: McGraw-Hill, 1970.

Menard, Orville D. *The Army and the Fifth Republic.* Lincoln: Univ. of Neb. Press, 1967.

Middleton, Harry J. *The Compact History of the Korean War.* New York: Hawthorn Books, 1965.

Millis, Walter, ed. *The Forrestal Diaries.* New York: Viking Press, 1951.

Millis, Walter; Mansfield, Harvey C.; and Stein, Harold. *Arms and the State: Civil-Military Elements in National Policy.* New York: Twentieth Century Fund, 1958.

Mills, Charles Wright. *The Causes of World War III.* New York: Simon and Schuster, 1958.

————. *The Power Elite.* New York: Oxford Univ. Press, 1956.

Montrose, Lynn; and Canzona, Nicholas A. *The Pusan Perimeter.* U.S. Marine Operations in Korea. Washington: Government Printing Office, 1954.

————. *The Inchon-Seoul Operation.* U.S. Marine Operations in Korea. Washington: Government Printing Office, 1955.

————. *The Chosin Reservoir Campaign.* U.S. Marine Operations in Korea. Washington: Government Printing Office, 1957.

Moore, John Norton. *Law and the Indo-China War.* Princeton, N.J.: Princeton Univ. Press, 1972.

Moore, Robin. *The Green Berets.* New York: Crown, 1965.

Morgenstern, Oskar. *The Question of a National Defense.* New York: Random House, 1959.

Moskos, Charles C., Jr. *The American Enlisted Man: The Rank and File in Today's Military.* New York: Russell Sage Foundation, 1970.

Moulton, Harland B. *From Superiority to Parity: The United States and the Strategic Arms Race, 1961-1971.* Washington: Brookings Institution, 1971.

Mylander, Maureen. *The Generals.* New York: Dial Press, 1974.

Nalty, Bernard C. *Air Power and the Fight for Khe Sanh.* Washington: Government Printing Office, 1973.

Newhouse, John. *The Cold Dawn: The Story of SALT.* New York: Holt, Rinehart, and Winston, 1973.

O'Ballance, Edgar. *The Arab-Israeli War, 1948.* New York: Praeger, 1958.

————. *The Sinai Campaign of 1956.* London; Faber and Faber, 1959.

————. *The Third Arab-Israeli War.* Hamden, Conn.: Archon, 1972.

Oberdorfer, Don, *Tet!* Garden City, N.Y.: Doubleday, 1971.

Osgood, Robert E. *Limited War: The Challenge to American Strategy.* Chicago: Univ. of Chicago Press, 1957.

————. *NATO: The Entangling Alliance.* Chicago: Univ. of Chicago Press, 1962.

Paige, Glen D. *The Korean Decision, June 24-30, 1950.* New York: Free Press, 1968.

Paret, Peter. *French Revolutionary Warfare From Indo-China to Algeria.* New York: Praeger, 1964.

Paterson, Thomas G. *Soviet-American Confrontation: Post-War Reconstruction and the Origins of the Cold War.* Baltimore: Johns Hopkins Univ. Press, 1975.

Pentagon Papers: *The Pentagon Papers.* New York: New York Times Publishing Co., 1971. / *The Senator Gravel Edition—the Pentagon Papers: The Defense Department History of United States Decisionmaking on Vietnam.* 4 vols. Boston: Beacon Press, 1971. / U.S., Department of Defense. *United States-Vietnam Relations, 1945-1967.* 12 vols. Washington: Government Printing Office, 1971.

Pike, Douglas. *The Viet Cong.* Cambridge, Mass.: MIT Press, 1966.

———. *The Viet Cong Strategy of Terror.* Saigon: U.S. Mission, 1970.

———. *War, Peace, and the Viet Cong.* Cambridge, Mass.: MIT Press, 1969.

Pursell, Carroll W., Jr., ed. *The Military-Industrial Complex.* New York: Harper and Row, 1972.

Pye, Lucien W. *Guerrilla Communism in Malaya.* Princeton, N.J.: Princeton Univ. Press, 1956.

Quester, George H. *Nuclear Diplomacy: The First Twenty-Five Years.* New York: Dunellen, 1970.

Rees, David. *The Age of Containment: The Cold War 1945-1965.* New York: St. Martin's Press, 1967.

———. *Korea: The Limited War.* New York: St. Martin's Press, 1964.

Ridgway, Matthew B. *The Korean War.* Garden City, N.Y.: Doubleday, 1967.

———. *Soldier: The Memoirs of Matthew B. Ridgway.* New York: Harper, 1956.

Roberts, Chalmers M. *The Nuclear Years: The Arms Race and Arms Control, 1945-1970.* New York: Praeger, 1970.

Rogow, Arnold A. *James Forrestal: A Study of Personality, Politics, and Policy.* New York: Macmillan, 1963.

Rosen, Steven, ed. *Testing the Theory of the Military Industrial Complex.* Lexington, Mass.: Heath, 1973.

Rostow, Walt W. *The Diffusion of Power.* New York: Macmillan, 1972.

Rovere, Richard H., and Schlesinger, Arthur M., Jr. *The General and the President and the Future of American Foreign Policy.* New York: Farrar, Straus, and Young, 1951.

Rowan, Stephen A. *They Wouldn't Let Us Die: The Prisoners of War Tell Their Story.* New York: Jonathan David, 1974.

Salisbury, Harrison E. *Behind the Lines—Hanoi.* New York: Harper and Row, 1967.

Sarkesian, Sam., ed. *The Military Industrial Complex: A Reassessment.* Beverly Hills, Calif.: Russell Sage, 1972.

Sawyer, Robert K. *Military Advisors in Korea: KMAG in Peace and War.* Army Historical Series. Washington: Government Printing Office, 1963.

Schandler, Herbert Y. *The Unmaking of a President: Lyndon Johnson and Vietnam.* Princeton, N.J.: Princeton Univ. Press, 1976.

Schell, Jonathan. *The Village of Ben Suc.* New York: A. A. Knopf, 1967.

Schelling, Thomas C. *The Strategy of Conflict.* Cambridge, Mass.: Harvard Univ. Press, 1960.

Schiller, Herbert I., and Phillips, Joseph D., eds. *Readings in the Military Industrial Complex.* Urbana, Ill.: Univ. of Ill. Press, 1970.

Schilling, Warner R.; Hammond, Paul Y.; and Snyder, Glen H. *Strategy, Politics, and Defense Budgets.* New York: Columbia Univ. Press, 1962.

Schlesinger, Arthur M., Jr. *A Thousand Days: John F. Kennedy in the White House.* Boston: Houghton Mifflin, 1965.

Schnabel, James F. *Policy and Direction: The First Year.* U.S. Army in the Korean War. Washington: Government Printing Office, 1972.

Schwarz, Urs. *American Strategy, a New Perspective: The Growth of Politico-Military Thinking in the United States.* Garden City, N.Y.: Doubleday, 1966.

Scigliano, Robert. *South Vietnam: Nation Under Stress.* Boston: Houghton Mifflin, 1963.

Sebold, William J. *With MacArthur in Japan.* New York: W. W. Norton, 1965.

Shaplen, Robert. *The Lost Revolution: The U.S. in Vietnam, 1964-1966.* New York: Harper and Row, 1966.

Sharp, U. S. Grant, and Westmoreland, William C. *Report on the War in Vietnam.* Washington: Government Printing Office, 1969.

Shore, Moyers S., II. *The Battle for Khe Sanh.* Washington: Government Printing Office, 1969.

Simmons, Robert R. *The Strained Alliance: Peking, Pyongyang, Moscow, and the Politics of the Korean Civil War.* New York: Free Press, 1975.

Slessor, Sir John. *The Great Deterrent.* New York: Praeger, 1957.

Smith, Jean Edward. *The Defense of Berlin.* Baltimore: Johns Hopkins Univ. Press, 1963.

Sorenson, Theodore C. *Kennedy.* New York: Harper and Row, 1966.

Spanier, John W. *The Truman-MacArthur Controversy and the Korean War.* Cambridge, Mass.: Harvard Univ. Press, 1959.

Steel, Ronald. *Pax Americana.* New York: Viking Press, 1967.

Stein, Harold, ed. *American Civil-Military Decisions: A Book of Case Studies.* Twentieth Century Fund Study. University, Ala.: Univ. of Ala. Press, 1963.

Tanham, George. *Communist Revolutionary Warfare: The Vietminh in Indo-China.* New York: Praeger, 1961.

——. *Communist Revolutionary Warfare From the Vietminh to the Viet Cong.* New York: Praeger, 1967.

Taylor, Maxwell D. *Responsibility and Response.* New York: Harper and Row, 1967.

——. *Swords and Plowshares.* New York: W. W. Norton, 1972.

——. *The Uncertain Trumpet.* New York: Harper and Row, 1960.

Thompson, Robert G. K. *Defeating Communist Insurgency: The Lesson of Malaya and Vietnam.* New York: Praeger, 1966.

——. *Revolutionary War in World Strategy, 1954-1969.* New York: Taplinger, 1970.

Trager, Frank. *Why Vietnam?* New York: Praeger, 1966.

Trewhitt, Henry L. *McNamara: His Ordeal in the Pentagon.* New York: Harper and Row, 1971.

Trinquier, Roger. *Modern Warfare: A French View of Counterinsurgency.* Translated by Daniel Lee. New York: Praeger, 1964.

Truman, Harry S. *Years of Decision.* Garden City, N.Y.: Doubleday, 1955.

——. *Years of Trial and Hope.* Garden City, N.Y.: Doubleday, 1958.

Tucker, Robert W. *The Radical Left and American Foreign Policy.* Baltimore: Johns Hopkins Univ. Press, 1971.

U.S., Dept. of the Navy, Naval History Division. *Riverine Warfare: The U.S. Navy's Operations in Inland Waters.* Washington: Government Printing Office, 1968.

Valeriano, N. D., and Bohannan, Charles T. R. *Counter-Guerrilla Operations: The Philippine Experience.* New York: Praeger, 1962.

West, Francis J., Jr. *Small Unit Actions in Vietnam, Summer 1966.* Washington: Government Printing Office, 1967.

——. *The Village.* New York: Harper and Row, 1972.

Westmoreland, William C. *A Soldier Reports.* Garden City, N.Y.: Doubleday, 1976.

Westover, John G. *Combat Support in Korea*. Washington: Combat Forces Press, 1955.

Whiting, Allen S. *China Crosses the Yalu: The Decision to Enter the Korean War*. New York: Macmillan, 1960.

Williams, William A. *The Tragedy of American Diplomacy*. Rev. ed. New York: Dell, 1972.

Willrich, Mason. *Non-Proliferation Treaty: Framework for Nuclear Arms Control*. Charlottesville, Va.: Michie Co., 1969.

Wohlstetter, Albert. "The Delicate Balance of Terror." *Foreign Affairs* 37, no. 2 (Jan. 1959):211-34.

Yarmolinsky, Adam. *The Military Establishment: Its Impact on American Society*. New York: Harper and Row, 1971.

Yoshida, Shiguru. *The Yoshida Memoirs: The Story of Japan in Crisis*. Westport, Conn.: Greenwood Press, 1973.

Ziemke, Earl F. *The U.S. Army in the Occupation of Germany, 1944-1946*. Army Historical Series, Washington: Government Printing Office, 1975.

Zink, Harold. *American Military Government in Germany*. New York: Macmillan, 1947.

Three

Army Programs, Activities, and Uses

Chapter 11

A Century of Army
Historical Work

Col. John E. Jessup, Jr.
and Robert W. Coakley

ALTHOUGH the historical organization and work of the U.S.
Army today are largely an outgrowth of World War II, the
beginnings go back more than a century. On 26 January 1864,
Senator Henry Wilson of Massachusetts introduced a resolution
in Congress "to provide for the printing of the official reports of
the armies of the United States." The ultimate result was the 128
volumes of *The War of the Rebellion: A Compilation of the
Official Records of the Union and Confederate Armies;* the first
volume appeared in 1878 and the last in 1901. This documentary
history, so useful to Civil War scholars today, was published
under War Department auspices at a cost calculated to be
$3,158,514.67. But it was not the first of the department's
historical publications. Between 1870 and 1889 The Surgeon
General had published six oversize volumes, *The Medical and
Surgical History of the War of the Rebellion,* providing a wealth
of medical and historical data for later generations and
establishing a tradition the Medical Department was to follow in
future wars.

In its later stages, the project of editing and publishing the
Civil War records fell under the aegis of The Adjutant General,
whose office also undertook to collect and publish records of the
American Revolution. This latter effort lapsed without productive issue in 1915 when appropriated funds ran out. The
beginnings of Army historical work of a more sophisticated
character grew out of establishment of the General Staff Corps in
1903; buried in the order establishing it was a clause charging the
corps with "the preparation of . . . technical histories of military
operations of the United States" (General Order 120, War
Department, 14 August 1903). No general-staff historical section
like that existing in most European countries at the time emerged

Colonel Jessup (USA, Ret., Ph.D., Georgetown), Chief, Histories Divisions, CMH,
from 1969 until 1974, has published numerous articles on Soviet military history
and is President of the U.S. Commission on Military History. (For Dr. Coakley,
see the first page of Chapter 7.)

until March 1918, however, when in the midst of World War I a Historical Branch was organized in the War Plans Division. Historical offices were also established in General Pershing's headquarters and in the Services of Supply in France. The impulse behind this historical activity was initially the belief that the War Department should prepare a multivolume history of American participation in the war that, as Chief of Staff Tasker H. Bliss put it, "would record the things that were well done, for future imitation [and] . . . the errors as shown by experience, for future avoidance."[1]

These hopes were not realized. Rapid and almost complete demobilization in the summer of 1919 forced reduction in Army headquarters offices, including the Historical Branch; and most of the civilian professional historians who had joined it, in and out of uniform, were lost. Then Secretary of War Newton D. Baker decided it would be wrong to try to produce a scholarly narrative history. Such a history, wrote Baker, "would be incomplete unless it undertook to discuss economic, political, and diplomatic questions, and the discussions of such questions by military men would be controversial . . . and indiscreet for treatment by the War Department." Thus, he ruled, "the work of the Historical Section should . . . be limited to the collection, indexing, and preservation of records and the preparation of such monographs as are purely military in character."[2]

This dictum was to govern and restrict the scope of Army historical activity in the interwar years, with the result that there was no comprehensive organized body of materials available on experience in World War I for use by American planners at the outbreak of World War II except in one specialized area. Following the precedent established after the Civil War, The Surgeon General sponsored the preparation within his department of a clinical and administrative history of medical experience in World War I, published during the 1920s.[3]

A central Army historical section did survive, and in 1921 it was attached to the Army War College. There a reduced staff collected World War I records for eventual publication, prepared and published a complete Army order of battle for World War I,[4] provided extensive reference services to other elements of the

---

1. Memo, CofS for SW, 2 Jan 18, in CMH GRB files 314.7 HS WPD (1914–19).

2. Memo, SW Baker for CofS, 4 Aug 19. Copy in CMH Gen Ref Files—Thomas File 3336-H.

3. *The Medical Department of the United States Army in the World War*, 15 vols. (Washington: Government Printing Office, 1921–29).

4. *Order of Battle of United States Land Forces in the World War (1917–1919)*, 3 vols. (Washington: Government Printing Office, 1931–49).

Army and to the public, and in 1924 acquired the function of determining the official lineages and battle honors of Army units. For a decade after the war a writing program consisting of monographs on "purely military" subjects persisted, but it finally collapsed in 1929 in the face of opposition by The Adjutant General to members of the Army writing any sort of history on World War I.

The work of the Historical Section nonetheless did result in some publications. As chief of staff, General Pershing had established a policy that encouraged writing military history for outside publication, and some of the outstanding soldier-historians who served in this office between the wars—notably Oliver L. Spaulding, John W. Wright, and Hoffman Nickerson—produced some excellent scholarly studies on the more remote past. And between 1927 and 1933 a small Battlefields Sub-Section conducted numerous studies of American battlefields, four of which (on battles of the American Revolution) were published as congressional documents. But this function of studying battlefields for purposes of historical preservation was transferred to the National Park Service in 1933.

With the outbreak of World War II, the Army War College Historical Section became heavily engaged in preparing historical background studies to support current general staff work. But it continued to devote its main effort to editing World War I records and performing general reference work including keeping a World War II chronology. When the World War I documents were finally published in 1948,[5] they were restricted to the American Expeditionary Forces (no War Department documents) and represented a far less ambitious venture than did the *Official Records of the Rebellion*. By that time the War College Historical Section had been absorbed by a new historical office specifically designed to write a multivolume history of the Army's role in World War II comparable in concept to that originally contemplated for World War I.

The Historical Program During World War II

The strongest impetus for the World War II historical program came from President Roosevelt, who on 4 March 1942 directed all executive departments and agencies to arrange for preserving records and for relating their administrative experience during

---

5. *The United States Army in the World War, 1917-1919,* 17 vols. (Washington: Government Printing Office, 1948).

the war.[6] A second impulse came from within the Army when the staff recognized the need for recording operational as well as administrative experience. The result was that in the technical services, the major zone of interior commands, and overseas theaters historical sections were established to collect materials and write preliminary monographs on the activities of their particular staff or command agencies. And in August 1943 the War Department established a new historical branch in the Military Intelligence Division (G-2) of the General Staff to give direction and purpose to the Army's World War II historical effort.

The decision to establish a new central historical office stemmed from the conviction of both civilian and military leaders that the Army should eventually prepare a comprehensive narrative history of its experience in the war and from a belief that the existing War College Historical Section was not equipped for such a task. Rejecting the position of Newton D. Baker after World War I, Assistant Secretary of War John J. McCloy was the moving force behind the decision to create the new section; and Lt. Col. John M. Kemper, a thirty-year-old West Point graduate with a master's degree in history, became its principal organizer and first head. At Kemper's suggestion, McCloy appointed a planning committee of three civilian and three military members to assist G-2 in forming the new organization. The committee was headed by James Phinney Baxter, president of Williams College, then serving as deputy director of the Office of Strategic Services, and its other members were eminent historians.

As a result of the committee's work, the Historical Branch, G-2, became responsible for all Army historical work on World War II, including determining the functions of the War College Historical Section and final approval and editing of all historical manuscripts prepared for publication by Army agencies. While headed by a military chief, the professional supervision of the historical work was assigned to a civilian chief historian, a post assumed by Dr. Walter Livingston Wright, former president of Roberts College. The planning committee was continued as a War Department Historical Advisory Committee.

The first assignment for the Historical Branch was a series of studies on specific military operations; General Marshall wanted them for circulation within the Army and particularly

---

6. Ltr, President Roosevelt to Hon Harold D. Smith, Director, Bureau of the Budget, 4 Mar 42, copy in CMH—HRC 228.03 OCMH Hist Prog—Presidential Directives.

for distribution to soldiers who had been wounded in the actions described. This assignment was one of the factors producing closer links between the Historical Branch and the overseas theaters. Historical teams went overseas to do most of the preliminary research and writing; they returned their drafts to Washington for editing and publication (see Chapter 13). Between 1943 and 1947 the branch published fourteen studies in the Armed Forces in Action series. In addition to these publications, the wartime historical work resulted in a large collection of unpublished manuscripts that came to rest in the Historical Branch as the wartime commands, both at home and overseas, were dissolved or drastically reduced in the great postwar demobilization.

The U.S. Army in World War II Series

The Historical Branch began to plan a comprehensive history of the Army's role in World War II while still a part of G-2. But since its officers and historians realized that there was no real affinity between intelligence and history functions, they and the advisory committee recommended and Assistant Secretary McCloy backed a reorganization of November 1945: The branch became the Historical Division, War Department Special Staff, with Maj. Gen. Edwin F. Harding at its head; the following year it absorbed the staff and functions of the Army War College Historical Section. Only three months after establishment of the Historical Division, the Chief of Staff and Secretary of War approved its plan for a narrative history of a hundred or more volumes in a series to be designated The U.S. Army in World War II.

The volumes were to be assigned to the War Department, the major wartime zone of interior commands (Army Air Forces, Army Ground Forces, and Army Service Forces), the technical services, and the overseas theaters. Special studies would examine other subjects. The plan underwent many changes in numbers and titles of volumes in the years following, but the basic divisions remained intact. With the separation of the Air Force from the Army in 1947, however, the seven-volume U.S. Army Air Forces in World War II became an independent series.

Preparation of the official Army series absorbed almost all the energies of the new Historical Division for some years after its foundation. Early in 1946 Dr. Kent Roberts Greenfield, former head of the history department at Johns Hopkins University and wartime chief of the Historical Section at Army Ground Forces, succeeded Dr. Wright as chief historian and general editor of the series. He served in that post until 1958 and saw much of the series through to completion. A series of able general officers who served as military heads of the organization and colonels who manned its executive levels provided the military leadership in what Dr. Greenfield described as "a happy marriage of the military and historical professions." A second feature of the happy marriage was the advisory committee, reconstituted in 1947 with representatives from the higher Army schools and more civilian academic members. By and large, the Historical Division recruited the civilian professional staff for the World War II series from historians who had served in uniform in the various wartime historical sections at home and abroad.

It was also established that the volumes should be accurate and objective, conforming to the best traditions of historical scholarship, and that authors should have access to all pertinent Army records. "The history of the Army in World War II now in preparation," directed General Eisenhower in 1947, "must, without reservation, tell the complete story of the Army's participation, fully documented with references to the records used." He charged all members of the Army staff with facilitating historians' access to the necessary records and stressed that the directive was "to be interpreted in the most liberal sense without reservations as to whether or not the evidence of history places the Army in a favorable light."[7]

In the combat volumes historians could include the enemy side of the story. Unconditional surrender meant the wholesale capture of enemy records and testimony from many of the most important enemy officers. Captured German and Japanese military records were brought to Washington. Under an interrogation and writing program in the European theater, German officers produced some 2,500 manuscripts. And a large group of Japanese Army and Navy officers prepared a comprehensive series of monographs on Japanese plans and operations, about 180 of which were translated and distributed for Army use. Within the Historical Division a foreign studies section took shape to prepare the enemy side of the story for use by authors of the U.S. Army in World War II series.

The anticipation had been that much of the research and

---

7. Memo, Gen D. D. Eisenhower for Dirs of Army Gen Stf Divs, Chfs of Army Spec Stf Divs, 20 Nov 47, sub: Policy Concerning Release of Info fr Hist Docs of the Army—w/Spec Ref to the Events of WW II. CMH GRB Files—HRC 228.03 Hist Prog—Pres Directives.

writing for the series would be done in the commands and technical services, with the final editing and publication handled by the Historical Division. Indeed, the series was launched in 1946-47 with the publication of two Army Ground Forces volumes that were basically products of wartime monograph work in that command. Except for the Army Air Forces, however, most of the other commands disappeared so rapidly that the work devolved on the Historical Division. Only the seven technical services remained responsible for preparing their own volumes (each was eventually assigned three or four). And the Historical Section of the Medical Corps, the largest of all the technical service historical organizations, soon had plans to publish independently its own multivolume series of clinical histories in addition to the administrative volumes it proposed to contribute to The U.S. Army in World War II. Apart from these clinical volumes, the Historical Division retained responsibility for review, editing, and publication of the technical service histories, and its chief was given supervisory authority over all technical service historical activity.

In mid-1947, with the series hardly under way, reduced appropriations threatened the staffs of both the Historical Division and the historical units of the technical services. Largely as a result of the urging of Col. Allen F. Clark, then executive of the Historical Division, the Secretary of War created a War Department Historical Fund—$4 million in nonappropriated funds, part of the undistributed post exchange profits of World War II—to finance the writing and publication of the World War II series. It was estimated that the series could be completed in five years, and most of the people working on it were assured employment for that length of time. Although most of the technical services managed to continue their work without reliance on the fund, the Historical Division had to take over the Transportation Corps and Signal Corps programs, and for a time it also carried the historian of the Ordnance Corps on its fund roster.

The assumption by the Historical Division of most of the responsibility for writing as well as editing and publishing the series produced a new and different requirement for editors. Initially historians had been employed as editors in the belief that much of the writing would be done in other agencies. With the system changed, historians editing (and criticizing) the work of other historians led to frequent clashes. The solution was to create a separate professional editorial staff, largely recruited from publishing companies.

Large though it seemed at the time, the War Department Historical Fund financed only part of the World War II histories. The series took much longer to prepare and publish than was originally forecast. The fund was seriously depleted by 1954, while work on the series continued to absorb an important, though diminishing, share of the Army's historical effort into the 1970s. By 1977 some seventy-three volumes of the seventy-nine finally scheduled had been published and the rest were approaching completion. The U.S. Army in World War II series stands today as the greatest single endeavor in Army historical work.

Other Historical Activities

In 1950 the Historical Division, War Department Special Staff, was redesignated the Office, Chief of Military History, and was known as OCMH for the next two dozen years. In January 1956 OCMH was placed under the Army's Deputy Chief of Staff for Operations, for administration and general policy supervision. Neither of the changes had any fundamental effect on the work of the agency. But it did receive other tasks besides the World War II histories as that war receded into the background.

In 1946 the Historical Division had inherited general reference, staff support, and lineages and honors functions from the old War College section. In 1949 it also became responsible for historical properties, mainly general administration of a collection of American soldier art of World War II and captured German and Japanese paintings; this responsibility later broadened to include some supervision of Army museums and their collections. (See chapters 14 and 15.) In 1951 OCMH assumed the task of compiling and publishing a series on the background and battle honors of individual units. The first volume, on infantry regiments and battalions, appeared in 1953.[8] The project was later enlarged and redesignated the Army Lineage Series, a major activity of OCMH (see Chapter 16).

In 1949, to meet a staff-need, an Applied Studies Division was established to prepare and coordinate Army historical studies apart from the main World War II series. Under the direction of retired Brig. Gen. Paul M. Robinette, this division absorbed the foreign studies activities and produced special monographs on German operations, eventually published in some twenty

---

8. *Army Lineage Book*, vol. II: *Infantry* (Washington: Government Printing Office, 1953).

Department of the Army pamphlets. The division wrote other historical studies (also published as pamphlets) covering mobilization, demobilization, replacements, and utilization of prisoners of war in the United States, as well a *Guide to the Writing of American Military History*. As an outgrowth of the studies of German Army operations, OCMH planned seven volumes on the German campaign in Russia, to be published in a format similar to the U.S. Army in World War II series.

Despite the general liquidation of command and staff historical activities outside Washington after World War II, Army historical sections did remain in the two major overseas theaters—Europe and the Far East—and in the Army Ground Forces command. The two overseas sections worked on the foreign studies, on monographs and annual reports on the occupation of Germany and Japan, and, in the case of General MacArthur's command, on a separate history of operations in the Southwest Pacific during World War II. The ground forces historians also produced monographs just after the war, but by 1950 that command had given way to a new agency, Army Field Forces, with a one-man historical staff. Although the Chief of Military History was charged with coordinating and supervising historical activities of all Army units, major commands, and theaters, this supervision was lightly exercised and hardly existed at all in the Far East.

The Korean War and After

While the main emphasis in OCMH continued to be on the uncompleted World War II histories, the Korean War required a program similar to that of World War II for current coverage. As was the case earlier, impetus for preparing Korean War histories came from the president and from within the military establishment. In a directive reminiscent of President Roosevelt's in World War II, President Truman ordered departments and agencies to prepare administrative histories of their activities "in the present emergency."[9] And again the Army felt the need for operational history. The Army's responsibility actually extended beyond its own activities; the Joint Chiefs of Staff had ordered it to prepare a history of the joint command in the Far East during the Korean War.

---

9. Ltr, President Harry S. Truman to Director of the Budget, 29 Jan 51, copy in CMH—HRC 228.03 Hist. Prog.-Pres Directives.

The Army sent military historical teams to the theater, and material was collected and monographs written at both Eighth Army and Far East Command levels (see Chapter 13). OCMH prepared two narrative-pictorial histories of the war and two studies of small unit actions in combat and combat support and planned a new nine-volume series, similar to that of World War II, tentatively entitled The U.S. Army in the Conflict With the Communist Powers. Five volumes in this series were to be devoted to the Korean War itself, four more to the cold war in general. The latter four volumes were considered to be, fundamentally, a response to President Truman's directive. Each of the technical services also planned a volume covering its cold war activities.

Most of the Army's regular staff historians continued their work on World War II. To cover the Korean War, reserve officers with historical training were called to active duty and other officers learned by doing. Most returned to civilian jobs or other military duties once the war was over, but a few joined OCMH, first as officers and some later as civilians.

The new series was added to the Army's historical program at a time of decreasing personnel and increasing demands. With the War Department Historical Fund nearing exhaustion, OCMH fell from a peak of 251 officers and civilians in mid-1951 to 122 in mid-1954. After President Eisenhower endorsed the Army's historical work in 1954, appropriated funds were made available to transfer many, but not all, fund employees to the civil service. But the 1950s was a time of belt tightening throughout the Army, and the attrition in OCMH continued; by mid-1961 there were only seventy-seven employees. The command historical sections in both Europe and the Pacific were also reduced. Only the technical service sections were able, for the most part, to hold their own.

Meanwhile, new tasks proliferated. The Korean War underlined the need for continuously collecting sources and recording contemporary Army history in a crisis that threatened to go on indefinitely. The experience of World War II and Korea had proved the value of collecting documents, gathering oral testimony, and writing preliminary accounts while events were still vivid in the memories of participants. As the cold war went on, coverage of current Army history seemed in order as a continuing function, despite meager resources. OCMH had started a historical reporting system during the Korean War; Army staff sections in Washington and Army field forces were required to produce annual summaries of major events and problems. This program continued in the years following and became the major vehicle for covering the current history of Department of the Army headquarters staff sections, including the technical services, and of the Continental Army Command created in 1956. The two major overseas commands, in Europe and the Pacific, submitted annual reports under a different system. Some of the technical services, as well as the European command, also conducted monograph programs on current topics. The current history program grew haphazardly with little supervision and limited monitoring by OCMH; current history work in that office generally concentrated on the Korean War.

The Army staff and schools also increased their demands on OCMH and other historical offices for information and studies prepared on short notice—for what may loosely be termed staff support. The loss of the Applied Studies Division in the general cutback threw much of this burden on authors responsible for volumes on World War II and Korea. The reorganization of Army combat units under the Combat Arms Regimental System placed a heavy additional load on those working on lineages and honors volumes; historical properties work created even greater demands as responsibilities broadened to include Army museums; and queries from both officials and the public absorbed the best efforts of a small General Reference Section. A project of particular note assigned to OCMH in 1955 was the preparation and periodic revision of an American military history text to be used in the senior ROTC course. The first text, ROTCM 145-20, *American Military History 1607-1955*, a cooperative endeavor that occupied the best talent in OCMH for some months, was published in 1956, with a revision in 1959.

All of these demands on a shrinking staff played an important part in delaying completion of volumes in the various OCMH series. A committee reevaluated and reduced publications requirements in 1960. A new program set the limits of the U.S. Army in World War II series at seventy-nine volumes, retained a five-volume U.S. Army in the Korean War series, eliminated the other volumes in the proposed U.S. Army in Conflict With the Communist Powers series entirely, and cut the proposed seven volumes on the German campaign in Russia to three. An Army Historical Series was created to accommodate volumes that might be produced outside the World War II and Korean War series, including the foreign studies volumes.

The Reorganization of 1962-63

In a fundamental reorganization of 1962-63, the headquarters of five of the seven technical services were abolished, an Army Materiel Command created to absorb most of their functions, and the responsibilities of the Continental Army Command redefined and divided with a new Combat Developments Command. Accompanying the larger reorganization, and partly in response to it, the Army's historical program was reorganized and revitalized. On the basis of a detailed review of the existing system and structure, the Chief of Staff directed the Chief of Military History to coordinate and supervise the whole Army historical effort. A new Army regulation on historical activities (AR 870-5) brought together a host of separate directives, standardized the system for preparing and using military history throughout the Army, and established programs for both long-range and annual historical work. Under the new regulation, all major commands were to prepare annual historical reports and undertake historical studies on current activities. And the regulation established much closer control by the Chief of Military History over historical properties held throughout the Army. Active OCMH supervision over Army museums dates from 1962.

OCMH took on most of the book writing functions and a few of the historians of the five discontinued technical service headquarters; only the Surgeon General and the Chief of Engineers kept separate historical offices, and one of the remaining engineer volumes on World War II was transferred to OCMH. Many of the technical service historians and current history functions went to the Army Materiel Command and its subordinate components. The new Combat Developments Command acquired a historical staff, and the section at Continental Army Command was considerably strengthened. New Army history offices were established in the Army Air Defense Command, in U.S. Army, Alaska, headquarters; and in what became the Southern Command in Panama. The result of these redistributions was a much better balanced historical coverage of the Army and a new emphasis on current historical work.

Throughout the 1960s and early 1970s OCMH continued to give first priority to preparing books for publication, including the World War II, Korean War, and Army Historical series. By 1976, three of the proposed five Korea volumes had appeared and one more was well on the way. A revised and much improved ROTC text, *American Military History*, edited by Maurice

Matloff, was published in the Army Historical series in 1969, with a partial revision in 1973. Other books in this series covered Army logistics from the Revolution through the Korean War, the German-Russian war, and the American military occupation of Germany. OCMH also assumed responsibility for a pioneer volume in a proposed Defense Studies series, a work on integration in all the armed services. And an examination of Army organization from the founding of the General Staff in 1903 to the reorganization of 1963 inaugurated a new Special Studies series, designed to accommodate more detailed, monographic works.

Both in OCMH and throughout the Army, nevertheless, historians devoted much more time to recent events and to staff support. OCMH established its own current monograph program, and its historians prepared studies of the Army's role in such events as the Berlin crisis of 1961–62, the Cuban missile crisis, and the civil disturbance at Oxford, Mississippi, in 1963. Demands for special work on short notice reached new heights as the Army staff turned to OCMH for background studies on matters of current interest, ranging from the Army's experience with the Civilian Conservation Corps of the 1930s to deployment procedures in World War II and Korea.

As an added aspect of current history work, in 1963 OCMH also began preparing the Secretary of the Army's annual report. Secretary of War John C. Calhoun had signed the first one in 1822. Since 1949, however, it had formed part of the Secretary of Defense's annual report. Although this practice was discontinued in 1972, the document had been a valuable source of basic, unclassified information, and the Army decided to continue with a somewhat similar compilation, the annual *Department of the Army Historical Summary.*

Later Changes, MHI and CMH

Despite some changes, the basic lines established in 1962–63 have governed Army historical activities since that time. On 12 June 1967 the U.S. Army Military History Research Collection was established at Carlisle Barracks, Pennsylvania, as part of the Army War College. In 1970 it became a Class II installation under OCMH, and in 1977 the name was changed to the U.S. Army Military History Institute (MHI). This was something new in the Army historical establishment, an institution devoted to preserving materials related to the military history of the

United States and making them available to both military and civilian researchers (see Chapter 12).

Then in 1973, in another general reorganization, the Office, Chief of Military History, was converted from a special staff agency into a field operating agency under the new name of the U.S. Army Center of Military History (CMH). Its commander retained the title of Chief of Military History, however, and as such continued to exercise staff responsibilities for military history. The research collection became an integral part of the new center though still located at the Army War College. The Deputy Chief of Staff for Operations retained staff supervision over the center, and its mission and functions remained the same. The main change was that CMH acquired control over its own budget.

In a broader reorganization of the Army in 1973–74, Continental Army Command and Combat Developments Command were abolished and replaced by a Training and Doctrine Command and Forces Command, with a realignment of functions. A Health Services Command, which absorbed some of the operating functions of the Surgeon General's office, was created at the same time. Historical staffs and responsibilities were realigned to go along with these new commands. Further reorganizations in 1974 abolished Army component commands in the Pacific, Alaska, and the Caribbean, and the Army Air Defense Command in the United States. The jurisdiction of Forces Command was extended into some of these areas; but in the Pacific, for instance, field historical coverage devolved on such formerly subordinate organizations as the Eighth Army in Korea and U.S. Army, Japan. All the major commands, including the Health Services Command, nevertheless, established historical sections that, at the very least, produced annual historical reviews. The Corps of Engineers also retained a separate historical section devoted mainly to the corps' civil projects, while coverage of its military activities was transferred to the Center of Military History. Then in mid-1975 the last of the old technical service historical offices, the one with the longest tradition, lost its independence when the Medical Department Historical Unit was transferred from the Surgeon General to the Center of Military History and became the Medical History Division of that agency.

The Program for the War in Vietnam

Writing on Vietnam began in OCMH in 1962, as part of the

current history program, with a special study reviewing the Army's activities in that area since 1954. When the Office, Secretary of Defense, called for a more detailed account by each service and by the Joint Chiefs of Staff of their activities in connection with Vietnam, OCMH prepared a long classified monograph on the Army's involvement through the end of 1963. Later OCMH extended this monograph to record events through June 1965, and the historical office of U.S. Army, Pacific, increased in size for this specific purpose, did likewise. In Saigon a Military Assistance Command, Vietnam (MACV), historical office was set up in 1964 to cover joint military activities in the area.

In July 1965 President Johnson announced plans for deploying large numbers of troops to Vietnam and for expanding the Army; at the same time General William C. Westmoreland, MACV commander, announced the establishment of a separate U.S. Army, Vietnam, headquarters. Army historical activity soon quickened as Chief of Staff General Harold K. Johnson directed that the war receive coverage of the same quality as World War II. In OCMH a special historical staff devoted to the war in Vietnam took shape. As part of an Army-wide monograph program, each of the major commands in the United States was required to record its role in the Vietnam buildup. In Vietnam the Army command established a historical office, and Washington sent military history detachments to serve Army divisions and brigades in the field (see Chapter 13).

The purpose of these efforts was twofold: first, to meet staff and field requirements for historical information and support; second, to ensure the preservation of records needed to prepare a definitive narrative history of the war comparable to the World War II series. Plans for such a history had emerged by 1976 and called for twenty-one volumes dealing with the background of involvement; Department of the Army policy, planning, and support; land combat in the theater; various aspects of logistical support; and the problems of press coverage and soldier morale, matters of great importance in the Vietnam War. The Center of Military History collaborated with the Adjutant General's Office and the National Archives in expediting the retirement of records from Vietnam to depositories in the Washington area where they would be available to historians.

In 1970, OCMH published a slim paperback volume, *Seven Firefights in Vietnam*, reminiscent in many ways of the World War II Armed Forces in Action series. That same year General Westmoreland, as Army Chief of Staff, established a Vietnam

monograph series on various specialized topics, to be written by
key Army leaders who were specialists in the areas covered. The
first to appear was *Communications-Electronics, 1962-1970*, by
Maj. Gen. Thomas M. Rienzi; eighteen more had followed by the
end of 1976 with two still in progress. The job of the Center of
Military History in preparing the monographs was to assist the
authors in planning and research, to make the necessary maps,
and to edit the manuscripts for publication. In this sense the
monographs were not products of the center but firsthand
accounts to be used in writing definitive works for the 21-volume
U.S. Army in Vietnam series.

Army History Today

Army history has come far in the past century, and is now a
solidly based function supported by Army leaders. The first
century of Army historical work was devoted mainly to
collecting, editing, and publishing basic records; narrative
histories came into their own during and after World War II and
have remained the principal form of Army history, not merely as
published books but also as classified monographs and special
studies prepared on demand to meet specific needs. All the
historical services functions—general reference, lineages and
honors, collecting and organizing historical materials, and oral
history—have also continued to grow.

Army Regulation 10-48, 1 September 1974, gives the mission
of the Center of Military History: to

> formulate and execute the Army Historical Program; coordinate and
> supervise Army historical matters including historical properties;
> prepare and publish histories required by the Army; formulate the
> historical background and precedents required for the development of
> military plans, policies, doctrine, and techniques; supervise the Army
> Museum system; maintain a repository for the collection and
> preservation of historical documents relating to the United States Army;
> and provide historical material and assistance to, and maintain liaison
> with, public and private agencies and individuals and stimulate interest
> and study in the field of military history.

Since the addition of the Medical History Division to the center,
responsibilities also include preparing and publishing medical
history and collecting and maintaining medical history materials.

The commanding general of the center bears the title Chief of
Military History and as such represents the entire Army on
historical matters with responsibility for advising the Chief of

Staff, the Secretary of the Army, and all components of the Army. The center conducts the historical program under the provisions of Army Regulation 870-5 (1977) that sets forth the responsibilities of all elements of the Army in its fulfillment. The Deputy Chief of Staff for Operations and Plans exercises general staff supervision over the center. The various parts of the Army historical program—the several series, the monographs, the annual reporting system, the work of the Military History Institute, medical history, special studies, organizational history, lineages and honors, general reference service, historical properties, and Army art—are detailed in a long-range historical plan (a ten-year projection) and in an annual historical program which sets goals for each fiscal year.

Within the center, following the system established after World War II, the Chief of Military History is a general officer. He is advised on professional and technical aspects of military history by a Chief Historian, a civilian responsible for the professional quality of Army history. A Department of the Army Historical Advisory Committee composed of four military representatives of the Army school system, representatives of The Surgeon General's Office and The Adjutant General, the Deputy Archivist of the United States, and seven civilian historians, meets annually and advises the Secretary of the Army, the Chief of Staff, and the Chief of Military History on the Army's historical program.

A Management Support Division provides administrative services within the center. The center's principal functions are carried out by four other elements, Histories, Historical Services, the Military History Institute (research collection), and the Medical History Division.

The Histories Division produces the most widely read and used products of the Army historical program, the major narrative histories in the various series. The division also handles historical reports and demand projects requested by the Army secretariat and staff and other sources.

The Historical Services Division establishes the official lineages and honors of units, compiles the volumes in the Army Lineage series, provides general reference service, works on some of the demand projects, and is responsible for historical properties, including Army museums, and the Army art program.

The Medical History Division prepares and publishes volumes, monographs, and special studies on Army medical services. Much of the work of the division is in clinical histories;

some thirty-three covering World War II have been published. Written by physicians who are prominent specialists, these clinical histories are usually collections of articles, similar to those published in medical journals, on one subject. Essentially the job of the Medical History Division is to assist the physicians in their research and writing and to assemble and edit the final product. In addition to the clinical books, the division prepares administrative histories written by professional historians rather than medical doctors. For example the Medical Department was allotted four volumes in the World War II series, two of which have been published.

The fourth part of the center, the U.S. Army Military History Institute at Carlisle Barracks, Pennsylvania, is treated in some detail in Chapter 12 of this *Guide.*

The basic Army regulation on military history and the annual programs provide for historical activities of departmental staff agencies and Army commands worldwide. Army staff agencies send unclassified material to the Center of Military History for the annual *Department of the Army Historical Summary* and compile classified annual historical reviews for their own use and for preparation of later histories. Major commands and some subordinate commands also prepare annual historical reviews and monographs on selected current topics. The Army encourages its leaders, commissioned and noncommissioned, to make full use of military history. Individual units preserve and use their own history to promote pride and self-esteem, and many Army installations have museums.

The Army's historical program is comprehensive with organizational threads extending from the secretariat through the departmental staff and Center of Military History to stateside and overseas commands, agencies, installations, and units. The program is designed to preserve and use the military record for the many purposes that history serves.

Chapter 12

The U.S. Army Military History Institute

Col. James B. Agnew and
B. Franklin Cooling

LOCATED at the U.S. Army War College at Carlisle Barracks, Pennsylvania, the U.S. Army Military History Institute (formerly the U.S. Army Military History Research Collection—redesignated 1 April 1977) is a complex of library and reference facilities, special collections, and archives, all of which deal in the main with American and, to a lesser extent, foreign military history. Since its inception in 1967, the institute has collected, preserved, and made available for use documents and materials pertinent to the history of the U.S. Army. Because of the many domestic and foreign influences that have shaped that history, the staff of the institute has interpreted its mission broadly. Substantial holdings relate to the U.S. Navy and Air Force, the reserve components, foreign military forces, and wars in which the United States was not involved. Many of the holdings predate any American army and provide sources on the evolution of the military art.

The institute began almost by accident. In 1966 its first director, Col. George S. Pappas, then a member of the Army War College staff and faculty, was directed to update the history of that institution. While searching for source material, Pappas came across some very old books on military history in the War College library in Upton Hall, the administrative and academic center for the college. Colonel Pappas asked the commandant, Maj. Gen. Eugene Salet, for space to secure and preserve the books in Upton Hall when the War College library moved into new quarters in Root Hall. He also requested authority to seek other rare books to add to the collection; the whole would become

Colonel Agnew (USA, Ret., M.P.A., Princeton), Director of the U.S. Army Military History Institute in 1974–77, also served as Assistant Professor of History at the U.S. Military Academy and wrote *The Egg-Nog Riot: Christmas Mutiny at West Point*. Dr. Cooling (Ph.D., Pennsylvania) is Assistant Director for Historical Services at the Military History Institute. His numerous publications in military and naval history include a biography of Benjamin Franklin Tracy and *Symbol, Sword, and Shield: Defending Washington During the Civil War*.

part of the War College library. General Salet agreed, provided the project would not conflict with the activities of the Army's Chief of Military History, at that time Brig. Gen. Hal C. Pattison. General Pattison endorsed the idea and suggested the addition of a much larger collection, 30,000 volumes on military history before World War II that had been culled from the National War College library by that institution's librarian, George Stansfield, with the help of Charles Romanus of Pattison's office, and placed in special storage. With this first donation, the idea of an extensive research collection took shape; space was provided in Upton Hall in the facilities vacated by the War College library, and in 1967 an Army regulation established the Military History Research Collection.

From these small beginnings, the institute's holdings have expanded to more than 350,000 bound volumes, and it has also collected over 8,000 boxes of diaries, manuscripts, letters, and other valuable personal references to the Army and its heritage. Museum collections of artifacts, accoutrements, and art work have also been acquired. The professional staff has expanded from three to thirty-three civilian and military librarians, historians, archivists, curators, and administrators.

Although the collection dates from September 1966, the first academic researcher did not arrive until July of the following year. Seeking information on the life of General George Crook, Professor James King of Wisconsin State University found Crook's diaries and other related papers in the archives. Since then scholars such as Martin Blumenson, Forrest Pogue, Russell Weigley, Theodore Ropp, Charles Burdick, and S. L. A. Marshall have used other original records. In addition, a growing number of undergraduate and graduate students as well as other interested persons, both military and civilian, have used the institute's resources. Funds permitting, MHI administers an advanced research program involving modest grants for research in the institute's holdings. And an intern program gives undergraduates from nearby colleges experience in archives and museum management, library science, and the preparation of bibliographies.

The expansion of services and acquisitions during the decade since the facility was established can be traced by some highlights. In June 1968 the collection instituted a survey of surviving Spanish-American War veterans which helped develop perhaps the best archival holdings extant on the personal experiences of soldiers in that war, the Philippine Insurrection, and the Boxer Rebellion. The survey added over

300 linear feet of documents to those archives. Four months later began a monthly evening lectures series, "Perspectives in Military History," which brought prominent historians to Carlisle Barracks. In August 1969 an additional 120,000 volumes were transferred to the collection from the National War College library. In 1970 the collection was designated an official repository for documents and materials on the Army's heritage, the Senior Officer Oral History Program was established, and the first in a continuing series of bibliographic aids, *The US Army and Domestic Disturbances*, was published. Recently the institute has sponsored military history courses for the War College and has appointed distinguished academicians to the Harold Keith Johnson Chair of Military History. New acquisitions have included the Civil War collection from the Massachusetts Commandery of the Loyal Legion of the United States, the Aztec Club files, the Tasker H. Bliss papers, and numerous donations from retired senior American officers.

A field element of the U.S. Army Center of Military History in Washington, the institute is officially associated as well with the Army War College, whose commandant is also designated Commanding General, U.S. Army Military History Institute. The institute thus benefits from close ties with the Army's official historical agency as well as its senior service college.

Services and Facilities

The civilian scholar, military officer, or history buff visiting Upton Hall will find a prodigious amount of material. An archivist, librarian, or member of the reference service will interview the scholar concerned with a specific topic and, if appropriate, provide a desk in the research area near the primary and secondary sources relating to that topic. An officer doing more general research for a staff paper, graduate thesis, or War College project may find the spacious reading room more agreeable. A reference assistant or librarian will bring any necessary materials. Either type of researcher may want to use some of the more than 55,000 pages of oral history transcripts collected since 1970 from such military figures as Matthew B. Ridgway, Maxwell D. Taylor, Harold K. Johnson, Ferdinand Chesarek, and Austin Betts.

If the casual visitor is a military buff or a tourist interested more in looking around than in research, he can go on a self-guided tour of the Omar N. Bradley Museum, the Hessian Powder Magazine, or the various temporary displays in the foyer and corridors of Upton Hall. Collections of heraldic art, photographs, uniforms, and equipment may also interest him. He may even offer to donate personal items from family records.

The institute provides such services as holdings, staff, and time permit. For resident or visiting scholars this usually includes access to and assistance with the bound volumes, archival material, periodicals, and special collections. Persons unable to visit the institute may borrow books through interlibrary loan (unless the volumes are rare or in poor physical condition). The institute will also fill at cost modest orders for reproduced pages. The scholar writing for specific information receives a description of the holdings on the subject and suggestions on the location of other sources.

Each year the institute publishes two or three bibliographies pertaining to its special holdings. The Special Bibliographic series includes such titles as *The Army and Civil Disturbances, The Black Military Experience, Unit Histories, The Spanish War Era, The Mexican War, Archival Holdings* (two volumes), *The Era of the Civil War*, and *The Colonial and Revolutionary Period*. Future bibliographies will deal with the U.S. Army in the west and both world wars. These bibliographies are distributed to military officials and organizations and may be purchased from the Government Printing Office.

Among the notable holdings at the institute are the World War I and World War II Signal Corps photo collections; the Massachusetts Loyal Legion collection of Civil War photographs, including many unpublished portraits and views of Army life and historic sites; audio archives of lectures, martial music, and reminiscences of veterans; American and European recruiting, propaganda, and war-loan posters from the major wars of the twentieth century; and microfilm copies of a number of doctoral dissertations on military history. The institute carries on an active acquisitions program and also welcomes donations from all sources. Staff librarians periodically screen the holdings of other libraries throughout the Army for materials that would be of greater value at Carlisle Barracks.

A Sample of the Holdings

A sample of volumes and document collections in the Military History Institute will suggest the amount and variety of material that can be found there. In the general stacks may be found a superb basic collection of narratives, biographies, and special studies ranging from ancient Greece and Rome to the modern nation-states of Europe, Asia, Africa, the Middle East, and the Americas. Among the collections on special periods are seven or eight thousand volumes on the American Civil War, including rare personal narratives and unit histories; and nearly ten thousand volumes, in five languages, on World War I, including the official histories of all major powers. War Department reports, technical and field manuals, general and special orders, bulletins, and studies are abundant, although not all Army publications are available. The well-known writings of strategists such as Saxe, Jomini, Clausewitz, Napoleon, DuPicq, Schlieffen, and Mahan are available in several languages.

Most volumes in the rare book room were originally in the old War Department library, started about 1840. Works such as original manuscripts of the Lewis and Clark expeditions, medieval treatises on artillery and siegecraft, early histories of the British Army, Wellington's dispatches, Continental drill manuals, a Revolutionary War orderly book, and numerous superbly bound early histories of the United States and leather bound illustrations of military uniforms and equipment—some 6,000 titles in all—are in this repository.

The archives contain such major collections as the papers of Matthew B. Ridgway, Lewis B. Hershey, Paul Carraway, and Harold K. Johnson; the Spanish-American War and World War I veterans survey holdings; an original War Department copy of Emory Upton's study on the military policy of the United States; and the curricular archives of the Army War College for 1907-60. Countless personal papers, diaries, and individual military records of Civil War soldiers have been added in recent years, as have thousands of pages of oral history transcripts from more than seventy retired American generals.

The periodical section contains over 30,000 bound publications, both domestic and foreign, most either military or technical. Ranging from older copies of civilian periodicals like the *Nation*, *Harper's*, and *Time* to recent unit newspapers from the Vietnam period, the holdings include the *Army and Navy Journal*, various journals of the branches and services of the U.S. Army, and foreign military publications such as *Allgemeine Schweizerische Militaerzeitung, Der Adler, Deutsche Wehr, La Guerre Mondiale, Journal des Sciences Militaires*, and the *Canadian Military Gazette*.

A separate room is devoted to unit histories (including many of the British and German armies), Department of the Army authority files, and unclassified documents from the Korean and Vietnam wars. The institute also has a biographical reference room and collections of insignia, uniforms, weapons, and equipment.

An Institution in Transition

The worth of a research establishment such as the Military History Institute lies in its programs and services as well as its materials. The years 1966–74 were a period of organization and acquisition; those since of consolidation and expanded use. Accessions, while continuing, have decreased from the time when the staff worked to build basic holdings. The institute continues to acquire important new publications as well as those which are becoming rare, and individual archival contributions are always welcome; but a policy of keeping duplicates out of the stacks has minimized the search for wholesale additions.

The institute staff advertises its resources to attract users, military and civilian, institutional and private. A number come from the military educational system—the service school faculties and students. A semiannual newsletter, published bibliographies, special studies such as the anthology *Some New Dimensions in Military History* and the series Vignettes in Military History, command and staff visits, the oral history program, and word of mouth attract researchers to Upton Hall.

The institute attempts to impress upon military officers the value of accumulated knowledge of the past in solving the problems of the contemporary Army. The staff contributes to the War College through the expanded military history elective program and through advice, case studies, bibliographies, and instructional assistance. Future conferences and symposia at Carlisle Barracks, hosted by the Military History Institute, will involve military and civilian academicians exchanging views on the research, writing, and teaching of military history. Staff members do research, write, lecture, and attend conferences to stimulate interest in the institute. The visiting professorship provides a link between the Army War College and the nation's colleges and universities.

The future of the Military History Institute appears bright, although it is certainly not without its problems. Possible staff cutbacks could reduce services. Space, adequate in 1967, will be at a premium as new holdings and new programs threaten to outgrow Upton Hall. Plans are afoot for expansion, but declining military budgets may prevent new construction. The natural aging of books, manuscripts, and artifacts makes preservation a bigger job than in the formative years. Still, the periodic review of programs and progress by an energetic and innovative professional staff promises to expand, not curtail, service to the military history community. The institute expects to maintain its position as a valuable repository for information on domestic and foreign military affairs of the past.

Chapter **13**

The Military History
Detachment
in the Field

Richard A. Hunt

RECOGNIZING the military value of history, the U.S. Army established a historical branch under G-2 of the War Department General Staff during World War II and made the new organization responsible for accumulating sources for an official history of the war. From then on, the Army dispatched historians in uniform to the field to preserve and supplement the historical record as it was created. The main instrument has been the military history detachment or historical team. Its mission is to ensure that primary historical documents generated in the field are collected and preserved for later writing of complete histories. This underlying mission has changed little from World War II through Korea to Vietnam, although its implementation and the configuration of the teams have varied from war to war.

Historical teams in each war have been made up of officers and enlisted men who handled historical and clerical duties, respectively. Typewriters and jeeps, standard items in World War II and Korea, were complemented in Vietnam by tape recorders. Military history detachments were either attached to subordinate units with command and control retained by the theater, army, or administrative commander, or assigned to subordinate units such as divisions with command and control of the detachments vested in those units. These arrangements have limited the Army's central historical office (variously the Historical Branch, the Office of the Chief of Military History, and the Center of Military History) to "technical" rather than command supervision of the detachments on historical matters. Providing a service neither used by nor primarily intended for the field units which support them but for a staff agency in Washington, the historical detachments can sometimes be caught between the conflicting needs of the ultimate users of the information they gather and the requirements of their immediate field commanders. In such cases, the latter have in the past taken precedence.

Dr. Hunt (Ph.D., Pennsylvania) of the Current History Branch, CMH, was a field historian in Vietnam. He is working on a history of the pacification program in that country.

Yet the separation of the staff agency and the field historian does not necessarily diminish the quality or objectivity of the detachment's historical work. While this arrangement reduces the control the Washington historical office exercises, it can allow field detachments freedom and flexibility. Having the advantage of guidance from Washington, and often being under the immediate direction of a staff officer with no vested interest in the collection and disposition of historical documents, the commander of a historical unit in the war zone retains in theory enough autonomy to pursue his assignment thoroughly and objectively.

World War II

The World War II field historical program began in the midst of that conflict.[1] The first teams trained by the Historical Branch were assigned to the headquarters of the North African Theater of Operations where they initially prepared pamphlets about earlier World War II engagements for the Armed Forces in Action series. Teams soon existed at almost all levels of command. Located in the European, Alaskan, Central, South, and Southwest Pacific theaters, they covered the activities of Army ground forces, air forces, service forces, and technical services. It became customary for divisions and regiments, and occasionally for battalions and companies, to appoint an officer as a part-time historian. In addition, the theater or army historical section sent out roving historians to obtain firsthand information.

The theater historian indirectly supervised historical teams attached to army groups, armies, and corps, served as staff adviser to the theater commander on military history, maintained close liaison with his counterparts from other countries and other U.S. services, and sought to ensure the preservation of records. Because of unconditional surrender, German and Japanese as well as U.S. records eventually fell under his care.

Although the Historical Branch had intended to retain control of the overseas historical teams, the theater commander assumed control when they entered his jurisdiction. The branch had a voice in the selection of officer historians, gave them preliminary indoctrination, corresponded with them regularly, and kept a representative in Europe. Yet such influence was not

---

1. The discussion of the World War II experience is based on the following sources: Bell I. Wiley, "Historical Program of the US Army 1939 to Present," CMH files; Lynn M. Case, "The Military Historian Overseas," *AAUP Bulletin* 24 (Summer 1948):320–33.

uniform. For example, the branch had no liaison with historians in the Southwest Pacific until the war was nearly over; that historical office was located in an allied theater headquarters, not an Army one.

To supplement historical work below theater headquarters, the War Department in April 1944 established numerous information and historical service teams composed of two officers and two enlisted men. Most of the officers were reservists or civilian historians who had been called to active duty or had volunteered. Some were regular and reserve officers for whom no other place could be found. Field army headquarters generally dispatched the teams to subordinate units. Although duties varied from command to command, the teams generally sought to preserve and retire documents, prepare studies, and interview key individuals. Their reports and information were sent to the theater historical sections which had jurisdiction over them.

The teams built upon the interviewing techniques of Lt. Col. S. L. A. Marshall. Assigned to the Historical Branch, Marshall went to the Pacific theater in the fall of 1943 to cover the island campaigns of the 7th Infantry Division. By interviewing groups of battle participants immediately after an engagement, Marshall could reconstruct events as vividly and completely as possible. His accounts of small unit action were noteworthy for their human interest and battlefield realism and his methods were adopted by historical officers in all theaters.

Field historical work in World War II had its problems. Field commanders with full appreciation of the value of history and the difficulties of historical research were rare; many were impatient with the amount of time thorough historical work entailed and used the historian as a tour guide for visiting officials, lecturer, statistician, or expert on local history and mores. Officer historians often had to prove their usefulness to unsympathetic, skeptical commanders, many of whom felt that their S-3s or G-3s could do the job as well. Once the historian had won the confidence of his commander, he had to keep his function clearly separated from the work of unofficial historians who were compiling laudatory unit histories paid for by the subscriptions of unit members.

There were also research problems. Because of security precautions and faulty filing, the historian did not have complete access to important operational documents. Sometimes important records were destroyed or integral file collections dispersed before he could get to them. Deaths, wounds, transfers, transportation difficulties, and the general pressure of events on important officers made it difficult to conduct interviews. Some of these problems reappeared in Korea and Vietnam.

Korea

Beginning in February 1951, the Army sent eight historical detachments to Korea and assigned them to Eighth Army Special Troops.[2] At first one detachment attempted to supervise by correspondence the activities of the remaining seven, which were widely scattered in the field. When this arrangement proved too unwieldy, control of the eight detachments was consolidated under the historian at Eighth Army headquarters. Toward the end of the war, the separate detachments were merged into one large detachment at Headquarters, U.S. Army Forces, Far East, a move which separated the historians from the units fighting the war and burdened them with additional staff duties.

As in World War II, the tasks were enormous. The eight detachments in Korea had to cover the activities of one army, three corps, and six divisions. Some major commands, such as logistics commands, and some corps had staff historians, however, and some divisions appointed part-time historical officers. The Army called up qualified reserve officers to command the historical detachments, but there were not enough of these and others had to be drawn from the personnel pipeline. The Office of the Chief of Military History (OCMH) gave two weeks of orientation to detachment members before they went to Korea.

Although OCMH could not supervise the detachments directly or even establish a uniform method for combat interviews, it could offer professional advice and request written reports. Based on after-action interviews, terrain analysis, and available documents, these reports focused largely on specific small unit actions which the detachments could cover comprehensively. Forwarded to OCMH through intermediate historical offices, the raw reports were intended as reference and source material for the official histories to come. As the war progressed, however, the Eighth Army historian emphasized reviewing and polishing

---

2. Information on the use of Historical Teams in Korea has been derived from Lt. Col. James H. Ferguson, "The US Army Historical Effort in Vietnam, 1954–1968," 1969, CMH files; Maj. Robert Fechtman, "The Value of Historical Detachments," 1952, CMH files; Interview with Mr. Billy C. Mossman, former history detachment commander in Korea, 22 May 1975.

reports as they passed up the chain of command. As a result historians spent more time behind desks and had less opportunity to get to the field.

Vietnam

Because its people served under the Military Assistance Command, Vietnam (MACV), a joint U.S. command, the Army could assign detachments to Vietnam only after large Army units arrived and Headquarters, U.S. Army, Vietnam (USARV), was formed in 1965.[3] Activated in Hawaii, the first history detachment reached the war zone in September. Headquarters in Vietnam initially expected it would need only five additional detachments, but had to request sixteen more in November to cover the rapidly expanding involvement and in September 1966 raised the total to twenty-seven. Ultimately all twenty-seven detachments, over three times more than in Korea, were deployed and assigned to subordinate commands and units. Because the command historian sometimes shifted detachments from unit to unit, a particular unit may have had a detachment assigned to it for only part of the war.

As in earlier wars, it was difficult to find enough officers with satisfactory backgrounds or training. In 1965 only seventeen officers on active duty met the qualification for military historian. But this time the Army sought its historians among officers already in uniform and called no civilians to active duty. Yet the scarcity of professionally qualified historians in the early stages of the war was less serious than it might appear. Since the detachment commanders' mission was to preserve records and interview participants rather than to perform research or write monographs, it was more important for them to have broad experience in the Army and a working knowledge of its mores and procedures than to be certified historians. And as the war progressed, more officers with historical backgrounds came on active duty and, once in uniform, were assigned as detachment commanders. Many of those selected received training at OCMH and an orientation at Army headquarters in Vietnam to overcome gaps in professional backgrounds and prepare them for their new commands.

In Vietnam detachments were assigned to field forces, divisions, separate brigades, and support commands. While the

---

3. The discussion of the role of Historical detachments in Vietnam is based on Ferguson, "Historical Effort in Vietnam"; DA Pamphlet 870-2, *The Military Historian in the Field*, 1969; interviews with former detachment commanders in Vietnam; and memoranda, reports, journals, and correspondence in CMH files.

USARV historian exercised "technical supervision," his influence on the historical work of the detachments was limited because the unit to which each detachment was assigned wrote the efficiency report of the detachment commander and because detachments were widely dispersed. Responding to complaints of isolation and insufficient historical guidance, the USARV historian in August 1967 raised anew the same question of command and control that had been raised in Korea and proposed centralizing control of the detachments in his office. Rather than assigning them to outlying units and commands, he proposed attaching them temporarily to specific units to perform specific tasks; commanders of host units would not have operational control of the detachments. The Chief of Military History demurred. Because of the rapid pace and scattered action of the war, he believed it was imperative for detachments to be in the field. If they were dispatched from a central headquarters such as USARV, transportation to the scene of action would be a constant problem, and field commanders would be less responsive and cooperative with outsiders from a higher headquarters. For these reasons all detachments continued to be assigned to outlying units until 1970 when some were reassigned to USARV headquarters.

This type of assignment, however, permitted diversion of detachment commanders to other duties. While occasionally assigned to study specific problems, such as the shipping backlog in 1965, they were routinely charged with preparing after-action reports and operational reports, lessons learned (ORLLs). In an attempt to upgrade the historical value of the operational report and supplement the historical information forwarded to higher headquarters, U.S. Army, Pacific, encouraged the USARV historian to strengthen the historical section of the report. This effort met with some success, but the reports still absorbed much of the energy and time of the USARV historian and the detachment commanders and limited their time for purely historical work.

The difficulties the USARV historian had in advising and assisting detachments were multiplied by time and distance from the ultimate users of their work, Army historical offices in Hawaii and Washington. The influence of these offices was limited to messages and periodic visits to Vietnam. The Chief of Military History also established a "pen pal" program in which historians in Washington corresponded with all detachments, offering technical advice and assistance as well as suggesting areas of inquiry, research topics, and names of people to be interviewed.

The field historical program in Vietnam enjoyed a technical advantage over those of earlier wars. The portable tape recorder proved invaluable in individual interviews and in the combat interview program, an integral part of the detachment's mission. Field historians recorded interviews with commanders and action officers on staffs and forwarded the tapes to the Center of Military History for storage and later use as source material for the official histories of the war.

Historical coverage had to be expanded to include the important work of those who advised Vietnamese units or programs. Detachments were not originally assigned to cover the advisory program because it was under the military assistance command, a joint command. Later in the war U.S. Army, Vietnam, assigned one detachment in each of the four corps or regions in South Vietnam to cover the advisory effort. While U.S. pacification advisers submitted periodic reports to the military assistance command, the scattered and constantly moving teams advising Vietnamese Army units found such reporting difficult. In general, advisory records were more complete at higher headquarters such as corps and field force, where staff and command journals were kept, and less complete at lower levels where reports were made informally by phone, by radio, or in person. Advisers at these lower levels could keep few written records because they were constantly on the move and had little access to office facilities.

After the Vietnam War ended, military history detachments continued to make an important contribution to preserving the record of the Army. Of the three detachments on active duty at this time, two are stationed in Europe where they cover the operations of V and VII Corps. The detachment located in the United States and assigned to Forces Command headquarters covered activities at the Fort Chaffee, Arkansas, and Indiantown Gap Military Reservation, Pennsylvania, refugee reception centers. Reserve detachments, attached to the division or command with which they would most likely serve on active duty, participate with them each year in field or command exercises for their two-weeks' training. In the event of mobilization, they are scheduled to be called to active duty and deployed quickly.

From its beginnings in World War II, Army and civilian historians have appreciated the field historical program for preserving historical documents and recording the views and recollections of participants. Although command and control arrangements have frequently allowed the diversion of historical detachments to routine staff duties, they have nevertheless proved invaluable. Without their work the compilation of recent military histories would have been more difficult and, in breadth and depth of coverage, impossible to match.

Bibliography

Case, Lynn M. "The Military Historian Overseas." *AAUP Bulletin* 24 (1948):320-34.

Fechtman, Maj. Robert. "The Value of Historical Detachments." Washington: CMH files, 1952.

Ferguson, Lt. Col. James H. "The US Army Historical Effort in Vietnam, 1954-1968." Washington: CMH files, 1969.

U.S., AR 870-5. "Military History—Responsibilities, Policies, and Procedures," 1977.

U.S., DA Pamphlet 870. *The Military Historian in the Field*. 1969.

Wiley, Bell I. "The Historical Program of the US Army, 1939 to the Present." Washington: CMH files, 1945.

Chapter **14**

The Army
Art Program

Marian R. McNaughton

THE U. S. Army Art Collection is a rich and often neglected source of material for research and study in military history. As the student of military history becomes acquainted with war art, he discovers that historical illustrations are useful in a variety of ways. Sketches from sight are frequently the most authentic and sometimes the only descriptions of important battles, uniforms, and equipment of the past. Furthermore, modern narrative military paintings provide valuable insights into the life, thoughts, and feelings of the American soldier in his own time.

Since man first marched off to war, battles and heroic feats have been popular subjects for painting and sculpture. Military campaigns were commemorated on the temple walls of Egyptian pharaohs and Khmer emperors and in the palaces of Assyrian kings. Sculptures, relief panels, and vases of the intellectual Greeks and Chinese as well as the richly carved columns and arches of the conquering Romans also bear eloquent testimony to man's desire to memorialize his achievements in combat. European art in the Middle Ages was almost entirely of religious subjects, but the Renaissance in Italy brought about both a resurgent interest in commemorative sculptures and the creation of the earliest battle paintings on canvas or wood panels. Until the twentieth century, in the United States military art was the independent activity of a disparate group of courageous and industrious individuals. Throughout its history, nevertheless, the U.S. Army has fostered art by permitting both soldier and civilian artists to accompany troops and make sketches as the spirit moved them.

Combat art has become important as historical document, source of patriotic inspiration, and, in some cases, expression of artistic genius. The artist has played a diverse role in attempting both to record and to interpret his experiences in war. The advent of the camera in the nineteenth century reduced his role as a reporter without diminishing the value of his art as

Mrs. McNaughton (B.A., American), a specialist on American military art, is the CMH Staff Curator of the Army Art Collection.

historical document. Since his function as a reporter was not as necessary as before, the combat artist had greater freedom to communicate his impressions through personal interpretation and to involve the viewer by appealing to his emotions. But the most successful military artists still maintained a balance between personal and visual reality.

Each American war since the Revolution has had its own artists. As aide-de-camp on the staff of General George Washington, John Trumbull drew scenes of the War of Independence which he later developed into full-scale battle paintings. A large number of painters and engravers recorded battle scenes of the War of 1812, but no one artist rose to prominence. James Walker trudged with the troops and sketched the battles of Contreras, Churubusco, and Chapultepec during the Mexican War; Winslow Homer supplemented the work of the great photographer, Mathew Brady, in recording events of the Civil War; while a soldier assigned to the 71st Infantry in the Spanish-American War, Charles Johnson Post viewed the bombardment of Santiago Bay from his transport and filled two sketchbooks during the Santiago campaign. Frederic Remington rode with the 5th Cavalry in the 1880s covering the Indian campaigns of the northern plains. Armed with sketchpad and pencil, these men and scores of others deepened our knowledge of the infinite drudgery, horror, courage, and even humor of warfare. Most of this art passed into private collections and by the later part of the nineteenth century began moving into the Smithsonian Institution and other museums.

Establishment of the Army Combat Art Program

In World War I, as a result of a War Department decision to make a pictorial record of the terrain, uniforms, equipment, and actions of the war, eight artists selected by Charles Dana Gibson went to France to record the activities of the American Expeditionary Forces. After the war the art work was deposited permanently in the Smithsonian Institution, and no lasting program evolved from the project.

There was a more extensive effort in World War II. Late in 1942, thanks to Assistant Secretary of War John J. McCloy and General Brehon Somervell, commander of the Services of Supply, the Corps of Engineers established a War Art Unit in its Operations and Training Branch, Troops Division. Associated American Artists, an organization founded in 1939 by the artist Reeves Lowenthal, recruited artists for the War Art Unit. In

1943, the War Department established an art committee, composed of leaders in the art world and military historians, to work closely with Associated American Artists and make the final selections of artists. Some of the most talented painters of the 1930s and 40s were chosen—Reginald Marsh, Jack Levine, Joe Jones, Mitchell Siporin, Aaron Bohrod, and Henry Varnum Poor, whose works are now much desired by major American museums. Through graphic arts, oil paintings, watercolors, and drawings, twenty-three military and twenty civilian artists set out to make a pictorial record of the U.S. Army in time of war. They were instructed to depict events of outstanding military importance, incidents in the daily life of the soldier in training, frontline operations, combat and service support, and characteristic views of the countryside in which operations were conducted. They sketched and painted people, places, and equipment and documented each piece of art with information concerning the military unit, object, and persons depicted and with the date and place of completion.

The artists were assigned to teams which usually consisted of an officer, a civilian, and two technical sergeants. Thirteen units went within four months to all theaters of operations, but the artists barely had time to reach their destinations when their tours were terminated for lack of funds. Although the program lasted for only slightly longer than six months, February to August 1943, approximately 2,000 pieces of art were produced. The War Department Art Committee screened these paintings and selected 1,500 as of sufficiently high artistic or military and historical value for retention by the Army. Works not selected by the committee were returned to the artists.

When Daniel Longwell, editor of *Life* magazine, learned of the program's end, he visited the Secretary of War and offered to employ some of the Army's civilian artists. *Life* paid their salaries, but the Army continued to furnish transportation and billeting. The Army reassigned some of the military artists to other Army duties where they continued to paint and organized others into a War Art Unit under the Historical Branch, Assistant Chief of Staff, G-2. Finally, however, questioning the propriety of diverting funds for the prosecution of the war to the administration of the Army's art project, Congress terminated the program in the Military Appropriations Act of 1945 which provided that

> no appropriation shall be available for payment to or expenditure on account of any civilian personnel employed outside continental United States to paint or otherwise produce war scenes except by means of

photography, or to paint portraits, or for payment to or expenditure on account of any military personnel within continental United States who engage in decorative art projects or painting portraits to the exclusion of regular military duties.[1]

Initially the work of the War Art Unit of the Historical Branch was given to the Corps of Engineers, but responsibility shifted to the Pictorial Division of the Public Information Division, and in February 1945 to the War Paintings Office in the Bureau of Public Relations. By May 1945 the War Paintings Office had received approximately 1,300 paintings, and an estimated 700 more were expected to come in from the field. A few months later, the Secretary of War transferred responsibility for the war art to the Office of the Army Headquarters Commandant where a Historical Properties Branch was established to provide for collecting, processing, and preserving Army paintings and other objects of historical interest. In 1950 the art activity was transferred to the Historical Division of the Special Staff, later renamed Office, Chief of Military History.

Present Holdings and Program

Pre-World War II Art: The Army Art Collection contains twelve small oil sketches of the battle of Chapultepec by James Walker who was in Mexico City at the outbreak of the Mexican War. When Americans were ordered to evacuate, Walker fled over the mountains to Pueblo, joined the American forces, and served as a civilian interpreter on the staff of Brig. Gen. William J. Worth. He remained with Maj. Gen. Winfield Scott's army until it captured Mexico City. During the Civil War, encouraged by General Scott, Walker accompanied the Army of the Cumberland and painted both the *Battle of Lookout Mountain* and the *Battle of Chickamauga*. The Army owns boths of these paintings together with Thomas Nast's *Saving the Flag*, the only other Civil War painting in the collection.

American World War II Art: The War Department Art Committee's selection of 1,500 paintings, watercolors, and drawings formed the nucleus of the Army's World War II art collection. Further pictorial documentation of the war was undertaken by Abbott Laboratories, a manufacturer of medical supplies. With Associated American Artists serving as consultants, Abbott sponsored seven different war art projects from 1942 to 1945. Under one of the war projects, Abbott produced, in cooperation with The Surgeon General's Office, a fine collection

---

1. War Department Bulletin No. 12, 1944, p. 5.

of Army medical paintings by such well-known artists as John Steuart Curry, Peter Blume, and Joseph Hirsch. In 1945 Abbott presented this collection of 144 paintings to the Army.

A miscellaneous group of 1,200 drawings and cartoons, including several "Sad Sack" and "Private Dave Breger" strips published in World War II editions of *Yank* magazine, formed yet another addition to the Army collection in 1946. In 1955 Bill Mauldin augmented this group by donating four "Willie and Joe" cartoons which had been published in wartime issues of *Stars and Stripes*.

Henry Luce formally presented the entire collection of 1,050 *Life* paintings, which included Army, Navy, Air Force, and Marine Corps subjects, to Deputy Secretary of Defense James H. Douglas on Pearl Harbor day, 7 December 1960. The paintings were placed in the custody of the Army's Chief of Military History, who agreed to preserve the collection intact and display it publicly.

German Art: Many of the countries in World War II, both allied and enemy, had war art activities, but from the outset Germany had the largest program, both in the number of artists employed and in their output. To supervise the program Hitler appointed Capt. Luitpold Adam, a World War I combat artist who took charge of the war painters and press artists in the Propaganda Replacement Center in Potsdam. The work of this group and the subsequent artists division of the German high command, also under Adam's direction, brought prodigious results. The quality of the German works is uniformly high, although they had to serve the purposes of Hitler, who favored monumental realism and opposed expressionism. Within the restrictive bounds of realism, nevertheless, the German artists appear to have insisted upon a certain latitude in their choice of subjects. In any case, the resulting works give an impression of authenticity because Adam insisted that the painters work at the front during combat.

At the close of the war, U.S. military government ordered that all art collections relating or dedicated to the perpetuation of Nazism be closed permanently and the works seized. The office of the theater historian in Europe began to collect all available art works in this category. Gordon Gilkey, an Army Air Forces captain who was assigned the task of gathering the art, gave a fascinating report of his search for paintings in several improbable hiding places. Part of the huge *Kunst der Front* (Front Art) collection owned by Hitler was concealed in storage bins in a salt refining plant, and the smaller paintings from his collection were found in a second-floor dance hall in a cafe in St. Agatha, Austria. Gilkey found watercolors and drawings from

Luitpold Adam's high command collection in the attic of an abandoned woodcutter's hut on the Czechoslovak border and Himmler's SS war art in the Kellheim Liberation Hall. The *Haus der Deutschen Kunst* (House of German Art) and the basement of the Hitler Building in Munich yielded parts of the private collections of Hitler, Himmler, and Bormann. In 1947 the Army assumed custody of over 8,000 pieces of German war art assembled by Gilkey, and three years later the collection received a smaller group of historical objects and paintings collected by Army historians in Germany. Included in the latter group were ceremonial swords, medals, memorabilia of Hermann Goering, and four watercolors painted by a youthful Adolf Hitler between 1914 and 1917. Between 1951 and 1956 this collection was reduced by the return to the German government of 1,600 pieces that were determined to be neither militaristic nor propagandistic, the donation of approximately 28 watercolors and drawings to Australia and 26 to New Zealand, and the transfer of 300 pieces of art to the Department of the Air Force.

Japanese Art: Japanese war artists produced enormous, often imaginary, land and sea battle paintings for display in military museums and other official buildings. As early as November 1945 Capt. Hermann W. William, chief of the Historical Properties Section, Military District of Washington, cabled U.S. Army Forces, Pacific, requesting that all available Japanese war paintings and drawings be collected and shipped to the United States for inclusion in an exhibition scheduled for January 1946 at the Metropolitan Museum in New York City. Captain Williams stated that the paintings would "be of permanent value to the War Department." The collection was assembled in the summer of 1946, too late for the New York showing, and no further shipping instructions were issued by the War Department. The paintings remained with the Chief Engineer, General Headquarters, Army Forces, Pacific, until the summer of 1951 when the Department of the Army directed that the war art be forwarded to Cameron Station in Alexandria, Virginia. The shipment, consisting of 154 paintings, was received in the Office of the Chief of Military History the following September and became part of the Army Art Collection.

The Japanese art was the subject of a number of discreet inquiries from representatives of the Japanese government in the years that followed, and in 1967 the Japanese embassy formally requested its return. In March 1970 the paintings were lent to the U.S. State Department which in turn forwarded them on indefinite loan to the Japanese government. They are presently located in the National Museum of Modern Art in Tokyo.

Korean War Art: Although the Army provided no funds for an official art program during the Korean War, Robert Baer, a civilian cartographer and painter, executed a number of drawings and paintings which were acquired by the Office of the Chief of Military History for inclusion in the Army Art Collection.

Vietnam War Art: As the Vietnam War began to escalate, the Chief of Military History looked toward an art program for that war. Basic to the program as it developed was the conviction that the art history of the war should be recorded by the young and impressionable soldier as well as the mature professional artist. Thus the program provided for pictorial documentation of Army activities by both civilian and military artists, selected from volunteers on the basis of competency by a Department of the Army art committee.

The Army Chief of Staff approved the civilian portion of the program in March 1966. Thereafter OCMH recruited professionals in the Washington area, and art societies recruited other artists in the New York and Boston areas. Selected artists traveled in an assigned area for a maximum of thirty days, observing and sketching with a view toward producing paintings after returning home. The Army paid their transportation and other expenses and furnished art supplies. As volunteers, however, civilian artists were not paid salaries and were not under contract to produce a specified number of paintings but were free to donate to the Army as many or as few works as they wished. The military portion of the program, announced in June 1966, called for the use of soldier artists, who were placed on temporary duty assignments of 120–35 days and worked in two- to five-man teams. The teams spent sixty days in Vietnam visiting military units and sketching and photographing the activities observed and then proceeded to Hawaii to translate their preliminary sketches into studio paintings. The program was expanded in 1969 to permit pictorial documentation throughout the world. Civilian artists completed assignments not only in Vietnam but also in Thailand, Germany, Korea, the Canal Zone, and the United States, including Alaska, while teams of soldier artists toured Vietnam, Thailand, and Korea.

Although the Army artist was instructed to document completely each sketch and painting, he was given few instructions on subject matter, style, and technique and was permitted almost complete freedom of expression. Consequently artists not only recorded firefights, swamp patrols, and village searches for hidden Viet Cong, but they also depicted with compassion and realism a wounded soldier, a bereaved Vietnamese family, and a relaxed fellow artist surrounded by fascinated Vietnamese orphans. Varied in form and expression according to the artist's individual interpretations, the Vietnamese collection presents a broad view of man's experience in war.

Portrait Programs: Portraiture also holds a significant place in the Army's pictorial archives. The earliest official program originated during the tenure of Secretary of War William Worth Belknap (October 1869–March 1876). With the centennial year in mind, Belknap and his assistants assembled portraits of all of the Secretaries of War who had served before that time. They compiled a list of forty former secretaries, including the two predecessors of the secretaries, Horatio Gates, President of the Board of War in 1777–78, and Benjamin Lincoln, Secretary at War, 1781–83.

They found only one portrait in the possession of the War Department—that of Timothy Pickering, who held office in 1795. Another painting, of Benjamin Lincoln, was purchased from a dealer in New York City. The remaining thirty-eight portraits were copied from existing portraits or painted from life by some of the most talented artists of the period—Daniel Huntington, Henry Ulke, Robert Weir, and John Wesley Jarvis. These portraits and those of succeeding secretaries presently adorn the Pentagon corridors.

In 1971 the Office of the Chief of Military History began a three-year program to commission portraits of all Army Chiefs of Staff from 1903, when the office was created, to the present. This program was made possible by the generosity of former Secretary of the Army and Mrs. Robert T. Stevens who, in April 1971, offered to finance the entire cost of the project. The twenty-six paintings, done by the best portrait painters available to the Army, hang in a special hall in the Pentagon.

Minority Art: The Army Art Collection contains a negligible amount of minority art devoted to military participation by black Americans, Indians, Mexican Americans, Puerto Ricans, Oriental Americans, and women. Because of a steadily increasing number of requests for exhibits of such material, the Chief of Military History developed a bicentennial project for a group of paintings on the military contribution of minorities and obtained the approval of the Army staff bicentennial committee. In the spring of 1975 eighteen artists who were themselves members of minority groups were commissioned to execute paintings showing acts of heroism or other significant military contributions by members of American minorities from the Revolution to Vietnam.

Use of the Collection

The Center of Military History maintains a comprehensive file on Army art as a research aid to students, writers, military historians, museum curators, and magazine and book publishers. A card index is cross-referenced by artist, title, size, and medium. A separate card index includes subject, geographical area, nationality, arm of service, theater of operations, and military organization. Another file of interest to scholars is the photographic index of art works in the collection; approximately one half of the collection has been photographed and prints are available in albums for easy reference. A continuing effort is made to search out and collect biographical information on all artists represented in the collection.

A conservation program involves both storage and handling of the active collection and the renovation of approximately 150 paintings each year. Exhibits of fifteen to thirty paintings each are available for temporary showings by such public and private institutions as museums, art galleries, schools, colleges, community centers, banks, department stores, and shopping centers. The art exhibits help to supplement written military history and encourage its study and use by stimulating the viewer's imagination. One powerful work of art can reflect vividly the significant functions and accomplishments of the Army. It can permit easy mental reconstruction of the atmosphere in which an historical event took place, and at the same time it can illustrate both the American soldier's experience and his spirit as perceived by the artist. Thus the art collection is used to stimulate *esprit de corps* and foster public awareness of the Army's role in peace and war.

Bibliography

Abell, Walter. "Industry and Painting." *Magazine of Art* 39 (Mar. 1946):83–85.
An Album of American Battle Art, 1755-1918. Washington: Library of Congress, Government Printing Office, 1947.
American Battle Painting 1776-1918. Washington: National Gallery of Art and The Museum of Modern Art, 1944.

The American Heritage Picture History of The Civil War. New York: American Heritage Publishing Co., 1960.

The American Heritage Picture History of World War I. New York: American Heritage Publishing Co., 1964.

The American Heritage Picture History of World War II. New York: American Heritage Publishing Co., 1966.

The Armed Forces of the United States as Seen by the Contemporary Artist. An Exhibition by The National Armed Forces Museum Advisory Board. Washington: Smithsonian Institution, 1968.

The Army at War: A Graphic Record by American Artists. Washington: Government Printing Office, 1944.

The Civil War: A Centennial Exhibition of Eye Witness Drawings. Washington: National Gallery of Art, Smithsonian Institution, 1961.

Craighead, Alexander McC. "Military Art in America." *Military Collector and Historian* 15 (1963):nos. 2, 3; 16 (1964):nos. 1, 2; 17 (1965):nos. 2, 3.

Crane, Aimee, ed. *Art in The Armed Forces.* New York: Hyperion Press, 1944.

Gardner, Albert Ten Eyck. *Winslow Homer: A Retrospective Exhibition.* Washington: National Gallery of Art, Smithsonian Institution, and Metropolitan Museum of Art, 1958.

Gilky, Gordon. "German War Art." Office of the Chief Historian, Headquarters, European Command, 1946.

Great Battles of The Civil War. New York:Time-Life Inc., 1961.

Ingersoll, L. D. *History of the War Department.* vol. 1. Washington, 1879.

Larkin, Oliver W. *Art and Life in America.* New York: Rinehart and Company, 1949.

"Life Magazine Presents War Art to the Department of Defense." *Quartermaster Review* 40 (Jan.-Feb. 1961):68.

Life's Picture History of World War II. New York: Time-Life, Inc., 1950.

Mackenzie, Dewitt. *Men Without Guns.* Philadelphia: Blakeston Company, 1945.

McNaughton, Marian R. "American Artists in Combat." *Army Digest* 21 (Dec. 1966):38-44.

———. "James Walker, Combat Artist of Two American Wars." *Military Collector and Historian* 9 (Summer 1957):31-35.

Meredith, Ray. *The American Wars: A Pictorial History From Quebec to Korea, 1755-1953.* Cleveland: World Publishing Co., 1955.

Morgan, John Hill. *Paintings by John Trumbull at Yale University.* New Haven: Yale Univ. Press, 1926.

Post, Charles Johnson. *The Little War of Private Post.* Boston: Little, Brown, 1960.

Rigg, Robert B. "Image of The War In Vietnam." *Army Digest* 20 (Dec. 1965):65-72.

Rose, Barbara. *American Art Since 1900: A Critical History.* New York: Praeger, 1967.

The Second World War. 2 vols. New York: Time-Life Inc., 1959.

Soldier Art. Fighting Forces Series. Washington: Infantry Journal Press, 1945.

Texas and The War with Mexico. New York: American Heritage Publishing Co., 1961.

"U.S. Army Art." Undated Information Sheet. Washington: Army Art Activity, Center of Military History.

U.S. Commission of Fine Arts. *Art and Government: Report to the President by the Commission of Fine Arts on Activities of the Federal Government in the Field of Art.* Washington: Government Printing Office, 1953.

Weller, Allen S. "The Armory Show to the Mid-20th Century." *Encyclopedia of World Art* 1:301–13.

Williams, Hermann Warner, Jr. *The Civil War: The Artists' Record.* Boston: Beacon Press, 1962.

"World War II—As the Soldier-Artist Saw It." *Army Digest* 20 (June 1965):28–38.

Top: *First Rhode Island Regiment, 29 August 1778*, by Jerry Pinkney (CC 102245)
Bottom: *Battle of Lookout Mountain*, November 1963, by James Walker (CC 45034)

Top left: *The Gatling Guns*, Cuba 1898, Charles Johnson Post (CC 103703)
Bottom left: *American Troops in France*, 1918, by Kerr Eby (SC 674237)
Top right: *Dummy Antiaircraft*, England 1943, by Byron Thomas (CC 34354)
Bottom right: *German Supply Train in Russia*, by Max Ohmayer (SC 434807)

Top left: *Lookout Post,* Pacific 1944, by Paul Sample (USAAVA CCA-37-6)
Bottom left: *The Morning After,* 1944, by Edward A. Reep (SC 674239)
Right: *The Villagers,* Vietnam 1966, by Augustine Acuna (CC 41230)

Top: *The Way Back*, 1944, by
Lawrence Beall Smith
(USAAVA 72 CCA–211–5)

Bottom: *Combat Artist at
Work*, Saigon 1966, by
Paul Rickert (CC 39381)

Chapter 15

Military Museums and Collections

Joseph H. Ewing

T HE student of military history should not confine himself exclusively to the study of books and written reference material, for he can become acquainted firsthand with the past in the collections of military museums. Like the library and archive, the museum is an important source of historical knowledge. A properly functioning historical museum systematically collects and preserves objects of historical significance, uses them selectively in the creation of exhibits for the general public, and makes its collection available for examination and study by the serious researcher and scholar. In visiting such a museum the student of military history may gain a fuller understanding of the problems and accomplishments of men in the past as he views such things as the clothes they wore, the tools and implements they used, and the objects they created. In the museum he may learn what he cannot learn elsewhere. He can appreciate, for example, what a Sherman tank is only when he has actually seen one. By viewing and examining a museum's artifacts he may discover, for instance, how difficult it was to load the 1808 Springfield musket or how heavy and awkward to carry was the SCR 300 backpack radio of World War II.

The power of the artifact in teaching military history is attested to by the chief historian of the Army:

> If one picture is worth a thousand words, as the proverb would have it, what shall we say about the value, not of a representation but the physical object itself—in its original shape, form, and even dress? . . . The writer can only bring his subjects back to life on a written page through documents and words; the curator can resurrect the objects themselves as they originally were, and has a built-in visual advantage.[1]

Although the restrictions inherent in a museum exhibit do not

---

1. Dr. Maurice Matloff, address delivered at Second Annual U.S. Army Museum Conference, Fort Sheridan, Ill., 3 May 73.

Mr. Ewing (B.A., Notre Dame) is CMH Staff Museum Curator and editor of the *Army Museum Newsletter*. He also wrote *29 Let's Go: A History of the 29th Infantry Division in World War II*.

permit the treatment of any subject in great depth, still a well-executed historical exhibit may stimulate the visitor to turn to written history to learn more about the subject he has encountered. On the other hand, some of the exhibits he sees in a museum may not actually broaden his knowledge but reinforce and clarify what he already knows.

For the sensitive visitor, a historical museum can create a sense of kinship with the past. The disposition of men to seek continuity with their ancestors and with life in earlier times may find its fulfillment in museums and at historical sites more than anywhere else. The coat worn by Wolfe at Quebec, a cannon surrendered by Burgoyne at Saratoga, the Lexington Green, or the Petersburg crater may produce a special awareness of a particular historical period, event, or person or awaken interest in military history in general.

There are three main groups of U.S. military museums—those maintained by the armed forces; by federal civil agencies; and by states, counties, municipalities, and private institutions.

Museums Maintained by the Armed Forces

It was not until 1962 that the Army established a formal policy of preserving material evidence of its history. With the publication of Army Regulation 870-5 in 1962, all existing Army museums were placed under the supervision of the Chief of Military History, who assumed ultimate responsibility for the collection, control, and preservation of all historical properties throughout the Army and established a central catalog of these artifacts. Previously such preservation depended largely upon the degree of interest of the post or organizational commander, and artifacts in untold number were abandoned or discarded over the years because their historical value was unknown or unappreciated. Many, nevertheless, did survive. As early as 1854 the Ordnance and Artillery Museum was established at the U.S. Military Academy; it later became the West Point Museum, today the oldest museum in the Army. The Army Medical Museum (now the Armed Forces Medical Museum) came into being in 1862. The Springfield (Massachusetts) Armory Museum dates from approximately 1871, the Rock Island (Illinois) Arsenal Museum (now the John M. Browning Memorial Museum) from 1905, and the Army Ordnance Museum at Aberdeen Proving Ground (Maryland) from 1919. Except for the Field Artillery Museum at Fort Sill, Oklahoma, founded in 1934, all other Army museums were established in the 1940s or later.

Approximately sixty-five museums make up the Army Museum System. With the exception of that at West Point, they fall into four fairly distinct categories—branch, post, arsenal, and organizational. The West Point Museum is exceptional by reason of the size and scope of its collection and the size of its professional staff. While many of its holdings relate to the history of the U.S. Military Academy, by far the larger part illustrates the history of the U.S. Army as a whole as well as the history of warfare through the ages. Thus, it tends to approach the concept of a national Army museum. The Army's museums are listed and their collections described in detail in the Guide to U.S. Army Museums and Historic Sites,[2] a publication of the Army's Center of Military History. A sampling of the holdings of some of the branch museums will give some indication of the scope and content and diversity of the Army's museum collections.

A branch museum is concerned with the history of a major arm of service within the Army, such as infantry, artillery, or quartermaster, and usually operates as part of a branch school. Among the larger museums of this type is the Field Artillery Museum at Fort Sill, contained in eight separate exhibit buildings, most of them historic structures on the National Register of Historic Places. The museum's collection includes U.S. and foreign field pieces from the sixteenth century to the present. In its "cannon walk," a 700-yard display of field artillery, is "Atomic Annie," the 280-mm. gun that fired the world's first atomic artillery round in 1953.

At Aberdeen Proving Ground, Maryland, the Ordnance Museum collection represents ordnance development mainly since the introduction of smokeless powder. In addition to small arms, the collection includes tanks, self-propelled and towed guns, and motor vehicles. U.S. armored vehicles are displayed in single file in the "mile of tanks" along a main road of the proving ground. The museum also maintains a Chemical Corps collection, which it acquired upon the closing of the Chemical Museum in 1972.

The Patton Museum of Cavalry and Armor at Fort Knox, Kentucky, treats the history of U.S. armored forces and their equipment. It has a large collection of armored fighting vehicles, both U.S. and foreign, some of which are maintained in operational condition and are used to stage demonstrations for the public during the summer. The museum displays the

---

2. Compiled by Norman Miller Cary, Jr. (Washington: Government Printing Office, 1975).

personal effects of General George S. Patton, Jr. for whom it was named, including his ivory-handled pistols, and the limousine in which he was riding when he suffered fatal injuries in 1945. The history of horse cavalry, as distinct from armor, is preserved and displayed in the U.S. Cavalry Museum at Fort Riley, Kansas.

The story of the American foot soldier is told in the National Infantry Museum at Fort Benning, Georgia, with weapons, uniforms, and equipment since colonial days. The museum also has a broad interest in the infantryman regardless of nationality, as indicated by thirty-eight foreign countries represented in its small-arms collection. Its Japanese weapons collection is believed to be one of the most complete in the world.

Among the holdings of the Quartermaster Museum at Fort Lee, Virginia, are collections of uniforms dating from the Revolutionary War, insignia and chevrons, and military saddles, this last one of the most complete in the country. Also on display is the caisson which carried the body of Jefferson Davis to his grave in Richmond in 1889.

Army transportation methods are shown in some dioramas at the Transportation Museum at Fort Eustis, Virginia, while others trace the evolution of transportation beginning with the Stone Age and progressing through the development of the wheel, balloon, coach, and canal barge. Helicopters, fixed-wing aircraft, experimental aircraft, railway cars and steam locomotives, trucks, and amphibious vehicles are found in the collection.

The Aviation Museum at Fort Rucker, Alabama, displays an extensive collection of fixed- and rotary-wing aircraft in telling the history of aviation in the U.S. Army. It has the largest collection of military helicopters in the world.

The Engineer Museum at Fort Belvoir, Virginia, preserves military engineer equipment, uniforms, insignia, flags, maps, and small arms. Among its items of special interest are maps prepared by French engineers at the siege of Yorktown in the Revolutionary War and the ship's wheel recovered from the sunken Battleship Maine.

The Army has more than twenty post museums at such stations as Fort Leavenworth, Kansas; Fort Huachuca, Arizona; the Presidio of San Francisco, California; Fort Bliss, Texas; and Fort Monroe, Virginia. The post museum is mainly concerned with preserving and depicting the history of the post and frequently the military history of the local region, even though that usually predates the establishment of the post. Where a branch museum exists, it is usually the only museum on post and may assume the function of a post museum. The Field Artillery Museum at Fort Sill, for example, devotes perhaps half of its effort to presenting the history of the post and local area. Many Army installations without museums have small collections of historical artifacts, an excellent example being the numerous old cannon displayed on the grounds at Fort Lesley J. McNair, Washington, D.C. Often smaller historical items may be displayed in an officers' club, chapel, or headquarters building.

Only four museums fall under the arsenal classification. First among these is the venerable Springfield Armory Museum, which holds one of the world's most complete collections of small arms. It is operated by the National Park Service, to which the U.S. Army Center of Military History lent the collection. The John M. Browning Memorial Museum (Rock Island Arsenal) uses part of its collection in special exhibits of Browning's automatic weapons. The Picatinny Arsenal Museum at Dover, New Jersey, maintains a collection of U.S. and foreign explosive ordnance; and the Watervliet Arsenal Museum, Watervliet, New York, shows the use of artillery throughout history and displays cannon, howitzers, and mortars, the earliest dating from 1742.

Organizational museums operate primarily for the benefit of troop morale and *esprit de corps* and are devoted almost entirely to unit history. The 82d Airborne Division Museum at Fort Bragg, North Carolina, and those of the 1st Cavalry Division and 2d Armored Division, both at Fort Hood, Texas, are such museums. There are a few regimental museums, such as the Old Guard Museum maintained by the 1st Battalion, 3d Infantry, at Fort Myer, Virginia.

The Navy's two principal collections are the Navy Memorial Museum at the Washington Navy Yard, Washington, D.C., and the U.S. Naval Academy Museum at Annapolis, Maryland. Two museums are devoted to submarine history, one at the submarine base at Groton, Connecticut, and the other at the submarine base at Pearl Harbor, Hawaii. A naval aviation museum is located at Pensacola, Florida. Other Navy museums include the Seabee Museum at Little Creek, Virginia, and the Museum of the Naval Training Center at San Diego, California.

At Wright-Patterson Air Force Base, Dayton, Ohio, is the U.S. Air Force Museum, the central museum of that service. It displays more than 125 aircraft and missiles, both U.S. and foreign. Other aviation museums are the Hangar 9 Museum at Brooks Air Force Base, Texas, specializing in aerospace medicine, and the Air Force Space Museum at Cape Kennedy, Florida, devoted principally to space exploration.

The U.S. Marine Corps Museum is situated at the Washington Navy Yard in the History and Museums Division of the corps headquarters. In its collection are uniforms, battle flags, weapons, dioramas, and substantial holdings of personal papers, photos, and documents. Smaller Marine Corps museums are at Quantico, Virginia; Parris Island, South Carolina; and Barstow, California.

The Walter Reed Army Medical Center, Washington, D.C., is the home of the Armed Forces Medical Museum, which exhibits items for both the general public and for pathologists and other medical professionals. At Albuquerque, New Mexico, the Sandia Atomic Museum, operated by the Defense Atomic Support Agency, displays unclassified nuclear weapons and associated equipment used by the Army, Navy, Air Force, and Marine Corps.

Although the Army National Guard is rich in military history and tradition, it has few museums recognized as such. The New York State Military Museum, its largest, occupies space on the first and second floors of the state capitol in Albany. Some other states display objects related to their military history in the capitol or other state buildings but have no organized museums; many old-line National Guard organizations maintain trophy rooms which display memorabilia related to the unit's past. Information concerning National Guard collections and museums should be requested from the various state adjutants general.

Museums Maintained by Federal Civil Agencies

Within the vast holdings of the Smithsonian Institution in Washington, D.C., are two distinguished military history collections. Its Museum of History and Technology displays an impressive store of military and naval artifacts, including firearms, edged weapons, uniforms, headgear, and insignia. The National Air and Space Museum of the Smithsonian, filling a large new structure on the Washington mall, includes an expansive collection of aircraft and missiles, many of them military. The National Park Service administers some seventy-five museums (visitors centers) at battlefield sites and old forts throughout the United States, most containing collections for study. Professional and technical support, including the design and production of all exhibits, is furnished these museums by the Park Service's Harpers Ferry Center at Harpers Ferry, West Virginia.

Museums Maintained by Other Agencies

Many museum collections are maintained by states, counties, municipalities, and private institutions. Thousands of such collections are found throughout the United States, a small number of which are primarily, if not exclusively, military. In this category, for example, are the Indiana War Memorial, Indianapolis, Indiana; the War Memorial Museum of Virginia, Newport News, Virginia; and the Admiral Nimitz Center, Fredericksburg, Texas. Some art and science museums display military artifacts, such as the splendid examples of old arms and armor in the Metropolitan Museum of Art in New York. State historical societies are prime sources of information concerning the location of museum collections in their respective states. Also, much detailed information is available in the latest *Official Museum Directory* and the *Directory of Historical Societies and Agencies in the United States and Canada.*[3]

Even though opportunity to visit them might be limited, the student of military history should be aware of foreign military museums; he may need to correspond with them for information otherwise unobtainable. In Ottawa is the impressive Canadian War Museum, a branch of Canada's National Museum of Man. England offers the museum visitor a rich experience in the extensive collection of the Imperial War Museum, The Tower Armouries, and the National Army Museum, all in London, and the National Maritime Museum in Greenwich. Among the outstanding military museums on the European continent are the Tojhusmuseet in Copenhagen, the Musée de la Marine and the Musée de l'Armée in Paris, the Heeresgeschichtliches Museum in Vienna, and in Stockholm the Armemuseum and the Statens Sjohistoriska Museum (National Maritime Museum). Other fine museums are the Wehrgeschichtliches Museum at Rastatt and the Bayerisches Armeemuseum at Ingolstadt, both in the Federal Republic of Germany; in Madrid the Museo del Ejercito Español and the Museo de la Real Armeria; the Musée Royal de l'Armée et Histoire Militaire in Brussels, and the Leger-en-Wapenmuseum, in Leiden, Holland. Perhaps the most useful guide to foreign military museums is the *Directory of Museums of Arms and Military History*, published by the International Association of Museums of Arms and Military History in Copenhagen in 1970.

---

3. *The Official Museum Directory* (Washington: American Association of Museums, 1976); Donna McDonald, ed., *Directory of Historical Societies and Agencies in the United States and Canada*, 10th ed. (Nashville, Tenn.: American Association for State and Local History, 1975-76).

Copies may be obtained from the secretary of the association, c/o the director of the National Army Museum, Royal Hospital Road, London S.W. 3, England. *European Military Museums*, by J. Lee Westrate,[4] is another excellent reference. The International Council of Museums, 1 rue Miollis, 75 Paris 15ᵉ France, operates the ICOM-UNESCO Documentation Center, which is able to furnish information on museums in all parts of the world.

Use of Military Museums and Collections

Military museums vary greatly in the size of their collections; in the size and adequacy of their physical plants, staffs, and financial resources; and thus in the extent and quality of the services they provide. Most museums serve the general public with interpretative exhibits that are both attractive and historically accurate, and answer written and verbal inquiries concerning objects in the collection. The military history student, or the specialist, naturally benefits from these exhibits, but he also may wish to examine and study specific objects in the collection. Within reasonable limits, most museums will give him access to the objects he needs and provide working space. In some cases a museum's own research on its collection may not be adequate because of what it considers the more pressing needs of public exhibitions, guided tours, and the like.

Few armed forces museums offer any formal educational programs. The most notable exception is the West Point Museum, whose staff members, using artifacts, conduct classroom lectures in military history at the U.S. Military Academy. Many military museums, however, conduct guided tours for the general public and for school, college, and professional groups. The *Guide to U.S. Army Museums and Historic Sites* (see footnote 2) lists all U.S. Army museums as well as Department of Defense, federal, state, municipal, and private military museums throughout the United States and briefly describes their collections.

Military Historic Sites

Throughout the United States numerous forts, arsenals, and battlefields recall the military past of the nation. The more important of these are listed in the *National Register of Historic*

---

4. Washington: Smithsonian Institution, 1961.

Places, issued by the Department of the Interior. Established by law, the register includes not only property of national significance but also districts, sites, buildings, structures, and objects of importance at the state and local levels.[5] Many of these sites, such as Kings Mountain, Fort McHenry, Gettysburg, and Fort Sumter, are operated by the National Park Service. Historic sites are frequently found on installations of the armed forces, and some of these are integrated with the local installation museums. Examples include the Rock Island Arsenal, Rock Island, Illinois; Fort Leavenworth, Kansas; and the National War College Building at Fort Lesley J. McNair, Washington, D.C.

The Council on Abandoned Military Posts,[6] a nonprofit organization interested in the identification, restoration, and preservation of old military installations, is another source of information. It publishes a monthly newsletter and a quarterly scholarly magazine. Additional information on military historical sites may be obtained from *The Official Museum Directory* and the *Directory of Historical Societies and Agencies in the United States and Canada* (see footnote 3).

In his contact with museums the student of military history may come to appreciate the almost limitless historical treasures within their collections. He may find that museums supplement and reinforce the knowledge derived from reading and documentary research and serve to intensify his interest in this field of learning. And he may find a degree of inspiration.

---

5. National Park Service, Department of the Interior, *The National Register of Historic Places* (Washington: Government Printing Office, 1976). Detailed information concerning historic sites on U.S. Army property may be found in the *Guide to U.S. Army Museums and Historic Sites*.

6. P.O. Box 171, Arlington, VA 22210.

Chapter 16

The Place of
Unit History

Stanley R. Connor

PROUD soldiers form the backbone of any successful military organization. Skillfully used by the commander, unit history can be most valuable in instilling a strong sense of pride in the members of a company, battalion, regiment, or other Army unit. The study of unit history has sometimes been compared to genealogy, and the analogy is not a bad one. Just as knowledge of ancestry often creates a sense of pride in one's forebears, awareness of a unit's past can help to create *esprit de corps* for an organization. Americans are exceptionally proud if they can trace their lineage back to the Mayflower, but many families, representing waves of relatively recent immigration, are quite new to the United States. It is much the same in the Army. Except for those organizations in the Army National Guard that can trace their lineage back to colonial days, the vast majority of all Army units began in this century.

Obtaining prepared unit histories is not always easy. Many are published in limited quantities, if at all, and are often soon out of print. Because the use of incorrect history could damage the morale of a unit, the authenticity of existing histories should be determined through careful examination before acceptance. The New York Public Library probably maintains the best collection of published unit histories. They are listed in *Histories, Personal Narratives, United States Army: A Checklist* by Charles E. Dornbusch (1967—includes some unit histories in other collections). The U.S. Army Military History Institute maintains another good collection of unit histories, both published and in manuscript, cataloged in *United States Army Unit Histories*, Special Bibliographic Series 4 (1971). The library of the U.S. Army Field Artillery School has a more specialized collection cataloged in *Artillery Unit Histories* (1955). The U.S. Army Center of Military History maintains bibliographies on all divisions, most combat arms regiments, and a few other

---

Mr. Connor (B.S., Mississippi State) is Supervisory Historian, Historical Services Division, CMH, and coauthor of Parts I and II, *Armor-Cavalry* (Army Lineage Series).

organizations; some bibliographies show the locations of the volumes. The center also has one-page summaries, available upon request, of the actions of each division in World War II. Other possible sources for unit histories are libraries, publishers, used book dealers, and veterans' associations. Current lists of known veterans' associations are maintained by the Community Relations Division, Office of the Chief of Public Affairs, Department of the Army, Washington, D.C. 20310.

Very few unit histories were published before the Civil War, and many of those were more in the nature of memoirs or journals. Examples are Teresa Griffin Viele's *Following the Drum: A Glimpse of Frontier Life* (New York, 1858), which pertains to the 1st Infantry; and Lawrence Kip's *Army Life on the Pacific: A Journal of the Expedition Against Northern Indians* . . . (Redfield, New York, 1859), which provides information about Company F, 4th Regiment of Artillery (now 5th Battalion, 1st Field Artillery). After the Civil War a multitude of unit histories appeared, most either written by men who had served in the organizations or sponsored by the states that supplied them. Bibliographies of these histories, by state or region, continue to be prepared by Charles E. Dornbusch in *Regimental Publications and Personal Narratives of the Civil War: A Checklist* (1961–). Historical sketches of Union organizations are in Frederick H. Dyer's *A Compendium of the War of the Rebellion* (1908, 1959). A good starting place for histories of Regular Army regiments in the late nineteenth century is *The Army of the United States: Historical Sketches of the Staff and Line*, edited by Theophilus F. Rodenbough and William L. Haskin (1896). Its sketches originally appeared as separate articles in the *Journal of the Military Service Institution of the United States* between 1892 and 1896.

By the turn of the century the War Department was taking a more active interest in the heritage of its organizations and prepared *A Bibliography of State Participation in the Civil War* . . . (three editions, 1897, 1898, 1913), which is quite useful. The Adjutant General's *Statistical Exhibit of Strength of Volunteer Forces Called into Service During the War With Spain* . . . (1899) includes some information about volunteer units in that war. The *Order of Battle of the Land Forces in the World War*, prepared in three volumes by the Historical Section, Army War College (1931–49), provides similar data for units during World War I, including more detailed information about divisions.

A great number of unit histories appeared in the years following World Wars I and II and the Korean War, again written mostly by unit members or sponsored by the organizations themselves. Most narrative unit histories today are similarly prepared, but some compilations or histories have been published by interested individuals not necessarily connected with the Army. In addition to the already mentioned volumes of Dyer and Rodenbough and Haskin, Fred A. Berg's *Encyclopedia of Continental Army Units* (1972) covers many of the organizations that served in the Revolutionary War. Bruce Jacob's *Soldiers: The Fighting Divisions of the Regular Army* (1958) is about Regular Army divisions in World War II. Some contemporary authors are producing histories of units in the past, such as Hugh Rankin's *North Carolina Continentals* (1971). And service journals, such as *Infantry* and *Army*, often note or review unit histories.

Not all unit histories appear in print. In addition to those manuscripts in the U.S. Army Military History Institute, the Center of Military History receives annual supplements from several active units, usually Regular Army and Army Reserve organizations. They vary from one-paragraph summaries to a few excellent histories. Students who are writing theses or dissertations often prepare unit histories. One example is Patrick Daniel O'Flaherty's "History of the Sixty-Ninth Regiment of the New York State Militia, 1852–1861" (Ph.D. dissertation, Fordham University, 1963). Many are listed in *Doctoral Dissertations in Military Affairs*, by Allan R. Millett and B. Franklin Cooling (1972—updated annually in *Military Affairs*).

Many units, especially smaller ones, have no written histories, but some historical information about them is usually available. Such unit records as muster rolls, operations or after-action reports, morning reports, and other similar documents are invaluable. Most of these records are now in storage at one of several records depositories, including the National Archives in Washington, D.C. The National Archives also holds the unit histories that The Adjutant General required regiments to prepare around the beginning of this century. Other sources include local historical societies, museums, former unit members, the state adjutants general for National Guard units, and, when active, the units themselves. Information concerning the various possible sources is included in a pamphlet, *Organizational History: Its Preparation and Use*, prepared and distributed by the Center of Military History.

The history of a unit manifests itself in many ways other than in written form—tangibly in such symbols as flags, colors, and standards, streamers for campaigns and decorations, distinctive insignia, shoulder sleeve insignia, and organizational historical property. Intangibly, special traditions and customs and the spirit of an organization also reflect its history. Each symbol, whether tangible or intangible, has an important role in unit *esprit*.

During the nineteenth century considerable confusion existed as to the accepted procedures and methods for determining the history of Army units and their entitlement to honors for participation in various campaigns. After World War I many units with long histories and numerous honors were demobilized. The Historical Branch, War Plans Division, General Staff, published its *Outlines of History of Regiments, United States Army* in 1921. And during the 1920s, to prevent loss to the active Army of those units with the most significant heritage, the Historical Section of the Army War College began determining unit continuity. The section also guided the War Department General Staff on unit historical matters and monitored unit history preparation. With the tremendous changes that occurred during and immediately after World War II, the Organizational History and Honors Section of the Historical Division, War Department Special Staff, was established in 1947 to continue the work of the Historical Section, Army War College. Today, after several reorganizations, the unit lineage and honors function is performed by the Organizational History Branch, Center of Military History.

The basic document showing a unit's history is the official Lineage and Honors Certificate, which is prepared and issued by the Center of Military History to all flag-, color-, and separate guidon-bearing units that are organized under a Table of Organization and Equipment. These certificates outline major organizational changes and list official campaigns and decorations for units of all components—Regular Army, Army Reserve, and Army National Guard. The original certificate is suitable for framing and prominent display within the unit's area.

The certificate is divided into two parts. The first traces the history of the unit, in brief outline form, from its beginning through its various reorganizations, redesignations, and other changes up to the present. The second portion lists the unit's campaign participation credits and decorations. (AR 672-5-1, 3 June 1974, Decorations, Awards and Honors—Military Awards, describes authorized unit decorations and lists recognized campaigns with inclusive dates.) In order of precedence, U.S. decorations for Army units are the Presidential Unit Citation

(Army—formerly Distinguished Unit Citation), the Valorous Unit Award, and the Meritorious Unit Commendation. The Valorous Unit Award, the most recently established, is authorized for actions on or after 3 August 1963 and so has been awarded only to units that were in Vietnam. The Presidential Unit Citation is authorized for actions on or after 7 December 1941, and the Meritorious Unit Commendation for those on or after 1 January 1944.

The U.S. Army Institute of Heraldry uses the historical data provided by the certificates in creating coats of arms displayed on unit colors and unit insignia worn on uniforms. The U.S. Army Support Activity, Philadelphia, uses the honors portions of these certificates as the basis for issuing campaign and decoration streamers and silver bands for display with unit flags, colors, or guidons. Asterisks are used on the certificates of regimental elements organized under the Combat Arms Regimental System to denote those honors for which an element is an "earning unit," and their streamers have an additional device or wreath. The Adjutant General furnishes certificates for each U.S. unit decoration awarded. Honors are also the basis for ribbons and emblems that unit members wear on their uniforms.

While Lineage and Honors Certificates are not intended to be full histories of units, they do form the framework around which more complete histories can be written. Because the meaning of many of the terms used on the certificates is often misunderstood, a glossary is included in most volumes of the Army Lineage Series prepared by the Center of Military History. The CMH pamphlet *Organizational History: Its Preparation and Use* suggests content and format for unit histories and provides references and sources for information about Army organizations. Although the Department of the Army neither prepares nor requires units to prepare unit histories, many major commands do. Those that are prepared should agree with the data shown on the unit's official Lineage and Honors Certificate.

The Center of Military History furnishes other certificates that assist in fostering *esprit de corps*—those for unit days, special designations, and memorial awards. A unit day, commemorating some noteworthy event in the life of the organization, is selected by the unit for annual celebration in ceremonies and special activities. The date may be the one on which the unit was first organized or on which it performed some outstanding feat. The 1st Air Defense Artillery, for example, celebrates 20 March to commemorate its actions as the 1st Regiment of Artillery at the battle of Churubusco in 1847 during the Mexican War. Unit special designations, or nicknames, are of two types: traditional—those associated with the unit for at least thirty years, and distinctive—less than thirty years. The 101st Airborne Division uses "Screaming Eagles" as its traditional designation, while the 7th Cavalry has "Garry Owen." An example of a distinctive designation is "Truck Masters," selected by the 24th Transportation Company in 1974. An organization with a particularly distinguished history may select a memorial award for annual presentation to a unit member. It is presented in remembrance of a combat action in which the unit participated or in the name of an outstanding former member.

Units down to the separate company, troop, or battery should accumulate and permanently retain all significant historical data. Units are required to establish an organizational history file for such items as unit histories, photographs, copies of Lineage and Honors Certificates, correspondence about unit lineage and honors, and other material relating to the unit's history and traditions. The file is never retired. During periods of inactivation or at other time when the unit is unable to care for it, the file is kept in a records storage facility and is returned whenever the organization can again maintain it. (See AR 340–2 and 870–5.)

Volumes of the Army Lineage Series prepared by the Center of Military History highlight the background and accomplishments of units. Each volume has a narrative history of a branch of the Army and, in compact form, the history and honors of each major unit within that branch. In addition to tracing the evolution of individual branches, this series presents a capsule history of the entire Army and gives insight into the reasons for most organizational changes. A prerequisite to an understanding of unit history in today's combat arms is a sound knowledge of the Combat Arms Regimental System, which is explained in recent volumes of the series. Each book contains illustrations and descriptions of the official coats of arms and distinctive insignia, as provided by the Institute of Heraldry, for major units. These volumes are useful at all levels of command, the Department of the Army staff, service schools, various training programs, and for the general public. Like other CMH publications, they are available for issue to authorized recipients through normal publications channels or they may be purchased from the Superintendent of Documents, Government Printing Office, Washington, D.C. 20402.

The first lineage volume, published in 1953 and covering the infantry, is now out of print. A revised version, *Infantry, Part I*

(1972), includes Regular Army infantry regiments. *Part II*, on Army National Guard and Army Reserve units, is scheduled for later publication. *Part I* of the *Armor-Cavalry* volume (1969) has historical data on Regular Army and Army Reserve regiments, while *Part II* (1972) covers those of the Army National Guard. Other volumes planned for this series will be on armies and corps, divisions and separate brigades, air defense artillery, field artillery, engineers, medical, ordnance, signal, military police, and possibly other service and support organizations. A special volume, being prepared in conjunction with the Army's participation in the bicentennial observance, is entitled "The Continental Army" and will include the lineages and honors of Continental Army units during the Revolutionary War.

Unit history has many uses. It can help the commander in inspiring members of his command to excel in garrison or in the field. Heraldic symbols are tangible illustrations of a rich heritage. In addition to members of the unit itself, unit history often serves others. Quite frequently it provides the historian, social scientist, or fiction writer with material for a study of a war or campaign, a biography or autobiography, a sociological study, or a novel or short story. A sense of community pride may even stem from a unit having been raised or having served in an area. And veterans use unit history in reminiscing about their service with relatives and friends.

Bibliography

The Army Almanac: A Book of Facts Concerning the United States Army. 2d ed. Harrisburg: Stackpole, 1959.

Berg, Fred A. *Encyclopedia of Continental Army Units: Battalions, Regiments and Independent Corps*. Harrisburg: Stackpole, 1972.

Danysh, Romana. "What's the History of Your Unit?" *Army Digest* 22 (Dec. 1967):12–15.

Dornbusch, Charles E. *Histories, Personal Narratives, United States Army: A Checklist*. Cornwallville, N.Y.: Hope Farm Press, 1967.

——. *Regimental Publications and Personal Narratives of the Civil War: A Checklist*. Cornwallville, N.Y.: Hope Farm Press, 1961.

Dyer, Frederick H., comp. *A Compendium of the War of the Rebellion*. Des Moines: Dyer, 1908. Reprinted in three vols., New York: Thomas Yoseloff, 1959.

Jacobs, Bruce. *Soldiers: The Fighting Divisions of the Regular Army*. New York: W. W. Norton, 1958.

Mahon, John K., and Danysh, Romana. *Infantry, Part I: Regular Army*. Army Lineage Series. Washington: Government Printing Office, 1972.

Millett, Allan R. and Cooling, B. Franklin. *Doctoral Dissertations in Military Affairs*. Manhattan: Kans. State Univ. Library, 1972. Updated annually in *Military Affairs*.

Rankin, Hugh. *The North Carolina Continentals*. Chapel Hill: Univ. of N.C. Press, 1971.

Rodenbough, Theophilus F., and Haskin, William L., eds. *The Army of the United States: Historical Sketches of the Staff and Line*. New York: Charles E. Merrill and Co. 1896.

Stubbs, Mary Lee, and Connor, Stanley Russell. *Armor-Cavalry, Part I: Regular Army and Army Reserve*. Army Lineage Series. Washington: Government Printing Office, 1972.

——. *Armor-Cavalry, Part II: Army National Guard*. Washington: Government Printing Office, 1972.

U.S., Army, Adjutant General's Office. *Statistical Exhibit of Strength of Volunteer Forces Called Into Service during the War with Spain . . .* Washington: Government Printing Office, 1899.

U.S., Army, Army Regulations: 340-2, Maintenance and disposition of records in TOE units of the Active Army and Army Reserve, 30 Sep 69; 672-5-1, Military awards, 3 Jun 74; 840-10, Flags and guidons: Description and use of flags, guidons, tabards, and automobile plates, 23 Aug 62; 870-5, Historical activities: Military history—responsibilities, policies and procedures, 22 Jan. 77.

U.S., Army, Artillery and Guided Missile School. *Artillery Unit Histories*. Fort Sill, Okla.: Artillery and Guided Missile School, 1955.

U.S., Army, Center of Military History. *The Army Lineage Book: Volume II: Infantry*. Washington: Government Printing Office, 1953.

——. "Organizational History Branch—Its Functions and Services," 1974.

——. "Organizational History: Its Preparation and Use," February 1975.

U.S., Army, Historical Branch, War Plans Division, General Staff. *Outlines of History of Regiments, United States Army*. Washington, 1921.

U.S., Army, Historical Section, Army War College. *Order of Battle of the United States Land Forces in the World War, American Expeditionary Forces*. 3 vols. Washington: Government Printing Office, 1931-49.

U.S., Army, Military History Research Collection. *United States Army Unit Histories*. Special Bibliographic Series, no. 4. Carlisle Barracks, Pa., 1971.

U.S., War Department. *Bibliography of State Participation in the Civil War . . .* 3d ed. Washington: Government Printing Office, 1913.

Chapter 17

Military History in the Army School System

Brooks E. Kleber, Col. Roy K. Flint,
and Charles S. Hall

In his letter to the Chief of Staff in 1970 that led to the establishment of the Department of the Army Ad Hoc Committee on the Army Need for the Study of Military History, Brig. Gen. Hal C. Pattison, then Chief of Military History, contended that in the 1950s the Army's higher schools had turned away from the teaching of military history, traditionally an integral part of officer education. The net result, he thought, had been that officers in the 1960s paid the price of "neglect of the lessons of the past."[1] General Westmoreland's mandate to the committee consequently placed heavy emphasis on the question of the place of military history in Army school curricula, and some of the most significant conclusions and recommendations of the committee concerned this subject.

The committee found General Pattison's contentions right, that while interest in military history on civilian campuses had increased over the preceding twenty years, the Army had "shown less interest in teaching the subject in service schools than it did before World War II." Its first general recommendation called for the U.S. Continental Army Command to introduce a "progressive coordinated history program into the Army educational system." (ANSMH Cmte Rpt, 1:51, 56.)

When the committee met in 1971, responsibility for most of the Army's service schools, the Command and General Staff College, and the Reserve Officers' Training Corps (ROTC) and associated programs resided with the Continental Army Command; in the 1973 reorganization of Army commands they were transferred to

---

1. Ltr, Brig. Gen. Pattison to Gen. William C. Westmoreland, CSUSA, 30 Jul 70, copy in CMH files. On the committee report (ANSMH Cmte Rpt) and its part in the genesis of this *Guide*, see above, Foreword.

Dr. Kleber (Ph.D., Pennsylvania), Chief Historian of the Army's Training and Doctrine Command, is coauthor of *The Chemical Warfare Service: Chemicals in Combat* (U.S. Army in World War II). Colonel Flint (Ph.D., Duke) is Professor of History at the U.S. Military Academy. Dr. Hall (Ph.D., Columbia) is on the faculty of the Army War College. His publications include *Benjamin Tallmadge: Revolutionary Soldier and American Businessman*.

the newly created U.S. Army Training and Doctrine Command. The United States Military Academy and the Army War College operated at the time and continued to operate in 1977 under the direct control of Headquarters, Department of the Army. The teaching of military history in all these educational settings came under the ad hoc committee's examination, and only in case of the Military Academy did the committee make no recommendations for changes and improvements in the teaching and use of military history. The following account sets forth the status of military history instruction in 1977 at all of these levels, with some emphasis on the committee's recommendations and how they were carried out. To some extent, of course, the whole system is, and perhaps always will be, in a state of flux.

United States Military Academy

The purpose of the Military Academy is to educate and train professional officers for the Regular Army, and military history has always held an important place in the curriculum. In order to meet the requirements of the Army for officers capable of assuming the diverse responsibilities inherent in a modern defense establishment and who also possess detailed knowledge in various areas, the academy seeks to strike a balance between breadth and specialization in its academic program. The cadet is required to take several courses in each major discipline but is allowed to choose an area of concentration in either basic sciences, applied sciences and engineering, national security and public affairs, or the humanities. While an area of concentration is not the equivalent of a college major, it can, when taken in conjunction with the broader offerings, provide a sound basis for future study at the graduate level. At West Point, history is offered within both the national security and public affairs and the humanities areas of concentration.

Each cadet, regardless of his area of concentration, must study either modern European, world, or American history during his sophomore year and take a course entitled "History of the Military Art" during his junior or senior year. The latter course indicates the Military Academy's professional as well as academic responsibilities; among the traditional university functions of education, scholarship, and service, the last is somewhat more strongly emphasized than at other academic institutions.

The academy has taught the history of the art of war in one form or another for well over a hundred years. The two-semester course, "History of the Military Art," as it is presently constituted began to take shape in the mid-1960s. While preserving the traditional focus on the evolution of the military art, this course now presents more of the political and societal context in which wars have been waged; i.e., the causes and consequences of wars now receive more emphasis. The cadet examines the conduct of wars as well as the peacetime activities of military institutions in light of the milieu in which they existed.

This complex material is presented in terms of evolutionary themes, referred to as threads of continuity. They include strategy; tactics; logistics; generalship; military theory and doctrine; military professionalism; technology; and political, social, and economic factors influencing the nature of war. The evolution of these factors, the relationships among them, and the reasons they have changed form the structure of the course.

A thematic approach provides several significant benefits. By studying military history over a broad time span, the student can isolate and analyze the critical reasons for changes at different junctures in history. Ideally, such a process sharpens the cadet's judgment so that he will better understand contemporary military developments; it also builds the foundation for a broader and deeper understanding of war that will help the graduate make sound decisions and give useful advice as he moves through positions of increasing responsibility in the Army.

"History of the Military Art" is divided into subcourses covering various periods: ancient and early modern warfare through the eighteenth century, the Napoleonic wars, the American Civil War, World War I, World War II in Europe and the Pacific, together with several military conflicts since World War II. Although the course offers a selective survey of the history of the military art, the cadet studies two operations, Napoleon's Jena campaign and the battle of Vicksburg, in considerable depth to give him a more realistic understanding of the events that transpired and to develop his ability to conduct a detailed historical analysis.

In addition to this required two-semester course, the Department of History also offers a number of military history electives, generally taken during the junior and senior years. These include two popular courses, "The History of Revolutionary Warfare" and "War in the Twentieth Century," which are offered each semester, as well as broader, nonoperational electives such as "War and Its Philosophers," "The Development of Air Power," "The Development of Sea Power," and "The American Military Experience," presented less frequently. Since the institution of a visiting professorship in military history in 1972, each holder of the chair has offered a one-semester course in his area of principal specialization or interest.

Perhaps the major difference between teaching military history at the Military Academy and other academic institutions is the low student-to-instructor ratio. Each instructor teaches approximately sixty-four students in four separate sessions of sixteen students each, a ratio which gives him the opportunity to conduct the class more as a colloquium than as a lecture. This allows the student to participate in give-and-take discussion with the instructor and to probe him for answers to questions; it also enables the instructor to know his students individually. Classroom discussions are enlivened by a variety of visual instructional aids and are supplemented by occasional lectures, films, television programs, and demonstrations of weapons and equipment by the curators of the West Point Museum.

Assigning active-duty officers as instructors has a number of advantages, particularly in teaching military history, but it also results in an annual turnover of one-third of the officers within the department. Because of the personal method of teaching in a small classroom, continuous attrition makes the selection of instructors a vital and time consuming task which shapes the character of the entire department.

The department head's criteria for selecting military history instructors include a strong desire to teach cadets, excellent performance in duty assignments, and potential for academic achievement and growth. In addition it is desirable for military history instructors to have attended the Command and General Staff College before reporting for duty; to date about ninety percent of the officer instructors have done so. Those selected as instructors attend graduate school, usually for two years, to study under noted historians with an interest in military history and to earn an M.A. degree. Some continue their work toward a doctorate and complete the requirements while at West Point. New instructors in military history also receive several weeks of instruction during the summer preceding their first year, including a tour of selected American battlefields. Thereafter the instructor's continuing education is a product of his own initiative and the needs of the department. In addition to educated cadets, the system of teaching history at the Military Academy produces middle-grade officers with a greatly increased understanding of war and peace.

Military history increases the cadet's understanding of how, through the whole sweep of history, man has used war to achieve his goals; helps him perceive the relationships between strategy and policy, between tactics and technology, and between the military profession and society at large; and, finally, helps him appreciate his place in the profession of arms as a newly commissioned officer. By causing him to reflect upon how military commanders and statesmen of the past handled their problems, the Military Academy can alert the cadet to the demands that will be placed upon him as he matures to higher commands and responsibilities.

Reserve Officer Training Program

The Reserve Officer Training Program was established by the National Defense Act of 1916, and from the beginning military history instruction was an integral part of the program. Privately printed manuals supported all ROTC instruction for many years, and they provided some coverage of military history. The manual for 1922, for example, contained 106 pages of military history concentrated primarily on military policy rather than campaigns. By 1932, however, the historical accounts had shifted to military operations exclusively.

The ROTC program was suspended during World War II and underwent extensive study and changes in the immediate postwar period. A major revision in the curriculum took place in 1951. The new 480-hour curriculum contained thirty hours of instruction in American military history which emphasized the principles of war and stressed the history of the Army and of leadership to add meaning to the detailed factual information presented. In 1956 the Office, Chief of Military History, first developed a text for the course (see Chapter 11).

Further revisions of ROTC curricula took place periodically during the 1950s and 1960s. Most of these changes resulted from pressures in the academic community to substitute academic courses for military subjects and to eliminate instruction which was not up to college level, such as training on crew-served weapons. In 1965 an Army advisory panel on the ROTC reviewed several proposals and recommended a new curriculum which included sixty classroom hours of world military history in the freshman year and ninety hours on national security and the concept of force in the sophomore year. The Department of the Army approved this as a developmental program, and in 1968 eleven schools adopted the new curriculum, which was known as Option C. Almost immediately work began on another revision, a flexible one that allowed more academic substitution. Half of the 360 hours then required would be professional military courses taught by military instructors. The other half would consist of academic subjects which could be taught by the academic faculty. Although American and world military history were two subjects which could be taught by the academic faculty, about fifteen or twenty hours of American military history were included in the first year course, "Fundamentals of Leadership and Management." The Department of the Army approved this curriculum as another option in 1969.

When the ad hoc committee met in 1971, colleges and universities could choose from five ROTC programs. Three included 30 hours of American military history; one (Option C) contained 60 hours of world military history; and one, the curriculum approved in 1969, had 15 to 20 hours of military history augmented by those history subjects (enrichment courses) taught by the academic faculty.

Most of the committee recommendations with regard to the ROTC curricula were general. The one precise recommendation, that the required hours of military history in the 1969 curriculum be raised to thirty, was not approved by the Department of the Army—doubtless because of a desire to maintain the flexibility so necessary for a changing educational philosophy and for the accommodation of a wide spectrum of institutions with ROTC programs. These were, after all, the reasons for having a choice of curricula in the first place. In any case, in school year 1975/76 the large majority of ROTC students did receive the thirty-hour block of American military history. For this course the Office, Chief of Military History, provided its revised and much improved text in 1969, with an updated version in 1973 to provide more current coverage of the Vietnam War (see Chapter 11).

The ad hoc committee recognized a basic prerequisite for an adequate ROTC program in military history, competent instructors, and it recommended the assignment of at least one officer with a graduate degree in history to each ROTC unit. As this recommendation came at a time when many military subjects were being phased out of the ROTC program, it coincided with increased demands from colleges for ROTC instructors with advanced degrees in several fields. The Army decided to rely on a broader program, an advanced degree program for all ROTC instructors, to improve academic qualifications of teachers of military science and tactics and so rejected the committee's specific recommendation. In the advanced degree program, instructors with a master's degree were to have a three-year stabilized ROTC tour; those not having that degree were to be permitted up to two years of study at a civilian institution to work toward it, followed by a two-year stabilized tour of instructor duty.

In terms of upgrading the academic qualifications of ROTC instructors generally, the program was highly successful. The proportion of professors and assistant professors of military science with advanced degrees increased from only 8 percent in academic year 1968/69 to 64 percent in 1974/75. As of February 1976 the figure was 66 percent. While no distinction was made as to the disciplines in which these degrees were earned, history undoubtedly received its share.

Meanwhile, a major study of the officer corps started in 1974 had significant impact upon the ROTC program. Under the Officer Personnel Management System (OPMS), the assignment of officers to ROTC duty no longer would be by grade and branch with graduate degree in unspecified disciplines. Rather, officers would be assigned by grade and OPMS specialty, with graduate degree requirements corresponding to that specialty. Although precise requirements had not been determined in 1976, there was no reason to assume that ROTC requirements for officers with advanced degrees would decline significantly.

As approved, committee recommendations called for participation of the civilian faculty in teaching ROTC cadets military history, either in the core curriculum or in enrichment courses. Some colleges and universities offered military history courses within their own history departments which served as appropriate substitutes for the ROTC requirement. Team teaching continued to be an effective device which combined the talents of military and academic instructors in the presentation of military history. Guest lecturers added variety and depth.

A six-week military history workshop, conducted since 1968 at the United States Military Academy, has also improved the qualifications of some ROTC military history instructors. This program includes seminar discussions, guest lecturers, library research, and the preparation of monographs. In 1972, the Department of the Army asked the Continental Army Command to restudy the workshop requirement, particularly in view of the expected impact of the advanced degree program, but its value was solidly reaffirmed. These workshops have served as excellent training vehicles for selected professors and assistant professors of military science to prepare adequately for their role as military history instructors.

Branch Service Schools

Although branch service schools date from 1824, when the Artillery School of Practice was established at Fort Monroe, the present system took shape after the reorganization of the Army in 1920. During the period between the two world wars, service schools stressed a broad education and included the formal study of military history in the basic and advanced officer courses. For example, in the early 1920s the Infantry School's basic course contained 66 hours of critical study of selected campaigns, and its advanced course had 91 hours of formal military history. Some schools studied military history in relation to the particular arm or branch. The Artillery School advanced course after World War I contained 25 hours of "lectures on selected campaigns with particular reference to Field Artillery." World War II forced the abandonment of such "educational" subjects as the schools stressed the accelerated training of large numbers of officers.

Post-World War II attempts by some branch schools to reinstitute military history in their curricula were thwarted primarily by more pressing teaching requirements. In 1954, a survey of fourteen branch schools revealed that only the Chemical Officer Advanced Course provided formal instruction in military history. By the early 1970s some basic courses did include one-hour periods on the history of the particular branch. Although branch advanced courses benefited from extensive use of historical examples integrated into regular instruction, there was little or no history in the core curricula, and, at the time the ad hoc committee met, only a few schools offered military history electives.

For the basic courses, the committee recommended a two-hour block of instruction on the importance and value of the study of military history and two hours on the history of the particular branch. Two military history electives should be offered in the advanced courses, one operationally oriented and the other emphasizing civil-military relationships. Realizing the futility of offering military history courses without qualified people to teach them, the committee recommended that a minimum of two spaces be validated for officers possessing master's degrees in history for each school conducting an advanced course.

The Department of the Army concurred in the recommended basic course requirements but eliminated any reference to minimum hours. It agreed that two military history electives, "of diverse sophistication," should be included in each advanced course curriculum. And it also agreed that "one or two spaces" in each branch school should be validated as graduate degree positions in history; incumbents would teach history and advise fellow faculty members on matters of military history.

In addition the committee recommended that the Continental Army Command (CONARC) develop some instruction for officer candidate school students who had not been exposed to military history as college undergraduates. This instruction, which should approximate the ROTC American military history course, should be given no later than the branch basic courses. This recommendation was never approved; neither the relatively short length nor the performance-oriented training characteristic of both OCS and the basic courses were conducive to teaching military history.

By school year 1974/75, CONARC and the Training and Doctrine Command had carried out the other recommendations. CONARC directed the Command and General Staff College to prepare instructional packets consisting of scope, outline, and bibliography for the two military history electives which were to be included in the advanced course curricula. One course was called Topical Military History, the other Advanced American Military History. While some schools used this material, others developed their own military history electives, an approach facilitated by the assignment of qualified instructors to the branch service schools. Even so, there was no precise uniformity in offerings. The Armor School, for example, offered but one military history course during school year 1974/75, as part of the core curriculum. The Field Artillery School offered five military history electives in its advanced course ranging from an evaluation of warfare through the ages to the role of the military in the modern world. The Air Defense School offered two military history electives, one a review of American military history, the other a reading seminar which examined generalship and technology in warfare. The Infantry School offered a well-received world military history elective, taught by an officer instructor who was a Ph.D. candidate in history at Duke University.

By 1975, however, a change in the length of branch school advanced courses was affecting the elective program. The Training and Doctrine Command determined that advanced courses would be reduced from thirty-six to twenty-six weeks. This change, which took place in the school year 1975/76, forced out all elective courses. A survey of branch schools in 1976 indicated that only one intended to retain military history as part of the core curriculum. Other schools planned to integrate military history into the instruction, although that subject would not constitute a teaching objective. The removal of formal military history presentations from advanced course curricula naturally eliminated the need for officer instructors with advanced degrees in history.

The whole matter of reducing the length of advanced courses became interwoven with the formulation of the Officer Personnel Management System which was taking place at the same time. One of the ramifications of the system was a review of the advanced degree program and a decision to limit civilian schooling requirements to skills and areas dictated by officer specialties.

The Command and General Staff College

In 1966, the Department of the Army's Haines Board, convened to review the Army's school system, described the Command and General Staff College at Fort Leavenworth as "the keystone of the Army educational system in the tactical application of combined arms and services." From its inception in 1881 as the School of Application for Infantry and Cavalry, this institution presented instruction in military history. Refinements in the curriculum resulted from the influence of Capt. Arthur Wagner immediately before the Spanish-American War and the stimulus of Elihu Root's sponsorship and Maj. John Morrison's instruction after that war. If the period preceding World War I can be characterized as the time of intellectual ferment in the teaching of military history at Fort Leavenworth, the 1920s can best be described as one of pragmatic, utilitarian endeavor. During World War I, Leavenworth graduates had served in high command and staff positions and had organized training schools based on the Leavenworth model. Confident of the soundness of the Leavenworth method as modified by their wartime experience, they returned to reestablish the Army school system. The National Defense Act of 1920 provided for the progressive military training of officers from West Point and the Reserve Officers Training Program through the branch service schools and the Line and General Staff College at Fort Leavenworth to the Army War College.

The prevailing post-World War I educational philosophy was best expressed by a colonel in a 1921 issue of the *Infantry Journal*. To be an active and intelligent participant in the era that had just begun, an officer "must know, not only the military condition of the United States, but he must know its history, its political, industrial, and financial conditions, and the hopes and aspirations of its people."[2] This kind of thinking ensured the place of history within the curricula of the Army service school system during the interwar years.

In 1923 the institution at Fort Leavenworth was renamed the Command and General Staff School, and the curriculum that had evolved by that time was to remain substantially the same until World War II. A course in psychology and leadership, emphasizing American characteristics, included general historical studies and studies that dealt more specifically with such American military leaders as Grant, Lee, Sheridan, and Sherman. A course in logic was later combined with one in military history, while courses in military geography, strategy, and legal principles drew heavily upon the study of military history. The school's annual report for 1921 indicated the rationale for such measures:

> Purely theoretical studies . . . even though they consist largely of the discussion of concrete situations, are not considered sufficient to adjust the officer's mind to actual conditions. In time of peace, Military History must be relied on for information as to the actual conditions of war. As a consequence . . . the course in Military History and Strategy is scheduled to proceed hand in hand with the course in Tactical and Strategical Studies, Corps and Army, for the purpose of illustrating the actual workings of the principles discussed in the latter course.[3]

Despite good intentions for broadening the scope of military history, courses stressed for the most part military operations in the field. Although course hours and content fluctuated during the years up to World War II, the objective of military history remained that stated in the 1921 annual report. In the last year before World War II disrupted the school's operations, 53 of 1,073 total classroom hours were devoted to military history.

The first special World War II streamlined course, which began in December 1940, contained 318 hours of instruction and 243 hours of applicatory exercises. Both formal instruction in military history and the use of historical illustrations were discarded entirely. Operational lessons learned were to be the only vestige of military history. The post-World War II Leavenworth curriculum was an extension of the wartime model. Formal instruction in military history did not reappear

---

2. Henry A. Smith, "General Staff College Course," *Infantry Journal* 18 (Jan. 1921):51.

3. General Staff School, *Annual Report 1920-1921* (Fort Leavenworth, Kans., June 30, 1921), p. 23.

until 1952, when historical examples were introduced into the core curriculum as a means of illustrating the principles of war. By 1957 the curriculum included 21 hours of historical examples and one hour on the history of Fort Leavenworth. In addition, each student spent about 55 hours on a leadership paper involving rudimentary historical research and some 16 to 32 hours of historical illustrations were written into lesson plans.

By 1960 the upward trend was reversed and formal instruction in military history was reduced to a three-hour course, the purpose of which was the encouragement of self-study. These three hours were eliminated in 1965 in favor of a more comprehensive elective military history course. The use of historical examples to reinforce general instruction continued, and ten hours of leadership case studies were introduced. In 1967, as result of a Haines board recommendation, the college expanded its program of electives, including those in military history.

When the ad hoc committee met in 1971, the core curriculum of the Command and General Staff College contained no formal instruction in military history, although case studies and historical examples continued to be used. The college itself offered three military history electives—"Military History," "Topical Military History," and "Development of Combat Divisions—Free World and Communist Powers." Ten history or history-related electives from the University of Kansas, Kansas State University, and the University of Missouri at Kansas City were also available. The lack of qualified instructors at the Command and General Staff College was a problem in the military history elective offerings in 1971. None of the eleven instructors who taught two of the military history courses had graduate degrees in history, although two had masters in other disciplines—English and mechanical engineering. A similar situation existed in the third military history elective.

Ad hoc committee recommendations approved by the Department of the Army included the following: improving the quality of current military history electives within the college as faculty expertise improved; introducing electives in the critical analysis of actual tactical operations and in strategic studies; validating at least three spaces as graduate degree positions in history; and encouraging nearby colleges to offer more military history electives. The Department of the Army deferred action on a recommendation for restudying the feasibility of a visiting professor in military history.

The large majority of these approved recommendations were

carried out. The catalog of resident courses for the academic year 1977/78 listed ten military history electives taught by the faculty, while five more history courses were presented by professors from the University of Kansas. The college faculty also taught 29 hours in the common curriculum, including an 18-hour block on the U.S. Army in the twentieth century. Equally important, historians were introducing a theater operations exercise and a two-major-corps tactical exercise. Three of the five officers teaching military history had masters in history, one had his Ph.D. in history, and one had met all doctoral requirements but the defense of his dissertation. The military staff was supplemented by two civilians with doctorates in history and by a visiting professor in the John F. Morrison Chair of Military History established in 1974.

The Army War College

Military history has traditionally formed an important part of the instruction for students at the Army War College. Studies of campaigns and leadership to derive lessons from the past can be found in the curriculum of the Army's senior educational institution from its inception at Washington, D.C., in 1901. This type of study, emphasizing military operations in the field, reached its zenith in the years between World War I and World War II, when much time, both in and out of the classroom, was devoted to analyses of earlier campaigns and battles and foreign military institutions. Students toured Civil War battlefields in Pennsylvania, Maryland, and Virginia, and distinguished military historians such as Douglas Southall Freeman lectured frequently at the college.

Unlike the Command and General Staff College, the War College closed its doors during World War II. When it reopened after the war it was at a new location, first at Fort Leavenworth, Kansas, and after 1951 at Carlisle Barracks, Pennsylvania—and with a new curriculum reflecting new concepts of professional education for senior officers. The emphasis had shifted from field operations to the realm of national military planning and policy and management problems. The approach was interdisciplinary, and the tools of study more frequently political science, international relations, economics, and psychology than military history per se. The formal teaching of military history that had characterized the interwar period disappeared from the curriculum, though the use of military history for illustrative examples as part of the interdisciplinary approach did not.

In the various curriculum changes since the early fifties, the study of military history has increased both in terms of formal instruction and as part of the interdisciplinary approach. The ad hoc committee report in 1971 concluded that coverage within the core curriculum was adequate. The committee proposed a threefold definition of military history that furnished a framework for War College curriculum planners and professors. The committee's definition included (1) operations (tactics, strategy, and leadership, to mention the most important aspects); (2) administration and technology, such as the functional and professional activities of armed forces, doctrines, organization, manpower, training, and weapons and their development; and finally (3) the military establishment and society, dealing with the national and international aspects of national strategy in war and peace, the elements of national power, and the role of the armed services strategies in achieving national objectives. Since the War College seeks primarily to educate rather than train, the educational aspects of military history have been emphasized.

For the past several years the curriculum at the Army War College has had two major elements: a Common Overview to provide the core of professional knowledge essential to each graduate, and an Individual Concentration (elective) phase to allow each student to meet individual professional needs. The Common Overview exposes the student to the historical backgrounds of the United States and the leading nations of the world to aid him in assessing the domestic and international issues that affect U.S. national security. The approach during these core courses is interdisciplinary, and history in general and military history in particular is woven into the fabric of instruction.

A much more intensive and extensive use of military history can be found in the Evolution of Military Strategy course of the Common Overview. Here the three elements of the definition of military history come into play: operational, administrative and technical, and the military and society. All students are exposed to the development of military strategy/military history with special emphasis on the "great captains" and military strategic thinkers here and abroad. Thus, a definite military historical framework for all War College students is part of the required course.

The Individual Concentration phase gives the student an opportunity to explore military history in greater depth. In this as in the Common Overview, the War College has received excellent cooperation from the U.S. Army Military History Institute (MHI—see Chapter 12). Since 1971 the institute's staff and since 1973 visiting professors at the institute have offered elective courses. Each visiting professor has conducted a seminar in military history as an elective for War College students in addition to other services, such as advising students and guiding study projects.

Elective courses provide a range of choices in the general field of history as well as specifically in military history. Among the specific military history courses a student might choose are: Contrasts in Command, Changing Nature of Modern Warfare, and Strategic Issues of World War II. General courses with historical content include: Arms control: An Element of National Security; Nuclear Strategy: Policy and Planning; Politico-Military Dimensions of National Policy; Contemporary Issues in U.S. Foreign Policy; and War and International Law: The Kaiser to Kissinger. Area courses also have historical content, for instance, Africa: Problems and Promises; China as a World Power; Middle East Political Dynamics; and Soviet Power and Policy.

Besides formal curricular offerings, War College students have other opportunities to study military history. The commandant conducts wide-ranging small group discussions with all members of each class, and distinguished active or retired members of the armed services who visit the college can draw on professional experience stretching back in some cases to before World War II. One of the highlights of the academic year is the Gettysburg Battlefield tour which is open to students, their families, and guests. A presentation on the strategy, tactics, and events leading up to the day of battle precedes the tour. During the academic year the Military History Institute sponsors a series of evening meetings, "Perspectives in Military History," in which some of the leading military historians here and abroad discuss their current research. The institute also provides publications and exhibits.

Perhaps the most interesting and rewarding experience is the Oral History Program sponsored by the MHI. An average of about twenty students per year debrief senior retired Army generals and other distinguished military and civilian leaders and analyze earlier debriefings. These interview sessions make the student keenly aware of the significance and importance of military history in the education of the professional officer.

In summary, the current War College curriculum represents an interdisciplinary approach to fulfilling the college mission. A strong undercurrent of military history flows through the Common Overview courses and especially the Evolution of Military Strategy course. Almost half of the Individual Concentration courses have a direct relation to history and to military history in particular. Other educational and professional opportunities also exist outside the seminar room at the War College for the student to pursue an interest in military history.

Chapter **18**

The Use of Military History in Staff Work

Walter G. Hermes

$\mathbf{O}$N the eve of the Civil War the Secretary of War received two communications. One—a treatise on camels and their use in warfare—was sparked by Jefferson Davis's interest in the possibility of importing camels and employing them in the American southwest in the place of horses and mules. The second came from a junior Engineer officer who pointed out that the system of coastal defenses along the Atlantic seaboard would be largely ineffective against a maritime power. In the process, he gave a short account of amphibious landings undertaken since 1400 A.D. to demonstrate how the state of the art had changed and how vulnerable the United States was to invasion from the sea. The treatise on camels argued that the old ship of the desert still merited a place in warfare, while the engineer emphasized the impact of modern technology, such as the introduction of new steam vessels and more deadly weapons, upon military planning.

Whether the issue concerns the retention of the old or the adoption of the new, the telling points are frequently drawn from military history. For generations staff officers have marshaled facts and figures to support the pros and cons of a case. Patently, the officer who is poorly grounded in military history will often operate at a disadvantage in the staff arena.

It is thus unfortunate that as a rule the young officer entering his first assignment on a staff will have little time to devote to the study of military history. In most cases, he will soon become an action officer responsible for a specific area and will be immersed in current operations. Working against deadlines, he will be under constant pressure to prepare the never-ending stream of reports and memoranda that are the lifeblood of staff work. In the hectic schedule of a working staff, military history will usually play a subsidiary role.

Yet that role is important. Many of the papers that staff

Dr. Hermes (Ph.D., Georgetown), Chief, Staff Support Branch, CMH, wrote *Truce Tent and Fighting Front* (U.S. Army in the Korean War series).

officers prepare become the bases for decision—some of major consequence. The proper use of historical materials and resources in the preparation of these papers is essential in arriving at acceptable solutions to many problems. How then can the staff officer take full advantage of his training and resources to ensure that his staff submissions are historically sound and can be supported with confidence?

The exposure to military history that young officers receive during the academic years may vary from almost none to a great deal. The fortunate ones will have a general background of knowledge in the field, although it may be of only limited assistance in attacking a specific problem. Similarly, the experience acquired in research projects during the school years should give many officers at least a basic skill in finding materials and in digesting, assembling, and presenting information in a logical fashion. Some officers have also had the benefit of postgraduate work to sharpen those skills.

How these skills can be applied to each problem will vary according to the time available. For the most part, the staff officer will be dealing with a brand of history that, in this era of convenience packaging, has received the rather appropriate title of instant history. In staff operations the deadline is the controlling factor and the amount of research that can be done in support of a project is usually quite limited. Frequently the staff officer will not have adequate time to do a thorough job in investigating the background of a problem.

If the deadline is extremely tight—a day or less—the officer will have to depend upon what is immediately on hand or easy to obtain. He must know the sources he can tap quickly. Upon his assignment to a staff section, he should become thoroughly familiar with the office records and should set up and maintain a complete and well-organized file on the subjects he is responsible for. Since very few problems are wholly new, background material will be available in previous studies, reports, and other documents. Frequently the major task will be simply to update this material by screening current records or by getting information from other staff sections. In the search for such material the command staff historian or the Center of Military History can often be of service. The command staff historian, who may work alone or with a small staff, is charged with performing historical functions for his command or agency. Either he or the center may have done some work on the subject and may be able to provide spot information, statistics, or other data from reference files. For the immediate demand project, however, there is little time for basic research, and the result is instant history at its worst.

The quality of the response should rise in proportion to the time allowed by the target date, but the depth of the research will depend a great deal on the complexity of the subject and the location of the records. In other words, a week may permit an officer to become familiar with the desertion problems that existed during World War II but would scarcely allow him to do more than begin his research on the handling of deserters in all American wars. It also follows that if all the required records are located in one place, the staff officer will be able to cover much more than he could if they were scattered among half a dozen sites.

A quick survey of the dimensions of the problem will help determine whether the staff officer should attempt to do the job himself or seek outside help. In most cases, consultation with the command staff historian or, if the officer is located in the Washington area, with the Center of Military History is highly advisable. Historians can provide information on what has already been done on the topic—in 1965, for example, a center study on the call-up of reserve forces during the Berlin crisis of 1961 proved to be of great help to the staff in planning for the use of reserves during the war in Vietnam. Historians may also suggest books, articles, theses, and studies that can be helpful reference sources. Frequently they may be able to furnish names and addresses of persons and organizations that can give additional information and assistance. The historical office usually can save the busy staff officer valuable time that otherwise might be spent in searching dead ends by guiding him promptly to the most rewarding sources. By cutting down waste motion the staff officer can do a more thorough job, and that thoroughness will be reflected in his final submission.

On occasion the staff officer will be assigned, either individually or as a member of a study group, to prepare a long-range study on a major topic such as Army promotion policies, the overhauling of a logistical support system, or Army planning for the mobilization of reserve forces. Depending on the urgency of the situation, the time allotted for studies of this importance will, as a rule, vary from three months to a year.

For a comprehensive study the first task is generally the development of an outline. In almost every outline the first section will be devoted to the background of the topic. To know where you are going, it is necessary to know where you have been. If the study is on promotion policies, the officer will have to become familiar with the policies of the past before he can discuss those of the present or recommend those of the future. The scope of the study will determine whether he need only study the policies of the past decade or must trace developments from the Revolutionary War to the present. Similarly, a consideration of the use of foreign ports in wartime may be limited to the experience in Vietnam or may span the period from World War I on. Whether the period covers a few years or centuries, the background portion of the study is essentially historical in nature and should be approached as a historical research project.

It is rare to discover that someone else has already done the bulk of the research and writing in response to an earlier requirement. More frequently, the bits and pieces that form the background mosaic are scattered in a dozen places and considerable digging may be necessary. Should the staff officer decide that he has both the time and ability to do the historical work himself, he would still be wise to consult the command staff historian or the center of Military History. There is no point in duplicating the work of others, especially if they have done the job well. In any event, the guidance and suggestions of the historian can help smooth and shorten the path of the do-it-yourself officer.

If the study topic is broad and complex or if the study clearly cannot be completed on time without assistance, the staff historian or Center of Military History may be called upon to prepare part or all of the background material. Preliminary consultation with the historical office is always advisable before a formal directive is drawn up. Since each historical unit has certain fixed requirements and capabilities, the priority of a new request must be established and the availability of qualified persons to do the task must be determined. A small historical office, for example, will not have the flexibility of the Center of Military History and may not be able to assume an additional load, no matter how willing it may be to help. In some cases, requests for historical assistance may have to go through command channels and be approved by the staff agency that supervises the historical office. An informal discussion with the historian in advance will reveal whether his office can handle the job and meet the deadline. It will also assure that the request is sent through the proper channels and that the directive to be issued is concise and acceptable to the historical office.

The preparation of the directive is important and should be done with care. The staff officer must assume that he will get what he asks for. If the request for a historical background section or chapter is vaguely worded and does not state the requirement clearly, the end product will probably mirror the indecision. The directive should set forth the purpose of the study, the topics to be covered, and the scope and time focus of the historical background so that the historian's research will put the subject into the proper perspective. The background chapter should not be cluttered with material that is not germane to the study. If the subject should be the mobilization of the National Guard in times of crisis, for instance, there may be no need to cover in any detail the call-up of other reserve forces or the expansion of active Army units during these periods. The directive, in essence, should be a blueprint for the historian to construct a sound, unbiased, and relevant base for the study.

If the agency or command to which he is assigned prepares an annual historical summary of its activities, the staff officer may also become directly involved in writing military history. Although the administrative details of assembling and packaging the annual summaries are usually performed by civilian action officers, many of the submissions concerning directorate, division, and branch operations are prepared by staff officers as an additional duty. To do the job effectively, they must become thoroughly familiar with the background of missions, accomplishments, and problems so that they can present an objective, well-organized, accurate account of the major activities of the past year. In the process they should acquire a good overview of their own operations as well as valuable experience in researching, writing, and organizing historical materials.

Thus far only the more usual circumstances under which the staff officer would come into contact with military history have been considered. A development of recent years may become more commonplace and important. It is instant history also, but with a different twist. In 1962 during the Berlin crisis, the Chief of Staff wanted a record of the events, since the call-up of two National Guard divisions and a number of other reserve units had resulted in a number of problems for the Army. The Office of the Chief of Military History sent a four-man team to the Pentagon to collect the necessary data from action officers scattered throughout the Army staff. The team worked from current files and filled gaps in the records by interviewing military and civilian staff members who held important positions. Shortly after the reserve forces were released from active service in mid-1962, the team finished a detailed study that covered the background of the call-up, the problems encountered in mobilizing and demobilizing the reserves and in expanding the active Army, and an analysis of the lessons learned during the operation.

Later that year OCMH sent a historian to the Pentagon to monitor the Oxford crisis, which developed when a black student attempted to enroll in the University of Mississippi. Working side by side with the action officers, he was on hand as the drama took place and was able to obtain copies of most of the important documents and telephone conversations as they were generated. With this valuable source material he was able to write a monograph on the incident within a few months after it ended. Similar uses of historians occurred during later crises, with the historians collecting and writing the story almost as it happened.

The advantages of preparing instant history of this kind are obvious. The historian can be on the scene while the records are relatively intact. He can screen the source documents and organize a historical file that should eventually contain the core material for his study. By being close to the action officers while history is in the making, the historian can absorb a sense of the drama of the stituation and a feeling for the atmosphere. He can also talk to many of the participants while everything is still fresh in their minds, before the fog of time begins to obscure the sequence of events and leads them to magnify their own roles.

For the staff officer this type of instant history can be extremely useful. Almost immediately he will have a handy reference tool available to answer questions, to prepare reports, and to tap for planning and experience data. But the attractions of instant history should not blind either the historian or the staff officer to its inherent weaknesses. Of necessity it will be limited in scope and will reflect mainly the information to which the recorder is privy. Many pertinent records will not be available until well after the events are concluded, especially those dealing with the high-level story and those held by other agencies. Perhaps the most glaring limitation of all is the lack of perspective. Writing so close to the action, the historian can hardly avoid some distortion. And, like the quick demand project that the staff officer is called upon to prepare, instant history is bound to reflect the haste with which it has been turned out.

Despite these disadvantages, instant history's plus factors appear to outweigh the minus. The collection and preservation of the records alone would be enough to commend it. Besides, in many cases the instant history may be the only reliable account available for some years. It serves as a useful reference tool until the passage of time and the accessibility of other records permit a more accurate and balanced account to be written.

In summary, the staff officer will come into contact with military history on numerous occasions during his tour but will probably not have much time to study it. He will have to rely mainly upon whatever general knowledge of the subject he acquired during his school years plus what he has picked up on his own in the interim. Ideally he should be familiar with the standard books and reference works in the field and with the historical publications of the Center of Military History before he is assigned to staff duty; time for extensive reading may be sharply limited during the tour, especially under crisis conditions. Then the officer will have to know how to exploit quickly the resources at his disposal. The deadline will be the prime factor in every action, and the officer must know where to go for assistance, both short- and long-range, and be keenly aware of the time restrictions that govern his response. He will usually have to make compromises between the desirable and the practicable to satisfy the requirement of the moment.

To help ease the pressure and increase the reliability of his staff submissions, the officer may turn to the historical office for guidance and assistance. The professional military historian may not always have all the answers, but he does know the best places to look for them. When time permits, the historian may also be requested to prepare historical background material for staff studies and reports, especially those of major importance. During crises the staff officer may encounter the historian on the job when they work side by side covering the emergency. With luck the officer will have a draft account of the events on hand shortly after they come to an end.

All in all, the staff officer will be exposed to military history frequently during his tour, and often, consciously or subconsciously, will be applying his knowledge to the solution of his daily problems. For those who plan to reach the top, military history can be a valuable aid.

Chapter 19

Military History and Army Records

Vincent H. Demma

THE writing of military history depends upon the preservation of the record of military activities. Preserved in various archives, libraries, and other depositories, that record enables historians today to reconstruct the military history of bygone centuries. Through accident, neglect, or even design on the part of those entrusted with it, part of the record of the past has been lost forever. In our own time, no less than in centuries past, preservation is a very real problem. At one time or another in his career, every officer is likely to face it. Simply stated, it is one of preserving the current record that will be of greatest use and value in the future without flooding repositories with an unmanageable volume of paper.

Army Records Management

In many respects the writing of contemporary military history depends on the good judgment of numerous civilian and military action officers, secretaries, clerks, records managers, and administrators. An extremely small portion of the approximately one million linear feet of records created annually by the Army survives as part of the permanent historical record. Most records are destroyed by agency or command records managers and others shortly after they are created and their temporary value has ended. Those remaining are retired to federal records centers. Screened in accordance with predetermined retention and destruction schedules, some of these are destroyed periodically. Very few finally reach the National Archives, and from these the history of the Army in our own time must be written.

Good records management helps create future archives, and adequate documentation makes possible the preparation of good history. Effective management during the entire life-span of

---

Mr. Demma (M.A., Wisconsin) of the Current History Branch, CMH, is preparing a history of 1961–65 Army operations in Vietnam.

Army records is a prerequisite for the preservation of future military archives and the preparation of future histories. Throughout the Army, from the small unit to the departmental level, records clerks, action officers, records managers, and official historians, serve as custodians of the Army's actions and thoughts, keepers of the institutional memory. Only through the guidance and work of records managers, with the cooperation of civilian and military personnel alike, will Army records of historical value eventually enter the archives to become available to future historians.

Good records management is the product of experience and professional training. Although military officers and records managers are introduced to the historical importance of Army records in their respective schools and training programs, this introduction is fleeting. Many officers and civilians, including records managers, never acquire a keen historical sense. Determining which documents should be saved and which can be destroyed requires an appreciation of the place of history within the Army. Professional training, orientation, and experience should imbue historians with this appreciation. Army officers, usually lacking the historian's special training, still need to recognize the historical value and potential scholarly uses of the documents that pass through their hands.

Recognition of the historical significance of the many documents created during World War II helped spur the creation of a formal records management program. The Army had to arrange and dispose of a mass of unorganized and unevaluated documents, so that those of historical significance would be retained for future reference. Army historians, in particular, were interested in records necessary for official histories of World War II and pressed for a systematic program of collection and preservation. The result of this general concern was the establishment in 1943 of the War Department Records Branch of the Adjutant General's Office. Redesignated the Departmental Records Branch (DRB) in 1947, it became a custodial facility for the Army's World War II records. Until these documents were transferred to the National Archives as permanent records, they were maintained at the branch where they were screened and arranged in proper order. In compiling inventories, indexes, and other finding aids, the records managers in the branch became thoroughly familiar with the documents. Their knowledge was invaluable to the historians who prepared the volumes in the U.S. Army in World War II series.

Although successful in organizing and preserving a voluminous quantity of Army documents, records managers realized that many of their difficulties stemmed from fundamental weaknesses in the Army's system of creating and maintaining records. Records keeping in the Army had undergone little change since the introduction in 1914 of the War Department decimal filing system and its scheme of subject files. Using this system, Army file clerks often exercised considerable latitude in selecting documents to retain and files in which to place them. As the staff of the DRB discovered, the separate Army bureaus and various agencies, offices, and divisions of the Army staff rarely followed common standards of records management. The branch staff had to review thousands of documents item-by-item to separate unimportant from important ones. At the same time, latitude enjoyed by Army clerks allowed considerable duplication. Historians happily discovered that files maintained in certain agencies were more comprehensive than similar files in the custody of the DRB.

Hoping to prevent the recurrence of these difficulties, records managers began planning a new, Army-wide system soon after the end of World War II. To avoid reviewing documents and files in an intermediate records repository like the DRB required a system for predetermining the value of every Army file, one segregating temporary from permanent records at the time files were created. Permanent records would then go directly from the agency creating them to a records repository, and the entire records retirement program would become decentralized and streamlined.

After reviewing over two thousand different subject files then being used in the Army and considering the legal, administrative, fiscal, and historical value of the documents involved, records managers devised standards to determine the disposition of each file. Instead of incorporating these features into the existing system, however, records managers decided to create an entirely new system. In this new filing system, files defined by the function or mission they served in the unit or agency creating and maintaining them replaced subject files. A new records management program, the Army Functional Filing System (TAFFS), incorporating decentralized records keeping and retirement, was introduced throughout the Army between 1959 and the end of 1962.

The functional system has not completely lived up to expectations. Surveys of Army records as recently as 1975 show that some Army staff agencies still fail to use the system properly. Lengthy and sometimes confusing regulations sometimes cause difficulties, and subject filing and the use of the War Department decimal filing system continue. Historians and action officers, in particular, find subject files more convenient. A general lack of confidence in the system contributes to acquisition and retention of documents for reference and working files, a practice that causes duplication and delays the retirement of important records. And without familiarity gained by working with the documents, records managers frequently do not appreciate the historical value of many documents and files routinely shredded or burned. Particularly susceptible to destruction are informal files of working papers, background files, and personal working files that rarely enter the records retirement system. Decentralized records keeping, which in essence makes every action officer in the Army his or her own records clerk, continues to encourage highly individual approaches to the job without assuring that important records will be retained for historical reference.

Vietnam Records

Army historians recognized that problems continued even after adoption of functional filing, but intensified combat operations in South Vietnam beginning in 1965 caused real alarm. Anticipating once again the need for adequate documentation to prepare official histories, historians discovered that the Army records management program was falling short of its promise and potential.

Even during peacetime the Army's records program suffered from a shortage of experienced and trained managers. And records personnel assigned to units in combat sometimes lacked even basic training in records management. Uncertain about the functional system, entertaining only vague ideas about what constituted historical records, and with short tours limiting experience, records clerks and administrators in Vietnam often found their task complicated, unrewarding, and occasionally overwhelming. Moreover, because of the viscissitudes of combat or the lack of guidance, many records were never created while others were prematurely destroyed. Unit records tended to suffer most as professionally trained records managers generally were assigned only to major command headquarters. It was difficult for them to visit remote, highly mobile units engaged in combat; such units usually did without professional guidance on records keeping.

Historians were especially concerned about basic sources of

combat history: the daily journal and the supporting documents constituting the journal file, as well as other planning, intelligence, and operational records. These records provide the gist for future histories; units that leave behind poor records or none at all receive little notice by historians. More importantly, such documents help evaluate and modify the Army's doctrine, tactics, and training.

Military historians serving with units in Vietnam and working with records managers made special efforts to see that combat records and other significant documents were prepared and entered the Army's records retirement system. Instructions to Army field historians from higher headquarters gave first priority to "developing and maintaining general awareness of the necessity for creation and preservation of accurate comprehensive records."[1] By monitoring the records program within the units he served, the field historian helped assure that sources required by historians were being created and retired; he often salvaged documents that might otherwise have been destroyed or lost. Provisions were made to acquire records of activities such as the pacification and advisory programs for which the functional filing system provided inadequate guidance.

That such extraordinary efforts were required by field historians contributed to The Adjutant General in 1968 suspending authority to destroy any records created by Army units in South Vietnam. Starting in that year, all records from the combat zone were retired as permanent regardless of previous functional filing designation. To facilitate use by Army historians, records were returned to the United States quickly. Many records from Vietnam, however, remain to be screened, evaluated, reorganized, and disposed of by Army records managers, a situation somewhat similar to that after World War II.

Headquarters Files

Combat naturally makes difficult the creation and preservation of records. yet even at larger, more stable headquarters to the rear of the combat zone, including Department of Army headquarters itself, records are susceptible to unnecessary destruction. Pressures of economy, space, and time continually jeopardize historically valuable staff documents. The tempta-

---

1. Hqs., U.S. Army Vietnam, USARV Reg 870-1, 28 Dec 1966. See Chapter 13 for additional discussion of military historians in the field.

tion to destroy records is very real at every level. In their zeal to win the "battle of the bulk," records managers and staff officers easily lose sight of the historical value of records, and destruction is easier than preservation with its time-consuming administrative tasks.

At all large headquarters, whether during peace or war, a chronic problem is the creation and unwarranted destruction of uncontrolled personal working papers or action officer files. Records managers have been slow to recognize that these files often contain documents of historical significance. Such documents, drawn from a variety of sources and usually related to a single subject, action, or case, help historians understand the how and why of major actions, decisions, and policies. They often make the difference between good and bad history and, in some respects, are as crucial as the basic sources for combat histories. Officers sometimes consider working papers personal property and destroy them upon reassignment, retirement, or completion of a particular action. Sometimes they are passed to a successor, but the files rarely are brought to the attention of the records manager or historian.

There probably is no simple solution to the problem of preserving action officer files. The functional filing system itself is ambivalent regarding their official status, and records managers have yet to devise a system to keep them intact. Conscientious application of the functional system contributes in part to the destruction of these files when agency records managers remove historically significant documents from the files because they are not considered records material or because they originate from another agency or office. Army historians occasionally resort to a variety of informal practices to compensate for this neglect. They often personally gain access to or acquire certain files pertaining to their current work. After crises, when historians have worked closely with action officers, working files and background papers have been entrusted by officers to staff historians for safekeeping and future reference. That the historian alone seeks out and preserves these valuable documents and files is symptomatic of a serious weakness in the functional filing system. Historians fully recognize that it is impossible and improper for them to act as records managers of working papers and action officer files, but occasionally the higher claims of history must take precedence over a system that inadvertently neglects important sources. Historians would prefer records management regulations that assure the retirement of these files.

Even if it were proper for historians to play an active role in obtaining action officer files, they cannot be expert in all the subjects addressed by a large staff. Volume alone makes difficult the identification of historically significant working papers. Judgments in many instances are often based upon intuition rather than expertise. Neither the historian nor the staff officer is immune from occasional professional astigmatism that inhibits his appreciation of less familiar subjects. In many cases the action officer is the expert who can guide historians and records managers, advising them of the existence of significant files and urging their retention. Being aware that files may have historical significance is the first step toward their preservation.

Selecting and Preserving Historical Sources

Without the professional acumen and guidance of an historian, archivist, or records manager, determining what documents to preserve is risky. In a field as catholic as military history, selection of sources may well reflect a variety of biases. For some historians and officers, operational records of battles and campaigns suffice; others with a larger view of military history want additional records. Yet difficult as it is to specify the nature of the records from which the history of the Army will be written, some general guidance can be tendered to the officer who has to wrestle with this problem. Whether in a field unit or a large headquarters staff, primary consideration should be given to preserving records required by the functional filing system. If applied with diligence and intelligence, the system generally will cover the most basic and important Army records. A leading archivist set forth a "basic rule" that "if records constitute the data upon which important decisions were made or illustrate the . . . decision making process, they are likely to be of historical importance."[2] This rule or reliance on the functional system alone can be restrictive, and any selection at all risks neglecting the narrow interest of a specialist. Nevertheless, records pertaining to the organization, mission, functions, operations, plans, and policies of a unit or agency will include those historical records serving the widest possible interests.

Familiarity with the functional filing system together with professional historical advice will identify many important historical records, but finding the more elusive Army documents requires thorough knowledge of an organization and its

---

2. Meyer H. Fishbein, "The Archivist Meets the Records Creator," *American Archivist* 28 (1965):195–97.

workings. Through contacts with key persons, historians often locate and acquire significant documents. Similarly, in the course of staff work an officer will become familiar with how decisions are made, who makes them, and where plans and studies are prepared. Action officer files contain pertinent documents, but individuals often possess diaries, memoranda of conversations, personal messages, and similar confidential communications. These can be extremely important historical sources. People who have documents like these sometimes are surprised to learn of their historical value. Once aware of the value, they may become reluctant to part with the documents because of their personal nature. Others part with them but insist that their use be restricted in one way or another, while some, fearing the disclosure of sensitive, critical, or embarrassing information, may seek to censor or suppress the documents. Suppression of information embarrassing to the Army is generally a disservice to the Army and to the cause of history, and historians discourage it. On the other hand, unless special provisions are made for the preservation of sensitive personal papers, they may be irretrievable. The Army has a special repository, the Military History Research Institute at Carlisle Barracks, Pennsylvania, for just such a purpose. At the institute even the most highly sensitive personal papers can be preserved until their use is approved by the donor. (See Chapter 12.)

Attention to the details of creating, maintaining, and retiring records not only helps assure their preservation but facilitates their use. Although lost in the anonymity of large bureaucracies, the Army's records clerks, file clerks, secretaries, and others play a vital role in preserving historical records. Historians and staff officers may find that these people know the records quite well. In the search for historical sources, their contributions can be as important as those of many decision makers and action officers.

Automatic Data Processing

With the introduction of computers, miniaturization, and sophisticated means of communication, records keeping and records management in the Army is becoming more complicated than the mere filing and retirement of pieces of paper. These rapidly expanding and highly technical fields are impinging on almost every aspect of modern records keeping. Although paper records are not about to be replaced entirely, they are but one medium for the transmission of information. And information conveyed by the records, rather than the nature of the records, is the historian's prime concern. Neither the records manager nor the historian has displayed an overwhelming concern about the historical value of new forms of documentation. The ramifications of these less traditional records for future historical research is still uncertain. Records managers and archivists are beginning to come to grips with some of the difficulties in identifying, evaluating, storing, retrieving, and preserving new forms of documentation. Military historians, likewise, are realizing that these records offer new opportunities for research and are seeking their preservation. Like many paper records, computer records and micro records are perishable, and much work remains to be done by historians, records managers, and archivists to make certain that they are available for future research.

Some of the Army's contemporary history will be difficult to write without computer records and computer analysis of historical data. Even combat history may require these records and techniques as the use of computers in tactical operations alters the nature and substance of operational records. Most reporting systems within the Army today depend at one stage or another upon computer operations, and historians using such reports are concerned about the possible loss of the raw data and the supporting documentation. Nearly every officer has already been or will be exposed to this new computer environment. A few will become experts, but even fewer will combine their expertise with an interest in military history. Until historians and records managers acquire the technical and specialized skills of computer experts, they will have to rely on advice and assistance from those individuals who can bridge the gap between computers and history. As with paper records, the first step toward preserving information for research and reference is recognition by those handling such information that it possesses intrinsic historical value.

Not many in the Army can make its historical programs and the historical aspects of records management a primary concern. Not even historians or records managers can devote their full attention to preserving historical records. But all Army officers can help make records management an effective adjunct to the Army's historical programs. This help may entail no more than becoming familiar with appropriate regulations and assuring that records are prepared, maintained, and retired. A more active role may be required when, for example, action officer files, personal papers, or records that escape the normal channels of retirement are involved. Motives for preserving historical documents vary from individual to individual. Pride in a unit's accomplishments or a desire to see that lessons are derived from a particular action are worthy motives, but most historical records do not have immediate value. As a sense of history and an appreciation of the role history plays in the Army grows, a feeling may also grow that a record of events is worth preserving for its own sake.

Few pat answers exist for the many problems in records management and its relation to military history. Other than current Army regulations, no manual tells officers or records managers how to recognize historical records. While the functional filing system is a starting point, and the historian's insight and intuition help in locating and evaluating documents, every officer should make certain that significant records in his or her custody are preserved. Command interest in and emphasis on records management and historical activities are important and necessary. Yet the success of the Army's historical programs depends on the cooperation of many people in saving today's records for generations of historians to come. This cooperation and the preservation of the Army's historical records serves not only one's unit, command, or agency, but also in the years to come the historical profession, the Army, and ultimately the American people.

Bibliography

To place records management in the larger context of its relationship to the archival and historical professions, there is no better starting point than H. G. Jones's *The Records of a Nation* (listed below), also the articles by W. Kaye Lamb and Philip D. Jordan. Still general but relevant to the problems discussed in this chapter are the articles by J. J. Hammit, Arnold Olson, and Gerald F. Brown.

Especially useful articles about records management are those of Everett O. Alldredge (1971), Ollon D. McCool, Maynard Brichford, Frank B. Evans, and Meyer H. Fishbein. Literature about the Army's records management program is limited. See Seymour J. Promrenze, Mable Deutrich, and Sherrod East. Army regulations pertaining to functional filing are also listed below. The impact of computer technology and other advances in information technology on records management is generating a tremendous amount of discussion, much of it highly technical. The following authors give a general introduction: Everett Alldredge (1965), Ben Cramer, Rodd S. Exelbert, Harry N. Fujita, Chester L. Guthrie, Morris Rieger, and Gerald J. Rosenkrantz.

Alldredge, Everett O. "Managing Records in a Computer Age." *Records Management Journal* 3 (1965):2–10.

––––––. "Trends in Records Management." *Information and Records Management* 5 (1971):15–16.

Army Regulations: AR 340-1, AR 340-2, AR 340-6, AR 340-18-1 to AR 340-18-5.

Brichford, Maynard. "The Relationship of Records Management Activities to the Field of Business History." *Business History Review* 46 (1972):220–32.

Brown, Gerald F. "The Archivist and Records Manager: A Records Manager's Viewpoint." *Records Management Quarterly* 5 (1971):21–22, 38.

Cramer, Ben. "New Horizons in Records Managements." *Records Management Quarterly* 6 (1972):5–6.

Deutrich, Mable. "Decimal Filing: Its General Background and an Account of Its Rise and Fall in the U.S. War Department." *American Archivist* 28 (1965):199–218.

East, Sherrod. "Archival Experience in a Prototype Intermediate Depository." *American Archivist* 27 (1964):43–56.

Evans, Frank B. "Archivists and Records Managers: Variations on a Theme." *American Archivist* 30 (1967):45–58.

Exelbert, Rodd S. "The Records Manager and Future Shock." *Information and Records Management* 5 (1971):6–7.

Fishbein, Meyer H. "The Archivist Meets the Records Creator." *American Archivist* 28 (1965):195–97.

Fujita, Harry N. "Is Records Management Dead?" *Information and Records Management* 4 (1970):28–29.

Guthrie, Chester L. "New Data to Shape History." *American Archivist* 30 (1967):323–31.

Hammit, J. J. "Government Archives and Records Management." *American Archivist* 28 (1965):219–22.

Jones, H. G. *The Records of a Nation: Their Management, Preservation, and Use.* New York: Atheneum, 1969.

Jordon, Philip D. "The Scholar and the Archivist—a Partnership." *American Archivist* 31 (1968):57–65.

Lamb, W. Kaye. "The Archivist and the Historian." *American Historical Review* 68 (1963):385–91.

McCool, Ollon D. "The Metes and Bounds of Records Management." *American Archivist* 27 (1964):87–93.

Olson, Arnold. "The Federal Paperwork Jungle—the Natives are Becoming Restless." *American Archivist* 27 (1964):363–70.

Promrenze, Seymour J. "Aspects of the Army's Records Management Program." *Records Management Journal* 9 (1971):18–25.

Rieger, Morris. "Archives and Automation." *American Archivist* 29 (1966):109–11.

Rosenkrantz, Gerald J. "What Should the Role of the Records Manager Be in the ADP Shop?" *Records Management Journal* 9 (1971):2–6.

Chapter **20**

Writing for Official and Unofficial Publication

Joseph R. Friedman

A distinguished astronaut came back from the moon and wrote a fine and lively volume about his experience on the ground and in space. His book could have been an overly technical hodgepodge of abstruse language, a dull history full of the nuts and bolts that made up his vehicle. The significant factor, for the person who wants to be published, can be found in the front matter of Michael Collins's book, one page after the dedication to his wife. On that page he thanks first his prep school English teacher, who taught him to write a sentence, then his editor, and then his typist. Now that is listing priorities right.

A number of years ago a historical manuscript full of interminable qualifying clauses, endless compartments of fuller amplification, and passive verbs that protected the doer of an unfortunate deed from exposure came to my desk. I asked the author, a gifted raconteur and a personable fellow, what he was trying to say. He told me, I took notes, gave them to him; he juggled them somewhat and produced something intelligible. His prose had become "muscular," as Samuel Eliot Morison counseled. Why, I asked him, didn't you do that in the first place? You catch your audience's interest immediately when you talk. You made your points clearly and strongly when you translated your prose for me. Why don't you write the way you talk?

His answer was simple. When I write, he said, I feel the hot breath of my fellow historians on my neck. When I talk, I feel freer to slide over the dull patches. This man had all the proper academic credentials, he had lived dangerously through World War II, he was by no means a dull pedant; but he feared the academic stilettos—and there are none sharper—of his fellow scholars.

You who read these words have been to the requisite military schools. You have had the courses in History and English

Mr. Friedman (B.A., Oberlin), CMH's Editor in Chief, 1952–76, does free-lance editing in retirement and is editorial consultant to the George C. Marshall Research Foundation.

considered necessary to attain your present state of grace. You may have had battlefield experience. Perhaps you wear a gold or silver bar. You might even sport twin bars or a gold oak leaf on your shoulder. Many of you have stars in your eyes. Having been exposed to appropriate education and training in how to study, and profit from, written military history, you have read the wise words purveyed in the preceding chapters of this book. Now you are presumably ready to advance your career to the point of producing fruits of your own that will nourish your colleagues and specialists in the broad acres of the field of military history.

How do you start producing? You start by using your own experience, your training, and your reading to give birth to ideas. As soon as the ideas mature enough, you start writing. Like truth and beauty, research can be its own excuse for being. But beauty, too blatant or contrived, is a drug on the market. Truth, told in unrestrained detail, can become tiresome. The most effective form of research consists of plucking the important verities of a situation from a confusing mass of items. This is the beginning of writing.

For purposes of this guide, research must be considered as a means to an end, and one of these ends is writing. There are those who find the act of writing so difficult and the fussy detail in research so fascinating that they put off the end and concentrate interminably on the means. This approach does not make for a high rate of production. The obvious answer, of course, is to get on with the writing as soon as possible. To do so will facilitate research as well as writing because the prose put down will undoubtedly expose holes. To fill in the holes more research is necessary, but this kind of research will be better directed and more meaningful as the inevitable gaps that must be filled become more readily apparent.

It is perhaps tarnishing the gilt on the lily to repeat what has been attributed to the late New Yorker editor, Harold Ross, that easy writing makes damn hard reading. The first thing to do to ease the burden of the reader is to establish a pattern. Is your material to be told chronologically? Is it to be told topically? Is it to emerge as a combination of the two, which is generally the case in anything more complex than a child's nursery rhyme?

Unless the end result is to amount to a gloworm without the glow, it must be given some sort of bone structure. The bone structure sets the pattern, and the pattern must be discernible under the fleshing or words, not too fat, not too lean, akin in many respects to the features of an attractive human being.

When the word writing comes up, it is inevitable that style

shoves its head in and must be dealt with. It is well known that most words in the English language have more than one definition—take the multiple meaning of the little word *get* for a sample. Style, in its most important definition, is impossible to teach. For it is the result of lifelong habits. It would be as rewarding to teach such a subject, and as fruitless, as to teach personality to an oaf or to stimulate a recognition of pitch in the ear of someone who is tone deaf. These components of the human character are built up from the time the baby rewards his mother and his deliverer by making his first outcry against the injustices of the world he is thrust into. His personality, his ear, his style are from that moment on the product of his genes, his conversations with his parents or whoever happens to have the job of rearing him, and his reading, his writing, and his ways of coping with or circumventing the traps that lie in wait for all creatures on earth. To teach style in this meaning would be as misleading and meretricious as to claim that ear training is a useful service in overcoming an inherent inability to distinguish sharp from flat. The claim is false. If one needs this kind of training, he might well consider a different outlet for his energies.

Too many tyros in the business of writing believe that a one-shot course in how to write is the answer to questionable evils. This is the approach of an overoptimistic dilettante who would survive neither a battlefield nor a skirmish with a publisher. It encourages people who should never have unslung their pencils from their hosters to use their weapons indiscriminately, indefinitely, ambiguously, and, more to the point, inaccurately.

Another kind of style, however, is teachable. It consists of what might be called the mechanics of writing. A good editor can be of immense service. But it would be helpful to him and to you to get a few things squared away before you embark on your literary endeavors. Not until you begin to write do you come up against the gadfly dilemmas of whether a number should be written out or not, an organization should begin with a capital letter or not, a last name should appear first in a footnote or not, a page of manuscript should be double-spaced or not, a simple comma should be inserted or not. These little problems are only the beginning. When, for example, does one use a plural verb with a collective noun? Most of the time in England, but only sometimes in the United States. When is the antecedent of a noun of doubtful parentage? When do you use the third edition of Merriam-Webster or the second edition? These are all fleabite questions, but readers scratch what they consider to be the wrong answer raw. The world is full of a number of things, but to the writer it sometimes seems to be populated by nitpickers. It should be remembered that nits are young lice, and manuscripts afflicted with them can justifiably be called lousy.

It would give the writer and his critics comfort to include here a style manual. But to do so could lull the reader of this guide into a false sense of security. Different publishers have different rules. If you are to appear under the aegis of Prentice-Hall and you wish to quote fifty or more words of copyrighted material from a single publication, you must secure written permission from the copyright owner. The same rule applies at the Army's Center of Military History. But if you are to be published by Harper and Row the magic number is five hundred words. Commas and other pieces of punctuation tend to be used or not used according to the house style. The strict (some might say old-fashioned) approach is to use a comma after even the shortest of dependent phrases, if these phrases open a sentence. Other firms disdain this grammatical nicety.

The Center of Military History has a style manual of its own. The one used by most commercial publishers in this country is the latest edition of *A Manual of Style*, published by The University of Chicago Press. If the Government Printing Office is to be your publisher, the latest edition of its *Style Manual* is required. If other publishers are involved, they should be queried as to whether they have a style manual or what their predilections are. If you are fortunate enough to have an understanding editor, he can supply much help.

The first thing a historian who intends to get into print should do is to look at the marketplace. The *Literary Market Place* (LMP) (New York: R. R. Bowker Company, published annually) is an obvious first choice. It can be obtained at virtually any library. Any good librarian of your choice can give you the names and addresses of other reference works that will help in determining possible publishers of your material. If you are near a large library, check the magazines in its current periodicals room. What kind of articles do they use? How long are they? Does a journal publish popular or serious material? Unlike books, articles usually have to be written with a particular publisher in mind. It goes without saying that if you have written *Jonathan Livingston Seagull* (New York: Macmillan, 1972) such help that is advised in these paragraphs is unnecessary. But the Bachs, both the best-selling literary type and the incomparable musician, both Richard and Johann Sebastian, are few and far between. This section is directed at those who do not possess extraordinary gifts.

The bibliography that follows may seem a bit slight. But not because of the canard that blossoming officers can digest only specially prepared portions. This assessment smacks of a slur on the brain cells and the intellectual digestive system of young people who wear a uniform. They can eat and drink of literature as well as their brothers and sisters who study and work in jeans.

Anyone who wants to write should read, in addition to the following, anything he can lay hands and eyes on: good and bad history, good and bad magazines, cookbooks, obesity cures, telephone books (mainly the yellow pages), even ungrammatical advertisements. He should live it up in words. Follett's *Modern American Usage* should be in his regimen as well as Fowler's *Modern English Usage*, which *is* on the list. The Bible and Shakespeare are omitted from it because they are staples of literary life. Like well-taught English courses, they are prerequisites for writing of readable prose, whether history or not.

It would be remiss for a chapter on research and writing to omit the title of probably the most helpful and therapeutic book on the subject: *The Elements of Style*, by William Strunk, Jr., and E. B. White. It is full of common sense, which is a commodity that writers can always use. The most indispensable tool of all, however, is the ability to read voluminously, to digest what is read, and to translate the acquired knowledge into articulate meaning for others. This is the tool that cuts to the heart of what research and writing are all about.

Selected Bibliography

Bartlett, John. *Familiar Quotations: A Collection of Passages, Phrases, and Proverbs Traced to Their Sources in Ancient and Modern Literature.* Edited by Emily Morison Beck. 14th ed., revised and enlarged. Boston: Little, Brown, 1968.

Bernstein, Theodore M. *Miss Thistlebottom's Hobgoblins: The Careful Writer's Guide to the Taboos, Bugbears, and Outmoded Rules of English Usage.* New York: Farrar, Straus and Giroux, 1971.

Collins, Michael. *Carrying the Fire.* New York: Farrar, Straus and Giroux, 1974.

Fowler, H. W. *A Dictionary of Modern English Usage.* Revised by Sir Ernest Gowers. 2d ed. New York: Oxford Univ. Press, 1965.

A Manual of Style. 12th ed., rev. Chicago: Univ. of Chicago Press, 1969.

Morison, Samuel Eliot. "History as a Literary Art." In *By Land and By Sea: Essays and Addresses.* New York: A. A. Knopf, 1953.

The Original Roget's Thesaurus of English Words and Phrases. Completely revised and modernized by Robert A. Dutch. New York: Longmans, Green, 1962.

Strunk, William, Jr., and White, E. B. *The Elements of Style*. 2d ed., rev. New York: Macmillan, 1972.

Wheelock, John Hall, ed. *Editor To Author: The Letters of Maxwell E. Perkins*. New York: Scribner's, 1950.

The Writing of American Military History: A Guide. DA Pamphlet 20-200. Washington: Government Printing Office, 1956.

Four

History Outside the U.S. Army

Chapter **21**

Military History in the Department of Defense

Romana Danysh

WITHIN the Department of Defense are several historical agencies and programs comparable to those of the United States Army. The Secretary of Defense, the Joint Chiefs of Staff, the Air Force, the Navy, and the Marine Corps all have historical offices. In fact, the Department of Defense is the largest employer of professional historians in the federal government. Each of the military services also teaches history in its schools and encourages the study of military history as a professionally rewarding activity, and many military officers have graduate degrees in history.

The Office of the Secretary of Defense

Recognizing the need for maintaining a historical record of the activities of his office and its associated boards and staffs, James Forrestal, the first Secretary of Defense, established the position of Historian, Office of the Secretary of Defense, on 8 March 1949. In December of that year Forrestal's successor, Louis Johnson, issued a directive outlining the major duties of the historian: collecting and preserving historical documents, writing a thorough and objective history of the Office of the Secretary of Defense, preparing the secretary's semiannual report to the president and Congress, and coordinating historical projects within the Department of Defense.

Over the years these functions have varied according to the specific assignments given by each Secretary of Defense, the changing requirements of the times, and the historian's interpretation of his responsibilities. The secretary's report, for example, was published semiannually until June 1958, on a fiscal-year basis from 1959 to 1968, and then discontinued. Recently, there has been much greater emphasis on writing the history of the

Miss Danysh (M.A., Stanford), of the Staff Support Branch, CMH, is coauthor of *Infantry, Part I: Regular Army* (Army Lineage Series) and is preparing Part II on the Army Reserve and National Guard.

Office of the Secretary of Defense. In addition to several volumes of this general history, a number of special studies are also being prepared for publication, including a two-volume history on prisoners of war in Southeast Asia, a history of military assistance, and a documentary volume on the organization of the Department of Defense from 1947 to the present. Professional historians, hired on a consultant basis, are writing most of these publications, since the small permanent historical staff, consisting of the OSD historian, his deputy, another historian, and a secretary, has many other duties.

Collection of historical documents remains one of the major missions, and interviews with important present and former Department of Defense officials are now being conducted to supplement the written records. The historical staff cooperates closely with the State Department in preparing for publication the documentary series, *Foreign Relations of the United States*. The staff also works on many special projects for the Secretary of Defense and other high officials, ranging from brief replies to simple reference questions to comprehensive historical studies on complex topics.

Although the OSD historian is responsible for coordinating historical activities in the Department of Defense, this coordination is largely informal. Even before his position was created in 1949, the Army, Air Force, Navy, Marine Corps, and Joint Chiefs of Staff already had historical programs of their own, and no attempt has ever been made to unify them into a single defense historical program. Nevertheless, the OSD historian maintains close contact with all historical agencies in the department and serves as the senior historian for the Department of Defense.

The Joint Chiefs of Staff

The Joint Chiefs of Staff created the JCS Historical Section on 2 October 1945, when they agreed to designate an Army officer and a Navy officer, of suitable background and ability, to write the official history of the Joint Chiefs of Staff. By the end of the year there were six officers in the new section. In December 1946 the Joint Chiefs named the heads of the War and Navy Department historical offices as the senior Army member and senior Navy member, adding a senior Air Force member in November 1950. Five volumes of the official JCS history were completed by mid-1954 when the section temporarily suspended work on the history because of an increasing number of higher priority tasks.

On 8 March 1955 the Joint Chiefs of Staff issued a charter for the Historical Section designating it as the agency responsible for all historical matters within their organization. The charter provided that the section would function under the Director of the Joint Staff and would no longer be subordinate to the group of senior service members. Except for a military chief, personnel were to be professional civilian historians. In 1958 the section was transferred to the Joint Secretariat and renamed the Historical Division; on 1 January 1961 it was reorganized to consist of a Histories Branch and a Special Projects Branch. Work on volumes of the official JCS history resumed in 1961 with the understanding that the division would continue to give priority to special projects. Since October 1964, a civilian historian has served as the chief of the Historical Division.

At present the main function of the Histories Branch is to prepare volumes describing the organizational development and major activities of the Joint Chiefs of Staff. The Special Projects Branch is responsible for producing special studies. It also furnishes staff historical support to other components of the Joint Chiefs of Staff and reviews the annual historical reports required of all unified and specified commands. Although JCS histories are primarily for internal use, copies are distributed to the chiefs of the military services and to the senior service schools. Once declassified, they are placed with the JCS records in the National Archives where they are available to the general public.

The Air Force

The Air Force historical program traces its origin to 1942 when a Historical Division was established in Headquarters, Army Air Forces, as a result of President Roosevelt's request that each government agency prepare an administrative record of its wartime activities. The program continued after the end of World War II and after the establishment of the U.S. Air Force as a separate service. In September 1949 the central historical office moved to the Air University at Maxwell Air Force Base, Alabama, leaving only a small liaison office in Washington, D.C.

During the two decades that the Historical Division remained at the Air University, it completed a seven-volume history, *The Army Air Forces in World War II*, edited by Wesley Frank Craven and James Lea Cate (1948–58), and published a history of the Air Force from 1907 to 1957, two volumes containing brief histories of Air Force combat units of World War II, and a volume on the

Air Force in Korea. The authors and editors of these publications were either division members or former Army Air Forces historians who had returned to academic life after World War II. The division also prepared a long series of monographs called USAF Historical Studies, worked on many special studies, projects, and reports, maintained a growing archival collection, and answered various requests for historical information. At the same time, it supervised a global field program covering current activities, which was the largest part of the Air Force historical program thoughout this period.

A major reorganization and a fundamental change in the objectives of the historical program took place in January 1969. The liaison office was absorbed by the Office of Air Force History, a new special staff agency of Headquarters, U.S. Air Force, headed by a general officer and manned by civilian and military historians, editors, and administrative personnel. This agency assumed responsibility for directing the Air Force historical program. Since 1969, the main goal of the program has been to publish comprehensive and scholarly historical accounts of Air Force activities which serve as guides for planning, training, and operations, preserve the history of the Air Force and its predecessors, and inform the public about the role of air power in peace and war.

Recent publications include a monograph on the battle of Khe San, an annotated bibliography on Air Force history, a chronology of the Army Air Forces in World War II, a four-volume documentary history of the Air Service in World War I, and an illustrated history of the Air Force in Southeast Asia. Several monographs and a series of narrative volumes on the war in Vietnam as well as major studies of air defense and strategic deterrence since World War II are currently in preparation. Within the Office of Air Force History, the Histories Division with its General Histories, Special Histories, and Editorial Branches is responsible for the publication program. The office also has a Support Division consisting of reference services and administration, and there is a special assistant for field history programs.

The former Historical Division at Maxwell Air Force Base, redesignated the Historical Research Division in 1969, is now an organizational element of the Air University, subject to the policy guidance and operational control of the Office of Air Force History. In May 1972 it was renamed the Albert F. Simpson Historical Research Center in memory of the man who served as the Air Force's chief historian from 1946 to 1969. The center is the principal repository for Air Force historical records. It collects and preserves historical materials of archival significance, determines combat credits and unit lineage, answers historical inquiries, prepares special studies and publications, conducts oral history programs, and furnishes other historical and archival services. The major portion of the center's extensive archival collection consists of unit histories and supporting documents that Air Force organizations have submitted periodically since 1942.

Although the publication effort now has top priority, the field work remains a significant part of the overall historical program. Each major command and numbered air force (or comparable organization) is required to maintain a separate historical office staffed by professional historians. Command historians, in the past usually subordinate to public information officers, now report directly to their commanders. They supervise all historical activity in the organization, prepare monographs and special studies, and submit annual histories. Quarterly historical reports are prepared by wing-level units and by independent groups and squadrons not reporting to a wing. The Air Force awards a special plaque to the "Wing Historian of the Year" for the best quarterly history over the preceding fiscal year.

There is also a field program called Project CHECO (Contemporary Historical Examination of Current Operations), which began in June 1962 in Vietnam as a type of after-action reporting in support of the Air Staff. The Office of Air Force History is responsible for establishing future CHECO field offices during wartime or other emergency situations in order to provide timely historical documentation of air operations.

At present, 145 colleges and universities have Air Force ROTC programs. The curriculum consists of a two-year general military course followed by a two-year professional officer course, with the second year of the general course devoted to the history of air power. The core curriculum at the Air Force Academy in Colorado Springs includes courses in history, one of which is a survey of modern warfare and society. In addition to the required courses, there are numerous history electives, several on military topics. The academy also offers a history major of particular value for cadets contemplating careers in operations, plans, or intelligence. In 1959 the annual Harmon Memorial Lecture in military history was inaugurated in honor of the first superintendent of the academy, Lt. Gen. Hubert R. Harmon. Each year the academy invites a leading military historian to present an original lecture in this distinguished series. Since 1967 it has also sponsored a series of military history symposia, currently on a biennial basis, designed to encourage interest in military history among the cadets, members of the armed forces, professional historians, and other scholars. The proceedings of the symposia are published jointly by the Air Force Academy and the Office of Air Force History.

None of the schools in the Air University at Maxwell Air Force Base teaches military history as an independent subject or separate study area, but history provides background for various study areas, particularly in the university's senior school, the Air War College.

The Navy

The origins of the Navy's historical program may be traced to President John Adams's directive in 1800 to the first Secretary of the Navy to establish a library, the initiation of a project in 1881 to collect and publish naval records of the Civil War, and the establishment of an Office of Library and Naval War Records in 1884. Between 1894 and 1922 that office and its successor, the Office of Naval Records and Library, published thirty volumes of *Offical Records of the Union and Confederate Navies in the War of the Rebellion*, with a general index completing the series in 1927.

To collect World War I historical material and record wartime operations, a history section was organized under the Chief of Naval Operations in 1918. The section was later transferred to the Office of Naval Records and Library, which published eight of the monographs written on World War I. After completion of the volumes of Civil War records, it published two other documentary series, one on the quasi war with France (seven volumes, 1935-38) and one on the Barbary wars (six volumes, 1939-44). The head of the office was also designated Curator for the Navy Department in 1930.

With the outbreak of World War II, the Office of Naval Records and Library began to systematically collect documents on the war. Early in 1942, the Navy commissioned Samuel Eliot Morison of Harvard University and assigned him the responsibility of writing a history of naval operations; in February 1943, Robert G. Albion of Princeton was entrusted with supervising the documentation of wartime Navy Department administration. To coordinate the preparation of wartime histories, a flag officer was designated Director of Naval History in 1944. After the war, his office merged with the Office of Naval Records and Library, which was renamed the Naval History Division in 1952. The main products of the World War II effort were about three hundred unpublished bound volumes of administrative histories, Morison's fifteen-volume *History of United States Naval Operations in World War II* (1947–62), and Rear Admiral Julius A. Furer's *Administration of the Navy Department in World War II* (1959). To provide coverage of the Korean War, James A. Field of Swarthmore College, under contract to the Naval History Division, wrote a one-volume history of naval operations.

The Director of Naval History gained added responsibilities when the Navy Memorial Museum opened in the Washington Navy Yard in 1963. Both the division and the museum are now parts of the Naval Historical Center established on 1 December 1971 at the Navy Yard. The Director of Naval History, a flag officer on the staff of the Chief of Naval Operations, is also Director of the Naval Historical Center, as well as Curator for the Navy Department. The Secretary of the Navy's advisory committee on naval history, composed of civilian scholars, reviews the programs and activities of the center and its members serve as consultants.

The Naval History Division has many functions and duties including research, writing, and publishing in American naval history. It maintains library, archival, and curatorial facilities that provide a wide variety of historical and staff services to the Navy Department, other official users, visiting scholars, and the general public. The Navy Department Library is one branch of the Naval History Division. Another branch, the Operational Archives, collects and services naval records relating primarily to operations, policy, and strategy from 1940 to the present. The division's Ships History Branch keeps files on all ships that have served in the Navy, prepares histories of these ships, and recommends names and sponsors for new ships. The Curator Branch has custody of thousands of artifacts, numerous prints and paintings, and a large collection of historic photographs. A fifth branch, the Historical Research Branch, concentrates on research, writing, and editing of naval documents for publication. Although each branch has certain specific functions, all branches share the division's general reference and staff support work and participate in its publication program.

Before World War II the Navy's historical publications consisted largely of collections of documents, but since the war they have become more diversified. The current Naval History Division catalog lists histories, biographies, chronologies, bibliographic and archival guides, illustrated paperback pamphlets, and historical prints, as well as documentary series. In the past, interpretive historical narratives were usually written by academic historians like Morison and Field or by professional Navy officers like Furer. Although not members of the Naval History Division, these authors were sponsored by that office, had full access to official records, and received research, editorial, and administrative assistance from the division. Recently, however, division personnel began to work on a major narrative history of the Navy in the Vietnam conflict. Another important publication now in preparation is the *Dictionary of American Naval Fighting Ships*. Of the projected eight volumes, six are in print, containing brief histories of all commissioned ships whose names begin with the letters *A* through *S*. A third major current project is the multivolume series entitled *Naval Documents of the American Revolution*, seven volumes of which (covering the period from December 1774 to February 1777) have been published to date.

The Naval Historical Center at the Washington Navy Yard also has administrative responsibility for the Department of the Navy Declassification Team. The team, which is Navy-wide and includes representatives from the Marine Corps, was organized in 1972 as a special agency for systematic review of classified records. Outside the Naval Historical Center are several full-time historians in some of the major commands, bureaus, and offices of the Navy Department, and all ships and commands are required to prepare annual histories.

Although the Navy's school system emphasizes technical and scientific subjects, some history is taught at every educational level. At the Naval Academy in Annapolis all plebes must take a semester of Modern Western Civilization and a semester of American Naval Heritage, and many midshipmen take other history courses as part of their humanities and social sciences requirements or as electives. A history major provides a basic background as well as the opportunity for specialized study in American, European, non-Western, naval, or military history. The academy held its first historical symposium on 8 May 1972, with twentieth-century American naval history as the theme and Samuel Eliot Morison as the guest of honor. Similar meetings were held in 1973 and 1977 and others are scheduled for the future.

Naval ROTC programs are currently conducted on fifty-eight campuses. The curriculum includes a required course on the history of sea power and maritime affairs and an elective in

American military affairs. Students selecting the Marine Corps option take two additional history-oriented courses on the evolution of warfare and amphibious operations. The Naval Postgraduate School in Monterey, California, places major emphasis on advanced degrees in science and engineering, but its Department of National Security Affairs offers several history electives, one of which covers recent insurgency warfare. The Naval War College at Newport, Rhode Island, teaches strategy and policy by means of a series of historical case studies starting with the Peloponnesian War. Among the chairs for visiting professors at the college is the Ernest J. King Chair of Maritime History, established after World War II in honor of the wartime Chief of Naval Operations and Commander in Chief, U.S. Fleet. Over the years, this position has been held by outstanding military and naval historians.

The Marine Corps

On 1 December 1971 the Commandant of the Marine Corps named a general officer as Director of Marine Corps History and Museums and put him in charge of the Historical Division with responsibility for the formulation, conduct, and supervision of the Marine Corps historical program. In the past, the historical office had been a section, a branch, and a division, attached from time to time to different parts of Headquarters, U.S. Marine Corps, while some historical functions had been assigned to other agencies, such as the Division of Information and the Marine Corps Museum.

The first Marine Corps historical office was organized in 1919. It operated largely as a reference service and a records depository until the end of World War II, when a sustained historical writing program was added to its reference and archival functions. Between 1947 and 1955 the office published fifteen monographs describing individual World War II campaigns from the defense of Wake Island to victory on Okinawa. These monographs served as preliminary studies for the official five-volume *History of U.S. Marine Corps Operations in World War II* (1958–71). A number of articles written by members of the historical office for the *Marine Corps Gazette* during the Korean War became the basis for another five-volume history, *U.S. Marine Operations in Korea* (1954–72).

On 15 October 1973 the Historical Division was redesignated as the History and Museums Division. It is a special staff activity of Headquarters, U.S. Marine Corps, and the director reports directly to the commandant. There are two deputy directors, one for each branch of the division. The Historical Branch supervises the preparation and publication of official Marine Corps histories and the preparation of historical studies in support of planning, some of which may be published for wider distribution. The branch plans and coordinates the writing effort, administers a comprehensive oral history program, serves as the principal research and documentation center for Marine Corps history, and prepares lineage and honors certificates for all Marine Corps units.

The publications of the Historical Branch range from simple pamphlets to multivolume histories. A definitive, thoroughly documented, and extensively illustrated history entitled *Marines in the Revolution*, published in 1975, was the Marine Corps' major contribution to the bicentennial celebration. Currently under preparation are several unit histories, a comprehensive chronology of Marine Corps history from 1775 to 1975, and a variety of narrative studies, including nine monographs on Marine operations in Vietnam. The monographs will be followed by an official multivolume history of the Marine Corps in Vietnam, comparable to the World War II and Korean War series. Authors of such publications are civilian historians, Marine Corps officers, or civilian-military teams that combine professional experience in historical research and writing with extensive military knowledge.

The second branch of the History and Museums Division is the Museums Branch. Its main function is to collect, preserve, and exhibit objects, memorabilia, artwork, and personal papers of lasting historical and traditional value to the Marine Corps. The branch provides technical support to Marine Corps command museums at various posts and stations and operates the Marine Corps Museum in the Washington Navy Yard. That museum is in the Marine Corps Historical Center, which houses the entire Historical Branch and most of the Museums Branch. The ordnance and aviation collections are located at the Marine Corps base in Quantico, Virginia.

Although the primary focus of the Marine Corps historical program is the Marine Corps itself, the program also emphasizes service to the Department of Defense and other government agencies, to the academic community, and to the general public. Most Marine Corps organizations, including all Fleet Marine Force and Marine Corps Reserve units down to the battalion and separate company level, submit annual or semiannual command chronologies. Marine Corps staff historians in the field prepare historical reports, collect historical documents, and conduct oral history interviews. The field program also includes collection of items of potential historical significance and other museum activities.

In the Education Center of the Marine Corps Development and Education Command at Quantico, Virginia, military history courses are part of the required program at the Basic School, the Communication Officers School, and the Amphibious Warfare School, while the Command and Staff College offers two electives in the field. On 8 April 1972 Quantico hosted the Marine Corps' first conference on military and naval history, which was modeled after the military history symposia of the Air Force Academy. Future conferences may be held at the Marine Corps Historical Center in the Washington Navy Yard.

The Coast Guard

Although the Coast Guard is in the Department of Transportation, it is one of the military services and operates as a part of the Navy in wartime. At present, the Coast Guard has neither a separate historical office nor an official historical program comparable to those of the other services. Its only professional historian is assigned to the Public Affairs Division, where his principal function is to provide a historical reference service for official and public use.

The Coast Guard's most significant historical publications to date have been a series of thirty monographs entitled The Coast Guard at War, which came out in limited editions between June 1944 and January 1954. They cover the entire range of Coast Guard participation in World War II, with each monograph devoted to a separate phase of the service's multifaceted wartime activities. The first monograph was prepared by the Statistical Division, while all the rest were written by the Historical Section of the Public Information Division. After the completion of that project, the Coast Guard had no historical staff until 1970, when a historian was appointed.

The historian has published an annotated bibliography listing books, monographs, and pamphlets dealing in whole or in part with the Coast Guard and its predecessors and a detailed, documented chronology of the evolution of the Coast Guard's aids to navigation. Recently the Public Affairs Division also initiated a publication program of historical works prepared by

Coast Guardsmen on their own time, including bibliographies, chronologies, transcripts of interviews, and monographs on various aspects of Coast Guard history. The first product of this program was an unclassified account of the activities of the Coast Guard in Southeast Asia, published in 1975.

At the Coast Guard Academy in New London, Connecticut, incoming cadets receive orientation lectures in Coast Guard history, and a semester of American history is part of the core curriculum. In addition, there are several elective history courses. No history major as such is offered, but the academy's government major includes history. Coast Guard history is also taught at the Officer Candidate School in the Coast Guard Reserve Training Center at Yorktown, Virginia.

Bibliography: General

Ad Hoc Committee, Department of the Army. "Report on the Army Need for the Study of Military History." 4 vols. West Point, N.Y., 1971. See "Military History in the United States Navy and United States Air Force," 1:43–44; and "Military History in the Other Military Services," Vol. 3, Annex M.

Higham, Robin, ed. Official Histories: Essays and Bibliographies From Around the World. Manhattan: Kans. State Univ. Library, 1970. See articles in the section entitled "Why Official History?" pp. 9–45, as well as in the section, "United States," pp. 528–640.

Leopold, Richard W. "Historical Advisory Committees: State, Defense, and the Atomic Energy Commission." Pacific Historical Review 44 (Aug. 1975):373–85.

Rundell, Walter, Jr. "The U.S. Government's Historical Programs." Congressional Record, 91st Cong., 1st sess., Dec. 18, 1969, pp. H12772–78.

———. "Uncle Sam the Historian: Federal Historical Activities." The Historian 33 (Nov. 1970):1–20.

Bibliography: Air Force

"The Air Force Historical Program." Aerospace Historian 19 (Sep. 1972):119.

*Air Force Regulation 210–1. "Regulation for Air Force Historians." 28 Jan. 1977.

*Air Force Regulation 210–3. "Air Force Historical Program." 10 June 1977.

Correll, John T. "In Pursuit of the Past." Airman 19 (Aug. 1975):12–16.

*Cresswell, Mary Ann, and Berger, Carl. United States Air Force History: An Annotated Bibliography. Washington: Government Printing Office, 1971. Includes publications of the Office of Air Force History and its predecessors.

Ginsburgh, Robert N. "A Fresh Look at History in the Air Force." Aerospace Historian 19 (Sep. 1972):114–18.

*Paszek, Lawrence J. United States Air Force History: A Guide to Documentary Sources. Washington: Government Printing Office, 1973. See "The Albert F. Simpson Historical Research Center," pp. 1–23.

"Shaping Things to Come." Airman 17 (Sep. 1973):7–10. Interview with Brig. Gen. Brian S. Gunderson, Chief, Office of Air Force History.

Simpson, Albert F. "The USAF Historical Division and Its Program." In *Official Histories: Essays and Bibliographies From Around the World,* edited by Robin Higham, pp. 603-19.

Bibliography: Navy

*Allard, Dean C., and Bern, Betty. *U.S. Naval History Sources in the Washington Area and Suggested Research Topics.* 3d ed., rev. and enlarged. Washington: Government Printing Office, 1970. See "Naval History Division," pp. 1-10.

Eller, Ernest M. "Naval History Division Documentary Publications." In *Official Histories: Essays and Bibliographies From Around the World,* edited by Robin Higham, pp. 528-35.

———. "The Navy's Historians." U.S. Naval Institute *Proceedings* 89 (Apr. 1963):96-109.

McElroy, J. W. "Office of Naval Records and Library, 1882-1946." Unpublished study (1946) available in Navy Department Library.

*Naval History Division. *United States Naval History: A Bibliography.* 6th ed. Washington: Government Printing Office, 1972. See pp. 89-91 for publications of the Naval History Division and its predecessors.

*"Naval History Division Publications in Print." Processed pamphlet. Washington: Naval History Division, Mar. 1977.

Bibliography: Marine Corps

Fortitudine: Newsletter of the Marine Corps Historical Program. Washington: Marine Corps History and Museums Division, 1972-. Published quarterly.

*Frank, Benis M. *Marine Corps Oral History Collection Catalog.* Rev. ed. Washington: Marine Corps History and Museum Division, 1975.

"Marine Corps Historical Program Progress Report." Washington: Marine Corps History and Museums Division, 1 July 1972-. Issued annually.

Marine Corps Historical Publications Catalog. Washington: Marine Corps History and Museums Division, 1975.

*Marine Corps Order P5750.1D. "Manual for the Marine Corps Historical Program." 11 Apr. 1972.

Shaw, Henry I., Jr. "The Historical Publications of the U.S. Marine Corps." In *Official Histories: Essays and Bibliographies From Around the World,* edited by Robin Higham, pp. 543-50.

*Wood, Charles Anthony. *Marine Corps Personal Papers Collection Catalog.* Washington: Marine Corps History and Museums Division, 1974.

Bibliography: Coast Guard

*Strobridge, Truman R. *United States Coast Guard Annotated Bibliography.* Washington: Government Printing Office, 1972. Includes official Coast Guard historical publications.

---

* Revised, updated, and reissued at irregular intervals.

Chapter 22

Official
Programs Abroad

Alfred M. Beck

AS long as rulers and governments have existed, they have recorded their memorable deeds, especially martial successes, in officially subsidized narratives. Among the earliest archaeological artifacts are clay tablets bearing cuneiform campaign histories of ancient Assyrian and Mesopotamian kings. Alexander the Great commissioned Eumenes of Cardia as chronicler of his military exploits. The historical record of human conflict relies heavily on officially sponsored, and therefore officially sanctioned, versions of events. The modern era extended the practice with the establishment of archives among the absolute monarchies of seventeenth- and eighteenth-century Europe, for preserving records of diplomacy, dynastic ambition, and military planning and warfare. The formal organization of military records in specialized collections facilitated their use in compiling summaries of campaigns and battles. Official military history thereafter was nearly exclusively the province of active or retired military officers, who sought tactical principles for aspiring officers or precedents supporting existing doctrine or staff procedures. Such battle studies, although meticulously detailed, gave virtually no consideration to the wider economic and social implications of warfare. This limited form of analysis and the organization to support it were nowhere so developed as in the Historical Section of the Prussian Great General Staff; its work was widely emulated in the post-Napoleonic armies of Europe.

Even within their narrow focus, the official histories raised controversy. Some works frequently ran beyond a simple establishment of fact or doctrinal lessons and sought justification or exculpation for tactical errors or faulty defense policies. Many studies were so self-serving that they soured the reputation of official history and contributed to the lingering suspi-

Dr. Beck (Ph.D., Georgetown), of the General History Branch, CMH, is preparing a study of U.S. military government and civil administration in the Ryukyu Islands, 1945–72.

415

cion with which it is still regarded in scholarly circles. The official program of the Habsburg empire was known for its irregularities. Litigation and even duels resulted from allegations made in some Prussian official histories in the nineteenth century; and Sir Basil Liddell Hart, having worked on the British official history of World War I, maintained long afterwards that "'Official History' is a contradiction in terms—the word official tends to qualify, and often cancels out the word 'history'."[1]

The sheer magnitude of the two world conflicts of the twentieth century made a heavy imprint upon official military historical programs abroad and led to developments which many of the leading programs share in some degree today. To deal with the massive record of both wars, some governments turned to civilian professionals for objective portrayals of the events, especially after World War II. The British and the Australian series fell under the jurisdiction of a general editor, an organizational innovation that also influenced the American official program after 1945. After 1918 the histories began to recognize that total war affects the whole of modern society. Official histories of World War II acknowledge further the burdens and accomplishments of the home front and explore the intricacies of the mobilization of societies and national economies for war. The number of volumes devoted to the home front in World War II has rivaled those devoted to combat, and far more serious consideration is given logistical and other technical support of combat forces, often in specialized subseries volumes.

New approaches in official historical projects were common after World War II. Among the major European powers and Japan, all except the French program were conceived as joint efforts of the armed forces. Although neither uniform nor everywhere permanent, this development contrasted with the American practice in which official history programs remained divided among the armed services, the Joint Chief of Staff, and the Department of Defense. Even a brief survey of some of the major official programs reveal distinctive characteristics.[2]

---

1. B.H. Liddell Hart, "Responsibility and Judgement in Historical Writing," *Military Affairs* 23, no. 1 (Spring 1959):35.

2. Unless otherwise noted, information on the national programs is drawn from Robin Higham, ed., *Official Histories: Essays and Bibliographies From Around the World* (Manhattan: Kans. State Univ. Library, 1970). It gives comprehensive studies of the national programs dealt with here.

Germany

The German effort, much changed since its re-establishment after the collapse of 1945, commands attention among European historical offices as the heir to a tradition envied and imitated among military staffs over a century ago. Though the tradition of official military historical writing was common among Prussian kings and army officers, it took a radical turn in 1807. With the reform movement that sought to redress the disastrous defeat at Jena the previous year, Generals Gerhard Johann Scharnhorst and August Neithardt Gneisenau employed extensive and self-critical historical analyses in adapting Napoleonic military and administrative genius to Prussian use.[3] Scharnhorst's pupil, Captain Carl Wilhelm von Grolman, preserved this methodology when he established the War History Section of the Prussian General Staff in 1816. Renamed the Department of Military History in 1824, the section combined writing branches, the war archives, and the production staff of the *Militärwochenblatt* (Military Weekly), which published supplements containing the department's battle and campaign studies and biographic material illustrating the principles of leadership. One branch of the department under the elder von Moltke turned out a history of the Seven Years' War, also the justly famous Moltke military studies and a quarterly magazine devoted to military arts and sciences. Officers in the program submitted articles to a continuing series, "Studies in Military History," and some fifty monographic campaign analyses had appeared by the outbreak of World War I.

The historical function declined during World War I; and with the disappearance of the Great German General Staff as a condition of the peace settlement, official military historical work came under the newly instituted Reichsarchiv, a civil agency under the Ministry of Interior. The Reichsarchiv collected documents from all branches of the government, but military records were its main concern in the 1920s. Prussian Army records, surviving as a collection separate from German army records of World War I, remained in the Heeresarchiv (Army Archives), but they were almost totally destroyed in 1945.[4]

The head of the Reichsarchiv worked in conjunction with a Reichskommission of German scholars, among whom was Hans

3. Hajo Holborn, "Moltke and Schlieffen: The Prussian-German School," in *Makers of Modern Strategy.* ed. Edward M. Earle (Princeton, N.J.: Princeton Univ. Press, 1943), p. 174.

4. Thomas E. Skidmore, "Survey of Unpublished Sources on the Central Government and Politics of the German Empire, 1871-1918," *American Historical Review* 65, no. 4 (July 1960):849.

Delbrück, whose critical approach to military history had already earned him a lasting reputation.[5] The intervention of an academic group in the military archives caused no small tension, but with the Reichskommission's advice and direction, the displaced military historians began work on an extended series, *Der Weltkrieg, 1914-1918* (The World War, 1914-1918). In addition to traditional campaign and battle narratives, it included volumes covering German railroads during the war, cultural life under the stress of the conflict, and the economic aspects of the home front and military mobilization. This series was still in progress when the Nazi regime assumed power, and the last combat volume appeared only in 1956 under the auspices of the Federal Republic (West Germany), although it had been set in type in 1942.

In April 1935, military historical functions returned to a Military Historical Research Institute of the Army, the seventh section of the resurgent German General Staff. In 1940, the High Command of the German Armed Forces (OKW) established a section for Wehrmacht history under Col. (later Brig. Gen.) Walter Scherff. Though the written output of the section during the war was negligible, Scherff collected military records from all German field commands and from the archives of overrun countries, a hoard microfilmed by American and British archivists and historians after the collapse of Nazism. A separate though parallel effort in the German documentation of the war was the war diary of the Oberkommando der Wehrmacht, kept by Helmuth Greiner from 1939 to 1943 and by historian Percy Schramm until the end of the war.[6]

Revived German military archival practice not only supplemented the work of the Historical Research Institute of the Army, but was also an indispensable adjunct to German staff planning. So strong was this tradition that one archivist, himself a product of German training, asserted after the stunning victories in 1940 that "the overwhelming success of the Germans was attributable to the fact that they had entered the war with a better filing system."[7]

---

5. See Chapter 4 on Delbrück, also Gordon A. Craig's "Delbrück: The Military Historian," in Earle's *Makers of Modern Strategy*, pp. 261-83.

6. Percy Schramm, ed., *Kriegstagebuch des Oberkommandos der Wehrmacht* (Frankfurt/Main: Bernard & Graefe Verlag für Wehrwissen, 1961) 4 (2d half):1772-74. See also Howard McGaw Smyth, *Secrets of the Fascist Era: How Uncle Sam Obtained Some of the Top-Level Documents of Mussolini's Period* (Carbondale: Southern Ill. Univ. Press, 1975), pp. 109 ff; and Helmuth Greiner, *Die oberste Wehrmachtführung 1939-1943* (Wiesbaden: Limes Verlag, 1951).

7. Ernst Posner, *Archives and the Public Interest* (Washington: Public Affairs Press, 1971), p. 87. Posner left Germany in 1939 and pursued a highly successful career in the United States.

Official historical work led a shadowy existence after the collapse of Nazi Germany until the establishment in 1957 of the Militargeschichtliches Forschungsamt (Military Historical Research Office), a joint staff element under the Bundeswehr [Federal Defense Force] General Inspekteur. The research office provides training material and runs informal programs in military history among troops and officers; it also manages the military records of the Bundesarchiv collection located at Koblenz.

The research office has undertaken research and publication in several areas, including a monographic series devoted to individual battles and a continuing series publishing older military records and documents of value. A reference work, *Handbook on German Military History from 1648 to 1939*, now over seven volumes, presents comprehensive bibliographies, while a more lengthy series, *Contributions to Military and War History*, has treated such topics as women in wartime, Army administration and promotion policy, a history of the development of the Luftwaffe, and an extensive analysis of the German General Staff from 1871 to 1945. Other projects seek to conclude work begun on German World War I air operations, and there has been some reworking of nineteenth-century histories of the Austro-Prussian War of 1866 and the Napoleonic campaigns. German official historiography has become far less nationalistic in tone since World War II while maintaining a commitment to the exposition of events in the conflicts involving Germany up to 1945. Recent reorganizations and revised policy have emphasized the histories of the development of the Bundeswehr as opposed to World War projects.

France

The present French official historical office claims a long heritage dating from an order of Cardinal Richelieu in 1637 to his secretary of war requiring the preservation of military state papers in a central archives. In one form or other, this document collection process has continued under military auspices since that time.

Official French production began after World War I with the series, The French Army in the Great War. Divided into eleven separate "books," each with a single title and each containing several subvolumes, the series dealt with operations in France and Belgium from 1914 to 1918. Primarily narrative, the works also include several volumes of maps depicting the areas covered in the histories. One "book" deals with theaters of war other than the main front in Europe—Gallipoli, Salonika, and Africa. Three other multivolume works appeared in the period between the two world wars recounting the military history of French colonies, protectorates, and mandates (nine volumes), French military conquest of colonies (ten volumes), and the contribution of colonial soldiers and officers serving in the French armies (two volumes).

Reappearing in 1953 after the wholesale destruction of French records in World War II, the official military historical office serves the French Army as the *Service Historique de l'Armée de la Terre* (Historical Service of the Army) under the Ministry of the Army. Charged with providing historical materials for all French military training, the service also handles heraldic records, libraries on French Army posts, and archives of French military affairs since the sixteenth century. The respected journal produced by the service, *Revue Historique de l'Armée* (Army Historical Review), usually devotes each issue to a specific aspect of the army such as communications, armor development, chemical warfare, or command and leadership.

Historical production since World War II has not been as extensive in France as elsewhere. The major continuing work has been a series on higher headquarters commands, published as *Les Grandes Unites Françaises: Historique Succincts*. One separate volume concerns the history of the army between the world wars, and a number of works have been published privately with the support of the service. Within the service schools, historical study is emphasized as training for staff work. Students generally have the opportunity to apply historical lessons in field exercises lasting from two to four weeks.

Great Britain

Early official historical work in Britain was frequently overshadowed by private publications such as Sir John W. Fortescue's *History of the British Army* (fourteen volumes), appearing at the turn of the nineteenth century. Generally considered the first official publication, however, is the compilation of the Royal Engineers and the Royal Artillery on their operations in the Crimean War, commissioned by the Secretary of State for War in 1855.

No permanent historical section remained as a result of this effort, but in 1872 the Topographical and Statistical Departments of the War Office collaborated in the translation of the official German volumes on the 1866 Austro-Prussian War. In the following year, the Intelligence Branch under the Topographical Department began functioning as a center for historical documentation and writing, and collected data on numerous colonial expeditions and campaigns.

The worldwide commitments of the British Army and the guiding influence of Sir Frederick Maurice in the last years of the nineteenth century and until World War I gave official British works a more cosmopolitan aspect than other national programs and produced considerably less imitation of the Germans than was the case in other countries. A three-volume history of the Russo-Japanese War made no analysis of tactics employed in the German-trained Japanese Army. Very little "doctrinal" history came from official British historians in this period.

By 1907, historical work was subordinated to the newly established Committee of Imperial Defense in a subcommittee for the control of official histories. Accompanying this change, the histories of World War I from 1920 to 1948 came to be connected with the name of one man, Brigadier Sir James E. Edmonds. They reflect Edmonds's dislike of politicians, and his mild treatment of battlefield blunders produced some conflict even among the official staff. The series, History of the Great War, amounted to five volumes on operations in western Europe and at Gallipoli and Salonika, supported by numerous maps and appendices of battle orders.

With the onset of World War II, the Committee of Imperial Defense became the War Cabinet Office; its secretariat managed the wartime historical staff, consisting after 1941 of an advisory committee of scholars from British universities. In 1946 the advisory committee decided upon a joint interservice history of the war and embarked as well on an extensive treatment of the civil aspects of the conflict. The entire production is divided into the United Kingdom Civil Series, with Sir William Keith Hancock as series editor, and the United Kingdom Military Series edited by Sir James Butler. A third, separate series deals with medicine in the war; it contains three subseries covering clinical services, combat medicine, and civilian services. The civil series devotes volumes to all aspects of civilian life and economy in wartime Britain, including food administration, social policy and services, industrial production and labor, weapons design, civil transportation, and overseas supply lines. The military series has volumes on grand strategy and conventional battle narratives on British ground, sea, and air campaigns around the world. It also includes a subseries on military administration, occupation policy, and civil affairs in conquered territories.

For all of the breadth and the reliance on original records from the British cabinet, from wartime administrative agencies, from industries, and from the armed services, source citations in all series are very scant. But for the American reader, the British history of the Second World War is a fine history in a familiar language, and the volumes are masterpieces of literary style. A shorter eight-volume history appeared as an interim popular work before the production of the two main series started.

In the active service today, the sense of history and tradition again centers in the separate services; in the army the traditional pride in the individual regiment survives. Regimental and retired officers' associations preserve the memory of past events by publishing unit histories and encouraging the study of military history in general.

Until 1971 British officers had to pass examinations that included questions in military history for promotion to the rank of major. Although this practice has been dropped, a "war studies" paper and a study on some aspect of international affairs remain mandatory. Formal study of military history continues at the Royal College of Defense Studies and at the Joint Services Staff College, and some officers have attended regular university courses in history. The British government has endowed chairs or fellowships in military history at civilian schools to stimulate and support interest in military affairs.[8]

Commonwealth Countries

The larger countries of the British Commonwealth have pursued historical programs of their own. Canada's and Australia's came into their own in the decade after World War I, and relied greatly on the collection of documents in Britain and on coordination with the British writing program. Canadian work began both in Ottawa and London during the conflict, and gradually evolved into the Historical Section of the Canadian general staff by November 1918. Early histories followed the French models somewhat in that documentation and maps in each volume far outweighed narrative material. After World

---

8. Ad Hoc Committee, Department of the Army, "Report on the Army Need for the Study of Military History" (West Point, N.Y., 1971) 3:pp. N-6, N-8.

War II the program came under the inspired leadership of Col. C. P. Stacey who guided to completion a combined civil and joint military history of the war. Stacey's experience as a history professor in American and Canadian universities contributed much to the program.

The Australian contribution to official historical programs is noteworthy. At the end of World War I, Prof. C. E. W. Bean was the first to make a formal statement of the idea of having joint service histories prepared by civilian scholars working with military professionals. He devised an operating structure that put all of the historical effort under one general editor. This system has been followed with some variations by successful programs in Britain, Canada, Germany, and the United States to the present day.

Even as Professor Bean saw the volumes of World War I concluded in 1943, research for the series on World War II began under Mr. Gavin Long as general editor. Though a journalist by profession, Long preserved his predecessor's approach and organizational concepts. The work on World War II relied to some extent on the documentary collections of wartime allies, and for the Pacific War upon interrogations conducted in occupied Japan. Mr. Long also initiated a wide-ranging interview program in 1943 to record the actual experiences of individual Australians. The resulting series, with the overall title *Australia in the War of 1939-1945*, consists of five subseries, the first three being traditional accounts of combat action in all theaters where Australian forces were engaged; the fourth subseries covers industrial mobilization and the government's prosecution of the war. A medical subseries completes the Australian official record, twenty-two published volumes altogether.

New Zealand's program on World War II borrowed much from the Australian project, but the output shows the influence of Maj. Gen. Sir Howard Kippenberger, chief editor, and Mr. E. H. McCormick, New Zealand's chief war archivist. Nearly fifty volumes fall into four distinct categories: document collections, illustrated and documented popular histories for use in the school system, campaign and battle histories, and unit histories. The series has also covered the story of women in the war, the war economy, medical and dental services, and treatment of New Zealanders held as prisoners of war.[9]

---

9. Ronald Walker, "The New Zealand Second World War History Project," *Military Affairs* 32, no. 4 (Feb. 1969:173-81.

Imperial Russia and the Soviet Union

As with some other countries, official history in imperial Russia had forerunners in battle histories written by officers working independently of any staff or institution, although allowed access to official records. This practice continued after the establishment of a historical section in the Imperial Russian General Staff in 1836 and contributed to the controversial nature of Russian official and semiofficial histories of the Crimean War. A history of operations in the Turkish War of 1828-29 was the first officially written and published work in which the historical section cooperated.

After 1900 historical functions centered in the so-called Military Historical Commission of the General Staff, which undertook a multivolume series on the Russo-Turkish conflict of 1877-78, a project still underway when World War I erupted. A second major work was on the Russo-Japanese War of 1904-5. Both of these efforts slowed during the war years, and ended altogether with the Bolshevik Revolution.

Soviet military history virtually ignored the Russian experience in World War I and concentrated on the events of the Russian Civil War of 1918 to 1920 and on operations during the Polish War of 1920. Active official historical work declined seriously by the mid-1930s, and in the Red Army came under Mikhail Frunze's early attempts to revolutionize military doctrine and historical events as well. During World War II and the twenty years thereafter, the functions of the Historical Administration of the Soviet Army General Staff extended far beyond what its name implied. During the war the section collected field reports on strategy, tactics, weapons, and unit organization. It had a strong influence on strategic planning and even on the equipment of troops; its directives became standard procedure, usually within three months after critiques and recommendations were issued.[10]

In the immediate postwar years, the administration's journal, Voyennaya Mysl' (Military Thought), restricted to military officers, showed some independence and professional outlook, but eventually it took the lead in establishing the approved and basic interpretations expected of all Soviet history. All credit for the strategic and much of the tactical direction of the war came to rest with Stalin. Even the disasters of the first two

---

10. Walter D. Jacobs, "Frunze Rides Again," Military Review 39, no. 3 (June 1969):16. U.S. War Department, TM 30-430: Handbook on USSR Military Forces (Washington, 1945), p. I-19.

years of the war were uniformly transmuted into manifesta-
tions of a Stalinist mastery of defensive concepts. The same
journal cautiously anticipated the revision of Stalin's role in the
war two years after the dictator's death and a full year before
Party Chairman Nikita Khrushchev debunked the Stalinist cult
in a speech at the Twentieth Party Congress in February 1956.[11]

After this "secret speech" Soviet histories spread credit for
the victory among Communist party leaders, military commanders, and the great Soviet people. But otherwise they still
followed the official Communist Party and Marxist-Leninist
line and therefore remain suspect.[12] The most ambitious single
work on the war to appear in the Soviet Union reflected the de-
Stalinization movement. In 1957 a committee of over two
hundred historians, many of them military men, began work on
a six-volume *History of the Great Patriotic War of the Soviet
Union*; the last volume was published in 1965. The history was
written for popular consumption under the auspices of the
Institute of Marxism-Leninism. Maj. Gen. E. A. Boltin, deputy
director of the institute, furnished ideological and technical-
military guidance for the research in articles published in
Voprosy Istorii (Questions of History), the official journal for
Soviet historians. The contributing historians used archives
scattered throughout the Soviet Union and the Soviet client
states of eastern Europe.

In 1966 the Supreme Soviet created an Institute of Military
History directly subordinate to the Chief of the Soviet General
Staff. Under a general officer who is a corresponding member of
the Soviet Academy of Sciences, the institute has published a
series of highly competent battle studies, including works on
the conflict with Japan along the Manchurian border in 1939,
about which relatively little was known in the west. Other
volumes deal with campaigns in the Caucasus and south-
eastern Europe during World War II. A one-volume history of
the war and a memorial edition on the ordeal of Leningrad were
also produced in popular versions. The institute is now publishing a twelve-volume history of World War II. The institute also
participated in the Thirteenth Congress of the International
Congress of the Historical Sciences in Moscow in 1970 and in a
similar conference at San Francisco in 1975 as a member organization of the International Commission on Military History.

---

11. Matthew P. Gallagher, *The Soviet History of World War II* (New York: Praeger, 1963), pp. 64-78.

12. Col. John E. Jessup, Jr., "Soviet Military History: Efforts and Results," *Military Review* 53, no. 6 (June 1973):22-23.

An apparently open-ended series of unit histories began appearing from a wide array of official publishing houses after 1962; they covered mainly the numbered armies and "fronts" of World War II. A companion series, started in 1968, examines the histories of local military districts in the Soviet Union before and during the war. Extensive publishers' lists of memoirs and accounts of single battles attest to the still-lively interest in World War II. A leading American bibliographer of Soviet military histories listed over 130 titles published in 1968–70. Beyond the public interest, Soviet military academies continue to emphasize military history in officer training. The average cadet at the Frunze Academy applies some twenty percent of his time to historical study and the preparation of papers in that field.[13]

Official historical programs in Soviet bloc states of eastern Europe parallel the Russian example to a large degree. Marxist-Leninist interpretations avowedly dominate the output, and the general staffs of the various countries or special organizations sponsored by the local Communist party have jurisdiction. Many of the military programs include research on national heroes and bygone wars, but the treatment of World War II follows the Soviet practice, with heavy political coloration and the necessary emphasis on the Red Army's role in the liberation of eastern Europe from Nazi oppression.

China

Exact data on historical activites in the Peoples' Liberation Army of the Peoples' Republic of China is very sketchy. Even though historical offices exist within the army and the Ministry of National Defense, various party organs have sponsored historical projects. The China Youth League solicited tens of thousands of personal memoirs from participants in Chinese revolutionary events from 1921 to 1950 and published over three hundred of them. Many of the vignettes describe small-scale military operations and individual acts of self-sacrifice performed in the name of the revolution. With contributions from Chairman Mao himself, and from other leaders such as one-time Premier Lin Piao and Army Commander Chu Teh, the collection

---

13. Michael Parrish, "A Selected List of Books From the Soviet Union on the Great Patriotic War Published during 1968-1970," American Committee on the History of the Second World War Newsletter, no. 5 (Sep. 1971), pp 10–12; Parrish, "Soviet Army and Military District Histories," Ibid., no. 8 (Sep. 1972), pp. 3–8. DA Ad Hoc Committee Rpt., vol. 3, p. N–3.

is a leading example of the use of ideologically embellished history for mass indoctrination.[14]

Japan

Information on Japanese official historical activities within the armed services prior to World War II is limited, but some German record-keeping practices accompanied the importation of German military doctrine in the late nineteenth century. World War II caused widespread destruction of Japanese records, either by Allied bombing or by deliberate Japanese action after the surrender. Official military history has labored under this handicap ever since, although efforts continue to amass materials still scattered among the wartime enemies of Japan.

As commander of occupation forces, General Douglas MacArthur began the first official program in postward Japan when he directed selected Japanese Army and Navy officers to write monographs on operations in China and Manchuria prior to 1941 and in the Pacific thereafter. The resulting series on the Pacific war, which the group concentrated on first, is highly uneven; some of the works barely outline events, and many of them were written only from memory. In 1951 the Far East Command established a Japanese research division to edit and rewrite some of the monographs and to analyze operations in Manchuria, as originally planned, again employing former Japanese officers. The Manchurian series is superior to the earlier efforts in organization, documentation, and quality.[15]

Since October 1955, the Japanese Self-Defense Force's Office for Research in Military History has produced joint histories of all of Japan's armed services. The office combines writing, editorial, and archival functions and has cooperated extensively with nongovernment researchers. Among the best products is the seven-volume *On the Road to War*, which recounts the political and military crises in the Far East prior to 1941. The *Asahi Shimbun* newspaper chain printed and distributed the series and now plans publication in English.

Published official volumes include studies of the Sino-Japanese War of 1894–95, a lengthy survey of Japanese intervention in Siberia from 1919 to 1922, and narratives on operations in China in 1928 and during the Shanghai incident of 1932.

---

14. Robert Rinden and Roxane Witke, *The Red Flag Waves: A Guide to the Hung-ch'i p'iao-p'iao Collection*, Center for China Studies, China Research Monograph no. 3 (Berkeley: Univ. of Calif Press. 1968).

15. Department of the Army, OCMH, "Guide to the Japanese Monographs and Japanese Studies on Manchuria, 1945–1960" (n. d.). American involvement in this program ended in 1960.

The Japanese program has also traced some of the convoluted history of the infighting between the Chinese Communists and the Kuomintang (Nationalists) in China from 1926 to 1936. Work continues on the history of Japanese operations in the Pacific during World War II.

Aside from its own research and publication, the Office for Research supplies teachers and materials for staff schools. Both civilian and military instructors provide the three hours per week in military history required of students at the triservice Japanese Defense Academy. To encourage officers to continue the study of history throughout their careers, the official Japanese program also supports an informal military historical council, which publishes historical papers in a monthly journal. Membership is open to officers and university scholars interested in military history.[16]

Smaller Powers

South Korea's War History Compilation Committee published a documentary and statistical record of the Korean War in five volumes, ending its six-year existence in 1956. In 1966, it was revived to edit historical narratives on the Korean War produced by separate historical staffs of the Korean Army, Navy, and Air Force. Available in English as *History of the U.N. Forces in the Korean War* (1972-), the series emphasizes the contributions of all the powers involved.

The Philippine armed forces headquarters has had a historical branch attached to its adjutant general's office since 1963, a successor to official writing programs that began in 1946. The branch devotes much attention to World War II events and leaders in the Philippines, but has also completed volumes on the postwar Huk insurgency, the Philippine revolution (1900), and the Korean War.

The Chinese government in Formosa maintains a history bureau of the Ministry of National Defense which has produced official compilations on Chinese wars with Japan in the 1890s and from 1937 to 1945, also the Chinese Civil War in the 1920s and late 1940s.

Indian official history after World War II followed the British format, relied heavily on British documentation, and employed British officers until full Indian independence in 1948. The official 24-volume *Indian Armed Forces in World War II* was completed in 1966.

The Israeli Defense Forces Historical Section, established in

---

16. DA, Ad Hoc Committee Rpt., vol. 3, pp. N-12—N-14.

1948 to document the Israeli war of independence, continues its accounts of more recent wars in the Middle East involving Israeli forces. The section's archival resources support both historical writing projects and constant efforts to revise or update military, naval, and air tactics and doctrine.

Each program represents in own peculiar amalgamation of scholarship, political ideology or the lack of it, and, inevitably, a government's willingness to expend resources on long-term research projects with somewhat intangible benefits. There is still some pursuit of "proven" lessons from the experiences of great military men. But as the leading scholar of the Canadian official program after World War II observed, officers should abjure the barren search for tactical devices that worked for Caesar, Napoleon, Suvorov, Patton, Manstein, or Zhukov, and concentrate on discovering those "qualities of heart and mind which go to the making of a great commander."[17]

The best of the recent programs, most notably the British, go beyond a mere summary of wartime documents with a cautious treatment of controversial issues. They make some effort "to inquire systematically into the relationships between military and political institutions, and to analyze the interaction of strategic policy and battle."[18] Though still criticized at home and abroad, they permit serious insight into the nature of individuals, institutions, and doctrines in the stress of conflict, victory, and defeat.

Bibliography

Ad Hoc Committee, Department of the Army, "Report on the Army Need for the Study of Military History." 4 vols. West Point, N.Y., 1971.

Craig, Gordon A. "Delbrück: The Military Historian." In *The Makers of Modern Strategy,* edited by Edward M. Earle. New York: Atheneum, 1970.

Gallagher, Matthew P. *The Soviet History of World War II.* New York: Praeger, 1963.

Higham, Robin, ed. *Official Histories: Essays and Bibliographies From Around the World.* Manhattan: Kansas State Univ. Library, 1970.

Holborn, Hajo. "Moltke and Schlieffen: The Prussian-German School." In *Makers of Modern Strategy,* edited by Earle.

---

17. C. P. Stacey, *Introduction to the Study of Military History for Canadian Students* (Ottawa: Queen's Printer, 1953), p. iv.

18. Peter Paret, "The History of War," *Daedalus* 100, no. 1 (Spring 1971):376.

Liddell Hart, B. H. "Respectability and Judgement in Historical Writing." *Military Affairs* 23, no. 1 (Spring 1959):35.

Paret, Peter. "The History of War." *Daedalus* 100 (Spring 1971):376.

Posner, Ernst. *Archives and the Public Interest.* Washington: Public Affairs Press, 1971.

Stacey, C. P. *Introduction to the Study of Military History for Canadian Students.* Ottawa: Queen's Printer, 1953.

Chapter 23

Military History and the Academic World

Ronald H. Spector

"**A**ND this I write that young men may learn, if they should meet with such trials as we met with there, and have not opportunity to cut off their enemies; yet they may, with such pretty pranks, preserve themselves from danger. For policy is needful in wars as well as strength." So wrote Lion Gardner in his 1638 *History of the Pequot Warres* (p. 32), perhaps the earliest military history written in America.

The writing of military history has thus a long tradition in the United States, and some of the most distinguished American historians, from William H. Prescott to Henry Adams to Samuel Eliot Morison, have turned their hand to it. Yet it has not been an academic tradition. If we accept Walter Millis's definition of a military historian as "a technically trained professional historian [who] . . . applies the interests and techniques of the general historian to the study of warfare" (*Military History*, p. 11), then it must be said that, until very recently, the academic historian of war hardly existed in the United States.

From the emergence of modern historical research in America, around the 1880s, until the end of the First World War, most of the serious writing on military history in the United States was the work of professional officers such as Alfred Thayer Mahan, author of the famous *Influence of Seapower Upon History* (1890), and Emory Upton, an Army officer who completed the manuscript of his pioneering *The Military Policy of the United States* in 1881 (published posthumously in 1904). In 1912 when the American Historical Association held a conference on military history in conjunction with its annual meeting, only two of the participants were professional historians.[1]

---

1. *Annual Report of the American Historical Association 1912* (Washington: American Historical Association, 1914), 159-93.

Dr. Spector (Ph.D., Yale), of the Current History Branch, CMH, is working on a history of the early U.S. military involvement in Vietnam. He has also published two books, *Admiral of the New Empire: The Life and Career of George Dewey* and *Professors of War: The Naval War College and the Development of the Naval Profession,* as well as numerous articles on military and naval history.

Far from stimulating American interest in military affairs, the First World War led to a widespread reaction in the 1920s and 1930s against all things military. During this period historians whose specialties were in other areas nevertheless carried on a fair amount of research in military history. The *American Historical Review*, for example, carried fifteen articles or notes on military history between 1920 and 1930 and eighteen between 1930 and 1941, a respectable number in a journal in which so many fields are represented. About six percent of doctoral disserations written in these two decades were also on military topics.

But few professional historians could or wished to concentrate primarily upon the history of war. Some of the most important work in the field was, in fact, done by persons without formal historical training, such as the journalist Walter Millis and the political scientist Harold Sprout. At the University of Chicago, scholars from a number of disciplines, including history, cooperated in a massive study of the causes of war begun in 1926 under the guidance of political scientist Quincy Wright. The Chicago project produced a large number of monographs, articles, and books culminating in Wright's own work, *A Study of War* (two volumes, Chicago: University of Chicago Press, 1942). But though Wright's study contained much to interest the historian, it was in no sense history. Wright himself had little use for military history, which he believed to be "less historical than technical in purpose and usually designed to assist the practitioners of the art."[2] Like many academics of the 1920s and 1930s, Wright believed that war in general could be understood without detailed study of any particular war.

World War II and the onset of the cold war enormously increased scholarly interest in the study of war, but historians generally did not share in this revival of interest in matters military. After 1945 social scientists largely preempted the field of military studies, particularly recent national security policy. While study of civil-military relations, military administration, strategy, and arms control flourished in departments of political science and sociology, military history continued to languish. In 1954 after polling 815 schools, Dr. Richard C. Brown found 37 colleges and universities offering courses in military history (*Teaching of Military History . . .*).

During the last two decades, however, there has been an unmistakable growth of interest in military history among

---

2. Quincy Wright, *The Study of International Relations* (New York: Appleton-Century-Crofts, 1955), p. 149.

American historians. This is most clearly reflected in the surprisingly large number of recent dissertations which deal wholly or in part with military subjects. Although there is no sure means of classifying or determining the exact contents of all of the hundreds of dissertations produced over the last twenty years, some ten percent probably fall within the general area of military history.

These dissertations are not confined to the study of operations but range over a wide area of subjects. Many explore new or neglected areas of scholarship or reexamine old topics from a new perspective. The new areas include the role of minorities in the U.S. armed forces, the Army and Reconstruction, the influence of war plans upon foreign policy, the armed forces and disarmament, the role of the military in developing countries, and the social ideas of professional military men. (See Millett and Cooling, *Doctoral Dissertations . . .*) The growth of interest in military history may be attributed in part to the impetus provided by the historical programs of the armed services after World War II. Distinguished academic historians like Kent Roberts Greenfield of Johns Hopkins University headed the Army's historical work, Samuel Eliot Morison of Harvard University produced the magisterial *History of United States Naval Operations in World War II*, and Wesley Frank Craven of New York University with James Lea Cate of the University of Chicago edited the seven-volume *Army Air Forces in World War II*. That none of these men had any connection with military history before World War II was symptomatic of the state of military history in the academic world in 1945. Two decades later, however, historians like Harry Coles, K. Jack Bauer, Martin Blumenson, Louis Morton, and I.B. Holley, who had begun their careers as Army and other official historians, were teaching and directing research in military history at a number of universities and colleges throughout the country.

At the same time ties between the Army and academic historians have grown closer, and visiting professorships in military history now exist at West Point, the Army War College, and the Command and General Staff College. Committees composed in part of distinguished academic historians advise the Army, Navy, and Air Force, and all of the services have established modest programs to support predoctoral research in military history. The prototype of these programs was the Center of Military History's Dissertation Year Fellowship Program established in 1970.

But increased interest in military history has not been

matched by a corresponding increase in the number of courses offered in the field. A 1962 study of 502 institutions of higher learning revealed that military history was offered less frequently than any other type of history course (Perkins and Snell, p. 76). The absolute number of course offerings, nevertheless, has almost certainly increased over the last decade. In 1969 Stetson Conn identified 110 colleges and universities listing courses in military history aside from those required for ROTC. (Brown's 1954 poll surveyed many more schools.) Of the twenty-five graduate schools rated as the leading institutions in the field of history in 1970, at least seven offered graduate courses or seminars in military history.[3]

Besides American and European military history, a number of history departments now offer such courses as "Comparative Military Establishments," "Technology and War," "Congress and American Military Policy," "War, Revolution, and Modernization," "The Military in American Life," and "War and Economic Change in the Twentieth Century." Courses concentrating on one of the two world wars are also increasingly popular. Military history still occupies a rather marginal and uncertain place in most colleges and universities, however. Many of the courses presently offered are a product of the personal interest and effort of the professor involved. If he leaves or retires, the military history course usually goes with him. Few history faculties feel a need to replace a lost position in military history as they would in, say, ancient history or diplomatic history. And most graduate advisers warn their students that military history is not a recognized specialty and offers extremely limited opportunities for teaching and publication.[4]

Only a handful of institutions accept military history as a major or minor field for the Ph.D. In some graduate schools the student who wishes to do his major research in the area of military history still faces an uphill struggle to convince his mentors of the feasibility or indeed the respectability of his project. That many are successful is attested to by the increasing number of solid dissertations in military history, many written at schools which offer no course work in the field.

The American attitude toward military history has always

---

3. Stetson Conn, "List of Universities and Colleges in the United States Offering Specialized Courses in Military History," Washington, CMH files. American Council on Education, *A Rating of Graduate Programs* (Washington, 1970).

4. Theodore Ropp, "Military History and the Social Sciences," *Military Affairs* 30 (Spring 1966):8. Louis Morton, "The Historian and the Study of War," *Mississippi Valley Historical Review* 48 (March 1952):608.

been ambiguous, and to this day the practitioners and critics of the art find themselves unable to agree on the proper approach to the subject. In the past many intellectuals feared that writing and teaching military history might contribute to the glorification of war and the spread of militarism. "In the process of militarizing minds," Alfred Vagts complains, "no small role has been played by the writers of military history" (*History of Militarism*, p. 23). Although this idea is seldom articulated, it is far from dead. As recently as 1957, Professor Arthur Ekirch ("Military History . . . ," p. 54) warned the American Historical Association that "contemporary military history involves the danger that its very bulk . . . may result in our literature as well as our society becoming further militarized." The critical and independent scholarship of such writers as Marcus Cunliffe, Walter Millis, Peter Karsten, and Alfred Vagts and the reputation of the U.S. Army's official histories for honesty and candor have done much in recent years to allay these fears.

A second approach to military history might be termed, for want of a better description, the utilitarian approach. Like Lion Gardener, many American writers of military history have sought *"lessons" useful to future generals and strategists or* illustrating the underlying principles which they believe govern the conduct of war. Others have addressed themselves not only to soldiers but to the informed citizen as well. They believed that the study of military history would enable the civilian voter to understand the military problems and needs of his country. In 1912, Maj. J.W. McAndrew of the Army War College told the American Historical Association (*Annual Report,* p. 188) that "the education of our people in our military history will be the best guarantee of continued peace."

A growing number of younger scholars, however, have abandoned this utilitarian approach to military history and begun to examine it as simply an important branch of general history. "Most of us have abandoned the military's definition of military history as lessons of command and strategy," Professor Allan Millett observed. "Rather we study the conduct of America's wars and the development of its military institutions in the . . . milieu which shaped them. I would guess we hope such study will give us a fuller understanding of American history rather than make us strategists." ("American Military History . . . ," p. 158.)

Like the utilitarian view, this approach to military history has a long ancestry. Sixty years before Millett, the distinguished journalist Oswald Garrison Villard criticized those who "confine in their minds the study of military history to the technical purpose of preparing men to take the field," and called for the study of military history "as a purely historical study" (AHA *Annual Report . . . 1912*, p. 173). But the idea of military history as an autonomous academic specialty did not take root easily in the United States. Unlike Britain and France, the United States has no tradition of civilian scholarship in military history, and until recent years eminent European students of war such as Hans Delbrück in Germany and Charles Oman in Britain had no American counterparts. Since 1945, however, academics such as William R. Braisted, Arthur Marder, Peter Paret, Theodore Ropp, John Shy, and Russell Weigley have gone far toward making military history a significant part of American historical writing.

The emergence of a self-conscious group of academic military historians since World War II has also led to new approaches to the study of military history. Professor Peter Paret (1971) has called for an end to the old compartmentalizing of history as "social, intellectual, or military" and suggested instead that historians in all specialties combine their efforts to explore such areas as the economic aspects of war, the interaction of war with science and technology, and the history of ideas relating to war. (For a defense of traditional operational history, see Dennis Showalter, 1975.) John Shy recently (1971) explored some of the implications of psychological theory, particularly learning theory, for understanding the American military experience in a pathbreaking article, "The American Military Experience: History and Learning," while Alan D. Anderson has pointed to the usefulness of systems analysis in the study of operational history (1972). Military historians have begun to participate in such interdisciplinary undertakings as the Inter-University Seminar on Armed Forces and Society and the section on military studies of the International Studies Association. The American Historical Association has a "Section on Peace Research in History" in which military historians have been active collaborators.

The trend toward a more autonomous, more academically oriented and less "militarized" type of military history in the United States does not, of course, mean that the study of history has ceased to be of importance to the professional officer. On the contrary, it may be argued that the more scholarly and independent a work of history, the more useful it ultimately is to the student of war. One would have to go far to find a better discussion of the problems of command than Douglas S. Freeman's *Lee's Lieutenants* or a more thoughtful discussion of commerce warfare than Henry Adams's famous chapter on privateers in his *History of the United States*. Yet neither of these men had any thought of writing specifically for a military audience.

Military history as an academic field has experienced an impressive degree of growth and development during the past two decades. Although it still has far to go to match the more established historical specialties, one might argue that it is at least moving in the right direction and has already contributed much to our understanding of American history.

Bibliography

Anderson, Alan. "An Experiment in Combat Simulation: The Battle of Cambrai 1917." *Journal of Interdisciplinary History* 2 (1972):229–47.

Annual Report of the American Historical Association 1912. Washington: American Historical Association, 1914.

Brown, Richard C. *The Teaching of Military History in Colleges and Universities in the United States*. USAF Historical Study No. 124. Montgomery, Ala.: Air Univ. 1955.

Ekirch, Arthur A., Jr. "Military History, a Civilian Caveat." *Military Affairs* 21 (Summer 1957):49–54.

Gardener, Lion. *A History of the Pequot Warres or a Relation of the Warres Between the Powerful Nation of Pequot Indians, Once Inhabiting the Coast of New England, and the English Inhabitants in the Year 1636*. Reprinted, Cincinnati, 1860.

Karsten, Peter. "Demilitarizing Military History: Servants of Power or Agents of Understanding." *Military Affairs* 36 (Oct. 1972):88–92.

Mahon, John K. "Doctoral Dissertations on Military History." *Military Affairs* 17 (Fall 1953):140–42.

Millis, Walter. *Military History*. Washington: American Historical Association Service Center for Teachers, 1961.

Millet, Allan R. "American Military History: Over the Top." In *The State of American History*, edited by Herbert J. Bass. Chicago: Quadrangle, 1970.

Millet, Allan R. and Cooling, B. Franklin. *Doctoral Dissertations in Military Affairs*. Manhattan: Kans. State Univ., 1972.

Morton, Louis. "The Historian and the Study of War." *Mississippi Valley Historical Review* 48 (Mar. 1962):599–613.

Paret, Peter. "The History of War." *Daedalus* 100 (Spring 1971):376–96.

Perkins, Dexter, and Snell, John L. *The Education of Historians in the United States*. New York: McGraw-Hill, 1962.

Ropp, Theodore. "Military History and the Social Sciences." *Military Affairs* 30 (Spring 1966):8–13.

Scheips, Paul J. "Military History and Peace Research." *Military Affairs* 36 (Apr. 1975):71–74.

Showalter, Dennis. "A Modest Plea for Drums and Trumpets." *Military Affairs* 39 (Apr. 1975):71–74.

Shy, John. "The American Military Experience: History and Learning." *Journal of Interdisciplinary History* 1 (Winter 1971):205–29.

Vagts, Alfred. *A History of Militarism*. New York, W. W. Norton, 1937.

Appendices

Reference Works:
A Select List

Thomas E. Kelly, III

I N either study or research the student of military history will need to consult standard reference works on general history and more specialized references on military history. In the listings that follow, the most useful reference works have been treated in three categories—bibliographies and guides, general reference works, and atlases—each category broken down between general and military history. Each type of reference has its own uses. In each category, a brief introduction discusses the most useful works, followed by an annotated alphabetical listing.

Bibliographies and Guides: General

Constance M. Winchell's *Guide to Reference Books* covers the humanities, social sciences, history, and pure and applied science. A. F. Walford's *Guide to Reference Material* is a useful supplement emphasizing material published in Great Britain. Helen Poulton's *Historian's Handbook* describes and analyzes the reference aids of particular importance for historians. Although published in 1961, the American Historical Association's *Guide to Historical Literature* is still valuable. The volume is annotated and under topical and geographical headings contains approximately twenty thousand entries. Each section of the *Guide* was prepared by a specialist. Another indispensable reference is the 1974 edition of the *Harvard Guide to American History* edited by Frank Freidel. This volume contains the most comprehensive bibliography of works in all fields of American history, with materials arranged topically in Volume I and chronologically in Volume II. There is nothing comparable in English for European, Asian, or African history.

American Historical Association. *Writings in American History*, published annually between 1902 and 1961 as a part of the *Annual Report of the American*

Mr. Kelly (M.A., Missouri), of the Current History Branch, CMH, is working on a history of the Army's effort in Vietnam.

Historical Association. Under topical subheads lists every book and article published during the year "that has any considerable value for study and research pertaining to the history of the United States from primitive times to the recent past."

Beers, Henry B. *Bibliographies in American History: Guide to Materials for Research.* New York: H. W. Wilson, 1942. Although dated is still the standard reference for material published before 1942.

Besterman, Theodore. *A World Bibliography of Bibliographies.* 4th ed., 5 vols. Lausanne: Societas Bibliographica, 1965–66. An alphabetical listing, under sixteen thousand subject headings, of bibliographies of all kinds with appropriate cross reference between subjects.

Boehm, Eric C., and Lalit, Adolphus. *Historical Periodicals: An Annotated World List of Historical and Related Serial Publications.* Santa Barbara, Calif.: Clio Press, 1961. Periodicals dealing with history and related disciplines arranged geographically by country of publication.

Dargan, Marion. *Guide to American Biography.* 2 vols. Albuquerque: Univ. of N.M. Press, 1949–52. Reprinted by Greenwood Press, Westport, Conn. in 1973. On prominent Americans who lived between 1607 and 1933.

Ferguson, Eugene S. *Bibliography of the History of Technology.* Cambridge, Mass.: MIT Press, 1968. Primary sources and secondary works classified and annotated; of particular value to those interested in the association between technology and warfare.

Fox, William T. R., et al. *Civil-Military Relations: An Annotated Bibliography, 1940-1952.* New York: Columbia Univ. Press, 1954. Prepared under the direction of the Committee on Civil-Military Relations Research of the Social Science Research Council. A survey of materials and introduction to research in the major areas of civil-military relations. Most of the material discussed deals with the United States but some with Great Britain.

Freidel, Frank, ed. *Harvard Guide to American History.* Rev. ed., 2 vols. Cambridge, Mass.: Harvard Univ. Press, 1974. The third revision of a guide prepared in 1896 by Harvard Professors Albert Bushnell Hart and Edward Channing. A comprehensive work, it attempts to serve the general reader, the student, and the scholar.

Howe, George F., et al. American Historical Association's *Guide to Historical Literature.* New York: Macmillan, 1961. Literature in all fields; although most of the works listed and annotated are in English, includes important books in foreign languages.

Kirkler, Bernard, and Laqueur, Walter. *A Reader's Guide to Contemporary History.* London: Weidenfeld and Nicolson, 1972. Ten bibliographic essays divided by geographic region. Each essay prepared by a competent British scholar.

Neiswender, Rosemary. *Guide to Russian Reference and Language Aids.* New York: Special Libraries Association, 1962. An annotated guide to Russian dictionaries, encyclopedias, bibliographies, language material, and other reference sources; originally an internal Rand publication.

Poulton, Helen T. *The Historian's Handbook: A Descriptive Guide to Reference Works,* Norman: Univ. of Okla. Press, 1972. A very helpful guide and analysis of reference works in history.

Schmeckebier, Lawrence F., and Eastin, Roy B. *Government Publications and Their Use.* 2d rev. ed. Washington: Brookings Institution, 1969. A basic descriptive guide to government publications and an analysis of their uses and limitations. Not a bibliography.

The Standard Periodical Directory. New York: Oxbridge Publishing. An alphabetical subject guide to more than 20,000 U.S. and Canadian periodicals; biennial.

Subject Guide to Books in Print. New York: Bowker. Has 65,500 subject
  headings, and 56,000 cross-references; published annually.
Ulrich's International Periodicals Directory. New York: Bowker. Lists by subject
  more than 62,000 periodicals published throughout the world. Revised
  biennially.
Walford, A. T. *Guide to Reference Material.* London: Library Association,
  1973-76. An annotated guide to reference works and bibliographies in all fields
  emphasizing material published in Great Britain.
Winchell, C. M. *Guide to Reference Books.* Chicago: American Library
  Association, 1977. An annotated guide to reference works in the humanities,
  social sciences, history, and pure and applied sciences. Considered the
  standard work in the reference field.

Bibliographies and Guides: Military

Robin Higham of Kansas State University has edited three
volumes that are very helpful for military history: *Official
Histories: Essays and Bibliographies from Around the World; A
Guide to the Sources of British Military History;* and *A Guide to
the Sources of U.S. Military History.* All follow the same general
format of an essay by a recognized scholar on a particular period
or topic and a listing of the important studies on the topic. Robert
G. Albion's *Naval and Maritime History: An Annotated Bibliography* covers books and theses in English on maritime and
naval history in its widest definition. Two Department of the Air
Force historians, Mary Ann Cresswell and Carl Berger, have
compiled *United States Air Force History: An Annotated
Bibliography.* It is organized both chronologically and topically
and lists significant books and articles on the Air Force since its
inception as part of the Army's Signal Corps. *Doctoral
Dissertations in Military Affairs: A Bibliography,* compiled by
Allan R. Millett and B. Franklin Cooling, was published in 1972.
It lists all dissertations written in the United States in the field of
military history. The list is updated yearly in an issue of *Military
Affairs.*

Air University Library Index to Military Periodicals (originally *Air University
  Periodical Index*). Maxwell Air Force Base, Ala.: Air Univ. Library, 1949-. A
  quarterly subject index of significant material appearing in seventy-one
  English-language military and aeronautical publications. Indexes periodicals
  not covered by commercial services.
Albion, Robert G. *Naval and Maritime History: An Annotated Bibliography.* 4th
  ed. Mystic, Conn.: Munson Institute of American Maritime History, 1972.
  Covers books and unpublished theses in English dealing with maritime and
  naval history in the broadest sense.
Blanchard, Carroll H. *Korean War Bibliography and Maps of Korea.* Albany,
  N.Y.: Korean Conflict Research Foundation, 1964. An extensive listing of

books and articles dealing with the political and military conflict in Korea, 1950–53. Lists foreign language materials as well as English.

Chandler, David G. *A Traveler's Guide to the Battlefields of Europe.* 2 vols. New York: Chilton Books, 1965. A brief analysis of 245 battles in Europe focussing on the period since 1500. Also treats the changes wrought in warfare by developments in weapons and tactics.

Craig, Harding. *A Bibliography of Encyclopaedias and Dictionaries Dealing with Military, Naval, and Maritime Affairs, 1577–1971.* 4th rev. ed. Houston: Rice Univ. Dept. of History, 1971. A selective listing, by year of issue, of military encyclopedias and dictionaries. Its strength is in foreign language publications, while its weakness lies in the selective nature of the English language material listed.

Cresswell, Mary Ann, and Berger, Carl. *United States Air Force History: An Annotated Bibliography.* Washington: Office of Air Force History, 1971. A chronological and topical listing of significant books and articles on the history of the United States Air Force.

Greenwood, John, comp. *American Defense Policy Since 1945: A Preliminary Bibliography.* Lawrence: Univ. Press, of Kans., 1973. A topical listing of writings on national security policy, 1945–72.

Higham, Robin, ed. *A Guide to the Sources of British Military History.* Berkeley: Univ. of Calif. Press, 1971. Twenty-five chapters, each prepared by a specialist in a particular phase of British military history. Coverage is from prehistoric times through and after World War II. Each chapter follows a standard format: a brief bibliographical essay followed by a listing of primary and secondary sources.

———. *A Guide to the Sources of U.S. Military History.* Hamden, Conn.: Archon, 1975. A publication in the same format covering all aspects of American military history.

———. *Official Histories: Essays and Bibliographies From Around the World.* Manhattan: Kans. State Univ. Library, 1970. A guide to official military history programs throughout the world with listings of works produced.

Lang, Kurt. *Military Institutions and the Sociology of War.* Beverly Hills, Calif.: Sage Publications, 1972. Five topical bibliographical essays followed by a classified bibliography of important literature in the field.

Larson, Arthur O. *National Security Affairs: A Guide to Information Sources.* Detroit: Gale Research Co., 1973. A topical listing of works on national security policy with emphasis on the period 1958–73.

Millett, Allan R., and Cooling, B. Franklin, comps. *Doctoral Dissertations in Military Affairs.* Manhattan: Kans. State Univ. Library, 1972. Dissertations completed in the United States up to 1970. Yearly updates have appeared in *Military Affairs* since then.

Nevins, Allan, et al. *Civil War Books: A Critical Bibliography.* 2 vols. Baton Rouge: La. State Univ. Press, 1967. A critical analysis of 5,700 books.

United States Naval History: A Bibliography. 6th ed. Washington: U.S. Naval History Division, 1972. A selective listing of important works from the Revolution to Vietnam.

Ziegler, Janet, comp. *World War II: Books in English, 1945–65.* Stanford, Calif.: Hoover Institution Press, 1971. A listing of 4,519 publications in English dealing with political, economic, social, and military aspects classified by subject. The American Committee on the History of the Second World War has published a supplement in pamphlet form, *A Select Bibliography of Books on the Second World War in English Published in the United States, 1966–1975.*

Encyclopedias, Dictionaries, and General References

To answer specific questions of who, what, where, or when, specialized reference works assist the student. One of the most useful is the *Encyclopedia of World History* edited by William L. Langer. A successor to Karl Ploetz's *Epitome of History*, Langer's work is both a chronological and geographic handbook. In addition to a chronological listing of important events, Richard B. Morris's *Encyclopedia of American History* has a separate section on socio-cultural and economic aspects of the American experience and short biographic sketches of five hundred American notables.

The difference between historical encyclopedias and historical or biographical dictionaries is not very distinct, but in general the dictionaries offer more comprehensive essays on particular persons, events, or institutions. The seven-volume *Dictionary of American History*, for instance, offers comprehensive essays on more than seven thousand subjects, each written by a specialist and including a brief bibliography. The one-volume *Steinberg's Dictionary of British History* is less comprehensive, although it presents a short narrative of important political, military, economic, and religious events from 1066 to 1970.

For biographical information on British and Empire personages of historical importance, the *Dictionary of National Biography*, commonly called the *DNB*, is the standard reference. Originally published in 1900, seven supplemental volumes have brought the coverage to 1960. Each article has been prepared by a specialist and includes a bibliography. The *Dictionary of American Biography (DAB)* is the counterpart to the *DNB*. The *DAB* was originally published in twenty volumes between 1928 and 1936. Five later volumes cover those who were deceased by the end of 1955. *Notable American Women, 1607-1950* (three volumes) has biographical essays on 1,359 women and is a useful supplement to the *Dictionary of American Biography*.

Adams, James T. *Concise Dictionary of American History*. New York: Scribner's 1962. A condensed version of the original Adams *Dictionary of American History* described below.

————. *Dictionary of American History*. Edited by Louise Bibelof Ketz. 7 vols. New York: Scribner's 1976. Over seven thousand items on all aspects of American history. The 1976 edition constitutes a thorough revision of the original five volumes edited by James Truslow Adams in 1940 to which a supplementary volume was added in 1961.

The Cambridge Ancient History. Series editor J. B. Bury. 12 vols. and 5 vols. of plates. New York: Cambridge Univ. Press, 1923-39. A standard reference ending with Roman Emperor Constantine's victory at Adrianpole in 324 A.D. Each volume has a bibliography broken down by subject.

The Cambridge Medieval History. Series editor J. B. Bury. 8 vols. London: Cambridge Univ. Press, 1911–36. A standard reference on the history of Europe from 324 A.D. through the fifteenth century. Each volume contains a subject bibliography.

The New Cambridge Modern History. Series editor G. N. Clark. 14 vols. London: Cambridge Univ. Press, 1957–69. An updating of Lord Acton's original Cambridge Modern History published in 1896–1912. Each volume covers a specific period from the Renaissance through the end of World War II. This edition does not, however, contain the usual Cambridge History bibliographies.

The Cambridge History of the British Empire. Series editor J. Holland Rose. 8 vols. New York: Cambridge Univ. Press, 1929–40. The standard work through World War I. Each volume has an extensive bibliography classified by subject.

James, Edward T., and James, Janet W. Notable American Women, 1607-1950: A Biographical Dictionary. 3 vols. Cambridge, Mass.: Harvard Univ. Press, Belknap Press, 1971.

Johnson, Allen, ed. Dictionary of American Biography. 20 vols. plus index vol. New York: Scribner's 1928–36. Five-volume supplement by same publisher, 1944–77.

Langer, William L., ed. An Encyclopedia of World History: Ancient, Medieval, and Modern, Chronologically Arranged. 5th ed. Boston: Houghton Mifflin, 1972. The standard American reference for historical facts relating to all periods of world history.

Laqueur, Walter, ed. A Dictionary of Politics. London: Weidenfeld and Nicolson, 1971. A concise reference work dealing with political developments since 1933. Gives the historical background of contemporary political problems and changes in terminology.

Morris, Richard B. Encyclopedia of American History. New York: Harper and Row, 1976. Part I develops the basic chronology, Part II the socio-economic aspects of American life, and Part III gives short biographic sketches of five hundred American notables.

Morris, Richard B., and Irwin, Graham W. An Encyclopedia of the Modern World: A Concise Reference History from 1760 to the Present. London: Weidenfeld and Nicolson, 1970. A geographic and chronological survey of political developments. A topical chronology traces economic, cultural, and legal developments.

Steinberg, S. H., and Evans, I. H., eds. Steinberg's Dictionary of British History. New York: St. Martin's Press, 1971. A brief narrative of important political, economic, and religious events in Britain and the Empire from 1066 to 1910.

Stephen, Leslie, and Lee, Sidney, eds. The Dictionary of National Biography. 22 vols. and 4-vol. supplement. London: Oxford Univ. Press, 1885–1971. Biographical sketches to 1960. An abridgement has been published in two volumes.

Tunney, Christopher. A Biographical Dictionary of World War II. London: J. M. Dent, 1972. Covers important figures, both military and civilian, in World War II.

Biographical Directory of the American Congress, 1774-1971. Washington: Government Printing Office, 1971. Short biographical sketches of past members of Congress.

Williams, Neville. Chronology of the Expanding World, 1492-1762. London: Barrie and Rockliff, 1969. Important events from the discovery of America to the end of the Seven Years' War. Events are listed chronologically on left-hand pages while achievements in such areas as science, the arts, and music are listed on the right-hand pages.

———. *Chronology of the Modern World, 1763-1865*. Rev. ed. Harmondsworth: Penguin Books, 1975. A listing in the same format as above.

Encyclopedias, etc.: Military

Of particular value is the *Encyclopedia of Military History From 3500 B.C. to the Present* edited by R. Ernest and Trevor N. Dupuy. Organized geographically within a chronological framework, it is the only relatively complete and reliable reference work surveying wars, warfare, and military affairs. The great value of the work is in its chronology, bibliography, and indices. Introductory essays in each chapter offer the authors' interpretation of events or periods described.

Boatner, Mark M., III. *The Civil War Dictionary*. New York: David McKay, 1959. Short articles on persons, events, operations, equipment, strategy and tactics, and most other subjects, all prepared by the author.

———. *Encyclopedia of the American Revolution*. Rev. ed. New York: David McKay, 1974. Similar to the *Civil War Dictionary*.

Dupuy, R. Ernest, and Dupuy, Trevor N. *The Encyclopedia of Military History From 3500 B.C. to the Present*. Rev. ed. New York: Harper and Row, 1977.

Effenberger, David. *A Dictionary of Battles*. New York: Thomas Y. Crowell, 1967. An alphabetical listing with short descriptive narratives of 1,560 individual military engagements from Megiddo in 1469 B.C. to Tow Morory in Vietnam in 1966. Gives commanders, numbers, strategy, tactics, and results. The emphasis is on land warfare although naval battles are included.

Farrow, Edward S. *Farrow's Military Encyclopedia: A Dictionary of Military Knowledge*. New York: Published by the Author, 1885. Valuable for terms and practices in the nineteenth century.

Peterson, Harold L., ed. *Encyclopedia of Firearms*. New York: Dutton, 1964. A guide to small arms throughout history, primarily describing the history and development of particular weapons.

Windrow, Martin, and Mason, Francis K. *A Concise Dictionary of Military Biography*. Reading, Eng.: Osprey Publishing, 1975. Brief sketches of two hundred world military leaders from 900 A.D. to 1975.

Historical Atlases: General

One of the best general references is the *Atlas of World History*, edited by R. R. Palmer. This atlas focuses on Europe and North America but does contain some coverage of the rest of the world. *The Atlas of American History,* edited by James Truslow Adams, contains 147 maps originally designed for use with the *Dictionary of American History.*

Adams, James T. *Atlas of American History.* New York: Scribner's, 1943.

Alexander, Gerard L. *Guide to Atlases, World, Regional, National, Thematic: An International Listing of Atlases Published Since 1951.* Metuchen, N.J.: Scarecrow Press, 1971. Of value in identifying the most useful atlas for any particular study.

Palmer, Robert R., ed. *Atlas of World History.* Chicago: Rand McNally, 1957. Concentrates mainly on Europe and North America. Most of the maps are devoted to changing political subdivisions, but some show economic, social, and religious trends or factors.

Paullin, Charles O. *Atlas of the Historical Geography of the United States.* Washington: Carnegie Institution, 1932. Arrangement of the 688 maps is both chronological and topical.

Wheat, James C., and Brun, Christian F. *Maps and Charts Published in America before 1800: A Bibliography.* New Haven: Yale University Press, 1969. An annotated guide to 915 maps published separately or as illustrations not only of America but also of the world. Arranged politically and geographically.

Winch, Kenneth, L. *International Maps and Atlases in Print.* New York: Bowker, 1974. Arranged by regions and countries.

Atlases: Military

For the military history of the United States, there is nothing comparable to Brig. Gen. Vincent J. Esposito's *West Point Atlas of American Wars.* With a concise narrative accompanying well drawn maps, it is an indispensable reference tool for the study of America's wars.

Banks, Arthur. *A Military Atlas of the First World War.* New York: Taplinger, 1975.

——. *A World Atlas of Military History.* Vol. 1 to 1500. London: Seeley Service, 1973-.

Esposito, Vincent J. *The West Point Atlas of American Wars.* 2 vols. New York: Praeger, 1959.

Young, Peter. *Atlas of the Second World War.* New York: Putnam's 1974. A commentary accompanies the maps.

Historical Journals and Societies

Thomas E. Kelly, III

THE student of military history should have some acquaintance with historical journals, professional associations which normally publish these journals, and other periodicals that frequently publish articles of historical interest. The two major historical associations in the United States are The American Historical Association and the Organization of American Historians; their publications, the *American Historical Review* and the *Journal of American History*, respectively, are the most important of the professional journals. The former concerns itself with all fields of history while the latter is limited to American history. In addition to the major associations, there are also regional associations such as the Southern and Western Historical Associations and specialized organizations such as the Economic History Association and the Society for the History of American Foreign Relations. In the field of military history, the major American organization is the American Military Institute. Two international organizations in this field are also of some importance, the International Commission on Military History whose American affiliate is known as the U.S. Commission on Military History and the Comité d'Histoire de la Deuxième Guerre Mondiale whose American affiliate is The American Committee on the History of the Second World War.

Moreover, each of the fifty states and the District of Columbia has a historical society, and literally hundreds of local groups are interested in the history of their cities, counties, or regions. The American Association for State and Local History acts as a central clearing house and publishes biennially a *Directory of Historical Agencies in the United States and Canada*. It also publishes a monthly *History News* containing information of current developments in the field of state and local history.

The following list covers the more significant historical periodicals published in English in the United States and abroad. (The only foreign language publications listed are the journals of the two major international organizations concerned with military history.) The list includes journals published independently as well as the more numerous organs of historical societies and associations and, in a separate category, some selected periodicals not devoted primarily to history that frequently publish articles of historical interest. To avoid excessive length, it does not include any of the publications of state or local historical societies.

History, Published in United States

American Heritage, sponsored by the American Association for State and Local History and the Society of American Historians, is the best known popular-history journal in the United States. It appears bimonthly and has articles on American history and culture.

The American Historical Review is published by the American Historical Association (see above). Prior to 1977, included once a year a classified bibliography of newly published artices in all fields of history. The bibliography is still compiled but must now be acquired from the association.

American History Illustrated, a popular-history magazine, is published in Gettysburg, Pennsylvania.

American Neptune: A Quarterly Journal of Maritime History is published by the Peabody Museum of Salem, Massachusetts; has articles and reviews on all areas of naval and maritime history.

The American West, a journal of the Western Historical Association, has articles on the historical and current development of the western United States.

Arizona and the West: A Journal of History has articles and reviews on the history of the trans-Missisiippi west.

Business History Review is the quarterly of the Harvard Graduate School of Business Administration.

Bulletin of the History of Medicine is the official organ of the American Association for the History of Medicine and the Johns Hopkins Institute of the History of Medicine. Carries occasional articles and reviews on military medicine.

Central European History is sponsored by the Conference Group for Central European History of the American Historical Association. Its articles and reviews deal exclusively with the German-speaking peoples of Central Europe.

Civil War History: A Journal of the Middle Period, published under the auspices of Kent State University, has many articles relating to the military history of the Civil War.

Civil War Times Illustrated is a popular-history magazine published in Gettysburg, Pennsylvania.

Diplomatic History is the journal of the Society for the History of American Foreign Relations. The first issue appeared in 1977. It will offer articles on American foreign relations from the early republic to the Cold War. In addition the editors plan to include essays on contemporary diplomacy.

French Historical Studies is the semiannual of the Society for French Historical Studies. In addition to articles and reviews, each issue lists recent books in French and English on French History.

Hispanic American Historical Review, the quarterly of the Conference on Latin American History of the American Historical Association, has frequent articles and book reviews on Latin American military history.

The Historian, the quarterly of the Phi Alpha Theta International Honor Society in History, contains articles and reviews in all fields of history.

History and Theory: Studies in the Philosophy of History is published by Wesleyan University Press. The journal has established a strong reputation for scholarship; its book reviews are detailed essays.

The Indian Historian, the journal of the American Indian Historical Society, carries historical and literary articles on the American Indian, his culture, and his relationship with American society.

ISIS: An International Review Devoted to the History of Science and Its Cultural Influences is a joint publication of the History of Science Society and the Smithsonian Museum of History and Technology. Each May issue contains a critical bibliography of books and articles published the preceding year.

The Journal of American History, published by the Organization of American Historians, has articles and reviews on all areas of American History only. Each issue contains a classified bibliography of recently published articles on American History.

The Journal of Economic History, the organ of the Economic History Association, has articles and reviews on all aspects of economic history. The March issue includes papers given at the association's yearly meeting.

Journal of the History of Medicine and Allied Sciences is published by the Department of the History of Medicine of the University of Minnesota. The journal has articles on the forces which shaped the development of American Medicine.

The Journal of Inter-Disciplinary History, relatively new, is published by the School of Humanities and Social Sciences of the Massachusetts Institute of Technology. Has attempted to use the methodology of the social sciences to deal with traditional historical questions and to raise questions previously unasked.

The Journal of Modern History, the quarterly of the Modern European Section of the American Historical Association, consists of articles and reviews on the history of modern Europe.

The Journal of Negro History is published by the Association for the Study of Negro Life and History. In addition to articles and book reviews, it occasionally prints documents relating to the history of Afro-Americans.

The Journal of Southern History of the Southern Historical Association has articles and reviews on the Southern states. Each May issue contains a classified bibliography of important articles on Southern history published the previous year.

The Journal of the West, now issued quarterly at Manhattan, Kansas, will be changing its traditional format. The new editor plans to have issues with a central theme and also to offer issues with general articles and book reviews on the history of the American West.

Labor History is published by the Taimiment Institute of New York University. In addition to articles and reviews, the fall issue has a bibliography of articles, dissertations, and research in progress.

Pacific Historical Review, the journal of the Pacific Coast Branch of the American Historical Association, stresses the trans-Mississippi West and U.S. involvement in the Pacific Ocean area.

Prologue: The Journal of the National Archives includes historical articles based in part on research in the records of the National Archives.

Reviews in American History and *Reviews in European History*, recently established quarterlies, review major books in their respective fields.

Speculum: A Journal of Medieval Studies, a publication of the Medieval Academy of America, often has articles on the military history of the Middle Ages.

Technology and Culture is the journal of the Interdisciplinary Society for the History of Technology.

Western Historical Quarterly carries articles and reviews on the history and culture of the American west for the Western History Association.

William and Mary Quarterly is published by the Institute of Early American History and Culture at Williamsburg. Stresses colonial history, but contains articles on the Revolution and the early national period as well.

History, Published Abroad in English

Balkan Studies, the semiannual of the Institute for Balkan Studies, in Thessaloniki, Greece, has articles and reviews in one of five languages: English, French, German, Greek, or Italian.

The Canadian Historical Review, the quarterly of the Canadian Historical Association, carries articles and reviews on all aspects of Canadian History.

The Canadian Journal of History, published three times a year, has articles and reviews in all fields of history except the history of Canada.

The Economic History Review is published by the Economic History Society of Great Britain. Although the review accepts articles in all fields of economic and social history, most of its writings are concerned with English, Commonwealth, or American history.

The English Historical Review is a privately published quarterly with articles and reviews on all areas of English History.

History Today, a popular monthly, appears in London and has articles and reviews by respected historians and includes suggestions for further reading on the topics of the various articles.

The Journal of African History is sponsored by the School of Oriental and African Studies of the University of London. Articles covering all aspects of African history may appear in English or French.

The Journal of Contemporary History, published for the Institute for Advanced Studies in Contemporary History in London, has articles on the main issues of Europe since 1914.

The Journal of Imperial and Commonwealth History is published three times a year by the Institute for Commonwealth Studies of the University of London.

Soviet Studies in History is a quarterly of translated, unabridged articles from Russian historical journals.

Military History

Aerospace Historian, the journal of the Air Force Historical Foundation, publishes articles and short reviews on all aspects of the history of airpower.

Military Affairs: The Journal of Military History, Including Theory and Technology is the quarterly of the American Military Institute. In addition to articles and reviews on all areas of military history, each issue contains a classified bibliography of important journal articles.

Military Collector and Historian, a publication of the Company of Military

Historians, has articles which emphasize the collection, preservation, and development of military hardware and insignia.

Military History of Texas and the Southwest is published by the Military History Press in Austin, Texas. It has articles on all phases of that area's military history. Periodically has reviews and bibliographies of recent material.

Revue d'Histoire de la Deuxième Guerre Mondiale, the periodical of the Comité d'Histoire de la Deuxième Guerre Mondiale, an organization of scholars interested in the history of the Second World War. Its U.S. affiliate is the American Committee on the History of the Second World War.

Revue Internationale d'Histoire Militaire is published by the Commission International d'Histoire Militaire. The U.S. Commission on Military History is its American affiliate.

By Valor and Arms: The Journal of American Military History is published by the Old Army Press. It has original articles and reprints significant work from sources such as the *Cavalry Journal, Army-Navy Journal*, and the *Journal of the Military Service Institution of the United States*. The magazine covers American military history from the Revolution to World War I.

Service and Service Related Journals

Air University Review may publish occasional articles on historical topics, but stresses contemporary national security issues.

Military Review, a monthly of the U.S. Army Command and General Staff College, emphasizes current military topics but frequently has articles on military history.

United States Naval Institute *Proceedings* is published eleven times a year by the U.S. Naval Institute. Although some military history articles appear, contemporary naval problems are the main subjects.

[U.S.] *Naval War College Review* carries occasional articles of historical interest but emphasizes current national security issues.

Parameters: The Journal of the Army War College publishes a few historical articles but stresses current national security.

Journals Publishing Some History

American Quarterly, published by the American Studies Association, seeks to give "a sense of direction to studies in the culture of the United States." Does not carry book reviews.

Armed Forces and Society, the quarterly of the Inter-University Seminar on Armed Forces and Society, has articles on civil-military relations and military sociology and is often organized around a central theme.

Foreign Affairs and *Foreign Policy* offer two divergent styles in their articles on international relations. The former is the publication of the Council on Foreign Relations and has a very traditional and scholarly approach. The latter publishes serious articles and attempts to find new directions for policy. Both accept essays which are "trial balloons" for changes in administration foreign policy.

The Journal of Asian Studies is published by the Association of Asian Studies.
  Formerly known as the Far Eastern Review, it publishes each year a classified
  bibliography of books and articles written the previous year.
The Journal of British Studies is the semiannual of the Conference on British
  Studies, the organization of American and Canadian scholars active in the
  study of British and Commonwealth history and culture.
Journal of Conflict Resolution: Research on War and Peace Between and Within
  Nations. Formerly offered a traditional interdisciplinary outlet for the study of
  international relations and global war. Since 1973, however, the journal has
  moved to a more quantitative approach; some knowledge of quantitative
  methodology is required to understand the articles and reviews.
The Journal of European Studies, founded in England in 1971, is an interdiscipli-
  nary quarterly with articles on the literature and history of the European
  Continent since the fifteenth century.
The Journal of Peace Research is published by the International Peace Research
  Institute in Oslo, Norway. While the American journal, Peace and Change, is
  historically oriented, this journal has a contemporary-problems approach.
JPMS: The Journal of Political and Military Sociology, a semiannual, has articles
  on values and social policy and relationships within political or military
  structures.
Latin American Research Review, the journal of the Latin American Studies
  Association, covers art, anthropology, history, politics, and sociology. Articles
  on the military in Latin America appear frequently.
Modern Asian Studies, published in Great Britain, carries articles and reviews in
  all the social sciences on China, Japan, and the countries of South and
  Southeast Asia.
Peace and Change: A Journal of Peace Research first appeared in 1972 and is
  sponsored by the Conference on Peace Research in History of the American
  Historical Association. Its articles and reviews are of particular interest to the
  military historian.
Political Science Quarterly, published by the Academy of Political Science, has
  articles on diplomatic and political history and also reviews major historical
  works.
Science and Society: An Independent Journal of Marxism is a quarterly which
  offers articles and reviews from a Marxist viewpoint of history.
Slavic Review: American Quarterly of Soviet and East European Studies is
  published by the American Association for the Advancement of Slavic
  Studies. Articles and reviews on the military history of the Slavs are common.
Soviet Military Review is an English-language Russian monthly which carries
  articles on military doctrine and weapons, military history, and soviet political
  theory.

Index

Index

G

H

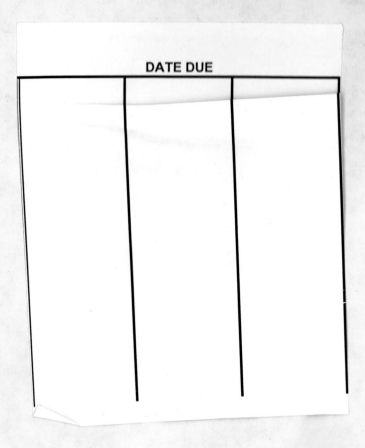

DATE DUE